FRANCE FROM 1851 TO THE PRESENT

FRANCE FROM 1851 TO THE PRESENT

UNIVERSALISM IN CRISIS

Roger Celestin and Eliane DalMolin

First published in 2007 by
PALGRAVE MACMILLAN™
175 Fifth Avenue, New York, N.Y. 10010 and
Houndmills, Basingstoke, Hampshire, England RG21 6XS
Companies and representatives throughout the world.

PALGRAVE MACMILLAN is the global academic imprint of the Palgrave Macmillan division of St. Martin's Press, LLC and of Palgrave Macmillan Ltd. Macmillan® is a registered trademark in the United States, United Kingdom and other countries. Palgrave is a registered trademark in the European Union and other countries.

ISBN-13: 978–0–312–29524–0
ISBN-10: 0–312–29524–3

Library of Congress Cataloging-in-Publication Data is available from the Library of Congress.

A catalogue record for this book is available from the British Library.

Design by Newgen Imaging Systems (P) Ltd., Chennai, India.

First edition: September 2007

10 9 8 7 6 5 4 3 2 1

Printed in the United States of America.

PERMISSIONS

- *The Bald Soprano* by Eugene Ionesco. Excerpt reprinted by permission of Grove/Atlantic Inc. Ltd.

- *Discourse on Colonialism* by Aimé Césaire. Excerpt reprinted by permission of Monthly Review Press.

- "Depth Advertised" from *The Eiffel Tower and Other Mythologies* by Roland Barthes. Translated by Richard Howard. Translation copyright © Farrar, Strauss and Giroux, LLC, 1979. Reprinted by permission of Hill and Wang, a division of Farrar, Straus and Giroux, LLC.

- *Nouvelle histoire de la France contemporaine. La France du XXe siècle* by Christophe Prochasson and Olivier Wieviorka. © Editions du Seuil, 1994 and 2004.

- *This Sex Which Is Not One,* by Luce Irigaray. Translated by Catherine Porter and Carolyn Burke. Translation copyright © Cornell University Press, 1985. Used by permission of the publisher, Cornell University Press.

- Gilles Deleuze. *Regarding the* nouveaux philosophes (*Plus a More General Problem*). In *Two Regimes of Madness. Semiotexte.* New York, Los Angeles, 2006. Excerpt reprinted by permission of *Semiotexte.*

- Jean-Marie LePen, Speech of May 13, 1984. Reprinted by permission of Jean-Marie LePen.

- "The French Language in the Face of Creolization" by Edouard Glissant. From *French Civilization and Its Discontents. Nationalism, Colonialism, Race*, edited by Tyler Stovall and Georges van den Abbeele. Lanham: Lexington Books, 200. Excerpt reprinted by permission of the publisher.

To
Simone, Sonia, and Cassandra
and
Raymonde, Andrew, Sophie, and Paul

CONTENTS

LIST OF ILLUSTRATIONS

ACKNOWLEDGMENTS

We would like to thank Mark Humphries, Eva Valenta, and Alyson Waters for their reading of the first draft of the manuscript. We would like to thank Bambi Billman for her help on the index, and Kristopher Tetzlaff for helping us getting through the permissions process. We are grateful to Farideh Koohi Kamali, Julia Cohen, and Kristy Lilas at Palgrave for keeping us on track at all steps of the publishing process. Our thanks also go to Norma Bouchard, Head of Modern and Classical Languages at the University of Connecticut for her support of this project. Finally, we are grateful for the support and patience of our families without whose love and understanding this book would never have seen the light of day.

Maurice Chevalier waiving his boater, or Edith Piaf—the Little Sparrow—alone on a dark stage, holding a note interminably while one or two melodies are dashed off on the accordion. These overexposed portraits are from a set of lingering 1950's clichés, most of them hovering under a striped café awning: the silly beret, the comical mustache, a toy poodle or two and intellectuals seated around outdoor tables bantering with women in low-cut dresses whose cleavages must be ogled with condescending concupiscence. Dispersed around the landscape is the perennial trio of perky French protuberances: the cigarette, the baguette and that frail filigreed phallus of an Eiffel Tower.

—Marcelle Clements, "Sighing, a French Sound Endures."
New York Times, October 18, 1998

The French will be like us, and as they become like the rest of us—Americanized, prosperous, modern, complacent—a great historical epoch will vanish from the earth, the epoch of Frenchness . . . Perhaps as you hold this volume in your hands, you will be experiencing the last few minutes of the existence of the French difference . . . You can be sure that when the urge to be different fades and the need to make that difference a common property disappears, the world will feel a bit relieved and deprived as well. For, as Victor Hugo said, without the French we will be alone.

—Richard Bersntein, *Fragile Glory. A Portrait of France and the French* (1990)

Today it is France that is isolated, and this temptation of a France alone is not only on the Left but also on the Right.

—Jacques Julliard. "France Alone." *Le Nouvel Observateur*, June 15, 2005
(two weeks after France's "no" vote to the European constitution
referendum, and two weeks before the International Olympic
Committee's "no" to Paris as host city of the 2012
Summer Olympic Games)

We are all in this. We are globalized. When Jacques Chirac says, "No" to Bush about the Iraq war, it's a delusion. It's to insist on the French as an exception, but there is no French exception.

—Jean Baudrillard, "Continental Drift." Interview.
New York Times Magazine, November 20, 2005

INTRODUCTION

In order to remain a great country, France must extend its language, its customs, its flag, its weapons, and its genius wherever it can.

—Jules Ferry, Speech to the Chamber of Deputies, July 28, 1885

France is only itself when it is at the forefront of nations . . . Only great projects can hope to compensate the seeds of dissent its people carry within themselves; our country, as it is, among others, as they are, must aim high and stand tall, lest it die. In short, in my view, France cannot be France without greatness [grandeur].

—Charles de Gaulle, *War Memoirs, 1940–1944*

So we do not have any regrets for the past? Will we not have to repent for having exchanged the banalization of France for simple material satisfaction? To abandon these old relics and to lose a part of our soul in the process; was this really the price to pay in order to be able to exist and to succeed in the great economic game? And are we prepared to continue in this direction? . . . Finally acquiring a sense of economics, have we fallen into line, after our loss of power, of our illusions, and a part of our soul? Are we condemned to be a middle-size nation like any other? Is God still French?

—Raymond Soubie, *Is God Still French?* (1991)

The above quotations span over one hundred years of French history and politics. In spite of the contrasting images of France they reflect—a secure, great, and ascending nation with a mission to extend itself over the globe (Ferry), a France that must remain true to its nature, that is, its *grandeur*, in order to exist at all (de Gaulle), and a France that is no longer great, has lost its power, and sacrificed its ideals to material imperatives (Soubie)—they all have one thing in common: France, whether dominant or in decline, is different from other nations. As a British scholar puts it, "The idea that France is somehow unique is deeply embedded in the nation's self-image. This is not just the routine rhetoric common to all nationalisms, nor even the inflated vanity typical of most great powers. It reflects the conviction that France has an exemplary, universal role as a civilizing force, that its aspirations are those of humanity at large" (Jenkins, 112).

One way of characterizing the present study of France from the mid-nineteenth century to the first few years of the third millennium is to consider it to be an exploration of the basic proposition—not necessarily the authors'—contained in the three quotes used as epigraphs above: France is different from other countries or, rather, France is *more different* from other countries. In academia and the media, this difference has been referred to as the "French exception" or "French exceptionalism." Recent studies have examined this exceptionalism, attempted to pin down its properties, and also considered its limits (Chafer and Godin, Silverman and Wirth). Others, while accepting the existence of a French exceptionalism at one time, have announced its demise as of two decades ago, at about the time when France was celebrating the bicentennial of its 1789 Revolution (Furet, Juilliard, and Rosanvallon). Another although in a tone at once more playful, ironic, and radical—the work in question is a novel—considers the issue a moot one and wonders whether "[the French realize that] they have been wiped off the map since 1945?" (Sollers, 200). Given that the author, Philippe Sollers, is French, alive, and well, and notoriously caustic, the question is to be taken with a grain of salt.

Our approach takes at least one thing for granted: the French have not been wiped off the face of the map. France's recent *non* to the European constitution in the spring of 2005, and its less recent *non* to the invasion of Iraq in the spring of 2002 are, whether we agree with these positions or not, ostensible signs of its continued existence and, even, resilience. To these *nons* we can add a list of more positive items that reflect France's continued power and influence today: Paris continues to be the principal destination of travelers to Europe, just as the Cannes Film Festival remains one of the major showcases of international cinema; France possesses the world's third-largest film industry (after India and the United States) and ranks second (after the United States) in food exports. On a more technological front, it was from Toulouse, the center of France's advanced aeronautics industry, that Airbus A380, the world's largest commercial aircraft, was built and started out on its maiden flight in the spring of 2005 and, in June 2005, Cadarache, a small town in southern France, was designated as the site of one of the most ambitious scientific projects ever undertaken: the International Thermonuclear Experimental Reactor (ITER).

A half-century ago, Cadarache was designated by Charles de Gaulle as France's national center for atomic research; there is thus a clear continuity between de Gaulle's idea of a France of *grandeur* and the country's present-day accomplishments. However, the world France was instrumental in creating, a world in which it was also a major political and cultural power, has changed. The result is obviously not the disappearance of France itself, but the disappearance of what we would like to call the *compatibility* between France and the world in which it exists, the disappearance of a basic congruence between its universalist principles and ideology, and those that obtain in the world today. In order to better understand this disappearance and its effects on the republic, it is necessary to take a closer look at what is meant by French exceptionalism and the essential place held by republican universalism in its definition.

French exceptionalism originates in the Enlightenment and the Revolution of 1789. The *philosophes* of the eighteenth century, among them Voltaire, Rousseau, and Diderot, perceived themselves as the harbingers of a new world in which arbitrariness, injustice, and the irrational, all associated with the Ancien Régime, would be vanquished by the forces of reason and progress. This would be true not only of France, but also of the rest of the world, for these notions of reason and progress were perceived as being universal.

The French Republic that was born of the Revolution of 1789 perceived itself as the enactment of these universal principles, as reflected, for example, in the revolutionary motto *Liberté, égalité, fraternité*. The republic created by the French Revolution was perceived as the particular embodiment of the Enlightenment's abstract universalism, a "universalist republic." The sovereignty and specificity of a particular nation were thus inextricably linked with principles that were considered universal. This meeting of the universal and the particular, of the universal *in* the particular, is at the heart of what has been referred to as French exceptionalism. Other elements also contribute to the construction of France as a modern nation: the secular republic recognizes only individual citizens and not members of particular groups—religious, regional, or ethnic, among other possibilities—that would have an identity over and above republican citizenship. A strong and interventionist state ensures equality before the law and, more generally, leads the way toward perpetual progress. Within its borders, the forces of arbitrariness, injustice, and irrationality give way to republican principles and a modern nation, a process Eugen Weber referred to as "turning peasants into Frenchmen" during the half-century that preceded World War I. Beyond its borders, the republic had a mission to advance the cause of universal reason and progress by spreading them throughout the world. This is the aspect of French universalism that laid the basis for France's massive colonial project, referred to as its *mission civilisatrice* (civilizing mission). Culture, and more specifically, a certain idea of cultural greatness, also lies at the core of the republic's mission both inside and outside its frontiers.

All of these characteristics of the universalist republic combine to create what is generally referred to as French exceptionalism. The first French Republic may have been the one that emerged from the Revolution of 1789, but universalism in practice, at its height, is traditionally associated with the period of French history known as the Third Republic (1870–1941). The year 1870 is the starting point for a number of recent cultural histories of France (Forbes and Kelly, Sowerwine). On the inside, the Third Republic's *instituteurs*—teachers sent out throughout France to inculcate republican principles to the masses—and, on the outside, its soldiers and colonists with their pith helmets in Asia and Africa, have become symbolic of French republican universalism in an ascending phase of its development. The Third Republic coincided with a period when the universal Enlightenment principles at the core of the French Republic were values that dominated on the international scene. This is what we have referred to above as the compatibility between French universalism and the world in which France existed. Further, the years of the Third Republic coincided with a period when France was a major military power and, as Jules Ferry, one of its emblematic figures formulates it above, France was in a position to "extend its language, its customs, its flag, its weapons, and its genius" to the far reaches of the globe.

Yet our study begins two decades earlier, in 1851. This choice is dictated by the need to delineate the passage from the republic that emerged from the revolution of 1789, which bequeathed universal principles that were philosophical, civic, and political, to a period when, at the onset of the conservative regime of the Second Empire (1852–1870), the notion of universalism went beyond this essentially political and ideological arena to become an overwhelming cultural force. It was from this moment on that Paris started to become the archetypal city of modernity, a modernity announced by the poet and art critic Charles Baudelaire as early as 1845: "The Heroism of modern life surrounds and pushes us further . . . That man will be the painter, the true painter, who manages to draw out the epic side from modern life, and to make us see and realize, by means of color or drawing, how great and poetic we are in our cravats and patent leather boots. May the true seekers give us next year that rare delight of greeting the advent of novelty" (407). It was the period during which impressionism made its first appearance, and the period that saw the beginnings of colonial ambition.

What of the year 1851 itself? That year, *universal* suffrage, a fundamental republican principle, which had been severely limited, was reinstituted; it was the year in which ordinary humanity entered the exclusive world of Art in Gustave Courbet's realist masterpiece *Burial at Ornans*; the year in which *the world was not enough* for the French who visited the first World's Fair held in London, but preferred to call it *exposition universelle* (*universal* exhibit—emphasis added), announcing their own qualifier for the exhibits they would organize throughout the following decades. The year 1851 was the year of President Louis Napoleon's coup d'état that led France out of the republic and into the empire, but also out of the age of cholera into that of a self-proclaimed age of progress and culture.

The exceptions to universalism and to "great culture" also became evident during this period, revealing the paradox of exclusion that is part and parcel of these concepts. Universal suffrage was "fully" restored but it excluded women. The impressionists appeared on the scene, but they would have to exhibit at the *Salons des Refusés* (Exhibit of the Rejected), a parallel exhibit outside of the official *Académie*-sponsored *Salon*. Baron Haussmann's project to transform and modernize Paris is commonly associated with the policies of the Third Republic, but it is as Prefect of the Seine from 1853 to 1870, appointed by Napoleon III, that he oversaw the modernization of the city and the changes brought to its social geography; the wide avenues and monuments of "Haussmannization," also entailed the relocation of the poor and working-class population to peripheral sectors of the capital.

After the defeat of the French Empire by Germany in 1870 and after the Third Republic was proclaimed that same year, modernity and French republican universalism followed parallel courses. The Third Republic's claim to universalism was, as we have seen, simultaneously a claim to modernization and progress. Those forces that could not be assimilated in the process were relegated to categories that bore a variety of names: the backward, the unhealthy, the mad, the criminal, the unpatriotic, the provincial, the unclean, and subversive masses, in a word, and in one uniform category, the "different." In the very process of affirming and extending themselves, French republican universalism and modernity thus both consist of a dual movement of assimilation and exclusion that designates a multiplicity of "others." Universalism and modernity have in common an imperative to delineate differences in order to advance or even exist at all. These developments did not occur exclusively in France, but, as Max Silverman suggests, there is something—that we will call exceptional—in the way they manifested themselves in that country: "Although this process of boundary-drawing was a fundamental feature of modernity in general, we might once again suggest that France was exemplary. For in which nation were rationality and the irrational, science and superstition, nation and race orchestrated so systematically as ideological opposites as in France?" (2).

The opposites were set up, but universalism prevailed. Until the advent of World War II, France the universalist, modernizing republic existed in a world where it was not only a major power but also one whose principles and ideology were made compatible with that world by its power. World War II may seem a rather exact marker to indicate the end of this compatibility, and indeed signs of a shift were present well before the German blitzkrieg in the spring of 1940 led to the collapse of the Third Republic and to the beginning of the infamous Vichy regime. The *expositions universelles*, for example, were not exclusively showcases where the republic displayed scientific advances and the successes of its colonial expansion and "civilizing mission" for the edification of its citizens; they were also venues of mass entertainment for the amusement of consumers, already announcing the Disneylands of America. They indicated a blurring of the separation between republican public sphere and consumerist private space, and they were also announcing the late twentieth century "Euro-Disney" built in the suburbs of Paris. The colonies were not exclusively vast tracts of land where the empire could spread its civilization and extend its trade, but also the source of other practices, other esthetics that would reappear in the center of the empire in the works of the great modernist artists like Picasso. The Russian Revolution of 1917 also constituted a spectacular counterdiscourse to the French Republic's universalism; it represented the paradox of *another universalism*.

On the eve of World War I, shortly before this "other revolution," French film production represented 70 percent of the world film market. While this was indicative of France's continued cultural prevalence, films made in the United States, that "other republic" born in the late eighteenth century, would soon begin to claim an ever-increasing share of the market. In fact, the film medium itself, at least a certain practice of this medium, already constituted a challenge to the universalist republic's traditional definition of culture, the "high culture" with which France is still commonly associated. "Hollywood movies," on the other hand, would become a fundamental component of mass culture associated with an American brand of popular culture. The calls to stop "American cultural domination" were not yet being heard, but the world in which French universalism was the dominant paradigm was being bypassed. To an ideology that placed the citizen's allegiance to republican principles above all else, the United States presented the challenge of a Fordist production model and a system where the consumer is king. During the same period, the Russian revolution held out the promise of a world in which the proletariat would rule.

All of this taking place in the aftermath of World War I strangely resembled the situation that would be prevalent in the aftermath of World War II, which was thus not a sudden limit marking the abrupt disappearance of compatibility between French universalism and the world. Rather, the post–World War II period reflected the crystallization of trends that had been evolving for decades. There is, however, a crucial difference between the two eras, between a time when the Ford Company was making the "Model T"—production lasted from 1908 to 1927—and the aftermath of World War II: thirty years after the Bolshevik revolution and twenty years after the last Model-T came off the assembly line, the United States and the Soviet Union emerged as the two superpowers while France, as Alain Soubie bemoans above, was becoming "a middle-size nation." This was the point where French political and economic power could no longer sustain or enforce the principles of French republican universalism on a planetary level. In addition, the two systems represented by the United States and the Soviet Union at that time offered alternative models that also presented themselves as "universal."

In this new distribution of power and influence France aligned itself with the neoliberal economies of the American-dominated North Atlantic sphere. It opted for the American modernization model in the three decades that have been called France's "Thirty Glorious Years," when it was transformed from a war-devastated country into one of the world's fastest-growing economies. In the midst of these transformations, de Gaulle attempted, during the years of his presidency (1958–1969), to maintain a "certain idea of France," to enact a policy of "grandeur." However, the increasing privatization of everyday life along consumerist patterns, and the disappearance of the French Empire were signs that, by then, the French republican universalist model had already reached a critical point. This passage from a paradigm in which France was dominant to one in which it no longer was paralleled what Silverman refers to as "the crisis of modernity" itself:

> If modernity was intricately connected with industrial society and class conflict [respectively symbolized by the Model-T and Revolution], the nationalizing mission of the state, colonialism, and the cultural avant-garde, then today's transformations in the industrial fabric of society, the attack on the so-called sovereignty of the nation-state from above and below (through globalization and localization), post-colonialism and the broadening of the cultural sphere to encompass what were formerly designated as the political and social spheres, all bear witness to the crisis of modernity. (4)

We acknowledge here the scholarship of others working in this area, Silverman's work in this instance, by stating that, before we read his *Facing Postmodernity: Contemporary French Thought on Culture and Society*, his introduction in particular, we had thought of *The Crisis of Modernity* as a possible title for this book. For we too see in the contemporary debates on French identity and French exceptionalism a reflection of the passage from a modern to a postmodern paradigm.[1]

However, our method and, as previously mentioned, our point of departure differ from those of previous studies. The aim of *France from 1851 to the Present: Universalism in Crisis* is to provide a chronological narrative and a broad historical sweep as a background against which we can examine France's claim to universalism through an exploration of politics, culture, and society over a 150-year span. To a certain extent, this study can be considered a cultural history, but one with a particular thesis. As is the case in cultural histories, we try to provide an overall account that includes as much information as possible; but we have also chosen to focus our narrative on the opposition or tension between a homogenizing and centralizing state and the resistance to its policies and ideology represented by different individuals, groups, and movements. In addition, we have taken into account a shift in the context of this opposition: in an initial phase, covered in the first five chapters, France's universalist ethos exists in a period where it dominates, and the exceptions to its principles can be relegated to the status of aberrations. In a second phase, covered in chapters six through ten, a phase whose beginnings we locate in the aftermath of World War II, it has become increasingly difficult for the republic to apply policies based on its claimed universalism. This is the phase where, internationally, it no longer dominates and, nationally, has to contend with the appearance of either previously repressed or newly emerging identities claiming their place. In order to maintain a hold on its founding principles in this second phase, the republic has had to make an increasing number of adjustments in its recognition of differences. *Universalism and exceptionalism had to make exceptions.* Whence our title and our approach: universalism in crisis. Gustave Flaubert's (1821–1880) sardonic definition of "exception" in his *Dictionnaire des idées reçues* (*Dictionary of Commonplaces*) gives us an idea of the intricacies involved in the transformation of French republican universalism in this second phase: "Exception: Say that it confirms the rule. Don't venture to explain how."

Since we do not claim to offer a totalizing or exhaustive account of France from 1851 to the present time, our argument has also directed and limited our selection of material. Rather than attempt to include a maximum amount of information at the cost of simply naming or mentioning people and events when there was no room for analysis or development, we have chosen, as much as possible, to include only material for which we could provide at least some background, while providing continuity for the reader. When this could not be done within the narrative, we have also included a number of "dossiers" as a means of developing particular events and trends. Our goal is to combine information and chronological continuity with a particular proposition. It is our hope that the readers of this study will not only find a general presentation of France over the past 150 years, but that they will also find in our approach a unifying framework for the many names and events they encounter in the process.

Note

1. We are aware of the sometimes contentious reception of the term "postmodern," but endorse it here as a means of summarizing a variety of developments. These range from the end of colonial empires to the replacement, in advanced industrial societies, of the old "smokestack" and assembly line industries by service and information oriented economies, with all of the social and political upheavals this entails; from the appearance of mass consumerism to the globalization of economic flows; from an admittedly problematic notion of ethnic homogeneity, to multicultural populations; from what the French philosopher Jean-François Lyotard has called "grand narratives," such as the discourse of the Enlightenment or of universalism, to a multiplicity of discourses.

References

Chafer, Tony and Emmanuel Godin, eds. *The French Exception*. New York, Oxford: Berghahn Books, 2005.

Flaubert, Gustave. *Dictionnaire des idées reçues*. Paris: Librio, 1997.

Forbes, Jill and Michael Kelly. *French Cultural Studies. An Introduction*. Oxford: Oxford University Press, 1995.

Furet, François, Jacques Juilliard, and Pierre Rosanvallon. *La République du centre: La fin de l'exception française*. Paris: Calmann-Levy, 1988.

Jenkins, Brian. "French Political Culture: Homogeneous or Fragmented?" In William Kidd and Sîan Reynolds, eds. *Contemporary French Cultural Studies*. London: Arnold, 2000, 111–126.

Lyotard, Jean-François. *The Postmodern Condition: A Report on Knowledge*. Geoff Bennington and Brian Massumi, trans. Minneapolis: University of Minnesota Press, 1979. Originally published as *La condition postmoderne: rapport sur le savoir* (Paris: Editions de Minuit, 1979).

Robiquet Paul, ed. *Discours et Opinions de Jules Ferry*. Paris: Armand Colin & Cie., 1897.

Silverman, Maxim. *Facing Postmodernity: Contemporary French Thought on Culture, and Society*. London, New York: Routledge, 1999.

Sollers, Philippe. *La fête à Venise*. Paris: Gallimard, 1991.

Soubie, Raymond. *Dieu est-il toujours français?* Paris: Editions de Fallois, 1991.

Sowerwine, Charles. *France since 1870. Culture, Politics and Society*. Houndmills, NY: Palgrave, 2001.

Weber, Eugen. *Peasants into Frenchmen: The Modernization of Rural France, 1870–1914*. Stanford, CA: Stanford University Press, 1976.

Wirth, Laurent. *L'exception française*. Paris: Armand Colin, 2000.

PART I

1851–1944: UNIVERSALISM TRIUMPHANT

Eliane DalMolin

CHAPTER 1

FRANCE AT MID-CENTURY

1851: The Year of the Universal

Until 1870, the French never ceased to claim that their singularity was to be bearers of the Universal.

—Françoise Mélonio, *Histoire culturelle de la France* (1998)

France has a passion for the universal.

—Pierre Bouretz, *La République et l'universel* (2000)

When he arrived in London for a quick visit to the World's Fair held at the Crystal Palace in Hyde Park in September 1851, French writer Gustave Flaubert was at a key moment in his personal and literary life. He had recently returned from a long trip to Egypt and Turkey, and he was filled with extraordinary memories and dreams of visiting the exotic lands of the "Orient." He had also just begun writing his master-piece, *Madame Bovary*, the sordid and tragic story of a bored provincial bourgeois housewife. The topic of this new novel alone reflected his critical sentiment toward the materialistic and disingenuous rising Western bourgeoisie, while his recent travels reinforced his enthusiasm for Eastern culture and beauty. His love of the East may very well have been a response to his disapproval of Western bourgeois life. What he saw in the conservative and status-driven French society of the mid-nineteenth century was far from the ideology of the egalitarian society imagined by the partisans of the 1789 French Revolution. So, when the first World's Fair opened its doors in London to an indisputably bourgeois public, he was the first to be surprised at how enjoyable the event was, and he was genuinely pleased to see the heteroclite display of artifacts from all over the world. Despite his general disillusionment with French bourgeois principles, he could not escape the "universal" feeling brought on by the international spirit of the great bazaar embodied by the 1851 London Fair. He would speak with admiration of the fair as a "very beautiful object [. . .] admired by every-body" (Seznec, 23). The fair was indeed a beautiful universal venue where a predom-inantly bourgeois crowd came to admire not only modern civilization, but also the wonders from faraway lands. Against all odds, Flaubert momentarily put aside his pro-found dislike of the bourgeois way of life and enjoyed being "like everyone else" as he went through the extensive display of novel and beautiful objects offered by the exhibit. More particularly, his inclination for the exotic was readily satisfied by the Chinese and Indian booths where he spent some time writing descriptions of the various exhibited artifacts: from India, a howdah-harnessed elephant, a sofa, a jacket, a sword, fans, and turbans; from China, folding screens, silk shawls, a sculptured ivory tree, a sampan. This Eastern bric-a-brac in the middle of a proper bourgeois setting did not strike Flaubert or any other visitor as odd or anachronistic; on the contrary, it suggested the beginning of an era when the Western world became increasingly fascinated with Eastern cultures in particular, and more curious about the rest of the world in general.

Under the roof of the Crystal Palace many different cultures converged. As a "multicultural" moment, the fair was indeed perceived by its contemporaries as the epitome of universal enlightenment. It was a gathering the French appreciated and even envied as they felt they were in a higher cultural position to hold this type of event and impress the world audience with their ability to host foreign cultures while showcasing their own.

For the French, the time for a universal gathering seemed propitious, especially so in the mid-nineteenth century when "universal" liberties earned after the French revolution seemed compromised by national contradictions and self-interest, and when the *Hexagone* suddenly appeared too small to realize the dream of Enlightenment and equality that had been formulated at the end of the eighteenth century. By 1851, the ideal universalism originally defined as a political principle of inclusiveness seemed more and more unattainable and questionable as it was increasingly overshadowed by exclusion. Despite the promise of comprehensive unity behind its basic definition, universalism had never been a perfect concept, but at the very least it represented hope for relative equality among citizens of a single nation. It is this idea of relative equality that had been eroded with time and political regimes during the first half of the nineteenth century, and finally seemed in real jeopardy with the debilitating "reforms" brought to universal suffrage in 1851. As it faced political failure, universalism came to mean "for all, with the exception of many," rather than "for all, with the exception of a few," but despite its inherent contradiction it nevertheless survived by reinventing itself through a radical shift toward the cultural domain. The World's Fair "format" presented the perfect venue to reassert universalism's all-embracing quality differently and to display cultural artifacts for all to see and share. The French felt that it was time to take the lead and to show the world their own cultural standards and their dream for a modern society. It would be a society where, ideally, life would be easier and healthier for everyone, for the rising bourgeois class as well as the growing working class. The French thus aspired to a model society resting on universalist principles of goodness and happiness for all classes. In addition, universalism also meant the development of a policy of cultural prestige to make France "shine," *rayonner* in French, throughout the world as a beacon nation for the arts and culture. In other words, universalism was defining both the domestic and international image of France.

As part of their policy of *rayonnement*, the French thought that an international fair of their own would introduce other nations to the high level of their culture while also giving them the opportunity to share their own ways of life. Thus, the London event showed that a fair was the ideal venue for giving foreign cultures visibility in the Western world, allowing their influence to make its way into Western arts, while also influencing them to respond positively to Western culture. The London Fair brought all these sentiments to the surface and prepared France psychologically for the next fair-like event, which would be held in Paris in 1855.

The fair appeared to Flaubert, as it did to others, as a place where East met West; a place where a nation was given the opportunity to shine as the host and ambassador of universal values and to exhibit the world's most remarkable and various cultural accomplishments under its auspices. At the end of the fair, the French learned the cultural power of the Universal and vowed to seize and multiply its effects at home in order to rise to what they felt was their destiny as "bearers of the Universal" (Mélonio, in de Baecque, 191).

We thus begin with the premise that 1851 may well be the pivotal year in the rise and establishment of a ubiquitous and already growing universalism, a universalism marred with exceptions and contradictions but filled with renewed cultural energy both within France's borders and beyond. It was the year when the Universal extended its far-reaching powers to the public, cultural, and artistic spheres of a French society in full industrial expansion, to citizens, who were now in the process of moving from predominantly agrarian and local ways to more urban and worldly lives. Beyond its own borders, France also appeared more clearly to the world as a country asserting its cultural position by constantly building upon two key principles in the constitution of its modernity: quality and equality: quality of life and relative equality in the human community both inside and outside of France. No doubt, throughout the years, many variations came to distort and even at times to negate this two-pronged theory but, like most social and cultural theories, the general intention and inner patterns of this dual view of French culture came to represent and project a certain image of France to the rest of the world.

Within the *Hexagone*, the question of equality was at the heart of France's constitutional battle over universal suffrage in 1851. The French were witnessing the end of the elusive and inflammatory Second Republic (1848–1852), a time when the conservative republican administration made the mistake of reducing the number of male voters, thus bringing chaos and dissent to French political life and facilitating the takeover of Napoleon III, then "prince-president" of the Second Republic. His coup d'état would, in turn, rapidly reinstall imperial times to France for the next eighteen years (1852–1870).

In terms of quality of life, as demonstrated during the 1851 fair and for many other fairs to come, the French imposed themselves on the bourgeois scene as the nation of taste and sophistication as well as of the esthetics of everyday life. The French shined with standards of excellence at the London Fair, and, beyond the event itself, the occasion gave them the impetus and the ambition to surpass the British event in subsequent years. Indeed, the 1851 fair inspired the French to do better in areas including industrial innovation, colonial exhibitions, and the general quality and presentation of the event itself. With a renewed sense of cultural confidence, they organized five individual events of enormous proportions during the second half of the nineteenth century. Each one of these shows was bigger and more spectacular than the preceding one. They were held in Paris in 1855, 1867, 1878, 1889, and 1900 in order to showcase France's continuous industrial advances, its high quality products, its relatively new and growing colonial empire, and its thoroughly revamped capital, which from that time on became a primary destination and an object of beauty and curiosity for the entire world. After the 1851 London Fair, the *exposition universelle* (Universal Exposition), as the French called it, became a huge event for France and the world. The success of the French expositions of the nineteenth century may be attributed in large part to an unparalleled effort by the French to satisfy the simultaneously materialistic and refined desire of a flourishing Western bourgeois population aspiring to a comfortable and practical life to complement their recently acquired social status. In responding to bourgeois demands, the French put their heart and soul into solidifying their long-standing attachment to high and tasteful standards of living while keeping up with the practical demands of an advanced modern culture. Throughout the nineteenth century, curious and fascinated world citizens flocked to Paris in ever-increasing numbers and watched in delight as culture and progress came together in a single place. French singularity was indeed of universal proportion as it attracted the world to see the splendor of its modernity. Not surprisingly, the showcasing of a highly modern France during this time firmly contributed to placing the French at the vanguard of world culture and universal ideals for many years to come.

The London World's Fair

The 1851 "London Universal Exhibition: The Great Exhibition of the Works of Industry of all Nations" occupied much of the year, opening on May 1 and closing on October 15. To display the best of the world for the first time required acts of cultural and architectural audacity and courage, and a certain amount of risk. The British wanted to show the world that they were ready to welcome foreign cultures with much enthusiasm and a complete sense of novelty. For the occasion they built the Crystal Palace in Hyde Park, a uniquely modern and disposable construction. In architectural history, it will stand as the first temporary large convention center: tall, spacious, and ephemeral. It was the fair's symbolic representation, built exclusively for the occasion and immediately pulled down at the end of the fair in order to restore Hyde Park to its original traditional configuration. The Palace was nonetheless in and of itself a magnificent construction fit for the most prestigious show on earth. Entirely made of glass and iron, two new construction materials, it looked like an immense transparent cage or a prodigious cut diamond receiving and reflecting light all day long and standing proud in the modern world of architecture. Its temporary presence added to its value by becoming the primal example of what, in 1859–1860, French poet and art critic Charles Baudelaire would call the "transitory nature of the modern world" and the "eternal quality" that can be retained from its fleeting conception (*Painter of Modern Life*, 12). The Crystal Palace appeared as the quintessential example of modernity, and the World Fair it harbored as the first and optimal world show.

The idea of expositions were not new to the French, as they were in fact the first to organize annual national industrial shows (1782–1804), but when Louis Joseph Buffet, minister of agriculture in 1848 and again in 1851, suggested that these events become international, the French government hesitated: it did not see any immediate benefits to internationalizing these events and was not ready to "globalize" them. The mood was unchanged until the London Fair actually began. By early May 1851, France's growing bourgeois society embraced the idea of universalism and of international competition embodied by the London Fair. The very idea of the fair was considered an innovation and privilege to show national and international treasures, and a prestigious means to confirm the status of France as one of the world's most developed and refined nations. Indeed, in 1851 the French realized that the concept of gathering national and international industrial and cultural novelties during an international event would lead to world recognition of their newly developed industry on the one hand and of the status of French culture on the other. The fair had the positive effect of making the French understand the crucial role that such an event could represent for the future of their country's highly respected culture. Through a fair or exposition of their own, they felt that they could lead the world "in matter of art and taste" a sentiment expressed by political economist Adolphe Blanqui (107), and assert their new industrial leadership in the "global economy" (Walton, 10).

Competition between major European countries became a factor in asserting cultural power. It played a leading role in the understanding of universalism, as by definition the concept invited open challenges and comparisons between different cultures and the desire for any country involved in such challenges to outdo the others. It also raised the bar for other "less-developed nations" to adopt the ways and to catch up with more industrialized nations. In this idealized universalism, free trade encouraged competition among nations and had the effect of bringing them together in the international brotherhood of economically competing cultures displaying their particular types of national novelties. For France, novelty was framed by bourgeois standards of quality. Elegant and popular goods were made with new and more practical, but no less beautiful, materials. For example, in the *orfèvrerie*, or French silver industry, Charles Christofle exhibited his popular line of silver-plated and gilded house items, which looked truly elegant but cost less than the solid silver items.

France had mixed feeling about free trade. The dominant bourgeois class, whose tastes dictated the choice of goods and exhibitors at the fair, wished to claim the exclusivity of their inclination for beautiful arts and crafts, while recognizing that mass-produced objects made them more readily available and less expensive to purchase. Whether on a small-scale or mass-produced, items of quality were the pride of many French artisans and manufacturers. This sentiment was, however, constantly jeopardized as they felt the pressure of British competition. Indeed, the unequivocal competition between France and Britain pervaded many aspects of the 1851 exhibit.

Dossier 1.1   The World's Fair as Viewed by the Press (1851)

In *Le Pilote de Londres*, a newspaper printed in French in London and distributed on the first day of the fair, May 1, 1851, the lead article displayed critical views on the uneven distribution of booths in favor of the British and consequently attempted to dissociate London from the universal objective of the fair: "The London fair is not a British fair but truly a universal fair [. . .] Hyde Park is a neutral ground where nationalities disappear and where all populations should receive equal treatment in relation to the size of their representation" (*L'Illustration*, 427, 272). The journalist appeals here to the very notion of universalism to claim equal and proportional representation for all nations at Hyde Park. Under his pen, universalism becomes the ultimate concept with which France defends its right to be a real competitor, a true player in the world game. Here, universalism applies only to French interests even when, in an effort to discredit the British occupation of the largest area of the fair ground, the writer aspires to see "all populations" fairly represented and gathered at the palace. This seemingly well-intended and idealistic notion that the fair could truly be a universal event is ultimately part of the French journalist's rhetorical style, a means of pointing to and frowning upon the British. In this publication, France justified its mission as an egalitarian and world-friendly nation by criticizing in universalistic overtones a world event for minimizing the French presence.

Emphasizing the universal character of the fair was the firm intention of Paulin, director and editorialist of *L'Illustration*, the most popular newspaper of the time, appropriately subtitled *Le journal universel* (The Universal Journal). In his inaugural article on the fair Paulin declared with optimism, zeal, and utopian energy that the World's Fair was indeed universal, with global repercussions for mankind, the changing face of the arts, and the sweeping progress of industry:

The moment, they say, is solemn. All countries in the universe are invited to measure themselves in the peaceful arena of labor. For the first time in the history of humanity, men from all countries of the world will be gathering. There is no denying it; this meeting of all populations at an industrial tradeshow is a revolution unheard of. It is the most complete victory of common interest and intelligence over prejudices. The Fair is the first universal council of mankind. It will have immense consequences for the future of the universe, for world peace, for the advance in the arts and the industry, and for the greatness of civilization. The glory of such an event will eternally be the honorific title of Prince Albert. Before the marvels of industry, men of State and economists will be forced to modify their opinions. They will have to tackle the most important international questions: free trade, the universal system of weights and measure, single currency, universal lettre de change, new measures of uniformity in trade agreement for all the countries of the globe, and a general system of prevention against commercial fraud and counterfeit. All these questions will be brought forth and will require an answer (L'Illustration, no. 427 [1851] : 274).

This printed media display of solemnity and grandeur promoting the universal character of the fair emerges here from a sincere desire on Paulin's part to see all global accomplishments as part and parcel of the catalyzing event represented by the fair.

It is important at this point to discuss the difference concerning the very name of the fair in English and in French: "World's Fair" in English becomes "Universal Exposition" (*exposition universelle*) in French. A quick sociolinguistic analysis of the two ways of naming the event reveals an essential difference in the way the two nations, France and England, constructed the respective cultural vision it embodied. In effect, the term "world" points to the way the British represented the international dimension of the fair. To them, the world was indeed the biggest geographical unit that would make the fair a true manifestation of and for all mankind, whereas the French conceived an even larger, infinite concept to represent the same event: "the universe." The term is both grandiose and unrealistic as it goes beyond the planetary possibilities of the event, but it also adds a touch of idealism and anticipation to the notion itself. In other words, the view from the French "universe" is greater and more futuristic than the one from the British "world," a distinction that followed the pattern of competition between the two countries, whereby the French felt it was their objective not only to catch up with the British, but to outdo them.

The comparison of the two labels for the event leads us to a contradiction in terms. The British "world" refers to a more limited space compared to the French *universelle*; in addition, the British "fair" points to the numerous fair-goers while the French *exposition* signals primarily the importance of the exhibitors, those who exposed. The paradox seems well entrenched in the language as well as in the divergent economic, social, and cultural motivations behind the different terms. The word "fair" used by the British evokes a place of pleasurable interaction designed to accommodate as many different people as possible. It implies the idea of a global mix of fair-goers, exhibitors, and specta-tors, while the word exposition used by the French refers directly to the actual exhibitors and only indirectly to the visitors. In the French label, the term exposition placed in cor-relation with the all-encompassing term "universal" projects a strange association between the great and overwhelming universe, to which the French hyperbolically aspire, and the particular and unique group of individuals responsible for its greatness, the exhibitors. This configuration reflects the first major contradiction inscribed in the very notion of "the universal," a fundamental fissure that will persist inside the official and ideal definition of the concept. This fissure will be the sign of a contradiction between desire and reality, between a desire to eliminate the barriers between all people and coun-tries, and the reality of a French culture envisioned as a universal show where the splen-dor of the spectacle, the magnitude of its display, and the means of this display, are of greater importance than the people to whom it should be, but in the end is not, entirely destined. At mid-century, French culture presents itself as universal at the very moment when it is *not* a universal culture, but a distinctly bourgeois one. However, despite its inner contradictions, this notion of a *universal French culture* would carry, in its many exports—ranging from luxury goods, music, and painting to architecture and literature— the seal of national "quality" and the desire for others to reach and adopt France's degree of cultural excellence.

The following example involving French composer Hector Berlioz during the 1851 fair points precisely to the undisputable reputation for the high quality of French manufactured products in the eyes of the international community. The composer was sent to the fair as the French representative on the international jury in charge of evaluating and voting on the best makers of the world's instruments. Berlioz's report is clear on the superiority of the French in the field: "The French member of the jury [Berlioz himself] should feel no embarrassment whatsoever in recognizing the immense superiority of French products in this contest open to all nations, since he was alone in defending the interests of his compatriots, while England counted four representatives and since, in the distribution of awards, the equity of rival nations has reserved the highest honors for the French exhibitors" (2). The unsurpassed expertise of the French in instrument making was therefore impartially recognized by a jury that counted four times more British jurors than those of any other nation. It was also in the spirit of fair and equal competition that the French won the most medals, thus ensuring and consolidating their unmatched reputation for excellence in the arts in general and in music in particular. From his experience as a member of a jury in which France was underrepresented, Berlioz's clear conclusion was far-reaching for French artistic culture: France was a highly respected artistic nation and its cultural prestige appeared as a universal trait understood by and among all other cultures.

The Second Empire and Universal Suffrage

At the close of the London Fair, France could not immediately organize its own inter-national industrial cultural event, as the country was facing a domestic problem of constitutional and "universal" proportions. Historically, 1851 is remembered as the year when the president of the Second Republic, Louis Napoleon Bonaparte, the nephew of Napoleon I, reestablished all-male universal suffrage after his December 2 coup d'état, thus obtaining the trust of the people and their votes to continue in his presidency. Restoring universal suffrage was a decisive political gesture on the part of the president who, as a result, was perceived by the people as a true defender of civil liberties. His minister of the interior and half brother, the Duke de Morny, highlighted with much conviction the president's resolute political will to restore universal suffrage, making it impossible to separate this particular presidency from universal voting rights.

Dossier 1.2   "Honor to Universal Suffrage" (1851)

Proclamations.

The President of the Republic and his government will do everything in their power to maintain order and guarantee the security of our society, but they will always listen to the voice of public opinion and the wishes of honest men.

They did not hesitate to alter the voting rules they had taken from historical precedents but which, in the present state of our morals and electoral habits, did not sufficiently ensure the independence of the voters. The President understands that all electors are completely free to vote as they see fit, regardless of whether they exercise a public function, and regardless of whether they pursue civil or military careers. Absolute independence, complete electoral liberty, these are the wishes of Louis Napoleon Bonaparte.

Paris, December 5, 1851.
Minister of the Interior.
De Morny. (2)

After the president's coup and a sustained campaign focused on enhancing his image as guardian of universal rights, it is not surprising that the people almost unanimously gave him the authority to continue holding office in spite of his forceful takeover. In fact, with the December 21 plebiscite (a direct yes-or-no vote from the people) to determine whether Louis Napoleon Bonaparte should be the lawful leader of France, the voters gave him a landslide approval vote of 7,340,000 "yes," against only 646,000 "no" votes (with 1,500,000 abstentions).

Before resorting to force, the prince-president had hoped to convince the conservative assembly of the Second Republic to prolong his presidency by revising the constitution, which did not allow the renewal of a four-year presidential mandate. When his request was turned down, he spent the remaining time of his mandate carefully planning to overthrow the republican government by first changing key cabinet positions and then by earning popularity with the intention of reforming the severely limited universal suffrage. Once ready, he organized a quick insurgency with his army and closest political allies on the night of December 2, 1851 and dissolved the assembly. The date, December 2, was carefully chosen. It was highly symbolic to the powers-that-be, as it recalled glorious moments from the reign of his uncle, Napoleon I: his self-crowning as emperor of the French on December 2, 1804 and his victory over the Russo-Austrian Army during his most glorious and resounding war effort, the battle of Austerlitz, on December 2, 1805. December 2, as a date representing a tradition of imperial and military greatness, was already well embedded in French national consciousness after these first two historical moments. The soon-to-be emperor, Napoleon III, reinforced the significance of these dates in order to impose respect and establish his authority. For years to come the emperor would enjoy the benefits of undisputed authority, an authority that he owed almost exclusively to his faithful defense of universal voting rights that culminated in the events of 1851. Universal suffrage was clearly understood as the pillar of civil freedom and democracy, and when it was first established in 1848, it was fairly liberal, as it aimed to register all men over twenty-one years of age who had lived at the same address for at least six months and had "no record of serious felonies" or "mental problems." An important civic campaign followed, calling all male citizens to vote in order to foster a strong sense of national identity. To turn a nonvoting nation into a well-greased voting machine required that the voting principles be carefully knitted into the very fabric of national identity. French authorities set to the task of making the right to vote an intimate and indistinguishable part of being a true French citizen. They strongly advocated and implanted the idea that he who voted would truly be French. In other words, a true sense of *Frenchness* was not a birthright but a privilege acquired through the very act of voting itself. With such a strong question of identity attached to the act and significance of voting, it was not surprising that the decision made by the conservative French Assembly of the Second Republic to toughen and reduce the scope of universal suffrage to 70 percent of all male voters in 1850 was perceived as a giant step backward by many, among them, French writer and social activist Victor Hugo, ardent defender of France's universal principles. In several speeches the famous author of *Les Misérables* underlined the definitive character of universal suffrage, a right that could never be taken away, changed or reduced. For example, in his address to the assembly on May 20, 1850, he strongly reaffirmed that universal suffrage had been created as a "capital deed, an immense deed, a considerable event, which introduced a new, definitive, and irrevocable element into the State" (*Actes et paroles 1*, 358). According to him, the adopted principle of universal suffrage had forever created an irrevocable "fixed point" in French constitutional rights and democratic foundation, a point representing "the national will, legally demonstrated" (367). Hugo's argument was that the universal right to vote was a confirmed and legal right within the French electoral system that could never be retracted.

The universality at the very heart of the civic and political right to vote did not, however, include women, who continued to decry the inadequacies of a "universal" system that, throughout imperial times up to the end of the Third Republic and the Vichy government in 1944, excluded a good half of its adult, tax-paying population. Feminist writer and public speaker Maria Deraismes often spoke in the 1860s of "a pocket-size universal, leaving out half of humanity" (Huard, 189). In 1851, after the prince-president's coup, along with many who opposed it, unionist and feminist Pauline Roland was arrested and deported to Algeria, where, unbroken by this forced exile and strongly attached to her political views, she refused to admit any alleged faults. Female writer George Sand intervened successfully to obtain Roland's pardon but, exhausted by her detention, Roland subsequently died on the way back home before she could see her children again in December 1852. Her deportation and death inflamed writers like George Sand and Victor Hugo. In her honor, Hugo wrote a poem where the closing lines are

> The human race was, for her, a family,
> As her three children were humanity.
> She cried: "Progress! Love! Fraternity!"
> She opened sublime horizons to the suffering.
> When Pauline Roland had committed these crimes
> The savior of Order and the Church took her
> And threw her in prison.
>
> (*Oeuvres Poétiques* II, 132)

In Hugo's poem, the savior of the church and order is Louis Napoléon who sent Pauline to prison for what Hugo ironically calls her "criminal" activities, that is, her goodness and love of humanity. After her death, the Pauline Roland episode was far from forgotten. For generations to come, her name stood for women's rights for many who were fighting for equality and, more specifically, for the right to vote. Her case made its way into the Third Republic in an important avant-garde feminist essay, a pamphlet written in 1878 by the suffragette Hubertine Auclert, entitled *The Political Rights of Women: A Question That Was Not Treated during the International Women's Conference*. Having been refused the right to give her speech at the 1878 Women's Conference where suffrage issues were perceived as a potential distraction from the discussions on women's rights, Auclert decided to publish it anyway. While she recalled Pauline Roland's courage in this speech, she also launched an attack on the republican ideology, pointing to the hypocrisy of those who claimed "liberty, equality, fraternity" and yet excluded women from the life and politics of the republic. Auclert argued that if "woman had no rights, she therefore had no taxes; I do not vote, I do not pay" (Hause, 71). To her, the situation concerning women's right to vote in 1878 had not progressed and was no different in the political discourse of the Third Republic from what it had been during the Second Republic, when universal suffrage was hailed by deputy Victor Hugo and his followers as the "fixed point" and the fundamental key to republican liberties: only an abstract principle, but far from true in the reality of the people's voting rights. As mentioned earlier, for the Second Republic to cut back universal male suffrage in 1851 reflected the major inconsistencies between the universalism-imbued republican discourse and actual political reality. For women of the same period and long after, these inconsistencies loomed larger still. For them, being "universal," that is, equal in civic rights to their male counterparts, continued to mean nothing at all if it did not include them.

Despite what seems unequivocal in the meaning of the word "universal," many French politicians justified the liberties they took with the universal right to vote by giving new and paradoxical definitions to the word itself. For example, during the debate on the restrictive laws on voters, the deputy Adolphe Thiers, leader of the conservative *Parti de l'ordre* (Party of Order) and strong supporter of President Louis Napoleon Bonaparte, simply and oddly declared that "universal" did not mean for everyone, but for the greatest number of individuals in the spirit of the constitution. According to him and to many other politicians sitting in the National Assembly, electoral lists had to be cleansed of what he nonchalantly called the *vile multitude*, the riff-raff, the dangerous mob, entire segments, in fact, of the poor, working-class population that, according to him, had no place in the voting system and whose opinion was not deemed legitimate. In other words, Thiers looked down with utter bourgeois contempt at the many men forming an otherwise urgently needed work force. These workers were living in appalling and unsanitary conditions, and moving in and out of crowded *garnis*, low-end rentals, usually small, shared rooms, as they could not afford permanent lodging. The "transient" nature of this population provided Thiers and his conservative fellow deputies with an opportunity to modify voting principles. They voted to deny the right to vote to working-class French citizens who could not establish a three-year continuous residency in any given region. Migrant workers employed in the expanded and prosperous industrial sectors brought about by the new industrial age were then cut off from their civic duties, and therefore also from a sense of national identity. In the end, despite their stated commitment to enforce the democratic principles of the French Revolution, the "inexperienced" leaders of the Second Republic ended up enraging the "universal man" that their predecessors of 1789 had first created, by taking away some of his universal rights, thus reducing his national and personal sense of *Frenchness*. The historical irony of this situation is that when Louis Napoleon Bonaparte challenged the censorship imposed on universal suffrage, he effectively fought a battle in favor of republican ideals in order to become emperor. Championing the universal character of his nation won him almost twenty years of liberal politics in a nonetheless autocratic empire. His rise to power proved that universalism had a solid foundation and a brilliant future in France and that December 2, 1851 would remain the symbolic date of this new order as reflected in his printed call to all Frenchmen to rally to his cause.

Dossier 1.3 Speech to the French People by Louis-Napoléon Bonaparte (December 2, 1851)

The current situation cannot continue any longer. Each day our country is facing more danger. The Assembly elected to represent order is now filled with traitors. Even its three hundred most patriotic members have been unable to stop this fatal tendency. Instead of preparing laws of common interest, it is heading for civil war; it is attempting to seize the power which I hold directly from the people, it is encouraging evil passions and compromising France's peace. I have dissolved it and I have asked the people to judge between the Assembly and me. As you know, the Constitution was drafted in order to weaken in advance the power that you were going to confer on me. Six million votes were a striking protest against it, and yet I observed it faithfully. Provocation, slander and outrage have not affected me. But now that the fundamental pact is no longer respected by those very representatives who continually invoke it, and when the men who have destroyed two monarchies want to tie my hands to overthrow the Republic, my duty is to thwart their treacherous schemes, to maintain the Republic at all costs and to save the country by asking the solemn judgment of the only sovereign I recognize in France: the people.

Therefore, with all my heart I call upon the entire nation, and I beg of you to choose another leader if you wish to maintain such a feeble situation which is degrading and compromising to your future, as I do not want any part of a power unable to spread goodness, refuse to be responsible for its unavoidable bad actions, and do not wish to be captain of a sinking ship.

If on the other hand you trust me, give me the means to accomplish the great mission for which you have appointed me. This mission consists in closing once for all the era of revolutions while satisfying the legitimate need of the people by protecting its interest from subversive passions. It also consists in creating durable institutions that will survive beyond this age in order to constitute the final foundations upon which men can build a solid future.

I submit the following points to your deliberations:

1. *A Head of State elected for ten years by universal all-male suffrage.*
2. *Ministers responsible only to the Head of State.*
3. *A Council of State composed of the most distinguished men.*
4. *A Legislative body; and*
5. *A Senate composed of illustrious men.*
   Louis Napoléon Bonaparte. (1)

This solemn speech clearly spelled out the reestablishment of universal male suffrage, the unconditional defense of the republic, the promise of peace, and, in general, it outlined the president's program for a new constitution made in the interest of the people and by a leader appointed by the people. In principle, it looked solid and appealing, but it was an almost perfect copy of the 1799 program proposed by Napoleon I before *his* coup. Would history repeat itself, would the prince-president seek to become emperor after appealing to the people, was the republic in danger of being replaced by an empire? For now, the people trusted the prince-president and liked his stand on universal suffrage, but the opposition led by Victor Hugo had already foreseen the similarities between the two Napoleons and the danger the prince-president represented to the current republic. On July 19, 1851, Hugo spoke loudly and clearly at the National Assembly about the looming empire incarnated in the prince-president. He tried to warn the deputies that the president's ambition was to become emperor, like his uncle, but that he would only be "little" compared to his "great" predecessor. Hugo asked rhetorically how "Napoleon the Little" could possibly be any better than his uncle. His fears and predictions caught up with reality when, on December 2, it became clear that the prince-president, borrowing his ideology from his uncle and designing a constitution in conformity with that of Napoleon I, would probably seek to become emperor. His speech alone projected the image painted by Hugo of a prince-president either "little" or at least with little political imagination, as he modeled his coup and his constitution after the "great" Napoleon I.

The day following the coup, Hugo immediately reacted by organizing spontaneous protests in defense of the republic that he knew was doomed if Napoleon were not stopped immediately. He put together a "Committee of Resistance" and called the prince-president an outlaw who needed to be removed by force. Some responded by building barricades; members of the bourgeoisie and deputies wearing tri-colored sashes marched in the streets, and more crowds gathered to fight the armed soldiers, but in general the rebellion was not united or well organized, and many workers did not see the point of fighting for what appeared to them to be a bourgeois cause. In *L'Education Sentimentale*, Flaubert wrote of the working-class sentiment toward the December 2 coup and subsequent protests when his main character, Frédéric Moreau, after having asked a worker to join in the protest, received the reply: "We're not so dumb as to get ourselves killed for the bourgeois! Let them deal with this by themselves" (446). Throughout France, it seemed that workers in general remained apathetic to the turmoil and did not answer the intellectuals' call to fight a battle that they did not feel concerned them. The rebellion remained mild and was easily crushed on December 4; some 10,000 prisoners were sent to Algeria, and Hugo also left France on a long exile, first in Belgium, then on the island of Guernsey in the English Channel. In Belgium he wrote and published a full version of *Napoleon the Little* in which he continued to attack Louis Napoleon, criticizing not only his politics, but also his physique and his character: "medium height, cold, pale, slow, who looks as if he were not quite awake [. . .] he is a vulgar, childish, theatrical and vain character" (30–31).

We shall see in chapter 2 that what he lacked in political skill and poise the future emperor would make up in cultural development, bringing immense respect and prestige to France by transforming its infrastructure and by launching a colonial campaign. At the time, however, Hugo's prediction proved to be true, as Louis Napoleon did become emperor on December 2, 1852.

Almost a year later, on November 21, 1852, the Second Empire was approved by plebiscite. Having been president of the Second Republic and now promising to be the emperor of a stable Second Empire, Louis Napoleon Bonaparte, now called Emperor Napoleon III, was unquestionably trusted by the majority of the people— the aristocrats, the bourgeois, and the workers together—to lead a long-awaited quiet political era, "to close the era of revolutions," and to carry universalism to its next level as a durable foundation for future regimes. On December 2, 1852, Louis Napoleon Bonaparte officially became emperor as had his uncle, Napoleon I, forty-eight years before him. For better or worse, "The dynasty of the Bonapartes" was back, this time by the will of the people who had overwhelmingly and almost unanimously voted for the political return of Napoleon III as an able and reliable leader with universal appeal.

Courbet's Realism: Art for All

As if carried by the same wave of sweeping universalism, the art world would likewise come to a crucial juncture in 1851. This was the year when Gustave Courbet's famous painting "Burial at Ornans"—painted in 1849 but exhibited in the winter of 1850–1851—became the subject of a roaring controversy on the universality of man in artistic representation. In the world of fine arts, a world defined by the old and venerated Academy of the Arts, founded in 1648 during the reign of King Louis XIV, not all creatures were created equal. In academic terms, only historical figures, men and women of the highest social consideration, or mythological characters were worthy of being represented on canvas. Paintings were first judged by the academy and then exposed at the official annual art exhibit called the "Salon" where the general public would go to admire them. There were no other recognized public or private venues for the effective circulation of art. Courbet had had a hard time getting his paintings accepted at the Salon. Between 1841 and 1847, only three of his paintings were exhibited, but more were shown in 1848 due to a glitch in the system: no jury was consulted that year. In 1849, he finally achieved his first measure of success with "After Dinner at Ornans," which received the gold medal. It was obvious from the start that Courbet's paintings were slightly different from the usual representations, as he painted a plain and simple provincial life inspired from his own upbringing in Ornans, a small town East of Paris. As a Parisian artist by adoption, he nonetheless felt a kinship with the simple farming world of Ornans, not forgetting that his father was a modest farmer.

As long as Courbet's commonplace representations were believed to be of a Romantic nature, no real offense to institutional art was deemed to have been committed. This situation would change when his alleged Romanticism all of a sudden became an unacceptable form of realism, identified and recognized by many conventional art critics with whom he quickly fell out of favor. In their eyes, art was a much too elevated cultural form to accommodate representations of everyday life, of "real" life from all of its inconsequential angles. The other "Ornans painting" by Courbet, "Burial at Ornans," opened the controversy about realism and about the choice of painting subjects and their relevance to the art world. The way "Burial at Ornans" acquired its status as realist art, and attracted the spite of many art critics, was largely due to the "intellectual" attention it received from a recognized literary and journalistic figure, Jules Husson—known by his pen name Champfleury—who, apart from being a novelist and an art critic, also became the leading apologist of the realist movement in France. Champfleury consecrated Courbet as the consummate realist painter when he reinforced his definition of realism as a new school of thought through the unique example of Courbet's paintings. Champfleury had already written favorable articles on "Burial at Ornans" in 1851. He admired the objectivity of the painter, his lack of interpretation, and the simple execution of the scene. He was one of the few journalists to acclaim the young painter who seemed so banal and vulgar to others. He subsequently developed his initial argument about Courbet's unassuming paintings into a full-scale conceptualization of realism when in 1855 he published in the journal L'Artiste an open letter to the writer Georges Sand on the subject matter. This article was considered the true manifesto of realism. The context for the article was the 1855 Paris Universal Exposition, where Courbet organized his own private exhibit within the perimeter of the exposition at his own expense, after two of his best paintings ("Burial at Ornans" and "The Painter's Studio") had been refused by the jury of the exposition. Champfleury supported Courbet's decision to show the paintings regardless of the jury's verdict. For the occasion, he rekindled his 1851 explosive praise of "Burial at Ornans" with even more passion than before: "What incredible gall, it is the subversion of all institutions as represented by the jury, it is a direct appeal to the public, it is freedom itself" (Du Réalisme, 67). The painting, described as an audacious assault on institutionalized art and a direct call to an all-encompassing public, ended up being symbolic of freedom according to Champfleury. It is true that in "Burial at Ornans" Courbet allowed a universal sense of freedom to enter the composition and interpretation of the painting. Not only did he give artistic consideration to all socioeconomic classes of human beings—all villagers from Ornans regardless of their social status, simple people and notables who are gathered to pay their last respects—but he also painted them life-size, a privilege until then reserved for religious, royal, and bourgeois figures. This "realistic" sizing of peasants and villagers shocked the bourgeois and their exclusive sense of "high" art, and critics spoke of the painting as a scandal that degraded art. Champfleury challenged these notions by presenting a modern view of real life and real size representation through a derisive comparison between the common man and the noble figure:

> Mister Courbet is seditious for having represented in good faith life-size bourgeois, peasants, and village women. This was his critics' first point. They do not want to admit that a quarry worker is as worthy as a prince: the nobility is upset because Courbet has given so many yards of canvas to simple people; only monarchs have the right to be painted standing up, with their medals, embroidered garments, and their official look. What? How dare a man from Ornans, a peasant in his coffin, gather a considerable crowd at his burial: farmers and people of lowly background, thus giving this painting the same development that Largillière himself gave to magistrates going to the Holy Spirit mass. When Velasquez painted great figures, they were Spanish lords and infantas, with silk and gold on their clothes, decorations and bouquets of feathers. Of course Van der Helst did paint life size bourgeois, but at least the appearance of their clothes saved these heavy Flemish from criticism. (*Du Réalisme*, 70)

There is a deeply felt irony in Champfleury's remarks about the presumed unthinkable representation of poor and simple villagers on Courbet's canvas when he cynically compares them to the noble figures of so-called classical merit by Largillière, Velásquez, and Van der Helst. Still ironically, Champfleury suggests that Courbet must indeed be "seditious," a rebel who dares to paint reality in classical format thus elevating the commoners to a place traditionally reserved for "great figures." In the world of art, the painting became associated with a fatal *coup de canon* (firing of the cannon) (*Du Réalisme*, 71–72) to the French artistic tradition. First, it was an unusually large canvas—seven by three and a half meters—representing forty-six common Ornansians gathered at a burial. Second, Courbet shocked the lofty and traditional world of the state-regulated academic arts by presenting not only the banality of everyday life but also what was considered a grotesque representation of the ugly, deformed, and alcoholic faces of the good people of Ornans, as they were described by the hostile press of the time. Representing the opposite viewpoint, the Socialist and art critic François Sabatier-Ungher, one of the very few favorable voices, wrote: "Here comes democracy in the arts" (Ferrier, 9–10). His was the explosive remark that made "Burial at Ornans" the talk of the town in 1851 and the first scandal in the world of modern art. More scandals would follow: for example, Manet's 1863 paintings "Luncheon on the Grass" representing two contemporary men realistically depicted while picnicking with a naked woman in a public park, and "Olympia" the Parisian prostitute staring at us from across the canvas with her piercing gaze while fully stretched out naked on her bed, and, a little later, Gustave Courbet's own "The Origin of the World" (1866), where the artist depicts a woman's naked lower body with her legs opened, and her sex exposed in a lascivious frontal position. For these paintings it was not the nude in and of itself that shocked the viewers, as the nude was an accepted form of representation in painting, but, rather, the nonchalant "realistic" and contemporary air they conveyed beyond the frame that made them unacceptable to art critics and connoisseurs.

Courbet shook the world of art with his unconventional representation of provincial people and was labeled vulgar by an embittered art press that could not place the painting in any known categories or recognized schools. In reality, the people gathered at the funeral in Ornans were no more "vulgar" than simply being themselves, painted in their natural milieu, in their natural light, without any other design than to present a slice of real life, simply as it was. However, it was still too early for a comfortable level of bourgeois tolerance toward the "popular" in the realm of the fine arts. Art remained in the bourgeois eye the exclusive domain of high culture, classical and preserved in its ivory tower by the strict censors of the academy. With Courbet, the word and the concept of "popular," defined as the life of simple, unromantic, and plain, everyday people captured in their natural environment, broke into the highly selective world of art; art would never be the same, and the "popular," meaning "of the people" would not either.

Population, Popularity, and the Popular

In 1851, the population of France was approximately 35,783,000 and the birth rate remained alarmingly low. The reasons for such a low birth rate are difficult to gauge, but it seems that in the nascent modern and industrial age of the mid-nineteenth century, children were perceived as costing more money than before, and families became conscious and wary of the additional financial burden brought on by a large family. In addition, the French, under the influence of early nineteenth-century Malthusian theory feared overpopulation. This theory contributed to setting the norm among middle-class families at an average of two children in order to ensure a more comfortable life for the family and a more secure social future for their children who, around the time and according to bourgeois spirit, began to acquire real individual and social status and value within the family context. Conversely, working-class families had many children, but crowded and unsanitary living conditions brought on a number of fatal diseases, tuberculosis being the most notorious. It would not be long before the miserable social conditions of the poor and their high rate of mortality would be seen through the lens of the dominant scientific discourse on natural selection, Darwin's *The Origin of Species* (1859). In light of Darwinian theory or, rather, of the uses made of it, the poor would thus form a "degenerate" category of human beings that needed to be controlled if the human race was to survive as a strong species and outlive the dangerous primitive conditions of the "inferior" classes. Darwin's view of the "survival of the fittest" permeated the Second Empire (1852–1870), but only became of primordial importance in regulating the "masses" during the Third Republic (1870–1940). Fear of degeneracy also found a name and a place in literature. It was called "naturalism," and it reduced the notion of realism to a theory of biological and social determinism against which only death could prevail. The writer Emile Zola led the naturalist movement and illustrated his philosophy in an impressive series of twenty novels in which he portrayed the demise of the working-class family during the Second Empire. The *Rougon-Macquart* series, subtitled "*Natural and Social History of a Family during the Second Empire*," 1870–1893, recounts the saga of a family that cannot escape its "natural" milieu and its biological destiny. Because his books were conceived and written as "real stories" of life during the Second Empire, they read more like scientific studies of social mores than works of fiction. Zola's work reflects the general status of poor people during the Second Empire, people whose conditions put them more at risk of dying young than the more socially protected middle class, despite and, as some believed, because of progress in science and industry. Based on the principle of scientific determinism, each volume of the *Rougon-Macquart* presented a society where materialism had replaced religious belief, especially in urban centers like Paris, which had so much *material excitement* to offer that religious practices became almost obsolete there. The waning of religion was accompanied by a decline in the population. Only regions like Brittany, the North, or the Center with strong attachments to Catholic princi-ples seemed spared by the slowing demographic growth as couples in these parts of France continued to have many children. In general, the French, especially the urban middle class were cautious about the number of members in the family. The result was a slow population growth in France that resulted in the desperate need to bring foreigners to compensate for the lack of manual laborers.

In 1851, immigration began to have a sizable impact on the dwindling French population. Fearing the economic consequences of a diminishing labor force, France could only, and effectively did, "welcome" these immigrants. Despite its unstated but fundamental social fear of others, France officially became the first country to allow massive immigration, a *terre d'accueil*, a land of both opportunity and shelter for foreigners in need of a new life, a new job, and, eventually, a new citizenship. To make its good intentions official, in 1851, the French government developed an accommodating reform of citizenship laws, instituting a double *jus soli*, a Latin term meaning double right of the soil, whereby a foreign individual born in France of foreign parents also born on French territory was automatically awarded French citizenship. With this new law, the borders were opened wide, facilitating the arrival of many newcomers. According to the 1851 census—the first accurate statistical pop-ulation survey done in France—immigrants, coming mostly from bordering coun-tries like Belgium, Italy, and Spain, constituted 1.05 percent of the population in 1851, for a total of 379,289 people. Official statistics reveals the French administra-tion's desire to adopt a more "scientific" basis for organizing and creating accurate records of its population. From 1851 on, questions of demography fell under the banner of universal scientific research. However, despite the real intention to elimi-nate the uncertainties of the old census, the new statistical methods of establishing scientific evidence of French demographics, while better in principle, still suffered from some degree of error.

Aside from the growing number of foreigners, numerous migrants from rural France also converged on city centers, where jobs were more lucrative and excite-ment and entertainment more appealing than in the countryside. Even with such movement toward cities, France remained economically dependent on its abundant rural and agricultural resources. Despite the upward demographic trend resulting from the population of new immigrants, the total number of Frenchmen remained low. However, population density, both French and foreign, increased around city centers, with the result that this new urban dynamic was not entirely consistent with the official statistics, which indicated that the population in France was still slowly shrinking.

For bourgeois society of mid-nineteenth-century France, booming industrial life was changing and modernizing everyday life, especially in cities, both because it improved the quality of the products offered to the people, and because it paved way for an efficient new communication and transportation systems. Merchandise and people travelled more easily and more rapidly during the Second Empire than ever before as the emperor recognized the urgency of building more roads and of extending the reach of the railroads in order to overcome traffic saturation within the existing transportation network. As a result of his vision for a highly efficient train system, the building of an important railroad network was undertaken. At 3,000 kilometers in 1850, it jumped to 17,000 kilometers in 1870, reaching 45,000 kilometers by the end of the century. In Paris, an important peripheral train line was inaugurated in 1851. The extraordinary development of a system of rails, bridges, stations, locomotives, and wagons called for an extraordinary budget, extraordinary resources in iron, steel, and energy, and a no less extraordinary mobilization of labor throughout France. France met this challenge head-on and the results were nothing short of a tour de force in industrial development. During these intense and prosperous times France became a major international economic player whose only real competitor was Britain.

The development of the railroad system gave a major boost to the tourist industry. It brought many people to French cities as well as to southern coastal resorts that were previously hard to reach. Leisure visitors, chief among them the British aristocracy and bourgeoisie, for whom France had always been a favorite destination, were now coming in larger numbers. As they preferred to spend their leisure time in picturesque cities like Nice on the French Riviera or in the streets and restaurants of the French capital more than at any other location, tourism was the only industry in which the British did not attempt to compete with the French. In the mid-nineteenth century, British tourists began arriving in large numbers by steamboats across the Channel and then by train all the way to Paris and other parts of France. Some British visitors came to spend a few days, while others came to stay much longer. Even prior to the French Industrial Revolution in the first half of the century, there was a general feeling among the British that Paris was "far superior to London" (Gerbod, 117), superior in the beauty of its monuments, its long and spacious avenues, its cafés and gardens. Around the same time, Mrs. Trollope, a popular British author, wrote about the streets of Paris, the Tuileries gardens, the Madeleine church, and in general, how she found the French capital "happy and luminous." These early visitors came at the very beginning of the transportation revolution, before the modern transformation of Paris by Baron Haussmann. Even so, their feeling of fulfillment as they came to the French capital reflected a sentiment that would endure among the British when considering their French neighbor's cities and resorts. The feeling that nineteenth-century France had more *quality* and more beauty to offer than England would become widespread among the British bourgeoisie who, when they came to France, enjoyed living, even momentarily, in a society "more free, more entertaining and more *égalitaire* than their own" (Gerbod, 121). For these British travellers, France seemed more modern, more open, and more flexible than their own society, which, oddly enough, was the most advanced in its industrial revolution.

Given France's booming tourist industry and the increasing population in and around city centers, it seems logical that the visitors as well as the ever-growing working-class population, along with the already flourishing bourgeoisie, would be searching for fresh venues to entertain themselves within the limits of their respective means. Home life had always been the privileged center of social activity for much of the aristocracy, and later for the bourgeoisie, who usually brought entertainers to their residence. It was also central for the peasants, who enjoyed their private life at the farm with their own family. With the excitement of industrial times, social life shifted to public space. City dwellers, especially, deserted their homes to go out for long walks and to sit at newly opened cafés and restaurants; they felt the enthusiasm of the times and were ready to be part of it. They were no doubt responsible for the boost in the number and the popularity of cafés and restaurants of all kinds, as demand exceeded existing availability. It is commonly accepted that the notion of cafés and restaurants often overlapped during these times. A café was often a restaurant offering food and drinks and vice versa. Eating out was more than ever before an option for nearly everyone with little or lots of money, regardless of social status. Workers and bourgeois ate out, albeit in different restaurants. There were simple restaurants where people of modest means "ate" a basic meal, and others where the bourgeois population "dined" in great style and consumed intimidating quantities. Le Véry in the neighborhood of the Palais Royal was highly sophisticated, while Restaurant Philippe offered an eighteen-hour feast each Saturday to a group of refined, big eaters named the "club of the great stomachs." "French cuisine" was not new, as it was a well-established French tradition, but eating in a public place—indeed even the term "restaurant"—was a fairly recent activity that dated only from the mid-eighteenth century. It is at the beginning of the nineteenth century that the fate of cuisine as a refined sense of human taste, coupled with the skills and talents of cooking, was sealed in the words and thoughts of the politician, lawyer, and gastronome Jean-Anthelme Brillat-Savarin who wrote the bible of culinary philosophy: The Physiology of Taste or Meditations on Transcendent Gastronomy (dedicated to Parisian gastronomes) in 1825. His work celebrated and consecrated cuisine as a French art form. Brillat-Savarin closely associates cooking and eating with basic human pleasures and happiness as reflected in one of his many aphorisms collected in the preface of the book: "The discovery of a new dish confers more happiness on humanity than the discovery of a new star" (4). Food is here presented as an extraordinary human discovery surpassing discoveries in the sciences. In fact, the sensation provided by taste also competes in Brillat-Savarin's words with physical love. In this light, he describes the mouth as the primary human organ for taste and pleasure, more complete in the sensations it provides than sex itself.

Having challenged science and sex, Brillat-Savarin's book on the pleasures of the table extended its reach to all humanity and indeed became a manifesto of universalism: "The pleasure of the table belongs to all ages, to all conditions, to all countries, and to all areas; it mingles with all other pleasures, and remains at last to console us for their departure" (3).

Brillat-Savarin's assessment of the "pleasures of the table" would subsequently be borne out by changes in French eating habits, as restaurants and cafés became privileged emblems of the "universal" character of the French. By the mid-nineteenth century, occasional visitors and customers became permanent and faithful patrons of cafés, an institution that we can qualify today as the national social space for all Frenchmen, old and young, rich and poor, bourgeois and working class.

However, despite his brilliant understanding of the need of human beings to rejoice in food, Brillat-Savarin did not make a strong case for their taste and desire for alcohol. In his 1851 article on "wine and hashish," refined dandy, flâneur, and wine-drinker Charles Baudelaire, the illustrious poet who actually devoted a full section of his (in)famous 1857 book of poetry, *Flowers of Evil*, to wine, remarked severely on the near absence of references to the drink in Brillat-Savarin's otherwise respected work. In contrast, he advocated the reading of E.T.A. Hoffmann's musical writings, *Kreisleriana*, where the German author establishes strong affinities between different types of music and different types of wine (*Oeuvres 1*, 378). In the mid-nineteenth century, drinking wine was a social activity highly respected and practiced mainly by the middle class. Yet, despite their appreciation for drinking, potential middle-class café clients were often more driven by the simple desire to "go out" and meet other people than by the need to have a meal or even a drink. The social quality intrinsically associated with the mere frequenting of cafés became more popular than the eating or drinking themselves, defining the very nature of the places where these activities took place.

The quality and clientele of the cafés were determined by the social status of the neighborhoods in which they were located. For example, in Paris, workers and people of modest means lived mainly on the left bank of the Seine river, while wealthy and cultivated people preferred the refinement of more opulent areas on the right bank like the *grands boulevards* (the main boulevards), the area around the Palais Royal, the Boulevard des Italiens, and, later on, the modernized Champs-Elysées.

Before ranking as the most fashionable and commercial thoroughfare in the world, the Champs-Elysées, created in the seventeenth century as an extension of the Tuileries Gardens, was, in the mid-nineteenth century, considered a connector between the capital and *en vogue* towns like Saint Cloud and Longchamp, where newly popularized horse races took place as early as 1856. Originally, the races attracted only upper-class crowds, but eventually became a more widespread pastime, opened to all classes with money to bet on horses. Along the Champs-Elysées as well as in other privileged sections of town, street configuration and life were transformed by the new placement of a great number of cafés. These cafés developed into elegant and mandatory stops on the way to the races that only the rich could afford. Soon, these stopovers became almost more pleasant than going to the races themselves. This was especially true when the Champs-Elysées was reworked into the most remarkable and scenic promenade in the city: spacious sidewalks still dotted with the legendary trees, and augmented with streetlights and fountains, thus proving that the Modern—gas lighting, sidewalks, new buildings, cafés—did not sprout in contradiction to the Natural—trees, gardens, clean water from fountains. The Champs-Elysées, with its café life and its urban and agreeable surroundings, served as the enviable model of a modern urban infrastructure, both cultivated and beautiful. It represented the ideal of all boulevards, a modern place where people relaxed in cafés and leisurely strolled around to see others and to be seen, a formidable gathering place, and, naturally, a place of historic proportions: it is there that the French national holiday ("Bastille Day") has been celebrated every July 14, since 1880, that General de Gaulle triumphantly entered the city when France was liberated in 1944, that major world sporting events are celebrated, like the 1998 French soccer victory at the World Cup, or where such events take place, such as the final stage of the world's most famous bicycle race, the "Tour de France." Finally, it is there that millions of Parisians and visitors go to feel the pulse of Paris. The *Champs*, as it is familiarly called, holds an important symbolic value for French cultural representation both inside and outside of France.

Cafés were not only an enhancement to rich bourgeois life, but also widespread places of gathering and entertainment for all classes. Smaller, simpler cafés were also sprouting up in less prosperous parts of town. In fact, the number of upper-class cafés did not grow nearly as fast as that of simpler cafés and sordid estaminets that proliferated significantly in modest and poor parts of the city and its suburbs.

Figure 1.1   Le Petit Mazas, cabaret in Levallois-Perret, northwestern suburb of Paris (1871)

Squalid and rough taverns were common in suburbs like Levallois-Perret and Clichy, and within Paris, as for example in sections of the left bank, such as on and around the rue Mouffetard, or in the neighborhood of the Faubourg Saint Marcel. Throughout Paris, there were cafés similar to this one in which ordinary people would congregate. Street people like ragpickers, ordinary women, and weary workers, all sharing long tables and rustic benches, some conversing and smoking their pipe while others looked as if they were drifting sadly in their own somber thoughts, as bottles of strong alcohol were readily available on every table. (© L'Illustration)

There, hard and cheap alcohols, like eau-de-vie, a sort of strong and cheap brandy, were often favored, providing quick and sustained intoxication to consumers searching for efficient and inexpensive ways to momentarily disconnect from their miserable lives. For the poor population, cafés were also a place where, surprisingly enough, everyone could get a safe drink, an alcoholic but noncontaminated drink, unlike the water available in these areas. Ironically, drinking hard liquor diminished the danger that the poor would become sick and even die from frequent and fatal epidemics brought on by contaminated water, such as the cholera epidemic that struck Paris twice during the nineteenth century. On the other hand, in the sophisticated cafés of the boulevards, artists, journalists, and wealthy people liked to gather in order to exchange political, philosophical, and artistic ideas while consuming wine and beer. In these establishments, as mentioned before, it was common to meet people more interested in talking than drinking.

Throughout the second half of the century, the social north-south separation of Paris would gradually change. In 1859–1860 the Paris city limits were extended beyond its center to officially incorporate districts and small villages around the inner Parisian belt, thus forming the Paris of today with its twenty arrondissements. From 1860 on, the socioeconomic division of the cafés reflected this new configuration of the city, and it gradually transformed into an east-west division. Western parts of the city, such as the newly annexed sixteenth arrondissement, would harbor a well-to-do population, while on the eastern side a modest to poor working-class population settled in areas like the twentieth arrondissement, also recently incorporated to the city. Throughout the nineteenth century and more so after the 1850s, café life and status greatly depended on the social and political movements within the city. The number and quality of establishments relentlessly followed the growing desire of the people to be socially connected or separated. Cafés followed and defined French people wherever they went.

During the mid-nineteenth century, the growing number of cafés and cabarets— as some of these cafés also offered music, shows, and public dancing—and their increasing popularity earned them the name *salons de la démocratie* (salons of democracy). This expression, first coined by journalist Hippolyte Castille, was rein- forced by sociologist Alfred Delvau who, in his 1862 *Anecdotal History of Cafés*, observed that they gather all Parisian social classes "the highest to the lowest, the most noble to the vilest" (vii).

Cafés became the new space of sociability for a new generation of modern Frenchmen, rich or poor who, for the most part, had replaced going to church with going to the café, where they discussed life, culture, and, especially, politics. In *Le Ventre de Paris* (*The Belly of Paris*, 1873) Zola gives an example of a political café, Lebigre, named after his owner, where opponents of the regime regularly meet to drink and plot a revolution against the empire. The language used to describe the café often compares and opposes modernity with traditional religious elements:

> Monsieur Lebigre was the proprietor of a very fine establishment, fitted up in the modern luxurious style. [. . .] The counter or "bar" on the right looked especially rich and glittered like polished silver. Its zinc-work, hanging with a broad bulging border over the substructure of white and red marble, edged it with a rippling sheet of metal as if it were some high altar laden with embroidery. [. . .] On the left, moreover, was a metal urn, serving as a receptacle for gratuities; while a similar one on the right bristled with a fan-like arrangement of coffee spoons. (144–145)

We see here the modern defined in terms of new materials like the glittering zinc, while the traditional is highlighted by the use of marble and embroidered cloth. Further on, beyond the strict context of the bar, the comparison between the bar and the altar points to the crucial moment when the culture of the church was being slowly phased out to be replaced by that of the café. Finally, the juxtaposition of the two urns, one for donations, as is commonly seen in churches, and the other presenting a display of coffee spoons, marks the overlapping of the two worlds as a cultural sign of transition from the religious to the modern, from the traditional to the new, from the solid and solemn marble of the altar to the shiny and exciting metal of the bar.

After the 1789 revolution, many churches were sold and destroyed, and attendance was essentially reduced to women and children while men gradually thronged to the cafés that did not seem to open soon enough. In all of France there were 100,000 establishments in 1789, compared to 500,000 in 1914. In Paris alone there were 3,000 cafés in 1789, and 22,000 in 1870. Their number stabilized around 33,000 in Paris alone at the end of the century; yet the demand kept on growing.

The café was a place the workers called home and where they could meet, speak, and even organize themselves politically, while also drinking and eating. In other words, for working-class café-goers, drinking was not the primary purpose either, gathering was. Eighty percent of all drinking establishments catered to the working class and were run by married couples using their children as servers, while bourgeois cafés, although larger and more flamboyant, were in the minority. There the setting was plush and comfortable, and professional waiters rather than relatives served a well-off clientele.

In 1851, *Le Divan Le Peletier*, situated on rue Le Peletier across from the Opera, near the Boulevard des Italiens, was a renowned literary café already in the last throes of its twenty-year stretch of popularity. Opened in 1809, it was insignificant until it was revamped in the mid-1830s to welcome the increasingly elegant crowd of opera-goers. Instead of becoming a post-opera place of entertainment, however, it attracted a steady stream of illustrious literary figures, like the Romantic writer and poet Alfred de Musset and assorted fashionable bohemians, who came more for the lively discussions than the fare being served. It is no wonder that this light-drinking crowd brought *Le Divan* to its decline and bankruptcy during the Second Empire, finally closing its doors in 1859. In 1851, one would most likely meet there the writer and bookworm Charles Asselineau, the poet and art critic Charles Baudelaire; also joining in were the poet Gérard de Nerval and the novelist Henry Murger. Still using the café as he had in the 1830s was the old and elegant bohemian editor Guichardet, who did not lose his manners despite his addiction to absinthe, a hallucinogenic drink in vogue in the mid-nineteenth century. At *Le Divan*, you would almost always meet the outspoken Jewish writer and intellectual Alexandre Weill, as well as the two novelists and historians, but also opinionated socialites, Edmond and Jules, the Goncourt brothers, and, later in the 1850s, their friend the renowned and brilliant journalist and polemicist Aurélien Scholl, who moved from the Bordeaux area to Paris in 1851 and successively worked at *L'Artiste,* *L'Illustration,* and *Le Figaro* before founding his own newspaper *Le Nain Jaune* in 1863. Apart from the nonstop conversations, one of the clientele's favorite ways of passing the evening at *Le Divan* was to play, for hours on end, the popular game of *misti* or *mistron*, a sort of poker game that could take its players through closing time. In their lifelong journal, the Goncourt brothers recall one of these evenings in May 1856 at *Le Divan*: "*Le Divan* on Peletier street. It's a stupid, nasty little place where at night bands of lowly gentlemen gather. They are to literature what paperboys are to journalism [. . .] There, we drink bad beer; we play a game of *mistron*. Gavarni, who only went there once, claims that this is place where gold canes' heads are sawed right off" (124). As *Le Divan* was not a first-class café, the Goncourts, used to lavish surroundings and austere social gatherings, saved appearances and status by first criticizing the very nature of the café as a "stupid, nasty little place" before letting themselves be conquered by the exciting ambiance, the bad beer and the game of *mistron*.

Dossier 1.4   Théodore de Banville's "Le Divan Le Peletier" (1852)

A frequent visitor to *Le Divan*, Théodore de Banville, poet, essayist, and leader of the Parnasse movement, the celebrated "art for art's sake" literary movement that brought together some of the most famous poets of the nineteenth century, wrote a poem in honor of the establishment, entitled "Le Divan Le Peletier" that immortalized the place and its *habitués*.

In the poem, Banville expressed how *Le Divan* was a place where *l'esprit moderne* (the modern spirit) was always a favorite topic of conversation and a major cause for argument among café-goers, as it was a novel concept that still needed to be sorted out, "winnowed."

Le Divan Le Peletier

This famous couch is a winnower
Where the modern spirit is been winnowed.
More absolutist than Yvan,
This famous couch is a winnower.
There, jokers from the Morvan
Overcome the Lernean hydra.
This famous couch is a winnower
Where the modern spirit is winnowed.
There, Guichardet, like a god,
Displays his worthy and vermilion nose.
Here, dwarfs without eyes;
There, Guichardet, like a god,
Murger, it is quite expensive,
Writes words for a hundred cents a line
There, Guichardet, like a god,
Shows his worthy and vermilion nose.

One sees the sweet Asselineau
Sitting near the savage Baudelaire.
Like a Muscovite in a sledge,
One sees the sweet Asselineau.
More bitter than a green almond,
While the other one is like an angry Goethe.
One sees the sweet Asselineau
Sitting near the savage Baudelaire.
There one also meets Babou
Who makes of this place his Capua.
With his quill like a bamboo,
There one also meets Babou.
On his left, a silly little poet

Dispatches a silly little ode.
There one also meets Babou
Who makes of this place his Capua.

Close to the harmonious Stadler,
Still shines La Madelène.
Emmanuel looks up in the air,
Close to harmonious Stadler.
Voillemot sees in a flash
The phantom of Helen.
Close to the harmonious Stadler
Still shines la Madelène.

The couch close to the Opera
Is an orchestra for discordant voices.
We do not know the magician who created
The couch close to the Opera.
When these immortal voices are gone,
We will pay to contemplate their graves.
The couch close to the Opera
Is an orchestra for discordant voices. (September 1852 [Oeuvres 1, 228–230])

As he made his own comments on the poem and the café it celebrated, Banville qualified the establishment as the "true circle of French literature" (372–373) and laments its closing and demolition in 1859. His poem would keep alive the spirit of the café and the sentiment of modernity that defined its multifaceted clientele. In his comments, Banville briefly identifies some of the figures he mentions in his poem: Guichardet, Musset's old friend; Stadler, the refined poet and dramatist; Emmanuel, the scientist who should have been treated as a contemporary Galileo but remained unknown to the history of Science; the journalist and writer Hyppolite Babou; writer and businessman, Henri de la Madelène; official painter of the Second Empire, André-Charles Voillemot; and, of course, famous writers like Charles Baudelaire and Henri Murger; and a motley array of anonymous customers, jokers, dwarfs, aspiring young poets, and drinkers who contributed to the diversity and the liveliness of the café. Bohemians, poets, scientists, painters, entrepreneurs, editors, everyday people, all met at *Le Divan*, all representing what Banville calls the "discordant" but nevertheless dynamic "voices" of modernity. Within the informal setting of the café, they discussed, wrote, and painted the rapidly changing face of the world and presented us with the new face of modernity, a new and visibly mixed multitude with contrasted social backgrounds.

Modernity for the People: *Les Halles*

Architect Victor Baltard's project of rebuilding the *grandes Halles*, the covered wholesale marketplace in the heart of Paris, was inaugurated by the prince-president, Louis Napoleon Bonaparte on September 15, 1851. In his inaugural speech, the president spoke of the building as a true benefit for Humanity. His words reflected his whole-hearted approval of the construction of such an essential building, where commerce and distribution throughout the city could be facilitated, helping thousands to have better produce and, in the long run, a better, healthier life. Louis Napoleon also spoke about the necessity of protecting from seasonal changes the numerous farmers and other food providers who brought their produce to Paris every day in increasing quantities in this period of industrial dynamism. In his speech, the president sounded genuinely touched by the workers' difficult working conditions, and seemed to want to make their trade more profitable for both themselves and the city they served. In effect, he was offering them the chance to rise to bourgeois status, and he referred to them as a large class that suffered daily in order to feed Paris. The president's desire was to make of *les Halles* an architectural example, merging the social and the practical, a place that would make Parisians' lives easier without compromising the style of the capital's buildings or the industrial sense of the time, a place for the enchantment and the well-being of the people, a place compared by the emperor to a great museum, as the "Louvre of the people." Further, this model was to be pursued and repeated on a much larger scale in the entire city, and , beyond it, to the entire nation. It was clear to Louis Napoleon that the transformation of the *urbanscape* went hand in hand with social reforms. "Les Halles" was one of his first projects, a concept that demonstrated his belief that transforming the city was a social issue as much as it was a scientific and an esthetic one. The president was thus in full agreement with the social and economic theories of the early nineteenth century thinker Saint Simon, an aristocrat and a Socialist, who believed that thinkers and scientists had the intellectual duty to allow everyone in society to benefit from developing industrialization and to make the new industry a science for social progress. Louis Napoleon saw himself as just such a thinker, practitioner, and leader of a social movement that put progress and science at the forefront of a great new construction program. Nothing but the latest and most advanced techniques and materials would satisfy his desire to see beauty and science meet in order to conceive a new type of public building. This may explain why, after his initial enthusiasm and as the construction of *les Halles* progressed, Louis Napoleon criticized the architecture that he judged too austere and too monumental for a modern population, preferring a modern iron construction to the classic stone that Baltard had begun. The president's fundamental belief that one ought to live within one's industrial and social times without discrediting artistry seemed in jeopardy. Subsequently, at the beginning of the Second Empire, the project was stopped, reevaluated, and restarted, with the help of the new Prefect of Paris, Baron Haussmann, with whom Baltard shared a similar educational background, and whose judgment he therefore trusted. Baltard now used iron as the main construction material. The final project was a ten-acre pantheon of iron and glass stretching over parts of four districts of central Paris. It was composed of ten pavilions set off by a configuration of streets connecting them to each other and to the rest of the city. *Les Halles* resembled a small city inside the city, a place built for the convenience of a busy, growing, and demanding new society, a place pulsating with life, where a constant flow of people and food mixed in all corners, from the early hours of each day until dark. It was truly a microcosm of modern economy. *Les Halles* was the new heart of the city, or its full and gurgling belly, to refer to the organic metaphor used to suggest the constant circulation of food taking place there, a metaphor that was later immortalized in Emile Zola's 1873 novel *The Belly of Paris* (also translated as *The Fat and the Thin*). Zola wrote this novel, the third in his series depicting the life of a family during the Second Empire, at the dawn of the impressionist movement.

Dossier 1.5 Les Halles: "Paris' Colossal Belly"; from Zola's *Le Ventre de Paris* (*The Belly of Paris*, or *The Fat and the Thin*) (1873)

In this passage, two friends, Claude, the starving artist, and Florent, a native of the neighborhood and recently back from the penitentiary, meander through the night into the early morning hours, walking in the newly developed neighborhood of *les Halles*.

They began chatting together as they went back towards les Halles. Claude whistled as he strolled along with his hands in his pockets and expatiated on his love for this mountain of food, which rises every morning in the very center of Paris. He prowled about the footways night after night, dreaming of colossal still-life subjects, paintings of an extraordinary character. He had even started on one, having got his friend Marjolin and that jade Cadine to pose for him; but it was hard work to paint those confounded vegetables and fruits and fish and meat-they were all so beautiful! Florent listened to the artist's enthusiastic talk with a void and hunger-aching stomach. It did not seem to occur to Claude that those things were intended to be eaten. Their charm for him lay in their color. Suddenly, however, he ceased speaking and, with a gesture that was habitual to him, tightened the long red sash which he wore under his green-stained coat.

And then with a sly expression he resumed:

"Besides, I breakfast here, through my eyes, at any rate, and that's better then getting nothing at all. Sometimes, when I've forgotten to dine on the previous days, I treat myself to a perfect fit of indigestion in the morning by watching the carts arrive here laden with all sorts of good things. On such mornings as those I love my vegetables more than ever. Ah! The exasperating part, the rank injustice of it all is that those rascally bourgeois Philistines eat all these things!"

Then he went on to tell Florent of a supper to which a friend had treated him at Baratte's on a day of affluence. They had partaken of oysters, fish, and game. But Baratte's had sadly fallen, and all the carnival life of the old Marché des Innocents was now buried. In its place they had the central markets of les Halles, that colossus of ironwork, that new, wonderful and so original town. Fools might say what they liked; it was the embodiment of the spirit of the times.. . .

The dawn was now rising. . . .

At present the luminous dial of Saint Eustache was paling as a night-light does when surprised by the dawn. The gas jets in the wine shops in the neighboring streets went out one by one, like the stars extinguished by the brightness. And Florent gazed at the vast markets of les Halles now gradually emerging from the gloom, from the dreamland in which he had beheld them, stretching out their ranges of open palaces. Greenish-grey in hue, they looked more solid now, and even more colossal with their prodigious masting of columns upholding an endless expanse of roofs. They rose up in geometrically shaped masses; and when all the inner lights had been extinguished and the square uniform buildings were steeped in the rising dawn, they seemed typical of some gigantic modern machine, some engine, some cauldron for the supply of a whole people, some colossal belly, bolted and riveted, built up of wood and glass and iron and endowed with all the elegance and power of some mechanical motive appliance working there with the flaring furnaces, and wild, bewildering revolutions of wheels. . . .

He now heard the loud continuous rumbling of the wagons that were setting out from les Halles. Paris was chewing and doling out the daily food of its two million inhabitants. These markets were like some huge central organ beating with giant force and sending the blood of life through every vein of the city. The uproar was akin to that of colossal jaws- a mighty sound to which each phase of the provisioning contributed, from the whip-cracking of the larger retail dealers as they started off for the district markets to the dragging pit-a-pat of the old shoes worn by the poor women who hawked their lettuces in baskets from door to door. . . .

For the last time he raised his eyes and looked at les Halles. At present they were glittering in the sun. A broad ray was pouring through the covered road from the far end, cleaving the massy pavilions with an arcade of light, while fiery beams rained down upon the far expanse of roofs. The huge iron framework grew less distinct, assumed a bluey hue, became nothing but a shadowy silhouette outlined against the flaming flare of the sunrise. But up above a pane of glass took fire, drops of light trickled down the broad sloping zinc plates to the gutterings; and then, below, a tumultuous city appeared amidst a haze of dancing golden dust. The general awakening had spread, from the first start of the market-gardeners snoring in their cloaks, to the brisk rolling of the food-laden railway drays. And the whole city was opening its iron gates, the footways were humming, the pavilions roaring with life. Shouts and cries of all kinds rent the air; it was as though the strain, which Florent had heard gathering force in the gloom ever since four in the morning, had now attained its fullest volume. To the right and left, on all sides indeed, the sharp cries accompanying the auction sales sounded shrilly like flutes amid the sonorous bass roar of the crowd. It was the fish, the butter, the poultry, and the meat being sold.

The pealing of bells passed through the air imparting a quiver to the buzzing of the opening markets. Around Florent the sun was setting the vegetables aflame. He no longer perceived any of those soft watercolor tints which had predominated in the pale light of the morning. The swelling hearts of the lettuces were now gleaming brightly, the scales of greenery showed forth with wondrous vigor, the carrots glowed blood-red, the turnips shone as if incandescent in the triumphant radiance of the sun.

On Florent's left some wagons were discharging fresh loads of cabbages. He turned his eyes and away in the distance saw carts yet streaming out of the Rue Turbigo. The tide was still rising. He had felt it about his ankles on a level with his stomach, and now it was threatening to drown him altogether. Blinded and submerged, his ears buzzing, his stomach overpowered by all that he had seen, he asked for mercy; and wild grief took possession of him in the very heart of glutted Paris, amid the effulgent awakening of les Halles. Big hot tears started from his eyes. (22–33)

Considering the near abusive use in this passage of adjectives such as "gigantic," "huge," "vast, "and "colossal" to describe the excessive physiognomy and human and inhuman excesses of *les Halles*, it seems fit to use the expression "colossal belly" to express the overwhelmingly organic outlook of Zola and Parisians in general toward the formidable new structure of the city market. Ironically, in a marketplace where so much food circulates, the two friends stroll along the buildings of *les Halles* hungry. *Les Halles* is a place for all social classes: for the overfed bourgeois (according to Claude), for the food retailers aspiring to becoming more bourgeois, for the daily and temporary workers on low wages, for the poor and homeless eating scraps from this giant food market and sleeping in the wide and deep cellars of its iron and glass pavilions. In Zola's novel, *les Halles* appears as a place where humanity in all its variety lives, a modern place for the people, all kinds of people. Everyone in the confines of *les Halles* finds some sort of individual fulfillment, if not with money or food, at least with friendship, but also with the esthetic appeal of the place and the sheer sense of wonder it sparks as one is confronted with its growing, hustling, and bustling everyday life, defining the energy and novelty, the constant movement behind the concept of modernity as it affects the city in transformation.

Despite his hunger, Claude finds pleasure in the everyday fleeting beauty of *les Halles*. He feasts with his eyes on the display of colors provided by the wide selection of fruits and vegetables, meat and fish, flowers and spices. The way he experiences *les Halles* is similar to an impressionist painter fascinated by the wonders of the modern era—by the industrial and commercial development of the city many impressionist painters captured on canvas, from steaming locomotives to iron bridges or the chimney stacks of factories (see chapter 3), as well as by the changing light that shows *les Halles* under different angles, in different moods, as if it were a modern object studied by the keen social observer represented by the artist. The way light seems to provide new creative potential for Claude reminds us of Claude Monet's studies of a single setting under different light conditions, for example, his cathedral of Rouen series or even his series depicting the Saint Lazare railway station.

As with all his other novels, he had conducted a thorough "scientific" social study of the place, of its commercial and human movement, while keeping in mind the cultural and artistic fashion of the time. In this novel (see dossier 1.5), one of his characters is genuinely inspired by impressionist ideas that foreshadow the famous avant-garde painters who would be so attached to the rapidly changing city and the artistic power of natural light, while another marvels at the modernity of the edifices of *les Halles*. These reactions take place as Zola simultaneously insists on the pervasive and very real physical hunger experienced by one of the two friends. Through fictional characters Zola thus manages to demonstrate that the real cruelty generated by poverty and hunger can be momentarily alleviated by the power of the gigantic, beautiful, and mechanical belly of *les Halles*. In this sense, he is not far from Louis Napoleon's social and cultural vision of the splendor and well-being inscribed in the modern concept of the new Parisian marketplace. The president's dream of a modern and beautiful structure to ease the suffering of the people while appealing to their sense of urban esthetics, and his progressive objective to serve humanity with the technological advances of his time did not find its fulfillment in the particular classical style of Baltard alone. The additional contribution of Baron Haussmann, whose simultaneously efficient and beautiful style would soon and forever change France's architectural image nationally and internationally, was also necessary. Baltard and Haussmann had begun the extraordinary transformation of a city of mixed beauty and population by giving it a new heart and a full belly with the construction of *les Halles*, but the capital's complete and modern new body was yet to come.

It was quite clear that, from 1851 on, France was *en route* to achieving its ambitious goal of becoming a leading modern society and nation, with a prestigious culture and a universal role to play on the world scene. Yet, however noble their notion of a grand modern nation may have been, the French were nevertheless advancing in the elaboration of their society and culture based on universalist principles that could only be distorted in the attempt to apply them concretely. In the project of making France a world cultural and political power, French universalism took on dimensions that resulted in exclusions and inequalities that stood out as contradictions to the ideal and abstract principles of universalism. Nevertheless, even in its warped application, universalism prevailed as a curiously defective but efficient concept. In 1851, at the twilight of the Second Republic, universalism emerged from the speeches of leaders, from the theories of artists and intellectuals, from the growing appetency of the middle class and, beyond the republic itself, in the era of empire, it continued to be the leading principle of France's ambitions.

In 1851, the project of building a world-class culture seriously began, undeterred by the contradictions inherent in universalism, better yet, encouraged by the concept's idealist energy. In fact, despite all its shortcomings, universalism was, against all odds, the dominant discourse of the time, and it set the nation on a path of cultural achievement that would, in principle, be good for all while also establishing France's own and particular preeminent international reputation for its "superior" culture and way of life, an enviable model to be imitated. In the end, this period of significant political, social, and cultural change, inspired by France's proclaimed mission to become an enlightened and egalitarian nation, came to a culminating point, making 1851 the year of the Universal, and France at mid-century a nation with an ostentatious commitment to modernity.

References

Abélès, Luce, ed. *Champfleury—L'art pour le peuple*. Paris: Réunion des Musées Nationaux (Dossiers du Musée d'Orsay), 1990.

Auclert, Hubertine. *Le droit politique des femmes, ou question qui n'est pas traitée au Congrès international des femmes*, 1878. In Y. Ripa, ed. *Les femmes, actrices de l'histoire, France, 1789–1945*. Paris: Armand Colin, 2002.

Baecque de, Antoine and Françoise Mélonio. *Histoire culturelle de la France: Lumières et liberté*, In Rioux and Sirinelli. Paris: Seuil, 1998.

Baudelaire, Charles. *The Painter of Modern Life and Other Essays*. Jonathan Mayne, trans. and ed. New York: Da Capo, 1986.

Berlioz, Hector. http://www.hberlioz.com/London/Berlioz1851.html, 2002.

Bouretz, Pierre. *La République et l'universel*. Paris: Gallimard (Folio-Histoire), 2000.

Bresler, Fenton. *Napoleon III: A Life*. London: HarperCollins, 1999.

Brillat-Savarin, Jean-Anthelme. *The Physiology of Taste or Meditations on Transcendent Gastronomy*. New York: Knopf, 1971.

Champfleury. "Le Réalisme." *L'Illustration* (414, Vol. XVII), January 31–February 7, 1851.

———. *Lettre à George Sand*, in *Du Réalisme: Correspondance*. Luce Abélès, dir. Paris: Cendres, 1991.

Clark, Timothy. *Image of the People: Gustave Courbet and the 1848 Revolution*. Princeton, NJ: Princeton University Press, 1981.

———. *The Absolute Bourgeois: Artists and Politics in France, 1848–1851*. Berkeley: University of California Press, 1999.

Delvau, Alfred. *Histoire anecdotique des cafés et cabarets de Paris*. Paris: Dentu, 1862.

Duclert, Vincent and Christophe Prochasson, eds. *Dictionnaire critique de la République*. Paris: Flammarion, 2002.

Ferrier, Jean-Louis. *Courbet: Un enterrement à Ornans*. Paris: Denoël-Gonthier, 1980.

Flanary, David. *Champfleury: The Realist Writer as Art Critic*. Ann Arbor: University of Michigan Research Press, 1980.

Flaubert, Gustave. *Oeuvres I*. Paris: Gallimard (Pléiade), 1951.

Flaubert, Gustave. *Oeuvres II*. Paris: Gallimard (Pléiade), 1952.

Fried, Michael. *Courbet's Realism*. Chicago: University of Chicago Press, 1992.

Garrigou, Alain. *Histoire sociale du suffrage universel en France (1848–2000)*. Paris: Seuil, 2002.

Gerbod, Paul. *Voyages au pays des mangeurs de grenouilles: La France vue par les Britanniques du XVIIIe siècle à nos jours*. Paris: Albin Michel, 1991.

Guy, Christian. *La Vie quotidienne de la société gourmande en France au XIXe siècle*. Paris: Hachette, 1971.

Haine, W. Scott. *The World of the Paris Café: Sociability among the French Working Class, 1789–1914*. Baltimore: Johns Hopkins University Press, 1996.

Hause, Steven. *Hubertine Auclert—The French Suffragette*. New Haven: Yale University Press, 1987.

Hemmings, FWJ. *Culture and Society in France (1848–1898): Dissidents and Philistines*. New York: Charles Scribner's Sons, 1971.

Huard, Raymond. *Le Suffrage universel en France (1848–1946)*. Paris: Aubier, 1991.

Hugo, Victor. *Napoléon-le-Petit*. Paris: Nelson, Editeurs. 1911.

———. *Oeuvres complètes: Actes et paroles 1—avant l'exil (1841–1851)*. Paris: Hetzel & Quantin, 1882.

Jones, Colin. *The Cambridge Illustrated History of France*. Cambridge: Cambridge University Press, 1994.

Labracherie, Pierre. *Napoléon III et son temps*. Paris: Julliard, 1968.

Langle de, Henry-Melchior. *Le Petit monde des cafés et des débits parisiens au XIXe*. Paris: PUF, 1990.

Le Wita, Beatrix. *French Bourgeois Culture*. J.A. Underwood, trans. Cambridge: Cambridge University Press,1994.

LeHir, Marie-Pierre and Dana Strand, eds. *French Cultural Studies: Criticism at the Crossroads*. Albany: SUNY Press, 2000.

Marx, Karl. *The Class Struggles in France (1848–1850)*. New York: International Publishers, 1935.

———. *The Eighteenth Brumaire of Louis Bonaparte*. New York: International Publishers, 1955.

Mélonio, Françoise and Antoine de Baecque. *Histoire culturelle de la France: lumières et liberté*. In Rioux and Sirinelli. Paris: Seuil, 1998.

Napoléon III and Duc de Morny. *Appel au peuple Français—Honneur au suffrage universel*. Paris: Bibliothèque Nationale, MSS BNF# LB55–2296, 1851.

Nochlin, Linda. *Realism and Tradition in Art 1848–1900*. Englewood Cliffs, NJ: Prentice-Hall Inc., 1966.

Paulin, Jean-Baptiste. "Exposition Universelle." *L'Illustration* (427, Vol. XVII), May 1–8, 1851.

Rioux Jean-Pierre and Jean-François Sirinelli. *Pour une histoire culturelle*. Paris: Seuil, 1998.

Rosanvallon, Pierre. *Le Sacre du citoyen: Histoire du suffrage universel en France*. Paris: Gallimard, 1992.

Seznec, Jean, ed. *Flaubert à l'exposition de 1851*. Oxford: Clarendon Press, 1951.

Smith, W.H.C. *Napoleon III*. London: Waylan, 1972.

Témime, Emile. *France, terre d'immigration*. Paris: Gallimard (Découvertes), 1999.

Whitney Walton. *France at the Crystal Palace: Bourgeois Taste and Artisan Manufacture in the Nineteenth Century*. Berkeley: University of California Press, 1992.

Zola, Emile. *The Fat and the Thin*. Alfred Vizetelly, trans. New York: Mondial, 2005.

CHAPTER 2

A CHANGING WORLD: THE SECOND EMPIRE AND
BEYOND (1852–1871)

Old Paris is no more (a town, alas, Changes more quickly than man's heart may change)

—Baudelaire, *Flowers of Evil* (1857)

These lines from "The Swan," a poem from the section entitled "Parisian Scenes" in Baudelaire's classic collection of poems *Flowers of Evil* indicate how rapidly the city was renewing itself and how traumatic and surprising this quick metamorphosis was to Parisians during the Second Empire. Here, the changes trigger anxiety in the poet's mind, caught between the "old" Paris he is so comfortable and familiar with, and the "new" one, thrilling, modern, but also frightening in its haste to reinvent itself. Like many others in this period, Baudelaire found himself at the very heart of the most active and dramatic demolition and transfiguration of Paris. The feverish changes did not suit his melancholy nature, even though, at times, he not only applauded the modernity and fleeting quality of the times, but also exulted in the city's strange, arresting beauty, in the fascinating transformation of its appearance and in the formidable new influence of the crowds of city dwellers in the vitality of this new hub of modernity. We examine here what is lost and what is gained in this massive transformation of the urban space—and eventually, of the rural space as well—in France during the period of the Second Empire. This transformation would affect and alter the lifestyle of the people of this era, turning them into modern citizens, mostly bourgeois in nature, living in renewed cities ideally designed and ostensibly built for the betterment of their lives. In reality, however, this transformation would leave many behind, physically separate the classes, and allocate them different social spaces. Whether it was intentional or not, the Second Empire's architectural idealism, which aspired to nothing less than the universal improvement of all mankind, ended up segregating the classes by empowering the bourgeoisie and excluding a number of others, most notably the working classes and the poor.

Building for the People

The vision of a newly designed and modern city serving the needs of its people while showing a style of grandeur reflecting the economic and industrial prosperity of the time was imagined by Napoleon III and developed by the great Parisian architect Baron

Haussmann. As early as 1853, with the support of the emperor, Haussmann began transforming Paris into a museum of modernity showcasing an era of extraordinary urban and social change. The city of mud (*Lutetia*, Paris' Roman name, from the Latin "Lutum" that means "mud") became the city of light. Light, both natural and gas-generated, became a social concern and a technical advance of daunting proportions in rethinking the massive makeover of Paris. First, in order to give breathing room to the crowded city, major streets and boulevards were reconfigured and rebuilt with natural light as the essential consideration. Light was the main component in Haussmann's attempt to successfully open up the city below to the sky above. This development included the construction of low-rise buildings, the widening of the avenues and the installation of parks and squares. Second, as early as 1856, three years after its appearance gas light was already twice as powerful as before, providing better illumination to the city at night and safer streets to its inhabitants, who could now continue to stroll after sundown. That same year, the number of street lamps tripled and the lamps themselves were "artistically" designed.

Figure 2.1 Paris (1860)

View from the busy and popular Pont Neuf, the oldest standing bridge in Paris conceived by Henri III and built during the reign of Henry IV whose equestrian statue stands in the middle of the bridge. In the mid-nineteenth century, the Pont Neuf received much-needed renovations and continued to be a favorite place for strollers who enjoyed its large sidewalks and recently installed street lamps. (© L'Illustration)

The novelty of gas–lit streets, which made French cities bright and attractive was but one of the many radical developments that took place from 1853 to 1870, approximately over the same period of time as the Second Empire. The motivation for such unprecedented urban change was quite different from that of other European neighbors who, while also involved in a number of important renovations, paid less attention to the architectural configuration of their cities than the French. As opposed to cities like London or Rome, which owed their face-lifts partly to fire and flood, the formidable reshaping of French cities was not motivated by natural disaster, but rather by a desire to make cities clean, practical, and modern in their entire infrastructure. French cities of the nineteenth century became places where people wanted to live or visit, places where they could walk for miles on newly built sidewalks, socialize in newly opened cafés, and where gardens, parks, and trees created a general feeling of well-being. Household waste and sewers were directed out of the open streets into an underground network of tunnels and galleries, thus insuring the cleanliness of the streets while preserving the good health of the people who no longer had to live with soiled and contaminated water. The task undertaken by Haussmann was much more than a local and partial reconstruction that made small advances by renovating the areas of the city that required it the most: it was a grand-scale metamorphosis of the entire urban landscape. Such changes would naturally not only transform the city but also the lives of its dwellers. Life would indeed forever change in city centers, and people reorganized their daily habits in relation to the new face of the city. Migration within each neighborhood, or from one section of the city to another—as certain previously impoverished areas became gentrified and attracted a new bourgeois population—or even from remodeled old parts in the center to peripheral sections seemed inevitable for those who could not afford living in the new apartment buildings of the city center. Most of the poor were negatively affected by the changes, as they were forced either to retreat to overcrowded areas still remaining within some central areas of Paris or to relocate outside of the city. Haussmann's work was criticized for the massive exodus of the underclass to the city's periphery, and for the new social segregation of all urban centers now almost exclusively limited financially to the bourgeois population. In any case, everyone, rich or poor, was concerned and touched by what could be called the structural "(r)evolution" of the capital.

The new Paris became the talk of the town. No literary or artistic figure of the time escaped the excitement or the disappointment associated with such drastic transformation of the city: Hugo, Flaubert, Huysmans, Maupassant, Zola, to name only some of the most famous. Some loved its new look, while others criticized the ruthless eradication of rundown but nevertheless settled and charming neighborhoods. For the latter group, Paris seemed to be vanishing all too fast.

The Vanished City

As with every major reconstruction of urban space, the transformation of nineteenth-century Paris implied the demolition or the elimination of important parts of *populaire* areas. Here *populaire* is used to designate the space where low-to-no-income people lived, usually in overcrowded and old buildings, in appalling *garnis*, or sparsely furnished small apartments found in rat-infested and decrepit buildings. Generally speaking, these areas were so filthy and unhealthy that they were often ideal breeding ground for the rapid proliferation of deadly epidemics like cholera. For example, in 1849 a particularly strong strain of cholera quickly spread among the Paris population living in areas situated mainly on the left bank of the Seine. Not only did rats constantly rummage through the trash thrown in the middle of the streets, but also shared the daily refuse with poor and starving street people. Gustave Flaubert's friend, Maxime Du Camp, one of the first travel photographers, writers, and witnesses to social conditions during the Second Empire, thought, along with the emperor, that Paris was on its way to becoming unlivable and that "its population was suffocating in the narrow, winding, rancid alleys where it was forced to live," and that "everything suffered from this state of things: hygiene, security, the speed of communication and people's morals" (*Le Paris du Baron Haussmann*, 9). This concern was not new; it was simply a cry for urgent attention in order to avoid the worst. It was not the first time that Paris had been criticized for not meeting very basic human needs. Du Camp echoed earlier social voices like the eighteenth-century philosopher Jean-Jacques Rousseau, who, in his *Confessions*, declared: "Entering through the faubourg Saint Marceau, I saw only small, dirty and stinking streets, ugly black houses, an air of filth, poverty, beggars, carters, sewing women, women hawking tisanes and old hats" (146–147). Du Camp also echoed as another contemporary of Rousseau, the Enlightenment philosopher Voltaire, who despised what he saw as a squalid and over-crowded city. Well before Haussmann's arrival on the Parisian scene, Rousseau had already dreamed and written about the arrival of an enlightened architect who would successfully rehabilitate "this now decrepit" city of kings. Almost a century later, Baron Haussmann, the new prefect of Paris, would be the man for the job.

Haussmann's comprehensive and radical project to transform the cities did not include renovating. He was in favor of an imperative demolition of the most squalid, dark, and narrow parts of the city. His program was indeed based on the complete annihilation of the most unsightly and constricted areas of Paris and on fully rebuild-ing them according to his ambitious plan. While it is true that Haussmann wanted to eliminate the asymmetrical layout of the old Paris, he nevertheless worked hard at preserving the spirit of neighborhood and its local feel, keeping it connected to the city as a whole through careful architectural planning delineating living space along with commercial streets, long avenues, gathering intersections, and pleasant green spaces. Paris was transformed into a complex yet harmonious arrangement of small and large streets, where each newly designed and defined section was bordered by large avenues that defined the community while also opening it to those around it. Each newly delimited neighborhood recalled the setting and life of a smaller town with its own church, monument(s), green and social spaces, a kind of township within a city, a district that, while belonging to the general environment of Paris, also developed local pride and culture.

In 1855, at the onset of the "Haussmannization" of Paris, the demolition sites were so extreme and numerous that many thought that the old city was literally vanishing, melting as it were. This was happening at such a rapid pace that many of the inhabi-tants grew nostalgic at the sight of the old Paris crumbling under their own eyes. However, beyond these laments over the disappearance of the old city, a sense of surprise took over when many destroyed buildings allowed historical monuments to reappear after being obscured for a long time behind "hideous shacks that were hiding them" (Gautier, *Paris démoli*, i). In fact, despite local criticism, the main resistance to

Haussmann's project was not esthetic but economic. This disapproval only surfaced in a major way in 1870, seventeen years after the beginning of Haussmann's urban transformation program, and was not concerned with the demolition of certain neighborhoods, but rather, with the additional funds Haussmann requested in 1867 for the completion of his ambitious project. It is under the critical pen of a young journalist by the name of Jules Ferry, who would later become the emblematic statesman of the Third Republic, that Haussmann's program was chastised for its high cost and dubious accounting procedures. Ferry's persuasive articles on the topic, a series entitled "The Fantastic Accounting of Haussmann" and published in the newspaper *Le Temps* in 1869 forced Haussmann into retirement. It is true that before being exposed by Ferry, Haussmann had enjoyed complete financial independence to do as he pleased. In order to help Haussmann carry out his reconstruction project, the emperor, who was very sympathetic to the idea, had in 1852 voted in a new law enforcing a program of automatic eviction from any housing in the line of new construction. He also facilitated generous loans for Haussmann, in addition to subsidizing his program with state funds. Once these laws and programs were in place, any potential social and financial difficulty was smoothed out, allowing Haussmann to successfully complete his program.

In addition to Ferry's articles, other voices also raised concerns about the forced segregation inherent to the eviction program that pushed poor and working-class people out to the city's periphery. In 1855, for example, the secretary of the Chamber of Commerce and political economist, Horace Say, son of the famous economist Jean-Baptiste Say, had this to say regarding the dispersion of the poor families of Paris during Haussmann's era:

> The circumstances that forced the laborers to move away from the center of Paris were generally considered to have had unfortunate consequences on their conduct and morality. In the past, they usually lived on the top floors of houses otherwise occupied by the families of industrial entrepreneurs or people of otherwise relative affluence. A sort of solidarity existed between different residents living under the same roof. Everyone helped each other out. In the event of sickness or unemployment, laborers had access to services and assistance; and on the other hand a sort of human respect stamped with regularity the habits of working families. By moving north of the canal St. Martin and even beyond the borders of the city, laborers live where there are no bourgeois families and find themselves left running wild and deprived of the help of those who were formerly their neighbors. (Report of Horace Say, June 15, 1855)

According to Say, one of the major consequences of the huge demolition program of central Paris was the "ghettoization" of the less fortunate, and by extension, what he called the lowering of the moral standards of these segregated groups. It is true that during this period the number of "zones," or shantytowns, increased throughout the few undesirable and marginal sections of Paris and its surrounding areas. But it is also true that Say is prejudiced when he judges the morals of ghetto dwellers. However, his expression "running wild" to depict the condition of the underprivileged after their spatial separation and social abandonment in outlying neighborhoods could describe the situation 150 years later that led *banlieue* (suburb) inhabitants, for the most part non-European and working class, to revolt violently against social and urban segregation (see chapters 9 and 10). Left unattended and uncared for, "running wild," the young *banlieusards* of 2006 intended to remind the French government that they existed. They went on a three-week rampage and destruction of the suburbs where their families had been "parked" and left in the rough for so long. It may be that Say's nightmare about the consequences of the forced displacement of low-income families outside the city finally came true in 2006. What is certain is that in 1855 the legal exclusion of the poor dramatically and for the first time separated socioeconomic groups and accentuated the differences in the living conditions of an already class-bound society.

Other voices were more lyrical and favorable to the demolition of Paris, praising the notion that beauty existed in and beyond the ruins of the city. This was the case for poet and journalist Théophile Gautier who dusted off an article he had written for the *Moniteur Universel* in 1854 to introduce a book on Paris' demolition with kind and hopeful words for the city of the past, present and future (see dossier 2.1). As Gautier points out, most of the old rundown Paris had vanished to give way to the capital we know today. He compared the memory of former edifices whose vestiges lie under the new Paris to the graves of the ancestors of France from which new life sprouted.

Dossier 2.1 Théophile Gautier: "Paris Demolished"

While Gautier understands the melancholy thinker who sees the disappearance of so much humanity and history, both personal and national, with each old building razed to the ground and each reconfigured street, he simply speaks of the universal and implicit law of the inevitable chaos out of which the beauty of modernity will rise.

It's a curious sight, these open houses with their floorboards suspended over the abyss, their colored or flowered wallpapers still tracing the forms of rooms, the stairs that lead to nowhere, the basements opened up to the sky, the bizarre collapses and violent ruins; dark tones apart, it calls to mind the collapsed edifices and uninhabitable architecture that Piranèse outlined in his etchings with a feverish needle. This upheaval is not without beauty; light and shadow play with each other to picturesque effect over the rubble, over the piles of stones and haphazardly fallen crossbeams. But now the terrain is swept clean and flattened, making way for new construction to sprout with all the whiteness of youth, allowing the city to don a palatial tunic embroidered with sculpture.

No doubt the thinker feels a sort of melancholy grow in his soul when he witnesses the disappearance of these buildings, hotels, and houses where preceding generations had lived. A piece of the past falls with every stone on which we read, under the rust of time, the tales of our ancestors. More than one memory we would like to keep is cut in two by the building line. A façade rises where a great event once took place; where there is now a street, an illustrious man once lived, an honor to France and to mankind. Perhaps a work of art rots beneath the vulgar plaster of rubble on a sketchpad touched by genius. Precious memories are being lost in this universal spring-cleaning . . . but what to do? [. . .] The earth's crust is but a superposition of tombs and ruins. Any man who takes a single step stirs up the ashes of his fathers; any building raised carries within itself the stones of its demolished forebears, and the present, for better or worse, walks on the past. [. . .] Civilization, which requires air, sun and space for its furious activity and perpetual motion, cuts for itself wide avenues in the black mazes of crossroad alleys, the impasses of the old city; it razes houses the way the American pioneer razes trees. In its own way, civilization also clears the way. [. . .] The modern demolitions, therefore, destroy naught but insignificant masonry, unsigned rubble the artist has nothing to regret; and besides, when they come upon a monument, say, the Tour-St-Jacques-des-Boucheries, for example, they stop and turn away, or surround it with an open square which enhances its value and effect; what they destroy is born anew in the pages of some refined, erudite book, like that of M. Edouard Fournier. (i–xii)

According to Gautier, the sacrifice of old buildings is well worth the benefit and advent of modernity. In order to accommodate the frantic movement of contemporary urban civilization, in order to allow the old city to breathe again, drastic and even painful changes to the city's configuration must be made. However, modernity was not to be senseless, emerging from a renovation frenzy that would mindlessly destroy. Architects of the new Paris treated with respect the unexpectedly discovered monuments and other precious city spaces that were previously hidden behind a network of old buildings. They adjusted plans and buildings around these sites in order to preserve and even to enhance these historical and cultural spaces.

Haussmannized Cities

Even though Paris constituted the primary site of the renovation and transformation project imagined by Napoleon III and carried out by Haussmann, during the same period other French cities underwent the same full-scale demolition, and reconstruction, and modernization. Cities like Lyon (1855), Marseille (1856), Lille (1858), Bordeaux (1854), and, to a lesser degree, Toulouse (1867), Rouen (1859), and Avignon (1856), also became the sites of important Haussmannization programs that followed the Parisian model. This architectural and structural model was conceived on several recurrent principles: the opening of wide and straight avenues and boulevards, the planting of more trees, the desired visual effect of a monument standing in the perspective of a new avenue, the construction of ornate bourgeois low-rise apartment buildings in *pierre de taille* (freestone) bordering the new thoroughfares, the creation of parks and gardens, the ubiquitous construction of large sidewalks, and the installation of an underground sewage system. Because of the full-scale national effort devoted to urban development, the transformation of France's cities has often been associated with the birth of modern urbanism. No other project since then has measured up to the enormous scale of Haussmann's endeavor. In fact, his model was also emulated in foreign cities, especially after the 1867 Universal Exposition in Paris, whose ambition was not only to present the wonders and discoveries of technological advances, but also to unveil proudly the new Paris to the rest of the world. The project was successful, as other European cities followed Paris' example and rebuilt according to Haussmann's model. Berlin, Brussels, London, Rome, and Vienna went through their own brand of the Haussmann revolution, and sometime after the transformation of the French cities, these foreign cities began their own metamorphoses. For all these cities, the modernization of their centers was more than just a significant face-lift of the urban environment, for it constituted at the same time a serious promotion of a more "hygienic" way of living. Haussmann was particularly insistent on the objective of his program, as a basic principle of his project was that no new city, no matter how modern, could thrive on old, unsalubrious grounds.

For Haussmann, the search for clean water and the question of the environment had been a lifelong commitment. Throughout a great deal of his childhood, Haussmann was a sickly child, and as a result, he grew up with both a strong phobia of unhealthy water and an obsession with cleanliness. Later on, water became one of his prime professional preoccupations as illustrated by the following anecdote. From February to November 1841, Haussmann briefly served as subprefect of the small town of Saint Girons in the southwestern Department of Ariège in the foothills of the Pyrénées that separate France from Spain. At first, he hated the appointment and felt it was a true disgrace for such a well-educated Parisian: "Saint Girons did not even deserve my disdain" (*Mémoires*, 161). However, while living in the Pyrénées, surrounded by natural beauty and the mountains' clean water sources and rivers, he became extremely sensitive to environmental issues. He was convinced that the safe and healthy mountain water running in Saint Girons and the efficient sewage system of this town made its population strong and healthy. This conviction never left him and guided him through his first task in the rebuilding of Paris that indeed began with the restructuring of the water and sewage system of the city: "It is in Saint Girons that I strengthened the now unshakable convictions to which Paris owes a network of redirected waters sources, pure and healthy" (*Mémoires*, 173).

It was clear to Haussmann that Paris had suffered from its contaminated and dangerous water for too long, as demonstrated by the devastating 1832 and 1849 cholera epidemics that caused a total of nearly 40,000 deaths (Kudlick, 25). Before Haussmann's water reform, the sewage and drinking water were often one and the same. This was the case for the people living in the vicinity of the small and now nonexistent Parisian river called the Bièvre, running in the east and south of the city, under the loop of the Seine that would later be referred to as the "left bank."

The Disappearance of the Bièvre River

One of the major open sewers of Paris was indeed a small river called the Bièvre. It ran for approximately thirty-five kilometers southwest of the Seine into the heart of the old Paris before reconnecting to the Seine by the botanical garden, the *Jardin des Plantes*. Refuse and excrement, animal blood and guts from local butchers and tanners, dyes, and chemicals from the Gobelins tapestry manufactory, the oldest industry in Paris—founded during the reign of Louis XIV, the "Sun King"—were some of the most common pollutants transported by the Bièvre, which spat them out into the Seine at the end of its course. It is true that even before absorbing much of this pollution, the Bièvre was naturally muddy. The murkiness of the water did not incite Parisians living and working on its banks to keep the small river clean. Not yet "environmentally educated," the population simply thought that the river was coming to them already dirty and thus felt no guilt in adding more garbage to it. The result was a much-polluted river that looked more like an open sewer than a brook running inside and outside the city limits, through surrounding villages and working-class neighborhoods. However, despite its filthy water, many nineteenth-century Parisian *promeneurs* (strollers) were attracted to its "interrupted" banks and stream. During the city's reconstruction project in the area where the river flowed *intra muros*, within the city limits, and, depending on the structural work being done, it was sometimes buried in galleries or rerouted through areas unaltered by construction, thus offering to the eye smaller sections of open stream as the century progressed and giving it more the image of a dotted river line. For a while longer and before the extension of the city in 1860, when a full belt of rural districts surrounding Paris was officially added to the city, it continued to flow freely through the countryside on the outskirts of Paris, from its source in the town of Trappes to its entry into Paris. It was part of a bucolic environment, as it offered the peaceful sight of a rural river running through a relatively untouched countryside still scattered with hills, mills, and bordering farms, as captured in the drawings of seventeenth-century artist Philippe de Champaigne; all of this at the very edge of the bustling capital. The small river provided the ideal location for the traditional Sunday stroll, a cultural and social activity that the Seine could not offer due to the busy commercial life of its waterways and its deteriorating banks and quays. In comparison to the agitated activities of the Seine, the quiet environment of the Bièvre charmed some Parisians, despite the undeniable murkiness of its waters, its unhealthy look, and its periodically nauseating stench. Still, there was something about the river that appealed to the melancholy *promeneurs* such as the writer Joris-Karl Huysmans who loved the baroque side of the city. He was utterly charmed and conquered by "its air of desperation and thoughtful look of one who had suffered," by this "moving rubbish dump" that still nourished the poplars of Paris, by these stagnant waters appearing "sclerotic and eaten away by leprosy." Like a sick organ, its belly spat out "long gods of melodies" and "conjured up in this vale of tears the voice of a pauper-woman" comparable to a "sobbing voice, the desolate howl of the poor suburbs themselves" that "grip you by the entrails" (*Parisian Sketches*, 93–95). Huysmans developed a love for the duality of this river, sometimes recalling a clean and serene past still present in some bends and bordering gardens, and at other times deploring the modern changes that transformed the Bièvre's life and raison d'être.

Huysmans was at first associated with the realist movement, and his prose reflected his refined sense of literary accuracy in describing the poverty of those who lived around the Bièvre, while also adding a striking touch of the grotesque and the decaying. Huysmans was a mystic and an introvert whose natural inclination went to the outlandish and the strange. Zola described him as a unique "language virtuoso," close artistically to Northern painters like Rembrandt and Rubens as he evoked in words the somber colors and languid moods these painters put on canvas. In addition, his poetic invitation to the muddy and putrid Bièvre brought him closer to the beautiful melancholy music of Schubert whose "desolate rhythms" (*Le Drageoir aux Epices*, 66) he hears with a strangely satisfying sadness as he walks on the river banks. Huysmans finds pure artistic and literary gold in describing the roughness and the poverty associated with the foul waters of the Bièvre. In one of his *Parisian Sketches*, he ascribed to the rancid and dirty waterway the melancholy feelings of "those who suffer" and whose sufferings are contained in the murky life of the river:

> The work have begun, soon limewash will mask the mottled sores of this ailing quarter with its uniform whiteness, and the silhouettes of the skinners and chamois-makers' open-air dryer against the grey skies will be obscured. Soon the eternal and delightful promenade so beloved by intimists, across a plain furrowed by the industrious and the miserable Bièvre as it toils on its way, will be lost forever. (96)

Making his way along the river's banks, the Sunday stroller encounters the reality of his rapidly changing surroundings, poised between detritus of poverty and the novelty of modernity. Huysmans considered the disappearance of the Bièvre to be as inevitable as the end of the secret and inner life of man. It was as if with the improvement made to the city and the condemning of the river, man was losing part of his spiritual self to the advances of modernity, as if, despite the ongoing demolition, the modern city always kept the memories of its bleak past, a feeling that Huysmans expressed through the image of the rich new "hotels surrounded by green gardens where the black ribbon of the Bièvre meanders" (*Oeuvres complètes* XI, 15). The new and the old, the modern and the decaying, all coexisted in Huysmans's evocations of the river flowing from the country into the city, but the Bièvre would not survive the modernization of Paris.

After much controversy, Haussmann decided on the elimination of the river in 1858: "The foul stream of the Bièvre will no longer pour its murky waters into the Seine" (*Sur les traces de la Bièvre parisienne*, 51). Sections of the Bièvre were subsequently transformed into a covered sewage system while others were simply dried out and paved over to become regular streets. The Bièvre was completely covered or drained by 1912, disappearing from the Parisian landscape and leaving few traces of its existence. The inhabitants of the thirteenth or the fifth arrondissements in the south of Paris say to this day that its sleepy and lazy waters continue to flow underneath the streets and buildings of Paris, and they say that they can still sometimes hear the Bièvre running under their houses.

Keeping Cities Clean: From Ragpickers to Trash Collection

[. . .] Let's contemplate one of those mysterious beings, living so to speak off the excrement of great cities; for there are some strange occupations around. [. . .] Here is a man whose task is to pick up all the rubbish produced in one day in the capital. All that the great city has thrown out, all it has lost, all it has disdained, all it has broken, he catalogues and collects. He consults the archives of debauchery, works through the confused *bric-a-brac* of rubbish. He makes a selection, chooses astutely; he picks up, as a miser seizes on treasure, the refuse which, when chewed over by the magic of Industry, will become objects of use or enjoyment. Look at him, in the dark glow of the street lamps whose light flickers fitfully in the night wind, climbing up one of the long winding roads on the Montagne Sainte-Geneviève where many poor families live. He is wearing his wicker shoulder basket, holding his number seven. Here he comes, shaking his head and stumbling over the cobble stones like those young poets who spend all their days wandering around in search of rhymes. He is talking to himself; he pours out his soul to the dark cold night air. It's a splendid monologue that puts to shame the most lyrical tragedies. (Baudelaire, *On Wine and Hashish*, 7–8)

A familiar figure to the urban landscape, the ragpicker, with his "wicker basket and his number seven" (his basket thrown over his shoulder and his hook shaped like a number seven), contributed to the unremitting quest to keep city streets clean. The nineteenth-century ragpickers collected, sorted, and "recycled" trash for a living. They were considered to be on the lowest level of society, along with beggars and prostitutes, below the working class, and even looked upon as outsiders. Nevertheless, they obeyed the rules of their self-made corporation and respected its unspoken but functioning hierarchy. They were a paradox: marginalized characters with a sense of order and responsibility. The city trash, deposited outside each day either in open buckets or simply dumped in the street, was collected in three rounds. First came the ranking ragpickers, the "aristocrats of the rag" who collected the "best" of the trash. Then came the apprentices, who were usually not working as part of a corporation and were thus lower in status than the senior pickers; they began their round after the top pickers, around four in the morning. They could only count on luck to find anything of value the first group might have missed or did not want. Finally, the municipal cart rolled by to pick up the rest. These carts were operated by municipal workers who opened the city waters in order to sweep the last scraps through the drainage gutter in the middle of the street, toward the main sewers. This type of open street drainage was in essence not different from that of the Middle Ages. Despite this triple operation, the streets still looked rather filthy. Nevertheless, in this chain of morning chores, the ragpickers were essential in contributing to keeping the streets of the city as clean as could be, before the invention of the trash can in 1883 by the prefect of the Seine, Eugène Poubelle (*poubelle* in French now means "trashcan"), and before organized trash collection—begun in 1884, but not officially regulated until the end of the twentieth century. The arrival of the trashcan in cities did not eradicate the ragpickers, but it considerably reduced their function, their usefulness and their numbers. So it is mainly during the Second Empire that the "profession" prospered and peaked.

The ragpickers traversed the nineteenth century like fireflies in the night: one could easily notice the furtive light of their lantern in the dark but could not discern their features. They were, however, familiar shadows, marginal characters, who fell outside the social order. They were out scavenging throughout the city from dusk to dawn, stooped under their dim lights, meandering from street to street. They appeared to the early observers of the century as romantic characters; by mid-century they were perceived as more mystical, even diabolical, and finally, by the end of the century, they survived as an example of urban pauperism that resulted from the sweeping changes to the city, a traditional and enduring *petit métier* (small profession) associated at mid-century with the opulent life of the modern and increasingly wasteful city.

Although the profession was passed on from father to son, the ragpicker also came from other walks of life. Some were ruined aristocrats, others failed university students, unsuccessful businessmen, or hopeless intellectuals. Without any hope for a better future, they were often melancholy and suicidal, with a hand-to-mouth existence. They survived psychologically thanks to their regular and plentiful consumption of eau-de-vie (literally, water of life) but in reality a strong and cheap brandy they drank in the many estaminets along their collection routes (see figure 1.1). There were both male and female ragpickers, as both sexes picked over the street garbage and also often met and partied in rough cabarets like the "Pot blanc" or the "Nectar de Bacu" (Nectar de Bacchus). Their equipment was simple: a lantern for night vision, a basket on their back to throw the daily "harvest" of waste, and finally, to rummage with ease and expertise through the garbage, a long metallic hook, an emblematic tool to which the ragpickers would eventually owe their familiar name, "knights of the hook." Lantern, basket, and hook were vital to their trade, alcohol was their just reward, and bourgeois life their assurance of a plentiful collection. The growing new middle class consumed in great quantity and consequently was throwing out much more than before, thus improving the quality of the scraps. The amount and quality of refuse made rag picking an increasingly profitable profession and a welcome activity for city dwellers. Without the ragpicker, the already pestilential city would have been overwhelmed by trash and the diseases associated with accumulating and rotting refuse. That was one reason why the rag-pickers survived the century without much trouble from the authorities. The worst ragpicker repression occurred in 1831 during what became known as the "ragpicking war," a sort of social movement organized by the ragpickers to stop a municipal decision to modify trash collection. Ragpickers were afraid that this reform would cause the disappearance of their trade. For a week, they fought against the police, and collection practices remained unchanged.

Undoubtedly, the rag pickers were of precious service to the cleanliness of the city, and better still, they represented one of the first models for recycling of modern history. Not only did they collect trash, but also sorted and cleaned it before reselling it, directly or indirectly through a "boss," to retailers who would put the goods back in circulation at a discount price. Rags, papers, books, letters, pieces of metal, glass shards, bones, corks (extremely valuable as they could be directly exchanged at wine dealers for a glass of wine) were some of the street treasures that one could find in their dilapidated dwellings. Trash represented literally their lifesavings. The recycled goods took on a number of new forms: glass shards were reconstituted into new bottles, newspapers into paper of all sorts, animal skins and furs into lady's scarves, cigarette butts into cigarettes, bread crumbs into bread pot pies (highly sought after by high-class restaurants), old ribbons into pillows, bones into canes, dice, and buttons.

Valuable as they were to the urban environment, the ragpickers were at the same time the undesirable "homeless" of the nineteenth century whose mere presence made the bourgeois population uncomfortable, even though most ragpickers operated only at night, remaining invisible during the day. General opinion about them was divided, especially concerning their assumed moral values. In the press they regularly appeared under the double light of useful professional street cleaners and individuals of low morals and were often described as "necessary parasites." In an article entitled "Les Chiffonniers de Paris" (The Ragpickers of Paris) published in the newspaper *L'Illustration* on November 27, 1858, the editorialist Ferré described the ragpicker as a fly feeding on dirt and scum and invading the city. Ferré criticized the ragpicker for having no human dignity, as he lived in the worst conditions in crowded shantytowns or small rooms, surrounded by trash and sharing mattresses with other men and women without any consideration of sexual difference. Ferré continued by deploring the ragpickers' moral abuses, especially the rapid pace at which they spent all their money on liquor, and concluded with their poor work ethic, as they seemed to "work only for drinking."

Alfred Delvau, an editorialist who specialized in Parisian social and popular life and specifically in the city underworld and lowly professions, wrote about his own experience as he stopped by a ragpickers' cabaret on the old rue Mouffetard. Despite his harsh metaphor in describing how he thought these men were born and bred, and would most likely die, on a pile of manure, he found some originality to their trade, which provided "precious information on the life of these philosophers of the night, human refuse often looking for its daily bread in social refuse" (*Histoire anecdotique des cafés et cabarets de Paris*, 63). Paul Imbert, also an editorialist of the period who wrote specifically about the ragpickers of the Butte-aux-Cailles, a newly added Parisian district, part of the thirteenth arrondissement, insisted that they be seen and respected as any other human beings, and tried to give an objective account of their profession.

The ragpickers were also portrayed in literature and art through the century. Numerous representations of the ragpicker are found in poetry with, for example, Baudelaire's *Le Vin du chiffonnier* (The Ragpicker's Wine, 1857) and poetic prose pieces like *Du vin et du haschich* (Of Wine and Hashish, 1851) in *Paradis artificiels* (*Artificial Paradises*), Tristan Corbière's "*Paris Nocturne*," a poem published in *Amours jaunes*, or in Lautréamont's *Les Chants de Maldoror*, where ragpickers frequently appear. The ragpicker is often the main character in plays such as the Socialist Félix Pyat's enormous success, *Le Chiffonnier de Paris* (*The Ragpicker of Paris*, 1847), which he later adapted as a dramatic series successively published in two papers *Le Radical* and *Le Cri du peuple* (*The Cry of the People*) from 1886 to 1887. In fiction, well-established authors such as Balzac in sections of *La Comédie Humaine*, Hugo in *Les Misérables*, and Zola in episodes of his *Rougon-Macquart* series incorporated the ragpicker in their depiction of everyday life in the nineteenth century. The ragpicker also appeared frequently in minor and popular literature, for example, Baron Michel de Rougemont's 1818 short stories "*Le Chiffonnier*" and *Le Bonhomme*, or Mie D'Aghonne's 1873 *Les Mémoires d'un chiffonnier* (*Memoirs of a Ragpicker*). He was also pictured in the press in the famous caricatures of Daumier and Grandville and in drawings and paintings by Manet, for example "The Absinthe Drinker" (1859) or "The Ragpicker" (1865–1869), and by Raffaelli's series "Ragpickers" in the 1880s. Ragpickers likewise drew much attention from nonfiction writers. French police administrator Henri Frégier associated them with criminals in his 1840 book, *Les Classes dangereuses* (*The Dangerous Classes*). Journalist Edmond Texier observed the hierarchy in the profession and the substantial material differences existing between all the social strata of the corporation in *Tableaux de Paris* (1853). Victor Fournel, another journalist interested in popular Paris, pointed out the ragpickers' similarity to the European Jews and gypsies, therefore asserting their social apartness, in his 1858 *Ce qu'on voit dans les rues de Paris* (*What One Sees in the Streets of Paris*). Finally, Alexandre Privat D'Anglemont, a well-known literary and social critic, described the ragpicker as a true homeless and marginal individual in his 1861 *Paris inconnu* (*Unknown Paris*). In opposition to these social representations, the ragpicker was often romanticized by some writers who saw in him a philosopher of modern times, or a dissident who rejected conventional life, a figure closely associated with that of the poet, as both also found themselves misunderstood and rejected by the new capitalist order and living off the scraps of an opulent and self-centered society. Victor Hugo in his *Memoirs* describes the ragpicker as a "hyphen between the beggar and the philosopher" (6). It is also as an unconventional philosopher of the Paris streets that writer Louis Lurine described him in his 1844 book *Les Rues de Paris: Paris ancien et moderne* (*The Streets of Paris: Old and Modern Paris*): "The rag picker is the practical philosopher of the Paris streets. In his absolute abdication of any form of social vanity, in his ceaseless nocturnal ramblings, in his profession pursued under the stars, there is a mix of strange independence and nonchalant humility, an in-between-ness connecting the dignity of the free man to the hopelessness of the abject man" (328).

Dossier 2.2   Liard, Ragpicker and Philosopher of the Rue Mouffetard

One ragpicker in particular became a street celebrity, as he epitomized the strange mix between beggar and thinker. His name: Liard. His profession: ragpicker/philosopher.

Who doesn't know, at least by reputation, the philosopher Liard, this rag picker who is simultaneously an educated man, an artist, a phrenologist, and an impressive orator. This philosopher on the antique mode knew everyone, from Beranger who gave him his books, to Travies, the newspaper humorist and caricaturist, who has so picturesquely drawn him.

Liard, besides his manifest superiority over other "common" rag pickers, typifies the many aspects of the corporation; Liard does not "drink" much; he despises wine and only touches eau-de-vie; he talks a lot but never fights. He is proud and yet accomplishes the most humble tasks; he has a high opinion of his dignity yet he is covered in rags. Liard is an orator [. . .], his tribune is the street, his audience the first passer-by, his subject probity. Sometimes he goes to the deputy assembly (that is how the rag pickers have named their meeting point at the Poissonnière gate), and there, he participates in interminable discussions. These estimable industrialists have rigorously imitated our honorable deputies: the milestones are called armchairs, the baskets tilburies; finally, to complete the similarity, the majority of the assembly does not understand a word of what the ordinary orators are saying but does its job in applauding vivaciously (Lurine, 328–329).

Lurine then points to the many talents of Liard and to his reputation in Paris, specifically on the popular rue Mouffetard where he was often spotted practicing his trade, but also in many other good cafés throughout Paris where it became fashionable to be seen in his company.

His reputation as a philosopher was superficial and popular by name only, as other writers and thinkers such as Charles Yriarte saw how he had a tendency "to dazzle his audience with the luxury of his many citations and to give a useless display of his science" (*Les célébrités de la rue*, 244).

About Liard's oratorical skills, Lurine adds with humor that despite his genuine knowledge of the literature of antiquity, much of what he says is not understood and is often a series of *non sequiturs*. In fact, various topics being discussed by ragpickers appear here as the popular counterpart to the political gibberish being exchanged at the official level. It was often the general public's impression that much of what was said during public hearings appeared incomprehensible to everyone, but the speeches were nevertheless applauded and approved as if politicians and their programs were only the dramatic sum of empty words. This impression of incommunicability between politicians and the people remains unchanged, and it reinforces the suspicion with which the French people regard their often elitist and well-spoken political representatives. This gap would become a cultural source of derision at the expense of politicians for years to come, as, for example, we feel the humor behind the "official" and Babel-like assembly of ragpickers described by Lurine.

As he searches for more information about ragpickers in general and Liard in particular for his book on Paris, Privat d'Anglemont, Baudelaire's friend, tried to sit with Liard and interview him on his life and profession. Liard did not stray from his aloof intellectual image, and all of his replies took the form of the recitation of verses from Virgil's *Aeneid*.

For poets, writers, and artists of the nineteenth century the ragpicker cannot be dissociated from the social and cultural environment of the time. That is why he appears in all their work with varying degrees of importance. Even if in the end the ragpickers' existence was still miserable and their social status unimproved, they were nonetheless a by-product of a society of high consumerism and high waste, reflecting in their own way as well as responding to the bourgeois ideology of wanting and wasting, of (over)consumption. However, despite their low social status, they survived and at times even prospered thanks to their own sense of commerce and trading, and their original entrepreneurship, until and even beyond the creation of the trashcan, and municipal collection and recycling. Their entrepreneurial spirit—when they could as easily have chosen to become criminals and thugs—is consistent with a wave of commercial fever that caught everyone, rich and poor, during the prosperous times of the Second Empire: the rich in the frantic rhythm of buying and consuming, the poor in general and the rag-picker in particular in the equally raging tempo of recuperating and recycling.

Commercial Life

Commercial life went through major changes during the Second Empire. Excited by the modernization of the cities, the prosperity of industry and the new capitalist power, the French, especially the middle class, became avid lovers of shopping, and, as much as possible, shoppers for products of quality, as their now legendary sense of taste was not to be undermined by the large number of products then available on the market. The Second Empire saw the appearance and expansion of grocery store chains, like the Felix Potin stores. As early as 1852, the commercial phenomenon of the department store was launched with the opening of the first large store, "Le Bon Marché" (figure 2.2), followed by "Le Printemps" in 1864 and "La Samaritaine" in 1867. Oddly enough, as successful and lucrative as the concepts of food store chains and department stores were, they did not destroy the prosperity of smaller business.

Figure 2.2 The Great Staircase of the *Bon Marché* Department Store (1875)

The store was the main inspiration for Zola's 1883 novel *The Ladies' Paradise*. Zola conducted an exhaustive research of the *Bon Marché* before writing his novel (see dossier 2.3). (© L'Illustration)

After almost 150 years in existence, the Felix Potin chain finally went bankrupt in 1996, only to be replaced by other, more modern small neighborhood convenience stores. Despite the final demise of Felix Potin, the concept of the street corner grocery store has survived into the twenty-first century in France. As for the department stores opened during the Second Empire, with the exception of La Samaritaine, which closed in 2005, they are still open today throughout Paris. In conjunction with this innovative commercial activity launched during the Second Empire, other small boutiques and shops continue to thrive in all French city centers today. They still provide the neighborhood atmosphere they did in the past. They are the welcome sight of the intimate shopping environment where the customer receives individual attention and feels a kind of provincial sentiment of local bonding, a tradition cherished by the French shopper.

Dossier 2.3   Emile Zola, *Au Bonheur des Dames* (*The Ladies' Paradise*) (1883)

At first glance, *The Ladies' Paradise* appears to be the story of Denise Baudu, a humble young woman from the provinces, who finds a job in a Paris department store and falls in love with the owner Octave Mouret, but in reality, the love story is secondary to the story of the extraordinary commercial adventure represented by the recent opening of department stores like the Bon Marché or La Samaritaine, and the immense success of the shopping concept they inaugurated in the new bourgeois world of Paris. In her introduction to the translation of *The Ladies' Paradise*, Kristin Ross sees the book as a "phantasmagoric hymn to the marvels of modern commerce" (v) and of the giant and excessive department store as the main character of the novel.

In Chapter 4, Denise's innocence and timidity are contrasted with the greed and shallowness of several frenzied female customers caught in a shopping craze. Two rich bourgeois women acquaintances, Madame Marty and Madame Desforges, meet in the crowded and fashionable department store, "The Ladies' Paradise," where a sale is going on. They have both been in the store for a while, and they have both gone overboard in their shopping expedition. Now, Madame Marty is looking for a fabric to make a coat, while she has already bought quite a few articles of clothing. Even though she promised her husband to be reasonable, she cannot resist buying, and she has one of the clerks follow her with an armful of items she has already picked up. It is not so much the actual purchase she enjoys as the opportunity to go through an array of selections, often in the company of a young, devoted, and, sometimes, flirtatious salesman who in reality feels exasperated by her whimsical and fussy behavior. Madame Desforges also enjoys the variety offered in the store, but above all she takes pleasure in testing her new bourgeois ranking with the personnel in a series of aloof and condescending attitudes and useless purchase; for example, she has already bought twelve pairs of gloves and is being fit for a thirteenth pair by an overly attentive and apparently fully subjugated clerk, whose behavior is described by Zola as that of a submissive lover. When they meet, the two women express great delight in sharing their impressions of the exhibit of Oriental rugs, as if they had just visited a stunning museum collection. But better still, they decide to visit the silk collection of the store called "Paris-Bonheur," literally "Paris-Happiness," where, surely, ecstasy awaits.

Beneath the flaming gas-jets, which, burning in the twilight, had lighted up the supreme efforts of the sale, everything appeared like a field of battle still warm with the massacre of the various goods. The salesmen, harassed and fatigued, camped amidst the contents of their shelves and counters, which appeared to have been thrown into the greatest confusion by the furious blast of a hurricane. It was with difficulty that one traversed the galleries on the ground floor, blocked out with a crowd of chairs, and in the glove department it was necessary to step over a pile of cases heaped up around Mignot; in the woolen department there was no means to passing at all, Liénard was dozing on a sea of bales, in which certain piles, still standing, though half destroyed, seemed to be houses that an overflowing river was carrying away; and further on, the linen department was like a heavy fall of snow, one run up against iceberg of napkins, and walked on light flakes of handkerchiefs.

The same disorder prevailed upstairs, in the departments of the first floor: the furs were scattered over the flooring, the ready-made clothes were heaped up like the great-coats of wounded soldiers, the lace and the underlinen, unfolded, crumpled, thrown about everywhere, made one think of an army of women who had disrobed there in the disorder of some sudden desire; whilst downstairs, at the other end of the house, the delivery department in full activity was still disgorging the parcels with which it was bursting, and which was carried off by vans—last vibration of the overheated machine. But it was in the silk department especially that the customers had flung themselves with the greatest ardor. There they had cleared off everything, there was plenty of room to pass, the hall was bare; the whole of the colossal stock of Paris-Happiness had been cut up and carried away, as if by a swarm of devouring locusts. And in the midst of this emptiness, Hutin and Favier were running through the counterfoils of their debit-notes, calculating their commission, still out of breath after the struggle. Favier had made fifteen francs, Hutin had only managed to make thirteen, thoroughly beaten that day, enraged at his bad luck. Their eyes sparkled with the passion for money. The whole shop around them was also adding up figures, glowing with the same fever, in the brutal gaiety of the evening battle. [. . .]

"How much, Lhomme?" asked Mouret.

"Eighty thousand seven hundred and forty-two francs two sous," replied the cashier.

A laugh of ecstasy stirred up The Ladies' Paradise. The amount ran through the establishment. It was the highest figure ever attained in one day by the draper's shop. (105–106)

In the passage, the crowds have left the store after a hectic day of sales. The clerks are described as tired soldiers and the store as a devastated war zone. The metaphor of war and its aftermath is powerful in creating a sense of pure destruction, which in any other circumstances would leave no room for any sort of excitement or hope if it remained true to the image of the disastrous ending of a conflict. Here, however, war and destruction do not trigger desolation and human despair; they have quite the opposite effect on the clerks who, despite their weariness calculate with avidity their total gain out of this "disaster." And the store then explodes in orgasmic laughter after the day's incredible revenue is announced. Zola's message here is that money has turned these low-wage, lower class citizens into capitalist opportunists whose ambition to acquire more money has transformed them into fierce competitors, egotistical and inhuman, feasting on "the brutal gaiety of the evening battle."

For clerks and bourgeois alike, the newly created department stores provided an ambiance of both entertainment and cruelty that, driven by the overwhelming power of consumerism, united social classes across the spectrum in an orgiastic destruction of human values in the insatiable desire for a new dress or an extra buck (or, in this case, franc). In this era of multiplied commercial and shopping venues, money, whether spent or earned, definitely became the new universal value of modern society. Zola observed the greed associated with such developments, and he feared a loss of humanity in such commercial success; at the same time he himself seems to be under the spell of the extraordinary array and artifice of colors and plentifulness associated with the extravagance of modernity. In the end, "The Ladies' Paradise," the inhuman giant store grinding down its competitors, accumulating record amounts of money and seducing with exotic fabrics, seemed to parallel the position of imperialist France, and Zola's novel may be read as a tale of "urban empire [with] traces of colonial narrative [. . .] perceptible in Orientalist fantasy and the whole eroticized display of Asian products" (Ross, xiv). In *The Ladies' Paradise*, Zola showed that he was sensitive to the variety of products coming from various foreign lands and to the way they complemented and stimulated the French national sense of good taste and its aptitude for elegance and fashion.

Fashion and Fashionable Times

There is no doubt that the wild and frenetic commercial life described by Zola in *The Ladies' Paradise* was linked to a renewed sense of fashion associated with bourgeois life. We see a previous example of this phenomenon in Flaubert's 1857 novel *Madame Bovary* where his fashion victim, the provincial new bourgeoise Emma Bovary, bankrupts herself in superfluous, beautiful, and fashionable garments and ultimately prefers death to destitution and shame. Throughout the book, Emma Bovary searches for commercial ways to distance herself from her provincial upbringing by buying extravagant dresses that would be more appropriate to wear in cosmopolitan environments and seem out of place in the small town in Normandy where she lives with her dull husband, who is an older man and a local doctor. His lack of ambition drives Emma to younger and more exciting men, and his small salary cannot cover her outrageous lifestyle. In the end, her insatiable desire for more dresses, coats, hats, all made of expensive fabrics, is responsible for both ruining her unsuspecting husband and causing her own death. Even though she never goes shopping at the newly inaugurated *Bon Marché* in Paris, she experiences the same frenzy as the women in Zola's *The Ladies' Paradise*. Ultimately, all these bourgeois women were convinced that the power of buying gave them fast access to a better social status and a new form of respect. For them, no sacrifice was big enough to step into bourgeois life, as is the case with Emma Bovary. At the beginning of the commercial era of the mid-nineteenth century, many women, caught in the frenzy combining the beautiful, the plentiful, the exotic, and the new, often overspent senselessly. In this nascent age of consumerism, spending seems to have been too *exciting* for some women to be able to control the impulse. Madame Marty and Emma Bovary's stories of uncontrollable spending were not isolated fictional account; they represented a type common in the period. However, despite the evils and abuses of the age, the power to buy momentarily freed women from domestic and social boredom while making them a new economic force.

The success of department stores was also related to the variety of products they sold, a hitherto unknown variety. Many women felt overwhelmed and excited by the abundance of newly arrived products, especially those coming from the colonies. The exotic appeal of the French colonies was felt on the cultural level of everyday bourgeois life in France, and products from faraway lands became highly desirable. Women were particularly fond of silk materials, carpets, and new fabrics that appealed to their tastes. Their product-related desire fit directly into the contemporary and growing awareness created by the new fashions of the times. In fact, a "fashion" discourse was undertaken by many nineteenth-century writers, a discourse that spoke not only of the trivial elements of style particular to high society, but society at large. During this period, fashion stepped out of the exclusive domain of the privileged, frivolous few to become a true societal paradigm.

Already in the early nineteenth century, Balzac had written in *Traité de la vie élégante* (Essay on Elegant Life) that "garments are the very expression of society" (Pléiade XII, 250). The society he was referring to was that of 1830, but his views on the way fashion reflected society, culture, and people of that time remained true even later. Like him, prominent writers and thinkers like Théophile Gautier in the 1850s, Charles Baudelaire in the 1860s, and Stéphane Mallarmé in the 1870s spent some of their valuable writing time on the topic of fashion considered as an art: one must "study fashion as an art form," suggested Mallarmé (831). In an 1858 article entitled "De la mode" (Of Fashion), Gautier defended the newly introduced crinoline dresses and praised women who turned a deaf ear to the constant criticism of the press for what, admittedly, looked like the most cumbersome outfit ever worn by women: "Women are right to continue to wear the crinoline in spite of the jokes, the caricatures, and the vaudevilles and snubs" (29). To Gautier, nineteenth-century society had to make structural changes, enlarge its salons, and rebuild its theaters to accommodate fashion, rather than the other way around.

Like many of his writer friends—Charles Baudelaire, Gérard de Nerval, Arsène Houssaye—Gautier was fascinated by the Orient as an alternative to the stifling industrial age of Europe and the capitalism of America. According to him, and specifically to his sense of "dandyist" esthetics, the greatest victim of this age of progress and technology was beauty. He asserted that women who were the very embodiment of beauty were now made ugly by European standards. To him, only the artifice of the Orient could return to women their fashionable appeal: "Adieu, old Europe, you who think yourself so young; try to invent a steam engine that manufactures beautiful women, find some new gas to replace the sun. I am going to the Orient: it's much simpler that way" (*L'Orient*, 219).

As he wrote about fashion, Gautier applauded the determination of women to hold on to their fashionable selves regardless of general criticism and bemoaned the failure of new artists to recognize beauty in their stylish attire. As a dandy, he found the new elegance of women both modern and artistic. He defended the fashionable image of women, whom he saw as more beautiful as well as more spiritual and purer when fully "costumed" by fashion, that is, artificially made-up and dressed in satin and moiré. Powdered, she had the marble look of a statue, and she also appeared more intelligent than other women whose natural coloring spoke about the baseness of their physical instincts. It is in the subterfuge and luxury of fashion and in the inspiration it acquired from various other cultures that, according to him, modernity would find beauty again.

In 1863, Baudelaire, also a dandy, concurred in an essay on fashion that he wrote for the paper *Le Figaro*, a piece that convincingly praised the use of make-up for modern women, who would be more beautiful, "magical and supernatural" (*Oeuvres II*, 712) under the unnatural artifice of rouges and powders. In 1874, Mallarmé, also captivated by women's fashion, created a whimsical fashion magazine called *La Dernière Mode* (The Latest Style), for which he was the only editorialist under the penname of Marasquin. As sole editor, he orchestrated the entire publication, assuming various personalities and writing under many different names like Miss Satin or Mme Marguerite de Ponty. Besides its unique editorial policy, the originality of this fashion magazine was that it spoke about the world of fashion from the inside. Eight issues of "La Dernière Mode" appeared in 1874, until Mallarmé gave up this schizophrenic but amusing journalistic charade. Mallarmé, the legendarily difficult poet, must have found some relief from the intellectual intensity of his usual writings when he launched his fashion magazine, thus creating a pleasant hiatus to his otherwise cerebral life.

Dossier 2.4   Crinolines and Empire (1845–1870)

The early crinolines appeared in 1845 but became fully fashionable during the Second Empire between 1852 and 1870. Roughly speaking, they rose and died during the time of the Empress Eugénie, wife of Emperor Napoléon III, who put them in fashion in 1854 and then out of fashion at the end of her reign in 1870 (see figure 2.3). Just like any other industry, women's fashion evolved with the advances and progress of newer material and modern mentalities, and crinolines were the result of a "scientific" re-conceptualization of fashion that kept women elegant, "their waists thin, their torso well defined, and their bodies graciously pyramidal" (Gautier, *De la mode*, 30). Not everyone was in agreement concerning the advantages and esthetics of the crinolines. Many saw a revival of the old and tasteless "paniers" and "vertugadins," doctors thought that the naked women's legs under the crinoline hoops would expose women to cold drafts, while on the contrary women found it liberating to be able to move their legs freely in the private space under their ballooned skirts. In addition, national pride and questions of taste were at stake in the highly fashionable times of crinolines. Indeed, some of the French felt that crinolines were yet another manifestation of British industrial advance over the French: crinolines were a British invention, developed by the British couturier Charles Frédéric Worth, who was first noticed and protected by the Princess of Metternich and then by the Empress Eugénie herself. He subsequently became French when he created his highly selective boutique on the rue de la Paix in Paris. Worth was also largely responsible for the disappearance of the crinolines in 1870. Crinolines were indeed a reflection of imperial French society, their general look imposed the power of an elegant and voluminous dress while allowing a new "hidden" freedom, one that was felt from under the dome of the dress but not seen by the public.

Besides their social status, crinolines were also the product of research in the fashion industry. They were conceived as a light cage made of flexible bone-like material on top of which elegant fabric cascaded down and followed the gentle movement of the body swinging gracefully with each step. Some saw a kind of similarity between the construction of Crystal Palace for the 1851 London World Fair and the structure of the crinoline cage, as if the age of architectural invention and new modern material had extended its vision and its wonders beyond the confines of its specific field.

Simultaneously modern, as they reflected the "grandeur" and elegance of the empire, and not modern, as they seemed to violate basic rules of comfort, the crinolines were often a target of derision. They were part of a larger trend of humor that seemed to find in their bulkiness and apparent discomfort a wide range of comic material. For example, Bertall, an editorialist at the newspaper *L'Illustration*, wrote a humorous illustrated series entitled "Fashion Victims," where images and comments reflected the humorous potential created by crinolines: the overwhelming multilayered dress in which women disappeared and husbands lost their fortunes—as women kept adding expensive skirts to the basic cage—or the hilarious situation of a woman trying to sit in regular seats on public transportation having to compress a hoop skirt that would eventually spring back out at people sitting next to her. "A multitude of unfavorable stories circulated concerning the new fashion; Mrs. X couldn't fit in to her opera box; Ms. Y was forced by the dimensions of her crinoline to give up trying to get into a carriage; at the flower market, an impertinent sparrow strayed under the bell of a crinoline, where it remained imprisoned" (*Histoire de la mode en France*, 180).

In the end, whenever the press poked fun at the crinolines it seemed that beyond criticizing the world of fashion itself, it was aiming at the times and society that fashion represented. Journalists had found an indirect way to ridicule the empire by comparing the gigantism of its ambition to the unwieldy and impractical world of fashion incarnated by the stylish Empress and all other bourgeois women who looked up to her as the model for the latest fashion.

The 1867 Universal Exposition

The World's Fair, the final blow in the Americanization of France, industry triumphing over art, the steam engine reigning in place of the painting.

—Edmond and Jules de Goncourt, *Journal*

This is becoming crazy and out of hand. We are threatened with a new Babylon.

—Gustave Flaubert and George Sand, *Correspondence*

On the occasion of the extravagant 1867 Universal Exposition in Paris the national and international press had an opportunity to observe, criticize, and praise women of the Second Empire for the unique and innovative fashion that caused a sensation during this international event. The crinoline fashion was luxurious and impressive, and seemed an indication of the high standards and the glamorous facade displayed by the French during the modern magic of the 1867 exposition. Modern magic was indeed part of the general settings of the exposition as described by Paul Pawlowski in a general introduction to the exposition: "Today, everything is set up, ordered, prepared; the windows glisten with riches; in the fields of mining and metallurgy, steam has set in motion a variety of machines designed for manufacture; it is the life man's genius breathes into inert matter" (3–4).

Held on the Champ de Mars in Paris from April 1 to November 3, 1867, the Universal Exposition was an important political affair for the emperor who wished to show off the newly reconstructed and fully modernized Paris to the world as a sign both of his own greatness as a modern emperor and of the superiority of his country fully invested in the industrial age. More exhibitors from more countries than in any prior expositions and fairs came to Paris for the occasion. It seemed that the entire world was meeting in Paris to enjoy the grace and wonders of the newly recon- structed city and to grasp a taste of French-style modernity. As described in the intro- duction to a pamphlet on the exhibition, the exposition grounds resembled a miniature world built as a lively and diversified city of many nations:

> A delightful park containing a veritable city amid the lawns and copses, an extraordinary city, the likes of which only the storytellers of *The 1001 Arabian Nights* seem capable of conceiving; an ensemble of structures where the most violent contrasts gave birth to a strange and unexpected harmony, transporting the wide-awake visitor to the region of dreams . . . Turkish, Egyptian, and Tunisian palaces, a mosque, a temple of the Pharaohs, a temple of the Mexicans . . . Russian, Norwegian, and Danish houses, just next to the Tyrolean chalets; a corner of Rome's catacombs, English cottages, laborer's houses, farms, lighthouses, a theater, a salon, hundreds of structures as disparate as they were graceful and magnificent . . . and restaurants everywhere, for all classes of visitor, cafés, songs, orches- tras; the toll of bells, the whistle of steam machines . . . such was the Park of the Champ de Mars during the Universal Exposition. (*Paris il y a cent ans*. Introduction).

The exposition covered 417,550 square meters in Paris with some large additional space opened for agricultural machines on Billancourt Island, southeast of Paris (642,520 square meters), which made the exposition ten times larger than the one that had been held in London in 1862 or in Paris in 1855. The main pavilion itself covered thirty-six acres. In all, the exposition welcomed approximately 4 million visitors, the most to any past expositions and fairs. It was also the most lucrative, as it made the greatest profit of all expositions held in the nineteenth century, including the ones that followed it.

One of the remarkable features of the exposition was what became known as the "universal boardwalk." The main exposition center was built in the shape of a huge oval palace bordered by a mile-long paved, sheltered, and gas-lit boardwalk. Along this boardwalk one would find all countries represented by booths displaying their national arts and crafts, as well as performers to entertain the crowds. The exposition catalogue insisted on the extraordinary nature of the boardwalk, underlining its grandiose, exotic, and truly universal nature. First, the multitude of spoken languages created an intoxi- cating and strange multilingual environment gathered in one single place: "All the lan- guages in the universe were mixing on the boardwalk in a bizarre concert" (ix).

Then, the walk provided so much international street entertainment that it was hard to resist feeling part of a global community filled with a fulfilling variety of differences and particularities as described in the official catalogue.

> Strolling along the promenade, which will remain forever famous, and which accorded the Exposition the animated aspect of an immense country fair, one could witness the convulsionary Negroes from the Aïssaouas tribe going to the international theater to display their epileptic exercises, or the Russian riders upon the prancing steeds of the Czar, or yet still the Nubians walking the camels of the Viceroy of Egypt along the heights of Trocadero. Here as well, at the Fanta Brasserie, the excellent orchestra of gypsy artists, under the direction of their chief Pattrikarius attracted a crowd where all

classes of people mixed to give their enthusiastic applause to the fierce and energetic music, the colorful and picturesque music. Finally, before leaving the promenade, let us give an honorable mention to the French exhibit, refuge of the frightening dentist, *Iron Mask (Masque de Fer)*, of the talking decapitated head, and of the Chinese giant, accompanied by his wife and a Tartar dwarf. We can see the Fair was truly worthy to be called "universal," since there you could find everything from dentists to acrobats. (ix–x)

The boardwalk offered the atmosphere of a country fair with its local entertainment and its sideshows—complete with extraordinary performances by the talking decapitated head, or the Chinese giant and the Tartar dwarf—but it also had the dynamics of an international event and more specifically of an exotic display with varied spectacles, from African dancers to gypsy musicians. Horses and camels gave the exposition an additional circus flair and Paris a surreal appearance: camels walking on the Trocadéro! But more importantly, the feeling, as you walked around the main palace, was one of a true universal gathering where not only the different races met, but also where all social classes mixed.

Indeed, the people of Paris were here to see the world in miniature brought to their door, a sort of astonishing amusement park with an unprecedented variety of entertainment and extraordinary machines. Many international guests were personally invited and greeted by the emperor and the empress for a diplomatic visit to the exposition and a proper introduction to the "new" Paris. They were also invited to introduce their own national products and arts at the exposition itself. All were stunned by the magnificent host city that Paris had become.

Figure 2.3   Universal Exposition (1867)

The imperial family pays an official visit to the Egyptian exhibit, a reproduction of the Edfou Temple, during the 1867 Universal Exposition. The emperor, the empress, the young prince imperial, and their entourage are greeted by the Egyptian viceroy and the official delegation from Egypt. (© L'Illustration)

Among them was the Sultan of Egypt, whose visit to France was his first. Egypt was particularly honored during the exhibit and Egyptian officials received the "royal" treatment. This came as no surprise given that France had become economically tied to Egypt with the construction of the Suez Canal. On this topic, we also read the following remarks printed in the fair's catalogue:

> One finds a certain number of astonishing buildings in the Park. From Egypt, a reproduction of the temple of Philoe was raised with, on the inside, an exhibit of ancient treasures directly imported from an Egyptian museum. One likewise finds a reproduction of an Egyptian house, as well as that of the palace of the Egyptian viceroy. There is the pavilion with the Isthmus of Suez, wherein one may study blueprints and models of the canal. But one can also see the reproduction of an Egyptian bazaar, complete with artisans and vendors. (*Catalogue de l'exposition universelle de 1867*, x)

In this excerpt, we see how pleasure and knowledge joined forces to comprise the essential recipe that would keep the curious and entertained visitors coming to the exposition. In this light, the exposition may be seen as the actual precursor to contemporary "Disney Worlds," "Parc Astérix," and "Epcot centers."

Foreign Policy and Empire

It was not surprising to see all the diplomatic efforts made by the imperial family toward the East and the Mediterranean countries during the 1867 Universal Exposition, as Napoleon III, originally only mildly concerned with colonization, radically changed his views and became, as of 1859, very interested in developing his own colonial empire. Besides the fashionable exoticism of the time and the economic interest in developing a colonial empire, his attention to the colonial world was also triggered by his desire to catch up with the British, who had already established a significant empire in Asia and had made it fully functional and profitable for the English crown. As opposed to the British, the French did not have a systematic colonial policy until 1859. In fact, prior to this date, the French colonies already in place were often essentially claimed for France by individual French entrepreneurs, explorers, and missionaries and not as part of a proactive French official colonial program.

In 1859, with the beginning of the construction of the Suez Canal, Napoleon III, fully immersed in his Saint-Simonian liberal and progressive phase, began to affirm his political interests by establishing the presence of France in the world. Ideologically, he felt that the world needed to be modernized and "civilized" in order to improve the lives of all people. France's mission then became clear: it proposed to bring civilization and religious teaching to as many world outposts as possible with the objective of creating a better life for all nations under French protection. In this respect, Napoleon III's views were radically different from those of the British, whose colonial ambitions were more oriented toward conquering and taking over for the economic benefit of the British crown.

Eager to extend the European commercial routes to the East, Napoleon III set forth to develop the ambitious plan first imagined by his uncle Napoleon I to dig a canal through the Suez Isthmus in Egypt in order to link the Mediterranean Sea and the Red Sea and thereby create a water passage to India and other Asian countries. Through the intermediary of Ferdinand de Lesseps, a French diplomat in Egypt and a relative of the empress in addition to being a personal friend of the Egyptian Khedive, the sultan's viceroy, the French were given executive powers by the Egyptians to build the canal under the direction of de Lesseps, who founded the universal Suez Canal company in 1855—the *Compagnie Universelle du Canal de Suez*—to supervise the project. Despite strong British opposition, work began in 1859 and ended in 1869, when the 160-kilometer canal was inaugurated in the midst of lavish international festivities. The canal would shorten commercial sea routes to Africa and the East by 8,000 kilometers. Despite the positive outcome of the creation of the canal for world commerce, the authority given to the French in this matter would continue to worry the British, who feared not only another Napoleonic-type takeover in Egypt—the conquest of Egypt by Napoleon I was still present in their mind—but also the possible dismantling of their heretofore unchallenged hegemony in colonial matters. In order to counteract the slow but very real French competition in the conquest of the colonial world, the British would rapidly regain financial control of the canal by buying all its stock.

Besides his immediate success in the Suez Canal venture, Napoleon III's ambitious colonial plan was to extend French presence in the Arab world from Algeria to Iraq and thus fulfill his dream of a French Arab Empire. He thus began to look closely at Algeria, which had been a French possession since 1830.

Napoleon III had briefly visited French-colonized Algeria in 1860 and was impressed by the stark beauty of the country, the kindness of its people, and the resources available. However, unlike the British colonial policy of social and civil segregation between the European settlers and the indigenous population, Napoleon III wished for a policy of assimilation. From the time of his visit to Algeria on, he actively pushed his foreign policy agenda and specifically worked with his emissaries to give equal citizenship rights to Arabs, whom he refused to call "indigenous" any longer. His agenda was clearly laid out in his 1860 speech to Algerians and European settlers in Algiers:

> Our first duty is to see to the happiness of the three million Arabs, that the fate of arms has brought under our domination. To instill in the Arabs the dignity of free men, to spread among them the benefits of education, all the while respecting their religion, to improve their existence by unearthing all the treasures buried there, but which bad governance would leave sterile, this is our mission: And we will not fail. (*Napoléon III et son temps*, 153–154)

His pronouncement in favor of the "happiness" of Arabs as a primordial duty ruffled a few feathers among the European audience. In order to introduce the Arabs to modern times, the emperor's program included education and military training. Naturally, his plan for treating Arabs as equals encountered strong opposition from the colonists, who never accepted the idea of educating Arabs or even of bringing the two peoples together. They dismissed the emperor's program by forcing the Arab population away from Algeria's fertile and prosperous coastline into the southern part of the country, near and even into the Sahara desert, where living conditions were extremely harsh.

For those in favor of his approach to colonization, the emperor's visit seemed to be a resounding success. However, his relatively liberal and controversial program met with radical opposition from many others. The Algerian colonists were clearly disappointed by their emperor who did not publicly support their interests. The sour mood of the French colonists toward the imperial authority were an echo of Victor Hugo's

1850 derogatory depiction of the emperor as "Napoleon the Little," or the small emperor who tried to be great but did not have the political gravitas or character to follow in the footsteps of Napoleon I. As a colonial emperor, "Napoleon the Little" did not gain the full respect of his people, and this was obvious during his Algerian trip.

Eugenia: Beauty and Intelligence

What could have further contributed to the emperor's diminished image may reside in the fact that he shared much of the imperial limelight with a woman of great personality and beauty, his wife, the empress Eugenia. In fact, for a time, many critics of the empire accused the empress of ruling the country through her husband, passing on her religious and political ideas and opinions to him. Behind her undeniable beauty and her leading role as a cultural icon, she was often thought of as the unsung leader of France, as the brain behind the empire, and consequently as the guilty party for unsuccessful political actions.

In 1853, the emperor had married Eugenia María de Montijo de Guzmán, a Spanish noblewoman, blessed with beauty and grace, but also a staunch Catholic with strong political convictions. She became known in France as the Empress Eugénie for those who liked and respected her, and *l'Espagnole* (the Spaniard) for those who disliked her *discreet* political influence over the emperor. As a highly visible woman of combined grace and spirit, she remained throughout the Second Empire the easy target of every possible criticism directed at the political affairs of the emperor, whichever way they went.

During France's Mexican campaign, Empress Eugénie was accused of being the Catholic voice advising the emperor to fight the Mexicans in 1863. However, it seems likely that the emperor was primarily motivated by his own imperial desire to cut himself a part of Latin America, to create a "Latin Empire" as it were, in order to install a French presence on a continent so heavily dominated by the United States. In 1863, the emperor was at the height of his colonization phase and had views on going West, as he had just fulfilled part of his Eastern dream with the recent acquisition of Cochinchina (1862)—a region located between China and India, later called Indochina, and known today as part of Vietnam. The Mexican campaign was part of this Western dream. It began as a coalition with Spain and England, but soon ended up as primarily a French expedition. Napoleon III's army was victorious in Mexico and the emperor, who was looking for diplomatic ties with Austria, named the Archduke Maximilian, brother of the Austrian emperor Franz Josef I, emperor of Mexico. This "Napoleon-like" effort could have been a remarkable victory for the French Empire but, instead, the ensuing four-year Mexican guerrilla war slowly wore out the French Army. As interested as he was in enlarging his colonial empire, the emperor nevertheless did not see the point in wasting soldiers' lives, especially at a time when he needed them in Europe to prepare for the impending face-off with a much more threatening enemy, Chancellor Bismarck of Prussia. Finally, when the United States, whose political and military attention had until then been diverted by its own Civil War (1861–1865), began to take note of the situation in Mexico, it provided weapons to the rebels led by Juárez in order to help the Mexicans overthrow the French Empire and establish their own republican government. The empire's military strength quickly declined, and the remaining French troops returned home leaving the Mexican Empire unprotected. Finally, in 1867, Emperor Maximilian was killed, and Mexico proclaimed itself a republic.

Despite historical evidence that Napoleon III went into the Mexican campaign with a plan of his own, the empress, according to her detractors, had her share of responsibility for this fiasco. She was blamed for listening to the Mexican Catholic lobbyists and for influencing her husband to wage the Mexican War against the divided Mexican government led by the anticlerical and liberal president Juárez. Even if historians largely agree that the war started over a financial debt, it is possible that the additional push from the empress helped the emperor make a final decision. Juárez, who owed money to the British, the Spanish, and the French, could not pay it back in the time frame he was given to settle his accounts. This unpaid debt prompted Napoleon to form an alliance with the British and the Spanish, as they were all eager to recover their money from Mexico.

Undoubtedly, the empress had a pragmatic mind that was concerned with the empire's affairs and gave her "modest" opinion to the emperor. Naturally, she took a leading role in cultural life, but she was also directly and indirectly involved in the political affairs of the empire. Eugénie was both a trendsetter for the fashion of the times and to many a model of good moral values and proper royal conduct. However observant and respectful of her traditional role as the emperor's wife, the devoted mother to the prince, and leader of the court, she was also undoubtedly more than just the pretty and stylish "first lady" bound to social outings and protocol, and she did play, openly or not, a role in the political life of her husband. She often sat at the Assembly as the official regent in the emperor's absence. During these sessions, she would sometimes voice her opinions, an act many deemed inconceivable coming from a woman, especially a woman of such imperial and mythical stature who was theoretically remote from earthly politics. But Eugénie was more concerned with reality than she was with her traditional or even mythical image. After fulfilling her maternal and imperial duty to produce a male heir in 1856, she became Napoleon's strongest influence, his trusted private political advisor. She was by his side during the official trip to Algeria and the main boulevard built along Algiers's sea border, the "Boulevard of the Empress" was named after her. She represented the interests of the empire on her own during the lavish inauguration of the Suez Canal in 1869. More significantly, she is said to have encouraged Napoleon not only to declare war on Prussia in 1870, but also to act as commander in chief and lead his army to the front himself. However, his appearance as leader was less than imperial, as he left for war in visible physical pain due to his kidney problems. This image of the emperor leaving for war pathetically hunched over his horse clashed with the official paintings, where he appeared glorious and dignified. Much of his authority and respect had previously been transposed onto the equestrian portraits that were painted of him during his reign, especially the Alfred de Dreux's canvas (1858) where he appeared tall and defiant, standing straight in his stirrups, in full command of his steed. His profile as a leader, sitting proudly on his horse, was literally built into these paintings just as Napoleon I's imperial identity had been captured by classical artists like David and Gros who had sealed the political image of Napoleon in his famous equestrian portraits. There was a tradition of power inscribed in the manner the Bonaparte dynasty was painted on its horses, an imperial tradition inspired by the representation of another powerful figure, Julius Caesar. In fact, Napoleon III had a Caesar-like ambition, one that earned him the label of "Caesarist," or authoritative political and imperial figure with popular support and democratic intentions. As a modern Caesar, both his actions and his image were important in positively influencing his subjects. Unfortunately, the statuesque and regal image of the emperor seemed now shattered for those in his army who saw him in pain and crumpled over when leaving for the front on July 28, 1870. This image of a diminished emperor going to war may be read as a foreboding sign of an equally diminished empire, and of looming radical changes in the future of France. Despite the respect the people had for her, many were quick to criticize Eugénie for the emperor's decision to go to war as a weak and weary warrior. In his *Confessions*, the famous publisher Arsène Houssaye confirms the dual feeling Eugenia generated among the French and the contradictions she embodied:

> Women have always been the demise of their kingdoms and empires. . . . Her beautiful, luminous brow said everything. You could read her soul on every page; it was a poem of beauty with all the verses of grace. She was criticized for her smile, now she is criticized for her tears. But what is one woman's pain compared to that of France, near fatally wounded and suffering for fifteen years? History will never forgive her, even with all the charms of her beauty and grace, even with the many paintings which depict her bent over the beds of the dying beneath a halo of charity.
>
> How could she, without trembling, take the hand of the emperor, already a ghost emperor himself, to make him sign this war declaration that was going to send so many Frenchmen to the grave? She must have believed that her son was under a good star. (145–147)

In the emperor's entourage, many who had been under the charm of the empress's femininity and beauty now blamed her for using her power to influence her husband's political affairs and thereby bringing on France's imperial troubles: war and the end of the empire. Indeed, the emperor appointed her as regent on July 23, 1870, thus giving her the authority to enforce his political will and pursue his imperial vision for France in his place during his absence, a heavy responsibility for anyone to bear.

The Duc de Gramont, a conservative member of the "Conseil," or the French Assembly, and French foreign minister, asserted that the decision to go to war against Prussia in 1870 came from the empress who had spoken to the Assembly on July 14, 1870 in favor of the attack. However, other members of the Assembly such as first speaker Emile Ollivier reported that she remained silent throughout the session.

The delicate topic at hand on that day was the inflammatory demand from Prussia that a Prussian prince, Leopold Hohenzollern, be the Spanish royal successor. Napoleon III, with the support of a majority of Republicans, categorically refused such a prospect for the future crown of Spain. Undoubtedly, the "Spanish" empress must have also objected to such a succession, silently or not.

This question of the Spanish succession became the diplomatic detail that pressured France into waging war on Prussia.

1870: The Franco-Prussian War

Not only did Napoleon III request the official withdrawal of Hohenzollern, he also wanted Prussia's full assurance that such a situation would never again arise. Prince Hohenzollern withdrew, but the Prussian chancellor Otto von Bismarck, whose ambition it was to unite all Prussian and German states into a great German Empire, saw here the opportunity to fulfill his ambition by showing how powerful, respected, and, above all, competitive a united Germany could be in the modern world. He disregarded the French diplomatic effort—to obtain satisfaction on the request that Prussia would never again try to impose its will without consultation—by short-circuiting an official meeting between King Wilhelm I of Prussia and the French ambassador and rewording the final report in provocative terms. This diplomatic "insult" was enough to create a rift between the two nations and war quickly ensued; too quickly for the French army, which was not ready for the massive attack.

When France declared war on Prussia on July 19, 1870, it was with a false sense of confidence in its own military capabilities. France's international prestige as well as its own army's reputation left no doubt in the minds of the French that Prussia would soon regret waging war against them. On August 3, 1870, an overly confident Gustave Flaubert wrote to his writer friend George Sand: "But maybe Prussia is going to get a good rubbing?" (*Flaubert—Sand*, 208). French people in all cities were chant-ing with enthusiasm that the Prussians would be sent back to Berlin: "Let's march, let's march on Berlin and strangle the Prussians" (Zénaïde Fleuriot, 54), while others were defiantly singing the "Marseillaise," the French national anthem written after the French Revolution and banned several times afterward, most notably under Napoleon III. For now, everyone expressed some form of excitement for what all expected to be a quick war and an unquestionable victory for France.

On the one hand, the emperor felt certain that his volunteers' army would be easily mobilized. He trusted that French soldiers would turn out in great numbers and would also be very eager to fight proudly in defense of the imperial crown. On the other hand, progress in the military industry had improved artillery capacities with, in particular, the invention of the *mitrailleuse*, the machine gun.

Unfortunately for the emperor's overconfidence in France's war-making capabili-ties, many trained French soldiers sold their military "status" and identity to poor young peasants without military experience who would go to war in their stead. In addition, a number of strategic and logistical mistakes led to further military disaster. In one instance, a full supply of brand new chassepot rifles were sitting in Dunkerque, a port on the northern coast of France, while the soldiers in Lyon, a city in the east of France, awaited them in their units. Inexperienced soldiers combined with disorga-nized leadership and poor coordination led the army to its slow disintegration and the emperor to his defeat. It did not help that the Prussians were advancing with a much larger and more devoted army of conscripts who had superior military capabilities, reinforcing the imbalance between the two warring parties and leaving France with virtually no chance for victory. Morale was at an all-time low as it became more and more obvious that France was losing the war. But the inevitable outcome of the war was also the ideal occasion for the emperor's sizeable republican opposition to seize the moment by making a decisive move in the direction of the democratic govern-ment of which they had dreamed for so long. When, on September 4, 1870, the news of the emperor's capture by the Prussians in Sedan on the Franco-Prussian border reached Paris, a provisional republican government, or Government of National Defense, was quickly formed and also welcomed by the population all over France. In Paris, a young politician named Leon Gambetta proclaimed the end of the empire and the beginning of the Third Republic. Adolphe Thiers, a moderate conservative who led the opposition during the empire, was named head of the new, still unstable Third Republic. His "moderate" politics earned him the trust of many from both sides of the political fence, monarchists and bourgeois on the one side, and workers on the other. Despite difficult beginnings, the Third Republic became somehow exemplary and successful, as it lasted seventy years, until 1940. Indeed, today the French still abide by the spirit of the founding principles proposed by the proponents of the Third Republic: a political regime both universalist in principle and emancipatory in practice, protected by the text of a legally supreme constitution that allowed all citizens to live, work, and prosper under its protection.

In a brief but opportune moment on September 4, 1870, as the empire fell, the Third Republic was born. The war, however, was far from over. Prewar ebullience was soon replaced by an offended and virulent sense of national pride, raising dangerous levels of passionate feeling in favor of vengeance against the victorious Prussians. France would not stand humiliated and could not psychologically bring itself to accept the many war concessions made to the Prussians. Many historians believe that it is this ingrained thirst for revenge that took the French from the edge of the Third Republic all the way to World War I in 1914, a war where France reclaimed the territory lost as a result of the Franco-Prussian War.

During the few months that followed the proclamation of the Third Republic in 1870–1871, the country was slowly being occupied by the Prussians, who were penetrating French territory from the north and from the east and winning battle after battle. The continuous string of military defeats demoralized the French, who could not admit that their prestigious and powerful nation was being overwhelmed by the Prussians. Upon hearing the capitulation of the emperor, Flaubert, who had been a bold and optimistic prowar believer before the war, thought that France had finally hit rock bottom, but that its true patriotic spirit would carry its discontent against the Prussians for a long time. On this last point he was right. For his part, the poet Mallarmé spoke about the unknown degree of misfortune and insanity that was pervading the atmosphere of the times. When, on January 28, 1871, the armistice was declared and peace signed a few days later, the French regions of Alsace and Lorraine were annexed to the newly constituted German Empire and a five-billion-franc debt was imposed on the French government. It is then that pride and patriotism turned into dangerous sentiments of pure hatred toward the Germans. In addition, humiliation came to a height when Bismarck arranged for King Wilhelm I of Prussia to be named emperor of the now unified Germany at Versailles, the historical palace of the French kings. With this last blow, it is not surprising to read what army volunteer, writer, and extremist politician Paul Déroulède wrote about the situation. His fanaticism went as far as devoting his public life to finding ways to avenge France's honor. In 1872, he published the collection of songs and poems *Soldiers' Songs*, where he violently expressed his hatred for the Germans (Prussians) and his thirst for revenge:

> I despise this Vandal people,
> These ruffians, these executioner—all the names apply;
> I despise them, I curse their fatal race,
> Prussia and the Prussians!
>
> May their King, crowned tyrant in victory,
> Reversing progress to Antiquity,

Gag on their joy, choke on their glory,
Prussia and the Prussians!

This is, above all, the dream of my youth;
For this alone do I live, to this alone do I hold,
That the nation in mourning rise up and only leave
Prussia to the Prussians!

(126)

On the other hand, some saw the dangers of such exacerbated patriotism and counseled moderation in disdain instead of revenge. This was the case of the young critic and essayist Remy de Gourmont, who was convinced that people from Alsace and Lorraine were not so unhappy under German rule, as they had been long accustomed to their neighborly presence along the Rhine, and even spoke Alsatian, a regional language more closely related to German than to French. He claimed that as part of the German Empire, they were now carrying on with business as usual and eating as well as they had before. In his article *Le joujou patriotisme* (The Patriotic Toy) published in March 1891, he wrote about the necessity of accepting the Franco-Prussian postwar agreement. He warned the sour French patriots about the destructive passions brought on by their hard-line position: "Let us cleanse ourselves of these humors; let us take a few pills of disdain to purge ourselves of this new virus named Patriotism" (*Pendant l'orage*, 120–121). His attack on excessive patriotism provoked such indignation in the general public that Gourmont was professionally punished by being dismissed from his position as assistant librarian at the Paris Bibliothèque Nationale (the National Library).

Between these two extreme sentiments, many criticized the Franco-Prussian War and its consequences as a way to deplore war in general and its disastrous effects on all humanity. This was the case of the prolific writer Guy de Maupassant, who, having himself been deeply scarred by this traumatic period in French history, described his feelings against the Franco-Prussian War in some of his stories and novels, like *Boule de suif* written in 1880.

The war had ended a full ten years before Guy de Maupassant wrote *Boule de suif;* a story about a group of people fleeing war-sticken Rouen in a carriage to go to Dieppe, a city on the western shore where they hoped to take a boat to England: among them the friendly prostitute called "Boule de suif." However, the subject of war was still fresh enough in his mind that he decided to revisit it in order to alert his readers to its perils. The Franco-Prussian War confirmed his antimilitaristic views, qualifying wars as inhuman and pointless, as they destroyed both human lives and, perhaps more importantly for Maupassant, human dignity. As other conflicts arose in the remaining decades of the nineteenth century, those in Tunisia and China, for example, Maupassant would continue to write in favor of peace, inspired as he was by his harrowing experience of the Franco-Prussian War. Like Zola, Maupassant was a naturalist writer who believed that fiction should reflect and reveal the truth about society in all of its most horrific details. The war he described in *Boule de suif* was real, the environment of the story was also real—the carriage travels from Rouen, to Tostes, to Dieppe—the characters appeared with recognizable professional and social traits of the times, their everyday life is accurately described, and their social rank is depicted as that which defines them. As a case in point, the character Boule de suif is a patriot and a prostitute, the only "good" person among this group of people in the carriage from various social backgrounds: a revolutionary, several shopkeepers, grand bourgeois, nobles from Normandy, two nuns, innkeepers, and a Prussian officer. With this group of characters, Maupassant recreates in miniature the social make-up of the time and is able to record and test their individual actions against the background of the Franco-Prussian War. In the end, Boule de suif, the prostitute, proves to be the most honorable human being of them all, as she reluctantly accepts to sacrifice herself for the sake of saving her French travel companions held captive by a Prussian officer occupying the inn where they have stopped. After being cajoled by the overly convincing and selfish members of the traveling group, including the absolving nuns and the hypocritical aristocrat, into giving up her principles by having sex with the Prussian officer as the only way to save both the group and the honor of France, she silently goes upstairs to sleep with the enemy. Her sexual self-sacrifice alone frees the group from the Prussians, and the coach resumes its route the next day. However, the passengers, so friendly the day before, will now show their indifference, selfishness, and disdain toward Boule de suif who after all, according to them, is just a lowly prostitute, unworthy of their attention and concerns. Boule de suif sobs quietly for the rest of the trip, allegorically representing the mistreated body and soul of France, "raped" by the Prussians but left unprotected and abandoned by the French church as well as the French bourgeoisie and aristocracy.

Maupassant chose to introduce the short fifty-page story with a meticulously detailed, seven-page description of the war. He sets the tone for the story in the real-ist depiction of the somber mood marking the departure of the disbanded and weary French army, the silence and fear preceding the impending arrival of the Prussians, and the slow but perceptible acceptance of the enemy's presence. However, in spite of a kind of cooperation, even collaboration, between the Prussians and the French, there was an "intolerably unfamiliar [. . .] odor of invasion" (4) that would drive unaccepting citizens to resist and to rebel. In the hands of this resisting faction, Prussian officers would sometimes be killed and drowned, and their bodies later found in the rivers outside of Rouen. Hatred for the Prussians would indeed create a sense of courage beyond reason, revealing that some "brave" men and women were absolutely "ready to die for an idea" (5). This scenario would subsequently be repeated in history, as the German occupiers during World War II would also invade and settle in French cities where some of the population collaborated with them, while others French resisted (see chapter 5).

The city of Rouen was occupied by the Prussians on December 4, 1870. Like many other French cities it was not able to hold out against the impressive and highly organized Prussian war machine. Only two cities resisted the Prussians until the armistice of January 1871: Le Havre, on the northwestern coast of France, and Paris. Le Havre held on despite the sad state and shape of its troops. Paris refused to give up fighting and the Prussians encircled the city, hoping that either heavy bom-bardments or starvation would win over the physical strength and the fighting spirit of the Parisians. The bombing and shelling began on January 4, 1871 and lasted for the entire month but did not deter the population from defending its city. As for supplies, after a four-month siege and despite the warnings of the mayor, Jules Ferry, to conserve food, famine was widespread and supplies were completely exhausted. Paris had been cut off from its food supplies since September 1870, and the population had to establish a rationing system if everyone was to survive under the circumstances. The city was reduced to eating dogs and cats, and even rats became a rare delicacy.

Figure 2.4   The Siege of Paris (1870–1871)

A food stall during the 1870 Franco-Prussian War. Due to the siege of the city the population relied on unusual meat ranging from domestic animals like dog and cat to common rodents like rats. The clientele is a social mix of modest and bourgeois Parisians. (© L'Illustration)

These unusual victuals became luxury items available only at high prices, affordable by the well-to-do. Perhaps the most extreme measure taken to fight starvation in the city was the decision to sacrifice zoo animals. Some of the animals in captivity at the Paris zoo, zebras, buffalos, and even the two popular elephants affectionately named Castor and Pollux, became the last resort for the starved city. In his journal, Edmond de Goncourt recalled how on December 31, 1870, four months into the siege, he went to Roos's, a butcher specializing in luxury items, with a shop on the fashionable Boulevard Haussmann:

> Out of curiosity I went into Roos's, the English butcher's shop on the Boulevard Haussmann, where I saw all sorts of weird remains. On the wall, hung in place of honor, was the skinned trunk of young Pollux, the elephant at the zoo; and in the midst of nameless meats and unusual horns, a boy was offering camel's kidneys for sale.
>
> The master-butcher was perorating to a group of women: "it's forty francs a pound for the fillet and the trunk . . . Yes, forty francs . . . You think that's expensive? But I assure you I don't know how I am going to make any profit out of it. I was counting on three thousand pounds of meat and it has only yielded two thousand three hundred . . . The

feet, you want to know the price of the feet? It's twenty francs . . . For the other pieces, it ranges from eight francs to forty . . . But let me recommend the *black pudding* (blood sausage). As you know, the elephant's blood is the richest there is. His heart weighed twenty-five pounds . . . And there's onion, ladies, in my black pudding."

I fell back on a couple of larks, which I carried off for my lunch tomorrow. (*The Goncourts Journal*, 179–180)

During the siege of Paris, every part of every living animal was consumable because nothing "fleshy" or "meaty" could be wasted in those harsh times of meager resources. Along with meat, blood and organs of all sorts had to be consumed without shame or disgust as these very desperate times called for desperate measures. In peaceful times, the upper and middle classes may have valued and even been amused by the consumption of unusual and rare food, like elephant blood sausage. In addition to simple hunger, it was this quirky and trendy bourgeois habit of consuming rare delicacies that socially enabled this privileged population to consider buying such unusual products and eating them with the same acute sense of taste as during times of plenty. While times were hard, eating unusual meat and organs on a regular basis was indeed a necessity, but it was one that was performed with a ritual sense of class propriety. In fact, the social reasoning for consuming all sorts of animal products was that if one had to eat elephant blood, it was with the conviction that such blood was an excellent product as long as it was delicately prepared—with a confit of onions, for example—thus rendering it fully appetizing and acceptable to bourgeois standards. Despite the difficulty and the food shortage of the times, bourgeois values remained unchallenged and appearances were maintained as much as possible. However, beyond appearance and social etiquette, restrictions did affect the entire population of Paris.

In addition to being starved, and short of every commodity, Paris resembled a giant army camp. Works of art had been safely put away in underground locations, while the Louvre became a temporary arsenal, the palace of the Tuileries an army barracks, and hotels and theaters hospitals.

The city resisted the Prussians until the newly constituted conservative government led by Adolphe Thiers, the newly appointed "Chief of the Executive Power of the Republic," in other words, the new French premier, called for an end to the hostilities and surrendered on January 28, 1871. Not everyone accepted defeat, however. Having shown their unconditional courage and patriotic desire to continue fighting against the Prussians during the war, many Parisians literally felt abandoned by their own "new" government at the time of the armistice. They felt that their fighting had been in vain and blamed the government for giving up. The city, especially its "popular" or lower-class residents, grew angry at the conservative Assembly of the French Republic, first because Thiers, weary of the unrest, decided to move its headquarters from the capital to Versailles, and second because of the budgetary hardship resulting from war reparation payments owed to the Germans. The French government immediately looked for available assets among the already financially squeezed and emotionally drained Parisian population. To seek money from a greatly impoverished city seemed arrogant and untimely, but the French government went ahead and sought release from its financial liability by requiring rents and debts to be paid immediately and by stopping the financing of the National Guard, the militia force of Paris that had wholeheartedly defended the city against the Prussians. To cut off the National Guard was more than a financial sacrifice; it also represented a political gesture, a way to get rid off potential trouble. Without a doubt, this voluntary militia was now perceived as a potential threat by the official French government in place. Indeed, the National Guard was still armed with rifles and cannons and represented a potentially independent military force that was making the French government all the more nervous about its very existence. Preoccupied by the firepower still in the hands of a politically agitated city and its unofficial security force, Thiers sent French government troops to seize the city cannons stocked in Montmartre, a neighborhood on a hill north of Paris, on March 18, 1871. The incident set off a spontaneous rebellion among the people who grew rapidly into an angry mob and fought the government army outside the city limits. This municipal revolutionary movement was called "the Commune" and lasted just over two months, from March 18 to May 28, 1871. However, this relatively short uprising became one of the most controversial and brutal moments in French history as it set French people against each other, the Parisians against the French government established in Versailles, creating a political rift between Paris and the provinces. Nevertheless, the Commune did have a collective impact on some of the French provinces, as other French cities also proclaimed their own Communes: Lyon and Marseille on March 23, Nîmes, Narbonne, and Toulouse on March 24, and Le Creusot on March 26. These attempted Communes in the provinces lasted from twenty-four hours to a week, but despite their short-lived momentum, they demonstrated a fair amount of solidarity with the social uprising taking place in Paris.

The Paris Commune: Celebrating and Fighting

Still weak from the desolation and misery left by the Franco-Prussian War, and under siege again, this time from the French government, a majority of defiant Parisians remained elated and hopeful about their own political future. As proud urban citizens, they felt stronger and more united than ever, wishing to build an independent city-republic. Many, from the working class to the working bourgeoisie (Jules Vallès: "The working bourgeoisie, honest and robust [. . .] is by its courage and by its anxieties, the sister of the proletariat" *Oeuvres completes 2*, 44), viewed Paris as a "free city": free from a large number of reactionary provincials who, for the most part, still marched to the tune of the priests and the nobles—"Paris will always be crushed by [peasant] ignorance . . . the brutal power of numbers" wrote le *Le Cri du Peuple* on March 24; or, already in this section of Victor Hugo's poem *Ils ont voté* "They Have Voted" published in *Les Châtiments*, 1853: "Do you really think that France is you! / That you are the People, you brutish beasts, / And that you ever had the right to give us our masters?" (*Poésie*, 523). These "working" Parisians considered themselves free from a conservative Assembly that had physically and psychologically abandoned the city by symbolically relocating to Versailles, the palace of kings (government officials were often described as "monarchists" or "Prussians of Versailles"), free from the idle and "parasitic" high bourgeoisie of Paris itself, nonworking bourgeois who lived by their capitalist ideals and selfish sense of ownership—"the vultures" as the *Communards* called them, or ironically, "*francs-fileurs*" (quick to flee) for those who fled the besieged city—and, finally, free from the Prussians who, on March 1, 1871, marched through empty streets and under occasional fire from Parisian snipers. The bulk of the Communards was made up of workers, teachers, clerks, journalists, left-wing intellectuals, and working bourgeois; in other words, they were all anticlerical active "producers" set against the Christian "idlers" and the ignorant and bigoted "rurals." Due to the spontaneous nature of the Commune, they had to quickly elect a municipal government with a majority of socialist reformers, influenced by Marxist ideology: followers of the revolutionary ideologist Louis Auguste Blanqui, or Blanquists, members of L'Internationale—the Marxist international association of workers—who came from varied professional branches, thus representing a wide array of the Parisian socioeconomic classes. Among the commission delegates were some familiar literary and artistic figures such as Felix Pyat, member of the Internationale and a famous dramatist who wrote and staged the immensely successful Le Chiffonnier de Paris in 1847 (The Ragpicker of Paris), Gustave Courbet, the Socialist and controversial "realist" painter (see chapter 1), and, as always, Jules Vallès, the young and brilliant journalist and upcoming literary figure, often imprisoned for his radical ideas and the founder of the highly respected and widely read Communard newspaper, Le Cri du Peuple. Vallès and Courbet were both at one point or another part of the Education and Art Commissions and were responsible for appointing an educational committee with, for the first time, female members, a committee whose urgent and initial task it was to reform schools, to make education free and secular and equally open to girls and boys. Vallès and Courbet also encouraged creativity and experimental projects as part of the foundation of a comprehensive and republican educational vision. Even though the Commune did not last long enough to see any significant results in these areas, the education commission still managed to open a "professional" art school for girls and was just about ready to open one for boys when the Commune was brought to an end. Despite the shortcomings due to lack of time for development and implementation, the commission's educational philosophy would nonetheless serve as an inspiration and a model upon which to build a republican school system that would last into the twenty-first century. For the Communards, the education project was clear, perhaps the clearest of all the reforms they sought.

On many social and political grounds, the Communards did challenge the current government by enacting immediate reforms for Paris: the adoption of the red revolutionary flag, the reintroduction of the revolutionary calendar, self-management by workers in all workshops and factories, separation of church and state, abolition of conscription to be replaced by popular voluntary militias, and of course, secular, free and mandatory education for all children. In fact, many of these reforms would carry over from the Commune to constitute some of the basic principles of the French Republic. But for the men and women of the Commune, these reforms were urgent and vital "socialist" changes inspired by the thrust of Marxist ideology. As these reforms came out of a spontaneous popular uprising and a popular desire to organize an equal society for all, they were the fruit of what Marx, in his book on the Paris events of the Commune, Civil War in France: The Paris Commune (1871) considered to be the first real example of a "dictatorship of the proletariat." It was the popularity of these reforms that would force the French Assembly to rethink the terms of the republic under construction. In effect, the "universal" ideology and social reforms of the Commune represented an exceptional historical and social moment with symbolic ramifications in all aspects of French life and culture today: it shaped the terms of the republic, specifically its secularism and universalism, while branding it with its own form of individual liberties. It seems almost impossible, even unbelievable, that a relatively small number of revolutionaries made such a difference in so little time, in actuality helping to reshape the ideology of French politics and culture, placing women at the forefront of political debates, and advancing the cause of education.

Dossier 2.5 The Commune. Two Eye Witnesses: Jules Vallès and Louise Michel (1871)

In order to better grasp the strong and varied sense of equal liberties that made the Commune such a unique event, we will follow the chronology of the events through two of its eye witnesses: a left-wing radical journalist of provincial origin, and a female school teacher. The first, Jules Vallès was a spirited journalist who expressed his overwhelming joy at the proclamation of the Commune. The second, Louise Michel, the so-called red virgin, who dedicated her life to fighting for the principles of the Revolution and vividly narrated the street fighting during the Commune in which she participated with passion and conviction.

The Spirit of the Commune: Jules Vallès

Among the eminent personalities of the Commune, Jules Vallès was notable in helping to spread communard ideas by founding its most faithful newspaper *Le Cri du Peuple* in February, 1871. Vallès also wrote some of the most realistic fiction about growing up in provincial France and being poor during the times of the empire, and later, about living through the turbulent times of the Commune. It is clear that, for Vallès, life and writing, or writing about life, came together under the momentum of the Commune. He was a member of the main group of elected officials who wanted a radical and unmediated socialist government for the city of Paris.

Vallès was a brilliant young man who developed an acute sense of social justice early in his life and fought against the 1851 coup d'état and the authoritarian rule of the empire. As an opponent of the empire, in Paris he used his skills as a journalist and a writer to pen strong socialist pamphlets that would later help him enter the world of politics. His political publications consistently denounced the regime's injustices against, or even its indifference toward, the disadvantaged population, the marginal and the poor. As he campaigned to become the Socialist deputy for the Paris neighborhoods of Bercy and Picpus, he declared: "I have always been the defender of the poor, I am becoming the candidate of workers, I will be the deputy of the needy" (*Oeuvres complètes I, 1725*). All his books portray social discrimination and his main characters are usually members of the poor, working, and indigent "classes" that Haussmann's renovation project had pushed outside the city center. Wanting to express his views on the "real" life of the poor and the abused, he found inspiration in his own life and wrote an autobiographical trilogy composed of *L'Enfant* (1878), *Le Bachelier* (1881), and *L'Insurgé* (1886). In the first installment, *L'Enfant*, he announces that the book recognizes and pays tribute to those who "died of boredom at school or who were made to cry at home, those who, during their childhood, were bullied by their teachers or beaten by their parents" (*Oeuvres complètes II, 139*). In *Le Bachelier*, he continues to follow his main character, who has now become a failed student and a revolutionary idealist. His material life remains uneven and difficult, going from times of plenty to utter poverty. Finally, in *L'Insurgé*, the young man becomes an avid defender of the Commune. Street-fights, battles, and executions make of this last volume the most representative portrayal of the bloody reality of the Commune.

In the journal he founded in February 1871, *Le Cri du Peuple*, it is with the exuberance and the optimism of his radical spirit and with the writing of a lyrical patriot that he produces the following editorial, simply entitled *La fête* (Celebration). The title of the paper *Le Cri du Peuple* (The (Out)Cry of the People) carries the double meaning of a "birthing" cry, that is "a moment of entry in the language" (Bouvier, 197) for the (unborn notion of) people that is now given a voice, and a printed venue, to express itself, and of an outcry for celebration and liberty at the prospect of a new life for the Communards. In both cases, whether interpreted as the first cry of the birthing people or its liberating clamor of joy, the idea of a new and "original" popular voice points to a universal organic and oral bond between all Communards born to what they hoped would be a new world of freedom for all and celebrating this moment in a binding uproar, an *outcry of the people* that Vallès' paper translates in written form:

Le Cri du Peuple, March 30, 1871

Celebration: The Commune is proclaimed !

It came out of the ballot box, triumphant and armed. The newly elected members walked to the old city hall, the same hall that had heard the drums of Santerre and the gunshots of January 22, on this square where the blood of our national heroes and the dignity of Parisians is wiped clean on this day of celebration by the dust of our victorious feet.

We will not hear the drums of Santerre any longer; guns will not shine at the windows of the Commune's Town Hall and, if we wish so, blood will not stain the square anymore. And don't we wish so, citizens ?

The Commune has been proclaimed. The artillery on the river banks was shooting salvos in the sun, turning golden the grey smoke on the square. Crowds stood on the barricades: men waving their hats, women their handkerchiefs, at the triumphant parade, while, humble and peaceful, the canons lowered their bronze mouths to avoid pointing at the happy crowd. Under the windows filled with a respectful audience, the National Guards cast their enthusiastic and proud look at the somber building facade where the clock had struck so many hours, centuries, and had seen so many events now inscribed in History. The officials elected by the People stood on the stage; good men and women filled with energy and seriousness. The statue of the Republic, white on the red cloth, gazed undisturbed at the bright harvest of bayonets sprinkled with shimmering flags on colorful poles, while the buzzing of the city, sounds of trumpets and drums, salvos and acclamations rose up to the sky.

The Commune is proclaimed on a day of revolutionary and patriotic celebration, a day of peace and happiness, of exhilaration and solemn declaration, of grandeur and joyfulness, worthy of other days lived by the men of '92, a day that will make up for twenty years of Empire and six months of defeats and treasons. The People of Paris up and armed have proclaimed the Commune that has saved the city from capitulation, from the disgrace of a Prussian victory. The Commune will make Parisians free just as it made them victorious.

It should have been proclaimed on October 31! Still! You who died at Buzenval, victims of January 22, you are now all avenged !

The Commune is proclaimed.

The batallions that spontaneously took to the streets, the river banks, the boulevards, filling the air with the sound of the clarions, shaking people's hearts with the rumble of the drums, came earlier to acclaim and greet the Commune, to give its official announcement with a great civic review defying Versailles, and now they are returning, weapons at ease, towards their neighborhoods, filling the great city, the buzzing beehive, with their own clamor.

The Commune is proclaimed.

Today is the nuptial celebration of Idea and Revolution. Tomorrow, in order to fertilize the newlywed and newly-acclaimed Commune, the soldier-citizen, still filled with pride but now free, will have to get back to work to his shop or on his docks. After the poetry of triumph, comes the prose of work. (Oeuvres 2. 51–52)

Undeniably, the Commune was no laughing matter, but beyond the reality of harsh fighting and numerous deaths, it would appear that a certain degree of high spirit and street momentum accompanied the insurgents, over and beyond the barricades, from the battle to the ball, from the fights to the festivities. It would appear that the streets of Paris had been transformed into a providential stage for a multisocial and festive crowd, which had taken on a rebellious role as if the entire city had become the actual theater for an experimental play performed spontaneously. Indeed, even during the very last week of the Commune, on May 21, 1871, while fighting was raging and tension mounting in many parts of the city, an enormous outdoor concert, in which many singers and musicians performed for 6,000 Communards took place at the Tuileries gardens. France would not rekindle this feeling of revolution and celebration until the events that led Paris into a cultural and political upheaval almost a century later in May, 1968 (see chapter 8). Like the Commune, the movement of May 1968 had significant consequences for future generations of students, intellectuals, and workers in particular, as well as for the French political scene in general. Both events were also carried by a similar sense of high energy and celebration that would almost make the serious and even deadly times of revolution disappear behind manifestations of exhilarating outbursts of energy, which could be read as signs of an overdue social liberation for a much-repressed population.

Here Vallès speaks about the celebration as also being a form of commemoration and a dedication to those heroes who died for Paris, like the 4,000 men who died unnecessarily during the January 19, 1871 battle of Buzenval, betrayed by their own general who led them to be massacred in order to prove to the French that Paris could not hold out against the Prussians and that capitulation was necessary. A few days later, on January 22, a large crowd of angered Parisians, among them Louise Michel, gathered in front of City Hall to show their determination to continue fighting against the Prussians when, from the building itself, the army fired on the rebellious crowd, killing many. As he recalls these two unfortunate events, Vallès sees the proclamation of the Commune as a just homage to their victims. However, Vallès' overall feeling is that this day of proclamation is not only a time to remember Paris' darkest hours, but also a time to cheer on the bright future of the people of Paris.

For the participants in the 1871 Commune (and in the events of May 1968) personal and political freedom and liberation could be achieved with immense joy and great popular spirit. However, Vallès remains acutely aware that after the "poetry of triumph," after the festive and fiery gatherings in the streets, after the speeches and parades, people would have to regain a sense of normality and advance their social cause by coming to terms with what he calls "the prose of workmanship," in other words, by reorganizing the workforce with the same sense of collective enthusiasm.

Women and the Commune: Louise Michel

For the 1871 Communards who organized the revolt, it was indeed, at least at first, a time to revel and rejoice, as they were given a chance to show France and the world their own political talent and capacity for self-government. For them, there was no doubting that at the end of the bloody revolution and the street celebrations, there would be a new set of political and constitutional reforms favorable to a socialist "free city" that would ideally set the example for the rest of France and, even, for the world. Unfortunately for the Communards, the fighting between them and Thiers' army would bring a somber verdict: bitter fights, death on the barricades, quick arrests, and immediate executions. Most of the deaths occurred during the "bloody week" of May 21–28, when Thiers' army attacked the Communards on all fronts in a gruesome show-down, thus putting an end to their dream of universal liberties and equality for Paris.

Women constituted an entire group of Communards who welcomed the oppor-tunity to finally demonstrate their desire to gain equality in a society that had so consistently avoided including and representing them. They were often angrier, more rebellious, more visible, and more violent than men during the Commune since they felt that they had nothing to lose. Some say that they were responsible for setting Paris on fire to stop the advance of the Versailles army. Paris was indeed burning: large and symbolic monuments like the Palace of the Tuileries—emblematic of the fallen empire—and the administrative offices of l'Hôtel de Ville (City Hall) were destroyed by fire. Even if both men and women among Communards claimed responsibility for these fires as symbolic acts of their rebellion, it did not stop the rumor that created the mythical figure of crime-thirsty women who "petrol"-bombed the city. As a result of many unclaimed arsons throughout the city, a legend of pyromaniacal women called *les pétroleuses* (petrol-bombers) was born. On the one hand, this was one of the most powerful symbols of the Commune, as it gave visibility to all women involved. Historians agree that this was a time when women made their mark as a social and political force to be reckoned with, as never before had women received so much attention as part of social and historical events. It could well be that the image of the *pétroleuses* as the leading but not sole representation of the "unruly women of Paris" (Gullickson) effectively fostered the official entry of all women onto the French social scene. On the other hand, the mix of many real and fictional accounts and represen-tations of women's insurrections also gave them the status of reckless insurgents, anarchical terrorists whose wild, unleashed force and uncontrolled actions were destructive and threatening. The image of the women of the Commune stretched from mythical, courageous fighters, to hysterical, dangerous menaces. In either case, women's lives came to the forefront of the social and political scene with considerable force. What was seen as great acrimony on their part was fueled by years of govern-ments and regimes that had kept them away from constitutional rights and social reform. Despite some growing political and cultural sympathy for their contribution to society and the arts, their involvement was never acknowledged or formalized in any meaningful way. Among some of the male artists of the period who acknowledged the

talents of women, revolutionary poets like the young Arthur Rimbaud and his friend
Paul Verlaine praised and applauded a future where women could equally share the
cultural and the literary stage with men. In his famous "letter of the visionary" written during the time of the Commune on May 15, 1871, Rimbaud invites women to
free themselves from men and to become poets. He writes: "When the endless servi-
tude of woman is broken, when she lives for herself and by herself, man—hitherto
abominable—having given her her release, she too will be a poet" (379).

As for Paul Verlaine, the recently appointed head of the press bureau for the
Commune, he counted many women revolutionaries among his friends. Specifically, he
recognized and paid great tribute to one famous female insurgent of the Commune,
Louise Michel, to whom he dedicated a poem, "Ballade en l'honneur de Louise Michel"
(Ballad in Honor of Louise Michel) in which he celebrates the woman and the fighter:

> She likes the poor, rough and open,
> Or shy. She is the sickle
> In the high wheat of the white bread
> Of the poor, and Saint Cecil;
> And the tough yet refined muse
> Of the poor, as well as the guardian angel
> Of this simple and untamed man,
> Louise Michel is truly good.
>   (*Louise Michel: La passion*, 18)

Indeed, Louise Michel was the double muse, "refined and rough," Verlaine saw in
her. She was a revolutionary and a writer, a thinker and a teacher with a legendary
sense of goodness, generosity, and justice for others to whom she gave all she had—
she was notoriously poor for giving out to others more than she could afford. In the
early 1850s, refusing to serve the empire, she opened her own "republican-like"
school outside of Paris and then directed a school in the Paris working-class district of
Montmartre in the eighteenth arrondissement, where she became politically active
until the time of the Commune, when she physically fought day and night until her
arrest by the Versailles army. In spite of her ferocious verbal attacks on the government during her trial, she was not executed but deported to New Caledonia, where
she lived to tell and write about her experience before coming back to France in 1880.

To her, writing was an activity that stemmed equally from the desire to speak out
about social injustice and from her very fascination and amazement at the power of
language. As a social activist with a literary gift, she related her experience during the
Commune in journal-like memoirs (*Souvenirs et aventures de ma vie*) partly translated as
The Red Virgin, where she retold the events as they unraveled and as she participated
in them. In an early chapter of her memoirs, she specifically portrays the events that
took place during the bloody week of May 1871 in Montmartre, a highly symbolic
place, given that it was here that the Commune had begun two months earlier.
Reading through this chapter suggests that Louise Michel might simply be lucky to be
alive after the atrocities of the night when Commune leaders and fighters were being
killed in massive numbers by the Versailles Army:

> I threw myself in the middle of the fighting, closely followed by a young student who
> fell to the ground almost immediately. Poor boy! He wanted so hard to fight, he did not

even have time to hold a gun. How long did the fighting last? I do not know. All I remember is that it was dreadful. We fought in hand-to-hand combat, cutting throats with our bayonets. All we could hear were the gurgling of dying men, and the wailing of pain and rage. (30)

After holding the barricade, until all men were killed and all ammunitions gone, Louise Michel was caught, beaten severely, and left behind by the Versailles troops. Passing for dead, she managed to make her way out of rows of corpses and escaped through the night in Paris that was "looking like a slaughterhouse" (32).

As she was running through the streets dressed in man's clothes, she could hear continuous volleys of gunshots behind her, and she understood that "summary executions had begun" (32), as they did in the afternoon of May 28, 1871 when approximately one hundred and fifty communards were lined up and shot against the wall of the cemetery *Le Père Lachaise*, that would be remembered as the *mur des fédérés*.

Despite the gory and brutal combat and executions that left many dead, courage was the dominant feeling among the Communards during the bloody week, most of whom remained nameless as they did not live long enough even to be identified: the young and eager student who died before even firing a shot at the Army, the tall and handsome captain of the federated forces of the Commune and the short man from Brittany who both disappear after being caught. In addition, Louise Michel tells the story of an innocent shopkeeper killed simply for being in the wrong place at the wrong time. In the chaos, she appears to be the only one to escape the massive firepower that kills her comrades, innocent bystanders, and eventually the Commune itself.

In addition to the nameless dead fighters, she also mentions people in high command by name: "La Cecilia" who, despite the female code name, is a male Commune leader in Montmartre; the Communard army captain, Jaroslaw Dombrowski, who, despite his dedication and talent as a commander, is so demoralized by so many unnecessary casualties that he gives up the fight and gets killed; and finally, General Gallifet, the bloodthirsty commander of the Versailles Army who heads the program to assassinate all suspicious Parisians, whether they have taken part in the Commune or not. On the other side, the Versailles army commander is depicted as the cruel and inhuman executioner who puts to death everyone indiscriminately and with no respect for any form of justice. Beyond the revolutionary energy displayed throughout the passage, death remains the prevailing "character" as it destroys the Commune and takes away "thousands of unknown heroes" (32).

Louise Michel was arrested, and during her trial showed her unbroken commitment to the revolution and her desire to avenge her dead comrades as she declared to the judges:

I do not wish to defend myself, nor do I want to be defended. I belong completely to the Social Revolution, and I declare that I accept responsibility for all my actions. I accept it completely and without reservations . . . . If you let me live, I shall never stop crying for revenge and l shall avenge my brothers . . . . I have finished. If you are not cowards, kill me! (*Red Virgin*, 85–87)

Throughout the rest of her life Louise Michel never stopped fighting against injustice and speaking in favor of the Commune. "Red" she was in her belief in the revolution, but a virgin perhaps not, as some studies showed that she may have had an affair with Victor Hugo. Whether or not her passion for Hugo was of a physical nature, she had undeniable strong feelings for him for two reasons: as a man and as a defender of republican principles. Repeating a similar pattern of twofold passion, she later both admired and fell in love with her "friend" Théophile Ferré, a Commune leader, who was executed and to whom she dedicated some of her poems. In December 1871, the post–Commune Hugo wrote a long poem, "Viro Major," honoring Louise Michel. The following excerpt expresses the general tone of admiration that permeates the entire poem:

> And those who, like myself, know you incapable
> Of all that is not heroism and virtue
> Who know that if asked: "Whence do you come?"
> You would answer: "I come from the night where there is suffering
> Yes, I come from that duty you have made an abyss."
> Those who have heard your sweet and mysterious verse,
> Your days, your nights, your care, your tears given to all,
> Your selfless ways to rescue others,
> Your words like the flames of the apostles;
> Those who know your home without heat, air, bread
> Your bed of ropes and pine table
> Your goodness, your pride as a woman of the people,
> The bitter tenderness sleeping beneath your wrath.
>
> (*Louise Michel: la passion*, 18)

Conclusion

As Louise Michel laconically declared at the end of the bloody week, "the commune was dead" (*Souvenirs et aventures de ma vie*, 32).

In two months, a staggering number of Parisians—historians argue that this number was between 20,000 and 40,000—most of them Communards, but also innocent citizens, some men but also women and children, were killed: 43,500 were arrested, a handful court-martialed and sentenced to death, many imprisoned, and around 5,000 deported mainly to New Caledonia, a French colony in Melanesia. This was the case of the red virgin who, despite her exile, continued her social and political activism in New Caledonia. Some Communards, fearing for their lives if they stayed in France, left on their own and went into exile in neighboring countries like Belgium, England, and Switzerland, where they were welcome and protected. In her short story *Babette's Feast*, Danish author Karen Blixen tells the story of Babette, a French woman refugee of the Commune. Her husband and son having been executed, she barely escapes her own death by fleeing to Jutland in Denmark, where she slowly reconstructs her life through her knowledge of and expertise in food and cooking, a trade that she had learned from her husband and that she practiced in a famous restaurant in Paris before her exile. Beside the elements used as the basic storyline, Blixen did not minimize the strong and unbreakable emotional attachment of the refugee to her homeland and her desire to share her "Frenchness" with others through her cooking, thus retaining her national particularity in a foreign land. Even if in the end Babette decides to stay in Denmark, her feeling of national inadequacy and her desire to preserve her identity were real and shared by many Communards, who fled to countries throughout the world after the fall of the Commune, but who could never really assimilate the culture and mores of their adoptive nations, some to the extent that they committed suicide while in exile. The bulk of the extradited and exiled communards would have to wait nine years, until 1880, for a general amnesty, forcefully called for by Victor Hugo, by then a senator, in order to finally return home safely.

Once the Commune was crushed, Parisian executive powers were suspended, and the capital was placed directly under national governance. Another official municipal election would not be held until over a century later, in 1977, when Jacques Chirac became the first elected mayor of Paris since Jules Ferry in 1871. Despite the official moratorium on Parisian mayoral elections through the years, some Paris constituencies ignored the national government and continued to stage their own elections. This was true, for example, of a district like Montmartre, where local elections were conducted, inviting both men and women to vote on local issues, even before the national right to vote for women became legal in 1944.

Figure 2.5   Municipal Election in Montmartre (1922)

Women voting in the free commune of the old Montmartre district in Paris during a municipal election. The year is 1929, fifteen years before the legalization of women's right to vote. (© Hachette Photo Presse)

Ever since the Commune, Parisians were perceived by the French government and by the majority of the French living outside of Paris, especially in rural areas, as potential troublemakers who needed to be watched and restrained. It is ironic that Paris, culturally cosmopolitan and historically setoff from the rest of the country, would in fact thrive as the ultimate symbol of French culture in the eyes of the international community. For this community, Paris defined then and continues to define today the universality of France through the particularity of a city on which the French government lavished monuments, boulevards, museums, a city of which, in short, it made a showcase, but a city that was also politically distrusted for a long time after the events of the Commune.

References

Alexandre, Arsène. *Jean-François Raffaelli, peintre, graveur et sculpteur*. Paris: Floury, 1909.

Baldick, Robert, ed. *The Goncourt Journal*. London: Oxford University press, 1962.

Balzac de, Honoré. *La Comédie Humaine*. Vol. 12. Paris: Gallimard (Pléiade), 1981.

Baudelaire, Charles. *Oeuvres complètes*. Vol. 1. Paris: Gallimard (Pléiade), 1975.

———. *The Painter of Modern Life and Other Essays*. Jonathan Mayne, trans. and ed. New York: Da Capo, 1986.

———. *On Wine and Hashish*. Andrew Brown, trans. London: Hesperus Press, 2002.

Bédollière de la, Emile. *Histoire de la mode en France*. Leipzig: Alphonse Dürr, Libraire-éditeur, 1858.

Benjamin, Walter. *Charles Baudelaire: Un poète lyrique à l'apogée du capitalisme*. Paris: Payot, 1979.

Blixen, Karen (aka Isak Dinesen). *Babette's Feast and Other Anecdotes of Destiny*. New York: Vintage, 1988.

Bouvier, Luke. *Writing, Voice and the Proper: Jules Vallès and the Politics of Orality*. Amsterdam: Rodopi, 1998.

Burton, Richard. *Baudelaire and the Second Republic: Writing and Revolution*. Oxford: Clarendon Press, 1991.

Bury, J.P.T and Tombs R.P. *Thiers, 1797–1877: A Political Life*. London: Allen & Unwin, 1986.

Catalogue général de l'exposition universelle de 1867. Paris: Commission impériale, 1867.

Delattre, Simone. *Les Douze heures noires. La nuit à Paris au XIXe siècle*. Paris: Albin Michel, 2003.

Delveau, Alfred. *Histoire anecdotique des cafés et cabarets de Paris*. Paris: Dentu, 1862.

Déroulède, Paul. *Chants du soldat*. Paris: Calmann-Lévy, 1880.

Durand, Pierre. *Louise Michel, la passion*. Paris: Messidor, 1987.

Fabre, Maurice. *Histoire de la mode*. Genève: Edition Service SA, 1966.

Faure, Alain. "Classe malpropre, classe dangereuse? Quelques remarques à propos des chiffonniers parisiens au 19e siècle et de leurs cités." In *Recherches* 29 "L'Haleine des faubourgs" December 1977: 79–102.

Flaubert, Gustave and George Sand. *Correspondence*. Francis Steegmuller and Barbara Bray, trans. London: Harvill Press, 1993.

Fleuriot, Zénaïde. *Les Mauvais jours*. Paris: Dillet, 1872.

Fournier, Edouard, ed. *Paris démoli*. Paris: Aubry, 1855.

Gautier, Théophile. *L'Orient. Voyages et voyageurs*. Paris: Charpentier, 1877.

———. *De la mode*. Paris: Actes-sud, 1993.

Goncourt de, Edmond. *Journal des Goncourt—Mémoires de la vie littéraire*. Vol. 1 and 4. Paris: Charpentier, 1890.

Gourmont de, Rémy. *Pendant l'orage suivi de Le Joujou patriotisme*. Paris: Armand Colin (collection L'Ancien et le Nouveau), 1992.

Gullickson, Gay. *Unruly Women of Paris: Images of the Commune*. Ithaca: Cornell University Press, 1996.

Harvey, David. *Paris, Capital of Modernity*. New York, London: Routledge, 2003.

Higonnet, Patrice. *Paris, Capital of the World*. Arthur Goldhammer, trans. Cambridge, MA: Harvard University Press, 2002.

Houssaye, Arsène. *Les confessions—souvenirs d'un demi-siècle, 1830–1880*. Vol. 4. Genève: Slatkine Reprints, 1971.

Hugo, Victor. *La Bièvre* in *Oeuvres Complètes XI*. Genève: Slatkine Reprints, 1972.

————. *Le Drageoir aux Epices* in *Oeuvres Complètes I*. Genève: Slatkine Reprints, 1972.

————. *Poésie*. Paris : Seuil (l'Intégrale), 1972.

————. *Memoirs of Victor Hugo*. McLean, VA: IndyPublish.com, 2002.

Huysmans, Karl-Joris. *[Parisian Sketches*. Brendan King, trans and ed. Sawtry, UK: Dedalus, 2004.

Jones, Colin. *Paris. Biography of a City*. New York: Viking, 2004.

Kirkbride, Ronald. *The Private Life of Guy de Maupassant*. New York: Frederick Fell Inc., 1947.

Kudlick, Catherine. *Cholera in Post-revolutionary Paris: A Cultural History*. University of California Press (Studies on the History of Society and Culture, 25), 1996.

Lhospice, Michel. *La Guerre de 70 et la Commune en 1000 images*. Paris: Robert Laffont, 1965.

Lowry, Bullitt and Elizabeth Ellington Gunter, eds. *The Memoirs of Louise Michel, the Red Virgin*. Alabama: University of Alabama Press, 1981.

Loyer, François. *Paris Nineteenth Century: Architecture and Urbanism*. Charles Lynn Clark, trans. New York: Abbeville Press Publishers, 1988.

Lurine, Louis. *Les Rues de Paris: Paris ancien et moderne*. Paris: Kugelmann, 1844.

Maclelian, Nic, ed. *Louise Michel*. New York: Ocean Books, 2004.

Mallarmé, Stéphane. *Oeuvres complètes*. Paris : Gallimard (Pléiade), 1945.

Maupassant de, Guy. *The Complete Short Stories*. Vol. 1. London: Cassell, 1970.

Michel, Louise. *Souvenirs et aventures de ma vie*. Paris: La découverte/Maspero, 1983.

Moncan de, Patrice and Mahout Christian. *Le Paris du Baron Haussmann—Paris sous le second empire*. Paris : Editions Seesam—RCI, 1991.

Nash, Suzanne, ed. *Home and Its Dislocations in Nineteenth-Century France*. Albany: SUNY Press, 1993.

Noël, Bernard. *Dictionnaire de la Commune*. Paris: Hazan, 1971.

Pawlowski, Paul. *La Clef de l'exposition universelle de 1867*. Paris: Alcan Lévy, 1867.

Prendergast, Christopher. *Paris and the Nineteenth Century*. Cambridge, MA: Blackwell Publishers, 1992.

Rimbaud, Arthur. *Completed Works, Selected Letters*. Wallace Fowlie, trans. Chicago: University of Chicago Press, 2005.

Romi. *Histoire des festins insolites et de la goinfrerie*. Paris : Artulen, 1993.

Rousseau, Jean-Jacques. *Confessions*. Michel Launay, ed. Paris: Garnier, 1968.

Thomas, Edith. *Louise Michel*. Penelope Williams, trans. Montreal: Black Rose Books, 1980.

Thombs, Robert. *The Paris Commune 1871*. New York: Longman, 1999.

Vallès, Jules. *Oeuvres Complètes I and II*. Paris: Gallimard (Pléiade), 1975.

Vitu, Auguste. *Paris il y a cent ans*. Paris: Jean de Bonnot, 1975.

Ward, Patricia. *Baudelaire and the Poetics of Modernity*. Nashville: Vanderbilt University Press, 2001.

Wellman, Rita. *Eugénie: Star-Crossed Empress of the French*. New York: Scribner's Sons, 1941.

White, Edmund. *Le Flâneur: A Stroll through the Paradoxes of Paris*. New York: Bloomsbury, 2001.

Yriarte, Charles. *Les célébrités de la rue: Paris 1815–1863 (Paris Grotesque)*. Paris: Librairie Parisienne—Dupray de la Mahérie, 1864.

Zola, Emile. *The Ladies' Paradise*. Kristin Ross, Intro. Berkeley: University of California Press, 1991.

CHAPTER 3

SCANDAL AND INNOVATION IN THE THIRD REPUBLIC (1871–1899)

> *It is by universal misunderstanding that all agree. For if, by ill luck, people understood each other, they would never agree.*
>
> —Charles Baudelaire, *My Heart Laid Bare* (1897)

> *A consciousness without scandals is alienated consciousness.*
>
> —Georges Bataille, *Literature and Evil* (1957)

> *Beauty is a sort of corpse. It has been supplanted by novelty, intensity, strangeness, all the* shock values. *(Emphasis in original)*
>
> —Paul Valéry, *Leonardo, Poe, Mallarmé* (1929)

Introduction

The scandals and innovations that marked the passage from one century to the next—more specifically, from 1871 to 1914, a period of relative peace and energetic republicanism—further demonstrate the paradox inherent in France's attempts to reconcile its own particularities with the universalist rhetoric of the Third Republic. This paradox is even more striking when set against the backdrop of the strong republican desire to create a "model French citizen," a morally sound, educated, and healthy individual without civic idiosyncrasies or social differences, be they political or sexual; a sort of universal social mind and body. Such a unique individual represented the "perfect Frenchman" (in the gender-neutral sense) for the republic, the ideological achievement of an idealized citizen to which the social and educational programs of the state would cater. However, the very real French men and women of the period were complex individuals whose fragmented reality was often at odds with this comprehensive image of republican perfection. As the fundamental defender of individual liberties and democracy, the republic constantly struggled with this dual ideal of universalism and individuality. As we examine the way the French became "republicans," that is, citizens of the republic, we must keep in mind that, beyond the historical factors and political figures that were attempting to shape both the citizen and the republican regime, average French men and women were becoming less average and more passionate about their individual liberties and projects, thus transforming the national landscape into a vast domain of renewed creativity. Despite the official universalist ethos of the times, which necessarily went against the grain of particularities and idiosyncrasies, French passions were well served and represented by exuberant and diverse creations, many of which were characterized as "scandals" by the press and the establishment.

In the arts, the impressionists enraged their academically established peers and elated the new generation of artists. The first cinematographers fascinated a public in awe of the new techniques. In communications, the press became affordable to all, more diverse and attractive—with shorter articles, more advertising, serialized novels, comics—more widely distributed to the newly educated and literate masses—one million copies for daily papers like *Le Petit Parisien* and *Le Petit Journal*—and carrying more up-to-date information thanks to such inventions as Alexander Graham Bell's telephone from the United States—which made a slow but steady entrance into French everyday life—as well as to advances in transportation. For example, the railroads were improved and extended, and the first underground metro opened for service in Paris in 1900, just in time for the Universal Exposition. The French became healthier thanks to scientists like Louis Pasteur and Claude Bernard, both pioneers of modern medicine. In 1878, Pasteur discovered the existence and properties of germs and developed a successful vaccine against rabies in 1885, while Bernard, inspired by Darwin's theory of evolution, became the father of experimental medicine. In 1865, he published his famous book on the topic, *An Introduction to the Study of Experimental Medicine*, in which we read the following:

> When we begin to base our opinions on medical tact, on inspiration or on more or less vague intuitions about things, we are outside of science and offer an example of that fanciful method which may involve the greatest dangers, by surrendering the health and life of the sick to the whims of an inspired ignoramus. True science teaches us to doubt and, in ignorance, to refrain (55). . . . Particular facts are never scientific; only generalization can establish science (91). . . . Generalization must proceed from particular facts. (26)

Bernard's conception of medicine is evident: a particular instance cannot be trusted but is nevertheless necessary in order to lead to a "generalization" or universal finding, a mirror-image of the contemporary political paradigm where the particular was essential to republican universalism but absorbed by its principles, or where the individual was absorbed into the single frame and universal model of the citizen.

The word "republican" in French politics is far from its modern American definition, and both terms should not be confused. In 1871 and until the "Dreyfus Affair" in 1894, a republican government simply meant that French officials were elected by all-male universal suffrage. In fact, the republican government favored "leftist" secular reforms in line with the Enlightenment project to educate and bring "freedom and reason" to all citizens. Republican politics were opposed in principle and in practice to the politics of the Right represented then by royalists and the church who believed in keeping a strong social hierarchy and division, and ruling by divine right. The political balance between the Left and the Right grew more complex by the end of the nineteenth century with the many scandals that forced the authorities to revise their republican objectives and with the emergence of new ideologies. These changes did not, however, alter the basic definition of what being republican meant: a universal citizen led by reason and education out of the divine and the irrational and into a democratic and modern way of life. Naturally, the Third Republic could not and did not match, in practice, the ideal definition of the universal and had to face countless changes and flaws throughout its existence. These challenges greatly impacted the totalizing image of the "ideal citizen" and, to a certain extent, resulted in politically and culturally diverse citizens.

From the establishment of the Third Republic until the outbreak of World War I in to 1914, a number of scandals shook the nation and the cultural world: the unjust punishment of the Jewish French army officer Alfred Dreyfus; the disparagement of paintings depicting prostitutes, like Manet's *Nana* (1876) or Picasso's *Demoiselles d'Avignon* (The Young Ladies of Avignon, 1906); the uproar in classical music and dance generated by exiled Russian composer Igor Stravinsky and his 1913 *Sacre du Printemps* (Rite of Spring), a musical celebration of pagan rituals boldly interpreted by the dancers of his compatriot choreographer Sergei Diaghilev—the Paris premiere developed into something of a riot, insofar as such a thing exists in classical music; and finally, the controversial construction of the Eiffel Tower in 1889 (see figure 3.1). At the time, these events caused much uproar and seemed vital enough that all bets were on the inevitable destruction of the republic, especially after the Dreyfus Affair, as the "young" and bold modern culture was roundly condemned by the establishment. As they rose to prominence together, both the republic and the Modern were often perceived as having been too hurriedly forged and, therefore, doomed by their many errors, inconsistencies, and their open defiance of tradition.

Against all odds, the Third Republic overcame its political tribulations, unsettling contradictions, unresolved exceptions and, contrary to expectation, consolidated its universalist foundations. Within its frontiers, the republic nurtured and enforced a constant belief in the civic power of universal suffrage, however flawed, and pursued a policy of educating the "standard" French citizen, while, beyond its frontiers, it pursued its colonial ambitions based on a policy of propagating "universal" and "civilizing" values. Having gradually consolidated its political ground, the Third Republic became the longest sustained political regime of modern France up to the present day.

Culturally, bourgeois values became highly desirable to the enlarged middle class, whose taste for art and technical progress was constantly challenged by the rapid changes in the cultural arena and in everyday life. The simultaneous rejection and embrace of the new, "scandalous" artistic and social movements did not, however, destroy France's elevated cultural image; instead, these developments helped place the country in a leading international position in the arts and in cultural life in general. During the tumultuous turn of the twentieth century, France developed a marked sense—and a style—of the modern and became the site of a uniquely rich and creative culture. This is the period that saw the appearance of some of the most characteristic emblems of French modernity, cultural exception, and quality of life: the Eiffel Tower and the metro, impressionism and cubism, perfumes and promenades, Paris and the French Riviera, Proust's *Belle Epoque* and Pagnol's Provence.

Figure 3.1   Universal Exposition (1889)

On the Esplanade of the Monumental Fountain near the Eiffel Tower, with the Trocadéro Palace in the background. A feeling of serenity marks the scene where crowds of middle-class *promeneurs* are enjoying the day. At dusk, the wonders of modernity came to life with the illumination and changing color of the fountain before a crowd of stunned Parisians. (© L'Illustration)

The next two chapters offer an analysis of this rich cultural context: a first chapter dealing with events and developments from 1871 to 1899, that is from the difficult beginnings of the Third Republic to the end of the Dreyfus Affair, a second concentrating on the period from 1899 to 1918, that is from the *Belle Epoque* to the end of the tragic events of World War I. In order to understand the close ties between the policies of the Third Republic and the rise of French modernity, the focus will be on the "scandals" and innovations of a fifty-year period ranging from the beginning of the Third Republic to the end of World War I. In the process, we will see how some of the totalizing and "universalizing" policies followed by the Third Republic paradoxically fostered individualism in a rising modern culture.

The "New" Republic

Declared on September 4, 1870 by an enthusiastic Gambetta and immediately put to the test by the civil war of the Paris Commune in 1871, the new republic was first entrusted to Adolphe Thiers, who was able to hold the French government together by assembling a conservative republican political regime (see chapter 2). This type of conservative republic still unleashed the anger of the monarchists in the Assembly, who had wished for the return to power of royalty, and who successfully put pressure on

Thiers, whom they found too moderate, to hand in his resignation in May, 1873. In its beginning, the republic was still controlled by a majority of hardcore conservatives, mainly aristocrats, and French political culture was not yet ready for the "necessary liberties" proposed by Thiers in a speech in 1864. They were even less ready for the "new social stratum" about which Gambetta first spoke in 1872 as the newest "class"—the quotation marks here are significant as "class" was precisely the term he did not want to use, insisting on the term "stratum" instead to identify the position and the property of the growing social group mainly composed of working bourgeois, as opposed to aristocrats or grand bourgeois—a social group born out of the industrial revolution, a rising and buoyant "middle class" coming from all levels of society and invested in earning, spending (and saving) money in the economic prosperity of the times:

> I foresee, I feel, I announce the coming and the presence in politics of a new social stratum which has been taking its part in politics for some eighteen months and which, to be sure, is far from being inferior to its predecessors" (Bury, 115) (Gambetta in Grenoble, September 26, 1872)

Both personally and socially, Gambetta himself embodied the "new social stratum" and the ideas of "true republicanism" he spoke about. Personally, he very much typified the rising small bourgeois to which he referred in his speech as the fastest growing demographic segment of society. Indeed, he was born and raised in the small provincial city of Cahors in southwestern France to a simple family of mixed origins. His father was an Italian immigrant who eventually became a local grocer and saved enough to finally buy his own convenience store. Gambetta's modest background explains in part that, throughout his brilliant career in politics, he would keep a down-to-earth point of view on the social situation of the French. When he finally "went up to Paris," as did so many ambitious young men from the provinces, his progressive politics, combined with his ebullient personality, attracted and intrigued many influential people, including quite a few from the highest social circles. Edmond de Goncourt, author and socialite, writes in his journal in 1877: "Right now, the bourgeois woman has an appetite for Gambetta. The fat politician is becoming a curious animal sought in all salons" (*Les Salons de la IIIe république*, 53). In part because of his naturally effervescent and unceremonious personality, he was more attracted to popular lifestyles, preferring noisy neighborhood cafés like the Procope to stuffy high society salons, and maintaining relationships with courtesans rather than society women. However, his public persona forced him to frequent political salons such as the one held by Juliette Adam, an influential and intelligent woman who was favorable to leftist republican politics and appreciated Gambetta's warm personality. Besides providing Gambetta with a valuable political network, she would also train the uncouth provincial in the rules of sociability, as she claimed, "you can be in the opposition in cafés, but you can only be in the government in high society circles" (*Les Salons de la IIIe république*, 53). It is interesting to see that in the minds of the French high bourgeoisie of the time, cafés were often associated with the life of the political opposition. They were thought of as the potential sites of rebellion against the establishment, that is, as gathering places for dissidents to meet, socialize, and, despite all appearances, organize themselves. Even though there were cafés of all styles for all types, bourgeois mentality dictated that "real politics" could be discussed only by a select few in the confines of the salons. Gambetta, who went from opposing the Second Empire to embracing the Third Republic, should have transferred his social life from the cafés to the salons, thus marking his move from dissidence to leadership. However, torn between his natural simplicity and acquired sense of sociability, he would not make a clear choice. His ambivalence toward the two worlds may have cost him the presidency in 1879. During different electoral periods, many saw him as occupying the social and political middle ground rather than as the bearer of a strong and clear political message. His speeches, however thought-provoking, endorsed this notion of being in the "middle," that is, in the "middle class" as well as midway between the conservatives in power and the oppressed peasants and workers.

During this period, it was often not the workers, but rather the peasants, who reflected social mobility by emerging from the lowest social rank and claiming a place in the lower middle class, from impoverished and disenfranchised farmers to ambitious employees of the republic. In fact, teachers were most often recruited from among the peasant class. Their social ambitions and strong work ethic were perfectly suited to the human and economic needs of the time. Gambetta, who knew firsthand the mentality of the French peasant was well placed to match the human resources of the peasantry with the republican need for hard-working individuals in all areas, from education to industry. He also realized how profitable this developing modern society could be for many of the ambitious poor and low-income individuals who wished to rise above their stations. In other words, he saw in the contemporary economic situation an opportunity for peasants to improve their lives. This reasoning earned him the label of political "opportunist," one that at the time, was without negative connotation. It was in relation to the world of the peasantry that the term "opportunism" was first adopted by many republican politicians, who also saw the good in "seizing the opportunity" of moving hard-working people out of their harsh daily reality into a potentially profitable economic future, in effect moving them out of poverty into the working class or even the lower bourgeoisie. Under Gambetta's leadership, the liberal "opportunists" placed much value on the notion of a well-deserved social reward for the hard-working man during these propitious times of an ebullient economy in need of efficient human resources. For example, it was Gambetta's thinking that peasants, who were used to hard work in the fields, would certainly put their skills and vigor in the service of the republic now that it needed a "few good men," civil servants, to develop successfully and strengthen its foundations. Convinced that work was one of the fundamental principles of success for the republic, the opportunists advocated the right to democracy and individual liberties for all who believed in a strong work ethic. In other words, he who worked could elevate himself in society and participate fully in a democratic system promoting freedom of expression and economic dynamism, rather than remain an exploited laborer in the service of an idle and profiteering conservative aristocracy. The political reality of this social movement was not always as clear-cut as it seemed, but it certainly brought to the surface a rising and hard-working new bourgeoisie, a socioeconomic group composed of small land owners, farmers, and small business owners who now had much at stake in the new economic environment. As this class or "stratum" grew in number and status, it provided a solid base for the republic, keeping it alive in spite of otherwise threatening political and cultural turmoil.

Needless to say, Gambetta's novel ideas, which included recognizing the influential presence of a new socioeconomic group and acknowledging the evolution of the class structure, did not appease the conservatives, who were still occupying much of the political stage at the time of Thiers's presidency (1871–1873). Consequently, in 1873, as a protective measure against the rising bourgeoisie, after Thiers's departure, the monarchist and military commander Marshal Mac Mahon was elected to the presidency by the National Assembly (1873–1879). A hard-line conservative, he instituted a government of "moral order" that took away some of the social and political advances achieved by the nascent Third Republic. He fostered religious propaganda, reduced freedom of the press, prohibited the annual July 14 celebration of the 1789 Revolution, and ordered the removal of all republican statuary in town halls throughout France. The restoration of the monarchy seemed inevitable. The most suitable potential king to return from political exile was Charles X's grandson, the Count of Chambord. With the aristocracy marching vigorously toward a takeover of power, the unsettled republic could have easily disintegrated but instead was saved by what might appear as a trivial affair, a symbolic detail that nonetheless epitomized the division among the monarchists—the traditional clerical nobles, called the "Legitimists," whom Chambord represented, versus the liberal "Orleanists" who were more in line with the new industrial society—and their subsequent political downfall. The detail was the color of the official French flag. The unremitting stubbornness with which Chambord insisted on the adoption of the traditional Bourbon white flag as the French national symbol was proof to many that the actual advances of a modern French society were not of great concern to the aspiring king. Looking backward to prerevolutionary times, Chambord's campaign for the adoption of the white flag symbolized his effort to reestablish the bygone era of the *Ancien Régime*. His plain refusal to accept the *tricolore*, that is, the blue, white, and red flag of the 1789 revolution, and thus his disdain for its liberating and democratic principles, proved to be an impossible hurdle for most republicans, even for monarchists of the Orleanist persuasion who could not bring themselves to back him up. Reluctantly, Mac Mahon had to accept the new republican laws put in place in 1875, constitutional laws that would lay the foundation of a parliamentary republic: the creation of a bicameral National Assembly composed of a *Sénat* (Senate) and a *Chambre des députés* (House of Representatives), and a presidential term of seven years. The president had little political power: he became head of the military and shared executive power with the Assembly. Antiparliamentary in principle, Mac Mahon eventually resigned from such a republican government in 1879 and Jules Grevy, a moderate Republican, was elected president (1879–1887). He immediately surrounded himself with influential opportunist Republicans like Gambetta (president of the House, then prime minister from 1881 to 1882) and Jules Ferry (minister of education and twice prime minister from 1880 to 1881 and 1883 to 1885), who quickly restored public liberties. In addition, following Ferry's election, many symbolic republican changes were made that were designed to boost public confidence and to reassure the French people of the democratic commitment of the new regime. Thus, in 1880, the government that had been moved to Versailles during the Franco-Prussian War finally returned to Paris. It showed leniency by giving amnesty to all exiled Communards, restored the French National holiday on July 14 and made the "Marseillaise" the French national anthem. A year later, in July 1881, freedom of the press and free and secular education were voted in by the Jules Ferry administration, while in 1884 freedom of association was restored and workers' unions were legally recognized by the government thanks to the Waldeck-Rousseau laws. By 1880, it seemed that, after a troubled decade during which liberal Republicans and opportunists faced-off with monarchists, the republic was back in full force.

Reforming Education

The opportunist Republicans, with Jules Ferry at the forefront, now focused their attention on something they perceived as a sine qua non of their progressive project: educational reform. From 1879 to 1882, Ferry enacted a series of fundamental republican laws finally making schools mandatory, secular, and free for all children between six and thirteen of age. It was Ferry's intention to create what the revolutionaries of 1789 had only dreamed about: a republican school where civic principles would be taught in order to transform French children into responsible young citizens. This paramount educational task was placed in the newly trained hands of primary school teachers, nicknamed *les Hussards noirs de la République* (the Black Hussars), a reference to the grey or black coveralls they wore in the classroom and to their loyal and unswerving devotion to the republic. Almost overnight the schoolteacher became the most important voice and servant of the republic, his profession the most respected, his words and wisdom the most revered. But respect and wisdom were not qualities that came with a high price tag. The schoolteachers were notoriously poor, as their salary often did not exceed that of an unskilled laborer. In 1901, a junior teacher made 100 francs per month while a metal worker made twice that amount. Nevertheless, these *missionaries*, as they were also called, lived with dignity and with complete devotion to republican ideology. In terms of social status, they were better off than the class from which they came, but still they occupied an uncertain social position, viewed as the "in-between class" Gambetta had identified in his speech on the "new social strata." They were not considered part of the working class, and while they were recruited from among the working and peasant classes, they felt estranged from their former milieu. Neither were they part of the bourgeoisie, a class whose members were keenly aware of the teachers' peasant and working-class roots, and often believed them to be political agitators. Preparatory schools for teachers, called *écoles normales* (normal schools) or centers for the teaching of *normalized* knowledge, were created and fully funded by the government. The instruction they received in these training schools was intellectual, practical, and moral, but most unquestionably it was anticlerical in every respect. Schoolteachers graduated from these schools with a newly acquired sense of civic duty, a general education adequate for teaching illiterate young peasants, and a complete distrust in the teachings of the church. They did indeed propagate the republican golden rule that school was a secular place where education could prosper only in a religion-free environment. Their devotion to republican ideology may not have made them rich, but it certainly gave them a certain amount of status in the communities in which they lived and worked. In towns and villages all over France the teacher came second in popularity only to the mayor, and sometimes stepped up to the mayor's position by popular demand, as if guided by a natural progression from educating citizens to representing them.

First metaphorically, then officially, after the final separation of church and state in 1905, teachers took over the privileged position that priests had held for so long in French society. They effectively assumed the priests' educational and moral functions.

Dossier 3.1   Marcel Pagnol, *My Father's Glory*

The following passage, from the memoirs of Provençal writer and filmmaker Marcel Pagnol describes the life of Proust's father at the turn of the century, a modest but devoted schoolteacher who would later become a lower bourgeois landowner while maintaining a staunch republican political stance:

In those days, the primary Normal Schools used to be true seminaries where the study of theology, however, was replaced by classes in anticlericalism.

The students were taught that the Church had never been anything but an instrument of oppression, and that it was the priests's task and purpose in life to blindfold the people with the black bandage of ignorance, while lulling them with fables of hell and paradise. . . . The curriculum of the Normal School students was not, however, confined to anti-clericalism and secularized history. There was a third enemy of the people, and one which was not at all a thing of the past: and that was Alcohol. . . . Apart from the fight against these three scourges, their program of studies was extremely wide and admirably conceived to turn them into teachers of the common people whom they understood so well. For almost all of them were the sons of peasants or workers.

They were given an all round education in general knowledge, more broad than deep no doubt, but which was quite a novelty; and they had always seen their fathers work twelve hours a day—in the field, the fishing-boat, or on the scaffolding—they congratulated themselves on their happy lot, because they could go out on Sundays and three times a year, had holidays which they could spend at home.

. . . The most remarkable thing was that these rabid anti-clericals had the souls of missionaries. To frustrate Monsieur le Curé (whose virtue was supposed to be a sham) they themselves lived like saints, and their morals were as inflexible as those of the early Puritans. "Like the parsons," my father used to say, "we work for the life to come. Only our concern is with other people—but down here." (My Father's Glory, 18–22)

Republicans knew that reforming education unilaterally through a standardized curriculum was a powerful way to unify all of future France and to reinforce its universalist principles. Thus, the curriculum was exactly the same throughout the country: besides teaching all children how to read and write, it included history, geography, civic and moral education, rudimentary political concepts, physical education, military exercise for boys and home economics, specifically sewing, for girls. Boys and girls were schooled in two different sections of the same building structure, which often also served as the town hall. This grouped spatial disposition of republican buildings consolidated the image people had of its major functions and formed a substantial local republican block that physically separated school grounds from church perimeters. In place of crucifixes and religious imagery, public schools displayed republican emblems: the tricolor flag floating in the front of the building, or the stone or marble bust of Marianne, the woman who came to officially represent revolution and liberty. All children were taught according to Ferry's ideology of a school system that did not include God. Yet religion remained a personal choice that republicans acknowledged by establishing Thursdays (today it is Wednesdays) as the day off from school for children who wished to continue their catechism. Up until 1905, when the church was finally barred from state politics, some references to god and religious symbols remained in textbooks, but thereafter these references were expurgated, while Thursday remained a day off from school for cultural activities or religious education. Republican values, praised and practiced within the education system, included a strong patriotic devotion to the country and a set of secular moral values that were adopted by the new bourgeois classes that Gambetta identified in his 1872 speech. These values comprised a strong sense of duty and order, an acute sense of the value of money and the merit of those who saved it, class-consciousness, moral order, including, for example, the active fight against "decadent lifestyles," such as prostitution and alcoholism. All these values were promptly incorporated in textbooks like the famous *Le Tour de la France par deux enfants* (*The Tour of France by Two Children*) subtitled *Duty and Country*, by G. Bruno (pen name of a woman writer, Augustine Fouillée) and first published in 1877. This fundamental textbook became an educational bestseller that would be used for almost 50 years, with over 6 million copies sold by 1901. Its contents made it the pedagogical tool of choice to transform ten- and eleven-year-olds from all over France into solid French Republicans. The book told the story of two orphan boys from Lorraine, a politically charged decision, as Lorraine had previously been part of eastern France, but was lost to Germany as part of the peace settlement after the French defeat in the Franco-Prussian War in 1871. Lorraine was central to the claims of *revanchiste* (revenge-minded) Republicans, as they were known, who had never been able to accept the loss of either Alsace or Lorraine to Germany and passionately wished to avenge that loss. In the textbook, the two "German" brothers have nine months to seek refuge in the French Republic, as stipulated by French immigration laws, and to find a remaining relative living in France in order to regain their French nationality and identity. They set forth in search of their French uncle, whose whereabouts are purposely unclear to justify the long and meandering journey. Each chapter begins with a moral statement and contains economic, geographical, historical, and civic instruction, all converging to make France an ideal country in all respects and instilling patriotism to last young readers for a lifetime.

Dossier 3.2   Preface to *The Tour of France by Two Children* (1877)

To know our nation is the very foundation of any true civic education.

We always complain that our children do not know their country well enough; the general voice of reason often says that if they knew it better, they would love it more and could serve it better. However, our instructors know how difficult it is to give children a clear idea of the nation, or simply of its land and resources. For a child, the word nation represents an abstract notion which, more than we wish admit, remains foreign to most of us throughout the greater part of our life. If it wants to impact young minds, the nation must be made visible and lively to them. With this objective in mind, we have tried to make good use of the interest that children have for travel stories. By telling the courageous story of two young boys from Lorraine who embark on a journey through France, we wanted to make children see and touch, so to speak, their country; we wanted to show them how two sons of the same motherland can profit from the riches of each region and how they learn through hard work how to make it yield plentifully even in areas where the soil is poor.

At the same time, this story offers to children examples of all forms of duty because our young heroes are not just touring France unconcerned: they must fulfill serious duties and run many risks. Following them in their journey, school children are gradually initiated to practical daily life, civic instruction, and, at the same time, to moral standards. They acquire basic notions of industrial and commercial economy, as well as of agriculture, the main sciences and their applications. They also learn about the interesting lives of great men from each province: each invention by famous men, every step of progress accomplished thanks to their wisdom become for the school child a true example, a kind of new moral in action, made more interesting when they are mixed in with descriptions of the places where these great men were born.

Thus, by attaching moral and civic knowledge to the idea of France, we wanted to introduce children to our nation in its noblest aspect, and to show them that its greatness comes with honor, work, and deep respect for duty and justice. (3)

Despite all republican efforts to *normalize* French individuals by teaching them the principles of the dominant bourgeois value system, a majority of children from rural and religious parts of France did not understand them. Sometimes religion and republic were kept side by side in the minds and daily routines of young school children. In his book *L'Argent* the Catholic writer and patriotic Republican Charles Péguy recalls how both school and religious teaching in fact coexisted without any "dissonance": "The Republic and the Church imparted diametrically opposed teachings. We did not mind as long as we were learning from both. [. . .] We loved the Church and the Republic together, and we loved them with the same heart, the heart of a child, that is, the immensity of the world and our two loves, glory and faith" (*Oeuvres 3*, 805). At other times, there was no reconciling the two camps as, for example, in this 1891 schoolteacher's report on how the harsh divisions between the two institutions played out on the everyday life of Castelmayran, a small southwestern town in the *département* of the Tarn and Garonne:

Castelmayran is home to two ferociously opposed clans: Republicans and Clericals. They keep their distance and have a profound hatred for one another. One clan drinks at the Café Bayron, the others go to Café Bouché; the leftist youth meet in a dance hall reserved for them, the right has its own hall. Similarly each clan has its own grocery store, its own butcher shop; everyone is labeled, ranked; you can socialize only with your side and must flee the other. (Allegret, 80)

In certain areas of France where everyday life was still governed by strong Catholic faith, religious fervor did little to help the republican cause and the turf wars between secular and religious traditions made it difficult to create effective citizens of the republic. Such dramatic divisions between the republicans, who believed in the separation of church and state, especially in matters of education, and the clericals, who held to the moral teachings of the church, could only lead to a political breach. These divisions also opened up sizeable social and cultural gaps between the different classes, who lived differently, socialized in different places, and learned under different moral paradigms, one secular and the other religious. This cultural rift translated into a pronounced mistrust between the classes, thus promoting a climate of conscious and visible class differences among the French, when, paradoxically, republican ideals aspired to establish a universal sense of citizenship and education.

In this social paradox, one point on which all agreed and on which the republican school insisted was the proper use of the French language. Children were expected to read, write, study, and speak standard French on school grounds, but they were also strongly encouraged to continue to use it outside so as to erase any linguistic differences among them and assimilate all French-speaking individuals into a single republican model of communication. Contrary to the republican desire for linguistic uniformity, however, school teachings, especially in the provinces, did not cross over to the social and family sphere. In fact each region continued to live within its specific identity by speaking its respective local dialect or native language on a daily basis: Occitan in the Southwest, Celtic Breton in Brittany, Auvergnat in Central France, and Provencal in the Southeast, to name only a few. In addition, many provincial children felt a cultural distance between the material taught to them and their own daily lives, between the reality of their provincial or rural environments and the urban culture of Parisian or city life. They often did not recognize themselves in the "average" Frenchman depicted in their textbooks and, as a result, continued to learn values and ideas with which they did not always identify, leaving them unmotivated and sometimes uninterested in learning any further. Ultimately, even if republican education failed to convince children throughout the regions that individual liberties resided in the progressive and anticlerical individualism promoted in their textbooks, it did achieve its main purpose of providing the basic learning skills to all Frenchmen who, ideally, would all be able to read, write, and count.

As early as the mid-1880s, the increasingly literate French population created a demand for printed material and facilitated the spread of news publications throughout the country. Literacy also made voters more knowledgeable about the candidates for whom they might vote, as opposed to the peasants of the Second Empire and early republic who, as reported in many anecdotes of the period, would vote by instinct, since they often could not read the names on the ballots, or were influenced by officials present at the polling booths. The rural population still represented more than half of the total despite the general demographic shift toward the newly industrialized cities. Indeed, while it did not empty the countryside of its population, industrialization nevertheless hastened rural exodus and brought agricultural laborers to the city where industrial jobs were plentiful. Work in the education sector also tempted newly educated peasants to leave their native villages in order to pursue a life of the mind and enjoy a slightly better economic situation elsewhere. However, republican politics and education did also make it possible for those peasants who remained on their farms and in their villages, the great majority of the population, to grow as modern individuals without jeopardizing their traditional values or without tearing them from their land. Still, despite a slow but consistent decrease in rural population, France would remain a primarily agricultural country well into the twentieth century.

The lives of villagers and peasants were forever changed by the arrival of the railroad, the greater autonomy of municipal politics, the improvement in agricultural machinery, and the comprehensive educational program for all children. This transformation of France from a backward and mostly illiterate country into a modern and educated nation-state is at the heart of Roger Thabault's 1943 book, *Mon Village: Ses hommes, ses routes, son école (Education and Change in a Village Community: Mazière-en-Gâtine, 1848–1914)*, a history of the social and economic transformation of the small village of Mazières in western France between 1848 and 1914. Rural awareness was also brought into literary circles by the celebrated 1904 biographical novel of a nineteenth-century "sharecropper" who lived through and remembered most of the historical events of the century from the empire to the Franco-Prussian War and the Third Republic; *La Vie d'un simple (Life of a Simple Man)* by the prolific "peasant" writer and union activist Emile Guillaumin, who spent all of his life on a farm near a small village called Ygrande in the Allier region of central France, relates the simple but hard life of a peasant named "Tiennon," his daily physical and emotional suffering, his feelings of educational and social inadequacy, his hardships as a farm worker, his feelings of shame and inferiority in relation to "city" people, including the working class and his "master," the owner of the farm. In his introduction, Guillaumin, whose literary ties to the peasantry were neither romantic nor naturalist, explained how he wrote this book as an insider, as opposed to "city writers" like Georges Sand and Emile Zola, who wrote about the rural world to "prove that peasants aren't as stupid as they [city people] imagine" (1). In this preface, Guillaumin also explains that his aim was to translate in "plain French" the spoken and regional French of Tiennon without changing the thinking behind it. In essence, Guillaumin, himself a peasant, an autodidact, and a self-taught writer, simply transcribed the full, "good and bad," confession of a peasant who had lived through the transformation of France in the nineteenth century, from an almost exclusively agricultural economy into a growing industrial power, and through the social changes brought about by that transformation. Some of the modern and universalist republic's reforms and projects ran counter to the way of life and character of Tiennon who, like countless other farmers and peasants, defiantly continued to live "the old way." Rather than being brought into the republican fold, many felt "ridiculous," inadequate, and alienated from the rest of the "educated" population. The human and social gap between rural and urban France thus widened, leaving the peasant an isolated individual misunderstood by city people. The intellectual and social isolation of the farmer, who nevertheless still continued to feed France, created a proud peasant caste that felt even more strongly attached to the land than before the industrial revolution. Peasants increasingly thought of themselves as social outcasts set apart for their backward ways by those they ironically fed daily, and forgotten by the authorities, conservative or progressive, imperial or republican. Even with noted industrial progress positively affecting part of the general agricultural activity in France, life and work on the farm, especially in the most remote parts of the country, remained intensely harsh and Tiennon's case speaks volumes of the peasants' continuous physical hardship and social isolation.

However, the education reforms and the general project of "turning peasants into Frenchmen" (Eugen Weber) was considered successful enough for Jules Ferry to apply them, to a certain extent, to another area of concern of the republic: the colonies.

Colonizing

Beyond the nation's borders, the task was now to transform the *indigènes* (natives), as they were called, into civilized individuals, to teach them the ways of the West in a great *mission civilisatrice* (civilizing mission). The French colonial attitude differed a great deal from that of the British, the uncontested imperial power. In opposition to the policy of *association* pursued by the British over its colonial Empire, *assimilation* was the stated aim of French colonial policy. "Assimilation" was a clear republican gesture specific to France and visible in its education program, whose aim was to assimilate all children into the republican model. It was not surprising to see at the core of the French colonial campaign principles of education that had been applied "at home." The French language was central to this endeavor. Within national borders, the republican government sought to alleviate and even erase "regional" differences and create a more homogeneous French population by teaching all children standard French: the same strategy would be applied to the education of "indigenous populations," thus facilitating their assimilation into the French republican model.

The ironic pronouncement of Joseph, the anticlerical schoolteacher in Marcel Pagnol's autobiographical novel *My Father's Glory*, comparing teachers to priests—"Like priests, we work to create a better future life" (see dossier 3.1)—reflected much of the general sentiment behind colonial policy, that is, the pedagogical and moral vocation of the Western world to educate the "natives." As Ferry formulated it in his 1885 speech to the French Assembly in an effort to justify colonization and motivate France to pursue its colonial ambitions and compete with other European nations for the conquest of the world, "[It is] the right and duty of superior races to educate inferior races" (in Chavan, 38).

The French already had a long colonial history beginning in the sixteenth century, notably with settlements in "New France," today the Canadian province of Québec, and then in the seventeenth in Saint-Domingue, today Haiti. A "second wave" of colonization was set in motion without much conviction or means during the course of the first half of the nineteenth century. This attitude changed when the French colonial program gained momentum during the Second Empire. Finally, colonizing became a significant political ambition and commitment for the Third Republic, which was actively seeking to enlarge France—in both territory and population—beyond the confines of the *Hexagone* from 1880 on. At the Berlin Conference of 1884–1885, the European powers, France among them, effectively split up the African colonial pie among themselves.

At first, France's colonial project could be subsumed under the label "civilizing mission"; commercial interests were not as systematically and overtly formulated as the scientific and anthropological ones; most of the "expeditions" were private, and the evangelizing component was strong. For example, in 1858, Henri Mouhot, a French explorer sponsored by the British Royal Geographical Society, arrived in Indochina where his first point of mooring was near a French cathedral: "We dropped anchor across from the cathedral of the French Mission and the modest palace of Monseigneur Pallegoix, a commendable archbishop who, after thirty years and only assisted by a handful of devoted missionaries, has managed in these faraway lands to establish respect for Christianity and for the name of France" (*Travels in Siam*, 45). In 1858, Emperor Napoleon III was not yet invested in a full-fledged colonial program, so for someone like Monseigneur Pallegoix in Indochina, there was clearly no official input from the French government, even if the France was benefiting from this extension of its reputation in "faraway lands."

France's reputation was to be taken to the four corners of the globe by way of its status as modern, industrialized, and scientific nation. In this still unsystematic and nonofficial phase of the colonial enterprise, however, the church saw in these new territories an outlet for its efforts to regain control of the moral education of the West. In this case, civilization was then simply equivalent to religion itself. This revival of the religious effort abroad attracted many more missionaries to the colonized world, where they taught the moral principles of Western religion to indigenous populations and often converted them to Catholicism. France was most successful in establishing Catholic communities in West Africa while England set up protestant strongholds in India. For the evangelized population of the colonies, civilization was intimately linked to religious teachings. Thus, the French desire to bring their secular culture and progress to primitive societies all over the world was preempted by a religious missionary effort before it became a resounding republican duty. As it became a "humanitarian" concept, the "civilizing mission" carried the double meaning of a republican moral and ideological effort inseparable from its already well-established religious component.

Beyond (or *beneath*) the two stated "missions"—to take the benefits of modern science to the "natives" and to evangelize the "pagans"—France's objectives, like those of other European nations involved in the colonial race, were commercial and military.

Later in his travel journal, Mouhot's observations shift from the "honorable work" of the French archbishop to the rising economic interest in Indochina. In particular, he speaks of the commercial enterprise launched by the French and the British in the region then called Siam (today's Thailand): "For a while now, Europe has heard about Siam, and based on agreements for trade and peace, based on inflated descriptions, several representatives of France and England have established commercial positions there . . . Bangkok has become the Venice of the Orient" (42–45). Mouhot's perception of the 1858 European mission in the Orient as shifting from humanitarian mission to commercial enterprise was consistent with the expansion of the "civilizing mission" into a full-blown colonizing program, developing educational but also strategic and economic ambitions.

As we saw, this comprehensive colonial program began in the second half of the Second Empire when Napoleon III promoted a colonial policy in Algeria (1860) and consolidated his diplomatic ties with Egypt over the construction of the Suez Canal (1859–1869). At the end of the Second Empire, colonial activities were momentarily suspended by an overly patriotic and nationalistic Third Republic, whose foreign interests in the 1870s were obsessively focused on France's mourning over the loss of the two French regions of Alsace and Lorraine to Germany and consumed by political strategies to regain control of these provinces. Gambetta was the first politician to redirect France's foreign interests outside of Europe and to argue for a concerted French colonial deployment to other continents. He was soon followed by the minister of education and Prime Minister Jules Ferry, who would also plead with French politicians to put an end to France's "mourning period" and instead to look into the potentially prosperous colonial future. A colonial party appeared, as well as a colonial superior council. In the council, Ferry was placed in charge of two provinces in

Indochina, Annam and Tonkin. His active campaign for a colonized Indochina (today's Vietnam, Cambodia, and Laos) would earn him the nickname of "Ferry the Tonkinese."

Dossier 3.3   Jules Ferry, "the Tonkinese"

Jules Ferry was brought up as a bourgeois and a freemason. He began his professional life as a lawyer and later became a journalist, coming into the limelight after writing a series of critical articles entitled "The Fantastic Accounting of Haussmann" for the newspaper *Le Temps* in 1869. The articles focused on what Ferry considered extravagant budget request by the famous prefect of the Seine, who wished to continue the ongoing architectural transformation of Paris. Strongly opposed to the Second Empire, Ferry entered politics as a leftist republican in 1870 and was briefly elected mayor of Paris during the Franco-Prussian War, when he became known as *Ferry la famine* due to his recommendation that while under siege, Parisians should conserve and ration their food. Later, he built a reputation as the architect of free, secular, and mandatory education and, like Gambetta, was an "opportunist" who, beyond French prosperity, wished for a greater place and destiny for France in the modern world. In a famous speech to the assembly on July 28, 1885 he declared, "France cannot simply be a free country, she must also be a great country, exercising on Europe the influence that she possesses, and she must spread this influence across the world, and carry wherever she can her language, her customs, her flag, her weapons, and her spirit" (*Identity, Insecurity and Image: France and Language*, 45). During Jules Grevy's presidency, Ferry occupied several important ministerial posts, allowing him to strengthen the image of republican France. His vision of a "great France" took his politics beyond national borders, to Africa and Asia, with a specific goal of developing a colonial empire in the Orient.

From 1882 on, Ferry was involved in France's commercial projects in southern China and in the negotiations of a peace treaty with the Chinese that would secure the French occupation of Tonkin and Annam. When China did not honor the treaty, France launched a victorious war against the Chinese. However, back home, Ferry's anticolonial opponents, especially a *revanchiste* leftist deputy named Georges Clémenceau, a future president, denounced what appeared to be a French defeat in Langson, North Tonkin, on March 28, 1885. He accused Ferry of high treason, of uselessly sacrificing troops that should have been used for a military buildup on the borders of Alsace and Lorraine; he demanded Ferry's resignation. Ferry was forced to resign as prime minister on March 30, 1885, and his popularity fell to its lowest point. Hence, the critical nickname he then received, "Ferry the Tonkinese," pointing to Ferry's alleged lack of true patriotism in his stubborn and apparently failed military engagement abroad. A day later, on March 31, the Chinese troops were beaten by the French and in the end the Tonkin was indeed secured for France, making the whole "Ferry the Tonkinese" incident a political mockery designed to exclude Ferry from the government. However, the damage to the prime minister's reputation could not be undone. Yet, even after resigning, Ferry remained in politics as a member of the Chamber of Deputies, as a representative of the Vosges department, remaining an active and vocal proponent of his own colonial policy. In 1885, only a few months after his forced resignation, he gave a key address on colonial issues in front of the full National Assembly. Addressing a skeptical audience of deputies still undecided about France's colonial empire, and under pressure from the anticolonial faction to look toward Alsace and Lorraine rather than overseas, he made three major and resounding points that did nothing less than convince his colleagues of France's colonial opportunities and its "duty" to colonize:

The policy of colonial expansion is a political and economic system . . . that can be connected to three sets of ideas: economic ideas, the most far-reaching ideas of civilization, and ideas of a political and patriotic sort . . . In the area of economics, I am placing before you, with the support of some statistics, the considerations that justify the policy of colonial expansion, as seen from the perspective of a need felt more and more urgently by the industrialized population of Europe and especially the people of our rich and hardworking country of France: the need for outlets . . . Gentlemen, we must speak more loudly and more honestly! We must say openly that indeed the higher races have a right over the lower races . . . I repeat, that the superior races have a right because they have a duty. They have the duty to civilize the inferior races . . . In our time, I maintain that European nations acquit themselves with generosity, with grandeur, and with sincerity of this superior civilizing duty . . . I say that French colonial policy, the policy of colonial expansion, the policy that has taken us under the Empire that has led us to Tunisia, to Madagascar-I say that this policy of colonial expansion was inspired by . . . the fact that a navy such as ours cannot do without safe harbors, defenses, supply centers on the high seas. . . . Gentlemen, these are considerations that merit the full attention of patriots . . . At present, as you know, a warship, however perfect its design, cannot carry more than two weeks' supply of coal; and a vessel without coal is a wreck on the high seas, abandoned to the first occupier. Hence the need to have places of supply, shelters, ports for defense and provisioning. And that is why we needed Tunisia; that is why we needed Saigon and Indochina; that is why we need Madagascar, and why we shall never leave them. (Robiquet, 199–215)

Ferry ended his speech by insisting that "spreading light" and educating the world was not enough if France wanted to compete as a strong economic power and that it needed to take action and be part of the "affairs of the world" (Robiquet, 218).

Commercial expansion in the colonies was far from the "civilizing mission" it was purported to be, and more like a brutal and repressive system forcing "indigenous peoples" into inhuman manual labor, as expressed here by Anatole France, one of the best-known writers of the period: "Our colonial policy is the most recent form of barbarity, or if you prefer the term, civilization" (*La France colonisatrice*, 224). The program of political assimilation, rife with moral and ideological contradictions, proved to be a nearly impossible task. Only Algeria would become somewhat "integrated" into France administratively, becoming an actual French *département*. This status, which, ideally would make of the Algerians "citizens of the Republic," in fact relegated them to that of "subjects of the empire." The French language continued to be taught to the indigenous populations, but the populations that were being taught this language were not socially or politically assimilated. Instead, in the great majority of cases, they were exploited while administered by the *Metropole* (mainland France) and subjected to its colonial laws of occupation. Different territories were subjected to different forms of colonial administration. In North Africa, Tunisia and Morocco, for example, retained more of their own administration, and were considered protectorates rather than colonies. As for the other French territories, they were largely regulated and exploited by France. This was, for example, the case for Senegal, the Ivory Coast, Upper Volta (today's Burkina Faso), Dahomey (today's Benin), French Sudan (today's Mali), French Guinea (today's Guinea), Mauritania and Niger, that together constituted what would be known as the French West African Federation in 1904 with Saint Louis, then Dakar as its capital. Similarly, in 1910, the Federation of French Equatorial Africa was created, gathering Gabon, Middle Congo (today's Congo), Ubangi-Shari (today's Central African Republic), and Chad. France also secured two additional colonies, on the East African coast: Djibouti in 1892 and the island of Madagascar in 1895. In Asia in 1887, the French asserted their sovereignty over the conquered south Chinese territories, which were composed of Tonkin, Annam, Laos, Cambodia, and Cochinchina, collectively renamed the "General Government of Indochina." In the Caribbean and South America, France had already established its colonies in Guadeloupe, Martinique, and French Guyana at the end of the Napoleonic wars, early in the nineteenth century. On the eve of World War I, France was the second-largest colonial empire, with 5 percent of the world's population, after England's (25 percent of the world population). At the onset of World War I in 1914, the French Empire was twenty-two times larger than France itself.

Despite its vast territory and abundant resources, the colonial empire was not as lucrative as Ferry had hoped, thus casting a cloud of doubt and uncertainty over the republic's decision to acquire and expand French colonial holdings. As had been the case for Haussmann's urban renovation project—denounced in Ferry's articles in 1869, budgetary issues created a rift among both proponents of and opponents to Ferry's colonial policy. Had France spread itself too thin through colonial expansion? Should it not concentrate its forces on the Franco-German border against the ancestral enemy? What was the purpose of sending troops to be slaughtered in hostile and "savage" lands, where France had no clear and immediate interests, such as the reclaiming of national territory lost in a recent war? Adverse reactions to colonial conquest came from the conservative Right as well as from the republican Left, and the arguments were political as well as ideological. At the time of his death, many ended up criticizing Ferry's colonial project.

Dossier 3.4   Séverine's "Obituary" for Jules Ferry (1893)

Perhaps no one criticized Jules Ferry's colonial legacy more openly and vehemently than Séverine, pen name of Caroline Rémy, a feminist and the first French woman journalist. She was the editorial assistant to Jules Vallès, the ex-Communard (see chapter 2) and an outspoken critic of what she saw as the racist foundations and immoral principles behind colonization and wrote countless articles on the topic.

In this scathing article, a highly unusual and caustic "obituary," Caroline Rémy wrote on the ruinous legacy Ferry would leave behind.

"Jules Ferry"

He is dead, he who slandered and executed Parisians; he who abused Christian minds; he who sent our dear soldiers, our sons, flesh of our flesh, to die of fever and torture in "yellow" countries . . .

The neighborhoods were cold and the boulevards indifferent; crowded as on a usual day, filled with curiosity but not with emotion . . .

I am not in the habit of insulting the dead, and my pen would be cruel if it did not recognize some form of sincere and profound but fragile feeling of pain for this dead man. But, believe me, the truth has to be spoken . . .

He was a domineering man; power hungry and authoritarian. To command, govern and manipulate in his powerful hands the destiny of races were actions that haunted him all of his life. Besides this, nothing mattered to him; he wallowed in blood, in lies, in intrigues; whether blamed or acclaimed, he was lost in his dream . . . insensitive and deaf.

If his ambitions were not vulgar, they were sterile from the start because they always were against public instinct . . .

As I write this article, I am looking at a piece of bread from the siege that I turned into a paperweight for my desk. I remember—in the snow, under fire, in below zero temperature standing in line in front of the bakery—the clamor rising against the mayor of Paris: "Ferry-the famine!" . . .

Wait there is more! Here comes the adventure in Indochina with all his failures, follies and crimes. "Ferry-the Tonkinese!" cry out all the crazed and tormented mothers, fiancées, sisters, widows whose loved ones were left out there in the wilderness: dead in the sun, blown out by bombs, faces smashed by enemy guns . . . and slowly, very slowly, tortured by the Asians.

Oh! What about his speech after the Langson disaster where he lied before fleeing, followed by the booing of his colleagues! On the Place de la Concorde, rue de Bourgogne, twenty thousand men were screaming: "Death to Ferry!" . . .

And now, on March 17, 1893, he is dead, almost in time for the silver anniversary of the Commune he disliked so much and in the wounds of which he drove his politician's pen. As a result the neighborhoods have prepared their present to him and he will never open fire on the locals again. (La France colonisatrice, 208–211)

Ferry received a state funeral, but was not buried at the Panthéon, the republican memorial monument in the heart of Paris where all "great men," who had served and honored the French nation were given a place. As a point of comparison, other prominent statesmen and literary figures of this period were honored and laid to rest at the Pantheon: Victor Hugo, Emile Zola, Léon Gambetta, and later, Jean Jaurès, the Socialist and pacifist politician, whose assassination in 1914 was the result of his antiwar campaign and the definite sign of the war that was about to begin.

The Shock of the New: Writers and Painters

For an artist, scandal is the best proclamation of success.

—Michel Conte, *Nu. . . comme dans nuage* (1980)

It is not surprising that in this turbulent political and cultural climate "shock value" would be central to French cultural and everyday life. In the arts, for example, many critics and their followers considered "shocking" some impressionist works from the 1860s and 1870s or those of the Cubists in the early twentieth century. While the artists from impressionist, postimpressionist, and cubist eras were all actively searching for new ways to paint the reality they saw around them and were experimenting with new techniques that would end up revolutionizing the art world, they were not deliberately and actively seeking to "shock"; the "shock value" of their art was thus almost an unintentional by-product of a desire to find new ways of seeing and using radically new techniques in their work. Beginning with Courbet and continuing with Manet and then Picasso, shock was mainly a value created and disseminated by critics who in fact did not obtain the negative result they expected for these disparaged artists and their art. Instead, the resulting notoriety contributed to bringing fame to artists who could well have remained relatively unknown. Once an "efflorescence" period passed, the initially "shocking" status became a legacy, fame being simply deferred, even if, for some of these artists, it came in their old age or even posthumously. Of course, this did not apply to those who were fully immersed in the academic dictates of the time, and enjoyed their celebrity while relatively young, as was the case for academic artists such as Alexandre Cabanel, who was carried into artistic stardom by his hugely successful 1863 "Birth of Venus." However, artists like Cabanel did not enter the "pantheon" of art history as did the impressionists or cubists. Today, names like Manet, Monet, Renoir, Degas, Gauguin, Cézanne, and Picasso have a resonance not found in those of Adolphe Bouguereau, Alexandre Cabanel, or Jean-Léon Gérôme, whose reputations remain confined to the traditional art of the period. The "shock of the new" attributed to impressionists and cubists projected them into the future of art history, eclipsing today the legacy of other contemporary, but less "scandalous," artists of the time.

This was, in effect, the itinerary followed by the impressionists. They were first rejected and even institutionalized as "rejects" or "refused" during the Second Empire when Napoleon III allowed the creation of a site to exhibit their nonacademic art known as the *Salon des Refusés* (Salon of the Refused) in 1863. Thus prepared, the critics could then go to this salon expecting the worst and be ready to demolish any "refused" artist who would exhibit there. Manet was one of these artists. In 1863, he showed his work in two diametrically opposed venues: at the official academic Salon organized yearly by the Arts Academy, and at the Salon des Refusés. That year, the impressionists were not yet born as an artistic group and movement. It was only eleven years later, on April 14, 1874, at a studio on the Boulevard des Capucines owned by Nadar, a famous Parisian photographer, that thirty artists, among them Boudin, Cézanne, Degas, Monet, Morissot, and Renoir, brought together a collection of paintings that today we call "impressionist." Immediately after this opening, the press was quick to create a scandal calling the artists "impressionists," a term whose use was meant to be derogatory and indicating a lack of the polished finish that was characteristic of dominant, academic style. This new art, according to the critics was not "finished" and closer to unworthy "impressions"; these "impressionist" works reflected the bad taste and the poor talent of artists who depicted a distorted reality through "sloppy brush strokes." In a vitriolic article published in the newspaper *Charivari*, journalist Louis Leroy sneered at Monet's painting, a seascape representing the port of Le Havre in Normandy in the very early morning light and entitled: "Impression, Sunrise" (1872). The display of this particular painting led Leroy to coin the word "impression" to identify Monet's style, a style the journalist compared to "wallpaper in its embryonic state" finding the wallpaper "more finished than the seascape" by Monet (Rewald, 323). A few days later, Jules Castagnary, a journalist and art critic who had been a friend and ardent defender of Gustave Courbet, wrote an article in which the term "impressionist" was used more constructively and favorably, and became the group's consecrated name: "If I want to characterize them with a single word that explains their efforts, one would have to create the new term of *impressionists*. They are impressionists in the sense that they render not a landscape but the sensation produced by a landscape" (Rewald, 330). Despite contention and disagreement, the movement and the term "impressionism" were born. The bright and mobile style of these impressionist painters, the simple and trivial scenes from everyday life they depicted, so distant from the lofty historical and romanticized mythical or romanticized rural scenes of academic painters, were now on the cultural map. It was as if painting had staged its own revolutionary coup by refuting the artistic tradition established by and for those in privileged positions, aristocrats and upper bourgeois, some of whom reduced the world of art to portraits of their own family, depictions of their own historical heroes, polished representations of their favorite mythical and romantic figures, and bucolic landscapes where they often had their estates, all painted to perfection. However, at the same time, some of the same wealthy patrons were able to look away from tradition, and appreciate and promote new art forms. They financially supported this new wave of artists who could not have survived without them.

The impressionists opened their canvases to life in its entirety as they painted hitherto "unworthy" familiar and popular scenes from the busy streets of Paris (Monet, "Boulevard des Capucines," 1873; Caillebotte, "Street of Paris," 1877; Pissarro, "Boulevard Montmartre," 1897), the industrial world (Guillaumin, "Sunset at Ivry," 1874; Monet, "Pont de l'Europe, Gare Saint Lazare," 1877; Pissarro, "Duquesnes Basin, Dieppe," 1902), and the countryside (Monet, "Poppy field at Argenteuil," 1873; Renoir, "Wild Poppies," 1876), all in the natural light of day or in the shadows of the night. More than scenery itself, light was crucial to the impressionists. They sought it out continuously at different times of the day, in cities and in the countryside, in luminous Provence and in dreary northern France. Monet produced several series—most notably "The Railroad Station," "The Haystacks," "The Cathedral at Rouen," and "The Waterlilies"—in which the same scene was painted at different times of the day or at different seasons in order to experiment with the play of light.

Modern life was making its way into the world of art. Art seemed now closer than ever to the people it represented, a veritable gallery of modern characters: the *flâneurs* or city strollers (Caillebotte, "Street in Paris in the Rain," 1877), clothes washers (Degas, "The Laundresses," 1884), butchers (Pissarro, "The Pork Butcher," 1883), dancers, both classical (Degas, "Ballet Rehearsal on the Stage," 1874), and popular (Renoir, "Moulin de la Galette," 1876; Toulouse-Lautrec, "The Dance at the Moulin Rouge," 1890), bartenders (Manet, "A Beer-Waitress," 1878–1879; "A Bar at the Folies-Bergères," 1882), drinkers (Degas, "In the Café (Absinthe)," 1875–1876), ragpickers (Manet, "The Ragpicker," 1865–1869), prostitutes (Manet, "Olympia," 1863; and "Nana," 1877). From casual and serene *flâneurs* to defiant prostitutes, from busy streets to quiet boudoirs, an entire array of characters and scenes culled from the incessantly and rapidly changing century was submitted to an astonished public and to scathing critics as daring representations of a new type of esthetic diversity that French impressionist painter Auguste Renoir called "beautiful irregularities." The impressionist painter saw beauty in imperfection and called for the creation of an esthetic principle centered on the notion of irregularity. According to Renoir the universal concept of beauty, reframed and reworked by varied new artists of the period, must comprise irregularities and flaws.

Visual Power

The impressionists saw and showed a modern and dynamic culture outside the institutionalized forms of representation; they welcomed and accepted modernity's "irregularities," subverted artistic norms and offered new ways of seeing. Simultaneously, they presented the viewing public with an inclusive cultural fresco: peasants and city dwellers, the countryside and industrial activity, leisure and labor, offering in the process a more *universal* view of the place and time in which they lived and worked. This universal quality intrinsic to the impressionist's subject matter goes a long way to explaining that, after the initial shock delivered by their style and content, a shock well propagated by the press, the world represented in their art began filtering through the politics of the time.

A visual culture informs and entertains through images, but also undoubtedly influences, through its visual power, the thinking about this particular culture. This is even more so when a nation is still far from being completely literate, as was the case for France in the second half of the nineteenth century. Image has, and is, power. While impressionists fell into this paradigm inadvertently, Republicans came to realize its potential and exploited its powers. More specifically, they embraced the democratic display of everyday life present on impressionist canvases. On the other hand, though it is true that impressionism presented a wider view of the world, artistic venues in general (museums, galleries) remained essentially a bourgeois space. Thus, in spite of its democratic, even universal quality, this new art primarily captured the interest of a certain bourgeois population, and mainly exercised its visual power over a restricted public, especially critics, that was responsible for pushing the impressionist adventure onward, from scandal to success.

The republic wanted to make full use of the persuasive and exciting power of "the visual" by multiplying public symbols like statues and monuments that best represented its values and cultural views. On the grand scale, statues like Aimé Jules Dalou's "The Triumph of the Republic" (1889–1899), and monuments like the Eiffel Tower (1889) (see figure 3.1), were part of the visual program serving the republic's civic and modernizing program. On a smaller but more widespread scale, busts of Marianne, the French symbol of republican principles, were placed in every government office and school, as part of the same plan to visually ingrain republican ideals in the collective French mind. Visual power was also invested in images used to educate the masses in transition between illiteracy and basic education. People who had only begun to learn how to read in the 1880s and thus, on the brink of entering reading culture, would still largely depend on the visual for information. This segment of the population, composed mostly of the poor and the peasantry, represented the bulk of the French population, did not share in the cultural sophistication of the bourgeoisie and had a different experience of the visual. Republicans understood this divergence and developed different visual strategies: the simplicity of cartoon-like images for the masses, and museum art for the bourgeois.

Bourgeois art, scandalous or not, as was the case for impressionism, remained "indoors," enclosed in the delimited bourgeois spaces: museums, galleries, and salons.

This type of art was easily accessible to city dwellers but largely unknown to the rural population. Cut off as it was from bourgeois art, the visual offerings available to this population was restricted to the images that appeared in the pamphlets, posters, books, and newspapers available in their towns and villages. These images, black and white or in color, were called *images d'Epinal* (images from Epinal), after the hometown of the craftsman who originally printed and produced them. They were extremely popular as they presented current events and history to those who could not yet read and who depended on this basic lithography. In accordance with its sweeping universal educational program, the republic used these images to reinforce its moral and patriotic principles in the minds of school children, and these images invaded textbooks and classrooms. Their childlike quality made them an effective pedagogical tool as they informed both visually and with simple verbal captions. The same qualities made them equally effective as political propaganda, especially at election time. They became ubiquitous in campaigning and political advertising either as single-image posters or series of images relating current events, and were plastered all over the French countryside by hired hawkers trying to rally the support of the rural population to a particular cause.

This practice was never more popular than during the rise to power of General Boulanger between 1886 and 1889 and, soon after, during the Dreyfus Affair, between 1894 and 1906. *Images d'Epinal* were used profusely by both friends and foes of these two military figures to relate their complex stories in simple terms and to stir popular interest and influence public opinion, in order to promote or attack the general in the case of Boulanger, or to discredit or defend the Jewish captain in the case of Dreyfus. Whatever the message conveyed, the style of the Epinal images was always that of exaggeration, presenting overly symbolic settings and caricatured characters. Boulanger was often represented by his defenders as sitting perfectly upright on his horse, recalling the imperial equestrian portraits of Napoleon I and Napoleon III, surrounded by flags and military or political men, commanding respect and inspiring confidence in his uniform. For his detractors, Dreyfus was represented either slumped over as if broken by his alleged unpatriotic acts, uncertain on his legs as a sign of weakness, and often with his rear end presented to the viewer thus invited to mock and symbolically kick him. He was often drawn with an overly huge nose to point to his Jewish roots and out of uniform to indicate his unworthiness to be in the military (see figure 3.2). These two "scandalous affairs" were brought to national attention through different channels and "media" (newspapers, speeches, sermons, etc.), but it was by way of the popular *images d'Epinal* that they reached a widespread audience throughout the republic.

The Boulanger Affair

Boulanger came into political focus at a time when the "opportunists" seemed to lose popularity over their colonial program, their economic policy and their social program for workers. On the one hand, *Revanchistes* from the Left and the Right, also known as nationalists as they placed the "nation" on a higher plane than the "republic," gained ascendancy over a French population that had grown more increasingly restive regarding the German annexation of Alsace and Lorraine. At the time, the denomination "Nationalists" included ideologically opposed groups; not only royalists, dead set against the universal principle of the republic, but also some Republicans, known as "radicals," who believed that the nation and the universal principles of the republic were not served adequately by the elected liberal opportunists, who, according to them, continued to pursue what they considered the useless and expensive colonial dream of a French Far East and a French coastal Africa. At the other end of the political spectrum, Socialists and newly formed workers' unions deplored the lack of reforms for the working class, accusing the opportunists of being politically selective by concentrating their reformist efforts on improving the lives of peasants and not that of other groups. The general feeling that the government was not doing anything to repair France's honor, left "bleeding" after the deep wound inflicted by the German annexation of Alsace and Lorraine—to paraphrase the dramatic terminology and metaphors of the period—seemed to be strong enough among men of different political stripes to find common ground in the public persona of General Georges Ernest Jean-Marie Boulanger.

Boulanger presented himself as the long-awaited man for the "revenge" against Germany, and was nicknamed "General Revenge." Despite his lack of clear political agenda, his popularity grew at the strategic time when the economy had slowed down, unemployment was growing, a time when many French people from all classes were in favor of "rescuing the nation" rather than expanding the colonies, which they believed to be a financial drain. The French were also losing respect for government officials, some of whom had been recently caught up in scandalous affairs. For example, the "scandal of decorations" involved President Grevy's son-in-law, whose corrupt practice of "giving away" military medals to undeserving individuals was brought into the open, forcing the compromised president to resign in 1887. He was replaced by Sadi Carnot, but the already weak presidential function came out of this scandal further damaged, reducing the president's role to mere ceremonial functions.

Boulanger was minister of war during Grevy's presidency and, as a military man, he represented stability and order at a time when the concept of antimilitarism did not exist and therefore did not inspire political opposition. His military persona also exuded a sense of protection for French people always wary of their German neighbors. Boulanger quickly rallied the dissatisfied French populace, and with the support and advice of extremist political associations like Paul Déroulède's nationalist "League of the Patriots" as well as with the general encouragement of the French population, he won his seat as representative of Paris in the elections of 1889. In a few months Boulanger's popularity had outgrown his own hopes to ever become a major political player. He was surprised by his own success. Soon after his quick and overwhelming electoral victory in Paris, nationalists from the Right incited him to take over the country by organizing a coup. At this juncture, Boulanger hesitated, and desisted. Explanations for his behavior range from military unpreparedness to pangs of conscience and advice from his mistress. He fled to Belgium where he committed suicide. The Boulanger episode made clear the extreme views of the nationalists and definitively isolated them politically from radical Republicans even if, for a while, during the Boulanger crisis, their common belief in the almighty and "sacred nation" had brought them closer. After the near success of the Boulanger coup orchestrated by the nationalists, the Republicans could no longer turn a blind eye to the danger they posed to republican principles. In 1889, the end of the veritable political craze known as Boulangism did not, however, put an end to the formation of nationalist groups. On the contrary, it marked the rise of a type of inflammatory right-wing nationalism, a fundamental political movement from the French Far Right that clearly distinguished itself from the rest of the political spectrum. The republic, having dodged the immediate nationalist bullet that Boulanger represented in 1889, celebrated with particular attention and with great pomp and circumstance its return to democracy and progress with festivities of massive proportions, like the highly symbolic celebration of the centenary of the French Revolution, with the hosting of the 1889 Universal Exposition and, for the occasion, with the inauguration of a "scandalous" and glorious monument that would soon outgrow its reality to become a legend: the Eiffel Tower (see figure 3.1).

Dossier 3.5   The Eiffel Tower (1889)

> The Tower is present to the entire world. First of all as a universal symbol of Paris, it is everywhere on the globe where Paris is to be stated as an image . . . It belongs to the universal language of travel . . . On the Eiffel Tower, one can feel oneself cut off from the world and yet the owner of the world. (Barthes, 237–250)

Despite its undisputed status today as the "universal symbol of Paris," at first the Eiffel Tower was an extremely controversial project. At first, it was considered by many to be a form of "irregularity," whether architectural monstrosity or exceptional edifice. Architect Gustave Eiffel's tower was then the tallest construction in the world, an extraordinary iron edifice that would gradually come to symbolize not only Paris, but France, sometimes Europe, even an emblem of "the universal language of travel" (Barthes, 237). Built to celebrate the centennial of the 1789 French Revolution and inaugurated at the 1889 Universal Exposition held in Paris, it was received with mixed feelings, and a group of concerned Parisians decided to vent their opinions on what poet Paul Verlaine called the "belfry skeleton," the essayist Leon Bloy the "tragic lamp post," and the writer Joris-Karl Huysmans a "hole-riddled suppository." Like these writers and intellectuals, Parisians felt that the tower would deface and degrade their beloved city. In fact, at the onset of the construction of the tower, a group of artists and writers, including Alexandre Dumas, Charles Garnier, Charles Gounod, Leconte de Lisle, Guy de Maupassant, expressed their anger publicly in the newspaper *Le Temps* on February 14, 1887, in a pamphlet addressed to the director of the 1889 Paris Universal Exposition:

We, writers, painters, sculptors, architects, lovers of Parisian beauty, untouched until now, come to protest with all our strength and indignation, in the name of the underestimated taste of the French, in the name of French art and history under threat, against the erection in the very heart of our capital, of the useless and monstrous Eiffel Tower, which our people has already christened the Tower of Babel . . . Must Paris associate with the baroque and commercial fancies of a builder of machines, thus making itself irreparably ugly and bringing dishonor? . . . To understand our argument one only needs to imagine for a moment a tower of ridiculous vertiginous height dominating Paris, just like a giant black factory chimney, its barbarous mass overwhelming and humiliating all our monuments and belittling our works of architecture, which will just disappear before this stupefying folly. And for twenty years we shall see spreading across the whole city, a city shimmering with the genius of so many centuries, we shall see spreading like an ink stain, the odious shadow of this odious column of bolted metal. (www.tour-eiffel.fr, 1)

Eiffel did not leave the protest unanswered and chose to respond in the same medium by granting the newspaper *Le Temps* an interview on the same day, February 14, 1887. In his response, Eiffel spoke of beauty and strength as the two principles that guided his engineering work. He also pointed to the innovative and bold gesture that led to the tower's construction. Finally, he pointed to the artistic act of defiance represented by the mere size of the tower, a "colossal attraction." "Colossal" was indeed the term that best depicted the tower itself while also reflecting its repercussions in the world of art, and its symbolic status as a sign of progress and modernity. No other monument would generate so much fascination for the millions of visitors to Paris, either then or for generations to come. In the end, history bore Eiffel out, as people came to realize and appreciate the beauty and strength of the tower as early as its inauguration and for years thereafter.

The Panama Scandal

In 1889, while France was busy reaffirming its republican faith through a grandiose celebration and the construction of the colossal Eiffel Tower, while the population was regaining confidence in the authority and the leadership of the Republicans and their ability to move the country forward, while most felt reassured by the reality of the nation's advances as they set eyes on the visual display of progress making headway throughout the entire nation, another scandal was brewing on the other side of the Atlantic, on the isthmus of Panama.

After great success as a diplomat, savvy negotiator, and a visionary entrepreneur at the time of the construction of the Suez canal, Ferdinand de Lesseps was placed in charge of another canal enterprise in the Colombian region of Panama, a small stretch of land seventy-five kilometers wide at its narrowest point of separation between the Atlantic and the Pacific oceans, an area which, if successfully pierced, could change the future of global commercial transportation. Lesseps's ambitious plan was to build a level canal that seemed a major engineering error to specialists—not surprising, since Lesseps was not an engineer—considering that the ground was hilly and uneven, in some areas, mountainous. A level canal, like the Suez Canal, is a lockless waterway, which, in the case of Panama, would have to be dug very deep to allow for and absorb the difference in sea levels from one ocean to the other, and to compensate for the uneven geographical terrain. Such a project would also require a great deal of "imported" manual labor, much more, in fact, than Lesseps had imagined. He planned to finish the canal in 8 years for the—already high—cost of 600 million francs. After his success in Suez, the French government had complete trust in Lesseps and readily approved his plan. In 1880 Lesseps thus founded the *Compagnie universelle du canal interocéanique de Panama* (Universal Interoceanic Panama Canal Company), and work began the following year. The originally popular project soon encountered difficulties: as expected, the tough, uneven terrain of the mountainous Panama region, the constant and deadly mudslides, a cholera epidemic, malaria and pox spreading easily among the physically unprepared workers, poor planning, and finally, the stubbornness and pride of Lesseps himself, who refused to accept failure and continued to run expenses above budget. Only halfway through, the cost of the construction was already in the red: 1,400 million spent instead of the

600 million initially announced. All these elements combined finally forced Lesseps to consider alternatives. In 1888, he called on the expertise of the popular engineer Gustave Eiffel, whose architectural merits were then highly appreciated by the government in light of his ongoing construction of the Eiffel Tower. The engineer reworked the canal plans, which this time included locks, and even lowered the final cost.

Lesseps also placed the financial investment of the project in the hands of two financiers, Cornelius Herz and Baron Jacques de Reinbach, whose mission was to influence public opinion in favor of the canal and to attract much-needed investors. Herz and Reinbach would resort to all sorts of methods to restore solvency to the project. Specifically, they made large illegal contributions to deputies who then influenced the general vote on a law allowing Lesseps to call for a new "lottery" loan. The two financiers also paid generous fees to members of the press, who often radically changed their tune from detractor to defender of the Panama project. At a time when the press had become a vital medium in an increasingly literate country, newspapers and politics seemed intimately related, if only pragmatically, since many newspapers reported parliamentary debates verbatim. In addition, newspapers often reflected specific political tendencies, from royalists and nationalists on the Right to Republicans and Socialists on the Left, even if not all papers were openly political. The most popular ones, called la presse à un sou (the penny press) were founded as apolitical papers, and attempted to remain as objective as possible (Le Petit Journal, Le Petit Parisien, Le Matin, Le Journal), while others were known for their clear political affiliations: La Justice, later renamed L'Aurore, one of the country's major newspapers, was directed by radical Republican Georges Clémenceau, Le Pilori was a royalist publication, Le Grelot Republican, and La Libre Parole openly anti-Semitic and nationalistic. Many reputedly republican papers were among those that accepted grafts from Herz and Reinbach, thus contributing to rebuilding optimism and encouraging investments for a project that, contrary to what the press was telling its readers, was already on the brink of bankruptcy.

Despite all efforts, legal and illegal, in 1889, the Panama Canal Company finally filed for bankruptcy, and angry but powerless shareholders lost up to 150 million francs. Many ministers and deputies were implicated in this affair, as they had accepted payments for passing laws favoring loans for the sinking project, or had agreed to publish enthusiastic reports about Panama in the press in which they also had stakes. One of these alleged "dirty" politicians was radical Republican Georges Clémenceau who always maintained his innocence, explaining that while he did accept money from Cornelius Herz for his newspaper La Justice, he did not know the actual financial disaster engulfing the Canal Company. Tainted by this scandal, Clémenceau would, for a time, fall from political grace.

The investors' loss was blamed on the corrupt government and allowed detractors of the republic to reemerge and expose what they labeled a "decadent" government, one infiltrated by those they insisted were corrupt Jewish businessmen, ruled by liberal politicians and a weak parliamentary system. The Panama affair, which had remained fairly unpublicized until 1889, was suddenly unearthed in great detail in a newspaper article published in La Libre Parole (Free Speech) in November 1892, by a nationalist extremist and a vocal enemy of the republic Edouard Drumont. Drumont had hoped that by publicizing this scandalous affair he would discredit the republican regime, gain the confidence of the public, and rally the nationalist movement. He had just founded his newspaper subtitled *La France aux Français* (France to the French), where he and his editorial staff expressed extremist views against the parliamentary regime and all foreign presence on French territory. According to him, Panama was "the greatest act of robbery" performed by the government thus far, a scandal filled with "gold, mud, and blood." Drumont denounced 140 officials, nicknamed the *chéquards* (for having accepted kickback "checks") in order to pass the 1888 law authorizing the lottery loans. Drumont also launched editorial duels with other editors, including Alfred Meyer of the conservative newspaper *Le Gaulois*, all offended by Drumont's virulent anti-Semitism. On August 12, 1893, *La Libre Parole* published a caricature summarizing Drumont's opinion of those directly involved in the Panama affair in particular and of the republic in general. The caricature was entitled *Ceux qui en sont et ceux qui n'en sont pas* (Those Who Are In and Those Who Are Out). It depicted Marianne, the symbol of the French Republic, guarding and protecting a darkened republic set in the background where officials, designated as Jews, exchanged bags of money and appeared to have a good time. However, the defiant Marianne was refusing entry and hospitality to another allegorical figure: France itself, represented by a weakened but proud monarch coming from the light with two tired but faithful peasants in her protective embrace. This caricature was accompanied by a dialogue-caption:

> *MARIANNE:* Who is there?
> *FRANCE:* The Nation
> *MARIANNE:* Don't know you! Do you have a check?

In the cartoon, France appears weak, as if doubly wounded, once by the German annexation of Alsace and Lorraine and a second time by its own decadent political regime dependent on kickbacks and dishonesty. However, her face remains proud and her resolve solid as she continues to help the peasants she is still holding dear. The nationalist message was clear: France in the hands of a decadent Marianne seemed to have no chance of regaining its dignity. The French peasants so close to France's heart were now destitute, while the deputies and their Jewish friends were celebrating the deceptive deal that was the Panama Canal.

Following Drumont's multiple public accusations in the press a number of politicians were brought to justice. Rienbach died shortly after the trial, Herz took flight, an already old Lesseps died of senility in the following years, while Clémenceau forcefully claimed his innocence. The affair was so extensive that not everyone could be tried. For those who were brought to justice, the verdict and sentencing were fairly lenient, ranging from a few months to five years in prison; only one minister admitted wrongdoing in this scandalous affair and was sentenced to five years. Everyone else benefited from either a reduced sentence or a presidential pardon.

The Panama affair was not only a watershed in French politics; it also reflected the extent to which the press had become a staple of everyday life. The "media war" that paralleled and often informed this period of political confrontation and major scandal was almost a form of entertainment for a generation of readers who enjoyed the newly granted freedom of the press (law of July, 1881), which finally allowed the publication of all divergent perspectives and opinions on current affairs. Reading the press had never been so exciting. Scandals made people buy newspapers, which in turn increased their print runs and influence.

The nationalists who had stirred the controversy so actively did not protest the courts' mild punishment and sentences for the responsible individuals in the Panama Canal affair with the same vehemence. For them, the affair had more important political implications, and their case had been made: the parliamentary system of the republic was discredited; French finances were in the hands of influential Jews and Jewish infiltration of all French institutions had to be stopped if France was to survive as a nation. The republic did not fall as a result of the Panama scandal but many of its politicians, moderate and radical Republicans, like Clémenceau, lost the favor of their traditional constituency who looked to the opposition, the nationalists and the Socialists, for better representation. One of the political repercussions of the Panama scandal was thus a strong resurgence of nationalism and anti-Semitism that would emerge spectacularly in the Dreyfus Affair. Simultaneously, in a country with an increasing population of workers organized in unions and calling for direct action and general strikes, the Panama scandal was also a call to leave the traditional republican movement and join the increasingly popular socialist program headed by Jean Jaurès.

In the end, the Panama Canal project was taken over by the Americans who reengineered the whole construction. Ironically, and as if the canal continued to bring bad luck to France, it is on the fateful date of August 3, 1914 that the canal was inaugurated by the Americans—the same day Germany declared war on France.

One could place the Panama scandal among the most culturally revealing events of the end of the nineteenth century. It revealed the new power of a recently liberated press, the active presence of a new socialist political movement, and a deep-seated anti-Semitism and xenophobia that would reemerge with the creation of nationalist leagues and the resounding scandal of the Dreyfus Affair.

Nationalism and Anti-Semitism

Before he became the founder and director of *La Libre Parole*, Edouard Drumont had demonstrated his particular brand of nationalism in writings where he expressed both his acquired attachment to a Catholic and monarchist France and his hatred of the Germans. He became better known as a successful essayist when, in 1886, he published a bestseller entitled: *La France juive: Essai d'histoire contemporaine* (*Jewish France: Essay on Contemporary History*). The reason for the commercial success of the book was a combined feeling of public curiosity for Drumont's extravagant ideas and the momentum behind the growing interest in nationalism. His main thesis was that the large presence and influence of the Jewish population in French commerce and finances was responsible for the poor state of its economy. In his book, Drumont showed a particular talent for capturing a common tendency that brought together social groups of different ideologies around the Jewish question. His anti-Semitism appealed naturally to the conservative Catholics, but also to part of the population that was frustrated and angered by what they saw as the unfair commercial and financial success of French Jews. In *La France juive*, Drumont defined, for example, the roles of the noble Aryan and of the greedy and destructive Jew, suggesting that past historical examples were an undeniable proof that the real allegiance of the Jew was to his money and not to the nation. From 1886 on, Drumont's rabid anti-Semitism would reach such heights that no French institution was safe from his diatribes and his conspiracy theory. He claimed that Jews were now "implanted everywhere," including in what he referred to as the "sacred arch," or the military, in order to destroy France's soul and spirit. Drumont's extreme views, and style, would scare away many nationalists who preferred to join other, less ostentatious, but no less anti-Semitic nationalists, like novelist and politician Maurice Barrès, who created the conservative league *La Patrie Française* (The French Fatherland) in 1898, or the writer and philosopher Charles Maurras, who revived the league called *Action Française* (French Action) in 1899. While Barrès praised the "cult of the ego" and made "romantic" claims to a return to traditional values, and specifically to the idea of French purity by soil and past sacrifices, a "nationalism of blood and soil," (*Nationhood and Nationalism in France*, 26) Maurras thought that immigrants and Jews alike did not have the "French instinct" and background necessary for a true commitment to the Nation. A real Frenchman could be born only on French soil, of French blood. Maurras blamed the democratic principles of the 1789 Revolution and the republic for what he saw as France's weakness—for example, during the 1896 Olympics in Athens, when French athletes were largely overshadowed by better prepared and stronger European competitors—and he looked enviously to the rigor and power of the British and the Germans. He thought that a prompt return to a monarchy was the solution to France's problems and its sure return to a position of world power. Contrary to other nationalists, he was an atheist who admired the order of the church, but whose faith was singularly invested in the literary and the political realms.

These three men, Drumont, Barrès, and Maurras were among the main leaders and "leaguers" largely responsible for reviving France's right-wing nationalism, despite some of their ideological differences, they were united on one issue: they were *anti-Dreyfusards*, that is, opposed to Captain Dreyfus and in favor of his conviction for high treason. The high-profile Dreyfus case held center stage for the next twelve years and shook France to the depths of its republican conscience, still idealistically aiming at universal justice and a fair society, but in reality deeply troubled by its own dehumanizing exceptions.

1894: The Dreyfus Affair

The year 1894 is only a point of departure for this case, simply referred to as "The Affair" with a capital A, a case of injustice motivated by anti-Semitic prejudice. The case originally came and went in the few months between 1894 and 1895, then, in light of new evidence, revived by the aging naturalist writer Emile Zola in 1898, to finally become a full-fledged scandal dividing France into two opposed camps, the *Dreyfusards* (partisans of Dreyfus) and the *anti-Dreyfusards* (enemies of Dreyfus), and did not fully conclude until Dreyfus's rehabilitation in 1906. Over the time of its development, the Affair had a huge impact as it affected to different degrees every man and woman, every politician and thinker, every institution and social class, every visitor to France. It seemed that everyone both inside and outside of France had an opinion about the case; it made enemies out of friends and friends out of enemies, but mainly it showed the extent of corruption in France's highest institutions, like the military and the Ministry of Justice, and the devastating effects of a deeply ingrained and collective anti-Semitism.

Captain Alfred Dreyfus had an impeccable record and a promising career in the military. After twelve years of unanimously excellent reports ("highly intelligent, educated, gifted, conscientious") and high marks at the elite military school, *Ecole Supérieure de Guerre*, he was assigned to the prestigious general staff reserved for top graduates. His well-deserved promotion was, however, a source of dissension and envy among his peers, especially in the wake of Drumont's attacks in *La Libre Parole* on the allegedly "dangerous presence" of Jews in high-ranking positions in the armed forces. Many officers frowned at the rapid professional climb of Dreyfus, and some misunderstood and envied his privileged relationship with the chief of staff, General Le Mouton de Boisdeffre. Between 1893 and 1894, reports from his superiors began to change, showing some signs of discontent, not toward his performance and intelligence, but in relation to his attitude, calling him "pretentious" and "a bit too sure of himself." This new and official perception of Dreyfus seemed to be generated by the same vein of anti-Semitism exhibited in *La Libre Parole*, but these negative evaluations alone could not be a pretext for putting Dreyfus on trial; only hard evidence of a serious nature could result in a court-martial. In the fall of 1894, an incriminating "note" (known as *le bordereau*) containing handwritten, secret information intended for the Germans emerged as the awaited evidence, but it was far from being hard and convincing. In a letter he wrote to his wife on December 18, 1894, right before his trial, for by then he had been brought up on charges of treason, Dreyfus was confident that, if based solely on the "note," the impending trial would rectify the injustice and bring an end to his suffering:

> My dearest one,
>
>   I finally come to the end of my suffering, to the end of my martyrdom. Tomorrow I will appear before the judges, my head high, my soul at peace.
>
>   The ordeal I have just undergone, terrible as it has been, has cleansed my soul. I will return to you better than I was. All the life that is left to me, I want to devote to you, my children, our dear families . . . .
>
>   I am ready to stand before soldiers, as a soldier who is beyond reproach. They will see on my face, they will read in my soul, they will be convinced of my innocence, as are all those who know me.
>
>   Devoted to my country, to which I have dedicated all my energy, all my ability, I have nothing to fear.
>
>   Sleep peacefully, my dear, and have no worry. Think only of the joy we will soon find in each other's arms . . .
>
>   A thousand kisses as we await that happy moment. (*France and the Dreyfus Case*, 38–39)

Despite Dreyfus's full trust in the military and the courts, despite his devotion to his career and his respect for high military command, a majority of witnesses from the office of the general staff testified against him. Only a handful of his peers spoke in favor of the captain. Thus, the case rested on the unsigned and undated "note" that Dreyfus was accused of writing and in which he would have passed on French secrets to the Germans. The convoluted explanation of the handwriting specialist placed all the blame on Dreyfus and "convinced" the judges who unanimously condemned Dreyfus to serve a life sentence on notorious Devil's Island off the coast of French Guyana, a colony in South America. A public degradation (figure 3.2) was organized in order to humiliate Dreyfus before he was to start his prison sentence.

Figure 3.2 Public Degradation of Captain Dreyfus (1895)

The full front page of the paper *Le petit journal* depicts a military official at the precise and symbolic moment when he snaps Dreyfus's sword in two before a large gathering of soldiers in the courtyard of the Paris Military School. This dramatic image is accompanied by the following caption: *Le traitre* (the traitor). (© L'Illustration)

Two years later, when enough solid evidence finally pointed to the real author of the "note," an officer of dubious repute named Ferdinand Esterhazy, the judges acquitted Esterhazy despite the overwhelming evidence against him. To rehabilitate Dreyfus and put Esterhazy on trial would have brought to public attention the injustice that had been committed by army officers, exposed weaknesses in the military, and thus constituted a "threat [to] national defense." The military establishment could not, however, prevent the case from taking a spectacular turn: a long, detailed, and defiant letter published in *L'Aurore* in January 1898 entitled "J'accuse. . . !" (I Accuse. . . !) by Emile Zola, who became the spokesperson for all of those who wanted to fight intolerance and bring justice for Dreyfus in the name of republican principles. Without Zola's letter, the Dreyfus Affair may have quietly been filed away in the archives of the Ministry of Justice, but it became a public manifesto, an act of defiance against the establishment that triggered a "republican reaction" on the part of intellectuals, and the subsequent revision of Dreyfus's case.

Zola's letter was addressed to French president Félix Faure, who had replaced Sadi Carnot, assassinated in 1894 by an Italian anarchist during a period when a number of revolutionary anarchists were terrorizing Paris by setting bombs in the buildings of a government with which they were at odds, preferring communal to national ownership, and no government at all to a scandal-ridden and corrupt one. The assassination of the president and the constant terrorist actions by anarchists should have captured more of the national attention than the Dreyfus Affair in 1894. Indeed, before Zola's intervention, the case had never really made any significant ripples as the newspapers were inundated with news of terrorist actions and threats. Since the beginning of the decade, much like the French government and the international community, the press had been in a constant state of alert imposed by the anarchists, who remained active until World War I, but whose actions culminated in the 1890s. It was in this context of international terrorism and fear that Dreyfus was brought to trial, just a month after the assassination of Carnot in 1894. Zola's letter was published in *L'Aurore* around the time when anarchists claimed responsibility for the killing of Spanish prime minister Del Castillo (in 1898, they would also kill the Austrian empress Elizabeth, King Umberto I of Italy in 1900, and U.S. president William McKinley in 1901). While the world was looking for ways to stop the wave of terrorism—twenty-one countries planned an "antianarchist international conference" in Rome for November–December, 1898—the officially closed Dreyfus case seemed unlikely to catch national and international attention. Yet, Zola's letter had an explosive effect that immediately refocused attention on the army's corruption; the famous author focused on the double standard that consisted of trampling universal principles of equality and justice in Dreyfus's case, while invoking the same principles to defend the nation and bring support to the world against acts of terrorism.

Dossier 3.6   "I Accuse. . . !" Open Letter to the President by Emile Zola (1898)

In December 1897, Zola had just written a "Letter to the Young" in which he called on the young generation to "fight for humanity" and begged them to rally to the cause of "justice and truth" (*France and the Dreyfus Affair*, 91). A few weeks later he wrote a "Letter to France" extending his call for justice to the entire country. Finally, on January 10, 1898, the author made the front page of *L'Aurore* with a full account of all the inconsistencies in the Dreyfus case and with a public accusation of all involved parties in the cover-up. The letter was extensive and it covered the entire front page, as if to show that nothing could possibly be more important than the "shouting of the truth." He proceeded to denounce the elaborate and deep injustice running through branches of the government and in particular the justice system, a system that brought the innocent Dreyfus to trial and condemned him to life in prison for a crime he did not commit. He ended the letter with a long list of official names responsible for the injustice and hardship endured by Dreyfus, and assuming full responsibility for his accusation, he added a paragraph acknowledging the fact that his words would certainly expose him to the same justice system he was accusing of corruption. In the name of justice and truth he was ready to face the law.

> *Sir,*
>
> *. . . My duty is to speak out; I do not wish to be an accomplice in this travesty. My nights would otherwise be haunted by the specter of the innocent man, far away, suffering the most horrible of tortures for a crime he did not commit . . .*
>
> *Truth and justice, so ardently longed for! How terrible it is to see them trampled, unrecognized, and ignored! . . .*
>
> *I accuse Lt. Col. du Paty de Clam of being the diabolical creator of this miscarriage of justice . . .*
>
> *I accuse General Mercier of complicity, at least by mental weakness, in one of the greatest inequities of the century.*
>
> *I accuse General Billot of having held in his hands absolute proof of Dreyfus's innocence and covering it up . . .*
>
> *I accuse General de Boisdeffre and General Gonse of complicity in the same crime, the former, no doubt, out of religious prejudice . . .*
>
> *I accuse the three handwriting experts, Messrs. Belhomme, Varinard and Couard, of submitting reports that were deceitful and fraudulent, unless a medical examination finds them to be suffering from a condition that impairs their eyesight and judgment.*
>
> *I accuse the War Office of using the press, particularly L'Eclair and L'Echo de Paris, to conduct an abominable campaign to mislead the general public and cover up their own wrongdoing.*
>
> *Finally, I accuse the first court martial of violating the law by convicting the accused on the basis of a document that was kept secret, and I accuse the second court martial of covering up this illegality, on orders, thus committing the judicial crime of knowingly acquitting a guilty man. . . .*
>
> *I have but one passion: to enlighten those who have been kept in the dark, in the name of humanity which has suffered so much and is entitled to happiness. My fiery protest is simply the cry of my very soul. Let them dare, then, to bring me before a court of law and let the enquiry take place in broad daylight! I am waiting.*
>
> *With my deepest respect, Sir.*
>
> Émile Zola, *13th January 1898. (France and the Dreyfus Affair, 93–102)*

The anger and indignation in Zola's letter were fully substantiated. It was suggested by anti-Dreyfusards that the letter was the product of a crazy and senile writer, who out of boredom decided to stir trouble. Even if it is true that Zola found himself in a literary slump around the time of the Dreyfus Affair, the facts and names he revealed about the unjust sentencing of the Jewish captain were not any less real and accurate. He referred to hard evidence to show that the Affair was a clear case of manipulation of the justice system, that it was a cover-up for a major military mess, and that bigotry was at the heart of the matter. In the end, Zola proved that the concepts of corruption and decadence that nationalists like Drumont and Barrès were so keen to identify as republican practices were very much part and parcel of the supposedly "sacred arch" of the military and the impartial justice system defending its principles. His public attacks on the French armed forces made Zola a very unpopular man with some ministers, deputies, and judges. As expected, he was immediately brought to justice for defamation, and at this point the entire nation became truly engrossed with his ten-day trial. While political activism gathered momentum outside the courtroom where anti-Dreyfusards screamed "Death to the Jews!" Dreyfusards argued for justice, and many onlookers joined the crowd to form what at one point was characterized as an "ominous" crowd of 6,000 people waiting to hear the verdict. This time, justice was "fairly" applied to Zola, who was sentenced to one year in prison and 300-franc fine. It is with Zola's trial that the entire effect of the Dreyfus Affair was felt both throughout the country and abroad.

At the time of the letter and the trial, Zola became a Republican hero for some and an enemy of France for others. Women, for example, despite being barred from holding public office and shut out of universal suffrage, did not refrain from speaking up either as feminists or as nationalists and enlisting the support of other women through the press. In a gesture of solidarity to Zola and Lucie Dreyfus—Dreyfus's wife, who was denied the right to join him in exile—the newspaper La Fronde, the first "feminist" paper created in 1897, reprinted Zola's letter the day after it was published in L'Aurore and began a series of petitions in favor of Madame Dreyfus's request to be with her husband. In the opposing camp, on the editorial staff of La Libre Parole, the novelist Gyp, a French countess, attacked Zola's supporters, calling them Izolâtres, a nasty neologism using the name of Zola with a pejorative suffix, implying that everyone supporting Dreyfus and Zola, Jewish or not, was in fact associated with the "dirty Jews." Besides her very offensive description of Jewish men and women, Gyp assigned to every Dreyfusard what she labeled as being Jewish traits. About Zola, she declared: ". . . by becoming the man of the Syndicate; by tearing to pieces, in concert with a handful of Jews, the country of adoption that had applauded his great talent, he has committed a vile and wicked act. Behind him, one smells the Jews . . . It is certain that abroad Herr Zola, Herr Reinbach, and the Izolâtres, are considered to be, for the moment, the elite among Frenchmen . . . But it is no mistake that in France the Izolâtres are not worth two cents" (France and the Dreyfus Affair, 116).

In fact, Zola did become valuable to many progressive French politicians, like Socialist deputy Jean Jaurès who, after some initial indifference to the case, finally spoke in favor of Dreyfus, extending his case to "humanity itself" (France and the Dreyfus Affair, 119). He also became exemplary to many intellectuals who immediately and for the first time organized themselves as a collective political force and formed a league of their own, the "League of the Rights of Man." Zola's words and actions represented huge political capital, as they generated concerted action from intellectuals who defended his argument for "truth and justice" in his fight for

Dreyfus's cause. In fact, Zola's letter and trial were instrumental in creating the modern notion of "the intellectual" as a politicized man of letters and a protector of universal rights. Intellectuals and writers had become involved in political matters in the past, most famously Voltaire, the Enlightenment *philosophe*, during the "Calas Affair" involving a Protestant, but the "composite" French intellectual who came out of the Dreyfus Affair and became the "conscience of a troubled nation" (Goetschel and Loyer, 15) was a new development indeed. In the twentieth century, at the onset of the "existentialist movement" (see chapter 6), the intellectual would be associated with *"engagé"* (committed or involved) men and women of letters whose convictions led them to take a stand in some of the most traumatic events of French history. But it was with the Dreyfus Affair that the worlds of literature and politics first met in full force. Writers, artists, scientists, university professors, among others voiced their opinion through speeches, petitions, newspaper articles in order to overturn the unjust condemnation of Dreyfus and to show solidarity with Zola. Oddly enough, this spontaneous, informal group that rallied around the Dreyfus case acquired its "intellectual" status through the desire to ridicule them coming from press attacks from the anti-Dreyfusard camp. This will to ridicule came most notoriously from Maurice Barrès who, as he tried to diminish the prestige of his intellectual opponents, called them "semi-intellectuals." In fact, the intended derision behind the word "intellectual" had unexpected consequences, since it consolidated the intellectuals' unanimity on the Dreyfus front, thus confirming the association of intellectuals with the fight for justice.

The Dreyfus Affair made it impossible for any public figure to remain neutral. Even for notoriously apolitical novelists, like turn-of-the-century writer Marcel Proust, the Affair was unavoidable and made its way into their writings. In his correspondence and his unfinished and "forgotten" novel *Jean Santeuil* begun in 1895, right after Dreyfus's first trial, Proust was quite clear on his position in defense of Dreyfus. In *Remembrance of Things Past*, his masterpiece, which presents a panorama of life during the Third Republic, he seems more ambivalent, placing literature and esthetic principles above and beyond political concerns. His belief that good writing is independent of political stances is evidenced by his dedication of one of the volumes of *Remembrance*, entitled *Guermantes's Way*, to Léon Daudet, a notorious right-wing journalist and advocate of *Action Francaise*, the nationalist league headed by Charles Maurras. As a writer committed to fiction and style and even fiction *as* style, Proust adopted a more removed position, by including politics in the social background of his masterpiece rather than advocating a particular opinion. In *Remembrance of Things Past*, written over the course of thirteen years, characters are for and against Dreyfus, sometimes changing their opinion about the case, sometimes solidly holding on to their positions, even if they run counter to religious belief or social status. Indeed, as in the real world surrounding the Affair, Proust shows that the division between Dreyfusards and anti-Dreyfusards was not clear-cut, and that no one could automatically assume that all anti-Semites, nationalists, and aristocrats were anti-Dreyfusards or that all liberals and Republicans were Dreyfusards. For some characters, to be a Dreyfusard means to believe in the universal principles of justice and truth, and for the sake of these basic principles to overcome religious, social, and political differences. The Catholic, anti-Semitic Prince of Guermantes is exemplary in this respect. Despite his positions concerning "pure blood and rank," the prince is engrossed by the Affair, reads the Dreyfusard press, and asks the priest, a Dreyfusard, to pray for Dreyfus. This is only one example, but many more unusual and unexpected views came to light and many daily habits were altered by the manner in which the Affair was interpreted, in this instance in bourgeois and aristocratic circles. There was no simple equation associating one milieu with one opinion. Proust's novel brought a measure of reality in his depiction of fin-de-siècle life and mentality, in the confusion and disarray produced by "scandals" and "affairs." At the turn of the century, it may be that the Dreyfus case brought this intricacy of French culture out into the open, a culture fractured by social and political differences, but ultimately kept together by an underlying and all-encompassing spirit of universalism that, in the end, made it possible for the republic itself to survive.

Dreyfus was brought back from Devil's Island for a new trial. In June 1899, he was handed a document explaining his change of status from convicted criminal to simple suspect and announcing a second court-martial. On September 9, 1899, Dreyfus was found guilty, but with extenuating circumstances, and received a ten-year prison sentence. About this second trial, Zola spoke of the most "detestable monument to human infamy," and the foreign press, shocked by the verdict, expressed its fear for the future of the French Republic weakened by what was qualified as "the greatest scandal of the century." French politicians immediately countered the potential destabilizing effects of the Dreyfus case by gathering official signatures for a presidential pardon that came swiftly on September 19, 1899. At the time, the pardon put the Affair to rest, but Dreyfus vowed to appeal the second verdict for a full rehabilitation. His wish came true when, in July 1906, he was publicly promoted to the rank of major and awarded the Legion of Honor in the same place where he had been degraded over a decade before, the courtyard of the *Ecole militaire* (Military School) in Paris.

Only after Dreyfus was pardoned in 1899 could France reaffirm its commitment to democratic principles and restore credibility to the republic. The public, saturated by the constant reminders of this long and painful case, was happy to see it end, even if only momentarily. With Dreyfus's pardon, the nation seemed finally appeased, international disapproval avoided, as French society entered into a seemingly peaceful and pleasurable period known as "*La Belle Epoque*" (The Beautiful Epoch) and began a new era and a new century with public displays of unity and progress.

References

Ager, Dennis. *Identity, Insecurity and Image: France and Language*. Philadelphia: Multilingual Matters Ltd., 1999.

Allegret, Roger and Patrick Roussel. *Histoire de la vie française*. Vol. 7. Paris: Illustration, 1972.

Barthes, Roland. *A Barthes Reader*. Susan Sontag, ed. and intro. New York: Hill and Wang, 1982.

Bataille, Georges. *Literature and Evil*. Alastair Hamilton, trans. Guilford: Calder & Boyars, 1973.

Baudelaire, Charles. *Oeuvres completes 1*. Claude Pichois, ed. Paris: Gallimard (Pléiade), 1975.

———. *Oeuvres completes 2*. Claude Pichois, ed. Paris: Gallimard (Pléiade), 1976.

Bernard, Claude. *An Introduction to the Study of Experimental Medicine*. New York: Dover Publications, 1957.

Bruno, G. *Le Tour de France par deux enfants*. Rpt; Paris: Librairie classique Eugène Belin, 1983.

Burns, Michael. *Rural Society and French Politics: Boulangism and the Dreyfus Affair, 1886–1900*. Princeton: Princeton University Press, 1984.

———. *France and the Dreyfus Affair—A Documentary History*. Boston, NY: St. Martin's, 1999.

Bury, JPT. *Gambetta and the Making of the Third Republic*. London: Longman, 1973.

Chavan, R.S. *Nationalism in Asia*. New York: Sterling, 1973.

Chiron, Yves. *Maurice Barrès: Le prince de la jeunesse*. Paris: Librairie Académique Perrin, 1986.

Colonna, F., ed. *Instituteurs algeriens: 1883–1939*. Paris: Presses de Sciences politique, 1975.

Conte, Michel. *Nu . . . comme dans nuage*. Québec: Presses Métropolitaines (Editions de Mortagne), 1980.

Ehrlich White, Barbara, ed. *Impressionism in Perspective*. Englewood Cliffs, NJ: Prentice Hall, 1978.

Eiffel   Tower.   www.tour-eiffel.fr/teiffel/uk/documentation/dossiers/page/debats.html, August 16, 2006.

Friedrich, Otto. *Olympia: Paris in the Age of Manet*. New York: Harper Collins, 1992.

Furet, François. *Jules Ferry, fondateur de la République*. Paris: Ecole des Hautes Etudes en Sciences Sociales, 1985.

Gavignaud, Geneviève. *Les Campagnes en France au XIXe siècle (1780–1914)*. Paris: Orphys, 1990.

Guillaumin, Emile. *The Life of a Simple Man*. Eugen Weber, ed. and intro. Margaret Crosland, trans. Hanover, NH: University Press of New England, 1983.

Goetschel, Pascale and Emmanuelle Loyer. *Histoire culturelle et intellectuelle de la France au XXeme siècle*. Paris: Armand Colin, 1995.

King, Mary Louise. *A History of Western Architecture*. New York: Henry Z. Walck Inc., 1967.

Martin-Fugier, Anne. *Les Salons de la IIIe République*. Paris: Editions Perrin, 2003.

Mendes-Flohr, Paul and Reinharz Jehuda, eds. *The Jew in the Modern World—A Documentary History*. New York/Oxford: Oxford University Press, 1995.

Mondrel, O. *Le Mythe de l'Héxagone*. Paris: Jean Picollec, 1981.

Mouhot, Henri. *Travels in Siam, Cambodia and Laos: 1858–1860*. Oxford: Oxford University Press, 1992.

Pagnol, Marcel. *My Father's Glory and My Mother's Castle (Memories of Childhood)*. Rita Barisse, trans. San Francisco: North Point Press, 1986.

———. *Oeuvres completes III—Souvenirs et romans*. Paris: Editions de Fallois, 1995.

Peniston, William. *Pederasts and Others—Urban Culture and Sexual Identity in Nineteenth-Century Paris*. New York, London, Oxford: Harrington Park Press, 2004.

Popkin, Jeremy. *A History of Modern France* (2nd ed.). Upper Saddle River, NJ: Prentice Hall, 2001.

Priollaud, Nicole, ed. *La France colonisatrice*. Paris: Liana Levy, 1983.

Rewald, John. *The History of Impressionism*. New York: Museum of Modern Art, 1973.

Robiquet Paul, ed. *Discours et Opinions de Jules Ferry*. Paris: Armand Colin & Cie., 1897.

Tannenbaum, Edward R. *The Action Française: Die-Hard Reactionaries in Twentieth-Century France*. New York: John Wiley and Sons, 1962.

Thabault, Roger. *Mon Village: Ses hommes, ses routes, son école*. Paris: Presses de la Fondation Nationale des Sciences Politiques, 1982. Translated by Peter Tregear as *Education and Change in a Village Community: Mazière-en-Gâtine, 1848–1914*. New York: Schocken Books, 1971.

Tombs, Robert ed. *Nationhood and Nationalism in France from Boulangism to the Great War, 1889–1918*. New York: Routledge, 1991.

Valéry, Paul. *Oeuvres 1*. Jean Hytier, ed. Paris: Gallimard (Pléiade), 1957.

———. *Oeuvres 2*. Jean Hytier, ed. Paris: Gallimard (Pléiade), 1960.

———. *Leonardo, Poe, Mallarmé*. Malcolm Cowley and James Lawler, trans. Princeton, NJ: Princeton University Press (Bollingen Series 65, 8), 1972.

Weber, Eugen. *Action Française: Royalism and Reaction in Twentieth-Century France*. Stanford: Stanford University Press, 1962.

Zola, Emile. *The Dreyfus Affair. "J'accuse" and Other Writings*. Eleonor Levieux, trans. New Haven: Yale University Press, 1996.

CHAPTER 4

FROM *LA BELLE EPOQUE* TO THE GREAT WAR (1899–1918)

> Today, France is peaceful and strong . . . She has justice and the law on her side. She expects the best from the future.
>
> —Etienne Lavisse. *Histoire, cours moyen* (1900)
> (Primary school history textbook)

> I don't think I have ever been so dirty. It's a thick and sticky mud that is almost impossible to wash away.
>
> —*Paroles de Poilus* (1915) (Letter from a
> World War I soldier)

Only fifteen years separate the two statements, fifteen years between the tranquility and the high expectations for the future of France evoked by Etienne Lavisse, historian and educator, to the thick layer of dirt and mud caked on the face of the soldier in the trenches facing at best a bleak future and at worst a degrading death; fifteen years from the prestige of the Universal Exposition to the horror of World War I, from the "Great Fair" to the "Great War." The *Belle Epoque*, the beautiful era, was indeed over as France entered a time of unspeakable horror.

In 1899, France seemed securely poised at the highest point of modernity, its cultural prestige at a peak, both nationally and internationally. The nation was continuing its triumphal march toward social, economic, and political progress. Despite the numerous scandals that had severely compromised the nation's republican ethos in the previous era, it was now refocused on those principles. Still, the inherent contradiction between the idealistic universal model, essentially a bourgeois model, and the barbarity of modern warfare grew increasingly obvious.

It is not surprising that, on the eve of the twentieth century, scarred by the long and traumatic Dreyfus Affair, the republic was now looking to regain momentum and reinforce its universalist base by expressing a unifying patriotic feeling through elaborate public demonstrations, memorable celebrations, and popular gatherings. These were carefully orchestrated events where the symbolic and the visual conveyed a commitment to republican spirit and unity.

1899: The Triumph of the Republic

One of the more memorable manifestations of unity and republican greatness came in the form of Jules Dalou's massive sculpture unambiguously entitled "The Triumph of the Republic," a work of art that had been completed in plaster in 1889 for the centenary of the French revolution and cast in bronze ten years later. The unveiling of the piece took place on the appropriately named "Place de la Nation" (*Square of the Nation*) and came pointedly two months after Dreyfus's pardon, at a time when it was urgent for the French people to feel united beyond their differences under the universal and protective eyes of the republic.

Dossier 4.1   Charles Péguy's "Triumph of the Republic" (1899)

The Catholic Socialist writer and editor Charles Péguy was in the crowd gathered at the unveiling. On January 5, 1900, in an article written for the first issue of the newspaper, *Les Cahiers de la Quinzaine*, he captured the feeling of unity that brought together the different political groups and the French people in general to celebrate the "Triumph of the Republic."

The Republic triumphed the day the people of Paris marched through the streets on Sunday the 19th, known as the Great Sunday. Just as Catholic priests reconcile and purify churches that have been polluted by blood and shame in purging ceremonies . . . three hundred thousand republicans walked towards reconciliation on the Place de la Nation . . . It was magnificent. Children, boys and girls, from school delegations and secular organizations marched by. Everyone made room for them to go by with sincere and universal respect . . . but, above all the conversations, all the stares, and all the noise, you could hear people singing. From the start and throughout the entire procession, people were singing. I did not know any of the revolutionary songs, except for the Carmagnole, whose refrain is designed to please every good artilleryman, a song that everyone sings. I only knew by name and reputation the great and grave Internationale. . . . The lyrics of Revolutionary songs, sung indoors, most assuredly do not have less unpleasant lyrics than comforting ones. When sung in the streets against the police or the armed forces, they must be passionately and vigorously performed in red-hot anger. Sung for the first time in the streets with the approval of the bourgeois republican government, these songs sounded refreshing and friendly, certainly not provocative. In this atmosphere, these passionate songs regained their freshness . . .

Suddenly clusters of men move in tighter together. The street procession is now separated from the crowd. Groups of republican guards get off their horses. Firefighting companies start to pay close attention. Here we go . . . No more soldiers, but only peaceful city employees in blue or green uniforms, guarding city parks and public gardens. Suddenly a loud roar rises up fifty steps ahead of us: "Long live the Republic!" . . . We are astonished by Dalou's Republic and also shout: "Vive la République!"[Long live the Republic!] Not the lethargic and official Republic, but Dalou's triumphant and social Republic, clear and golden, rising up against the clear blue sky, in the light of the setting sun.

It must have been past four o'clock. All this in a single cry, in a single word: "Vive la République!" spontaneously let loose in view of the monument . . . So when the monument loomed before us, clearly outlined above the clear water of the fountain below, we did not see the details of the monument, nor did we see the square itself . . . We saw the triumph of the

Republic, yet we did not pay attention to the means or the architects of this triumph, nor the two lions in front, the blacksmith, Blind Justice or the little children. The triumphant Republic, rising on her orb, could easily be isolated from her servants. We were praising her, and had eyes only for her, so majestic and unique, as we passed by quickly, for the steady stream of people had to keep flowing . . . I will never forget what was the best part of the day: walking down through the Saint-Antoine neighborhood. The evening was advancing, and night was falling. As ignorant as we all are about past revolutions, which always mark the beginning of the next social revolution, we all know about the glorious legend and history of this old district. We were walking on the paving stones of this past glory. Gravely and slowly, the bearers of La Petite République walked at the head of this new procession. People from the neighborhood were coming up closer, reading and spelling out "La-Petite-République socialiste," "Neither-God-nor-Master," they applauded, cheered us on, and joined in. The procession was now indistinguishable from the crowd of people. The people were drawn into the crowd and feeding off it. Again, we sang the old Marseillaise, recently discredited in the eyes of the revolutionary socialists by nationalist bandits. The entire neighborhood was walking together into the night, in an extraordinary surge without hatred.

We finally separated on the Place de la Bastille . . . Street dancing was soon to begin. (Oeuvres 1, 299–316)

Dalou's sculpture portrays Marianne, the allegorical representation of the republic wearing her revolutionary Phrygian cap and her torn peasant's clothes, sculpted as if walking on a globe as round as the generous food-giving Earth. Dalou wanted to have her standing alone on top of the world, her distinct silhouette standing tall, and perfectly outlined against the Paris sky, the supreme mistress of the universe. Below her, determined lions pull the chariot representing the Nation. She is surrounded by other allegorical characters: Work on one side and Justice on the other, Liberty in front and Peace behind, all surrounded by myriad children reaping the educational fruit of her passage. They all accompany her in her symbolic ride through the abundance of effort and plenty, and the entire procession demonstrates the unity of all men, women, and children living under Lady Republic.

Dalou, the "Communard curator" of the Louvre in 1871, had obtained second place for this work when he presented it at the city competition in 1879 for a sculptured representation to honor another Paris square, the *Place de la République*. His work and his past as a sympathizer of the Commune seemed too unconventional, too risky, for the young and conservative republic of the times, and the academic Morice Brothers were given first place for their sculpture, "The Republic." However, despite Dalou's work taking the second place, the city decided to acquire "the Triumph of the Republic," as the officials had further plans for it. These are the plans that came to fruition at the 1899 unveiling. The notable presence of many government officials who, for this occasion, braved terrorist threats by showing up in numbers—government officials had cancelled their appearance at the inauguration of other monuments earlier in the decade, especially at the height of anarchist terrorism—combined with the organization of street balls attracting people of all social backgrounds made that Sunday fully emblematic of a typical republican celebration. It had begun as an organized parade composed of different press organizations. Jean Jaurès, Socialist editor of the newspaper *La Petite République*, wanting to ensure the participation of the people of Paris, had printed an invitation in the paper. Given the government's reconciliatory objective, the authorities did not object to this "mobilization" of the masses. In his article, Charles Péguy (see dossier 4.1) would write about the odd mix of banners and ideologies present during the parade, the disparate political and patriotic songs sung as the group marched to the *Place de la Nation*, the display of symbolic colors like black (anarchy) or red (socialism), and, of course, the red, white, and blue flag of the republic, the various and opposing political slogans chanted even by children, all symbolic details marking the presence of adversarial groups and ideologies that could have easily soured this street celebration and turned it into a chaotic political upheaval. That day, however, everyone exercised restraint, and all political differences seemed to vanish, especially when the flow of people arrived in front of Dalou's statue, a sight that spontaneously generated the unanimous cry: "Long live the Republic!" The sight of the statue served as a great equalizing force, even if only for a moment, for this diverse and massive street gathering reminiscent of a similar gathering during the Revolution of 1789, which moved from the Place de la Nation through the Faubourg Saint-Antoine. In that oldest neighborhood of Paris, the memory of the angry Parisian mob marching toward the Bastille prison, ready to storm it, ready to topple the monarchy, to finally proclaim the universal principles of the republic, was singularly alive. Following in the footsteps of the ancestors of the revolutionaries of 1789, this 1899 November Sunday served as a consecration of the universalist spirit of the day and constituted a reenactment of deep-seated republican principles. In November 1899, people in the streets felt as if they were both exercising a right and indulging in a celebration, a dual activity where political divergence was resolved in a common space where one could shout, sing, and dance in the name of the republic.

1900: The Paris Universal Exposition

More celebration, but this time a celebration of the modern, was to follow, as France was preparing for yet another Universal Exposition, its fifth in fifty years. It opened in Paris on April 14, 1900 and closed on November 12. Many questioned the merit of yet another exposition. The bourgeoisie was hardly keen on the idea of being subjected to yet another flurry of construction, or to the dust, mud, and noise that would inevitably accompany it. The poor were unlikely to warm to the prospect of having once more to relocate either within or outside of the city. In addition, new construction required a larger workforce, and Paris would have had to accommodate the massive influx of workers from the provinces. While France's status as a host nation was not in and of itself at issue, many wondered why the exposition had to be held specifically in Paris again. Other French cities were discussed, but Paris always emerged as the best candidate to serve the interests of the Nation in the belief that it "attracted intellectuals and engineers from every corner of the world, and [that] innumerable visitors took back home with them a prestigious vision of the celebrating city" (Prochasson, 97). The universal attraction of the prestigious city was a winning argument that was not opposed for very long, and confirmed that Paris was indeed the best example of French culture and of France's distinguished international image.

Even thirty years after the Franco-Prussian War (see chapter 2), the choice of Paris for the exposition was also a question of national pride, especially when news of a projected event in Berlin for the same year surfaced in 1892. This piece of news alone consolidated the feeling that no other city, least of all a German one, could compete with or surpass the elegance and the readiness of Paris for this specific event. Moreover, the timing of this particular event took on additional symbolic weight scheduled as it was for 1900, the "bridge" between the nineteenth and the twentieth century. Paris still basked in the rich artistic and urban legacy left by Haussmann, while other capitals, certainly Berlin, Prague, but more pointedly Vienna, were challenging Paris' status as the metropolis of modernity. In light of such challenges, the organizers felt that it was Paris' universal vocation to host this particular exposition and to reaffirm its cultural supremacy. The world came in great numbers to the exposition, more than 50 million visitors as opposed to the 30 million in 1889. France would exhibit more than anyone else (43 percent of the exhibitors were French) and display more technical and artistic accomplishments than any other nation, even if in the end no profits were made and the books closed on a slight loss: prestige had its price. The poor financial results did not prevent the exposition from boosting French national pride and reaffirming the country's commitment to its culture, at home and abroad.

The narcissistic mode through which Paris was presented *as* France to the foreign visitors was evident during this particular exposition which made the French capital the main theme of the event, as opposed to previous exhibits where the focus had been to showcase a variety of cultures. The paradox of the 1900 exposition was that Paris was hosting an international event called Universal Exposition, when in reality the emphasis was placed on Paris and Parisian life. The focus on all aspects of Paris could only transform the visitor's vision of the city as the universal hub of all contemporary cultures. In a nation anchored in the ideal of universalism, the capital celebrated *itself* as the privileged center of cultural and scientific modernity of both the old century and the new. With this objective in mind, French exhibitors insisted, for example, on making the cabaret, the epitome of French entertainment, one of the main themes of the fair. They recreated a typical Paris street from the picturesque Montmartre neighborhood complete with restaurants, theaters, cafes, and cabarets, places of pleasure and entertainment, while much less emphasis was placed on what had been so prevalent in the previous exhibits: reconstruction of foreign cultural artifacts and scenes, such as the Cairo street recreated during the 1889 exposition. As for the arts, the Petit Palais and the Grand Palais, two new exhibition halls built for the occasion in the spirit of the predominant decorative form of the time, *Art Nouveau* (also sometimes referred to as the *style 1900* in French), presented a retrospective of French arts. The newly inaugurated first metro line, in spite of its utilitarian function, did not escape the artistic development of the period, and each entrance was distinctively styled by architect Hector Guimard in *Art Nouveau* fashion with wrought iron frames and glass awnings. Guimard's flower motifs and soft, "organic" designs, like climbing, and twirling ivy, meshed the artistic and the functional in the decorative: glass awning and metro entrance, metro entrance and station building, and on to the rest of the city. *Art Nouveau* restored unity among art forms, painting, architecture, and decorative arts (interior design, furniture, ceramics, glass work, and jewelry, among others), connecting all aspects of urban life through extravagant decoration, and using new materials like cast iron, even extending its reach to posters and advertising. *Art Nouveau* had an all-encompassing and universal feel adapted to a modern lifestyle. It extended the reach of art beyond the confines of the museum or other delimited spaces as it invested people's homes as well their streets. This successful modern art form gave urban surroundings a beautiful and "binding" look that came appropriately at a time when the nation, in the throes of modernity, was also in search of a unifying force. *Art Nouveau* seemed to fulfill the esthetic requirements of everyday life posited on a modern and universalist paradigm. *Art Nouveau* was not a French invention but a European artistic movement that dominated the creative and urban scenes in cities like Munich and Vienna. This did not prevent Guimard's metro entrances and awnings as well as numerous objects ranging from teacups to posters and vases from being presented as peculiarly *French* productions of the ubiquitous movement and as emblems of the country's commitment to culture and prestige.

The feeling that France was the leading "cultural nation" was widespread during the organization, development, and proceedings of the Paris exposition. In fact, the concept of "high culture" now appeared inextricably linked to the reputation of France. Press accounts of the time reflected the general opinion that France had achieved an unchallenged status that many other countries regarded as the epitome of the modern and the beautiful, allied to republican ideals, all embodied in the 1900 Universal Exposition. The April 15, 1900 issue of the popular newspaper *Le Petit Parisien* published the following on opening day:

> The exposition is open!
>
> Since the time when, after cruel setbacks, a new France was formed, this is the third universal exposition that opens its doors in Paris today. In thirty years, our nation has shown three times to the world the shining display of its people's achievements. She can legitimately look back like a climber reaching the highest peak and say: "I have climbed well!" What an impressive journey! For approximately ten years, universal expositions have been the memorable stages in our national existence . . . Now that the century is closing, France proclaims the peaceful interlude of work, progress, and civilization . . .
>
> "What is a universal exposition? Asked Victor Hugo on the eve of the 1878 event. It's all the neighborhoods of the universe! A place where all come to compare ideals. In appearance, a convergence of products; in reality, a convergence of hopes."
>
> The 1900 exposition crowns the nineteenth century with the glorification of peace; may the sun of the new century rise on the world in a cloudless sky!

This article was representative of the hopeful mood that pervaded French life and culture at the turn of the century. Its naive idealism was tempered by its mention of "cruel setbacks" a veiled and isolated reference to events such as the Franco-Prussian War, the Panama Scandal, and the Dreyfus Affair. Ultimately, however, its tone remained one of pride and hope. President Emile Loubet's banquet, held on September 22, 1900, echoed the same note of optimism and celebration in true republican fashion: Loubet invited all the mayors of France to this huge banquet held during the exposition and under the roof of the Grand Palais to celebrate the anniversary of the proclamation of the First Republic. This banquet was yet another typical republican event whose objective was the reaffirmation of the republic's principles. The lavish dinner was thrown for the nation's representatives from all corners of the *Héxagone*, officials who would later return home with a renewed sense of being part of a great whole, the republic, as well as with a sense of national pride at the magnificent exposition they had experienced in its capital.

The period of almost fifteen peaceful years, the *Belle Epoque* that was continuing with the new century, appeared as one of relative material ease, especially for the bourgeois world, but also a period of continued scientific progress and artistic renewal.

Perfume: A Scent of Progress and Art

Perfume is one of the best-known products of French "high culture." During the *Belle Epoque* France and perfume became synonymous in the eyes of the rest of the world, thus creating a lasting cultural stereotype. The enormous transformation undergone by perfumes in France at the time can serve as an example of how a particular commodity becomes associated with a culture and how the superfluous meets the scientific, the esthetic, and the durable industrial to create a lasting national artifact. Indeed, still today, and despite the undeniable presence and influence of other international perfume industries, perfumery remains closely associated with French culture. At first confined to the aristocracy and the upper class, perfumes were transformed by progress and science at the turn of the century, making them available to a still relatively select but now much larger bourgeois class.

During the Renaissance, the town of Grasse in the southeast of France just off the Mediterranean coast became the "world capital of perfumery" as it benefited from a climate and a flora offering many natural fragrances that were used in perfume-making. Through the ages, perfume has been the rare encounter and perfect mix of natural scents and it remained mainly an artisanal process. As perfect fragrance was a rare occurrence and natural aromas limited, real perfumes were few and far between ; hence these remained a luxury product, for a long time an aristocrat or bourgeois must-have, often more expensive than jewelry. Only at the end of the nineteenth century, with the discoveries in synthetic chemistry and new scientific methods of aroma extraction, which increased the number of scents and prolonged the durability of the fragrance—therefore offering more original and less expensive products—did perfumes enter the modern era. A perfumer from Grasse, Léon Chiris, first invented the process of chemical extraction and synthetic reproduction of natural fragrances. In 1889, with the House of Guerlain, perfumers since 1828, the art of "nosing"—a *nez*, or nose is a 'professional of scents' and aromas whose talent and expertise is to recognize and distinguish natural scents in order to create olfactory harmonies—and the science of chemistry successfully joined to produce the first commercial modern perfume, "Jicky," a combination of natural essences and chemical processes.

Dossier 4.2 The Science of "Nosing." J.K. Huysmans, *A Rebours (Against the Grain)* (1884)

In his 1884 novel *A Rebours*, the Decadent novelist Joris-Karl Huysmans gives a short narrative history of perfume at a time when natural scents were being recreated chemically.

He betook himself to his study. There, beside an ancient font that served him as a wash-hand basin, under a long looking-glass in a frame of wrought iron that held imprisoned like a well-head silvered by the moonlight the pale surface of the mirror, bottles of all sizes and shapes were arranged in rows on ivory shelves. He placed them on a table and divided them into two series-first, the simple perfumes, extracts and distilled waters; secondly composite scents such as are described under the generic name of bouquets.

He buried himself in an armchair and began to think.

Years ago he trained himself as an expert in the science of perfumes; he held that the sense of smell was qualified to experience pleasures equal to those pertaining to the ear and the eye, each of the five senses being capable, by dint of a natural aptitude supplemented by an erudite education, of receiving novel impressions, magnifying these tenfold, coordinating them, combining them into the whole that constitutes a work of art. It was not, in fact, he argued, more abnormal that an art should exist of disengaging odoriferous fluids than that other arts should send sonorous waves to strike the ear or variously colored rays to impinge on the retina of the eyes; but, if no one, without a special faculty of intuition developed by study can distinguish a picture by a great master from a worthless daub, a motif of Beethoven from a tune by Clapisson, so no one, without a preliminary initiation, can avoid confounding at the first sniff a bouquet created by a great artist with a pot-pourri compounded by a manufacturer for sale in grocers' shops and fancy bazaars.

In this art of perfumes, one peculiarity had more than all others fascinated him, viz. the precision with which it can artificially imitate the real article.

Hardly ever, indeed, are scents actually produced from the flowers whose name they bear; the artist who should be bold enough to borrow his element from Nature alone would obtain only a half-and-half-result, convincing, lacking in style and elegance, the fact being that the essence obtained by distillation from the flowers themselves could at best present but a far-off, vulgarized analogy with the real aroma of the living and growing flower, shedding its fragrant effluvia in the open air.

So, with the one exception of the jasmine, which admits of no imitation, no counterfeit, no copy, which refuses even any approximation, all flowers are perfectly represented by combinations of alcohols and essences, extracting from the model its inmost individuality while adding that something, that heightened tone, that heady savor, that rare touch which makes a work of art.

In one word, in perfumery the artist completes and consummates the original natural odor, which he cuts, so to speak, and mounts as a jeweler improves and brings out the water of a precious stone. (213–214)

"I seek new perfumes, ampler blossoms, untried pleasures" (*Against the Grain*, 100). These words borrowed from Gustave Flaubert's *La Tentation de Saint Antoine* will become the mantra of Des Esseintes, the protagonist of *A Rebours*. For Huysmans, a Decadent writer of the end of the nineteenth century, the art of creating perfumes was clearly more than just a simple extraction of fragrance from flowers; it involved solvents and essence, and a talent worthy of the best of jewelers. However, one last element was missing from this combination to make perfume the quintessential modern artifact of the twentieth century: the bottle.

It was at the beginning of the twentieth century, with the advent of the "totalizing" style of *Art Nouveau*, that perfume would come to fascinate the world through its alliance of industry and art. It was the time when the esthetics of the bottle took on as much importance as the luxury of its contents. In 1907, perfumer François Coty found the perfect formula when he partnered with the glass artist René Lalique. Together they produced the famous "Ambre antique," an exquisite perfume in a beautiful bottle, offered at a reasonable price. It was a pleasure for the eyes and the nose, and a pleasure that the women of both the middle and upper bourgeoisie could now afford. A decade later, the French designer and perfumer Coco Chanel would seal the future of perfume as a sign of modern woman when she declared that women without perfume were women without a future. Chanel thus contributed to the mythical quality of perfume as the perfect invisible apparel, the "only" indispensable feminine attribute, especially with her 1921 creation "Chanel No. 5" that later became Marilyn Monroe's perfume of choice and, as she proudly announced, the only thing she would use to feel truly feminine.

Perfumes brought France some of its international fame as a country whose established sense of good taste was now its undeniable cultural trademark. Naturally, the France that had steadily worked at developing its prestige in the major realms of politics and culture enjoyed the additional attention and the label of quality it acquired with the developments in its luxurious fragrances. Despite the fact that the pleasures of the scents were limited to women—and men—of aristocratic and high bourgeois status, and that the great majority of French people of the period were not buying or using perfume, in the eyes of the world, perfumes fell into the category of essential "things French." The fact that this particular stereotype has kept its "French aura" longer than many others may be attributed to the prosperous and peaceful times during which it came into being. For the perfume industry, the *Belle Epoque* was an extraordinarily rich and creative era, a time when science (chemistry), talent ("nosing"), and art (*Art Nouveau* bottles) united to create a luxury product. It is as if the perfume industry developed during the *Belle Epoque* created the solid foundation for an everlasting modern fantasy that could be universally shared.

The Visual Arts: Painting and Cinema

The same sense of excitement and discovery that characterized the perfume industry of the *Belle Epoque* was also evident in other cultural domains of the fin-de-siècle: cinema and painting.

Impressionism, so badly received by the press and the general public in the 1870s, had finally acquired some degree of success and also quickly evolved into a more personal form, called "postimpressionism" by the 1880s, with artists like Van Gogh and Gauguin and, a decade later, with "Pointillists" like Seurat and Signac. Impressionism and postimpressionism both triumphed around 1900 with Monet's garden scenes and water lilies, the bright and sunny Provençal paintings of the prematurely deceased Van Gogh, or the serene leisure scenes of Seurat. With a new generation of artists, like Vincent Van Gogh, Paul Gauguin, and Paul Cézanne, impressionism seemed to be in constant transition. While "nursed" in impressionism, they departed from its representations of urban bourgeois modernity, and scenes of the exuberant industrial age or the serene countryside around Paris. Van Gogh left Paris for Provence where he developed a more "expressionist" style; Gauguin also left the French capital, at first for Brittany and then for Tahiti where his style was informed by "primitive" shapes and colors, while Cézanne departed from impressionism to already announce the geometrical style of Cubism. Unlike a painter like

Claude Monet, perhaps the best known of the impressionists, who around 1900 was able to find relief from the "crazy" pace of modern life in his peaceful and beautiful garden of Giverny, in Normandy, Van Gogh, Gauguin, and Cézanne seemed to perceive the current modern environment differently as they individually entertained visions of a more personal, simple, and primitive nature. These new artists were still looking at the modern world and at the light and colors of changing landscapes; they still took their easels outside, fascinated as they were by nature, but the serenity and happiness of the environment evoked by the colors and motifs of Monet or Renoir were replaced by a more foreboding feeling that modern culture was not all that satisfying and presented something to be feared. It is as if these artists reflected another side of the modern era, the realization that "ever faster and newer" could be a dangerous formula for the soul and spirit of modern man. Fearing the potentially disastrous consequences of the worship of speed and efficiency, many artists, as well as writers and intellectuals of the period, did not feel engaged in the generalized euphoria brought on by the industrial and modern world, the sense of jubilation provoked by various extravagant Parisian projects like the universal expositions, new spectacular constructions, like the splendid Alexander III bridge over the Seine, and, close by, the Eiffel Tower, or new electrical inventions, like the *trottoir roulant* (moving walkway). In order to escape urban renewal, industrial progress and social snobbery, they looked outside of the Parisian bubble to rekindle their sense of humanity. Cultural historians have found their attitude consistent with a growing sense of "neurosis" (Forbes and Kelly, 33) emerging from all areas of culture and sciences and a generalized sense of anxiety directed at modernity.

As early as 1888, both Van Gogh and Gauguin fled away from something that was not yet named "consumer capitalism," Van Gogh to Arles, a small city in southeastern France, and Gauguin to the village of Pont-Avent, on the rugged coast of Brittany, where daily life seemed untouched by modernity. From the tormented mind of Van Gogh, an artist who saw himself as an introvert "living nature from the inside," exploded the bright Mediterranean sky, sun-drenched fields, bright sunflowers, and twisted olive trees, all rendered in vivid colors and tortuous brushstrokes. Gauguin, the extrovert loudly rebelling against the evils of the very bourgeois society of which he was a product, wished to return to a more primitive and more spiritual way of life. He first found it in the backwardness of religious and traditional Brittany and, later, in the faraway islands of Tahiti and the Marquesas in the South Pacific. Despite their clashing personalities—at one point Van Gogh attacked Gauguin with a straight-razor— the two artists established a connection as they shunned modern materialist society. In the end, Van Gogh's intense personality and mental instability did not allow him to relieve his "neurosis"; to make matters worse, his utter poverty forced him to live in dehumanizing conditions. This combination may well be the reason why he committed suicide in 1890, having sold but a single painting in his lifetime. Gauguin, who had stayed with him a few months in Arles, remembered in his autobiographical account, *Writings of a Savage*, Vincent's impassion for the South, the color yellow, and also how, "beyond the shadow of a doubt, that man was mad" (246–248). When Van Gogh died "with love for his art, without hatred for mankind" (257), Gauguin also felt that he was himself dead to the West, and like Van Gogh on his death bed, he approached his own symbolic death to the modern world with the "love for art and mankind," he had learned from Van Gogh and that he took with him on his voyage out, to the South Seas.

Dossier 4.3 Gauguin's Life as a Savage

Paul Gauguin left Europe behind when he took a ship to the South Pacific in 1891. To him, physical displacement was the only way out of the complexity and tyranny of modern civilization, as he made plain to the writer and journalist Octave Mirbeau on the eve of his departure: "I am leaving in order to have peace and quiet, to be rid of the influence of civilization. I only want to do simple, very simple art, and to be able to do that I have to immerse myself in virgin nature, see no one but savages, live their life, with no other thought in mind but to render, the way a child would, the concept formed in my brain and to do this with the aid of nothing but primitive means of art, the only means that are good and true" (*Writings of a Savage*, 48). Arriving at first in Papeete, the capital, he eventually moved to the remote Northern part of Tahiti. One of the first decisions Gauguin had made in disconnecting from his bourgeois past was to abandon his Danish wife and children, in order to "marry" young Tahitian girls that he tirelessly painted. He also simplified his material life and felt content to live in a hut that became the center of his universe: "My hut was Space, Freedom" (*Noa Noa*, 17). *Noa Noa* was written as an account of his transformation from "European native" to "primitive man." It was also a book meant to provide an explanation for his much criticized "Tahitian art" exhibited in France in 1893, during Gauguin's two-year return. He finally ended up in the even more deserted island of Fatu Hiva in the Marquesas. In July 1901, suffering from syphilis and the consequences of several strokes and various accidents, he wrote to his friend Charles Morice how isolating himself in the Marquesas would in fact bring hope to his life: "I think that there, the altogether wild element, the complete solitude will give me a last burst of enthusiasm which will rejuvenate my imagination and lead to the fulfillment of my talent before I die" (*Writings of a Savage*, 211).

It is in *Noa Noa* that we find the most sincere account of his transformation. He meant for the book to be written by a "savage," in fragments of dream-like scenes of his life that would only be "civilized" for the European public by the complementary writings of French poet Charles Morice whom he trusted would not distort the original, bringing the account together with appropriate transitions. The following passage is from Gauguin's manuscript.

Every day gets better for me, in the end I understand the language quite well, my neighbors (three close by, the other at various distances) regard me almost as one of them; my naked feet, from daily contact with the rock, have got used to the ground; my body, almost always naked, no longer fears the sun; civilization leaves me bit by bit and I begin to think simply, to have only a little hatred for my neighbor, and I function in an animal way, freely— with the certainty of the morrow [being] like today; every morning the sun rises serene for me as for everyone, I become carefree and calm and loving. I have a native friend, who has come to see me every day, naturally, without any interested motive. My paintings in color [and] my woodcarvings astonished him and my answers to his question taught him something. Not a day when I work but he comes to watch me. One day when handing him my tools, I asked him to try a sculpture, he gazed at me in amazement and said to me simply, with sincerity, that I was not like other men; and he was perhaps the first of my fellows to tell me that I was useful to others. A child . . . one has to be a child, to think that an artist is something useful.

The young man was faultlessly handsome and we were great friends. Sometimes in the evening, when I was resting from my day's work, he would ask me the questions of a young savage who wants to know a lot of things about love in Europe, questions which often embarrassed me.

One day I wished to have for a sculpture a tree of rosewood, a piece of considerable size and not hollow. "For that" he told me, "you must go up the mountains to a certain place where I know several fine trees that might satisfy you. If you like, I'll take you there and we'll carry it back, the two of us."

We left the next morning, early. The Indian paths in Tahiti are quite difficult for a European: between two un-climbable mountains there is a cleft where the water purifies itself by twisting between detached boulders, rolled down, left at rest, then caught up again on a torrent day to be rolled down further, and so on to the sea. On either side of the stream there cascades a semblance of a path: trees pell-mell, monster ferns, all sorts of vegetation growing wilder, more and more impenetrable as you climb towards the centre of the island.

We went naked, both of us, except for the loincloth, and axe in hand, crossing the river many a time to take advantage of a bit of track which my companion seemed to smell out, so little visible [it was], so deeply shaded. Complete silence—only the noise of water crying against rock, monotonous as the silence. And two we certainly were, two friends, he a quiet young man and I almost an old man in body and soul, in civilized vices: in lost illusions. His lithe animal body had graceful contours; he walked in front of me sexless . . .

From all this youth, from this perfect harmony with the nature that surrounded us, there emanated a beauty, a fragrance (noa noa) that enchanted my artist soul. From this friendship so well cemented by the mutual attraction between simple and composite, love took power to blossom in me. And we were only . . . the two of us.

I had a sort of presentiment of crime. The desire for the unknown, the awakening of evil. Then weariness of the male role, having always to be strong, protective; shoulders that are a heavy load. To be for a minute the weak being who loves and obeys.

I drew close, without fear of laws, and my temples throbbing.

The path had come to an end . . . we had to cross the river; my companion turned at that moment, so that his chest was towards me. The hermaphrodite had vanished; it was a young man, after all; his innocent eyes resembled the limpidity of water. Calm suddenly came back into my soul, and this time I enjoyed the coolness of the stream deliciously, plunging into it with delight "Toe toe," he said to me (it's cold). "Oh no," I answered, and this denial, answering my previous desire, drove in among the cliffs like an echo. Fiercely I thrust my way with energy into the thicket, [which had] become more and more wild; the boy went on his way, still limpid-eyed. He had not understood. I alone carried the burden of an evil thought, a whole civilization had been before me in evil and had educated me.

We were reaching our destination. At that point the crags of the mountain drew apart, and behind a curtain of tangled trees a semblance of a plateau [lay] hidden but not unknown. The several trees (rosewood) extended their huge branches. Savages both of us, we attacked with the axe a magnificent tree that had to be destroyed to get a branch suitable to my desires. I struck furiously and, my hands covered with blood, hacked away with the pleasure of sating one's brutality and of destroying something. In time with the noise of the axe I sang:

"Cut down by the foot the whole forest (of desires)
Cut down in yourself the love of yourself, as a man
Would cut down with his hand in autumn the Lotus."

Well and truly destroyed indeed, all the old remnant of civilized man in me. I returned at peace, feeling myself thenceforward a different man, a Maori. The two of us carried our heavy load cheerfully, and I could again admire, in front of me, the graceful curves of my young friend—and calmly: curves robust like the tree we were carrying. The tree smelt of roses, Noa Noa. We got back in the afternoon, tired. He said to me: "Are you pleased?" "Yes"—and inside myself I repeated: "Yes."

I was definitely at peace from then on.

I gave not a single blow of the chisel to the piece of wood without having memories of a sweet quietude, a fragrance, a victory, and a rejuvenation. (24–28)

In the early twentieth century, another young painter named Pablo Picasso became prey to the same phobia that had affected Gauguin and was animated by a similar desire to flee what he perceived as the decay of the time. Leading the life of a fashionable and promiscuous bohemian artist, Picasso did not follow the example of Gauguin's physical self-removal from civilization and the "Tahitian" painter's discovery of a primitive self and art in faraway lands. But, like Gauguin, he injected his fascination for the primitive and his alienation from his society into his paintings. His 1906–1907 painting, "Les Demoiselles d'Avignon" (the Young Ladies—Girls—of Avignon) scandalized critics and intellectuals who had become fervent defenders of impressionist and postimpressionist art, and whose taste and artistic values were now guided by color and light. Picasso forced them and the limited public that actually saw the painting at first to look again at the power of the line, at the genuine invention of the artistic geometric shapes, and at the puzzle-like perspective as part of what would later be called "Cubism." Picasso himself was consumed by his own creation and made hundreds of studies and variations before submitting the final but unfinished result, initially titled "Philosophical Bordello." The later title, "The Young Ladies—Girls—of Avignon," was more ambiguous, and the five represented women it referred to could either be seen as sick and suffering prostitutes, or as unspoiled—or primitive, in Gauguin's interpretation of the term—young girls. Even though they appeared naked and exposed, the five women could be as virginal and wholesome as the term "demoiselles" suggested, or just as easily sick and tainted as their deformed geometrical bodies indicated; both notions of the natural/primitive and the corrupted/decadent intersected and coexisted on the canvas as they converged in the double translation of the word "demoiselles." Some art historians, like David Lomas, have privileged the meaning of "prostitutes" for the "demoiselles" and, moreover, prostitutes to be feared as they carried and spread fatal venereal diseases like syphilis. Lomas presents the similarities between Picasso's treatment of the demoiselles's bodies and faces and the scientific studies conducted at the end of the nineteenth century on body shape and proportion by physical anthropologists who had joined the research on "degeneration" by elaborating theories on physical measurement for the bodies of criminals and prostitutes (Green, 104–127). Clearly, these scientific studies were intended to justify and maintain the exclusion of marginal individuals, like vagrants and prostitutes, among others, considered as sick and dangerous. Under the Third Republic, laws were introduced to "cleanse" the country of "such evils": prostitution itself was not banned, as it was still a major part of the bourgeois man's life, but regulated, that is, housed in licensed and controlled brothels—which continued to exist officially until 1946—where "working girls" were under medical scrutiny. The question that Picasso's controversial painting seemed to ask may be related to these ladies'/girls' health or lack thereof. Were their deformed, mask-like faces signs of the disease that many prostitutes carried inside their bodies? Or did they reflect Picasso's attraction to "primitive," African art, an art that had influenced his work and that he opposed to the urban, industrialized world that surrounded him? The answers to these questions can be found in part in the apprehension the bourgeois establishment felt as it faced the growing power of the newly educated masses and their tendency toward "low culture." "Urban decadence" was blamed on the appearance of a new social mix, and on this new public's predilection for "popular" forms of art and entertainment deemed responsible for the lowering of moral standards and for bringing "aberrant behavior" to the surface of everyday life. This bourgeois anxiety found its way into Picasso's painting, even though, ironically enough, Picasso himself was leading a typical bohemian and "decadent" Parisian existence. In any case, the style and content of his *Demoiselles d'Avignon* had no chance with the crowd that first saw it in 1907. As a result, this modernist masterpiece ended up rolled up in a collector's attic and was never again seen in France. It became "public" again outside of France, after it permanently entered the Museum of Modern Art in New York in 1939, more than thirty years after it was first exhibited. In the first decade of the new century, Picasso's artistic genius expressed a radical innovation in form that could not be fully grasped by his contemporaries, and also brought to the surface the underlying fear of degeneration and decadence expressed by cultural and political authorities. For the moment, the controversial painting needed to be put away so as not to spoil the prestige of a nation celebrating the century under the aegis of progress and reason.

The invention of cinema was in line with the positivist notion of progress that came to complement French cultural life with the advent of modernity. In December 1895, in a café on the *Boulevard des Capucines*, the first film was shown to an astonished public. Cinema as art and public entertainment was born. We owe this first public screening to the Lumière brothers, two industrialists in the photography business who had long been interested in developing the techniques of cinema. Averaging ninety seconds each, their short features were embodiments of technological advance. They also showed the world as it was and, in this sense, the Lumière brothers, who brought every day life to the screen, were the first documentary makers. One of the shorts showed a train coming into a station, which put the audience in a state of mental and physical shock as they thought the train was crashing into them. Slices of domestic life were also put on screen, such as happy parents feeding their baby, or the amusing sequence of a gardener sprayed by his own hose. Life in the factories also found its place on the 1895 list of screenings as one of the films showed workers leaving the Lumière brothers' factory. Their films were primarily a demonstration of the progress of technology in the field of visual entertainment, the actual contents being only secondary to their technological objective. Nevertheless they made others realize the importance of using the new medium to show what was happening in the world; the tradition of the newsreel owes much to the Lumière brothers' pioneering work.

Around the turn of the century, the brothers were joined in the new field of cinema by the magician, George Méliès. With Méliès, a theater owner and master illusionist, cinema displayed its intrinsic value as a source of entertainment. After the initial "shock of the new," people were no longer coming to the theater to see the "pictures move," to marvel at the technological wonders that made the "movies" possible; they were now past the initial amazement at the technology and came to the theaters precisely to plunge instead into a world of wild fantasies and entertaining stories. Méliès's success in the field of fantastic films was sealed in 1902 with the projection of a twelve-minute futuristic comedy, *The Trip to the Moon*. The film is extraordinarily advanced in "special effects," such as disappearing bodies and objects, slow motion, and superimposition and portrays the comic exploration of space by a group of European scientists, dressed like wizards, who arrive on the moon only to realize that all their scientific knowledge has not prepared them to meet the indigenous population that takes them as prisoners. In addition to its comic content, the situation presented by the film displays the dangers of foreign and exotic lands, and the authorities' inability to deal with their populations. Méliès's science-fiction farce about the exploration of other worlds could easily be construed as a criticism of the colonial enterprise, of the arrival of "civilized" men to foreign lands and their failure to either conquer or educate the "natives." While this notion of failed conquest can be construed as an anticolonial message, the film also evokes the possibility of going into space. For a society in the midst of rapid scientific advance, such an exciting fantasy represented more than a crazy idea. Basking in the ideology of constant progress, the French turn-of-the-century public felt that everything was now possible and that men would be able to walk on the moon and explore the universe one day.

Health and Sports

At the beginning of the twentieth century, sporting events contributed to the international spirit of the modern world. Sport was the "esperanto of the races," or the universal language, according to French writer and dramatist Jean Giraudoux in his sports chronicles, in which he wrote about the benefits of sport for the body and about the international dimension of competition. However, in France, while many sports like soccer and gymnastics were widely practiced and athletic facilities were built everywhere using state funds, the spirit of competition was not part of the national attitude toward sports. Republicans developed the notion that sports served three main purposes: they provided leisurely and family-oriented activities for the masses; they linked physical health to mental well-being—according to Pierre de Coubertin, an avid sportsman and athlete who founded the International Olympic Committee in 1894, it purified the mind and the body from vices such as sex and alcohol—but most importantly, sports were supported by the Ministry of War, eager to build a military force in the—increasingly likely— event of war. Always with a watchful Germany, and determined to regain Alsace and Lorraine, the French military associated the practice of sport to the training of future soldiers. This association of sport activities with military exercise had been at the heart of the creation of many sporting and gymnastics clubs in central Europe as early as the second half of the nineteenth century. The broad and well-established European trend of building healthy nations through sports influenced the French Republicans in their effort to build a strong nation.

Before the advent of the Third Republic sports often existed as activities reserved for the elite, such as golf, horseback riding, and sailing. Beginning in the 1870s and 1880s, they gained in popularity and were officially introduced into the lives of the citizens through education, when schools included in their curriculum "military" training for boys, and municipalities organized games and events specifically designed to showcase the benefits of gymnastics or of a newly arrived English sport, football. Situated on the Channel coast and receiving much of the English maritime transport, the port city of Le Havre in Normandy was always first to be influenced by Britain. At a time when England was a highly developed sporting country, Le Havre, by virtue of its geographical location, was naturally first to feel the impact of British football (soccer in the United States) and the city created the first French *club de football* (soccer team) in 1872.

As early as 1873, with the creation of the Union of French Gymnastics Societies, a program of physical activities combining gymnastics and shooting clubs was developed by the State to encourage the nation to become stronger and healthier, and skilled in the handling of firearms, confirming that an essential goal of developing sports was military preparation, not mere competition. This initial martial practice of sports was responsible for the deeply engrained noncompetitive feeling that pervaded French sports in general. It may have produced a nation of underperformers and, compared to the British and American sports fans, relatively unenthusiastic crowds of supporters and uncommitted fans. Sport in France was generally understood as a way to show to the world a nation of willing and strong athletes who were also worthy individuals with a national conscience: "Whether they were seeking to strengthen the sense of civic pride, to 'give Marianne muscles' to combat physical and moral degeneration or to provide physical training for future soldiers, physical activity was not an end in itself: it was undertaken in the service of a greater cause: the fatherland" (Mignon, *The French Exception*, 181). The discourse about sports was, however, as contradictory as war and peace. On the one hand, Marianne was "flexing her muscles" and showing the world a militarily trained nation, and on the other, "she" proudly reintroduced the Olympics to the world, a peaceful international event that would serve as a model for international unity. In the area of sports as in the political arena, the national effort to prepare for war was at odds with the international intention to promote peace through "friendly" competition. At the beginning of the twentieth century, this contradiction was also at the heart of the more general waning of the concept of universalism as an active tool of nation building.

"Universalism" took on a transitional aspect when the Olympic Games were organized as an international event with universal ambitions. The French aristocrat, Baron Pierre de Coubertin, who believed that sports were a universal value that could be enjoyed and shared by all different nations in a peaceful context, revived the original Greek Olympic Games at the end of the nineteenth century.

The last games had been organized at the end of the fourth century in 394 BC in Greece, and de Courbertin thought that the first modern games should be organized in Athens, where they took place in 1896. Paris was the host for the 1900 games, which were overshadowed by the extravaganza represented by the Universal Exposition being held in the French capital the same year. Still, the convergence of these two international events in Paris, on the highly symbolic year 1900 was testimony to the prominence France and its capital had achieved. Whether you were in Paris for the exposition or for the games, the city was indeed the place to be.

The universalist ambition of the Olympics involved setting representatives of different, and often antagonistic, nations against one another in the context of friendly athletic competition. The games would then serve humanity in a safe climate of respect for each other's differences, be they political, racial, or religious. They were meant to celebrate the athletic body, to offer a peaceful forum where athletes were able to perform heroic tasks, to display strength and talent in action, but also to demonstrate human values and justice for the enjoyment, the admiration, and the education of a large and varied public, from the wealthiest to the poorest classes. It has been suggested that by supporting the global initiative of reinstating the games, the French Republic took on the role of "universal teacher" making sport "a contribution to education and a possible recourse for those confronted with the decline of religion and the ideological battles of the day . . . Where society was imperfect, sport proposed, within the Olympic doctrine, a countermodel that was a synthesis of the virtues that were in decline." Some of these virtues applied to the Olympics included "fair play, commitment, selflessness, respect for one's opponent, justice, chivalry, generosity and a concern for education" (Mignon, *The French Exception*, 185).

According to French philosopher and critic Roland Barthes (see chapter 8), who wrote about the "myths" of daily life in modernizing France of the 1950s, a certain brand of displaced "chivalry" was and continues to be part of some sports, bicycling among them. Concerning the international French bicycle race, the Tour de France, Barthes would wonder about the "ambiguous morals" of an event that displayed "chivalrous codes continuously mixing with the brutal reminder of a pure desire to win" (*Mythologies*, 130–131). Born in 1915 and brought up and educated in the republican tradition himself, Barthes appreciated the superior physical effort demonstrated by the riders and found the bicycle race worthy of intellectual consideration. His essay on the Tour de France refers in particular to the sacrifice of the team for their leader, a team of individuals who worked and "pedaled heroically" to help the leader win. Barthes saw this sense of "chivalry" clashing with flashes of the brutish and individualistic spirit of competition when a rider would let his desire to win overcome his sense of sacrifice. In the first Olympics and other sports events of the same era, the spirit of competition was seen as the evil component of the sporting world, a much different view from the contemporary notion of competition perceived as a positive force and built in the psychological training of the athletes.

At first, as sports were becoming state-sponsored activities, the spirit of competition was considered to be more a personal "rage." The Olympic organizing committee interpreted it as an "excess" and running counter to the educational *noblesse* and peaceful international mission of the games. The discourse emanating both from de Coubertin's writings about sports and from the French Republic supporting his efforts did not openly promote a spirit of competition.

The First Tour de France. 1903

The modern bicycle was popular with many modest to upper bourgeois families who could then afford it—there were one million bicycles in France in 1900. Biking was also a leisurely activity that was not reserved to men, as women also enjoyed riding. For women of the *Belle Epoque*, bicycling represented a step toward emancipation as the bike allowed them the freedom of riding and of wearing comfortable long pants instead of the usual constraining corset. In addition, by the end of the nineteenth century, the promotion of sports in general as a spectacle for the masses—bicycling, but

Figure 4.1   First Tour de France (1903)

Photo taken during the second stage between Lyon and Marseille (381 kilometers=237miles) in the city of Valence. We see the leading rider Hippolyte Aucouturier, nicknamed "the Terrible," in front of the *peloton* encouraged by the heavy crowds of men and children, some of whom came with their own bike. (© L'Illustration)

also boxing, was developed with this goal in mind—manifested itself in the inception of bicycle races between two cities, *Le Paris-Roubaix* in the North of France *Le Paris-Brest* and *Le Paris-Bordeaux* in the West. People from cities and villages situated along the race's course, some of whom had never attended any major event, sporting or otherwise, were all of a sudden treated to a "free" spectacle right outside their doorsteps. They came in large numbers to the side of the road to applaud and encourage men competing on their "amazing metallic machine," and felt that they were finally witnessing a concrete combination of progress and physical achievement. With the organization of road races, cycling in particular, the world of sports in general was introduced as both spectacle and practice to a wider population. Watching in awe as the bikers rode by, many onlookers felt motivated to join the cycling craze, and made the purchase of their first bicycle.

The Tour de France was also a direct consequence of the upheaval that surrounded the Dreyfus Affair. The Dreyfusard director of the first French sporting newspaper *Le Vélo* (*The Bicycle*), Pierre Giffard, and its main financial investor, the anti-Dreyfusard Count of Dion, went their separate ways as a direct result of their respective positions on the "Affair." Giffard continued to edit the green-paged daily *Le Vélo*, while Dion hired a crafty director, Henri Desgrange, for his new yellow-paged *L'Auto-Vélo*, and published its first issue in October 1900. In court, Giffard sued Desgrange to remove the word *vélo* from the title of his publication. The paper simply became *L'Auto*, but continued to report and sponsor cycling events. However, Desgrange wanted to keep an edge over his direct competitor and, thanks to the ideas of a young collaborator named Géo Lefèvre, he launched the Tour de France, a 2500-kilometer race looping around the central part of France and running through some of its major cities: Paris, Lyon, Marseille, Toulouse, Bordeaux, Nantes, and back to Paris. The Tour was such an instant success that it catapulted *L'Auto* to the top of the sports periodicals, but at the same time and thanks to its geographical spread, it also increased the number of French people from the capital and from the provinces interested in the event. With football, bicycling had become the top spectator sports in the country. From the start, the Tour was also an international event with the inclusion of riders from Belgium, Switzerland, and Germany in 1903. As the number of participating countries grew with the years, this increasing international presence placed the Tour on the world map. A majority of French riders won the race in the first decade, but as with any other sports, riders and spectators were looking for more than a competition. Spectators loved the excitement it brought to their home towns, and the spectacle of the muddy and tired cyclists crisscrossing the country filled them with a profound sense of admiration for what seemed a truly Herculean task. Riders, who for the most part were of popular stock, had the unique opportunity to become heroes for a short eighteen-day period. The crowds chanted their names, helped them find shortcuts, feeding their heroes on the road and going as far as poisoning challengers, and worse. Onlookers trapped and sometimes beat a rider they did not like. The Tour truly became what the cultural critic and semiotician Roland Barthes would later call a "myth" of French society, and produced a steady stream of literary pieces produced by fascinated writers and intellectuals (Colette, Louis Aragon, Antoine Blondin, Roland Barthes, and many more) and films by major directors (Louis Malle, Claude Lelouch), which contributed to making the Tour a cultural phenomenon of "epic" proportions (*Mythologies*, 125).

Dossier 4.4   Colette's "End of a Tour de France" (1913)

This text, wrongly dated 1912, reports on the 1913 Tour in which 158 participants began the race and only 21 made it to the finish line in Paris. Colette is in a car following the race and gives us a taste of the emotions and the excitement surrounding riders' passage. People have been waiting all day on the side of the dusty roads and have brought along their picnics, making a special daylong occasion out of the event. It is clear from Colette's account that many of these roadside supporters had waited a little too long and picnicked a little too much as their sobriety was noticeably impaired. In the end, more than the loud arrival of the riders in the *vélodrome* [bicycle track] of the Parc des Princes stadium in Paris, it is mainly the active and frenzied road experience of the Tour that left Colette "deafened, [her] head throbbing."

Get away from there, you, for Heaven's sake! They're coming, they're coming! We don't budge. We stay silent and disdainful in the motorcar drawn up by the side of the road, near the train crossing at Villennes. An hour's waiting has taught us the worth of that warning, hurled at us by passing cyclists. They are red-faced, excited, sweating; they have flags on their handlebars and pedal very rapidly, shouting peremptorily. They are not the official announcers they are simple Sunday riders who try to disturb the peace of this farmed landscape, without success.

From Poissy to Villennes the dusty roadside serves as a carpet for placid families, unpretentious cyclists shoe laced with string and a few Sunday boozers. Some of them have lunch while awaiting, like us, the return of the riders of the Tour de France.

The breeze sways the asparagus seeds, the onion flowers and the ears of corn still standing, bringing with it the abominable stench of fertilizing sewage.

From time to time a youth scorches by on two wheels, coattails flying, and shouts with his eyes popping out of his head some dramatic invented news:

"Someone's just been killed!"

"There's only three of the Peugeot team left! All the rest have cracked!"

The road rises like white flour behind them, like the cloud of smoke that conceals an evil spirit conjured up in the theater . . .

But here come some other folks, also mounted on two wheels; no longer red in the face, but strangely yellow, they seem to belong to another species. Their faces are obscured, their moustaches matted by a paste of sweat and dust; their hollow eyes, between caked lashes, make them look like rescued well diggers.

"Now those are the serious amateurs," says my companion, "the racers can't be far off . . ." While he is still speaking a low cloud gleams white at the bend of the road and rolls down on us. We are blinded, suffocated; we move off cautiously; a pilot car howls at our heels like the siren of a sinking ship; another brushes by with the daring sinuous dash of a giant fish; a frenzied shoal of cyclists with ashen lips, half glimpsed through the dust, clutch at the wings of the cars, skid and crush . . .

We follow, enmeshed in the race. I see passing in front of us, suddenly swallowed up in thick swirls of dust, three slender racers: black and yellow backs carrying red numbers, three creatures who might as well have been faceless, spines arched, heads down to knees, under a white cap . . . They disappear very quickly, the only ones to be silent in this uproar; their haste to forge ahead, their silence seem to isolate them from what is happening here. They don't seem to be competing against each other, rather to be fleeing from us, to be pursued like a hunted game by an escort lifting thick dust mixed with shouts, horn-blowing, acclamations and peals of thunder.

We follow, nourished by fine crisp flint, our nostrils scorched. In front of us, in the cloud, there is the vague shadow of an almost invisible car, yet near enough for us to be able to touch its hood; we climb on the seat to see, behind us, another phantom car and others behind that; we feel the waving arms hear the shouts that swear at us and demand that we move along. Everywhere around us there is danger, the suffocating heavy odor of something burning, wild fires starting up; there is in us and everywhere around us the demoniacal lust for speed, the imbecile and invincible "desire to be first."

Meanwhile the silent racers—modest heads in this deafening procession—have brought us as far as the railway, where the closed gate momentarily stops the race. A crowd bright and dressed in its Sunday best, waits and cheers; there, again, the little black and yellow men carrying a red number thread their way through the pedestrians' gate, cross the track and vanish. We stay penned up behind the gates, furious and frustrated. The cloud of dust momentarily lowers to let me see a triple line of impatient and powerful cars marked with the color of the road, the color of mud, piloted by brick-colored as if masked drivers, who stalk the car in front, all set to pass with a possibly fatal swerve . . . On my right two men are standing up in their car, outstretched like gargoyles above their driver's head. In the car on the left another man black with oil and grease, squats on his heels, feet on the cushions and darts glances over the road from his bulging glasses. They all seem ready to leap, to strike, and the lenses of their many cameras pointed upward like black guns feel ominous . . . It's hot. A stormy sun broods over all this anonymous ferocity. . . .

The whole length of Poissy, a cordial, jovial crowd awaits the racers with whom we are now catching up. A fine sturdy old fellow, a little drunk, wants to show his enthusiasm by embracing one of the black and yellow automata, riding at a slow pace; the faceless automaton suddenly plants a terrible fist in the stout fellow's bloated face before disappearing in his cloud like a god avenged . . .

Avenue de la Reine, in Boulogne . . . The crowd, denser than ever, has invaded the middle of the roadway and in its inconvenient enthusiasm, makes barely enough way for the winner, who nevertheless raises his head, showing his exasperated eyes and opens his mouth, may be swearing with rage . . . They let him through but, as we follow him, the crowd reforms before us just as a field of packed wheat reforms after a squall. A second rider brushed against us, equally impeded by the welcoming multitude, and his fair face, also furious, looks intensely at a fixed point in front of him: the entrance to the velodrome [bicycle track] . . .

It's over. Now there's only the vast track of the Parc des Princes, filled with a scattered crowd. The shouts, the applause, the music are only a breeze compared with the storm that swept me here, and from which I emerged deafened, head throbbing. But I can still see over the track, rising and falling like the two minuscule untiring cranks that sufficed to stir up this mechanical tempest, the two shapely legs of the winner. (620–623)

Colette's experience and accurate description still hold partly true today; the Tour continues to attract hordes of people who wait all day, sometimes in horrendous weather, with fervent expectations and also marvel at the lightning-quick passage of these "god-like men" on their slick machines, a feeling recaptured every year in July along the French roads. The Tour became a veritable tradition that was only interrupted during the two wars between 1914–1918 and 1939–1945. The quasi-mythical status gained by the Tour helps us understand why the recent doping scandals caused such disappointment to contemporary fans, even if doping was suspected to be a common practice among the riders for quite a while. In his 1957 *Mythologies*, Barthes speaks of doping as "criminal and sacrilegious" (129). Since the "Festina Affair" of 1998, in which the Spanish watch company Festina team's *soigneur* (trainer) was picked up at the border between France and Belgium with a drug cargo destined to the entire team, a revelation that caused all its members to be banned from the Tour, cultural attitude toward biking have noticeably changed. The incident underlined the fact that, in the contemporary practice of sports, commercial and selfish motives often come before any notion of "fair play," "chivalry," or "good citizenship."

The "Festina Affair" was far indeed from a time when French children practiced sports in school to fulfill one of the nation's educational and political ambitions, by providing it with a future military force that could be trusted in case of a potential conflict. When French cyclists covered in sweat, blood, and mud were admired as national heroes, they were perceived with pride by the spectators who identified them with gods, but also as potential soldiers. When Pierre de Coubertin offered a model of "peaceful" international gathering with the revival of the Olympics, he pointedly encouraged friendly competition between all participating countries. Thus it seemed that in the unusually active world of sports of the early 1900s, the French were reproducing a cultural pattern consistent with a nation's preparation for a possible war, first pragmatically with the military-minded physical education of schoolboys, then psychologically with the population's loyal and proud feeling for its sports heroes. The revival of the international Olympics Games can itself be seen in the context of diplomatic efforts to encourage peaceful coexistence between countries with divergent and potentially explosive ideologies.

In many ways, the complexity and contradictions of the world of sports, as entertainment, public health project, potential war machine, *and* as pacifist effort, was at odds with the deceptive sense of beauty and tranquility of the last years of the *Belle Epoque*. The serenity of an afternoon walk on a Normandy beach and the happiness of a childhood spent in the back mountains of Provence were more in tune with a time that was ending as war approached.

The Beauty of the *Belle Epoque* in the Provinces

By the turn of the century Paris had established itself as the capital of modernity and was the scene of some of its most ostentatious manifestations: the Universal Exposition, the Olympics, the invention of cinema, the advent and display of electricity on the capitals' wide boulevards and the beauty and efficiency of its *Art Nouveau* metro. The serenity usually attributed to the *Belle Epoque* is arguably better rendered in memories of a time past spent in the provinces like Normandy or Provence, far from the bustling capital. Many novels and paintings set outside of Paris presented the quiet and pleasant times between the Dreyfus Affair and World War I. The images of moments of happiness came into being retroactively in contrast with the shame of scandals and the horrors of war. The concept of the *Belle Epoque* was thus created post facto and designated the years following the troubling Dreyfus Affair and preceding World War I (1899–1914). The name *Belle Epoque* itself, which could be translated as "beautiful epoch/era" but is better rendered as the "good old days" was only attributed to this fifteen-year period, after World War I, as physically and emotionally scared survivors of the war remembered with nostalgia the innocence and the beauty of a period that they had left behind and could never retrieve. The concept of the *Belle Epoque* thus emerged out a collective nostalgia after the gruesome war years. The devastation left by the war clearly changed the perspective of the French toward the prewar era. Had it not been for the Dreyfus scandal and the war, the period would have been simply recognized as an economically and culturally prosperous time, especially for the bourgeois class.

Marcel Proust's 1919 novel *Within a Budding Grove*, a classic of twentieth-century French literature, was awarded the Goncourt prize, the most distinguished French literary award. The decision was one of the most contested in the history of the Goncourt prize. It opposed those on the jury who favored Proust and those who wanted the Goncourt to go to another contender, Roland Dorgelès, a war veteran whose *Les Croix de bois* (*The Wooden Crosses*) they deemed more worthy than the "impressionistic" *Within a Budding Grove* written by an author who had not fought in the war for health reasons (Proust was an asthmatic). It may be that in 1919 the crowning of *Within a Budding Grove* as the novel of the year reflected the need of a therapeutic interlude from the ghastly words and images of war, an interlude to be found in peaceful memories of a prewar society when nonchalant promenades and chance encounters had defined much of the social life and spirit of a carefree segment of the population.

Dossier 4.5   Proust's Normandy, *Within a Budding Grove* (1919)

In the following passage we feel the gentle appeal of a lazy afternoon stroll on a pier where a concert has been set up in the open and is just about ready to begin, while a young man touched by the beauty of a group of healthy and happy, even giddy, young ladies walks by the seaside. The setting is reminiscent of Boudin's paintings of the beach resort of Trouville in Normandy, among them "The Beach at Trouville" (1865) and "Bathers on the Beach at Trouville" (1869). Although Boudin did not live to see the *Belle Epoque*, he captured the kind of lazy and nonchalant feel of the gatherings of the bourgeois families on vacation on the fashionable coast of Normandy. The mood in Boudin's paintings was similar to Proust's representation of the *Belle Epoque*, even if the painter and the writer were working at different times, sometimes as many as forty years apart. Boudin's representation of women in crinoline dresses on the beach called attention to the fashion of the Second Empire, a trend that had almost completely disappeared after the 1870s; bicycles were entirely absent from Boudin's paintings as they had only recently appeared as bourgeois commodities that were naturally part of the Proustian representation of the period. We feel the insouciance marking the scene where the only concerns of the day are related to a highly critical upper bourgeois sense of decorum far from the actual harsh reality of life, especially the life of the working class and the poor. The vacationing bourgeois of Trouville in Boudin's painting or Cabourg in Proust's novel had worries of a more psychological and privileged nature than those of the working class concerned with basic daily necessities. They lived in a world where what you did and wore, and who you knew, determined who you were and who you might become. The general context of Proust's story is an environment where modern life and anachronistic mores and codes of propriety contributed to the bourgeoisie's seemingly carefree but neurotic way of life. In this excerpt, Proust's intent is to write about the deep tension felt by an extremely status–conscious bourgeois society torn between newly fabricated and traditional representations of modern happiness, driven by a conflicted desire to appear both proper and fulfilled.

It was the hour at which ladies and gentlemen came out every day for a stroll along the front, exposed to the merciless fire of the lorgnette fastened upon them, as if they had each borne some disfigurement which she felt it her duty to inspect in its minutest details, by the senior judge's wife, proudly seated there with her back to the band-stand, in the middle of that dread line of chairs on which presently they too, actors turned critics, would come and establish themselves, to scrutinize in their turn the passing crowds. All these people paced up and down the esplanade, reeling and lurching as heavily as if it had been the deck of a ship . . .

In the midst of all these people, some of whom were pursuing a train of thought, but then betrayed its instability by a fitfulness of gesture, an aberrancy of gaze as inharmonious as the circumspect titubation of their neighbors, the girls whom I had noticed, with the control of gesture that come from the perfect suppleness of one's own body and a sincere contempt for the rest of humanity, were advancing straight ahead, without hesitation or stiffness, performing exactly the movements that they wished to perform, each of their limbs completely independent of the others, the rest of the body preserving that immobility which is so noticeable in good waltzers. They were now quite near me . . .

It was not perhaps mere chance in life that, in forming this group of friends, had chosen them all so beautiful; perhaps these girls (whose demeanor was enough to reveal their bold, hard and

frivolous natures), extremely aware of everything that was ludicrous or ugly, incapable of yield-
ing to an intellectual or moral attraction, had naturally felt a certain repulsion for all those among
the companions of their own age in whom a pensive or sensitive disposition was betrayed by shy-
ness, awkwardness, constraint, by what they would regard as antipathetic, and from such had
held aloof; while attaching themselves, conversely, to others to whom they were drawn by a cer-
tain blend of grace, suppleness and physical elegance, the only form in which they were able to
picture a straightforward and attractive character and the promise of pleasant hours in one
another's company. Perhaps, too, the class to which they belonged, a class which I should not
have found it easy to define, was at that point in its evolution when, thanks either to its grow-
ing wealth and leisure, or to new sporting habits, now prevalent even among certain elements of
the working class, and a habit of physical culture to which had not yet been added the culture of
the mind, a social group comparable to the smooth and prolific schools of sculpture which have not
yet gone in for tortured expression produces naturally and in abundance fine bodies, fine legs, fine
hips, wholesome, serene faces, with an air of agility and guile. And were they not noble and calm
models of human beauty that I beheld her, outlined against the sea, like statues exposed to the
sunlight on a Grecian shore? . . .

By this time their charming features had ceased to be indistinct and jumbled. I had dealt them
like cards into so many heaps to compose (failing their names, of which I was still ignorant): the
tall one who jumped over the old banker; the little one silhouetted against the horizon of sea with
her plump and rosy cheeks and green eyes; the one with the straight nose and dark complexion
who stood among the rest; another, with a face as white as an egg in which a tiny nose described
an arc of circle like a chicken's beak—a face such as one sometimes sees in the very young; yet
another, also tall wearing a hooded cape (which gave her so shabby an appearance and so con-
tradicted the elegance of the figure beneath that the explanation which suggested itself was that
this girl must have parents of high position who valued their self-esteem so far above the visitors
to Balbec and the sartorial elegance of their own children that it was a matter of the utmost indif-
ference to them that their daughter should stroll on the front dressed in a way which humbler peo-
ple would have considered too modest); a girl with brilliant, laughing eyes and plump, matt
cheeks, a black polo-cap crammed on her head, who was pushing a bicycle with such an unin-
hibited swing of the hips, and using slang terms so typically of the gutter and shouted so loud
when I passed her (although among her expressions I caught that tiresome phrase "living one's
own life") that, abandoning the hypothesis which her friend's hooded cape had prompted me to
formulate, I concluded instead that all these girls belonged to the population which frequents the
racing-tracks, and must be the very juvenile mistresses of professional cyclists. In any event, none
of my suppositions embraced the possibility of their being virtuous . . .

For an instant, as I passed the dark one with the plump cheeks who was wheeling a bicycle,
I caught her smiling, sidelong glance, aimed from the centre of that inhuman world which
enclosed the life of this little tribe, an inaccessible, unknown world wherein the idea of what I
was could certainly never penetrate or find a place. Wholly occupied with what her companions
were saying, had she seen me—this young girl in the polo-cap pulled down very low over her
forehead—at the moment in which the dark ray emanating from her eyes had fallen on me? If
she had seen me, what could have I represented to her? From the depths of what universe did
she discern me? It would have been as difficult for me to say as, when certain distinguishing fea-
tures in a neighboring planet are made visible thanks to the telescope, it is to conclude there from
that human beings inhabit it, and that they can see us, and to guess what ideas the sight of us
can have aroused in their minds . . . I knew that I should never possess this young cyclist if I
did not possess also what was in her eyes. And it was consequently her whole life that filled me

with desire; a sorrowful desire because I felt that it was not to be fulfilled; but exhilarating
because, what had hitherto been my life having ceased of a sudden to be my whole life, being
no more now than a small part of the space stretching out before me which I was burning to cover
and which was composed of the lives of these girls, offered me that prolongation, that possible
multiplication of oneself which is happiness . . .

I had looked so closely at the dark cyclist with the bright eyes that she seemed to notice my atten-
tion, and said to the tallest of the girls something I could not hear but that made her laugh . . .

Was, then, the happiness of knowing these girls unattainable? . . . Indeed the pleasure I
derived from the little band, as noble as if it had been composed of Hellenic virgins, arose from
the fact that it had something of the fleetingness of the passing figures on the road. This evanes-
cence of persons who are not known to us, who force us to put out from the harbor of life in which
the women whose society we frequent have all, in course of time, laid bare their blemishes, urges
us into that state of pursuit in which there is no longer anything to stem the tide of imagination.
(Within a Budding Grove, 846–853)

In *Within a Budding Grove* Proust writes about the ageless thrill of a first encounter that he compares to a carriage quickly taking away dreams of potentially rewarding love. But beyond the universality of desire at work in his novel, we also experience the narrator's perception of social propriety in his contemporary, modern world. As a romantic filled with platonic images of women, the narrator can express only confusion when these images become examples of modernity shaped by the technical and physical attributes of the new era. He mentions several times the flexible and athletic bodies of a group of girls being observed, bodies that reflect the relatively new consciousness regarding sports. Despite the official exclusion of women from the republic's sports project, women caught in the general spirit of the time promoting physical activities, especially "liberated women," biked and practiced a number of other sports. However, for the class-conscious narrator, this physical education made manifest in the shape and beauty of the modern female body produces some anxiety as to which class these girls really belong. For a refined young bourgeois man, recognizing someone's class by intuition is an essential sixth sense acquired throughout his upbringing. Being unable to indulge successfully in such discrimination becomes traumatizing. Confused and anxious as he is to try to determine as best he can each girl's virtue and class by looking at her behavior and her clothes, he remains sure that the one girl pushing a bicycle can be only of the lowest stock. Cyclists may be heroes on the racing road to victory, but off their "racing" bikes, they remain "invisible" working-class people. The narrator's attitude toward sports in general and biking in particular is consistent with others of his class. In keeping with his upper bourgeois upbringing, he has respect for the image of the untouchable "mythical hero" riding in the blazing sun or through torrential rains, but only has scorn for the actual man as well as for whoever associates with the biking crowd: "I concluded instead that all these girls belonged to the population that frequents the racing-tracks, and must be the very juvenile mistresses of professional cyclists. In any event, none of my suppositions embraced the possibility of their being virtuous." However, his preconceived judgment soon proves fragile and untenable as his contempt for the leisurely cycling modern woman quickly transforms into a burning desire to be part of her life. It is as if he would admit to experiencing excitement in association with lower-class activities and with those practicing them. What Proust explores in this particular episode of *Within a Budding Grove* is the narrator's partial relinquishing of his acquired bourgeois habits for a more accepting view of the modern world. After much hesitation, he eventually finds beauty and appeal in the young female cyclist who in a later volume of *Remembrance of Things Past* will become the love of his life. Solidly anchored in his "universal" bourgeois world where everyone is ranked and classified in terms of class and propriety, he nevertheless seems to come to terms with the leveling of social differences that were part and parcel of modernity. Without destroying the mythical image of the classic woman, he now admits to his fascination with athletic bodies shaped by physical activities like swimming and biking. As if captivated by the new modern woman, by her daring allure and free spirit, by her fit and slender body, he is able to find a happy medium between the image of the classic virgin of the Greek statue and the image of the athletic seductress in the woman of the *Belle Epoque*.

Marcel Pagnol's Provence

While much attention is usually given to canonized writers like Zola and Proust who wrote primarily about Parisians' way of life or, in the case of Zola about major social and political events, Provençal writers seem to hover on the margins of canonized literature as they keep a faithful attachment to a more local and less political, some would say "less serious" representation of France. However, today it is their local color that keeps them high on readers' lists. The qualities of their characters and the beauty of their countryside have consistently attracted a wide readership nationally and internationally, establishing Provence as a place where an "authentic" French life could still be found. The region seems to have retained more strongly than other places in France the nostalgic sentiment of authors looking back at the *Belle Epoque* as the "good old days." Indeed, a symbol like "quaint and sunny" Provence is often tested by significant rapid industrial and social changes similar to those that occurred during the *Belle Epoque*. The delicate combination of wholesomeness and folklore upon which the cultural image of Provence rested became vulnerable when confronted with the inevitable outside forces of modernity.

While real fear of the outside world emerges regularly in the plots of his novels, Marcel Pagnol (1895–1974), the southern French writer, filmmaker, and member of the French *Academy* is always careful not to reduce his literary Provence to a region of pigheaded peasants with immutable atavistic traits, refusing progress and modernity in order to keep nature, beauty, and traditions intact. On the contrary, in *Childhood Memories*, Pagnol demonstrates with the character of Joseph, a modern agnostic and Republican teacher, that one could hold progressive political ideas while remaining true to one's local heritage. Pagnol's sense of literary drama is heightened by the inevitable tension between traditional life in Provence and the disruptive national and international influences brought to the region. The geographical and social environment Pagnol describes could not be more different from the world described in Proust's *Remembrance of Things Past*. No rich Parisians are here, but the almost simplistic and touching story of a modest provincial family of authentic "republican stock." There are no fancy dresses or high bourgeois standards in Pagnol's world, but rather a genuine insistence on strong political support of the republican system and on the greatness of education at all times: "One must never lose an opportunity of acquiring knowledge" (*My Father's Glory*, 165), says Joseph to his son Marcel. Joseph is a schoolteacher of peasant background; he makes little money, but like the archetypal schoolteacher of the Third Republic, he is dedicated to his teaching job and to his family. His wife, Augustine, is a pretty but physically fragile seamstress for whom her family is everything. Like a "good republican family," especially at the key historical time of the official separation of church and state, which was instituted in 1905, they do not go to church, and the local priest is viewed as the "enemy" of progress and education. They believe in modern civilization, medical and technological progress, and in the life of the mind.

Dossier 4.6   Marcel Pagnol's *In My Mother's Castle*

In this second volume of Pagnol's *Chilhood Memories*, published between 1957 and 1959, it is both life and history's twisted fate that breaks the cycle of happiness that is omnipresent in the trilogy. First, Marcel's mother Augustine dies at a young age, and Lili the local peasant from the hills and Marcel's best friend dies on the battlefields of World War I.

> *Time passes and turns the wheel of life, as waters turn the mill wheels.*
>
> *Five years later, I was walking behind a black carriage, whose wheels were so high that I could see the horses' hooves. I was dressed in black, and young Paul's hand was gripping mine with all its strength. My mother was being borne away forever.*
>
> *Then little Paul grew very tall. He had outgrown me by a whole head and he wore a beard, a silky, burnished frill, but he had kept the bright blue eyes of childhood and its sunny smile.*
>
> *Along the Hills of L'Etoile, which he could not bear to leave, he drove his herd of goats . . . he was the last of Virgil's goatherds.*
>
> *My dear Lili did not walk at my side as I accompanied [my brother] to the little graveyard at La Treille, for he had been waiting for him there for years, under a carpet of immortelles humming with bees; during the war of 1914, in a black northern forest, a bullet in the forehead cut short his young life, and he had sunk, under the falling rain, on a tangle of chilly plants whose names he did not even know . . .*
>
> *Such is the life of man. A few joys, quickly obliterated by unforgettable sorrows.*
>
> *There is no need to tell the children so.* (339)

In both Proust and Pagnol's novels, as well as in other works by writers of the *Belle Epoque* and beyond, the war definitely put an end to the prosperity and the innocence that characterized the period, at least for some. The era's dominant bourgeois values perceived through a universalist prism were challenged by the appearance of "Others" made "visible" by colonialism, anti-Semitism, and class struggle, among other developments. The Great War, with its bloody trenches and casualties on an "industrial scale," would confirm the reality of this challenge. In the end, the abstract principles of republican universalism could not eliminate the inevitable and increasing dissemination of social, political, and cultural differences that were now openly becoming part of the foundation of a truly modern society.

While the inconsistencies between the stated goals of universalism and the growing sense of difference were felt through the strange and glossy veneer of the *Belle Epoque*, they came crashing down in the *grande boucherie* (the great butchery) of World War I.

Letters from the Front: The Great War (1914–1918)

"Farewell"
Letters Send me some letters my darling
We love to receive them in our batallion
One a day at least one at least I beg you.
(Apollinaire, *Poèmes à Lou*, January 4, 1915)

In 1915, Guillaume Apollinaire's poem "Farewell" could very well have served as the general heading to all the letters and poems written by soldiers of World War I; as if these written words were a farewell, as if each time a letter was sent home it brought news of a soldier's last thoughts and final wishes. Apollinaire fought the entire war but did not die on the front. Some might say that he was one of the lucky ones for returning home at the end of the war. However, he had to be trepanned after being wounded in the head by an exploding shell in 1917 and, ironically, died of Spanish influenza a few months later in 1918. Apollinaire was both a poet fighting in a war and a soldier with a gift for poetry; in addition, the poet-soldier was in love. For Apollinaire, love and language transformed the pain and horror of war into a strange lyrical world where exploding shells became blooming mimosas and soldiers' blood flowed like a fountain of joy. *Poems to Lou* is a collection of love letters written in the form of poems sent by a soldier on the frontline to the woman he loves. The soldier is easily identifiable as Apollinaire himself, a man whose feelings for the war and motivation to enlist in the French army were atypical as he volunteered for what, oddly enough, he thought at one point in 1915 was "a charming war." "Charming" would not be a common qualifier to speak about the war, but it may be that Apollinaire saw the military conflict just beginning with attenuated terror because he lived and fought it with the passion of his love for Lou in his heart. To him, World War I also represented a formative time for the bohemian and untroubled poet that he was. He felt the powerful appeal of danger and death as a way to become more than just a soldier, but above all a man toughened by warfare, death, and great destruction. In other words, to Apollinaire war was not only a "bloody butchery," but also a rite of initiation and the fulfillment of a certain ideal of masculinity. The year 1916 was also the year Apollinaire became a French citizen, a status he had keenly and persistently pursued (he was born Wilhelm-Apollinaris von Kostrowitzky in Rome in 1880, the son of a presumed Italian army officer and an aristocratic Polish mother). A man "reborn" in the crucible of war and a "citizen of France": the two converged for him in 1916. A year before, as an homage to the nation to which he felt profoundly attached, he honored France both as a poet and a soldier in a poem entitled *Chant de l'honneur* (Song of Honor): "I interpret for all the sweet sound of tree notes//that an oriole-like cannon sings when you sob" (*Calligrammes*, 175). Elsewhere in the poem, honor and respect are represented in images revealing the simple beauty of his fallen companions: "But here as elsewhere I know that beauty//can be found nowhere else but in simplicity//how many dead have I seen in the trenches//who were left standing with their head tilted//simply leaning against the parapet" (*Calligrammes*, 173). Here, the dead soldiers were depicted not lying in the mud, not dead in atrocious and humiliating conditions, but standing in the trenches looking as if they were casually leaning on the rail of a pier or of a balcony and talking with their friends. The simplicity of the evoked scene

Figure 4.2   Soldiers in the Trenches (1915)

After the fighting in the Argonne, on June 30, 1915, soldiers remove dead bodies from the roughly dug out trenches, while the wounded lay still in the narrow path and wait for their turn to be rescued. (© L'Illustration)

allowed for a beautiful and touching representation of these men caught in a peaceful moment of their everyday life rather than as casualties of war. Further in the poem, the night sky is illuminated with deadly fire from shells and cannons and Apollinaire still reassures himself that the raging battle has the appeal of a "beautiful night" filled with "cooing" and fireworks: "This night is so beautiful when gun shots are cooing//and a constant flock of shells above our heads are flying//Sometimes a rocket illuminates the sky//It is a flower that opens and fades in the sky" (*Calligrammes*, 174).

For Apollinaire as well as for thousands of other soldiers living the daily engagement of war in the trenches, words, written and received, lyrical or graphic, tender or distressed, sad and hopeful, were the only "joy" they possessed, the only way to remain connected to the world they knew as human beings, as farmers or teachers, writers or workers. Words often took on the symbolic role of the food and blood they needed to survive the hellish horror of the trenches.

> I write to you O my Lou from the reed hut
> Where nine men's hearts pound with love and hope
> Cannons are shooting shells continuously
> And I hear the whimpering of the birdless woods.
>   (*Poèmes à Lou*, 153)

Even for someone who went to war with enthusiasm like Apollinaire, the contrast between love and suffering must have held an additional tragic dimension that made the war almost more difficult to bear in his own writing than in straightforward accounts. It was as if Apollinaire embodied the passage from a serene moment in history to its radical opposite, from the carefree ease of the *Belle Epoque* to the harsh reality of war.

By early century many European intellectuals who had expressed doubts about France's frantic transformation saw in this devastating conflict a true moment of crisis for the European mind. To them the war indicated the cultural incapacity, the absence of an adequate intellectual response to the effects of modernization. War became the somber reminder that modern man was a vulnerable being, and that modernity did not automatically produce peace, or an answer to the most basic questions faced by humanity. In an open letter, the poet and intellectual, member of the Academy, Paul Valéry wrote about the stark reality of a modern civilization so quickly brought down to its knees: "We later civilizations . . . we too now know that we are mortal" (23).

As we have seen, from the second half of the nineteenth century to the beginning of the twentieth, the concept of modernity took over French culture in an unstable and deceptive climate of anxiety and euphoria, carrying in its wake eclectic new forms of thinking, new artistic practices and scientific discoveries, embraced by some and dreaded by others. To describe the confusion of modern Europe, Valéry proposed the image of a European Hamlet lifting one famous skull after another and failing to put them in order:

> Our Hamlet of Europe is watching millions of ghosts. But he is an intellectual Hamlet, meditating on the life and death of truths; for ghosts, he has all the subjects of our controversies; for remorse, all the titles of our fame. He is bowed under the weight of all the discoveries and varieties of knowledge, incapable of resuming the endless activity; he broods on the tedium of rehearsing the past and the folly of always trying to innovate.

He staggers between two abysses—or two dangers never cease threatening the world: order and disorder. (29)

In these "neurotic times" of rapid transformation, modern society lacked a unifying force, a deep structure of understanding. The new century was literally blinded by the glitter of the modern as Valéry points in "Crisis of the Mind":

Europe in 1914 had perhaps reached the limit of modernism. Every mind of any scope was at a crossroad for all shades of opinion; every thinker was an international exposition of thought. There were the works of the mind in which the wealth of contrasts and contradictory tendencies was like the insane displays of light in the capitals of those days: eyes were fatigued, scorched . . . How much material wealth, how much labor and planning it took, how many centuries were ransacked, how many heterogeneous lives were combined, to make possible such a carnival, and to set it up as the supreme wisdom and the triumph of humanity?" (28)

Had the Western world indeed reached the "limit of modernism?" Was it now, in 1914, at a critical junction, between an overflowing of ideas and discoveries and the inability to channel them through new modes of thinking? There seemed to be no overarching structure to accommodate the differences, particularities, and individualities that had appeared with the advent of modernity. With the arrival of the war, the peculiarly French notion of universalism took a dramatic step backward as modern culture entered a destructive phase. The notion took on a strange revival at the beginning of the war in the form of a unifying patriotism, but its bankruptcy became evident as war turned out to be a demoralizing and dehumanizing catastrophe. Facing the reality of the carnage, it was inevitable that the damaged French population would emerge from the war with incredulity, to say the least, about France's cultural status as "universalist" world leader.

While the France of the *Belle époque* was basking in the false illusion of a long-lasting and peaceful era, political tension had been escalating in Europe and in the world between liberal and democratic countries like France and England, and authoritarian empires like Germany and Austro-Hungary. Nationalism was on the rise and, in France in particular it was well ingrained in the heart of citizens and in the actions of politicians who since 1870 had cultivated a deep feeling of revenge against Germany. Despite opposition from the proponents of peace like Socialist Jean Jaurès, it was the single overwhelming political obsession of the French republican government to regain the ex-French territories of Alsace and Lorraine. More than a world conflict, France saw the war as a national revenge against Germany. In 1914, war seemed inevitable, as dialogue became increasingly difficult and the precarious balance between what Valéry called "order and disorder" was at the mercy of the smallest incident. For France, a combination of two incidents, one international and one national, led the country into the war.

Just over a month after the assassination of the Austrian Archduke Franz Ferdinand and his wife Sophie in Sarajevo on June 28, 1914, the international event that triggered the Great War, Jean Jaurès, the French political voice for peace, the Socialist deputy, founder of the leftist paper *l'Humanité* (1905), and defender of workers' reforms, was shot in the head while eating in a Parisian restaurant. The young man who killed him believed, like many other revanchistes, that Jaurès's appeal to negotiations with the Germans and a diplomatic resolution to the growing conflict meant that he was an enemy of France. In July 1914, the general outcry of "Jaurès is dead!" was a sign to the people in the streets that the world was on the brink of a major showdown. For many, his death meant that any hope for peace was lost and that war was truly inevitable. On August 4, the day of his funeral, Leon Jouhaux, head of the Socialist labor union, the *Confédération Générale du Travail* (CGT, General Confederation of Workers), spoke about the necessity for workers to obey the order to mobilize, issued by the French Government on August 1, in order to keep the country unified in a time of crisis, while remaining true to Jaurès's ideals of "human reconciliation" and the "pursuit of social happiness." Jouhaux's speech would revive the deep-seated principles of universalism that continuously guided France's republican mission at home and abroad, when he called on "soldiers of liberty" to fight in harmony with one another, despite any and all social differences, and to aim at restoring freedom to all nations of the world. His words echoed those of the president of France, Raymond Poincaré, who in a message to his parliament on the same day, coined the expression *l'Union Sacrée* (the Sacred Union) to describe the imperative for political and religious groups to look beyond their differences in order to present a united front to the enemy. On August 3, war was officially declared and French soldiers were immediately deployed to the Northern front where German troops, having crossed over to Belgium despite the country's neutrality, were already marching toward Paris, hoping to quickly reach the coastal area along the Channel. Stopped by a barrage of fire from the French and British armies, they would never reach the sea, and from that point on, the configuration of the war changed dramatically from an offensive and mobile war to a war of position and attrition. The front remained practically static for the rest of the war, cutting a deadly line in the northern part of France, where most of the casualties occurred.

In this army of spiritually united and motivated French soldiers, the Socialist Catholic poet Charles Péguy left without hesitation. His patriotism was consistent with the principles of the "Sacred Union" and with his own religious beliefs that Jesus' exemplary death should guide men on the battlefield. In his long classical poem written in 1913—7,644 lines, divided into 1,911 quatrains—entitled *Eve*, he evoked the patriotic sentiment that made death during a "just war" a happy return of a man's body to the goodness of a blessed earth. In the stanza made famous for its surge of patriotic appeal, Péguy borrowed a literary style developed by nineteenth-century popular songwriter Béranger and national poet and Republican politician Victor Hugo in his early *Odes and Ballads*. Inspired by a popular and lyrical literary heritage, Péguy thus wrote a poem where republican principles and Christian faith merged. *Eve* symbolized the possibility that ideological and social differences could be absorbed in the noble and universal virtues that were part of the shared heritage of all Frenchmen:

> Happy those who died for this carnal earth,
> But provided that it was in a just war.
> Happy are those who died for four corners of earth.
> Happy are those who died a solemn death.
> (Pléiade, 1028)

In a sense, the poem epitomized, albeit in a lyrical vein, the official rhetoric of the French Army, which presented war as a glorious moment for the Nation. According to this rhetoric, the time for revenge against Germany had finally arrived, but war was not, in the end, the heroic and chivalrous endeavor of official discourse. Yet, fearless and wrapped in his "Christian universalism," Péguy died in battle soon after the beginning of the conflict.

Immediately following the declaration of war, ruthless and bloody combats broke out leaving soldiers stunned by the unexpected brutality of the conflict, with a massive death toll resulting in part from a clear discrepancy between logistics and new developments in weapons technology: "Firepower for killing people had developed faster than transport for moving them" (Sowerwine, 107). Indeed, since the 1870 Franco–Prussian War, military power had grown significantly with the industrial age. Firearms were perfected, cannons were more accurate, tanks were invented in 1915 and deployed in 1916, and chemical warfare made its appearance. World War I was not a "mechanized war": common soldiers were on foot, while ranking officers used horses. In addition to the lack of protection for the troops, the often wet and cold climate in and around the northeast of France where the heaviest fighting took place was particularly rough during the war years, with colder than usual winters and rainy springs and falls. The battlegrounds were transformed into huge mud fields were men lived month after month in their frozen or flooded trenches (see figure 4.2).

Dossier 4.7   Jean Rouaud, *Fields of Glory* (1990)

World War I left lasting effects on French literature, from the poetry of those who, like Charles Péguy, died in the conflict, to contemporary fiction novelist Jean Rouaud's *Fields of Glory*, in which he tells the story of a present-day family still marked by the deep impact of the war. The novel won the prestigious Goncourt literary prize in 1990. In the following passage, Rouaud describes a new and deadly morning when the effects of biological warfare changed the color of daylight itself.

Earth ceased to be the magnificent blue ball that can be wondered at from outer space. Above Ypres a horrible greenish spot spread. Oh, admittedly the methane dawn of the world's first days was not exactly hospitable, the blue for which we are envied, the diffracted sunlight as we see it, is no more eternal than our lives. According to nature's seasons and man's inclemency, it will veer to purple or saffron, but this pistachio tinge along the Yser betokened an evil intention. Now the chlorinated fog infiltrates the network of communication trenches, seeps into dugouts (mere sections of trench covered with planks), nestles in potholes, creeps through the rudimentary partitions of casemates, plunges into underground chambers hitherto preserved by shells, pollutes food and water supplies, occupies space so methodically that frantic pain-racked men search vainly for a breath of fresh air. The first reflex was to bury your head in your jacket, but the bit of oxygen that it gives you is exhausted in three breaths. Out comes your head, you hold your breath as long as you can, before inhaling the horrible mixture. We have never really listened to those elderly twenty-year-olds, whose testimony would help us to retrace the paths of horror: the intolerable burning in the eyes, nose, and throat, the suffocating pain in the chest, the violent cough that tears the lungs and the pleura and brings bloody froth to the lips, the acrid vomiting that doubles up the body, the fallen whom death will soon garner, trampled by their strong comrades trying with their hands on the edge of the trench to hoist themselves out of it, to escape from this swarm of human worms, but their feet get tangled up in the telephone wires stapled to the parapet, and the resulting landslide uncovers tatters of last autumn's summarily buried bodies. Once above the ground, men struggle desperately through the green mist and the fetid mud. Suddenly a leg is sucked into a hole in the soft clay, the effort of pulling it out racks the lungs. Men fall into putrid puddles, their hands and feet coated with freezing mud, their bodies shaken by burning rales. And then, once out of the caustic green mist—O fresh transparent air—the time-honored methods of warfare took over, and the survivors are raked by an intense bombardment. (123–124)

A similar setting representing the bleak violence and hopelessness on the battlefields of World War I appears in French director Jean Jeunet's *A Very Long Engagement* (2003). A young woman whose fiancé is declared missing in action refuses to believe that he has died, and begins investigating the few clues that would help her reconstruct the story of his battalion and the events that led to his disappearance. Many graphic scenes take the viewer to moments similar to those described by Rouaud, while Jeunet's use of sepia tones remind us of Rouaud's palette of gangrenous greens and toxic yellows that typified the gas-infected landscape. Shades of unhealthy yellows also dominated British painter John Singer Sargent's 1918–1919 *Gassed*. The painting was commissioned by the British government, which saw in Sargent's impressionist style the appropriate approach. With *Gassed*, Sargent was far from his usual representation of bourgeois British society. The painting depicts two rows of blindfolded and exhausted soldiers protecting their eyes from the deadly gasses, while many more lay dead or dying on the already saturated ground.

The British suffered many casualties and held the unenviable record for fighting, with some help from the French army and its colonial regiment one of the bloodiest and most merciless battles of World War I, the Battle of the Somme (1918), where on the first day alone 60,000 lives were lost to German machine guns. In 1916, the French fought an equally bloody 10-month battle in and around the northeastern town of Verdun in which 360, 000 French and 335,000 German soldiers died. The French had to constantly evacuate their dead, sometimes at least 3,000 per day, and brought new soldiers to Verdun through a narrow corridor, the only open road, renamed the "Sacred Way," leading in and out of an almost completely surrounded Verdun. General Philippe Pétain, who would become premier of France after the German occupation of France during World War II, was the commanding officer. The battle began on February 21, 1916 and escalated into a series of bloody offensives that resulted in a horrendous number of casualties, as the official strategy of the German army was "to bleed France to the last drop." So many French soldiers were killed that the army was happy to receive reinforcement from the colonial infantry from Morocco, which helped win a battle for France, as the Moroccans defended and gained one of Verdun's strategic outposts at Douaumont. At the end of the war, France would recognize its debt toward the colonial armies of Africa, Asia, America, and Oceania. In a 1918 commemorative poster drawn by artist Victor Prouvé and entitled "What We Owe to Our Colonies," the text accompanying the drawing of an Arab horseman ready for battle reflects the French government's defense of its colonial policy. The poster publicly recognized the support of France's colonies in times of war, and concluded on a hopeful note regarding the future relations between the colonies and the *metropole*: "In common effort will grow common affection." Here again, we hear the universalist voice of the republic that seems to have erased the differences between the races and between the colonizer and the colonized.

Over the course of war, death was color-blind and universal indeed. At Verdun, after almost a full year of ferocious attacks by both sides, and despite the higher number of casualties on the French side, France held on to its territory and declared victory over the Germans, but close to 800, 000 soldiers had died in a battle in which no real advance was made.

Throughout the twentieth century, some of France's most respected writers conveyed the sense that World War I had left a gaping wound in the French collective memory. We can read evidence of so much hardship in literature throughout the century, from Marcel Proust's *Time Regained*, published in 1927 (see dossier 4.8), Louis-Ferdinand Céline's *Voyage to the End of Night* (1932), Jules Romains in *Verdun* (1938), to the recent *Fields of Honor* by Jean Rouaud (see dossier 4.7).

Dossier 4.8   Marcel Proust, *Time Regained*, Saint Loup's last letter (1927)

In Marcel Proust's *Time Regained*, the posthumously published final installment of *Remembrance of Things Past*, the narrative is almost entirely set against the background of World War I. The narrator remembers the village where he spent his summers, his walks, the presence of German soldiers and the devastation of his favorite places. Paris has also changed even if elegant society seemed to continue to live in style. Count Robert de Saint Loup has chosen to leave Paris and his aristocratic milieu and to go to the front. In his letter to the narrator, Saint Loup expresses the sentiment that war has revealed the beauty of all men, their fraternity and heroism, as if fighting in a French uniform offered a universal brotherhood and eliminated class differences. The word commonly used to refer to the French soldiers of World War I *les poilus* (the hairy ones), points less to the boorishness of rough and dirty men than to their courage and virility. Bound by heroism to men of humbler social classes on the battlefield, Saint Loup becomes a perfect example of the social unity that existed between soldiers under the banner of the "Sacred Union."

My dear boy,

If you could see every boy here, particularly the men of the humbler classes, working men and small shop keepers, who did not suspect what heroism they concealed within them and might have died in their beds without suspecting it—if you could see them running under fire to help a comrade or carry off a wounded officer and then, when they have been hit themselves, smiling a few moments before they die because the medical officer has told them that the trench has been recaptured from the Germans, I assure you, my dear boy, it gives you a magnificent idea of the French people, makes you begin to understand those great periods in history which seemed to us a little extraordinary when we learned about them as students. The epic is so magnificent that you would find, as I do, that words no longer matter . . . At the touch of such greatness, the word poilu has for me become something of which I no more feel that it may originally have contained an allusion or a joke than one does, for instance, when one reads about the chouans. But I do know that poilu is already waiting for great poets, like other words, "deluge," or "Christ," or "barbarians," which were already filled with greatness before Hugo, Vigny and the rest made

use of them. As I say, the people, the workingmen, are the best of all, but everybody is splendid.
(Time Regained, 775)

At a time when France was fighting to regain Alsace and Lorraine from the Germans and when Germans were the object of intense hatred, Saint Loup opts for the argument of the universality of men beyond French borders, and attenuates military oppositions by evoking the universal power of justice which will prevail for the French as well as for the Germans: "We know that victory will be ours and we are determined that it shall be, so that we can dictate a just peace, I don't mean 'just' simply for ourselves, but truly just, just to the French and just to the Germans" (754). The concept of a "just peace" as part of the "universalism of war" is consistent with Péguy's own notion of a "just war" mentioned above.

Neither Proust nor Péguy, in spite of the latter's willingness to die in battle, presented themselves as apologists for a nationalist political agenda. Such was not the case for Maurice Barrès who openly promoted his vision of a glorious war fought for the honor and glory of France in his *Chronique de la Grande Guerre* (*Chronicle of the Great War*, 1915), a work where the human component seems to have disappeared behind a wall of patriotic fervor. Barrès's exacerbated nationalism and his vision of war as glorious enterprise, and the more idealistic images of a community of soldiers were offset by more realistic depictions of war, such as pacifist writer Henri Barbusse's *Under Fire*. Published in 1916, the book was an instant international success and was awarded the Goncourt. Subtitled "The Diary of a Squad," Barbusse's novel is a grim account of the appalling experience of life in the blood and mud of the trenches; it is devoid of the grandiose rhetoric of Barrès's *Chronicle* and the lyricism of brotherhood that one encounters in Péguy's poetry or Saint Loup's letter, and rings vividly true.

The literature about World War I thus reflected a range of positions. While some writers and intellectuals advocated war as a duty and as an act of heroism, inflaming the minds of young men with statements such as this one from French philosopher Henri Bergson, "All the world knows that the struggle against Germany is civilization against barbarism" (in Strachan, 1123), others perceived inflated nationalism and the presentation of war as glorious or chivalric mission, to be dying political strategies and values. Oddly enough, "universalism," in one form or another pervaded the discourse of all parties. In opposition to Péguy and Proust, "universalism" for Barbusse could not be found in the heroic and the sacred, or in the leveling of class distinctions, but rather in the *indiscriminate* and senseless waste of human lives that defined this war. In an episode of *Under Fire* when, after a ferocious battle, the exhausted remaining soldiers retreat to the back trench Barbusse writes: "The universal noise of destruction was silent" (97); men from both sides had fallen on the "universal field of death" and could no longer be distinguished from one another:

> From very close, we notice that the heaps of dirt sitting on top of the ruins in this narrow path are human beings. Are they dead? Maybe asleep? No one knows. One of them opens his eyes and is looking at us while shaking his head. We ask: "French?" then "Deutsch?" He doesn't answer, closes his eyes and returns to his abyss of sorrow. We never found out who he was. (268)

German and French soldiers were *equally* united in death, and their experience *universally* unbearable and inhuman regardless of their nationality, as demonstrated in this famous passage from German soldier and writer Erich Maria Remarque's *All Quiet on the Western Front*:

> I am young, I am twenty years old; yet I know nothing of life but despair, death, fear, and fatuous superficiality cast over an abyss of sorrow. Through the years our business has been killing—it was our first calling in life. Our knowledge of life is limited to death. What will happen afterwards? And what shall come out of us? (266–267)

Before so much despair and such a bleak future, the only glimmer of hope often resided in the letters soldiers exchanged with loved ones. To maintain the morale of the troops, mail was delivered regularly and soldiers were encouraged to write. While it is true that much of this two-way correspondence kept soldiers "alive"—letters from home kept a number of soldiers from committing suicide— as they were able to relate their ordeal in writing, the reality of the situation was challenged by the inadequacy of language to represent it.

The barbarity of war and the loss of human identity was a common theme in many soldiers' accounts: "We were going over there, where you die, where your face is mangled, your body dismembered and torn to pieces" (Henri Aimé Gauthié, *Journal de guerre*, in *Paroles de Poilus*, 14); "You cannot identify these poor creatures" (*Under Fire*, 268). Many soldiers found it impossible to even put their experience into words: "How can you describe it? What words can you use ?" (*Paroles de Poilus*, 50).

Words seemed insufficient to describe the atrocities of war, "over there," on the front and in the trenches, where the butchery of bodies robbed the soldiers, both French and German, of their chance of being recognized and claimed by loved ones. Death was painful enough, but to make matters worse for families at home, additional suffering was caused by the impossibility of identifying dismembered and disfigured bodies, twisted flesh, mutilated bodies without names.

To write about the war was difficult; to represent its gruesome reality seemed impossible. If letters from the front carried a certain reality, an individual materiality, they described more than just facts of war, namely a variety of feelings that would not otherwise be expressed. In the end, when words could not capture events that seemed so contrary to reason, many soldiers wrote letters inspired by a world of domestic fantasy. Letters often drew on a style that borrowed its language and images from an imagined world of a perfect domestic situation, thus creating a fantasy of wives patiently waiting for their heroes to return and of men swearing their eternal love to women they had left behind.

At the end of the war, the idealized world that had been created in letters did not materialize when men returned home to a new domestic environment where women, having gained an active social status by working during the war, felt that they now had an economic say in family life. Where returning soldiers felt unappreciated for their act of heroism and traumatized by the horrors they had experienced, their wives felt equally misunderstood in their newly gained economic independence. The letters to and from the front had reinforced a myth of domestic happiness for soldiers at the very moment when it was being destroyed by the economics of wartime, which played a major role in the emancipation of women and, inevitably, to a reassessment of French universalism.

Women during and after the War

France lost 1,358,000 men, while over 4 million were declared war invalids. This represented the highest number of casualties of all fighting nations, with Germany coming in a close second. Globally, nearly 10 million perished during the 4-year war. Death, injuries, and absence deeply changed the balance of European societies. In wartime France, from Dunkerque to Marseille, from Nantes to Lyon, women began a "forced emancipation" by working outside the home, thus keeping the French economy afloat while men were fighting. It is ironic that the ferocious reality of war rather than the long-established political demand for women to become voting citizens had created an opportunity for social progress, while the nation was mourning its war victims, and morale was at its lowest. It is even more ironic to consider the official invitation women received to become workers during the war, when many still remembered the admonition of nineteenth-century French historian Michelet about the "horrifying" association of women and factories:

> How much more guilty are those who took women, who opened to the wretchedness of the city girl, to the blindness of the peasant, the fatal resource of an exterminating labor, and the promiscuity of factories . . . woman worker! Operative! an impious, sordid word, which no language ever had, which no period could have ever understood before this iron age, and which alone could counterbalance all our pretended progress. (*Woman*, 23)

In 1914, the war effort put the nation's economy in a state of emergency that required gender considerations be set aside. Women became workers in spite of pre-existing social interdictions. In fact, both women and children were officially called to serve the nation and honor their fighting husbands and fathers by working in the fields, factories, and offices in order to make up for manpower shortage. At the onset of the war, in a very eloquent speech rife with the same patriotic overtones of other speeches calling men to war, President René Viviani invited women to become the economic backbone of the nation and to volunteer at hospitals and charitable organizations. Women responded en masse. While they were praised for their work during the war, by the end of the conflict, they were being condemned for not returning to their prewar condition. Some women did gladly return to their domestic lives, but others found it difficult to give up the independence they had gained during the four-year separation from their men.

One of the most widespread notions of the postwar was that professionally active women would now adopt styles that made them less feminine. After the war, the tendency for many women was to wear more comfortable and sober clothes; they started smoking and many adopted a shorter hairstyle, a sort of neckline bob, which became the rage of the 1920s and replaced the long hair that had characterized femininity up until then. Dréan, a popular singer and comedian of the postwar period had great success with his song *Elle s'était fait couper les ch'veux* (She'd had her hair cut short) in which a stunned man tells the story of his wife, mother, and grandmother's new short hairstyles. The chorus repeated how pleasant, comfortable, and fashionable short hair was for women who now enjoyed dressing—and "acting like men." In 1922, *La Garçonne*—translated as *The Bachelor Girl* or *The Tomboy*—a novel written by Victor Margueritte, created a scandal with Monique, its "boyish" main character, an emancipated and freethinking woman who, after being abandoned by her fiancé, changes her style, cuts her hair, smokes cigarettes, and embarks on a series of sexual escapade. Her multiple lesbian experiences shocked French conservatives who went so far as to demote Margueritte from his honorific title of Knight of the Legion of Honor, an order created in 1802 by Napoleon and awarded each year to exemplary individuals who performed exceptionally in a military or civil service. To be deknighted by the Chancellor of the Order was a rare sanction, but this did not prevent Margueritte from being acclaimed by the French people who made *La Garçonne* one of the bestsellers of 1922. However, Margueritte's intention was far from writing a "feminist" manifesto or even a book promoting the "liberation" of women; his objective was to challenge censorship. He opened the novel with a warning expressing his disagreement with women's liberation: women who sought liberation would fall to vice and depravity.

The year 1922 was also the year when the Senate turned down a proposal granting women the right to vote, a proposal that the Deputies of the Assembly had adopted in 1919. French women were infuriated, wondering why they could not be taken seriously as citizens by their own government, especially when a majority of modern and western nations had already granted women the right to vote— immediately after the war, in England, Germany, Poland, and Russia, and in 1920 in the United States. French women would not be granted the right to vote until 1945. After the Great War many women felt betrayed, as it seemed obvious to them that their effort during the conflict would never be rewarded by an ungrateful and conservative administration. While culturally manifest in certain instances, their "liberation" would remain politically inconclusive, and so-called universal suffrage would continue to exclude women. Universalism felt more and more like an idealist notion rather than a concrete practice.

References

Agulhon, Maurice. *Marianne au pouvoir*. Paris: Flammarion, 1989.

———. *Quand Paris dansait avec Marianne*. Paris: Editions Paris-Musées, 1989.

Agulhon, Maurice and Pierre Bonte. *Marianne, les visages de la République*. Paris: Découvertes-Gallimard, 1992.

Apollinaire. *Calligrammes*. Paris: Gallimard, 1966.

———. *Poèmes à Lou*. Paris: Gallimard, 1969.

Bard, Christine. *Un siècle d'antiféminisme*. Paris: Fayard, 1999.

Barthes, Roland. *Mythologies*. Paris: Seuil, 1957.

Bredin, Jean-Denis. *L'Affaire*. Paris: Julliard, 1983.

Colette. *Oeuvres II*. Paris: Gallimard (Pléiade), 1986.

Coubertin de, Pierre. *Olympism: Selected Writings*. Lausanne: International Olympic Committee, 2000.

Forbes, Jill and Michael Kelly. *French Cultural Studies: An Introduction*. Oxford: Oxford University Press, 1995.

Frollo, Jean. "Les trois étapes." *Le Petit Parisien*, April 15, 1900.

Gauguin, Paul. *The Writings of a Savage*. Danile Guérin, ed. Wayne Andersen, intro. Eleanor Levieux, trans. New York: Viking Press, 1974, 1978.

———. *Noa Noa*. Nicholas Wadley, ed. Jonathan Griffin, trans. Salem, NH: Salem House, 1985.

Green, Christopher, ed. *Picasso's Les Demoiselles d'Avignon*. Cambridge: Cambridge University Press, 2001.

Huard, Raymond. *La Naissance du parti politique en France*. Paris: Presses de Sciences Politiques, 1976.

Huysmans, J.K. *Against the Grain*. Havelock Ellis, intro. New York: Illustrated Editions Company, 1931.

Laget, Serge. *La Saga du Tour de France*. Paris: Gallimard (Découvertes), 1990.

Leroy, Géraldi. *Péguy entre l'ordre et la revolution*. Paris: Presses de la Fondation Nationale des Sciences Politiques 1981.

Margueritte, Victor. *La Garçonne—La femme en chemin*. Paris: Flammarion, 1922, 1949.

Michelet, Jules. *Woman—La Femme*. J.W. Palmer, trans. New York: Rudd and Carleton, 1867.

Mignon, Patrick. "Sport and Politics: Another French Exception." In Emmanuel Godin and Tony Chafer, eds. *The French Exception*. New York, London: Berghan Books, 2005, 179–192.

Paroles de Poilus—Lettres et carnets du front (1914–1918). Jean-PierreGuéno and Yves Laplume, eds. Paris: Radio France—Librio, 1998.

Pagnol, Marcel. *My Father's Glory and My Mother's Castle (Memories of Childhood)*. Rita Barisse, trans. San Francisco: North Point Press, 1986.

———. *Oeuvres completes III—Souvenirs et romans*. Paris: Editions de Fallois, 1995.

Péguy, Charles. *Oeuvres en prose complètes 1*. Paris: Gallimard (Pléiade), 1987.

Perrot, Michelle. "Preface." In F. Thébaud, ed. *La femme au temps de la guerre de 14*. Paris: Stock, 1986.

Prochasson, Christophe. *Paris 1900: Essai d'histoire culturelle*. Paris: Calman-Lévy, 1999.

Proust, Marcel. *Remembrance of Things Past: Swann's Way, within a Budding Grove*. Vol. 1. C.K. Scott Moncrieff and Terrence Kilmartin, trans. New York: Random House, 1981.

———. *Remembrance of Things Past: The Captive, the Fugitive, Time Regained*. Vol. 3. C.K. Scott Moncrieff, Terrence Kilmartin, and Andreas Mayor, trans. New York: Random House, 1985.

Remarque, Erich Maria. *All Quiet on the Western Front*. Boston: Little and Brown Company, 1929.

Rioux, Jean-Pierre and Jean-François Sirinelli. *Histoire culturelle de la France. Le temps des masses: Le vingtième sciècle*. Paris: Seuil, 1998.

Rouaud, Jean. *Fields of Glory*. Ralph Manheim, trans. New York: Arcade Publishing, 1992.

Sowerwine, Charles. *France from 1870 to 2000*. New York: Palgrave, 2000.

Stamelman, Richard. *Perfume: Joy, Scandal, Sin—A Cultural History of Fragrance from 1750 to the Present*. New York: Rizzoli, 2006.

Strachan, Hew. *The First World War*. Oxford: Oxford University Press, 2003.

Tartakowsky, Danielle. *Le Pouvoir est dans la rue*. Paris: Aubier, 1998.

Valéry, Paul. *Collected Works, Vol. 10—History and Politics*. Denise Folliot and Jackson Mathews, trans. London: Routledge & Kegan Paul, 1956.

Winock, Michel. *La Belle Epoque. La France de 1900 à 1914*. Paris: Perrin, 2002.

CHAPTER 5

FROM THE "CRAZY YEARS" TO THE "DARK YEARS" (1918–1944)

The universe exploded. The artillery shell was coming, and I knew it was coming. Enormous, as huge as the universe. It filled the finite universe exactly. It was a convulsion of the universe itself. . . . Men who no longer know how to sculpt statues or write operas are only good for cutting iron into little bits.

—Drieu La Rochelle, "The Artillery Lieutenant" (1934)

Little ladies more
than dead exactly dance
in my head, precisely
dance where danced la guerre
—e.e. Cummings, *Poems* (1923)

After the "Great War"

The contrast between France in wartime, when "the universe exploded," and in the exciting post-war years was dramatic and extreme. Where war had savagely killed, "little ladies" were now dancing. Exhilarating pleasures and discoveries had quickly replaced the gloomy horrors of war. France was entering *les années folles*, the "crazy years."

However ebullient the 1920s seemed, they were also a therapeutic necessity for a traumatized and reckless post-war generation ready to live again after a deadly war that had shown the bankruptcy of Western values and institutions. For those who lived during this "post-traumatic" period, recovery by way of personal and creative "craziness" seemed a necessary exorcising step before life could resume a more "normal" pace. The young Parisian revelers of the 1920s were living through a transitional period of exhilaration and experimentation, a time when they were breaking the rules after the dark interlude of war.

While Paris provided young people with all the freedom they craved for, despair was still hovering in the air. Some French writers, who aspired to restore the glory of prewar France, did not hide their bitterness toward their country's failure to maintain its status as both pre-eminent and "exceptional" nation, a truly universal republic. This ideal seemed to have met its limits in the trenches of World War I.

The disaster of war had irremediably broken through the illusion of endless "progress" that had been central to the advent of modernity. The war also represented a spectacular refutation of some of the basic principles of French universalism, leaving in its wake a fragmented nation and a host of new cultural trends and political ideologies, ranging from surrealism to communism. The concept of a culturally and politically dominant French nation was now displaying its limits. In fact, republican universalism sometimes seemed to be in direct contradiction with the reality of the times. France's dominant status had received a major blow with World War I and, while the country continued to be an important player on the world scene, it was becoming increasingly clear that the Third Republic's dream of building an "exceptional nation" had entered a critical phase that would culminate during World War II.

Negotiating the Peace

With the armistice of November 11, 1918, the Great War was finally over, leaving the world with more than 9 million dead, 17 million wounded, many permanent invalids having to adjust to their new physical challenges and deformities, like the easily recognizable *gueules cassées* (broken faces or disfigured mugs) who wore their veteran status on their frightfully mangled faces. In France, one out of six mobilized soldiers did not return home, for a total of about one and a half million casualties. The war had killed 10 percent of the French male population. Such a crippling massacre prompted many to believe—naively, as it turned out—that this war was to be *la der des der*, the last of the last, the war to end all wars. Few could fathom that such a devastating experience could occur again, especially if the right measures were taken to ensure the security and cooperation of all parties. The Peace Treaty of Versailles turned out not to be such a measure. It was signed on June 28, 1919 by the "winners," France, Great Britain, Italy, and the United States. Germany was not invited to the negotiating table, and contested the terms of the treaty. Many Germans never recognized the legitimacy of the treaty, which they considered a shameful "diktat." In his memoirs Chancellor Prince von Bülow expressed the bitter feelings of Germany toward the treaty:

> Never, on no other people, has so crushing, so ignominious a peace been so brutally imposed as was the shameful treaty of Versailles . . . But such an un-negotiated agreement as this dictated Peace of Versailles is as little a true agreement between nations as would be a transfer of property for an individual whom a footpad had knocked down and forced to give up his purse. (*Memoirs*, 350–351)

As per the terms of the treaty, Germany lost all its colonies; and France regained the eastern regions of Alsace and Lorraine; Poland was given the Danzig corridor, thus separating East Prussia from the rest of Germany; the German army was reduced to a maximum of 100,000 men; the Ruhr Valley, situated near Germany's new border with France and an area rich in energy resources, was demilitarized, and the Rhine river banks were to be occupied by the Allied military forces for the next fifteen years. Germany was also required to pay substantial war reparations to France. What seemed a permanent amputation of German political power and economy was the result of a compromise reached by the four presiding nations, each protecting national interests before ensuring international peace, thus demonstrating that the stated objective of world peace might have just been a face-saving diplomatic decoy to justify the treaty's stringent provisions. Contrary to the spirit of peaceful understanding and balanced negotiations, each nation acted in its own interests and with deep suspicion of the others: Great Britain did not want to see France emerge from the war as perhaps the most powerful European nation; Italy was unhappy for not receiving the Austrian regions it was promised during the war—it obtained Trieste but not Fiume-Rijeka; the Americans were watching the new political developments in Russia closely after the successful takeover by the Communist revolutionaries in 1917, and American public opinion was not favorable to any formal involvement in Europe. With so many divergent interests at stake it is not surprising that Treaty of Versailles did not survive very long in its original form. The major point of contention was the degree of punishment to be inflicted on Germany when, at the same time, communism was rapidly gaining ground.

In this unpromising international context, a number of European and American politicians nevertheless hoped to establish the bases of a lasting international peace. The creation in 1920 of the League of Nations, a precursor to the United Nations, was a step in this direction. Under the terms of the covenant drafted in the light of American president Woodrow Wilson's "Fourteen Points," "Any war or threat of war, whether immediately affecting any of the Members of the League or not, is hereby declared a matter of concern to the whole League, and the League shall take any action that may be deemed wise and effectual to safeguard the peace of nations" (article 11, in Green, 5). The League of Nations lost one of its major supporters when Wilson was voted out of office in 1920, and the United States, after lobbying for the creation of the League of Nations and helping define its main principles, withdrew into isolationism. Germany, on the other hand, was finally allowed to join the League in 1926. Aristide Briand, a prominent French politician and diplomat, who would win the Nobel Peace Prize that same year, saw the entry of Germany into the League of Nations as a momentous occasion. In his Geneva speech delivered at the headquarters of the League of Nations, Briand spoke about the "universal peace" and the emotions surrounding the diplomatic effort that had made it possible for Germany to join the League of Nations:

> It is such a moving, edifying, and comforting spectacle that only a few years after the most terrifying and overwhelming war the world has ever known, and while battlefields are still humid with blood, that people, the same people who clashed so violently, could meet in this pacifist assembly and reaffirm their common will to collaborate on the work of universal peace. (Wieviorka, 285)

"Universal" peace remained, however, more an abstract concept than a political reality as the European powers remained in disagreement on a number of international issues, especially "the German question." As for the Americans, their absence from the League of Nations would soon be offset in the area of culture by the grand arrival of their writers, jazz musicians, and entertainers on the European scene.

The Americans Are Coming

If you are lucky enough to have lived in Paris as a young man, then wherever you go for the rest of your life, it stays with you, for Paris is a moveable feast.

—Ernest Hemingway, *A Moveable Feast.*

If the pretense of universalism still had a tight grip on the political institutions of France in the years after World War I, it was quite the opposite in the area of culture, where the only universal value was to refuse a failing universalism. Artists and writers who had lived and suffered through the war reinvented a postwar culture more in tune with their mix of disillusionment and energy. They claimed their rights to individuality and originality however "crazy" they might appear, and declared their own war on the Arts. After World War I, French culture looked for inspiration beyond its borders. Poetry became "surreal," painting "mechanical" and "abstract"; common objects were celebrated in "ready-mades"; classical symphonic music incorporated the everyday sounds, jazzy rhythms, and "disharmonies" of a new musical esthetic.

"Craziness" was definitely in the air and it ignited every foreigner who came to Paris. As Ernest Hemingway recalled in his Parisian memoirs (*A Moveable Feast*), "But this is how Paris was in the early days when we were very poor and very happy" (211). Hemingway was one of a number of American writers from the United States who had converged on Paris after the war. During this period, many of them made their home-away-from-home in Montparnasse, in the fourteenth arrondissement of the French capital. Located on the left bank, it was a popular hangout for many Americans who would gather in cafés like Le Dôme, Le Select, La Coupole, and La Closerie des Lilas. Montparnasse had replaced Montmartre, a neighborhood situated on a northern hill of Paris in the eighteenth arrondissement, site of the beginnings of the 1871 "Commune" (see chapter 2). In the last decades of the nineteenth century and the first of the twentieth, a veritable colony of artists and writers, among them, Gauguin, Apollinaire, and Picasso, lived and worked in the village-like atmosphere of Montmartre with its surrounding fields and vineyards. At the end of the war, the growing need for large and cheap living and working space gradually brought many of these artists and writers to more modern and central Montparnasse where the mood was, as it had been in Montmartre, cosmopolitan, but this time with a strong American flavor. The success of jazz and the daring nude dance performances by the black American entertainer Josephine Baker was then sweeping through Paris on a wave of American popular culture referred to as "*la folie américaine*," or "American madness" (Goetschel and Loyer, 41).

Americans, including political luminaries Thomas Jefferson, Ben Franklin, and Thomas Paine, all of whom inspired by France's social and political history, had been regularly coming to France since the eighteenth century. Throughout the nineteenth century, a less political and more literary and artistic contingent including the novelist Henry James, and Impressionist painters John Singer Sargent and Mary Cassatt, spent a great deal of time in France. More Americans came before World War I: independent-minded women such as novelist Edith Wharton (*The Age of Innocence*, 1920) and writer and art collector Gertrude Stein whose portrait was painted by Picasso. Stein presided over a famous "salon" in her Parisian apartment in the rue de Fleurus, close to the cafés and bars of Montparnasse: "26 rue de Fleurus" became one of the emblematic meeting places of the 1920s generation of both established and unknown American writers and artists. During the war came poet e.e. Cummings (*Vive la folie*, 1926), novelist John Dos Passos (*Journey Between Wars*, 1928) and bookshop owner and publisher Sylvia Beach who opened her bookstore-lending library "Shakespeare and Company" in 1919 and was the first to publish James Joyce's *Ulysses*, in 1922. After the war, future American literary giants like Ernest Hemingway and F. Scott Fitzgerald became regulars at Gertrude Stein's apartment and acquired fame through publications such as Hemingway's *The Sun also Rises* (1926) and Fitzgerald's *Tender Is the Night* (1934) and short stories like "Babylon Revisited" (1931). Others would follow: Henry Miller in the 1930s, James Baldwin in the 1940s, and the Beat generation in the 1950s.

What was the attraction for these writers and other Americans? At the end of the war, many young Americans were fascinated by the spirit of artistic—and sexual—freedom and creativity that permeated Paris. Postwar Paris, bohemian and glamorous, represented something of a rite of passage for many newcomers who were escaping the puritanical and commercial environment of the United States. For Gertrude Stein, who had been living in the city since 1902, Paris was simply the place where art and literature of the twentieth century would be reinvented.

During the war, the so called literary ambulance drivers became the first significant generation of American writers to experience the horrors of war firsthand. John Dos Passos and e.e. Cummings worked as ambulance drivers for volunteer organizations that became associated with the U.S. Medical Corps in Paris when the United States entered the war, while Hemingway did the same for the Red Cross in Italy. Women were not allowed directly on the front, but Edith Wharton and Gertrude Stein did volunteer to work on war-related tasks. Stein drove for the *American Fund for French Wounded* and helped relocate French families, and Wharton drove Red Cross supplies to hospitals near the Western Front, even going to Verdun; she described her experience in her 1915 essay *Fighting France*. Apart from these writers, there was also a large group of war journalists adding to the number of Americans in Europe in general and in France in particular.

These prewar and wartime generations of Americans in Paris created a vibrant American community that outlasted the war itself. As this community gained a sort of notoriety, new visitors, whether artists or tourists, came to Paris, hoping to meet any member of the "lost generation," as they had been labeled by Gertrude Stein in a tense exchange with Hemingway, which he relates in *A Moveable Feast* (see dossier 5.1). They often came with pages of a first or unfinished novel, or a few poems in their luggage, and visited the salons of Gertrude Stein or Edith Wharton, when invited or introduced by a "regular"; or they stopped by Sylvia Beach's bookstore or visit its French equivalent, Adrienne Monnier's (Beach's lifetime partner) bookstore. There, the newcomers could meet writers, especially American, British, and Irish and attend their readings. There clearly was an American "literary Paris" but mainly the tourists and "hangers-on" who came to the French capital in the post-war 1920s simply fell in love with the city of all possibilities, an ebullient urban center filled with charm and excitement. In Paris one could come across characters like "Kiki" the sexually liberated model and actress who lived and entertained in Montparnasse, sang, posed nude, and became the muse of many painters, sculptors, and photographers like the American Surrealist photographer and filmmaker Man Ray: "I met an American who makes pretty photos. I will pose nude for him. I like his accent and his mysterious look . . . He is now my lover . . . To me, Montparnasse is the country of all liberties. People here are very liberal. It is so picturesque and colorful. It seems that people from around the world have settled here, yet it feels like a great big family" (*Souvenirs*, 168). Kiki's memoirs, translated in 1930, with an introduction by Hemingway, was not authorized in the United States until the late 1970s, as it was judged too risqué by American standards. There is no doubt that Paris in the 1920s symbolized sexual liberation for many puritanically educated young Americans like the self-declared repressed virgin e.e. Cummings, or for the conflicted and inhibited small-town Americans described in novels by Sherwood Anderson (*Winesburg, Ohio*, 1919), but also for gays, lesbians, and bisexuals like the Gertrude Stein and her companion Alice B. Toklas, or the jazz composer Cole Porter. Paris, in short, was a haven from the world ironically described in Sinclair Lewis' *Babbitt* (1922) in which the eponymous main character declares:

> Most important, our Standardized Citizen, even if he is a bachelor, is a lover of the Little Ones, a supporter of the hearthstone which is the basic foundation of our civilization, first, last, and all the time, and the thing that most distinguishes us from the decayed nations of Europe. I have never yet toured Europe—and as a matter of fact, I don't know that I care to such an awful lot, as long as there's our own mighty cities and mountains to be seen—but, the way I figure it out, there must be a good many of our own sort of folks abroad. (185)

Those who came and stayed in Paris for a while, the expatriates, or "expats," formed a large network of Americans who had come to reinvent themselves or simply to bask in the city of modernity. In Hemingway's 1926 novel *The Sun Also Rises*, one of the characters, clearly not the authors' favorite, defines the expats as lost souls whose experience in Europe has ruined their sense of morals, their sense of an American identity defined by work and productivity: "You're an expatriate. You've lost touch with the soil. You get precious. Fake European standards have ruined you. You drink yourself to death. You become obsessed by sex. You spend all your time talking, not working. You are an expatriate, see? You hang around cafés" (115).

Dossier 5.1   Ernest Hemingway's *A Moveable Feast* (1952)

For Hemingway, poor and restless in the Paris of the "early days," the city offered the possibility of long, physically taxing, but satisfying walks. Like the French nineteenth-century poet Arthur Rimbaud, Hemingway walked everywhere for the energy and the exercise, but like the dandy French poet Charles Baudelaire he also walked as a *flâneur*, a leisurely and aimless wanderer in the great modern city. To him, the winding Seine was a beautiful sight as well as an interesting fishing spot. The cafés were places to write, drink, and stay warm during the winter.

It is during one of his many visits to Gertrude Stein's apartment on rue de Fleurus that he picked up, not without some criticism, the expression "lost generation" from Stein's depiction of Americans in Paris.

It was when we had come back from Canada and were living in the rue Notre-Dame-des-Champs and Miss Stein and I were still good friends that Miss Stein made the remark about the lost generation. She had some ignition trouble with the old Model T Ford she then drove and the young man who worked in the garage and had served in the last year of the war had not been adept, or perhaps had not broken the priority of other vehicles, in repairing Miss Stein's Ford. Anyway he had not been sérieux and had been corrected severely by the patron of the garage after Miss Stein's protest. The patron had said to him, "You are all a génération perdue."

"That's what you are. That's what you all are," Miss Stein said. "All of you young people who served in the war. You are a lost generation." "Really?" I said.

"You are," she insisted. "You have no respect for anything. You drink yourself to death . . ."

"Really?" I said . . .

"Don't argue with me, Hemingway," Miss Stein said. "It does no good at all. You're all a lost generation, exactly as the garage keeper said." (34–35)

Hemingway's apparently simple, pared-down style would prove to be a major turning point in American realism and gained him a mythical standing. Hemingway himself laconically declares in *A Movable Feast* that all one had to do was to "write one true sentence. Write the truest sentence that you know" (12). Hemingway also claims in these memoirs that he learned to "write like a painter" in Paris, specifically after he saw post-Impressionist painter Paul Cézanne's work: "I was learning something from the painting of Cézanne that made writing one simple true sentence far from enough to make stories have the dimensions that I was trying to put in them. I was learning very much from him . . . it was a secret" (13). The simple geometrical compositions and the repeated motifs of Cézanne's landscapes, portraits, and still lives became a guiding and underlying force behind Hemingway's "post-Impressionistic prose." Hemingway also learned much from Cézanne's perspective shifts. Beyond Cézanne and Hemingway, this French influence can be generalized to include an entire generation of American expatriate writers who found a place to live and work in post-war Paris. It could be said that France found a subtle place in American culture by way of this "lost generation"'s artistic, cultural, and human experience of the city.

Where American writers "filtered" the experience of France through their work, the French imported the popular culture of America. The French were fascinated by American popular culture, which was growing rapidly as an industry and offered an impressive variety of entertainment. The appeal was irresistible and America became the forerunner and disseminator of a recognizably "modern" popular culture in France and other parts of Europe.

From the 1920s on, American popular culture began its remarkable foray into France especially by way of jazz, nightclub entertainment, and a "second wave" would begin with the arrival in 1930 of the Mickey Mouse comic strips published in the French newspaper *Le Petit Parisien* and with the introduction in 1934 of the *Journal de Mickey*, a children's magazine fully dedicated to Mickey and his Disney family, and still in press and as popular as ever today.

Figure 5.1 Josephine Baker (1926)

Born from a poor family in Saint Louis, Minnesota, she came to Paris in 1925 where she became an overnight sensation at the cabaret known as La Revue Nègre (the Black Review). On stage, she often danced in a banana skirt, and not much else, a daring yet amusing outfit that made her famous. Baker was probably the most celebrated cabaret artist of the time in France. (© L'Illustration)

Josephine Baker, "the Black Venus," was a young American entertainer who came to Paris in the 1920s and conquered the French music hall scene first with the dance company the *Revue Nègre* and then with the famous *Folies Bergères*, where she danced frenetically, some said "savagely," and topless, wearing the bare minimum—her skimpy feathered costumes or the banana skirt she made famous. The French public was taken aback by her "untrammeled instinct, her animality" but also by a unique "modern" persona that had not yet been seen onstage (Rearick, 81). In 1931, she introduced her signature song *J'ai deux amours* (I Have Two Loves). The "two loves" of the song are Paris and her "country," a nameless land over the ocean that many were quick to associate with the United States but that could also apply to the beautiful "savanna"-like country she alludes to in the song, somewhere in the Caribbean or Africa. Baker's "exotic" nudity and her love for France made her a Parisian icon, as famous and cherished and admired as another French music hall star, the less "exposed" but no less sensual and at the time older Mistinguett, or "Miss," whose acrobatic style "suited a sports-loving era" (Rearick, 72). Mistinguett had already acquired star status before the war and was particularly known to the public for her famous legs and her dramatic feathered appearance on stage. She continued to dazzle after the war when, at forty-seven, she came out with her hit song *Mon Homme* (My Man) in 1920. Both women were successful stars but, unlike the French "Miss," American Josephine Baker was the "black pearl" whose appeal to the French audience went well beyond Paris and the familiar to also include what can be called the French "colonial unconscious." While she was received with mild success in the United States, she was the ultimate star in France; there, her blackness was indiscriminately associated with the prosperity and cultural export from the colonies, and simultaneously a unique, "modern" beauty imported from the United States. Her appearances on stage in "tiger-style" costume or in "safari décor," her pet leopard, the syncopated beat of the jazz to which she danced, all connected her in the eyes of the public to a colonized yet still untamed Africa. She represented "a floating signifier of cultural difference . . . many different things to different people . . . she could evoke Africa, the Caribbean, the United States, France, by turns or all at once as the occasion required" (Ezra, 99). As an exotic black beauty, she mesmerized many like Picasso and Hemingway.

In France, American "popular culture" occupied a place that, to a large extent, had been left vacant by the Empire and Third Republic's thriving notion of culture as mainly "high culture." In addition, French "high" cultural activities were largely concentrated in Paris, thus leaving aside the "traditional France" that was found to be "quaint" and "charming" but not representative of the grandeur—a word that would be taken up by President Charles de Gaulle after World War II—of the *Hexagone*. Ironically, this provincial culture is one that many French and foreign tourists are seeking today while continuing to see Paris and its bourgeois infrastructure as the grand token of French culture: "In the 1920s French high culture remained an essentially Parisian culture" (*French Cultural Studies*, 62).

French culture in the 1920s and 1930s seemed divided into two distinct areas, "high" bourgeois culture and "low" mass culture, a pattern that followed the social segregation of rich and poor, bourgeois and working class, city-dwellers and peasants, and thus confirmed that France in the 1920s was, more than ever, a class-bound society. Only in areas of mass entertainment like sports and cinema were cultural barriers crossed. Sports like cycling, soccer, rugby, and boxing were hugely popular with bourgeois and working classes alike. A mix of classes went in droves to films like Louis Feuillade's enormously successful series *Fantomas* or *Les vampires*, and feature films like Julien Duvivier's *Poil de carotte* (1925), and Marcel L'Herbier's *L'Argent* (1930). Theaters were ubiquitous in large cities as well as in the countryside where films were also shown *en plein air* (al fresco) on large screens hanging over the wall of local town halls.

In other areas, bourgeois culture remained firmly compartmentalized. Reading Marcel Proust's *Remembrance of Things Past*, for example, was not a "popular pastime," nor were opera or museums and galleries, which were primarily sites of high culture, even if they had been originally conceived as places where all could partake of "culture" *tout court*. Dada and surrealism (see below) were certainly revolutionary and antiestablishment movements, but they remained essentially avant-garde experiments and never had a mass circulation or impact, even if many of the Dada and surrealist artists, writers, and intellectuals were at one point or another members of the Communist Party (created in France in 1920). These two movements (Dada and Surrealism) definitely challenged the world of bourgeois high culture but only from within an already rarefied realm of "high" culture, even if their members would not recognize their ideas and practices in this label. Such avant-garde movements indeed managed to break the dominant cultural patterns of thinking and creating, yet they never quite engaged the masses in the same way as American popular culture did. In France, these movements remained primarily a rebellious and innovative component of "high culture," and a Parisian phenomenon.

Americans had brought their brand of popular culture to France, but it was received with mixed feelings. While a majority embraced American imports like jazz music and Hollywood films, a strong resistance was simultaneously voiced by some who saw the influence of America on everyday French life as a threat to "authentic" French identity and culture. Among those "resisters" was Georges Duhamel, a novelist, Academician and tireless apologist of French culture who would become the president of the famous *Alliance Française* after World War II. In his 1930 *America the Menace*, he expressed his distress about the coming of American culture to Europe:

> America may fall, but American civilization will never perish; it is already mistress of the world. Are we also to be conquered, we people of ordinary lands? . . . There are on our continent, in France as well as elsewhere, large regions that the spirit of old Europe has deserted. The American spirit colonizes little by little such a province, such a city, such a house, and such a soul. (214–215)

Duhamel denounced what he perceived as a new "mechanical age" whose destructive effects he had witnessed firsthand as an army doctor during World War I. His despondent post-war views led him to condemn any "global civilization" that could only invade national cultures and level differences. American culture in particular symbolized this new age and future nightmare. "In material civilization, the American people are older than we, a people prematurely old perhaps, who never properly matured, but who even now are enacting for us many scenes of our future life" (xiv). Cinema, certainly one of the most dynamic vectors of the new American popular culture, one hailed by the surrealists as the art form of the future, was a target of predilection for Duhamel:

> Cinema is a pastime for slaves, an amusement for the illiterate, for poor creatures stupefied by work and anxiety. It is the skillfully poisoned nourishment of the multitude . . . It

is spectacle that demands no efforts, that does not imply any sequence of ideas, that raises no questions, that evokes no deep feeling, that lights no light in the depths of any heart, that excites no hope, if not the ridiculous one of some day becoming a "star" at Los Angeles. (34)

Duhamel was not representative of the majority of French people, who delighted in the "movies" and other "products" of American popular culture. He was well aware of this and expressed his sadness at the "thousands who hailed [American culture] with loud shouts" (xiv). To Duhamel, the "American invasion" was all the more dangerous that it insinuated itself in the hearth of every French home and in the heart of every French citizen, and his apprehension takes the shape of vehement declarations such as the following: "At this point of the debate, each of us, westerners, must denounce with honesty all American things in our house, our clothes, our souls" (xvi).

Were the French, especially the French masses, at risk of "losing their soul" and their identity under pressure from American popular culture, or would they be able to maintain their specifically "French" character? This question entered the French national mindset of the interwar period and would emerge again even more spectacularly after World War II (see chapter 6) when the United States' influence both politically and culturally would become even more pervasive.

Even with American culture looming large on the horizon, throughout most of the 1920s and the 1930s French culture, both politically active and creatively rebellious, remained central for other nations, including the United States. With their specific brand of rebelliousness primarily directed at bourgeois life and culture and the universalist values of the republic—a culture and an ideology that had taken shape with nineteenth-century modernization and centralization—movements like Dada and surrealism kept France at the forefront of cultural debates.

Against Bourgeois Universalism: Dada and Surrealism

The period between 1918 and 1931 in France was described as the "crazy years " to a large extent because of the determination of a generation of artists and intellectuals to undo the past, to work against the grain, against all the values that had led to the war. Reinventing the arts was a way of expressing their disillusion with supposedly humane and universal values. Artists and writers came from all corners of the globe to experience the consuming energy of a generation that lived and created as if there were no tomorrow. As twenty-year old Raymond Radiguet wrote in his 1923 controversial novel *Le Diable au corps* (*Devil in the Flesh*): "I was in a hurry, on fire . . . like someone condemned to die young who works twice as hard" (162). Ironically, Radiguet died the same year.

World War I with its corpse-strewn fields and its bloody and muddy trenches was the great symbol of the failure of bourgeois values that had dominated the past. The future, if it was to be, lay in a total rejection of these values. The "Dadaist Manifesto" of 1918 is emblematic of this spirit:

DADA; knowledge of all the means hitherto rejected up to this point by the sexual prudishness of easy compromise and good manners: **DADA**; abolition of logic, dance of those who are incapable of creation: **DADA**; every hierarchy and social equation established for values by our valets: **DADA**; every object, all objects, feelings and obscurities, every apparition and the precise shock of parallel lines, are means for the battle of: **DADA**; the abolition of memory: **DADA**; the abolition of archaeology: **DADA**; the abolition of prophets: **DADA**; the abolition of the future: **DADA**; the absolute and indisputable belief in every god that is an immediate product of spontaneity: **DADA**; . . . to respect all individualities in their folly of the moment, [. . .] Freedom: **DADA DADA DADA**; shrieking of contracted colors, intertwining of contraries and of all contradictions, grotesqueries, non sequiturs: LIFE. (156–157)

So what exactly was Dada? Dada was pure and raw post-war energy, a kind of anti-movement and "anti-esthetic" that arrived from Romania through Switzerland in the shape of its "leader" Tristan Tzara. Dada was decidedly international as it attracted artists and writers from throughout the world, among them the Frenchmen Louis Aragon and André Breton, the German Max Ernst, the Franco-Spanish Francis Picabia, and the American Man Ray, who preferred to think of themselves as men without nationality bound together by the objectives of the Dada manifesto. By way of the manifesto, they chanted their anarchical desire to destroy all bourgeois values, and to erase the establishment and its institutions, which they accused of being responsible for the war. The Dadaists' call to forget individual nationalities and live in an international community of free and spontaneous thinkers went with the notion that, in order to start anew, there had to be a clean slate. However, the Manifesto stopped short of proposing concrete alternatives; Dada did entail prescribing rules of common understanding among its members, even if it nevertheless implicitly pointed to the possibility of total individual freedom through initial rejection. In that sense, the Dada manifesto was an antimanifesto, as it recommended nothing for the future of its newly created "counterculture."

If Dada could be said to have a goal, it lay in the complete dismantling of bourgeois values. Dada also expressed the frustration of artists who could not escape the system in which they existed but relentlessly and nihilistically attacked its institutions, as in Francis Picabia's *Manifeste cannibale dada*: "Hiss, shout, kick my teeth in, so what? I shall still tell you that you are half-wits. In three months my friends and I will be selling you our pictures" (in Ades, 4). In the end, Dadaists could not continue to seek inspiration in nihilism and Dada disintegrated as a movement; this seemed in tune with its refusal to propose or condone any specific alternatives to the establishment it had so vehemently condemned. In its very vehemence, however, Dada had pointed the way to possible strategies in the radical challenge to the political and esthetic standards of the establishment. A number of these strategies would find more concrete expression in surrealism.

The surrealist movement was launched in 1924 by yet another manifesto, written by its leader, the French poet André Breton who, inspired by the recently translated works of Freud, explored the creative powers of the unconscious in all art forms. Surrealism, like Dada, was an intrinsically internationalist endeavor. For example, it attracted to Paris a new generation of avant-garde painters from Catalonia, like the eccentric Salvador Dalí with his "melting" and dreamlike scenes, and Joan Miró with his twisted forms that hovered between paramecia and geometric design. From Spain also came the filmmaker Luis Buñuel who shocked audiences with sensational and dream-like films created in collaboration with Dalí, of which the *Andalusian dog* (1928), with its notorious image of a woman's eye being sliced by a razor blade, is the most famous. All were caught in the fever of surrealism defined by André Breton as "psychic automatism in its pure state by which one proposes to express the actual functioning of thought. Dictated by thought, in the absence of any control exercised by reason, exempt from any aesthetic or moral concern" (*Manifesto of Surrealism*, 26).

The affinities between the two avant-garde movements, Dada and surrealism, are explicit in this statement made by Buñuel, one the major figures of the latter: "The real purpose of Surrealism is to explode the social order, to transform life itself" (Buñuel, 107). Surrealism proposed to abandon conscious, logical reasoning, the very basis of a civilization that had shown its murderous capacity in World War I. In its place, thinking and behavior would be opened up to the rich territory of the unconscious, especially as it manifested itself in dreams. In proposing that the unconscious was at the core of human creativity, a means of tapping into a vast reserve of "hidden" or "latent" forces, surrealism was placing itself in the tradition inaugurated by Sigmund Freud's psychoanalytic theories. As stated in the *Manifesto of Surrealism*, "Surrealism is based on the belief in the superior reality of certain forms of previously neglected associations, in the omnipotence of dream, in the disinterested play of thought" (26). This entry into a superior reality, a "*sur*-reality," or *over*-reality by way of dreaming was illustrated by the surrealist Belgian painter René Magritte's 1929 *La Femme cachée* (The Hidden Woman) in which words and image meet on a canvas representing a naked woman, both an object of desire and an unattainable muse for the surrealist male artists who attempt to capture her image. The interrupted sentence spelled out in the painting "I do not see the [blank] hidden in the forest" leaves a space for the visual representation of the woman in place of the truncated section of the written sentence, precisely when the words announce that she cannot be seen, thereby suggesting that she could only appear in dreams. Magritte illustrated this with a photomontage of the painting framed by individual shots of sixteen members of the surrealist group, all with their eyes closed, as if sleeping and dreaming. In this dream state, they would have access to the unconscious, to what is unattainable to them in wakefulness.

For the surrealists, visual representations emanating from the depth of the human psyche became the "language" of choice to communicate and explore a renewed sense of creativity that challenged the logic of conventional language. Surrealist poetry, while still attached to some basic lyrical principles of versification, relied on the unlikely meeting of two opposite or incongruous images, as was the case in the series of images that constituted French André Breton's long 1931 poem *L'Union libre*. Literally *union libre* translates as "free union" meaning living together without being married, but in Breton's poem, the term also refers to the "free association" that was at its core. The central figure, again a woman, is presented in a patchwork of uncanny metaphors forcing the reader to visually free associate sets of images unlikely to meet in any other "logical" circumstances in order to create his own marvelous and fantastic "surreal" being:

> My wife with the lips of a cockade and of a bunch of stars of the last magnitude . . .
> My wife with the tongue of a stabbed host
> With the tongue of a doll that opens and closes its eyes . . .
> My wife with shoulders of champagne . . .

My wife with fingers of luck and ace of hearts
With fingers of mown hay . . .
My wife with breasts of a marine molehill . . .
My wife with buttocks of sandstone and asbestos
My wife with buttocks of swans' backs . . .
With the sex of an iris
My wife with the sex of a mining-placer and of a platypus . . .
My wife with savanna eyes.

                                        (*Clair de Terre*, 93–95)

Whether viewed as an erotic male fantasy—a criticism that was often leveled at the surrealists—of a woman's body blended in a strange mix of fauna and flora, or even as a game consisting of creating comical and freakish associations between body parts and the natural universe, surrealism succeeded in liberating poetry from strict linguistic or even symbolic interpretation through the "free union" of multiple images. This type of freedom empowering the reader/dreamer was at the very heart of surrealism, and "automatic writing" as well as free association were its means, its raison d'être, its weapons to emancipate art from the constraints of tradition, of reality itself.

Negritude

Surrealism had a strong impact on the Négritude Movement that the Martinican poet Aimé Césaire defined in 1935 in the newly founded journal *L'Etudiant Noir* (*The Black Student*). Central to the Négritude project was the recovery by black people everywhere of their African roots as a primary means of ending their alienation from dominant Western culture: "Black youth want to act and create. They want to have their poets, their novelists . . . they want to contribute to universal life, to the humanization of humanity" (*Cahier*, xxx). The political voice of Négritude and the liberated unconscious inherent in surrealism come into contact, even before their respective two leaders met during the early years of World War II when Breton lived in the United States and visited the West Indies. In Martinique, he met Césaire whom he called the "great black poet." There, he formally welcomed the author of *Cahier d'un retour au pays natal* (*Notebook of a Return to the Native Land*), published in 1939, to surrealism. Breton, who would later write an introduction to the New York edition of *Cahiers* in 1944 and to the New York–Paris edition in 1947, invited the poet to continue making surrealism his artistic "weapon" of choice to attack the white citadel that imprisoned the African spirit that Césaire and his fellow Négritude writers and activists, Senegalese writer Leopold Sédar Senghor, and Haitian writer Léon Gontian Damas, wished to restore. In an interview with Haitian poet René Depestre, Aimé Césaire declared: "Surrealism offered me what I sought in a confused sort of way. I welcomed its influence less as a revelation than as an aid to mutual intent. It was like dynamite to the French language. It was shaking everything up to the roots. This was very important because the traditional weighty, overused forms were holding me down" (Davis, 72).

Négritude represented the challenge of "another universalism" to "French universalism," especially as it had manifested itself in France's colonial enterprise. While one of the stated aims of French universalism was the assimilation of the colonial population, Négritude aimed, precisely, at undoing this cultural assimilation, and the alienation it necessarily entailed. The Négritude movement's "universal call" to all black people to create a boundless black culture had found a poetic voice inflected by the figures and rhythms of surrealism in Césaire's *Cahier* well before he actually met Breton.

> [. . .]
> And these tadpoles within me hatched from my prodigious lineage!
> Those who have invented neither gunpowder nor compass
> Those who have never tamed stream or electricity
> Those who have explored neither oceans nor sky,
> But know in its innermost recesses the country of suffering
> Those whose journeys have been uprootings
> Those who have become pliant with kneelings
> Those who have been domesticated and christianized
> Those who have been inoculated with debasement
> Tom-toms of empty hands
> Jejune tom-toms of resonant sores
> Burlesque tom-toms of a wasting betrayal
> [. . .]
>
> (Davis, 47–48)

The surrealist influence on Césaire's writing was also evident in his next collection of poems, published in 1946, entitled *Les Armes Miraculeuses* (*Miraculous Weapons*), whose incongruous images recall Breton's *L'union libre*:

> With small steps: shower of caterpillars
> With small steps: gulp of milk
> With small steps: ball-bearing rolls
> With small steps: earthquake tremor
> The yams in the ground stride with giant steps: a breakthrough of stars
> A breakthrough of night a breakthrough of Holy Mother of God
> With giant steps: a breakthrough of speech in the throat of a stammerer
> Orgasms of holy miasmas
> Allelujah.
>
> (Davis, 77)

According to Césaire, surrealism enabled him to access the "forces of the unconscious" that he located in the fundamental (re)discovery of Africa identified as the encrypted figure of a black psyche. As it aimed at exploring and enlightening the "darkness" of the African unconscious, Négritude was as poetically creative as it was politically engaged. In the labyrinth of the unconscious, it sought personal modes of expression as well as a universal mode of reckoning for all black men and women.

The "miraculous weapon" that surrealism offered to Césaire's poetry, a weapon to better "explode" the French language, had been used by French another Martinican writer René Maran who, short of reaching the yet undiscovered surrealistic *merveilleux* (marvelous), nevertheless used various African languages in his novels to empower and liberate black identity in Afro-French literature of the 1920s. Maran thus preceded Césaire's "collective African unconscious" with a similar engagement to "black universalism" that he transcribed in his 1921 novel *Batouala: Véritable roman nègre* (*Real Negro Novel*).

While negritude was most active from 1935 to 1960, it is indeed in the early 1920s with René Maran that a black humanist movement had its first significant stirrings. As a young man, Leopold Sedar Senghor had written in the 1935 issue of *L'Etudiant noir* an article entitled "Humanism and Us: René Maran" about Maran's "rational penetration" into African life. According to Senghor, Maran, a French-educated black humanist, was able to represent Africa in a manner the West could understand, but also with the advantage of an inherent "African spirit." While Senghor praised Maran's novel for bringing together "black soul and white writing," others saw this blend as an obstacle to recognizing Maran as a "real negro writer." Suspicious of his motives, his critics saw in him the very incarnation of the contradictions that Négritude would later denounce. A French writer of Caribbean descent, René Maran published what he called the first "real negro novel," a controversial phrase he insisted on using as a subtitle to his *Batouala*, the story of the rise and fall of an African patriarch in the colonized region of Ubangi-Shari of the Central African Republic where Maran had lived and worked as a civil servant for the French Colonial Ministry. Many asked whether *Batouala* was indeed a "real negro novel," accusing Maran of "aiming at exoticism" and calling him "an opportunist" who wrote a supposedly "negro novel" and "hoping for a previously unpublished originality," as the journalist J. Ladreit de Lacharrière put it in his 1922 review of the book in *L'Afrique Française*. This controversy about whether this novel was "truly black" ignited a debate that would later inform the more systematic investigations and formulations of the Négritude movement. In a 1963 article, Senghor placed *Batouala* at the origin of Négritude and declared Maran as the undeniable "precursor" to the movement. According to Senghor, everything about Afro-French literature and about a worldwide "black soul" was already in place in Maran's literature and political writings. In the 1920s, Maran had befriended the African-Americans of the Harlem Renaissance movement: Alain Locke, Langston Hughes, W.E.B. Du Bois, and many more who considered him a leader in the crafting of universal rights for black people. Besides his participation in black organizations in France, organizations such as the "Universal League for the Defense of the Black Race" and the "Committee for the Defense of the Black Race," Maran contributed numerous articles to political and literary journals like *La Revue du Monde Noir* (Review of the Black World), in which he published a seminal article that would become an intellectual credo for the generation of black writers and thinkers of the Négritude movement. Maran explained the aim of the *Revue* in the following terms: "To create among the Negroes of the entire world, regardless of nationality, an intellectual and moral tie that will permit them to better know each other, to love one another, to defend more effectively their collective interests and to glorify their race" (Cameron, 5). As we have seen, Négritude's universalism, as it was seeking the entitlement of the black race throughout the world, resonated both in parallel with and in contradiction to the republican universalism that, at least in principle, also sought to build a brotherhood of men outside of all differences, specifically outside distinction of gender or race. The two universalist systems, the French Republican one and the one promoted by Négritude were prey to similar contradictions. Both advocated the rallying around a set of abstract principles that, in practice, would exclude a number of groups and identities. We have seen how French universalism created and excluded in its wake a number of "Others" ranging from women to colonial subjects; in similar ways, Négritude's supposed universal and humanistic message could not sustain political coherence partly due to the inevitable differences among black people of different nationality, from different cultures, with divergent national interests. The idealism inherent to Négritude rested in fact on the monolithic figure of a mythical "Africa" in which many black people did not recognize themselves. Decades later, the general decline and fragmentation of ideologies would be reflected in the emergence of movements that would incorporate the diversity inherent in apparently unified or homogeneous cultures. This would be apparent, for example, in the "Creolité" movement—launched by a group of Martinican writers and intellectuals—which promoted the reality of *métissage* or *hybridity* rather than the reclaiming of "African authenticity" advanced by Négritude (see chapter 10).

Dossier 5.2   René Maran, *Batouala* (1921)

In 1921, Batouala was awarded the most prestigious French literary prize, the Goncourt, as had Henri Barbusse's *Le Feu* (Under Fire) in 1915, Georges Duhamel's *Civilisation* in 1918, or Marcel Proust's *A l'ombre des jeunes filles en fleur* (Within a Budding Grove) in 1919. If the publication of the "true negro novel" itself did not shock the public, the top honors it received from the highly respected Goncourt Academy created an uproar in literary and cultural circles. The press of the time stirred up the polemics regarding the controversial choice made by the Goncourt committee with an assortment of condescending remarks about Maran and the Academy. In their mildest form of attack, some critics simply accused the Academy of having selected Maran's novel to the detriment of real quality, in order to help a sluggish book industry that was seeking sensationalist "best-sellers" rather than accomplished works of literature. Others, ignoring the political dimension of Batouala, saw the novel as a return to a nineteenth-century form of exoticism, a romanticized view of life in Africa. The most virulent critics, among them the editorialist at *Le Temps* Paul Soulay, did not disguise their anger at a French institution that was giving literary recognition to an anticolonial novel at a time when the empire was considered a primary symbol of French universalism and grandeur. Soulay, like many others, had read the scathing preface to the novel in which Maran exposed and attacked the abuses of the French colonial administration in Africa as "an indictment of the colonials that will make every Frenchman and every European blush with shame" (Cameron, 16). Another journalist referred to Batouala as "obscene, ill-composed, devoid of interest, . . . a scandal of our time" (Cameron, 17). His harshly criticized novel was banned in the French colonies of Africa.

As a "non-European" novelist, Maran founded a language and a style that would indeed go against the grain of a cherished French literary tradition, as he would not only try to write about Africa from the point of view of an African or at least from the perspective of a black Frenchman trying to state "the facts" about Africa, but also wrote in a "nonacademic" French. This had to be a difficult task for someone so profoundly and academically educated in the French tradition. Maran used an abundance of words transcribed from various African languages and a syntax imitating rhythms from the African oral tradition. He interspersed African words, explained by means of circumlocutions, within the basic structure of the French language, thus creating an "Afro-French" novel of mixed linguistic horizons. This tour de force in itself represented a remarkable achievement and went a long way to explaining the novel's success. About Maran's language, Senghor declared: "After *Batouala*, we can no longer make the Negro work, love, cry or speak like the white man. It is no longer a question of making him speak *petit-nègre* [pidgin] but rather Wolof, Malinké, Ewondo, and French" (in "René Maran, précurseur de la négritude," 410).

The following passage is the account of a "Ga'nza," that is, a celebration of fertility in an African community. During the Ga'nza, adolescents are excised and circumcised in order to respectively become symbolically mature women and men. The celebration reaches its full paroxysm with a series of inflamed and entrancing dances between men and women of the village.

The ceremony was beginning.

The two old people spat on a flat stone, then carefully sharpened their knives on it. Already, sticks raised, the assistants rushed to the first patient, who staggered under their blows. If a bit of suffering were enough to fell him, it showed that he was unworthy to become a man and, by custom, should die of a beating.

But, disappointing their bloodthirsty hope, the new ga'nza joined their group. The blood from the wound ran down his legs, spattering his neighbors at each of his jump. Nevertheless he had to pretend to ignore the pain and began singing and dancing to prove his courage . . .

Ga'nza . . . ga'nza . . . ga'nza . . . ga'nza! . . .

That only happens once in your life . . .

Ours, women! Ours, men!

Now you are ga'nzas.

Ga'nza . . . ga'nza . . . ga'nza . . . ga'nza! . . .

Each operator wiped his knife, then excised the last girl and circumcised the last man. The tumult now reached its height. All that had gone before was nothing by comparison. All those outcries and confused actions were only preparation for the event they were all anxiously awaiting: the great dance of love, the one that is never allowed except on the evening of the ga'nza.

And during this glorious dance all things are permitted, even perversions and sins against custom.

The li'nghas, the balafons and the koundés competed frenetically. The toucans sniggered wickedly, and the night birds of prey busied themselves, bewildered, above the yangba, their hooting drowned by the outburst of the crowd's madness.

Two women made their appearance at just that moment. The more beautiful of the two was Yassigui'ndja, the wife of Batouala the mokoundji. The other had never known a man.

Both were naked and shaven. Glass necklaces adorned their necks, rings hung from their noses and from their ears, and bracelets jangled on their wrists and ankles. Their bodies were covered with dark red glaze.

Yassigui'ndja wore, besides these jewels, an enormous painted wooden phallus.

It was held by strings to the belt encircling her waist, a male symbol which indicated the role she was going to play in the dance.

At first, she danced only with her hips and her loins. Her feet did not really move, but the wooden phallus bounced with her every hip movement.

Then, slowly, she glided towards her partner. The girl drew back in fear. This woman did not want to give in to the male's desire! Her gesture and her leaps expressed her fear.

Disappointed, Yassigui'ndja, as the male, stepped back and renewed her advance, stamping the ground violently.

Meanwhile, having overcome her irrational fear, the maiden now offered herself from afar. She offered little resistance. She threw off all restraints, and melted to the ardor of the phallus as a fog melts in the rising sun, covering with her hands sometimes her eyes, sometimes her sex parts. . . .

A strange madness suddenly seized the confused human throng surrounding the dancers. The men tore off the pieces of fabric that served as loincloths; the women also removed the rest of their clothes.

The breasts of the women bounced. A heavy odor of genitals, urine, sweat, and alcohol pervaded the air, more acid than the smoke. Couples paired off. They danced, as Yassigui'ndja and the girl had danced. There were fights and raucous cries. Bodies spread out at random on the ground and all movements of the dance came to fruition. The children imitated the movements of their elders.

Sexual drunkenness, increased by alcoholic drunkenness. Immense natural joy, released from all control. Blood flowed freely from splendid abuse. Desire was the only master. (79–87)

Batouala recognizes one of the couples making love freely as his first wife and the handsome young hunter Bissibi'ngui. He gets angry and threatens to kill her and castrate him. The couple runs away and, by chance, is saved by the unexpected arrival of the white commandant, back from his mission earlier than expected. The crowd quickly scatters, well aware that the ceremony was not allowed by the French colonial authorities.

The initiation love dance performed by Batouala's wife and the young virgin has similarities with the frenetic dancing that the beautiful nude dancer Josephine Baker would perform a decade or so later. Josephine Baker's wild dance, wearing her banana skirt and stamping her feet on the music hall stage in Paris can be seen as both the "commodification" of colonial reality, its transformation into easily accessible entertainment, as well as the black entertainer's way of connecting with an African reality that she had never experienced firsthand.

The 1931 Colonial Exposition

The unprecedented success of the 1931 Colonial Exposition in Paris confirmed France's colonial status as a major colonial power. Completely dedicated to the colonial world, it opened its doors in May 1931 and welcomed close to 35 million visitors, making it the second most popular exposition after the Paris 1900 Universal Exposition with 50 million. The exposition took place in a 270-acre area of the Vincennes forest on the outskirts of Paris. It was advertised with slogans like "Visit Greater France" or "Around the World in One Day," plastered on posters and programs representing in various styles and compositions "model characters" from North Africa, Sub-Saharan Africa, Asia, and the Americas. In some cases, the exposition posters used one emblematic individual whose "typical traits" served to represent the larger colonial community. For example, a flamboyant and dynamic representation of Josephine Baker was used on a poster inviting Italians to travel directly to the fair. The minister of Colonial Affairs, Paul Reynaud, spoke about the event as an "apotheosis":

Colonization is the greatest feat of History. Is it possible that today we celebrate an apotheosis? Never before have the momentum and outpouring of thought been as powerful for us as they are now. Many believed that the extension of French power in the world would dilute it, weaken it, render it less capable of facing the ever-threatening perils of the world. But in tragic times, the colonies stood by the side of the Motherland, and the union of our Empire was tested in pain and in blood. Aside our old colonies, these family jewels scattered over the Atlantic and Indian oceans, is African France, as vast as Europe itself. (*Mémoires*, 301–302)

In spite of the official welcome to the "extended French colonial family" and the sense of equality expressed by the French exposition planners and other administrators, the distant "relatives" of France were presented at the Colonial Exposition as oddities that were exposed in their garb and habitat in order to be introduced to the world and to educate those Europeans who still harbored fears about the unknown men and women from the far reaches of the empire. In the spirit of Reynaud's concept of a "colonial conscience," the "natural environment" of the recreated "villages" of natives had largely replaced the cages and gated exhibits of the human zoos displayed in previous fairs. Displaying humans as anthropological oddities dated back to 1841, when the American P.T. Barnum launched these kinds of exhibits at the American Museum in New York. In 1874, the German Carl Hagenbeck revamped the idea of "ethnological spectacles" by adding the association of man with animal, thus creating the concept of "human zoos." The success of these displays was such that they became a featured section for more than thirty international fairs. By 1931, however, the notion of "human zoo" had lost much of its appeal, especially with the French colonial establishment more intent on illustrating and justifying its "civilizing mission" than offering titillating spectacle. The irony of a "more humane and dignified display" of people did not seem to enter its calculations. The idea was that men and women from the colonies were to be considered and presented as human beings in their "native environment" and not as animals. They were invited to act as if they were living in their homeland in front of a European audience. The hope was that by simply displaying the daily gestures of their domestic life, their frightening reputations as wild and barbaric individuals would fade and be replaced by a tame even if "exotic" one in the eyes of the curious Europeans. According to Paul Reynaud, the official voice of the French administration in these matters, the colonial subject was to be recognized as a "family" member of "greater France":

> Today the colonial conscience is in full ascension. Millions upon millions of Frenchmen have seen the splendors of Vincennes. For them, our colonies are no longer merely unknown names with which we have overloaded their school-time memories. Now they know the grandeur, the beauty, the resources: they have seen them alive right before their very eyes. Every one of them now feels like a citizen of greater France. (In Wilder, 37)

France's imperial influence was now extended to all areas of the world from Indochina to the Caribbean, and the exposition aimed to show the many wonders, customs, and curiosities of this expansive new French world as well as the other European nations' empires.

The Vincennes location was perfect for such a project as it offered a large area and varied landscapes. There, the exposition was carefully laid out among gardens, lakes, and hills. The French Empire occupied the most impressive area of the exposition.

Some of the most spectacular attractions were built on and around the "Great Avenue of the French Colonies" where one could find in particular the exposition's *pièce de resistance*: the reproduction of the temple of Angkor Vat surrounded by twenty-five colorful pavilions with a wide range of exhibits, material and human, from Southeast Asia. In the temple itself, groups of 500 visitors each could successively see women working with silk, miners extracting coal, rubber-tree bleeders, rice pickers, and much more. A tower from Annam represented the importance of education in the region, while Khmer statues were shown in the grand gallery. Further along the Avenue, visitors could stop at Djenné, the reproduction of an African village from Niger built around the "Tata," or fortified palace, and the mosque, surrounded by indigenous houses on and off the water, with several displays of Africans cooking and dancing. The visit continued on with the reproduction of an ancient city door and a theater from the city of Antananarivo, in Madagascar. The Moroccan pavilion began with a garden sprawling around cypresses and waterways where Moorish boutiques and cafes seduced the Orientalists-at-heart, before leading them to an impressive palace in which an advanced and different image of Moroccans turned them back into modern men and women. The colonial administration perceived Morocco as a country where both the traditional and the modern cohabitated, and the exposition emphasized both. Inside the palace the modern predominated, and even replaced the notion that Morocco was simply a large bazaar: a miniature reproduction of Casablanca's modernized harbor, exhibits displaying the advances the colonized country had made in road construction and electrical equipment, as well as countless photos of a modernized agriculture reflected the industrial benefits of the "civilizing mission."

Scattered along the avenue, the presence of the many Protestant and Catholic missions of the colonial world was also highlighted, with reproductions of churches, chapels, towers, and hospitals that marked the strong presence of spiritual, educational, and medical groups in the colonies.

The exposition was a huge success, despite the economic crisis and the particularly cold and rainy spring of 1931. Most unexpectedly, it made a huge profit, a rare occurrence in the history of universal exhibitions whose objectives were prestige and visibility rather than economic viability, and often lost money or broke even.

The exposition was also the occasion for a few "cross-cultural encounters." A journalist for *Paris-Soir* wrote the story of Deodat H'Oumlouh, the lieutenant of a tribal chief in French Guyana, whom the French journalist took along for a night out in Montmartre. First, Deodat had to be persuaded to give up his "national costume" the "Calembé," or *cache-sexe* (hide-sex), a "fig leaf style" underwear, to wear Western clothes. At the café where they ordered drinks, Deodat downed in one gulp his much too "litl" glass of port and by accident broke the glass, in his culture, a sign of bad luck. He began a very demonstrative prayer to conjure the evil eye that did not fail to attract the attention of the curious Parisian drinkers around. His tattoos and braids were also a source of curiosity in the restaurant where they later dined. As they finished the evening with a stop at the famous cabaret, the Moulin Rouge, Deodat came upon two aging ladies of the night who, in his views, had put too much "painting" on their faces. He concluded his reflection on Parisian women by these words: "Oh Massa! W'men in Guiana, when they old, only stay quiet in hut to smoke pipe. These ugly, old w'men ugly, ugly" (Hodeir, 95). The comparison was telling of the world of difference separating Deodat from his "friend," a difference described again and again by the journalist, as primarily incumbent on Deodat whose odd native behavior and thoughts could only make him an exhibit and a "Savage in Paris" as announced by the title of the article. According to the journalist, he received no wisdom from Deodat and the whole excursion turned out to be nothing more than an amusement for the evening.

It was this condescending attitude toward the colonized indigenous peoples and the sought-after feel of exoticism, falsely infused into colonial life through the many displays of the exposition, that was rejected by the organizers of a "counter-exhibit." The *contre-exposition* organized by surrealists, Communists, and Socialists, among them André Breton, Paul Eluard, and Louis Aragon, showed the "other side" of the colonial endeavor. Graphic and sordid photographs of colonial wars were put on display as well as works of art from the colonies that did not make it to the exposition jury. The organizers launched their anti-exposition with a flyer whose text began with the slogan: "Do not visit the colonial exposition!" and demanded France's "immediate pull-out from the colonies." Considering its limited means, the anticolonial exposition had measurable success and was a clear sign that the overwhelming display of colonial power that France staged for the world to see in 1931 did not go unchallenged. In a poem about the exposition entitled *Persécuté persécuteur* (Persecuted Persecutor) Aragon invoked the contradiction underlying the concept of a universalism-based "civilizing mission" in the colonies, a contradiction as discordant as the simultaneous presence of sun and rain in the poem:

> Sun sun from beyond the seas you render angelic
> The excremental beard of the governors
> Sun of corals and ebony
> Sun of numbered slaves
> Sun of nakedness sun of opium of flagellation
> Sun of fireworks in honor of the taking of the Bastille
> Above Cayenne a fourteenth of July
> It rains it pours on the Colonial Exposition.
>
> (216)

It was literally and metaphorically raining on Vincennes where France was hosting its last glorious "colonial exposition" before the political scene and world events turned unifying republican ideals into dividing national tensions, hurling a fragile France into another world conflict.

The Rise of Ideologies

In the 1930s the French economy was hampered first by its slow modernization, especially in the area of agriculture, and second by the world financial crisis that followed the 1929 Wall Street crash. Economic hard times crisis facilitated the development of political extremisms as the country began to experience a surge in ideological attacks from the Right and the Left. The hard-line Communist Party and the Far Right "leagues," both relatively new on the political and social stage and both embittered by the ineffectual economic policy of the government of Radical-Socialists, the political party of moderates.

On the left, the Communist Party created in 1920 hardened its political line and refused any cooperation with any other parties from the left. It considered the French Socialist Party (SFIO, *Section française de l'Internationale Ouvrière* or French section of the Workers International) a party of traitors taking sides with republican politics and ignoring the rights of workers. To the Moscow-aligned Communists, the more moderate socialist ideology stood in contrast to the Communist Party's strict belief in the unique power of the proletariat and its violent takeover of the government through revolution. As a result, the Communist Party enforced an uncompromising policy of political noncooperation labeled *classe contre classe* (class against class).

The increasingly popular paramilitary leagues of extreme right-wingers also promoted the radical transformation and even the dissolution of the parliamentary system; in its place they wanted the return of a strong and autocratic regime. The leagues had began their activities during the Boulangist era and the Dreyfus Affair (see chapter 3), voicing both their acute anti-Semitism and their desire for the return of some form of royalist or military leadership. They included *Action Française* led by the ideologue Charles Maurras who believed in taking direct action and praised the use of violence, and a newer league born in 1927, *Les Croix-de-Feux* (The Crosses of Fire) mainly composed of ex-servicemen, and the *Francistes* who marched in their blue-shirts and uniforms imitating Hitler's and Mussolini's Fascism in style and ideals. The increased number of leagues in the 1930s was related to a strong and renewed current of opposition to what the Far Right perceived as the dangerous rise of the Left as experienced in the Soviet Union, as well as to the frustration of the general public at the "corrupted" Radical government, which was implicated in a series of scandals. The leagues' audience grew steadily, especially among the confused and disenchanted middle class, which was not only affected by the economic depression, but also weary of government corruption, such as the infamous "Stavisky Affair." Stavisky was a notorious financial swindler flaunting a lifestyle of glamour and luxury when most in France were struggling with the economic hardships of the 1930s. When he was found mysteriously dead in the exclusive Alpine ski village of Chamonix, two theories emerged: either he had been killed by the corrupt government police before he could talk and compromise high officials, or he was the victim of his own conscience and committed suicide. Corruption and foul play were a more likely explanation for his death, which brought the affair into the public eye, especially when connections between Radical Prime Minister Camille Chautemps' family and Stavisky seemed to point to an undeniable case of government corruption. In the end, the ensuing trial could not firmly inculpate any government officials related to Stavisky, but the Chautemps government did not survive the scandal and a new cabinet was formed with Edouard Daladier, another Radical, as the new prime minister. The leagues exploited the situation in inflamed and passionate speeches in which they advocated "cleansing" France of the poor morals and corrupt actions they associated with republican politics. They were quick to seize upon the political uncertainties of the time by offering compelling arguments concerning the dangers of democracy, a discourse in line with the fascist ideologies of the time. They also rapidly transformed their words of discontent into "direct action," specifically into violent street riots. On February 6, 1934, they gathered enough sympathy and momentum to call for a massive demonstration in Paris. They were hoping to occupy the Palais Bourbon, which housed the French National Assembly, and to topple the Daladier government. Even hardcore Communists responded to the call for demonstration against the latest case of corruption, as they were just as eager as the leaguers to seize the opportunity to discredit the government. The combined force of these two groups from opposite ends of the political spectrum was potentially explosive. Menacing crowds demonstrated all day long on the Place de la Concorde and the adjacent bridge right across the street from the National Assembly building until things got out of hand, and by early evening the police began to shoot directly into the crowd, creating pure chaos and leaving fifteen dead and thousands wounded. American writer Henry Miller, who happened to be in the vicinity of the demonstration, described the events in a letter to a friend:

> I thought at first, seeing the streets so empty, so sinisterly bare, that a parade was taking place. Gradually, it dawned on me that something *real* was about to happen. I was at Richelieu-Drouot, on the Grands Boulevards, hemmed in by police and soldiers. Had the queer sensation (so true when you are in danger) that I was a target. Saw the mob pressing me flat against the walls and the bullets mowing us down. Realized that I was in a net. Looked frantically about for an exit. Got home just as the thing broke loose. And you know by this time that the fight at the Place de la Concorde and all along the Boulevards was very very real. Paris changed in those few hours tremendously. One could feel all over again the bloody drama of the Revolution. The crowd was ugly. Had the Cabinet not resigned I think the city would have been burned down. Terrific damage occurred in a few hours. (*Letters to Emile*, 144–145; emphasis in original)

Miller, an expatriate who had settled down in Paris in 1930 was shaken out of his nonchalant Parisian life by the "very real" moment of the February 6 riots. To him on this day, the romantic, permissive, and bohemian city that so many of his compatriots had celebrated now appeared under a new, scary cloud. The next day, the fatal use of police firepower was bitterly criticized by the press and the population demanded the immediate resignation of the recently appointed prime minister, Edouard Daladier, who had no choice but to step down, to be replaced by the aging conservative Radical, Gaston Doumergue.

It is noteworthy that Daladier became the first official of the Third Republic to step down under pressure from the "streets." By having an immediate impact upon the direction of French politics and despite the tragedy of the dead and wounded, the politically and socially diverse masses who had invaded the streets of Paris rediscovered a sense of their own power. Their action had directly affected the course and institutions of the bourgeois republic and the political parties representing its interests by forcing the prime minister out of office. On February 7, Daladier explained his resignation as a fundamental gesture to save the republic from bloodshed or even from the possibility of a civil war. With this resignation as the last and noble option to protect republican principles and citizenship, it now appeared that the universalist French Republic was no longer able to sustain its illusion of political grandeur and could only salvage the basics. The republic was undergoing its deepest crisis yet, and basic humane sentiments and democratic principles became the last resort to save failing republican authority: this was the reasoning behind Daladier's resignation. Facing such a crisis, the republic was indeed forced to deal with and accommodate new individualities, opinions, and differences, even if extreme, in order to restore relative peace and its own authority.

The bloody events of February 6, 1934 also represented the "fateful turning point" of a failing Third Republic, the moment when the weakness of an aging universalism became patent. Angry mobs in the streets demanded radical changes in authority that would be more in line with their individual special interests, and, as a massive and threatening political force, they almost succeeded in overturning the democratic principles of the republic. The events resulting from the "Stavisky Affair" clearly indicated that the very fiber of French society had changed and that only a pluralistic government in which everyone was represented could successfully carry out the final act of the Third Republic's utopia of universalism.

What was unique in the demonstration of February 6 was that it guaranteed no particular political party, not even the majority of the conservative rioters, that their words and actions would become the new language of French politics and set the country's course. This was particularly true of the royalists, who naively thought of the crisis as a way to reclaim power, a sort of coup d'état as the Duke de Guise, in exile, declared: "French men of all parties and of every sort, now is the hour to rally to the principle of the monarchy, on which was founded over the centuries the grandeur of France and which alone can assure peace, order and justice" (Shirer, 223). The Duke's declaration was in fact a lone voice among leaguers, which were not political parties and therefore had no organized agenda to "take over." This *acte manqué* on their part left the republic intact, albeit standing on uncertain ground. What could have been fatal for French republican democracy, that is, the very real possibility of the creation of a fascistic order in France, fell short thanks to the lack of a strong leadership from extremist elements or a long-term plan to establish an authoritarian regime similar to the Fascist and Nazi regimes in Italy and Germany.

The 1934 riots were demonstrably a high point for the leaguers in particular and the Far Right in general. They clearly sounded the alarm that fascism was indeed on the rise in France. Thus, rather than rallying popularity to the political message of the leagues and sympathy to their cause, the riots had precisely the opposite effect of sounding a political alarm for the deeply republican French, who realized that the growing threat of the Far Right could possibly swing France into the fascist camp. "Fascism is at the door," declared Léon Jouhaux, head of the CGT (*Confédération Générale du travail*, General Confederation of Workers) the powerful labor union. His warning was heard by many Frenchmen who were afraid, not without cause, of a possible political takeover by a homegrown brand of fascism. The fear of such a takeover resulted in a rallying of the left around the principles of the republic. To ensure basic democratic principles, channels between the different leftist parties were reopened and even the Communists overcame their differences with the Socialists. Together they organized a common march against fascism on February 12, 1934, only six days after the deadly riots of the Place de la Concorde. From that time on, the leftist coalition grew stronger as it became clear that a political victory could be achieved only with the support of other leftist constituencies as well as with the collaboration of the influential workers' unions. In 1935, a full alliance of the different leftist factions introduced the program of the "Popular Front," which was led by the Socialist Léon Blum, whose strong democratic principles earned him the respect of the other coalition members, Communists, Socialists, and Radicals. However, Blum's Jewish background exacerbated the anti-Semitic leaguers who did not hesitate to print slurs in the press such as these slogans from Charles Maurras *Action Française* in 1936: "The Blum guy must be seen, understood, fought and killed like a Jew" or "As a Jew he must be shot in the back." The campaign against Blum took a particularly nasty turn when on

February 13, 1936 he was violently attacked in the streets by leaguers who beat him so severely that he had to be hospitalized for six weeks. Despite these outbursts of violence from the leagues, France's Popular Front continued working to secure its political future by way of a coalition of the Left as it prepared for the 1936 legislative elections. The final touch to the Popular Front victory came with a famous radio broadcast by Maurice Thorez, the leader of the French Communist Party, who advocated complete republican unity by calling on all of France to unite in voting for the coalition for peace and reconciliation. The speech became known as *La main tendue* (the extended hand): "We call upon you all: workers, peasants, intellectuals, young and old, men and women, all of you, people of France, to fight with us for happiness and against misery, for freedom and against slavery, for peace and against war" (Alexander and Graham, 21). The French people responded to Thorez's republican appeal during the May 1936 election by aligning their second-round vote—the first round divided the votes along party lines—behind the Socialist Party, led by Léon Blum. The Front won the elections, the Socialists had the most seats—376 out of the possible 618—and Blum, as leader of the Socialist Party, became prime minister. However, and despite their help in electing the Popular Front and their support for Blum, the Communists declined to participate in the new government, which was mainly composed of Radicals and Socialists.

The *Cultural Revolution* of the Popular Front

With Blum as the first Socialist prime minister in the history of the Third Republic, the winds of French politics shifted and brought long-awaited social reforms. The Blum government quickly passed a series of reforms that would forever change the lives of the working class, while also reshaping the cultural identity of all French social classes. By reducing the workweek to forty hours, increasing salaries, and granting workers two weeks paid vacation, the Popular Front government not only improved their lives, but also stirred up a revolution in the cultural sphere. This was a moment of pure euphoria for millions of French working families, who had never been on vacation before, never been on a train, never seen the ocean, and never visited friends and family living far away. Blum often spoke of the elated spirit of the Popular Front, as in this radio speech in which he addressed the nation on December 31, 1936:

> Hope has returned, and with it a taste for work, a taste for life. France looks and feels different. Blood courses more rapidly through a rejuvenated body. In France, it is as though the human condition itself has been improved. New social relations are being established; a new order is being developed. We can see that equity and freedom are in themselves beneficial and salutary. (Lacouture, 281)

Blum's "healthy" France was also the beneficiary of an ambitious cultural program. Léo Lagrange, under-secretary of sport, culture, and leisure, initiated a full recreation program with the opening of youth hostels, the creation of new local theaters, and the opening of film theaters in the smallest villages. These novelties were part of a more general plan to educate and entertain all strata of the population, and especially the much-neglected youth for whom summer vacation, sports, cultural activities, and low-budget traveling replaced, for a while, the daily routine of work. Not all children could take advantage of Lagrange's plan, but the opportunities were there. In addition, willing or not, parents were forced to allow their children to be educated a while longer when the Popular Front government raised the mandatory school age from thirteen to fourteen. Books were now traveling to the readers with the creation of the *Bibliobus*, a state-financed library on wheels stopping in many neighborhoods of large cities, as well as in towns and remote villages in the French provinces. For many workers of the period, "everything seemed possible," an expression that would become the motto of the Popular Front, and which was first coined by the Socialist Marceau Pivert, a fervent member of the coalition, who declared right after the election: "In the atmosphere of victory, of confidence and discipline that flourishes in this land, yes, all is possible for those who dare" (*Nouvel Observateur*, 18). Everything seemed possible indeed for Maurice Habib, then a young apprentice tailor in Paris, caught in the fever of the cultural changes of the period. In a special 2006 issue of the magazine *Nouvel Observateur* on the occasion of the seventieth anniversary of the Popular Front, Habib reminisced about his life in 1936. He recalled his trip in the metro on a weekend in the direction of a lovely outdoor spot by the water in a forest just outside of Paris. He still remembered how his exuberance and happiness seemed to frighten the proper and quiet-mannered bourgeois crowds going for their traditional stroll in the woods and did not know what to make of this new energy "from below." He also decided to take advantage of night classes and studied what he could not before the reforms. He describes the cultural euphoria of the period in the following terms: "We were discovering life. We were thinking. The return to the earth, the free rides on public transport . . . we were dreaming. It was our very own Year One, with this intoxicating feeling that anything was possible, that we were going to drop everything and rewrite life itself" (Maurice Habib, in *Nouvel Observateur*, 9).

There was cheerfulness in the air, with more popular music, singing, and street dancing than ever before, and even the workers' strikes were called "strikes of joy." This general sense of popular enthusiasm was reflected in everyday culture: popular songs by artists like the "heartthrob with a Corsican accent," Tino Rossi, singing the hit song *Marinella*, as well as the dramatic and soon to become world-famous "Little Sparrow" in black, Edith Piaf, singing *Mon Légionnaire* about a handsome young soldier of the Foreign Legion, were on everyone's lips.

The adult population, especially from the working class newly empowered with some measure of time and money, could enjoy leisure in a way it never had before. National infrastructure naturally followed suit to accommodate a new "leisure class" in need of reasonably priced places to stay, affordable means of transportation, and entertainment. As early as August 1936, discounted train tickets were made available to working-class tourists who could finally travel at a reasonable fare to their first vacation destination. Within the first years of the implementation of the paid vacation reform, it was mainly the unmarried workers or the young couples who could afford to travel away from home on vacation. They were particularly interested in traveling to warm spots and beaches, traditionally the exclusive playgrounds of the bourgeois and upper class.

For the privileged, this mixing of classes on the beaches, mountain resorts, and other places that had hitherto been exclusively reserved for their exclusive use was not always welcome. They often resented the presence of workers around them, this time as vacationers and not servants, and soon developed a language of intolerance to describe this "newly visible" class. A common term used to speak about workers was *salopards en casquette* (dirtbags in caps). In fact, the workers' cap may be said to have become the "national headwear," replacing in sheer number the sophisticated fashionable hats created by Coco Chanel, the wide brimmed sun hats worn by women at the beach, or even the (now) stereotypical "French berets" that leaguers from the *Croix-de-Feu*, for example, had adopted as part of their uniform. The workers' cap was the cultural sign of the thirties, a sign that France had entered the era of social changes for the masses. The cap made a significant appearance in popular films of the period, like Julien Duvivier's *La belle équipe* a film strongly informed by the social optimism of the time. Duvivier's film tells the story of a group of unemployed working-class friends who, having won the lottery, decide to open a cooperative dancing-café, a *"guinguette"* on the banks of the Seine. Jean Gabin, France's answer to the Hollywood star, a mix of Bogart and Brando, played a kind of archetypal French working-class hero with his cap on his head, his cigarette hanging from the side of his mouth, and his rough yet endearing Parisian working-class accent.

The general euphoria of the Popular Front period stood in sharp contrast with the growing power and belligerence of fascism in Europe and the feeling that another war was imminent. Some writers attempted to ward off the impending catastrophe through their work. The pacifist playwright, Jean Giraudoux, rewrote Homer's *Illiad* in his play *There Will Be No Trojan War* (1935) in which Hector thinks he can avoid the war through diplomacy. Giraudoux could not ignore, in the end, even in his play, the rise of extremist ideologies that were pushing France into an inevitable conflict. Despite Hector's immense efforts at avoiding the clash of the Trojans and the Greeks, the gates of Troy finally open at the end of the play, a sign that war is imminent.

For most French men and women, the news of war came over the radio, as the advent of radio broadcasting had become a successful economic and cultural reality in the 1930s. The growing popularity of radio broadcasting was due to the medium's monopoly in a pretelevision age, as well as to the increasing population of listeners avid for serials and popular music. The majority of new listeners were from the working classes, and their tastes were taken into consideration in the general programming. As historians Pierre Albert and André-Jean Tudesq wrote in their history of radio and television, the 1930s were the starting point for the successful "radio era." It was a time when radio began to be regarded as a crucial tool by governments that saw its potential to educate and inform—and manipulate—, as well as be a leisure industry that understood its entertainment potential. In the 1930s, radios became less expensive, the quality of reception was improved, and advertising was authorized on private stations as early as 1934. This transformation of an amateurish field into a professional one soon translated into the creation of many new national and private stations, both in Paris and the provinces. In 1939, there were 5.5 million radios in French homes compared to 500,000 ten years earlier. These numbers were far behind the United States with 26 million radios, or even Britain and Germany, with approximately 8.5 million each, but they reflected the rapid growth of interest in radio in France. Those who could not afford to buy a radio often gathered at a more fortunate friend's house to listen to their favorite programs, ranging from educational lectures from the Sorbonne to popular songs performed in "street" French. Energized producers innovated constantly as they rode the tidal wave of radio success and responded positively to a wide range of demands from the audience. There was a significant change in the

1930s as lectures on literature and history, conferences, classical music, readings of plays and poems, while still maintained on the air, were soon overrun by popular music, games, singing competitions, and series like *La famille Duraton* (The Duraton Family) about the daily life of a fictional and "typical" French family; the series was extremely successful and lasted until 1966. Not everyone was happy about what was perceived as the commercialization and debasement of the medium, a waste of its potential, as noted by the classical French actress Cécile Sorel, "Radio could have been an instrument to educate the masses, but instead it makes them more ignorant" (in Rioux, 315). National radio continued to educate and inform the listeners while private stations made it a point to mainly entertain. Private radios, like the popular and innovative Radio-Cité, where *La famille Duraton* was broadcast, did not however neglect to keep its listeners informed with the latest news bulletins and did not hesitate to interrupt regular programming to bring serious news reports, like the historic live transmission of German troops entering Vienna in March 1938.

1940–1944: Voices on the Radio

In 1936, the voice of Maurice Thorez announcing his policy of national reconciliation had given France the optimism it needed at a time of political uncertainty. Events would soon change the voices and the contents of the messages coming through the radio.

The Popular Front government lasted until 1938, when the Radical Daladier returned to power and the leftist coalition disintegrated. However, the reforms it implemented became a social "given" never to be revoked under the republic. Pessimism nevertheless returned, but despite signs of an impending war, talks about "peace" continued to dominate political discourse. In order to avoid war, the French (and British) leaders preferred to follow a policy of appeasement rather than confront Germany head-on. At the end of September 1938, after the Munich Conference, Prime Minister Daladier justified the annexing of Czechoslovakia by Hitler as a collaborative effort on the part of the French and the British to "save the peace" by choosing diplomacy over force. At the same time, in London Prime Minister Neville Chamberlain was announcing "Peace for our time" to the British population. In reality, Hitler was bullying leaders reticent to go to war and who wanted desperately to believe in the possibility of peace.

Peace was the last international illusion to go when war finally broke out on September 1, 1939, as Germany invaded Poland. The offensive against France only began in May, 1940, after an eerie sense of quiet along the northern borders, a sentiment that made the puzzled French troops call the war a *drôle de guerre* (weird or funny kind of war). This feeling of uncanny tranquility quickly disappeared as the attack from German troops swiftly and brutally began on May 10. The Franco-British troops thought they were relatively secure behind the newly created Maginot line, a concrete defensive wall and bunkers built on the French side of the Franco-German border. However, Germans' tank divisions detoured around the Maginot line, through the Netherlands and Belgium, in a *blitzkrieg* (lighting war), with all their military forces engaged all at once, in order to achieve massive annihilation and a quick victory. Six weeks later, on June 14, 1940, German troops entered Paris. The feeling of social and cultural euphoria inspired by the Popular Front had disappeared and German troops marched by the Arc of Triumph, Napoleon's tribute to French military glory, and then made their way down the Champs Elysées.

Within twenty four hours, between June 17 and June 18, 1940, radio brought contradictory news of both the end and the continuation of war; news of "two Frances," one collaborating and another resisting the enemy. On June 17, 1940, the "legal voice" of France, that of Marshal Pétain, the trusted and aging hero of World War I who became French prime minister on June 16, announced that France would stop armed combat and declare an armistice. Half of France, including Paris, was occupied and directly administered by Germany until 1942, then all of France until the end of the war (see figure 5.2).

Figure 5.2   Occupation of Paris (January 1944)

German SS soldiers are standing in front of the Opera Garnier while an elegant Parisian crowd passes them by with clear hostility in their eyes. In the background temporary road signs indicate the direction and location of various German outposts and fronts throughout France. (© Hachette Photo Presse)

During the Occupation, the French government relocated to the spa town of Vichy where its cabinet became known as the "Vichy government." On June 18, 1940, the French heard another voice, this time from the London studios of the BBC, that of the recently appointed minister of defense, General Charles de Gaulle. The general called on the French to refuse the armistice and to join him in continuing the fight. His speech, referred to as the *L'Appel* (the call, but also the appeal), has become one of the most significant acts of modern French history. From London, de Gaulle galvanized and rallied the official resistance to Germany and Vichy France by calling on more troops to join him in England where he eventually received long-term political asylum from Winston Churchill after being court-martialed in absentia and sentenced to death for high treason against Vichy. London became the general headquarters for the new "Free French Army" commanded by de Gaulle. On June 17,

Pétain, recalling the savagery of World War I, had announced that France had to give up combat in the national interest. The next day, de Gaulle spoke about continuing the fight: "Must hope disappear? Is defeat final? No! . . . Whatever happens, the flame of the French resistance must not be extinguished" (Wierviorka, 369). In his first dramatic broadcast, De Gaulle announced with a solemn voice that France had only "lost a battle, not the war." He also inaugurated the notion of "resistance" and promised the French people to keep in touch by radio from his London outpost. From that point on, his broadcasts became the voice of hope that made many French people contemplate the future possibility of better days and gave them the courage to organize a resistance movement from within France.

So close together in time, these two opposing voices presented the French with a dilemma. Should they trust Pétain whose age and whose service to the nation in World War I inspired trust, but who was nevertheless capitulating to the enemy? Should they cast their lot with a government that seemed to be on the way to ratifying Germany's vision of a strong, economically powerful, hardworking, and racially stratified Europe? Or should they hold on to de Gaulle's vision of an autonomous France that would reclaim its frontiers, independence, global ambitions, and republican politics and culture? The answers given to these questions and the proportion of the population that "chose" one side over the other, the extent to which the French committed to one side or the other, are issues that are still being debated today (see chapter 6).

At first, Pétain's policies seemed to be a means of obtaining terms of peace that would be as advantageous as possible for France, but the "collaborationist" reality of the Vichy government and its espousal of nazi ideology became increasingly clear. The Vichy policy of "moral order" under the slogan *travail, famille, patrie* (work, family, homeland) was itself an extremely nationalistic and overtly anti-Semitic program that promoted a "blood and soil" ideology that could not always be distinguished from the nazi agenda.

Because they lived during a time of occupation and in constant fear of being denounced by their own if they did not follow the Vichy directives, the average French men and women became immensely suspicious of everyone, including members of their own family. Some felt that it was their duty as citizens of the French State to report Jews, Communists, or members of the Resistance to the legal authorities of Vichy; others hesitated, still others fought secretly to protect these "undesirable elements." Whatever their allegiance, locked in a strange paradigm of suspicion and secrecy, no one felt free to express their true feelings toward the two radio messages and the different ideas they conveyed.

Popular Front workers initially had to exchange their caps for war gear, and then for working clothes again when, in 1942, a majority of able-bodied Frenchmen was required to work in Germany. French Jews had to "register," wear a yellow Star of David on their sleeve, and were socially and professionally ostracized, all procedures that facilitated deportation when it actually began in 1942. That same year, fearing an attack from the Southern borders of France after the Allies had landed in North Africa, Hitler decided on a total occupation of French territory. Barred from any form of national decision-making and reduced to a symbolic role, the Vichy government still remained entitled to maintain and enforce a rigid moral order over the French population. More than ever, France was under the strictest watch by Germany and Vichy, and its social and cultural life was resolutely affected by the controlled and controlling environment imposed by the Occupation.

French films were heavily censured and many retreated into stories of the past where fantasy was the favored style. American films were banned and French cinema momentarily profited from this absence of competition from Hollywood, while German films spread the anti-Semitic message of the nazi ideology. During these difficult times when food was rationed and energy scarce, French theaters provided a rare warm place to forget, if only for a few hours, the hardships of the Occupation. Films like the 1941 dramatic romance *Remorques* (*Stormy Waters*) by Jean Grémillon, featuring the reigning couple of French cinema, Jean Gabin and Michèle Morgan, the 1943 *Le Corbeau* (*The Raven*) directed by Henri-Georges Clouzot, a *noirish* feature about a serial denunciator bringing an entire town to general hysteria, and Marcel Carné's 1945 masterpiece *Les Enfants du paradis* (*Children of Paradise*), an epic and a love story set in the world of theater in nineteenth century France, were all hugely successful and provided the French with at least momentary respite from the harsh reality of the Occupation.

As always, the voice of hope kept coming from London over the radio waves and competed with French radio stations under German control. The collaborators of the Vichy Government were naturally given most of the airtime in France. They continuously voiced their sympathies with Nazi Germany and called upon good French citizens to spy on those French men and women who silently refused to abide by the new nazi or Vichy policies. Many of those who resisted left for London to join de Gaulle, and others joined the underground Resistance that came to be known as *le maquis*. While used as a major instrument of propaganda by Nazi Germany and Vichy France, the radio also continued to serve the French Resistance from both inside and outside France. Singer Edith Piaf, who was secretly a member of the Resistance, was regularly heard on the waves. During the war, she came out with her famous love ballad "*La Vie en Rose*," which became a huge success and continues today to be emblematic of French *chanson* in particular and French "romantic culture" in general throughout the world. Piaf's voice and lyrics, speaking of passionate romance and of another life to all those affected by the war, seemed to have a truly universal appeal. German officers and soldiers stationed in France became fascinated by French culture, cabaret and music hall in particular, and above all they loved Piaf's voice, her Parisian street accent, and her romantic songs. She reluctantly sang for them, but in exchange obtained permission to sing for French prisoners of war, some of whom she helped to escape and join the Resistance. Americans loved her too. Steven Spielberg would feature her soothing and sad voice in his 1998 *Saving Private Ryan* before the final battle in which most of the American soldiers defending the fictional town of Ramelle are killed. The group of GIs we have followed throughout the film are depicted in a rare moment of quiet, softly lulled by Piaf singing a song that one of the soldiers translates into English for his comrades. This scene, set against the backdrop of a bombed out French town, harks back to a bygone era of universalism, for, in the midst of the rubble, Piaf's nostalgic and hopeful voice is the only intact archetype of a dominant France left "rising" among the ruins.

While most French radios played nazi-vetted love songs and continuous propaganda condemned in the famous rhyming slogan introduced by the Resistance: *Radio-Paris ment, Radio-Paris est Allemand* (Radio-Paris Lies, Radio-Paris Is German), the BBC continued to broadcast the voice of Free France. Daily programs like *Les Français parlent aux Français* (The French Are Speaking to the French) broadcast news bulletins as well as coded messages to members of the Resistance in France. These strange messages were either personal information or general calls for military action; they brought individual and collective hope to those who waited for a sign either to wait for the safe return of a loved one, or to prepare for action. This was done in mystifying phrases like: "John has a long moustache" or "Marguerite is a kinky girl." It is one of these messages that informed the French Resistance of the impending Allied landing in Normandy. This momentous piece of information took the shape of the first verses of *Chanson d'automne* (Autumn Song) a famous poem by the nineteenth-century French poet Paul Verlaine: *Les sanglots longs// des violons// de l'automne// blessent mon coeur// d'une langueur// monotone* (The long sobs //of violins//in the fall//hurt my heart//with their languid tone). A poem known by every school child in France became the news of liberation that so many had been waiting for. The Allied troops landed on several Normandy beaches on June 6,1944 and waged fierce and bloody battles to push the Germans back from Normandy to Paris, and eventually back to Germany where they surrendered in 1945. Along the way, in the newly liberated villages and towns, the message was now clear and joyous as people chanted "the Americans are coming" and women kissed GIs leaning from their tanks. Paris was liberated on August 25, 1944, and the disincarnated voice of de Gaulle that had given hope to the French for four long years was finally replaced by his tall figure descending the Champs Elysées, greeted by hundreds of thousands of cheering Parisians.

References

Ades, Dawn. *Dada and Surrealism*. New York: Barron, 1978.

Albert, Pierre and André-Jean Tudesq. *Histoire de la radio-télévision*. Paris: PUF (Que sais-je?), 1981.

Alexander, Martin and Graham Helen. *The French and Spanish Popular Fronts: Comparative Perspectives*. Cambridge: Cambridge University Press, 1989.

Anderson, Sherwood. *Winesburg, Ohio*. New York: B.W. Huebsch, 1919.

Andrew, Dudley and Steven Ungar. *Popular Front Paris and the Poetics of Culture*. Cambridge, MA: Harvard University Press, 2005.

Aragon, Louis. *Persécuté, Persécuteur* in *Oeuvre Poétique*. Paris: Livre Club Diderot 1975.

Bancel, Nicolas, Pascal Blanchard, Gilles Boetsch, Eric Deroo, and Sandrine Lemaire. *Zoos Humains, de la Vénus hottentote aux "reality shows"* Paris: Editions la Découverte, 2002.

Baxter, Annette Kar. *Henry Miller: Expatriate*. Pittsburgh: University of Pittsburgh Press, 1961.

Biondi, Jean-Pierre. *Senghor ou la tentation de l'universel*. Paris: Denoël, 1993.

Breton, André. *Clair de Terre*. Paris: Gallimard (Poésie), 1966.

———. *Manifestoes of Surrealism*. Ann Arbor: University of Michigan Press, 1969.

Bülow (von), Prince. *Memoirs, Volume III, The World War and Germany's Collapse: 1901–1919*. Geoffrey Dunlop, trans. Boston: Little, Brown, and Company, 1932.

Buñuel, Luis. *My Last Sigh*. New York: Alfred A. Knopf, 1983.

Cameron, Keith. *René Maran*. Boston: G.K. Hall & Co., 1985.

Campbell, James. *Exiled in Paris Richard Wright, James Baldwin, Samuel Beckett, and Others on the Left Bank*. Los Angeles: University of California Press, 2003.

Césaire, Aimé. *Cahier d'un retour au pays natal*. Abiole Irele, ed. Columbus: Ohio State University Press, 2000.

e.e. Cummings, *Tulips and Chimneys*. New York: Liveright, 1923, 1976.

Davis, Gregson. *Aimé Césaire*. Cambridge: Cambridge University Press, 1997.

Dos Passos, John. *Journeys between Wars*. New York: Harcourt, Brace, 1934.

Drieu La Rochelle, Pierre. "Le lieutenant de tirailleurs." *La Comédie de Charleroi*. Paris: Gallimard, 1934.

Duhamel, George. *America The Menace: Scenes from the Life of the future*. New York: Arno Press, 1974.

Firmage, George, ed. *e.e. Cummings: A Miscellany Revised*. New York: October House, 1965.

Fitzgerald, F. Scott. *Tender Is the Night*. New York: Charles Scribner's Sons, 1934.

Forbes, Jill and Michale Kelly. *French Cultural Studies: An Introduction*. Oxford: Oxford University Press, 1995.

Goetschel, Pascale and Emmanuelle Loyer. *Histoire culturelle et intellectuelle de la France au XXe siècle*. Paris: Armand Colin, 1995.

Golsan, Richard. *Vichy's Afterlife: History and Counterhistory in Postwar France*. Lincoln: University of Nebraska Press, 2000.

Green, L.C. *The Contemporary Law of Armed Conflict*. Manchester: Manchester University Press, 1999.

Hemingway, Ernest. *A Moveable Feast*. New York: Charles Scribner's Sons, 1967.

———. *The Sun Also Rises*. New York: Charles Scribner's Sons, 1926.

Hodier, Catherine and Michel Pierre. *L'Exposition coloniale*. Brussels: Editions Complexe, 1991.

Holman, Valerie and Debra Kelly, eds. *France at War in the Twentieth Century: Propaganda, Myth and Metaphor*. New York: Berghahn Books, 2000.

Jack, Belinda. *Negritude and Literary Criticism: The History and Theory of "Negro-African" Literature in French*. Wesport, CT: Greenwood Press, 1996.

Jackson, Julian. *The Popular Front in France Defending Democracy. 1934–38*. Cambridge: Cambridge University Press, 1988.

Kennedy, Gerald and Jackson Bryer. *French Connections: Hemingway and Fitzgerald Abroad*. New York: St. Martin's Press, 1998.

Kiki. *Souvenirs*. Alice Prin, ed. Paris: Henri Broca, 1929.

Knight, Christopher. *The Patient Particulars: American Modernism and the Technique of Originality*. Lewisburg: Bucknell University Press, 1995.

Lacouture, Jean. *Leon Blum*. George Holoch, trans. New York: Holmes and Meier Publishers, 1982.

Lebovics, Herman. *True France: The Wars over Cultural Identity, 1900–1945*. Ithaca: Cornell University Press, 1992.

Leiner, Jacqueline. "Entretien avec A.C. " In *Tropiques*. Vol. 1. Aimé Césaire, ed. [facsimile reproduction]. Paris: Éditions Jean-Michel Place, 1978.

Levenstein, Harvey. *We'll Always Have Paris: American Tourists in France since 1930*. Chicago: University of Chicago Press, 2004.

Lewis, Sinclair. *Babbitt*. New York: Harourt, Brace and Co., 1922.

Maran, René. *Batouala: A True Black Novel*. Washington, DC: Black Orpheus Press, 1972.

McMillan, James. *Modern France: 1880–2002*. Oxford: Oxford University Press, 2003.

Miller, Henry. *Tropic of Cancer*. Paris: Obelisk Press, 1934.

———. *Letters to Emile*. Georges Wickes, ed. New York: New Directions Book, 1989.

Mouré, Kenneth and Martin Alexander, eds. *Crisis and Renewal in France, 1918–1962*. New York: Berghahn Books, 2002.

Ngandu Nkashama, Pius. *Négritude et poétique: Une lecture de l'oeuvre critique de Léopold Sédar Senghor*. Paris: L'Harmattan, 1992.

Nouvel Observateur. Vol. 2164 (April 27–May 3, 2006). Special Issue: "Il y a 70 ans: Le Front populaire."

Pellisier, Pierre. *6 février 1934, la République en flammes*. Paris : Librairie Académique Perrin, 2000.

Radiguet, Raymond. *Le Diable au corps*. Paris: Grasset, 1923.

Rearick, Charles. *The French in Love and War: Popular Culture in the Era of the World Wars*. New Haven, CT: Yale University Press, 1997.

Reynaud, Paul. *Livre d'or de l'exposition coloniale*. Paris: Librairie Ancienne Honoré Champion, 1931.

———. *Mémoires: Venu de ma montagne*. Paris: Flammarion, 1960.

Rioux, Jean-Pierre and Jean-François Sirinelli. *La Culture de masse en France de la Belle Epoque à aujourd'hui*. Paris: Fayard, 2002.

Rydell, Robert. *World of Fairs: The Century-of-Progress Expositions*. Chicago: University of Chicago Press, 1993.

Scharfman, Ronnie. *"Engagement" and the Language of the Subject in the Poetry of Aimé Césaire*. Gainesville: University of Florida Press, 1987.

Senghor, Léopold Ségar. "René Maran, précurseur de la négritude" *Homage à Maran*. Paris: Présence Africaine, 1965.

Shirer, William. *The Collapse of the Third Republic: An Inquiry into the Fall of France in 1940*. New York: Simon and Schuster, 1969.

Stein, Gertrude. *Geography and Plays*. Madison: University of Wisconsin Press, 1993.

Tropiques, 1941–1945 (Collection complète). Paris: Jean-Michel Place, 1978.

Tzara, Tristan. *Approximate Man and Other Writings*. Mary Ann Caws, trans. Detroit: Wayne State University Press, 1973.

Vaillant, Janet. *Black, French, African: A Life of Léopold Sédar Senghor*. Cambridge, MA: Harvard University Press. 1990.

Wharton, Edith. *The Book of the Homeless*. New York : Scribner, 1916.

———. *Age of Innocence*. New York, Appleton, 1920.

———. *Fighting France: From Dunkerque to Belport*. Kila, Montana: Kessinger Publishing, 2004.

Wieviorka, Olivier and Prochasson Christophe, eds. *La France du XXe siècle*. Paris: Seuil, 1994.

Wilder, Gary. *The French Imperial Nation-State: Negritude and Colonial Humanism between the Two World Wars*. Chicago: University of Chicago Press, 2005.

Williams, Patrick and Laura Chrisman. *Colonial Discourse and Post-colonial Theory: A Reader*. New York: Columbia University Press, 1994.

Wiser, William. *The Crazy Years: Paris in the Twenties*. London: Thames & Hudson, 1983.

———. *The Twilight Years: Paris in the 1930's*. New York: Caroll & Graf, 2000.

PART II

1945 TO THE PRESENT: THE FRENCH DECLINE?

Roger Celestin

CHAPTER 6

FROM THE LIBERATION INTO
THE FIFTIES (1944–1955)

In the early days [of the Liberation] when the American army was first passing by, in jeeps and trucks the Americans used to say to me but they do not seem to get used to us, we have been right here over a week and they get just as excited when they see us as if they had never seen us before. You do not understand, I said to them you see every time they see you it makes them know it is not a dream that it is true that the Germans are gone and that you are here that you are here and that the Germans are gone. Every time they see you it is a new proof, a new proof that it is all true that the Germans are really truly completely and entirely gone, gone gone.

—Gertrude Stein, *Wars I Have Seen* (1945)

More than the arrival of American soldiers in their jeeps and trucks described by the American writer Gertrude Stein, who had continued to live in France throughout the war, the most emblematic images of the end of World War II and of the end of the German occupation for the French are probably those of General Charles de Gaulle as he made his way from place to place in Paris on August 25, 1944, from the Montparnasse train station where the headquarters of General Leclerc—the commander of the French military forces fighting with the Allies—were located, to a triumphal walk down the Champs Elysées, surrounded throughout by crowds of hundreds of thousands of cheering Parisians celebrating the liberation of their city after four years of occupation.

Dossier 6.1   De Gaulle in Liberated Paris (August 25, 1944)

The Parisian insurrection against the occupying German forces began on August 19, 1944. Charles de Gaulle, de facto leader of what was quickly becoming liberated France arrived in the capital six days later. De Gaulle, as always acutely conscious of the symbolic value of public events, carefully chose his itinerary. His first stop in the capital was Gare Montparnasse, one of Paris' main railroad stations, housing the headquarters of General Leclerc, commander of the second Armored Battalion, which has taken part in the city's liberation. De Gaulle himself had actively lobbied the Allied commanders to include French military forces in the liberation of Paris; he had felt particularly vexed by the fact that the free French forces had not been allowed to take part in the Allied landings on D-Day, June 16, 1944. Thus, making Leclerc's headquarters the first stop of his victory itinerary through Paris was a way of highlighting, as he also would in his speech later on in the day, the role played by the French—pointedly not the *Allied*— forces in this phase of the war. It was crucial for him at this stage to depict France as a free republic, or, more precisely, a republic freeing itself on its own steam. De Gaulle's next two stops were the War Ministry and Central Police Headquarters. He made it a point of going first to these two places before visiting City Hall, seat of the interior Resistance and Communist-dominated city government. There again, the emphasis was placed on the fact that France, although on the brink of victory, was a nation still fight- ing to rid itself of its occupiers, while the visit to police headquarters already prefigured the internal settling of accounts that must necessarily occur after four years of occupa- tion during which many French citizens had become implicated with the enemy. De Gaulle's speech at Paris' City Hall, in front of the CNR (*Conseil National de la Résistance*, National Council of the Resistance), the *Comité Parisien de Libération*, and the crowd of Parisians, alluded to some of these issues but focused on French unity.

Why should we try to hide the feelings welling up in us, men and women who are at home here, in Paris that has risen up to liberate itself and knew how to do so with its own hands. No! We will not hide this deep and sacred emotion. We are living through moments that transcend each of our small lives. Paris! Paris outraged! Paris broken! Paris martyred, but Paris liberated! Liberated by itself, liberated by its own population with the help of France's armies, with the support and help of all of France, of fighting France, of the only France, of true France, of eternal France. Well! Since the enemy that held Paris has capitulated, France has come home, to Paris. She enters bloody, but resolute. She enters enlightened by an immense lesson, but more than ever certain of her duties and of her rights. I say of her duties, and I will summarize them all by saying that for now, they are duties of war. The enemy is reeling but he is not yet vanquished. He remains on our soil. It won't be enough that, with the support of our cherished and admirable allies, we have chased him from our home for us to feel satisfied after what has occurred. We want to enter his territory as victors, as it should be. This is why the French vanguard has entered Paris to the sound of canons. This is why the great French army in Italy has landed in the south of France and is quickly making its way up the Rhône Valley. This is why our cherished and brave interior forces are going to equip them- selves with modern weapons. It is for this revenge, this vengeance and this justice that we will con- tinue to fight till the last day, until the day of total and complete victory. This war duty, all those present here today and all those who are listening to us in France know that it demands national unity. We, those who have lived the greatest hours of our History, we can want nothing other than to show ourselves, until the end, worthy of France. Long live France!

At the outset of the speech, all-encompassing and unifying declarations bring together into a single entity several disparate elements: the "me" that is de Gaulle, the "us" of the French people, "men and women, here, in their home," then "Paris" and finally "France." The Allies are clearly excluded from the speech's first and emotional acknowl- edgment of the forces that have liberated Paris, only to be briefly alluded to in the fourth paragraph and then only as "with the support of our cherished and admirable allies." Paris is liberated not by others but by "itself," "by its people," "with the help of France's armies," "with the support and help of all of France." Also excluded from this increas- ingly inclusive—from "me" to "France"—but exclusively French series is Vichy and those who collaborated and do not belong to the "France that is fighting [against the enemy, instead of collaborating with it]." This France is the only one that matters; it is above and beyond historical contingencies even as it belongs to history; it is the "only

France, eternal France," a simultaneously Platonically removed and centuries-old notion reaching back to the dawn of France's history—to Clovis the king, Charlemagne the emperor, and Roland the knight—that no amount of betrayal and hardship can ever obliterate. The people who have not fought and who are not fighting the enemy do not belong in this France. However, this appeal to a removed entity untarnished by recent and contemporary events and faraway in time, does not mean an absence of clear, present, and concrete measures for, in the speech, there is also a call to continue the fight. De Gaulle specifically refers to the French advance army's entrance in Paris, to the "great French army [that has] landed in the South and quickly coming up the Rhône Valley," and, finally, to the—also French—"forces of the interior that are going to equip themselves with modern weapons." The objective of this gathering of exclusively French forces is, of course, "total; and complete victory," but, more specifically, it is "revenge, vengeance and justice." It is not quite clear—indeed it is quite unclear—whether this is aimed exclusively at the German occupiers or also at those who collaborated with them. The word "collaborationist," or even any direct allusion to French men and women who would not be not part of "the eternal France" or even of this accomplishment of the "war duty" is scrupulously left out of de Gaulle's speech. This confirms a pattern already evident in other speeches made by de Gaulle throughout the war, in which he systematically operates a division between the "true French" and those he considers traitors, an aberration; for example, in a speech made the previous month, on July 2, 1940, de Gaulle uses historical figures culled from the French tradition from the Hundred Years' War to the World War I to make his point: "Would Joan of Arc, Richelieu, Louis XIV, Carnot, Napoleon, Gambetta, Poincarré, Clémenceau, or Marshal Foch ever have consented to deliver France's entire stock of weapons to their enemies so that they could be used against her allies?" (Holman and Kelly, 107). The Vichy government is taken to task here; however, as we have noted, in his August 25, 1940 speech, de Gaulle avoids any direct mention of or reference to Vichy and collaboration. Instead, the emphasis is placed on the sine qua non of "national unity," and the ultimate and rallying point of reference, remote and unchanging, above the fray, is France: "Long live France!"

De Gaulle, the de facto leader of France at that point—he was head of the provisional government of the French Republic—would later write in his memoirs that he had "brought back to France independence, the empire and the sword" (Rioux and Sirinelli, 216); the reference to the "sword" is in opposition to the "shield" that would passively protect France, whereas the sword, armed action whether from inside or outside France, constitutes a dynamic resistance against the occupier. This declaration and de Gaulle's policy in general in the immediate postwar period projected the image of an ascending France, ready to reclaim its position as an unoccupied, independent, united republic, as well as a military and colonial power. To a certain extent, this image was accurate. Political normalization, ranging from the épuration—the "purging" or "cleansing" of the nation through different degrees of punishment for those who had collaborated with the enemy—to the establishment of a new government, was followed by reconstruction and record economic growth; France, an independent republic after the nazi and Vichy interlude was, thanks to a large extent to the de Gaulle's persistent diplomatic and military efforts, among the victors; the empire seemed intact; indeed France's overseas colonies had been used as a power base and bridgehead by de Gaulle. Yet, his phrase containing the trio of "independence, empire, and the sword" did not reflect the new order inaugurated by the end of World War II, a world in which the European powers, or "old Europe"—a phrase pointedly brought out into the media limelight by Donald Rumsfeld, the American defense secretary in the Bush administration during the United Nations deliberations on the invasion of Iraq in 2003 (see chapter 10)—whether they were on the losing or winning side, could no longer determine the terms of international politics or economics. In this new distribution of power becoming increasingly evident in the postwar era, the fault line was no longer between European democracies and the nazi and fascist regimes, but between adversaries in a cold war waged by the two powerful and ideologically opposed main victors, the United States and the Soviet Union. In addition, it was a world in which the major colonial empires were already in the process of disintegrating. Ironically, de Gaulle, the victorious general who had brought "the empire back to France" in 1944, but resigned from political leadership in 1946, would only return to power in 1958, as a result of the Fourth Republic's inability to deal with what can be called an imperial crisis: the Algerian War. It is also ironic that, after a phase of reconstruction and concentration on heavy industry, France would find itself fully entering the consumer age (see chapter 8) at the same time as it entered a phase of decolonization, its empire on the wane (see chapter 7).

*   *   *

As World War II ended in 1944–1945, the primary goal of the provisional government headed by de Gaulle was to retain national unity and ensure political transition, even before concentrating on food supplies or rebuilding the country's industrial infrastructure. In de Gaulle's mind it was absolutely necessary to show that the Vichy regime had been an illegal and illegitimate aberration. On the day of the liberation of Paris some expected him to proclaim the beginning of a new republic, but his answer was "The Republic has never ceased to exist. Free France, Fighting France, the French Committee on National Liberation, each, in turn, incorporated it. Vichy always was, and remains, null and void. I myself am president of the Government of the Republic. Why should I proclaim it?" (*Mémoires de guerre, II*, 308; quoted in Novick, 197). De Gaulle ascribed legitimacy exclusively to the successive shapes taken by the movement he himself led from the moment Marshall Pétain signed the armistice, an act that, in de Gaulle's view, automatically rendered the Vichy government illegal, "null and void." In strictly legal terms, de Gaulle's position may have not been quite as clear or tenable but, in the aftermath of the occupation and in the heady weeks that followed the Liberation, it certainly carried the day. This position also raised a number of problems, the first of which was how to deal with those who had simply "gone along," or actively collaborated with Vichy and the occupying German forces to varying degrees. The most obvious place to start from a political point of view was to replace the Vichy officials and administration. There, de Gaulle had to move quickly, having to contend not only with the representatives of the Vichy regime, the illegal and illegitimate aberration, but, on the winning side, also with the interior Resistance, a powerful and, to some degree, revolutionary force. More specifically, the Communists, who had been particularly active in this interior Resistance—as a result, the Communist Party, *le parti des fusillés* (the party of the executed), was to become the most popular party in the aftermath of the war—wanted a series of reforms carried out from the bottom up and constituted a political and popular force to be reckoned with. In addition, de Gaulle still had to contend with the Allies, England and the United States, whose initial plan had been to occupy France militarily, with American and British generals in charge; coins and notes had already been made, and de Gaulle himself was to be dispatched as governor of Madagascar, then still a French colony, in the Indian Ocean, far from Paris. The Anglo-American Allies did not recognize De Gaulle's government until October 23, two months after his triumphant entrance into liberated Paris.

De Gaulle's tactic relied on systematic speed: as the liberating armies advanced in French territory, his *commissaires de la République* (commissioners of the republic) quickly replaced the Vichy administrators throughout the country; in late August at a meeting with the CNR he informed its leaders that it was now "part of the glorious history of the Liberation, but would have no further raison d'être as an organ of action" (*Complete War Memoirs*, 675; quoted in Sowerwine, 226); in other words, the nation recognized their heroic services during the war and occupation, and they would be honored , but they represented no legal power in postwar France; the army of resisters, the *Forces françaises de l'Intérieur* (FFI, French Forces of the Interior), a force of about 150,000, was incorporated into the regular French army, under de Gaulle's command. This was obviously part of de Gaulle's strategy of reestablishing governmental structures, and among the first steps in achieving his goal, the parallel armed forces that had taken shape during the occupation had to be dismantled.

Even if it was being incorporated into new ruling structures whose policies it did not always agree with, the interior Resistance shared an essential policy with de Gaulle's provisional government: after four years of occupation during which many had passively or actively collaborated with the enemy, there had to be a reckoning before France could return to any kind of reconstruction and even normalcy. The question of guilt and the extent of guilt, the manner of determining that guilt and the degree of punishment was of primary importance. And, here, the points of view diverged widely.

For de Gaulle, since Vichy was an aberration, the French people in their great majority had proved to be true to the ideals of "eternal France, fighting France" (see dossier 6.1) while only a few actively collaborated with the enemy. In April 1944, he declared in a radio broadcast from Algiers: "A few traitors may have directly served the enemy. A few cowards may have voluntarily and easily associated themselves with the collaboration of these unworthy leaders . . . but the immense mass of the French . . . are only unhappy brothers and must be combatants brought together to save the fatherland" (Sowerwine, 229).

This official discourse explained in part or at least rationalized by the need to regain dignity, unify, and rebuild, is subverted by a series of nonofficial discourses. For example, a differing version of the same period may be seen in Marcel Aymé's novel, *Uranus*, published in 1948, and made into a film in 1990 by Claude Berri. The novel is set in the immediate postwar; here the main character, an engineer in Blémont, a town in central France, is by himself and reflects on the changes:

> He was thinking about all these hypocrites, among whom he placed himself. Going beyond the limits of Blémont, he considered the question on the scale of the *département*, and then of the entire nation. The hypocrites could be numbered in the millions now. In all the provinces of France, in all the villages, in the big cities and in the small ones, he saw two-faced people swarming about . . . This wave of hypocrisy he thought he saw sweeping over France now took on grandiose proportions. That all the newspapers

pretended to ignore that there existed millions upon millions of individuals holding this opinion [that Vichy had done the right thing] or reduced their number to merely tens of thousands of idiots and sellouts amounted to a colossal lie, he thought. (37)

The truth probably lies somewhere between de Gaulle's official narrative, which could be justified by the imperatives of the times—keeping order and rebuilding dignity at a crucial juncture in the history of France—and the unofficial one offered by Aymé in novelistic form. In any case, throughout France, whether they believed in one version or the other, people exploded in sometimes extremely violent acts of revenge and punishment. In this spontaneous purge about 10,000 were summarily executed. Short of the firing squad—although sometimes those women who were considered to be "hard cases" also ended up being killed—the shearing of women who had been found guilty of "horizontal collaboration" or, as Gertrude Stein put it, "keeping company with the Germans," was a particularly widespread means of public humiliation and punishment. A journalist for the newspaper *Le Crapouillot* describes the first day of the Liberation in Clermont-Ferrand, a city in central France:

> The hunt began, for men and for women. They were dragged from their homes, found if they were hiding, brutally taken away. The men were arrested and the women, facing the crowd's invectives, were led to different places in the town where the shearings were carried out. The procedure did not last very long. And afterwards one could see these women's shaven heads above the crowd where they were exhibited through the whole town, gathered in carriages like those condemned by the Terror. (Brossat, 93)

This scene would be repeated hundreds, even thousands of times by some estimates (there simply are no official figures), throughout the cities and villages of France. Many commentators today see in this scene a reaffirmation of masculinity on the part of men who "had failed in the key tasks of manhood as defined at the time: they had lost the war and had failed to protect their families" (Sowerwine, 228). Indeed some among the Allies who also witnessed many of these public humiliations and usually stood by while they took place, although not officially condoning them, perceived these Frenchmen in the process of shearing "their women" as the same who, in their opinion, had given in much too quickly to defeat and occupation, and much too easily and actively to collaboration. The shearings have also been perceived as an "evident misogyny intrinsic to all forms of carnival" (Forbes, 100). The word "carnival" is one that harks back to the medieval past of France, a moment when established order temporarily disappears and chaos, for a while, reigns. In this particular instance, *Le Crapouillot's* journalist does not go back in time quite that far but links up the scene to a more recent one in the past: the period of the terror that follows the Revolution of 1789: men and women of the aristocracy, Marie-Antoinette being the most famous of all, being led to the guillotine on carriages, standing above the crowd on the way to their execution. It is ironic that, during the period when these events, with their misogynous overtones, were taking place, women were granted the right to vote in an ordinance signed by de Gaulle in October 1944. Five years later, Simone de Beauvoir's monumental *Le deuxième sexe* (*The Second Sex*), a founding text of feminism, would explore a number of issues not unrelated to the shearing of women in the immediate postwar (see dossier 6.4).

To this date Alain Resnais' *Hiroshima mon amour* (1959) by the novelist Marguerite Duras is the only film to deal with the subject, even if years later and in retrospect. The time is the late 1950s and a French woman meets and has a passionate affair with a

Japanese man at Hiroshima, where she is participating in the making of an antiwar film. Years before, during the occupation, in Nevers, a small town in central France, the woman had been in love with a young German soldier, shot by a French sniper while on his way to one of their encounters in the surrounding fields and ruins. At the Liberation, she is shorn by the townspeople, and her ashamed parents lock her in their home's basement. This aspect of the past of a "girl who was so young in Nevers" is revealed only toward the end of the film, a catharsis that brings together for the audience of 1959 the seemingly private trauma of the shearing of one young woman in 1944, the 105,000 dead and 94,000,000 surviving victims of Hiroshima and Nagasaki in August 1944, and the fear of nuclear holocaust, a continuation of the cold war beginning in 1947 and lasting into the 1960s. In her pronouncement against the act of shearing a woman, Duras comments on this link between private history, national history, and international history in her scenario: "To shave the head of a girl because she has truly loved an official enemy of the state is absolute horror and stupidity [*bêtise*] . . . It's as if the disaster of a woman shorn in Nevers and the disaster of Hiroshima echoed each other exactly" (quoted in Brossat, 53). Although left unmentioned here by Duras, the Algerian War (see chapter 7) with its own horrors, a war in which France is deeply engaged the year the film is released, 1959, no doubt constituted a kind of present but invisible and mute background to the events that were taking place in the film. When

Figure 6.1 Shearing of Women after the Liberation (1944)

The caption reads: *The punishment reserved for those who have collaborated with the enemy. A woman accused of having collaborated with the German occupier has her hair shorn by an FFI.* Behind, along the wall, other collaborators have already been shorn. The photographer is not identified. (© Hachette Photo Presse)

we know that some of the soldiers who had served in World War II were now serving in the Algerian War when *Hiroshima mon amour* was released, the link between these two traumatic moments in French history becomes even more immediate.

The woman from Nevers could be one of the women depicted in the photo, one of the many casualties of the nonofficial purge that followed the Liberation. There was no official approval of the shearings, even if regular army personnel from both French and Allied contingents were often present and did not intervene; one possible reason for this unofficial tolerance, if not approval of these actions by de Gaulle's provisional government, was that by allowing the public to engage in these temporarily unrestricted but limited actions, a more terrible bloodbath was being avoided. At one point, however, the government would have to deal directly with the designation and punishment of collaborators. Neither the shearing of women nor the summary executions could stand in for the general settling of accounts that had to take place, lest the actions of those who had been responsible for the most important aspects of collaboration should be ignored or diminished. This is what the poet Paul Eluard, who had been actively engaged in the Resistance, refers to in his *Raisons d'écrire* (*Reasons For Writing*) in August 1944 upon witnessing the aftermath of a series of shearings in Paris:

> Angry reaction. I see again, in front of a barbershop on rue de Grenelle, a woman's beautiful head of hair lying on the street. I see once more pitiful idiots quaking with fear facing the crowd's laughter. They had not sold out France and they had often not sold out anything at all. In any case, they had never preached to anyone. Whereas the apostle-faced hoodlums the Pétains, the Lavals, the Darnands, the Déats, the Doriots and the Luchaires have left. Further, some of them, confident of their power, remain peacefully at home, hoping to start all over again soon. (Brossat, 69)

The incorporation of the FFI into the regular army occurred at the beginning of the official purge and indicates political transition and stabilization. The summary executions and the shearing of women began to be replaced by trials and court-ordained executions, prison terms, and a number of lesser types of sentences, such as those of "national degradation" (loss of civic rights for varying periods). At the top of the power pyramid, Pétain and Laval were both tried, found guilty, and received the death sentence. De Gaulle commuted Marshall Pétain's sentence to life imprisonment, while Vichy Prime Minister Laval's own sentence was carried out. A number of historians have pointed out that this dual procedure at the very top amounted to a double standard and contributed to the creation of a myth of *résistancialisme*, already reflected in de Gaulle's speech from Algiers in 1944 quoted above. The version presented in this speech is that some of those actually condemned, the great majority, were less guilty than others and had collaborated out of necessity and had resisted as much as they could, while others, like Laval, the very small minority, had betrayed the ideals of the republic and actively collaborated with the nazi occupier. It should also be mentioned, however that, in Pétain's case, once the death penalty had been arrived at, justice could be assumed to have been served, since French law forbade the application of the death penalty in the cases of people over eighty; Pétain was eighty-nine at the time of his trial and would die while under house arrest at ninety-five, on the Ile d'Yeu, an island off the Normandy coast. Laval's outburst at his trial, accusing those who were conducting it of having themselves served the Vichy regime—he was right at least inasmuch as they had held the same positions they now held—is indicative of the difficulty of sorting out the guilty from the innocent. Of the tens of thousands of civil servants who made up the Vichy administration, fewer than 12,000 were punished, and "leniently" so, according to at least one historian: "4000 were dismissed, but with their pensions; the rest were slapped on the wrist by transfers, demotions, or temporary suspensions." As for the army itself, "only seven hundred officers were dismissed—and its structures were unchanged" (Sowerwine, 230). On the whole, some 30, 000–40, 000 individuals were tried and sentenced to different punishments ranging from prison terms to execution; between 700 and 800 were executed; 50,000 received sentences of "national degradation." Rather than a sharp break with the past and Vichy, the purge thus resulted in relative administrative continuity, informed partly by what can be called national and practical expediency. Putting on trial, let alone sentencing and carrying out the sentences of all those who had participated in the Vichy "national revolution" would have brought France to a standstill at a time when national unity and economic reconstruction were the order of the day after five years of war and occupation. The cases of particularly prominent and active supporters of Vichy such as René Bousquet and Maurice Papon, who would not be brought to trial for their role during the occupation until the 1980s and 1990s (see chapter 9) are indicative of this trend. On the other hand, practical expediency could not alone account for this delay. At work was also a more abstract and deep-rooted constant we have seen in de Gaulle's victory speech (dossier 6.1) as well as in his speech concerning the few collaborators and the great mass of resisters: eternal France, the France that harks back to a glorious tradition as well as to the republic born in 1789, this France remains untainted and unscathed by the aberrations of those who are not part of it and have not acted in its name.

In a culture where arts and letters have played such a major role in constructing "the glorious tradition," the fate of writers and intellectuals who had become compromised with the Vichy regime was particularly problematic. At a time when the idea of *responsibility* could not be avoided, their peculiarly crucial position in French society was all the more critical. As Jean-Paul Sartre, the most prominent intellectual of postwar France, paradoxically expresses it, "We were never more free than during the German occupation." He goes on to explain: "We had lost all our rights, beginning with the right to talk; everyday we were insulted to our faces and had to take it in silence . . . and, because of all this, we were free . . . Because an all powerful police tried to force us to hold our tongues, every word took on the value of a declaration of principles; because we were hunted down, every one of our gestures had the weight of a solemn commitment" (Novick, 21).

It is against this background, this time of crisis when words count *more than usual* that writers and intellectuals would face the *épuration*. Because of their dual position— on the one hand their central position in French society and, on the other, the particularly critical historical context in which their role is being played out—they would be held accountable in a different way. As the cultural historian Tony Judt writes, they "were singled out for much more attention than was ever given to lawyers, generals, businessmen and high civil servants whose services to the occupying forces had been unquestioningly more significant." Echoing Sartre's declaration and paraphrasing de Gaulle—respectively, the postwar preeminent intellectual and political figures—Judt goes on to offer at least one possible explanation of this particularity: "As de Gaulle later noted in his memoirs, in literature as in everything else, talent is responsibility. The capacity to express a point of view in a way calculated to convince others, the skill in dressing up an unacceptable act in respectable moral clothing, confer on the writer not only a great power but also a duty" (60). This is especially so when the writer's power is exercised in a time of great crisis. The German occupation certainly constituted such a time; as Alice Kaplan puts it in her thorough study of the Brasillach trial (see dossier 6.2) during the occupation, "the written word had a new status, a new power to do evil and good. Writers and intellectuals, whether they liked it or not, were read politically. Every decision they made about writing was political: what to publish, where to publish, and whether to publish" (34). In the field of letters, the purge was heavily influenced by these considerations. The case of Robert Brasillach, tried and executed for "intelligence with the enemy" (Article 75 of the French penal code) in February 1945 is particularly illustrative of the complexity of the issue.

Figure 6.2   Frenchmen on the Eastern Front with the German Army (1943)

Robert Brasillach, editor in chief of *Je suis partout*, Jacques Doriot, leader of the fascist Parti Populaire Français, wearing the Nazi uniform of the league of French volunteers in the German army, and Claude Jeantet, a journalist from *Je suis partout*, on the Eastern Front in 1943. Looking at Brasillach's petition for pardon after the writer received the death sentence in 1944, de Gaulle is said to have thought Brasillach and not Doriot was wearing the Nazi uniform, which may have played a role in his decision not to pardon Brasillach. (© Hachette Photo Presse)

Dossier 6.2   The Trial and Execution of Robert Brasillach (January and February 1945)

Robert Brasillach was born in 1909 at Perpignan in the Pyrénées Orientales; he attended the Ecole Normale Supérieure in Paris, traditionally the institutional foundation for the French intellectual elite. A writer of talent who produced literary criticism as well as poetry and novels, Brasillach was also a polemical journalist and a fervent advocate of fascism. In one of his articles written during the occupation he declared: "For a long time, in this 20th-century, fascism, both inside and outside [of France], will embody destiny itself. For Europe, of course. For Germany. For France. One does not take destiny lightly" (*Je suis partout*, October 20, 1942). He became a journalist with the Action Française (a right-wing movement founded by Charles Maurras at the turn of the century, advocating reversion to monarchical government) in 1931 and, after contributing sporadically to the anti-Semitic newspaper, *Je suis partout*, became its editor in chief from 1941 until August 17, 1943. He was tried by the French High Court, found guilty of treason on January 19, 1945, and executed on February 6, 1945. The government's case against Brasillach was based to a large extent on his writings in *Je suis partout*, of which the following are excerpts.

The Seven Internationals. September 25, 1942 "Quoting" an anonymous "highly placed foreign official" Brasillach writes: "Against the new world, the world of the 20th century there are seven Internationals," which he proceeds to enumerate and develop in his article: the Communist International, the Socialist international, the Jewish international, the Catholic International, the Protestant international, the Masonic International, and the financial International. Quoted here is the part of the article dealing more specifically with the so-called Catholic International:

There is, fourthly, the Catholic International. We are very careful in writing these words, and it is obvious the Catholic faith itself is not in question here. I believe that almost all the members of this newspaper's staff are baptized Catholics, and several are practicing Christians. All are respectful of Church tradition and of what our fatherland owes to Roman and Orthodox power. But all are also disturbed by the attitude taken by an important faction of the clergy (and of the high clergy in particular) concerning national issues. They are, admittedly, not too disturbed: political differences, whether in Italy, Germany, or Spain, have always been settled through mutual arrangements, conventions and legal agreements with the Church. But one must admit that that it is odd to allow a few prelates to quasi openly attack the new order. The archbishop of Toulouse protests against the measures adopted against the stateless Jews in the non-occupied zone and accuses the Marshall's government of taking his cue from foreigners! He talks of brutality and of separations that we are all ready to disapprove of, for we must separate ourselves from the Jews en bloc [all together, in one fell swoop] and not keep the little ones; human kindness is here in agreement with wisdom: but he forgets to say that these brutalities are the work of provocateur police agents who want to induce pity in foolish Aryans. And even if these accusations were true, why hasn't Monsignor, contrary to several courageous bishops, spoken out against the British massacres? Why has he, like so many of his acolytes, venerated Léon Blum? Why this bishop's shameful silence, with a few admirable exceptions (Monsignor Baudrillart, among others), at the time of the Popular Front, of the [Spanish] Civil War, etc.? Today, there is total silence on the war on the Eastern front (and silence even at the Vatican, where Pius XI had publicly blessed Franco), total silence regarding the alliances with Bolchevism "cursed" by several popes, opposition to the salubrious laws on youth and race. There exist "smuggling" convents that send men to de Gaulle, and one dares say that Franco-German collaboration has adversaries in a clergy guided by ultramontane interests that hide foreign interests. This in no way impugns the Catholic religion, but where, in all this, is the church's political position? We have no choice but to answer that it is not on the right side.

"Lets Give France a French Regime." June 30, 1941. As the German army advances on the Soviet Union in 1941, Brasillach writes the following: *The first aspect [of what the French position should be regarding the Soviet Union and communism] is the communist danger. This is no laughing matter. Communism must be mercilessly hunted down. The most forceful action must be taken against the leaders and the propagandists. We know that since July 1940 about four thousand provocateurs have been sent to concentration camps in the occupied zone, and thirty thousand in the free zone. Still, these should not be revengeful or unjustifiable actions. The main thing is to strike at the head. According to Le Soir of Brussels, Maurice Thorez, living in Switzerland, goes regularly to the non-occupied zone to give out orders and subsidies. Centers of activity of the old Popular Front continue to exist everywhere. Jacques Soustelle, assistant director of the Musée de l'Homme, was stripped of his French nationality, and that's well and good, but Soustelle is outside of France, while Monsieur Luc, friend of Masons and communists, is still director of technical education.*

"No mercy for the Murderers of the Fatherland." October 25, 1942. The overwhelming *majority of the French people, the commander-in-chief of the occupation has already said it, condemn with horror these criminal attacks that Marshall Pétain denounced a month ago. But a minority, alarmed by foreigners, gets intoxicated on crimes and on—an at least passive—complicity. These men who are arrested, sometimes in the most bourgeois circles, for illegal distribution of tracts and unlawful activities, are indeed morally guilty of complicity. What is one [What are we] waiting for to strike them? What is one [what are we] waiting for to execute the communist leaders already in prison? And also these grand bourgeois who, at night, by the light of their reading lamps, cut out metro tickets in the shape of Gaullist insignia? Against those who want the death of peace and the death of France, everything is legitimate. Their criminal relentlessness has been proven countless times. These most serious attacks bring new and irrefutable evidence. No mercy for those who want to murder the fatherland, whoever and wherever they may be!*

No to the Fretful. May 30, 1942. The new commissioner for Jewish Affairs, Monsieur *Darquier de Pellepoix, is completely convinced of the need for propaganda, especially in an area where the French public has been very badly informed. That racial issues be publicly debated, that the public be informed are primary obligations. But in order to achieve these goals, the State must display courage, determination, and intelligence. It is not by hiding the Jewish question from students that we will make them understand even the laws that already exist. If we say nothing to them, they will be led to find these laws unnecessary or unjust (while they are timid). Loyalty and obedience must be based on an understanding of the objective to be reached.*

Brasillach was found guilty and executed for "intelligence with the enemy," another way of saying "for treason." The most damning evidence against him was constituted by his calls to pursue, imprison, and execute. These calls were variously directed against a wide spectrum of groups, organizations, and individuals ranging from Jews, communists, Gaullists, and resistance fighters, to priests, Masons, Sorbonne professors, and even students who had torn a picture of Pétain at a Parisian high school. What made the articles in *Je suis partout* most pernicious and effective, that is, having concrete, directly measurable effects, was that often Brasillach's calls targeted not only an entire group such as the Jews, but became as specific as naming individuals and, in effect, condemning them to death. For example, the oft-quoted sentence from one of the articles above proposing "we must separate ourselves from the Jews *en bloc* and not keep the little ones," in spite of its viciousness stops short of naming particular individuals. This is not the case in the following from the weekly *Je suis partout*: "The Jew David Rubiné, naturalized French at the dawning of the Popular Front, went by the name Davidovici Ruben before May 1, 1936. He set up medical practice in Couches in 1935, before he was given French nationality. Now that a decree of Marshall Pétain takes away the benefit of that nationality from him, the Jew Davidovici plays dumb. He continues to practice. Perhaps it will be enough to point out this very curious anomaly to the Prefect of the Eure, responsible for carrying out the law?" (Kaplan, 32). This, in a context where Jews were being systematically deported from France, constituted a death warrant; 76,000 Jews were deported from France during the occupation, most of them were foreign Jews who had come to France in the 1930s as nazi policy toward them became increasingly clear. Of these some 2,600 returned from the concentration camps.

The same pattern of general to specific denouncing is evident in the case of other groups. "Communists must be hunted down" becomes a few lines further "Monsieur Luc, friend of the Masons and Communists is still director of technical education." While not naming specific names, Brasillach's notorious call in the article entitled "No Mercy for the Murderers of the Fatherland" is also clearly directed at immediately identifiable individuals: "What is one [or: what are we] waiting for to strike them? What is one [or: what are we] waiting for to execute the communists leaders already in prison?" Finally, Brasillach's denunciation of "an important faction of the clergy" becomes, in parentheses, the high clergy in particular, to focus on "the Archbishop of Toulouse [who] protests against the measures adopted against the stateless Jews . . ." Brasillach himself summarizes the overall policy he recommends and supports when he writes "Against those who want the death of peace and the death of France, *everything* is legitimate" (*Je suis partout*, October 25, 1942; emphasis in original).

The "legitimacy" Brasillach claims here raises a question that looms large in postwar France: that of the legitimacy of the Vichy government itself and, beyond it, the question of who can act and speak in the name of France. Ultimately, the question becomes that of *which* France is being paid allegiance to, a question that displays the existence of competing narratives vying for legitimacy.

As we have seen, de Gaulle's answer is categorical: Vichy is "null and void" and the "Republic has never ceased to exist." Beyond Vichy, however, Brasillach seems to be claiming allegiance, as did de Gaulle, to yet something else that would be the "true France"; when asked by the prosecutor at his trial why he did not stop his writings when he understood that they would serve the enemy, Brasillach answered: "I believed that my writing served my country above all" (Kaplan, 157), and when, at another point, he is accused by the prosecution of calling the Gaullists "traitors," he answers: "Today I do not blame those who chose to fight for their country, against their native soil, but I ask that it be recognized that those who chose their native soil back then were acting in the direct line of a certain French tradition" (Kaplan, 152). Beyond the trial of a particularly visible writer and intellectual during the occupation, what is at stake here is the very definition of what constitutes "France" itself. With the victory over Nazi Germany and the ensuing purge, de Gaulle's discourse, based on a definition of France as an old nation and a republic with universalist principles, defeated the fascist "blood and soil"–rooted nation narrative proposed by Vichy and its ardent defender Robert Brasillach. It is in the name of the writer's responsibility, especially at a time of crisis, and in the name of this vision of France that de Gaulle refused to commute Brasillach's death sentence, even after being presented with a petition with signatures of some of France's most illustrious writers and intellectuals, among them François Mauriac and Albert Camus who would win the Nobel Prize for literature in 1952 and 1957, respectively. Jean-Paul Sartre, who would also win, but refuse the Nobel Prize in 1964, declined to sign the petition. In his presentation of *Les Temps Modernes*, the journal he founded in 1945 with Simone de Beauvoir (see dossier 6.4), he, like de Gaulle, invokes the writer's responsibility. We should note that for de Gaulle the idea of responsibility is linked to the idea of the nation, but for Sartre the responsibility is ultimately to one's own individual ethos even as the writer necessarily plays out his part in history:

> The writer has a place in his age. Each word has an echo, as does each silence. I hold Flaubert and Goncourt responsible for the repression that followed the Commune because they did not write a single line to prevent it. It was none of their business, you may say. But then was the Callas trial Voltaire's business? Was Dreyfus's sentence Zola's business? Was the administration of the Congo Gide's problem? Each of these authors, at a particular moment during his life, lived up to his responsibility as an author. The Occupation has taught us our responsibility. ("Presentation," *Les Temps Modernes*, October 1945)

In her in-depth study of the case, Alice Kaplan asks: "Why was Brasillach killed when René Bousquet, the head of the Paris police who masterminded the massive roundup of Jews at the Vél d'Hiv got only two years of 'national degradation,' which were suspended on the grounds that he had aided the resistance?" The Vélodrome d'hiver was an indoor bicycle track where the Germans, with the collaboration of Vichy and the Paris police, rounded up 13,000 French Jews, including about 4,000 children, who were all sent to concentration camps a few days later. Kaplan proposes that one crucial reason that Bousquet's punishment was effectively delayed until the 1990s was (see chapter 9) because, as opposed to Brasillach who was found guilty of "intelligence with the enemy," his crime, "crimes against humanity," was not yet codified in 1945 (Kaplan, 228). The same argument can be made in the case of Maurice Papon, a Vichy official who, in spite of having signed off on the rounding up of 1560 Jews, including 223 children, from Bordeaux and its surrounding areas, all later sent to the Drancy transit camp and then to Auschwitz, later became Paris Police prefect under de Gaulle, and budget minister during the Valéry Giscard d'Estaing presidency (1974–1981); he was brought to trial only in 1994 (see chapter 9).

In addition to the nonexistence of a codified crime in the French penal code of the time, one must take into consideration the fact that what lay between collaboration and resistance, these two ostensibly diametrically opposed courses of action, often became a grey area during and after the occupation. The case of François Mitterand who, in 1981, was to become the president of the first leftist government since the Popular Front of 1936, reflects the difficulty of determining who was on the "right side," and when. Mitterand was made prisoner during the German offensive in 1940 and, on his third attempt, succeeded in escaping to join Vichy where he became head of the Prisoner Reclassification Section, a position he occupied until 1943; he was awarded the "Francisque," a decoration reserved for good service to Pétain and bearing the marshall's portrait. On the other hand, when the Reclassification Section clearly became a collaborationist fiefdom, Mitterand resigned and joined the Resistance, eventually making his way to Algiers, this time to join de Gaulle and fight against Vichy. After the war, Mitterand founded the National Movement of Prisoners of War; he was awarded the Legion of Honor, the Croix de Guerre, and the Rosette de la Résistance. In 1946, as the Fourth Republic was founded, he became its first government's youngest cabinet member. Not until the 1990s did Mitterand's "Vichy past" become widely known.

As the occupation ended, the writers and intellectuals who had collaborated with Vichy and the Germans, had profited from this collaboration, replacing those who had been excluded or eliminated, were suddenly on the losing side. Parallel to the purge conducted by government officials, writers and intellectuals, many of whom had been dismissed from their positions, forced into silence or into the underground, now organized themselves in the CNE (*Comité national des écrivains*, National Writers' Committee). The CNE could not itself put any one on trial and thus referred the most blatant and serious offenders to the official courts. Among the most prominent was Pierre Drieu La Rochelle, one of the leading writers advocating collaboration; he had become director of the prestigious NRF (the Gallimard publishing house's *Nouvelle revue française*) after the German occupation began; he committed suicide at the Liberation. Céline, pen name of Louis Ferdinand Destouches, the author of *Voyage au bout de la nuit* (*Journey to the End of Night*, 1932), who had become increasingly and intensely anti-Semitic and collaborationist during the occupation, was tried in absentia and was later amnestied. Unlike Brasillach who stayed on in Paris after the Liberation, Céline left France with Pétain and went with him and a number of other Vichy officials to Sigmaringen, a castle in Germany, and then on to exile in Denmark. Charles Maurras, one of the founders of Action Française, who had played such a major role in the anti-Dreyfus camp earlier on in the century, and had found in the occupation an ideal setting for his ideology, a mix of royalist nostalgia, fascism, xenophobia, and anti-Semitism, was tried and found guilty of collaboration with the enemy; he was sentenced to five year's imprisonment and "national degradation" crying out as he was being led out of the courtroom after sentencing, "It's the revenge of Dreyfus!" Other than Pétain, Maurras was the only member of the Académie française to be put on trial. The Academy had been solidly Pétainiste throughout the occupation; even after the Liberation, it allowed the two seats left by Pétain and Maurras to remain vacant until their deaths, as a form of protest against what it perceived as the unfairness of the purge.

The CNE did not play an active role in these official proceedings but nevertheless constituted a highly visible means of ostracizing, and effectively boycotting writers who had sympathized with Vichy, by publishing their names in its journal *Les lettres françaises*. Not everyone at the CNE agreed on the names to be included on this list, leading to well-publicized resignations beginning in 1947, among them that of Jean Paulhan and that of a number of the CNE's more conservative members.

Even if they do not reduce the purge to a movement of revenge by the former losers, now turned winners, some contemporary historians do agree that writers had been dealt with differently from others who had also been accused of collaborating. Tony Judt for one proposes that "The treatment of writers and artists who had collaborated was notoriously unfair—not so much because some of them did not deserve the punishment they received (many did), but because it was so selective. Many intellectuals who had published in the collaborationist press redeemed themselves by their later part in the intellectual Resistance and then turned with a vengeance on their former colleagues" (60). On the other hand, Alice Kaplan sees in this position a certain amount of myth in the making: "Despite the myth that 'writers took the fall' for collaboration, very few writers had actually gone to their deaths, and those who did—Chack, Suarez, Ferdonnet, Luchaire, and Brasillach—were tried as propagandists" (Kaplan, 214).

The fact that that such luminaries of the prewar intellectual establishment as André Gide, winner of the Nobel prize in 1947, for example, published literary criticism during the occupation in the *Nouvelle revue française*, whose director was the German sympathizer Pierre Drieu La Rochelle, helps us understand the difficulty of determining what "intellectual collaboration" consists of. Is it exclusively *what* one wrote, *where* one published it, or a combination of the two? Was the refusal to write or publish anything that was in any way controlled or supervised by the occupying forces the only option?

These questions, which we can only leave unanswered, also raise the question of which version of the *annés noires* (dark years) is the "correct" one. First, the "resistancialist" version, the one that confines collaboration to what de Gaulle's called "a few traitors . . . unworthy leaders, and . . . the few cowards who easily and voluntarily associated themselves" with the Vichy project, while the "immense majority" was composed of "unhappy brothers" who would, when the time came, take up arms against the enemy and against Vichy. Then, there is the version of a collaboration out of necessity or even out of a will to maintain France as *intact* as possible in the face of the occupier's orders and requisitions; this can be called the Pétainist version; ultimately this would be a *patriotic collaboration* exemplified by Pétain's declaration "Day after day, a dagger at my throat, I struggled against German demands" (Paxton, 47). Finally, there would be the version of an actively and willingly collaborating France that sympathized with the nazi project and even went beyond the occupier' wishes in enacting certain policies, such the rounding up of Jews, the execution of hostages, the recruitment of French citizens to serve in the nazi war effort, or providing increased industrial output—for a corresponding increase in profits—toward the same war effort.

What is at stake in opting for or favoring one version over another is enormous since it involves passing judgment, today, on an entire country that was going through one of the major crises of its history. In many ways asking this question is analogous to asking whether *all* or *a few* Germans *actively* or *passively* supported Hitler's policies. One historian's opinion on this issue strikes us as a well-balanced answer in the case of France during the occupation:

> Much of [France's] state apparatus, many of her police, civil servants, judges, and lawyers cooperated with the Germans; many supported Pétain and his policy of collaboration, especially in the early years of the Occupation. If, however, the Germans found people willing to collaborate, they also encountered serious resistance and principled opposition. German historians have been more hesitant than Anglo-Americans to condemn France. Those who have not known invasion, occupation and totalitarianism need to consider carefully whether their own country would do better in similar circumstances. (Sowerwine, 232)

In the concluding paragraphs of his influential study of the period, *Vichy France: Old Guard and New Order*, Robert Paxton offers a possible explanation for collaboration, something he calls a ". . . more subtle intellectual culprit [than] bureaucratic inertia and blindness to considerations beyond the efficiency of the state" or even "attraction to Pétain's National Revolution." For Paxton that culprit is "fear of social disorder as the greatest evil. Some of France's best skill and talent went into a formidable effort to keep the French state afloat under increasingly questionable circumstances. Who would keep order, they asked, if the State lost its authority? By saving the state, however, they were losing the nation" (382). However, this observation does not lead Paxton to assume a stance of moral superiority that would be conferred by hindsight: "It is tempting to identify with the Resistance and say, 'That is what I would have done.' Alas, we are far more likely to act in parallel situations, like the Vichy majority" (383).

Whatever judgment is passed on occupied France, inasmuch as judgment should or can be passed, it is not difficult to understand why, once France was liberated, de Gaulle would promote such a version to serve his policy of national unity whether he actually believed in the "resistancialist" version or not. At a critical juncture, de Gaulle's narrative enabled him to galvanize the French when challenges had appeared against those notions of a strong, centuries-old entity, *and* modern republic built on universalist principles: the defeat of 1940, the occupation, Vichy and collaboration, the Allies' refusal to include de Gaulle at Yalta or Potsdam, where the "Big Three," the United States, the Soviet Union, and Great Britain, were already planning the shape of postwar Europe, their project to occupy France and send de Gaulle to Madagascar, the relatively late recognition of the provisional government, and the incorporation of France into the North Atlantic capitalist bloc. Throughout the war and at the Liberation, the possibility of referring to both a long tradition with roots that go back to Antiquity *and* to a modernity that France had been crucial in creating is what gives many of de Gaulle's calls to the population its peculiarly French character; in other words, these speeches rely on the famous *exception française*, the French exception; for example, this excerpt from a speech of June 6, 1943:

> From the depths of our nation has risen the vital instinct that for nearly 2000 years has so often saved us from the abyss. This was the instinct that turned Clovis's Franks and Gauls to Christianity, when barbarians flung themselves onto the ruins of their pagan society. This was the instinct that stirred Joan of Arc and led Frenchmen to build a centralized state around the king when it seemed that feudal anarchy was delivering us up to domination by a feudal power. This was the instinct that made the nation stand up against its enemies and their accomplices at the time of the revolution, and dictated the great principles of the Rights of Man and Democracy, to save it. This is the instinct that today leads all Frenchmen concerned for the future of their country and her greatness, to desire and prepare for the Fourth Republic, bringing national renewal. (Holman and Kelly, 108)

Some of the essential aspects of the *exception française* are gathered in this speech to serve de Gaulle's objective of rallying the population: the call to the past and to tradition, the reference to the particularity of France as crucible of universalist principles, and the Jacobinist principles of a democratic, centralized nation. Although not at all the Jacobin revolutionary, de Gaulle would, when facing the damages in postwar France, inscribe himself in that centralizing tradition usually associated with more revolutionary or leftist politics. Rather than an aberration, however, this course of action on the part of political figure more to the right of the spectrum is illustrative of his affiliation with something removed from concrete political situations: an abstract entity named *France*. As James Corbett puts it, "The father of nationalization and modern *dirigisme* was not a Socialist or a Communist, but the conservative General de Gaulle, which proves, if anything, that state control of industry owes more to the French obsession with centralization than to Bolshevism" (300).

Beyond immediate political action, centralizing policies would indeed be enacted to deal with the bleak state of France at the Liberation: 210,000 soldiers had died in battle; 150,000 civilians had died, whether fighting in the Resistance, or through bombings or executions. In 1946, the population was at 39.8 million as opposed to the 41.1 million of ten years earlier; 1 million families were homeless; half the country's bridges and rails had been destroyed; in general there was extensive damage to the country's industrial and housing infrastructure; as the architect and urban planner Le Corbusier wrote in June 1945, *L'escargot France n'a plus de coquille*, "The French snail has lost its shell" (Rioux and Sirinelli, 230). As a result of the badly damaged transportation system, supplying the country in everything ranging from meat to charcoal was a major difficulty, especially since many items were in short supply. The official ration stood at 1200 calories a day at the end of the war, while bread rationing continued into 1949. A character in Alphonse Boudard's 1986 novel *La fermerture* [*The Closing*] comments on the effects of the shortages: "And then always, now, for six years, these eternal questions of grub [bouffe] . . . the ration cards . . . the meat, the milk, the cooking fat missing from the frying pans of France, liberated but with an empty stomach" (quoted in Ross, 72). Newspapers throughout the country were filled with articles and editorials covering the difficulty of keeping the public fed and warm. The front page of the *Parisien Libéré* dated Wednesday, January 17, during the bitterly cold winter of 1945 contains a variety of information on shortages and supplies expressed in tones ranging from the purely factual to the vehement: "We asked yesterday that, if necessary, the trees be cut down in the Bois de Boulogne, and the Bois de Vincennes [parks in Paris], as well as in the suburbs of Paris. As we've written, it is not possible to let children, the sick and the old die of cold." Beneath this column could be found a regular list of which items would be arriving on the market. The entry for January 20 reads: "American chocolate—As of January 20, the DS ticket dated December (E J1, J2, J3 category) will be invalid. Arrival of horsemeat, coal, preserves, heating oil, cooking fat. Eggs: to be distributed as supplies arrive; use January D5 tickets." The particular vocabulary and denominations reflect the administrative system put in place. Yet another story, still on the front page, is entitled: "Increase in the number of Infantile Bronchial Pneumonia Cases." An article from the same paper, entitled "WE WOULD LIKE MATCHES AND LAUNDRY SOAP," dated February 28, 1945 suggests that the problems are not always due to war damages: "It is still impossible to find matchers unless one is well connected with the tobacco shops. As far as we know, the Germans did not sabotage all the factories before they left." Indeed, the population was competing for a reduced number of goods, while the increased money supply put in circulation during the occupation due to the German demands resulted in rampant inflation, 27 percent in 1944 and reaching 63 percent in 1946. This was a prime situation for the development of a vast black market where everything was bought, sold, and bartered.

Since industrial production in 1945 was 29 percent of the 1929 level—a level it would not reach again until 1955—the shortages applied not only to the most basic food items but to consumer goods as well. Françoise Giroud, a journalist and cofounder of the newsweekly *L'Express* describes a situation that would remain difficult until focus was shifted from heavy industry to consumer goods, beginning in the early 1950s: "Anyone who wasn't in France in those days cannot understand what it means to be hungry for consumer goods, from nylon stockings to refrigerators, from records to automobiles—to buy a car you had to purchase a permit and then wait for a year . . . It's very simple: in 1946 in France there was literally nothing" (quoted in Ross, 72).

Some of the immediate measures adopted by de Gaulle's provisional government as well as those enacted during the early stages of the Fourth Republic broke as much as possible with a number of the initiatives taken by Vichy while laying the groundwork for economic reconstruction. Louis Renault, owner of the car company, was imprisoned as a result of his wartime collaboration with the Germans and his company was nationalized. The coalmines were also taken over and later merged into a single government-run company, which was one means of showing workers that the owners who had collaborated with the occupier were no longer in charge. Airlines were also nationalized and formed into one company, Air France, while the major banks and insurance companies representing the majority of this sector were also brought under government control. Beginning in 1946, gas and electricity production and distribution were provided by the newly formed national companies, EDF (Electricité de France) and GDF (Gaz de France). What Corbett called "the French obsession with centralization" was at work in these initiatives, and it is no accident that these economic endeavors were perceived in a larger context that included a certain place for France in the world. As proclaimed in the National Resistance Committee's program, published in March 1944, all the political movements and parties united in the CNR state as their first objective "to establish the provisional government of the republic formed by General de Gaulle in order to defend the nation's political and economic independence." Immediately following this, however, the objective was "to reestablish France in its power, its *grandeur* and its universal mission" (Prochasson and Wierviorka, 398). A political spectrum that ranged from the Gaullists to the Communists agreed on this charter, reflecting their common vision of an independent, strong, unique, and universalist France. For all the members of the CNR, political and economic renewal could not be perceived independently of a particular image of France. The renewal of postwar France can be perceived as one of those "great projects" that de Gaullle refers to in his *War Memoirs*: "France is only itself when it is at the forefront of nations . . . Only great projects can hope to compensate the seeds of dissent its people carry within themselves; our country, as it is, among others, as they are, must aim high and stand tall, lest it die. In short, in my view, France cannot be France without greatness [grandeur]" (Wirth, 21).

It is with this image of France's grandeur in the background that the CNR's charter laid the groundwork for many of the reforms that were undertaken in the post war years; the Charter proposed, among a comprehensive series of goals, the "establishment of a true economic democracy, necessitating the eviction of the large financial and economic feudalities from the running of the economy . . . the reestablishment of independent trade unions . . ." and ". . . a comprehensive social security program." On the whole, these directives were enacted in part through the centralization and nationalization measures detailed above. This was facilitated by the consensus around de Gaulle who ruled until January 1946 as a benign dictator by consent. The French were united in those two years after the end of World War II in their rejection of the political past—96 percent voted against the continuation of the Third Republic—and in the possibility of a better tomorrow. Far from sharing de Gaulle's political views, the secretary general of the Communist Party, Maurice Thorez, nevertheless encouraged the workers to accept sacrifices in the name of economic reconstruction. The Communist Party had then relinquished the principle of a takeover of the government through violent means, opting instead to "work within the existing political framework." The party's directives to the workers were to avoid strikes and to increase production. This was indeed a kind of compromise for a party that gathered 26.1 percent of the votes when the first constituent assembly was elected in October 1945, making it the largest party in France. The other major winners were the *Mouvement Républicain Populaire* (MRP, Christian democrats without the Christian label) heavily influenced by the progressive ideas of the Christian philosopher Emmanuel Mounier that garnered 25 percent of the vote, with the Socialist Party receiving 24 percent. If the Socialist and Communist parties were to form a coalition, they would effectively be able to control the government, but fear of being overwhelmed by the Communists led to the inclusion of the MRP in a government coalition that came to be known as "tripartism."

The election of this first Constituent Assembly marked the beginning of the end for de Gaulle's unchallenged leadership. With his policies and political line increasingly questioned by the Assembly, the general resigned in January 1946. In addition, the new constitution of the Fourth Republic adopted in October 1946 was nothing like de Gaulle's ideal constitution which would favor a strong executive, that is a president "above the parties" and appointing a prime minister. Instead, the Fourth Republic form of government had as its centerpiece a fractious legislative Assembly allied to different political parties with divergent political and ideological interests. Tripartism could not last long in such a context and ended with eviction of the Communist ministers on May 1947. This effectively put an end to the temporary rallying of all the political factions under the aegis of Resistance ideals, and also underlined the increasing realignment of French politics along the broad lines of the cold war. The Fourth Republic's twenty-three governments would change at an average rate of one every six months from January 1946 until de Gaulle's return to power in 1958, inaugurating the beginning of the Fifth Republic.

In spite of its structural political deficiencies, the Fourth Republic would oversee the initial phase of the *Trente glorieuses* (The Thirty Glorious Years), as the historian and economist Jean Fourastié named that period of unprecedented economic growth in France, both in its early phase of concentration on heavy industry and the beginning of a consumer society in the late 1950s and early 1960s (chapter 9). The Fourth Republic would also have to contend with the beginnings of a decolonization process that would ultimately lead to its demise and de Gaulle's return (chapter 8).

France's entry into consumer culture originated in measures and programs established and developed during the period 1944–1958, during, that is, the lifespan of the Fourth Republic. As the end of the war became more distant in time and the Fourth Republic began its troubled tenure, the Gaullist narrative of a France united in its fight against the occupier gradually became a narrative of economic reconstruction in which all Frenchmen and women would be willing to make sacrifices for the greater good of the nation. The concentration on heavy industry at the expense of consumer goods and housing for a few years was at the heart of two of the most concerted efforts to rebuild and modernize. The first was the establishment of a Planning Commission, created in 1947 under the directorship of Jean Monnet, a businessman who had followed de Gaulle to London, and had spent time in the United States both before and during the war. The "Monnet Plan" charted priorities to be set and specific goals to be met by different sectors, such as heavy industry, transportation, and energy. The objective was to rebuild while modernizing and simultaneously opening French industry to outside competition that would further stimulate innovation and growth. Although it had in common with Soviet-style type centralized economy the setting from above of production goals for designated economic sectors, the French "planned economy" relied on voluntary rather than imposed cooperation between business, labor, and government experts. A second initiative, the European Coal and Steel Community, established in 1951, was a logical extension of the Fourth Republic's goals of reconstruction and modernization coupled with the opening up of economic frontiers. This organization, uniting France, West Germany, Italy, Belgium, the Netherlands, and Luxembourg established among its members free trade of two vital components and resources of heavy industry, coal, and steel. Beyond its immediate effects on the respective economies of its members, the community laid the groundwork for the extended Common Market that would be created in 1957 by the Treaty of Rome. By then France would be well on its way into the consumer society (see chapter 9).

In a first stage, however, the French economy could not have been rebuilt and modernized at the rapid pace it experienced without direct and massive input from the American-financed Marshall Plan. The plan, which was to bear his name, was announced by Secretary of State George Marshall in June 1947, almost exactly one month after the Communist ministers were ejected from the French government on May 1. The Marshall Plan, a program of grants and loans to be invested in the recovering economies of Europe, was initially offered to all European countries, including the Soviet Union and what was quickly becoming the "Eastern communist bloc." The offer was rejected by these countries, which perceived it as part of an overall scheme to counter communism in Europe and, in its place, to extend American influence on the continent. France's acceptance of American aid through the Marshall Plan—a total of $15 billion in grants, loans, and credit—enabled it to fully implement the Monnet Plan, and also clearly put it in the American camp, on the other side of the "iron curtain [that] has descended across Europe" (Winston Churchill in his speech at Fulton, Missouri, in March 1946). Economic collaboration with the rest of Western Europe in general, and Germany, the recent enemy, in particular, was a basic condition of France's participation in the Marshall Plan. The country's participation in NATO (the North Atlantic Treaty Organization), which France ratified in 1949, a military organization that gathered the same participants as the Marshall Plan in a military alliance, contributed to the further polarization of French politics in the postwar and beyond. Rather than a monolithic discourse that gathered all French men and women in a political project, such as expelling the occupier from the nation, or an economic one, such as all making sacrifices for the reconstruction of the national economy, clashing discourses along political, economic, and ideological lines became the norm.

The Marshall Plan, welcomed by the French "Atlanticists" as an economic boon and a rampart against the Soviet camp, was denounced by the Communist Party and many of its sympathizers as a tool of political and cultural American influence and domination. The debates around the Blum-Byrnes agreement, signed in 1946 by Léon Blum, president of the French *Conseil*, and by James Byrnes, the American representative (beginning in 1947, Byrnes would become chief legal counsel for the Motion Picture Association of America) reflects these tensions. The agreement, made before the actual implementation of the Marshall Plan in fact conditioned American economic aid on the opening of the French market to American film production. For France who took pride in its contribution to the creation of cinema and whose films occupied over 75 percent of the world's screens until the eve of World War I, agreeing to a quota of American films to be shown of French screens, was a particularly sensitive issue. If we add to this the economic and political stakes in an industry whose personnel was widely sympathetic to the Communist Party—many of its well-known actors, actresses, and directors, such as Yves Montand, Simone Signoret, and Louis Daquin, were members—and the fact that Hollywood "peddled a way of life" (Ross) to a French population on the eve of entering the consumer society, the stakes were high indeed. At first, the French government agreed that in exchange for those pre–Marshall Plan loans an allowed quota of American films could be shown for nine of every thirteen weeks; the remaining four weeks of each trimester would be reserved for French films while further restrictions would apply to American films. Since American films had been proscribed from the French market by Vichy, and some barriers had been maintained by de Gaulle, a considerable number of American films stockpiled during the occupation, including films ranging from super productions like *Gone with the Wind* to smaller budget "films noirs" like *The Maltese Falcon*, began to flood the French market. From 91 in 1946, French film production dropped to 78 in 1947, while 338 American films were shown on French screens during the first three months of 1947 alone. The campaign against the Blum-Byrnes agreement, which had taken the form of editorials, articles, marches and press conferences by personalities of the French film industry, peaked in a protest march on the Grands Boulevards of Paris on January 4, 1948. Ten thousand people marched, among them the filmmakers Jacques Becker and Yves Allégret, and the film stars Jean Marais and Simone Signoret. The Blum-Byrnes agreement was subsequently revised, setting at 121 the number of American films that could be imported annually, and adding a fifth week of exclusivity on national screens for French films. In addition, the revisions allowed for the French government to vote a law establishing subsidies for national cinema, to be financed by a 7 percent tax on all ticket sales (including tickets to American films). Beginning in 1949 French film production had reached its prewar level of 107 (George, 4).

The Blum-Byrnes episode illustrates several interrelated aspects of French life in the postwar period, appropriately named a period of "cold war culture" by a number of French historians. This episode clearly reflects the rift between two ways of life competing for attention and adoption on French territory: on the one hand, the Communists who were considered to be the defenders of the working class and the promoters of a more just society, especially after the inequities of the Vichy period and the nazi occupation. On the other, the "American way of life," market economy, modernization *à l'américaine*, American-style modernization for which Hollywood movies, in this particular instance, were a showcase.

The Blum-Byrnes episode underscored the political importance and influence of the Communist Party, a party without government ministers in the Fourth Republic as of May 1947, but still a party with elected representatives that gathered a good quarter of the votes and, perhaps more importantly, a party representing a major ideological and cultural force. Its influence was particularly felt in an era when French politics were polarized by the cold war. The surrealist poet Louis Aragon, a high-profile member of the party and its "cultural czar" made the following comment highlighting this antagonism between two camps when a statue of Victor Hugo was temporarily removed from a Parisian square in 1951 and replaced by a new Ford:

> A Ford automobile, the civilization of Detroit, the assembly line, the atomic danger, encircled by napalm . . . here is the symbol of this subjugation to the dollar applauded in the land of Molière; here is the white-lacquered god of foreign industry, the Atlantic totem that chases away French glories with Marshall plan stocks . . . The Yankee, more arrogant than the Nazi iconoclast, substitutes the machine for the poet, Coca-Cola for poetry, American advertisement for la *Légende des siècles*, the mass manufactured for the genius, the Ford for Victor Hugo . . . a civilization of bathtubs and Frigidairs. (Kuisel, 41)

Aragon was only one of many well-known artists, writers, and intellectuals ranging from Pablo Picasso and Jean-Paul Sartre to Fernand Léger and Albert Camus who, to different degrees, ranging from card-carrying and unvaryingly staunch supporters of Party policy, to occasional sympathizers, were identified with the Party. Among those in the first category who faithfully and publicly supported Party policy and directives even when they sometimes privately disagreed with them, were Aragon, Picasso—who painted the dove of peace for posters advertising the Party's "Peace Congress" held in 1949— the writer Elsa Triolet (Aragon's wife), and the film director Georges Sadoul. In the other category of *compagnons de route*, "fellow travelers" who often were not members but who supported a number of the Party's positions—support for national liberation movements in France's colonies or opposition to the American presence in Korea, for example—were Jean-Paul Sartre, Simone de Beauvoir, Albert Camus, Paul Ricoeur and Maurice Merleau Ponty. This undeniable attraction of communism for these men and women, called a "major cultural fact of the cold war" (Sirinelli) justified to a certain extent the Party's self-labeling as "the party of intelligence."

This position was criticized by the sociologist Raymond Aron, Sartre and de Beauvoir's former classmate at the Ecole Normale Supérieure. Unlike them, he staked his position not only against the French Communist Party but also against the adoption of Marxism itself as a philosophy adequate to the needs of France at the particular historical juncture of the postwar. As he writes in *The Opium of the Intellectuals* (1955), "How is it that philosophers, who claim to be interested in the concrete, can reaffirm, in the middle of the twentieth century and after two World Wars, the Marxian prophetism concerning the proletariat—especially in a country like France which has more peasants and petty bourgeois than proletarians?" (80) Further, Aron asks, how can the proletariat as conceived in Marxist terms fulfill its function of subverting and eventually destroying bourgeois capitalist society as it is itself increasingly absorbed and transformed beyond recognition by that very society through industrialization and modernization? Here he also criticizes the intellectuals who continue, in his view, to conceive of such a role for the working classes: "Idealist revolutionaries assign to the working class the superhuman mission of putting an end to the all too tangible evils of industrial society. They have not the honesty to admit that the proletariat, as it becomes gradually and inevitably more bourgeois, loses the virtues which seemed to make it worthy of this high calling" (90). Aron, who does not consider himself an "Atlanticist," does not systematically analyze in his essay—to be fair, this is not its objective—the fact that what he perceives as the gradual transformation of the proletarian into the bourgeois is filtered through France's alignment with the United States and, by extension through modernization à l'américaine. Indeed, the gum-chewing GIs who arrived in France in June 1944 on the beaches of Normandy and were riding their tanks down the Champs Elysées a few weeks later were only one of the most spectacular signs that the United States had ended its policy of isolationism, and had emerged as one of the two superpowers of the post war era. As we have seen, in the wake of the GIs came the Marshall Plan and, with it, an entire array of manners and customs, and institutions ranging from American multinational companies to Hollywood films, jazz, and . . . Coca-Cola.

The resistance to what some considered a veritable onslaught against the French way of life did not come exclusively from the Communists. Although the label "Coca-colonization" was a communist coinage—a November 1949 article in L'Humanité, the Communist Party's official daily was entitled "Will we be cocacolonized?"—it was taken up in one way or another by a variety of publications and personalities from across the political and ideological spectrum. In the Catholic daily, Témoignage Chrétien, of March 3, 1950, one columnist writes: "We must label Coca-Cola for what it is—the avant-garde of an offensive aimed at the economic colonization against which we feel it is our duty to struggle." In the left-of-center Le Monde, the editorialist may be less focused on Coca-Cola but the United States remains the target: "What the French criticize is less Coca-Cola than its orchestration, less the drink itself than the civilization—or as they like to say, the lifestyle—of which it is a symbol" (Kuisel, 64–65).

Since the call to struggle against American "economic colonization" was taking place at the height of the cold war, at a time, that is, when the perceived possibility of nuclear Holocaust or Soviet tanks replacing the American ones of a few years before on the Champs Elysées was part and parcel of daily life, some felt that they had to choose one "side" over the other, as does Le Monde's eminent political commentator, Maurice Duverger, in August 1948: "The American threat remains at the moment less urgent, less serious, and less dangerous than the Soviet menace . . . Between the invasion of the Gletkins and the invasion of Digests, we certainly prefer the latter; however, in the long run, the civilization of Digests will kill the European spirit just as surely as the civilization of Gletkins" (quoted in Kuisel, 45). During those crucial years of the cold war, American economic and cultural policies combined the implantation of American multinationals in France and in Europe in general with positive images of "American lifestyle" through the distribution of American films and documentaries, mass circulation glossy monthlies, and radio programs, among other channels. The objective was to undermine any discourse, from the Left in general and the Communist Party in particular, that presented an image of the United States as a basely materialistic and imperialist power with an agenda of cultural and economic domination, and to present it instead as a modern, democratic, benevolent nation with no design on French markets or the French way of life.

On the other side, the Soviet Union, through its status as the preeminent Marxist state represented an alternative and the promise of a more egalitarian society where modernization would not be achieved at the expense of the working class, where all would not be sacrificed to the profit motive and the private sphere. Clearly, the 25 percent of the vote regularly garnered by the French Communist Party during those same years reflected a belief in the party's objectives and an adherence to leftist ideals that went well beyond the ranks of the intellectual class. As for the intellectuals of the period, they found themselves having to make choices that were not as clear to them as those of the recent past, between Nazis and Fascists on the one hand and resistance on the other, for example. For some, like Raymond Aron, it must be said that the choice *was* clear and made against the background of reports of the Soviet labor and prison camps, which began to filter into France in 1949, and the takeover of power by Communist parties throughout Eastern Europe: "The intellectuals of Poland or of East Germany have lived though the Soviet reality. They have the choice between submission, a hopeless resistance, or emigration. The intellectuals of the West are free" (Aron, 112). For others, the choice was not quite as evident and was experienced as an anguishing dilemma: to choose what Duverger called the "Atlantic Empire" was to endorse the politics and economics of capital and to estrange themselves, even betray the working class; on the other hand, to choose Marxism at that historical juncture was to endorse the increasingly publicized repressive policies of its most prominent representative, the Soviet Union. For those who believed that communism offered the best hope for a better society, it was not a simple task to disassociate Marxism from the Soviet State and its more negative practices in order to arrive at a choice that would be absolutely clear and justified. Emmanuel Mounier, founder of the review *L'Esprit* (1932) and the proponent of a politically committed and left-leaning Catholicism, eloquently summarized this dilemma: "The Absolute is not of this world and it is not commensurate with this world. We never commit ourselves except in debatable struggles for imperfect causes. Yet to refuse commitment is to refuse the human condition" (Cohen, 116). When we consider that a papal decree of 1949 forbade Catholics to cooperate in any way with Communists, under pain of excommunication, the political and ideological stakes become all the more obvious. Mounier's "Catholic personalism" became a way for many Catholic intellectuals to reconcile the spiritual with active engagement in the political and cultural life of France and gained vast influence through its dissemination in catholic schools and colleges as well as a wide network that included "Catholic newspapers, magazines, *ciné clubs*, [and] adult education classes" (Forbes, 114), among other venues. Catholic personalism was an innovative ideology in the sense that it undermined the traditional conservative doctrine of the Catholic Church, which maintained a separation between spiritualism and politics and culture.

In proposing that the "Absolute is not of this world" but that one must nevertheless not refuse commitment, Mounier displays Catholic personalism's similarity with what was the postwar era's most influential philosophical and cultural movement: existentialism. The crucial similarity lay in the emphasis on commitment, which became "engagement" in the existentialist framework. There was also a crucial difference between the two: if for Catholic personalism the "Absolute is not of this world," for existentialism there is no Absolute, or, in other words, there is no God. Jean-Paul Sartre, until the end of the war an obscure *lycée* (high school) teacher, found the basis of existentialism in the works of Edmund Husserl and Martin Heidegger, two German philosophers whose works explored the nature of reality and perception, and the relations between the two. Like Husserl and Heidegger, Sartre begins from the premise that there is no other reality behind or beyond the materiality of phenomena. In the mass and drift of things that make up the world, however, man possesses an attribute that sets him apart from " a moss or a fungus": a consciousness, a subjective life. This particularity does not redeem or make man any more fitting or justified than any other phenomena in the world; on the contrary, as the hero of Sartre's 1938 existential novel *La Nausée (Nausea)* discovers, his being is "contingent" and not justified or made necessary by any overarching or master plan; again, there is no God. And, if there is no God, the existential corollary follows, "man is free." Sartre developed the implications of both the absence of a metaphysical realm and the resulting independent existence of man in the world—"Existence precedes essence," as he famously summarized it—in his massive philosophical treatise *L'être et le néant (Being and Nothingness).* The book was written when Sartre was a prisoner in a German camp (it was published in 1943), a context in which the act of choosing or committing one's self to a particular cause or side, in the absence of any ultimate or objective justification, was all the more urgent. Existentialism's austerity as well as its ultimate optimism and its intrinsic humanism, as Sartre would argue in a lecture delivered in 1947 (see dossier 6.3), made it a philosophy that matched the mood of a country exhilarated by Liberation and the promise of a new start, but that was also rapidly confronting the end of the idealism of the Resistance, the horrors of the Holocaust, nuclear conflagration, and the reality of the cold war.

Dossier 6.3   Jean-Paul Sartre, *Existentialism and Humanism* (1945, 1947)

This short book is the written version, published in 1947, of a conference Sartre gave in Paris in October 1945. *Being and Nothingness* had already been published and had already exposed, in a much more strictly philosophical language the essential aspects of existentialism. Yet Sartre felt compelled to give a more accessible version of his philosophy, one that would also insist on its humanist component—the original title in French of this short text is *Existentialism Is a Humanism* (emphasis added). Only a year after the Liberation, the Resistance ideals still prevailed; parties and groupings from the entire political spectrum were still in a mood of compromise and sacrifice for the higher good of the nation in dire need of all its citizens for its reconstruction. This was also the official Gaullist discourse of the provisional government. In this context, Sartre's atheistic existentialism was attacked from all sides. Existentialism was perceived as an individualistic, pessimistic, even cynical philosophy; it was attacked by the Catholics for its materialist, atheistic side, and by the Communists, in whose clandestine publications Sartre had until recently been writing; the latter accused him of "subjectivism," of bourgeois individualism in the face of collective needs and historical necessity. At a time of apparent unity in the face of national need, Sartre's position appeared like a counter-discourse, a dissident voice. As Arlette Elkaïm Sartre put it in her introduction to a recent edition of *Existentialism and Humanism,* "'After the cataclysm of war, "people," as one of [Sartre's] critics declared,' were more preoccupied with a definition of man in conformity with historical exigencies, making it possible to get beyond the present crisis . . . In the mind of many people, Sartre was becoming the antihumanist par excellence; he demoralized the French at a time when France in ruins was most in need of hope." Sartre's conference, and then his text, thus bears the traces of a general exposition of what existentialism consists of and an explanation specifically directed at the Communists.

Atheistic existentialism, of which I am a representative declares with greater consistency that if God does not exist there is at least one being whose existence comes before its essence, a being that exists before it can be defined by any conception of it. This being is man or, as Heidegger has it, the human reality. What do we mean by saying that existence precedes essence? We mean that man first of all exists, encounters himself, surges up in the world—and defines himself afterwards. If man as the existentialist sees him is not definable, it is because to begin with he is nothing. He will not be anything until later, and then he will be what he makes of himself. Thus there is no human nature, because there is no God to have a conception of it. Man simply is. Not that he is simply what he conceives himself to be, but he is what he wills, and as he conceives himself after already existing—as he wills to be after that leap towards existence. Man is nothing else but that which he makes of himself. That is the first principle of existentialism. And this is what people call its "subjectivity," using the word as a reproach against us. But what do we mean when we say this but that man is of greater dignity than a stone or a table? For we mean to say that man primarily exists—that man is, before all else, something that propels itself towards a future and is aware that it is doing so. Man is indeed a project that possesses a subjective life, instead of being a kind of moss, or a fungus. (27–28)

If, however, it is true that existence is prior to essence, man is responsible for what he is. Thus, the first effect of existentialism is that it puts man in possession of himself as he is, and places the responsibility squarely upon his shoulders. And when we say that man is responsible for himself, we do not mean that he is responsible only for his own individuality, but that he is responsible for all men . . . (29) There can no longer be any good a priori, since there is no infinite and perfect consciousness. It is nowhere written "the good exists," that one must be honest or must lie, since we are now upon the plane where there are only men. Dostoyevsky once wrote: "If God did not exist, everything would be permitted. Everything is indeed permitted if God does not exist, and man is in consequence forlorn [délaissé], for he cannot find anything to depend on either within or outside himself. He discovers forthwith that he is without excuse. For if indeed existence precedes essence, one will never be able to explain one's action by reference to a given and specific human nature; in other words, there is no determinism—man is free, man is freedom. Nor, on the other hand, if God does not exist, are we provided with any values or commands that could legitimize our behavior. Thus we have neither behind us, nor before us in a numinous realm of values, any means of justification or excuse. We are left alone, without excuse. That is what I mean when I say that man is condemned to be free. Condemned, because he did not create himself, yet he is nevertheless at liberty, and from the moment that he is thrown into this world he is responsible for everything he does. (33–34)

Beyond an exposition of existentialism, Sartre's objective is thus to reconcile individualism with collective action, freedom with conscious, responsible choice. From a more concrete perspective, his aim is to show the Communists and the Communist Party, which embodied the ideals of the working class, that there was no contradiction between existentialism and Marxism. As he writes in *Existentialism and Humanism*,

The word "subjectivism" is to be understood in two senses, and our adversaries play upon one of them. Subjectivism means, on the one hand, freedom of the individual subject, and, on the other, that man cannot pass beyond human subjectivity. It is the latter which is the deeper meaning of existentialism. When we say that man is responsible for himself, we do not mean that every one of us is responsible strictly for his own individuality, but that in choosing for himself, he chooses all men. (29)

This declaration would seem to resolve the supposed contradiction, but Sartre's efforts at creating a bridge between existentialism and Marxism nevertheless encountered strong, even vehement resistance, especially on the part of the most orthodox Communists. In some instances, Sartre chose to disassociate himself from any party line but nevertheless to take part in the social and political issues of the day. *Les Temps Modernes* (*Modern Times*, also the title of Charlie Chaplin's 1936 film), the journal founded in 1945 by Sartre, Simone de Beauvoir, and Maurice Merleau-Ponty, became a tribune for *littérature engagée*, literature that would bear witness and actively, lucidly contribute to the transformation of society. As stated in the "Presentation" of the first issue of *Les Temps Modernes*, this would be achieved without pledging allegiance to any particular political party: "We are on the side of those who want to change both man's social condition and the conception he has of himself. This is why, concerning upcoming political and social events, our journal will take a position in each case. It will not do so *politically*, that is, it will serve no party . . . at least for us, literature again becomes what it has never ceased to be: a social function." Later on, as politics were increasingly defined by the cold war and by the taking of sides for the United States or the Soviet Union, Sartre attempted, with Mounier, to create a middle way by forming an actual political organization, the *Rassemblement démocratique révolutionnaire* in 1948. As opposed to *Les Temps Modernes*, which is published to this day, the RDP could not maintain the middle ground it sought to achieve and soon disbanded, while existentialism continued to be a dominant ideology and even a cultural phenomenon that went well beyond the borders of France.

In spite of its austere worldview and specialized philosophical vocabulary, existentialism also became a veritable popular trend. Its most complex propositions were taken up by a variety of groups ranging from journalists to students and became ready-made phrases or slogans for a generation emerging from the catastrophe of war and occupation, followed by the discovery of the Holocaust and the destructive possibilities of nuclear power.

In its popularized version, existentialism was most ostensibly linked with the Parisian left bank neighborhood of Saint Germain des Prés, with its cafés, most famously the Deux Magots and the Café de Flore, where Sartre and de Beauvoir could regularly be seen writing or conversing with a seemingly endless stream of people ranging from fellow writers and philosophers to students and American jazz musicians. In fact the association between existentialism and Saint-Germain des Prés also extended metonymically to jazz, played in the *quartier*'s many *caves* or cellars, by musicians ranging from Charlie Parker to Duke Ellington. Sartre was indeed an avid jazz fan and connoisseur who had gone to performances in New York during the war, most notably by Charlie Parker and Coleman Hawkins in the jazz clubs of fifty-second street.

Figure 6.3   Duke Ellington Arrives in a Jazz Club in Saint Germain des Prés (1946)

Duke Ellington is welcomed to one of the most famous of the *caves*, the Club Saint Germain des Prés, by Boris Vian, a prolific writer, poet, and musician, chronicler of postwar Saint Germain, who had been a student of Sartre's at the Ecole Normale Supérieure and published articles on jazz not only in specialized journals such *Le Jazz Hot*, but also in Sartre's *Les Temps Modernes*. Also welcoming Ellington, next to Vian, is Juliette Gréco, an actress and singer associated with the more popular dimension of existentialism; the second woman is Maria Casalis, owner of the club and well-known "troglodyte" as the frequenters of these caves were called by the press. In spite of a coincidental resemblance, the man behind Duke Ellington is not Jean-Paul Sartre. (© Hachette Photo Presse)

Jazz had been proscribed during the nazi occupation and the black musicians living in Paris before the war had been forced to flee. Now, simultaneously with the rise of existentialism, jazz knew a rebirth that coincided with the influx of a number of black American musicians in postwar Paris' Saint Germain, epicenter of the "existentialist scene." African American writers also flocked to Paris, which became once again the stage for a veritable community of American artistic and intellectual expatriates. This time, however, as Tyler Stovall writes, "Black writers constituted the most important literary group of any color in the French capital. If the 1920s were the era of Fitzgerald, Hemingway and Stein, then the 1950s belonged to [Richard] Wright, [James] Baldwin, and [Chester] Himes" (*Paris Noir*, 182). These black American writers and musicians came to symbolize in postwar and then cold war France both the best and the worst of the superpower that the United States had become: they simultaneously embodied the repressive and racist America of Jim Crow and the modern, vibrant culture that produced jazz. Sartre's appreciation of jazz and his praise of American novels and cinema did not stop him for writing that "America has rabies" after the execution of Ethel and Julius Rosenberg in 1953.

Albert Camus was also associated with existentialism by the public and by the press but consistently denied being a member of any philosophical movement or, indeed the practitioner of any ideology. Nevertheless, the affinities with his thought and Sartrian existentialism are sometimes striking. Camus's concept of the "absurd" can be used as a convenient shortcut to examine these similarities. Camus explores and develops this concept in what is sometimes referred to as the "cycle of the absurd," three works he published during and immediately after the war: the novel *The Stranger* (1942), the philosophical essay *The Myth of Sisyphus* (1942), and the play *Caligula* (1944). Like Sartre, Camus begins with the absence of any ultimate or metaphysical meaning in the world: the universe is simply *there* and, to man's questioning consciousness, it only offers silence. For Camus it is neither the universe nor man that is absurd, it is this very confrontation between a yearning consciousness and a silent universe. Thus, rather than an attribute of either the universe or of man, the absurd is a *tension* between the two. As Camus famously declared in the very first lines of *The Myth of Sisyphus*, in the face of the absurd the only truly serious philosophical question is suicide: "To judge whether life is worth living or not, is to answer the fundamental question of philosophy." Camus's fictional characters repeatedly confront the question of what to do in the face of the absence of any ultimately justifying meaning. Meursault, the protagonist of *The Stranger*, set in colonial Algiers where Camus was born, faces an Arab man on a beach and can be said to *enact* the absurd: "The whole world seemed to have come to a standstill on this little strip of sand between the sunlight, the sea, the twofold silence of the reed and stream. And just then it crossed my mind that one might fire, or not fire and it would come to absolutely the same thing" (72). In his decision to shoot the man, not out of revenge or anger or racism, but because, ultimately, both options, to shoot or not to shoot, are rendered equivalent in a world devoid of absolute, overarching meaning. Meursault embodies the absurd hero; he does not actively or even consciously kill the man, "the trigger gave." In this sense Camus's absurd protagonist is different from Sartre's existentialist hero who consciously chooses "all men" and actively establishes a hierarchy of meaning in the process. However, Camus's absurd protagonists only represent a stage in his philosophy, whether Sisyphus, condemned to roll a boulder up a mountain only to see it roll down again throughout eternity, or the Roman Emperor Caligula who, endowed with considerably more power than Meursault, the anonymous clerk in Algiers, also enacts the absurd by enforcing a complete overturning of his empire's laws and rules of behavior—criminals are released and rewarded, the "just" are punished, and so forth. In his 1944 novel, *The Plague*, the inhabitants of Algiers besieged by the epidemic and its rats *choose* to fight and, ultimately, win, as the plague recedes and disappears, even if, like Sisyphus's boulder it will appear again one day. Thus in both schemes, Sartre's and Camus's characters make conscious choices in the face of an ultimately meaningless world as they themselves had chosen during the nazi occupation to fight in the Resistance and not join forces with Vichy.

A crucial difference between Camus's and Sartre's thought may well be the different ways in which they determine the very nature of the struggle or of action. In spite of his sometimes antagonistic relations with Marxism, Sartre nevertheless attempted to find a middle ground with the Communists; even if he never joined the party, he saw in Marxism a means of political *engagement* that could be justified. Camus, on the other hand openly criticized "the Marxists and their followers likewise [who] think they are humanists, but for [whom] human nature will be formed in the classless society of the future." For Camus,

> This proves that they reject at the present moment what we all are: those humanists are accusers of man . . . They reject the man of today in the name of the man of the future. That claim is religious in nature. Why should it be more justified than the one that announces the kingdom of heaven to come? In reality, the end of history cannot have, within the limits of our condition, any definable significance. It can only be the object of faith and of a new mystification. A mystification that today is not less great than the one that of old based colonial oppression on the necessity of saving the souls of infidels. (*The Myth of Sisyphus and Other Essays*, 208–209)

Beyond this interview, Camus formulated his criticism more systematically in his essay *The Rebel* (1951) leading to well-publicized responses and counterresponses and, ultimately, to a breach with Sartre. Although the two would find common ground in their strongly anticolonialist stands, the most urgent and important political issue for French intellectuals of their generation, the breach was left unresolved when Camus died in a car accident in 1960.

Simone de Beauvoir, (see dossier 6.4), the author of *The Second Sex* (1949), cofounder of *Les Temps Modernes*, was, with Camus and Sartre, one of the most influential intellectuals of postwar France. Although not an "existential work," *The Second Sex* clearly applies some of the principles of that philosophy to what it means to be a woman. De Beauvoir's famous answer to the question "What is a woman?" subverts, as does existentialism, the very notion of a stable essence that would define human identity once and for all: "One is not born, but rather becomes, a woman."

Dossier 6.4   Simone de Beauvoir, *The Second Sex* (1949)

"Few bibles are written in the history of humanity," writes Benoîte Groult, the contemporary writer and essayist, in her introduction to Simone de Beauvoir's *The Second Sex*. Groult goes on to explain that very few books meet the dictionary definition according to which "Bible" means "THE BOOK, the revelation, the message." Published in 1949, only five years after women received the right to vote in France and forty years before the creation of the *Mouvement de libération de la femme* (MLF, Woman's Liberation Movement), the book for which de Beauvoir is best known is indeed *the* women's book, the founding work of modern feminism. Feminism, however was not a movement nor a concept de Beauvoir championed in 1949. In the very first few lines of her own introduction to *The Second Sex*, she writes that "the quarrel of feminism has made enough ink flow: let's not talk about it anymore. Still people are talking about it. It does not seem that the voluminous nonsense spurted out during this past quarter century has shed any light on the problem. In fact, is there a problem? And what is it?" For de Beauvoir, the issue at the time she wrote the book is, rather, to be formulated in another question: "What is a woman?" At a time when women had become an active group both in the workforce during the war and in the Resistance, the question had particular resonance. In answering this question, de Beauvoir draws up, in the one thousand pages or so of *The Second Sex*, a veritable philosophical, historical, anthropological, psychological, sociological, and literary masterwork that, for the first time ever, systematically explored and defined women and the status of women in terms that went beyond any "objectively" or "essentially" given difference from a universal point of reference that would be "men." The affinities of her overall approach with some of the major concepts of existentialism become evident in the passage below. It is no accident that de Beauvoir, who at twenty-one became the youngest *agrégée de philosophie* (recipient of a degree conferred after a highly competitive postgraduate examination) in France, should have become associated with and influenced by existentialism, the most influential philosophy of the postwar years. She met the major proponent of that philosophy, Sartre, while they were both studying for the *agrégation* examination and eventually became lifetime companions—a relationship based on absolute freedom and what Sartre at first defined as a temporary and renewable contract—and intellectual partners; they founded the influential journal *Les Temps Modernes* together in 1946 and participated jointly in some of the major debates of their time. Although *The Second Sex* is her most celebrated work, de Beauvoir published widely in a variety of genres: among others, the novels *L'invitée* (1943), *Les Mandarins* (1954) for which she received France's most prestigious literary prize, the Prix Goncourt, and a series of autobiographical volumes ranging from *Mémoires d'une jeune fille rangée* (*Memoirs of a Dutiful Daughter*, 1958) to *La cérémonie des adieux* (*Adieux. A Farewell to Sartre*, 1981) that focuses on the last years of Sartre's life. Her autobiographical work describes the life of a girl born in 1908 in a Catholic upper middle class family living, to a great extent, according to a traditional codes that were closer to nineteenth-century norms than contemporary ones, and gradually but surely extracting herself from that milieu; from *jeune fille rangée* (dutiful or well brought up young lady) to major author, public intellectual, and feminist icon. When *The Second Sex* was published, it created a scandal, disturbing as it did both men's and quite a few women's intellectual comfort and sense of decorum and, more importantly, dealing with issues that never had been dealt with in quite that way before, sexuality in particular. It was even placed on the Vatican's Index of Prohibited Books.

The book is divided into two parts. The first deals with the facts and myths of biology, psychoanalysis, and history. There, de Beauvoir proceeds with a veritable dismantling of the sexism and essentialism of these disciplines and concludes with an analysis of the representation of women in literature written by men. The second part, entitled "Women's Life Today" illustrates de Beauvoir's thesis that, rather than objectively and eternally *given*, what makes a woman is *constructed*, a social product. The book's last chapter, "Toward Liberation," calls for a common effort by men and women toward a more just place for women in the world, and also relies on socialism to achieve this goal.

This excerpt is from part II, chapter XII, "Childhood."

One is nor born, but rather becomes, a woman. No biological, psychological, or economic fate determines the figure that the human female presents in society; it is civilization as a whole that produces this creature, intermediate between male and eunuch, which is described as feminine. Only the intervention of someone else can establish an individual as an Other. (281)

Marriage is not only an honorable career and one less tiring than many others: it alone permits a woman to keep her social dignity intact and at the same time to find sexual fulfillment as loved one and mother. It is thus that her entourage envisages her future, as does she herself. There in unanimous agreement that getting a husband—or in some cases a "protector"—is for her the most important of undertakings. In her eyes man incarnates the Other, as she does for the man; but this Other seems to her to be on the plane of the essential, and with reference to him she sees herself as the inessential. She will free herself from the parental home, from her mother's hold, she will open up her future, not by active conquest but by delivering herself up, passive and docile, into the hands of a new master. (346)

[De Beauvoir has just quickly developed the idea of sports for boys as "an apprenticeship in violence, when their aggressiveness is developed, their will to power, their love for competition . . ."] Moreover, in many countries most girls have no urge towards sports; since scuffles and climbing are forbidden, their bodies have to suffer things only in a passive manner; much more definitely than when younger, they must give up emerging beyond what is given and asserting themselves above other people: they are forbidden to explore, to venture, to extend the limits of the possible. In particular, the competitive attitude, most important to young men, is almost unknown to them. To be sure, women make comparisons among themselves, but competition, challenge, is something quite different from these passive comparisons: two free beings confront each other as having on the world a hold that they propose to enlarge; to climb higher than a playmate, to force an arm to yield and bend, is to assert one's sovereignty over the world in general. Such masterful behavior is not for girls, especially when it involves violence.

In the adult world, no doubt, brute force plays no great part in normal times; but nevertheless it haunts that world; many kinds of masculine behavior springs from a root of possible violence: on every street corner squabbles threaten; usually they flicker out; but for a man to feel in his fists his will to self-affirmation is enough to reassure him of his sovereignty. Against any insult, any attempt to reduce him to the status of object, the male has recourse to his fists, to exposure of himself to blows: he does not let himself be transcended by others, he is himself at the heart of his subjectivity. Violence is the authentic proof of one's loyalty to himself, to his passions, to his own will; radically to deny this will is to deny one's self any objective truth, it is to wall one's self" up in an abstract subjectivity; anger or revolt that does not get into the muscles remains a figment of the imagination. It is a profound frustration not to be able to register one's feelings upon the face of the world.

In the United States it is quite impossible for a Negro, in the South, to use violence against the whites; this rule is the key to the mysterious "black soul"; the way the Negro feels in the White world, the behavior by which he adjusts himself to it, the compensation he seeks, his whole way of feeling and acting are to be explained on the basis of the passivity to which he is condemned. In France during the occupation those who had made up their mind not to resort to violence against the forces of occupation even under provocation (whether through selfish prudence or because they had imperative work to do) felt a profound alteration in their status in the world: the caprice of others determined whether they were to be changed into objects; their subjectivity no longer had means of concrete expression, being only a secondary phenomenon.

In the same way, the universe does not wear a similar aspect for the adolescent boy who is permitted to give imperious notice of his existence and for the adolescent girl whose sentiments have no immediate effectiveness. The one constantly questions the world; he can, at any moment, rise up against whatever is; and he therefore feels that when he accepts it, he actively ratifies it. The other simply submits; the world is defined without reference to her, and its aspect is immutable as far as she is concerned. This lack of physical power leads to a more general timidity; she has no faith in a force she has not experienced in her body; she does not dare to be enterprising, to revolt to invent; doomed to docility, to resignation, she can take in society only a place already made for her. She regards the existing state of affairs as something fixed. (347–348)

The first sentence of this passage, "One is not born, but rather becomes, a woman" has often been quoted to encapsulate the essential thesis of *The Second Sex*: there is nothing "natural" or immutable about what makes a woman. In existential terms, this is echoed by Sartre's "existence precedes essence": a human being defines himself/herself through his/her actions since there is no metaphysical, ahistorical a priori to determine this definition. What de Beauvoir does in *The Second Sex* is to show that there is a difference in the way men and women *historically* fit in this configuration: where a boy, having been educated, trained to perceive himself as endowed with the capacity to question and challenge his surroundings, a girl, as a result of the education and general socializing she receives is "doomed to docility." In approaching a philosophical construct from the particular point of view of women, and in showing that women, like "the Negro in the South" have been reduced to the status of objects through no fault of their own but by a materially superior power, de Beauvoir has, as Toril Moi puts it, "surreptitiously tacked on a form of materialism to Sartre's tragic ontology." It is fitting that for de Beauvoir economic independence becomes the first step toward the improvement of women's condition. As Moi points out, "it does not follow that economically independent women automatically achieve emotional and intellectual freedom as well: patriarchal conditioning is likely to be more recalcitrant than that. Beauvoir's point is simply that economic liberation is the sine qua non of every other form of liberation" (Hollier, 985). These other forms of liberation would lead de Beauvoir into increasingly specific strategies of involvement, ranging from her account of the torture of a young girl, Djamila Boupacha, by French forces during the Algerian War, to her support for the legalization of abortion in France. De Beauvoir would also increasingly abandon her initial ambivalent attitude toward feminism and write in the fourth volume of her memoirs *All Said and Done* Published in 1972: "I declare myself a feminist." In the United States and in England, where millions of copies of *The Second Sex* were sold, women such as Betty Friedan, Kate Millett, and Germaine Greer did not wait for this declaration to make of Simone de Beauvoir's best-known work one of the major references of the feminist movements.

Albert Camus, Simone de Beauvoir, and Jean-Paul Sartre were far from constituting a seamless intellectual front, even if the intervening years between the postwar and our time have contributed to a mythologizing image of the three united under the banner of existentialism. The differences in their philosophies, politics and approaches were sometimes considerable, as we have seen. Sartre and de Beauvoir were certainly in favor of a neutral socialism in the sense that they kept their distance from the Communist Party while remaining *compagnons de route*, believing the revolutionary potential of Marxism would lead to undermining, eventually eliminating bourgeois class structure and, particularly for de Beauvoir—as evidenced in the concluding part of *The Second Sex*—to radical improvement of the condition of women. As noted above, Camus, who called de Beauvoir's *The Second Sex une insulte au mâle latin* (*an insult to the Latin male*) denied being an existentialist, and, especially in *L'Homme révolté* (*The Rebel*, 1951) presented a critique of revolution as ultimately leading to authoritarian dictatorship. What the three clearly did have in common, however, was a certain didactic quality in their fiction and plays partly due no doubt to the particular political imperatives and conditions of the postwar period: the more urgent necessity of taking political position than in times of peace and prosperity, a more urgent necessity of taking and illustrating a philosophical position in the wake of the nihilistic catastrophe whose itinerary was marked by World War II and nazi occupation, the Holocaust, Hiroshima, Nagasaki, and the cold war. Thus, Camus's *The Plague* illustrated the possibility of action in the face of the absurd—the plague symbolizing a meaningless universe where events occur with no warning or explanation—or, as it was interpreted by some, the possibility of resistance in the face of occupation (the plague symbolizing the Nazis); de Beauvoir's *Le sang des autres* (*The Blood of Others*) published in 1944 also serves as philosophical stage where the heroine gradually arrives at existential and political awakening, "existentialism applied to the Occupation" as Charles Sowerwine describes it (246). Sartre's *Les Mouches* (*The Flies*) staged during the occupation, is in fact a representation of some of the essential aspects of existentialism presented through ancient Greek myth and theater: Euripides' *Oresteia*, a recounting of the story of the House of Atreus. In Sartre's version, Orestes assumes his absolute freedom by negating the gods' power over men: "I am neither the master nor the slave, Jupiter. I *am* my freedom!" He then consciously assumes this freedom by choosing to kill his mother in revenge for his father's murder. Like Camus's Caligula and Sisyphus, Sartre's Orestes may be the symbol of a new philosophy, a new way of being in the paradigm of uncertainty that comes out of World War II, but, also like them, he evolves on a stage and in a type of theater that remains formally traditional. As Geneviève Serreau wrote in her *Histoire du "nouveau theâtre"* (*History of the "New Theater"*): "Moralists before being playwrights, they only see in the theater an efficient means—but not the only one for them—of illustrating their philosophical options. At no time do they try to revolutionize its forms and structures, heedlessly pouring their new wine into the old bottles of traditional theater" (26). Others see in this traditional aspect of "existential theater" a strategic and necessary choice: "For a theater which set itself an instructive goal in engaging with ethical issue there would have been a counter-productive risk of diverting public attention by introducing arresting new techniques" (Forbes, 157). This was clearly also the case for overtly political theater, such as Roger' Vailland's *Le colonel Forster plaidera coupable* (*Colonel Foster Will Plead Guilty*) staged at the height of the Korean war and which equated the American army with Hitler's Nazi battalions. Both existential theater and political theater were thus focused on illustrating a philosophy or taking a concrete political position; and they did so through characters and techniques that served this objective. What Serreau calls the *Nouveau Théâtre* focused instead on reflecting and rendering the new state of affairs— a world from which traditional concepts of meaning and subjectivity had been obliterated—through the very treatment of theatrical form and language itself. The precariousness and relativity of reality and of the place of human beings in the universe certainly remain major concerns of this theater, but, there, the protagonists in their Greco-Roman garb and backdrop have disappeared, just like their often lyrical and didactic soliloquies; they have been replaced by tramps who fart, English families whose members all have the same name, and English clocks that sound out seventeen "English" strokes, before a Mrs. Smith, in the first line of a play, declares: "Well, it's nine o'clock." The plays referred to respectively here are Samuel Beckett's *Waiting for Godot*—in which no one named Godot ever appears—first staged in 1953, and Eugene Ionesco's *La cantatrice chauve, The Bald Soprano*—in which there are no sopranos whether bald or hairy—first staged in 1950. The two plays are two of the most celebrated of this "new theater" that, within a few years, was to reach a public well beyond the small left bank theaters where they appeared originally, and become modern classics staged in the most established theaters of France and throughout the world.

Samuel Beckett, an Irishman who had come to Paris as a young lecturer at the Ecole Normale Supérieure and remained in France for the rest of his life, wrote what is arguably the iconic work of this nouveau theâtre that some saw as a third great age of theater (the first two being Greek, and then Elizabethan, and French classical theater— Shakespeare, Molière, Corneille, Racine): *Waiting for Godot*, staged in January 1953 by Roger Blin at the small Théâtre de Babylone, in the same Saint Germain neighborhood where the "existential cafés" and "troglodytes" were to be found. The usual sets have disappeared, and with them the whole notion of the well-made play: rational expectations and answers reflected in clear exchanges between characters, a linear narrative dominated by the classic dramatic arc. Instead, Vladimir and Estragon, two tramps—some of their clothes, belongings, and statements in fact suggest clowns—stand on an almost bare stage, a solitary tree the only thing breaking the emptiness; and there they will pass the time waiting for someone they have never met but hope will come. In the meantime, they wait; they pass the time talking, sleeping, eating, scratching. Neither tramps nor clowns, Vladimir and Estragon are, as Martin Esslin writes, "merely two human beings in the most basic human situation of being in the world and not knowing what they are there for." The existential predicament is thus at the heart of the play but the way in which it is represented is what has radically changed. The human predicament of being thrown in a meaningless universe is not so much *conveyed*, in the form of a message spoken by the characters for example, as *embodied* in the new theater and in *Godot* in this instance. Realistic theater has been stripped to its bare bones so that the most basic questions can be asked once again: Who am I? What am I doing here? Where classic dramatic arc and narrative offer a linear progression, a crisis and a resolution, Becket gives us circularity, the very *thereness* of people who cannot go anywhere and will find no answer. By the "end" of *Godot*, the two who have ineffectually tried to kill themselves once already, using the rope that holds up Estragon's trousers, simply *remain*:

ESTRAGON: We'll hang ourselves tomorrow. (*Pause)* Unless Godot comes.
ESTRAGON: And if he comes.
ESTRAGON: We'll be saved.
[*Vladimir takes off his hat (Lucky's) peers inside it, feels about inside it, shakes it knocks on the crown, puts it on again.*]
ESTRAGON: Well? Shall we go?
VLADIMIR: Pull on your trousers.

ESTRAGON: What?
VLADIMIR: Pull on your trousers.
ESTRAGON: You want me to pull off my trousers?
VLADIMIR: Pull ON your trousers.
ESTRAGON: (realizing his trousers are down). True. He pulls up his trousers. Silence.
VLADIMIR: Well? Shall we go?
ESTRAGON: Yes, let's go.

[*They do not move.*]

CURTAIN

Beckett won the Nobel Prize for literature in 1969 while Ionesco became one of the forty "immortals," a member of the French academy, in 1970: the theatrical avant-garde that had emerged in the early 1950s in the wake of existentialism had by then become classics of the international repertoire.

Eugene Ionesco, like Beckett, came to the French language "from the outside": born of a French mother and a Romanian father he went to live early on with his family in Bucharest, returning to France to pursue university studies, making Paris his home thereafter. It is perhaps Ionesco's particular relation to the French language, influenced as it was by Romanian, that helped produce the kind of playful obsession with language *as* language that characterizes all his plays. Ironically, learning English from a beginner's manual was the catalyst for the first of his "antiplays," *The Bald Soprano* (staged in 1949). In *his Notes and Counter-Notes* (1962), Ionesco later explained how, gradually, the run-of-the-mill, banal sentences and constructions of basic English slowly became emptied of meaning for him, leading to a moment of the complete dismantling of language, now laid bare. This encounter with language signals a major shift to a more formal, less psychological or ethical framework that would become increasingly manifest in later trends in literature and the social sciences such as the *Nouveau roman* (the New Novel) and structuralism (see chapter 8). As the postwar receded in time the dominant ideology of existentialism increasingly gave way to what would become known as the "linguistic turn." Typically, in the existentialist framework, the encounter is with reality, things, and the ensuing contingency of the protagonist, the meaninglessness of his existence, as in Antoine Roquentin's encounter with the brute *thereness* of things in front of the root of a chestnut tree in Sartre's existential novel *La Nausée* (*Nausea*, 1938) or Meurtsault's encounter with "the Arab" on the beach in Camus's *The Stranger*. The language used by Sartre and Camus, and their protagonists *logically* expresses and articulates the encounter of a consciousness yearning for objective meaning and the absence of that meaning, whereas Ionesco has us meet, for example, Bobby Watson, this gentleman who has been dead for four, three, or two years, in short "a good-looking corpse [who] did not look his age" and whose wife, daughter, aunt, uncle, cousin, grandmother, and others, are also all called Bobby Watson. The falling apart is the falling apart of language, *enacted* in a zany, impossible world in which the rules of logic and method no longer hold sway. For Ionesco and his characters, the discovery of contingency is expressed *in* language itself rather than through concepts and modes of behavior simply expressed in a realistic mode by language. As Ionescco writes about *The Bald Soprano*, "For me, it was like a falling apart

of reality . . . I saw myself as having written something like *the tragedy of language.*"
And everything else follows: the nonsensical, absurd—but in a sense very different
from Albert Camus's use of the term in *The Myth of Sisyphus*—concatenation of
encounters and events that make up Ionesco's world, one in which, as happens in *The
Bald Soprano*, a man and a woman discover after a long conversation that they are
husband and wife.

Dossier 6.5   Eugene Ionesco, *The Lesson* (1950)

The same "logic" is again at work in Ionesco's next play *The Lesson*. As the play
opens, the student is sitting with the professor in his kitchen where the lesson is to
take place:

MAID: Yes, Sir. I've found the plate I was looking for. I'm just going . . .
PROFESSOR: Hurry up, please, and go back to the kitchen.
MAID: Yes, Sir, I'm going. [Offers to go, then] I beg pardon, Sir, but please do be careful.
Not too much excitement
PROFESSOR: Don't be so ridiculous, Marie. Nothing whatever to worry about.
MAID: But that's what you always say.
PROFESSOR: Your insinuations are entirely without foundation. I am perfectly capable of
behaving myself. After all, I'm old enough.
MAID: That's just it, Sir. But don't you go telling me I didn't warn you.
PROFESSOR: I'm not interested in your warnings, Marie.
MAID: Monsieur must do as he thinks best.
[She goes out]
PROFESSOR: I'm sorry about this stupid interruption, Mademoiselle . . . . You must
understand that this poor woman is always afraid I shall tire myself. She's worried about my
health.
PUPIL: Oh, it really doesn't matter, Sir. It shows she's devoted to you. She must be very fond
of you. Good servants are hard to find.
PROFESSOR: She really goes too far. It's stupid to be so nervous. Let us get back to our
arithmetic sheep.
PUPIL: I follow you, Sir.
PROFESSOR [wittily]: But still sitting down, I see!
PUPIL: [appreciating the joke]: Just like you, Sir!
PROFESSOR: Good! Then shall we arithmetize a little?
PUPIL: I'll be pleased to, Sir.
PROFESSOR: Then perhaps you wouldn't mind telling me.
PUPIL: Not in the slightest, Sir. Please go ahead.
PROFESSOR: What do one and one make?
PUPIL: One and one make two.
PROFESSOR [astounded by his pupil's erudition]: But that's very good indeed! You're
extremely advanced in your studies. You'll have very little difficulty in passing all your Doctorate
examinations.
PUPIL: I'm very pleased to hear it, Sir. Especially from you.
PROFESSOR: Let us proceed a little further. What do two and one make?
PUPIL: Three.

PROFESSOR: *Three and one?*
PUPIL: *Four.*
PROFESSOR: *Four and one?*
PUPIL: *Five.*
PROFESSOR: *Five and one?*
PUPIL: *Six.*
PROFESSOR: *Six and one?*
PUPIL: *Seven.*
PROFESSOR: *Seven and one?*
PUPIL: *Eight.*
PROFESSOR: *Seven and one?*
PUPIL: *Still eight.*
PROFESSOR: *Very good answer. Seven and one?*
PUPIL: *Eight again.*
PROFESSOR: *Excellent. Perfect. Seven and one?*
PUPIL: *Eight for the fourth time. And sometimes nine.*
PROFESSOR: *Magnificent! You're magnificent! Sublime! My warmest congratulations Mademoiselle. There's no point in going on. You're quite first-rate at addition. Let's try subtraction. Just tell me, that is if you're not too tired, what is left when you take three from four?*
PUPIL: *Three from four . . . Three from four?*
PROFESSOR: *Yes, that's what I mean to say, what is four minus three?*
PUPIL: *That makes seven?*
PROFESSOR: *Stop there, Mademoiselle. Which number is the greater? Three or four?*
PUPIL: *Er . . . three or four? Which is the greater? The greater number out of three and four? In what way greater?*
PROFESSOR: *Some numbers are smaller than others. In the greater numbers there are more units than there are in the smaller ones.*
PUPIL: *Than in the smaller numbers?*
PROFESSOR: *Unless, of course, the numbers are made up of smaller units. If all the units are very small, there may be more units in the small numbers than in the big ones . . . that is, if they are not the same units . . .*
PUPIL: *In that case small numbers can be bigger than big numbers?*
PROFESSOR: *Yes, well, we won't go into that. That would take us much too far: I just want you to realize that there are other things apart from numbers . . . there are sizes, too, and totals, and then there are groups and heaps, heaps of things, like ducks and drakes and cabbages and kings, etc . . . etc.*

The language is deceptively simple, everyday, like the phases of a beginner's manual for learning a foreign language, but, behind the banality of declarations such as "Good servants are hard to find," it has fallen apart, taking everything in its wake, and although there is something that looks like a plot—ultimately, the "lesson" goes awry and the professor ends up stabbing and killing the student—what Serreau wrote about *The Bald Soprano* remains true here: "There are no longer any characters, or any plots, only pure theatrical mechanism running on empty, or, rather, chewing up language, the only hero of the play, comically manhandled to agony" (41). The "absurd" in the sense of the *Nouveau théâtre* is in the nonsequiturs, the fact that "seven and one" can be "eight four times in a row," but "sometimes nine"; it lies in the complete subversion of everything that usually combines to create the illusion of a "normal" reality. The very taxonomy of the world is thrown topsy-turvy: ". . . there are sizes . . . and totals, and then there are groups, and heaps, heaps of things, like ducks and drakes and cabbages and kings, etc, etc." Once revealed, this absurdity will, like the heroes of *Waiting for Godot*, remain. Indeed the circularity, or eternity, that was to be depicted in *Godot* a few years later is already established in *The Lesson*: after the student's body is removed from the scene, the professor calls out the play's last line: "Next." *The Bald Soprano* and *The Lesson* play nightly to this day at le Théâtre de la Huchette, a small theater on the left bank.

Existentialism and the Nouveau Théâtre were certainly not the only literary, philosophical and theatrical trends of the period that followed World War II and continued into the cold war. The Théâtre National Populaire, for example, under the directorship of Jean Vilar, was one of the major cultural venues of that time. One of its primary objectives was the "popularization of theater," or, rather, of its audience: to bring those who lived in the Parisian "red belt," the outlying working-class suburbs, to theatrical performances. The TNP's program was made up of classics, both French and foreign: Molière, Racine, and Shakespeare rather than the "avant-garde" works of Ionesco and Beckett. At a time when the government itself made the decentralization of culture and its use as "social cement" one of its primary cultural policy objectives and heavily contributed to such projects, we must be careful not to overestimate the importance of existential theater and the nouveau théâtre, which are to be perceived in the more general cultural context of the period. In that sense, existentialism and the *Nouveau Théâtre* can be seen as counterdiscourses to a more official and state-sponsored culture: existentialism with its ascribing of responsibility to the free human agent, perceived as a counterhumanist project, and the *Nouveau Théâtre* with its bums, clowns, and its breakdown of language and sweeping away of the props of traditional theater, perceived as going against the grain of the order and decorum of classical French theater and its three unities. Still, in a first stage, it was existentialism, and Jean-Paul Sartre in particular and, later, the *Nouveau Théâtre*, Becket and Ionesco in particular, who were instrumental in providing Paris with its renewed position as international cultural capital. At a time when France emerged as a nation that could no longer be considered a major world power, or "super power" as the United States and the Soviet Union had become, it "continued," as Rioux and Sirinelli formulate it, "to shine through its culture" (220). In the twenty years that followed the end of World War II, five Frenchmen won the Nobel Prize for literature, among them Camus (1957) and Sartre, who refused the prize in 1964. As Tyler Stovall writes, Paris also "achieved prominence as an (and in some ways *the*) intellectual center of the postwar world, and academic polemics originating on the left bank were followed avidly by writers, professors and students from Argentina to Yugoslavia" (*France*, 64). Even if some of the writers, artists, and intellectuals mentioned above can be considered to form counterdiscourses to official national policy and objectives, they nevertheless contributed to what de Gaulle called "a certain idea of France." And it is this idea of France as locus of culture and ideas that continued to dominate even as France was confronting its reduced political and economic status on the world scene. This "certain idea" of France is, as we have seen, not only posited on de Gaulle's notion of a France as an old nation with its roots in a distant, venerable past; it is also a France with values of universalism born in the crucible of the Enlightenment and the French revolution; it is the France of the Third Republic's policies of centralization and modernization as well as of its colonial "civilizing mission," obviously linked in turn to the same Enlightenment universalist notions and France's perception of itself as a model that could (and should) be "exported." As France was beginning to shift from the first phase of economic reconstruction with its emphasis on heavy industry in the early 1950s, it is precisely this "certain idea of France" that would increasingly be challenged by a number of developments that signaled the advent of postmodernity: decolonization, with its challenge to the hierarchical and idealized structure of the French Empire; consumer society itself already the harbinger of "globalization," with its challenge to traditional and colonial France where exchanges with empire dominated foreign trade, and where, at least in the official national discourse, the idea of the "citizen" preceded the idea of the "consumer." The 1950s and 1960s were, to paraphrase Eugene Weber's phrase, "from peasants into Frenchmen," the years during which peasants had already become Frenchmen and now became consumers. Among these consumers, young people emerged as a particular group with its own challenges to tradition, challenges that would culminate with the explosion of May 68 (see chapter 8).

References

Aron, Raymond. *The Opium of the Intellectuals*. Lawrence Kilmartin, trans. New York: Norton Library, 1957.

Aymé, Marcel. *Uranus*. Paris: Gallimard, 1948.

Becket, Samuel. *Waiting for Godot*. London: Faber & Faber, 1955.

Brossat, Alain. *Les tondues. Un carnaval moche*. Paris: Editions Manya, 1992.

Camus, Albert. *The Myth of Sisyphus and Other Essays*. Justin O'Brien, trans. New York: Knopf, 1967.

———. *The Stranger*. Stuart Gilbert, trans. New York: Alfred A. Knopf, 1946.

Cohen, William, ed. *The Transformation of Modern France. Essays in Honor of Gordon Wright*. Boston, NY: Houghton Mifflin, 1997.

Corbett, James. *Through French Windows. An Introduction to France in the Nineties*. Ann Harbor: University of Michigan Press, 1994.

De Beauvoir, Simone. *The Second Sex*. H.M. Parshley, trans. and ed. New York: Knopf, 1953.

Duras, Marguerite. *Hiroshima mon amour*. Paris: Folio, 1973 [1959].

Forbes, Jill and Michael Kelly. *French Cultural Studies. An Introduction*. Oxford: Oxford University Press, 1995.

George, Eric. "De l'exception et de l'exemption culturelles à la diversité culturelle. De l'internationalisation à la mondialisation supranationale des économies?" *Colloque Panaméricain. Industries culturelles et dialogue des civilisations dans les Amériques*, April 2002.

Hollier, Denis ed. *A New History of French Literature*. Cambridge, MA: Harvard University Press, 1989.

Holman, Valerie and Debra Kelly, eds. *France at War in the Twentieth Century*. New York, London: Bergham Books, 2000.

Ionesco, Eugene. *Four Plays by Eugene Ionesco*. Donald M. Allen, ed. New York: Grove Press, 1958.

Judt, Tony. *Past Imperfect. French Iintellectuals, 1944–1956*. Berkeley: University of California Press, 1992.

Kaplan, Alice. *The Collaborator. The Trial and Execution of Robert Brasillach*. Chicago, London: University of Chicago Press, 2000.

Kuisel, Richard. *Seducing the French. The Dilemma of Americanization*. Berkeley: University of California Press, 1993.

Novick, Peter. *The Resistance versus Vichy. The Purge of Collaborators in Liberated France*. New York: Columbia University Press, 1968.

Paxton, Robert. *Vichy France. Old Guard and New Order*. New York: Columbia University Press, 1972.

Prochasson, Christophe and Olivier Wierviorka. *La France du XXième Siècle. Documents d'histoire*. Paris: Editions du Seuil, 1994.

Rioux, Jean-Pierre and Jean-François Sirinelli. *Histoire culturelle de la France*. Vol. 4: *Le temps des masses. Le vingtième siècle*. Paris: Editions du Seuil, 1997.

Ross, Kristin. *Fast Cars, Clean Bodies. Decolonization anmd the Reordering of French Culture*. Cambridge, MA, London: MIT Press, 1995.

Sartre, Jean-Paul. *Existentialism and Humanism*. Philip Mairet, trans. and intro. London: Methuen, 1966.

Serreau, Geneviève. *Histoire du "nouveau théâtre."* Paris: Gallimard, 1966.

Sowerwine, Charles. *France since 1870. Culture, Politics and Society*. New York: Houndmills, 2001.

Stein, Gertrude. *Wars I Have Seen*. New York: Random House, 1945.

Stovall, Tyler E. *Paris Noir. African Americans and the City of Light*. Boston, NY: Houghton Mifflin Company, 1996.

———. *France since the Second World War*. Harlow, London: Pearson Eeducation Ltd. 2002.

Virgili, Fabrice. *La France virile: Des femmes tondues à la Libération*. Paris: Payot, 2000.

Wirth, Laurent. *L'exception française. 19e–20e siècles*. Paris: Armand Colin, 2000.

CHAPTER 7

(DE)COLONIZATION (1944–1962)

They grabbed what they could get for the sake of what was to be got. It was just robbery with violence, aggravated murder on a great scale, and men going at it blind—as is very proper for those who tackle a darkness. The conquest of the earth, which mostly means the taking it away from those who have a different complexion or slightly flatter noses than ourselves, is not a pretty thing when you look into it too much.

—Joseph Conrad, *Heart of Darkness* (1902)

Not so very long ago, the earth numbered two thousand million inhabitants: five hundred million men, and one thousand five hundred million natives. The former had the Word; the others had the use of it. Between the two there were hired kinglets, overlords and a bourgeoisie, sham from beginning to end, which served as go-betweens. In the colonies the truth stood naked, but the citizens of the mother country preferred it with clothes on: the native had to love them, something in the way mothers are loved. The European elite undertook to manufacture a native elite. They picked out promising adolescents; they branded them, as with a red-hot iron, with the principles of western culture, they stuffed their mouths full with high-sounding phrases, grand glutinous words that stuck to the teeth. After a short stay in the mother country they were sent home, whitewashed. These walking lies had nothing left to say to their brothers; they only echoed. From Paris, from London, from Amsterdam we would utter the words "Parthenon! Brotherhood!" and somewhere in Africa or Asia lips would open ". . . thenon! . . . therhood!" It was the golden age.

It came to an end.

—Jean-Paul Sartre, Preface to Frantz Fanon's *The Wretched of the Earth* (1961)

Jean-Paul Sartre's preface was written toward the very end of empire. It was published in 1961, at a time when France was entering consumer society and its empire was entering its final phase in bloody battles fought in the mountains and cities of Algeria. Joseph Conrad's *Heart of Darkness* is set closer to the beginning of empire. It was published in 1902, at a time when the views expressed above by Marlowe, the novel's protagonist-narrator, seem to run against the grain of a period of European history, the turn of the century, when colonialism was generally viewed in positive terms. Rather than "robbery with violence," or "aggravated murder on a great scale," empire was commonly viewed in terms of the "white man's burden," the title of Rudyard Kipling's 1899 poem encouraging the United States to imitate Europe in its mission to "take light to the dark places of the world," essentially, in the case of Europe, to the "natives" of Africa and Asia. Marlowe's statement would seem to be an absolute condemnation of the colonialist project viewed as a positive, even heroic endeavor. In fact, it ultimately leaves the traditional justification of colonialism unchallenged, for in his condemnation Marlowe is only referring to men he perceives as aberrations, exceptions to the general rules and goals of colonization; he is referring to men like the novel's dark center, Kurtz, "men who were not colonists," men whose actions were not ultimately governed and redeemed by "the idea." For what redeems colonialism for Marlowe is, as he puts it, "an idea at the back of it; not a sentimental pretence, but an idea; and an unselfish belief in the idea—something you can set up, and bow down before, and offer sacrifice to . . . What saves us is efficiency—the devotion to efficiency" (31–32). For him, in short, colonialism is ultimately justified and even redeemed by its noble goal of taking civilization to those places that do not have it, at least in the conquering nation's definition. In the French tradition this is referred to as the *mission civilisatrice*, the civilizing mission of a universal model, with its roots in the Enlightenment that produced the Revolution of 1789 and the modern French Republic.

The positive view proposed by Conrad's protagonist was, in general, the one still held by the overwhelming majority of the French people as World War II was ending, leading to what Tyler Stovall calls "the paradox of a republican empire" (47): a nation founded upon the principles of the Revolution of 1789, the principles of "liberty, equality, fraternity" and universal citizenship, but a nation that, at the time of its own liberation from nazi occupation in 1944, ruled over 60 million colonial subjects in places spread from the Caribbean Sea to the Indian Ocean. However, the postwar world was very different from the one in which Marlowe, a half-century before, could confidently view "true colonization" in a positive light. The conditions that had made France's extensive colonial empire possible had changed and the stage was set for its disintegration. At the heart of this disintegration lay a challenge to the very basis of France as the supposed origin and repository of universal values that could be exported throughout the world. The challenge was twofold. It lay first in the following proposition, formulated by a number of "natives" themselves: if there is such a thing as a universal citizen, then we are all free, it is a status that belongs de facto to all humanity, including the colonial subjects, the "natives." In this case, colonization, which demands a hierarchy (and thus de facto inequality), is an aberration that cannot be maintained. This proposition leaves the framework of universalism intact, only implying that it be taken to its logical end by being extended to all. The challenge also lay in another, more radical dismantling of the ideological basis of colonization, formulated as follows: there is no such thing as a universal model or a universal citizen, there are only historical agents; the universal citizen is both an abstract and arbitrary notion that leaves no (equal) room for "others"; the only solution is for "other" identities to manifest themselves *as such*, outside of any hierarchy, indeed outside of any supposedly universal framework. As Franz Fanon, the black French writer from Martinique, put it in his anticolonial treatise *The Wretched of the Earth* (1953), "The natives' challenge to the colonial world is not a rational confrontation of points of view. It is not a treatise on the universal, but the untidy affirmation of an original idea propounded as an absolute" (33). Of course, as Conrad's protagonist already clearly saw even half a century before, the "conquest of the earth" was, foremost, an economic enterprise, "the taking [of the earth] away from those who have a different complexion or slightly flatter noses than ourselves." When added to the economic component, affective, psychological factors, as well as strategic and geopolitical imperatives, together formed a powerful combination that made the idea of decolonization extremely undesirable and even unthinkable for many segments of French society in the aftermath of World War II. This meeting of an increasingly untenable system and the incapacity or unwillingness to eliminate it would lead to the "untidiness" referred to by Fanon. This "untidiness" would take different shapes in the close to two decades (1945–1962) following the end of World War II, ranging from war in Indochina and Algeria to a less violent granting of independence to Morocco and Tunisia, to a relatively peaceful granting of independence to the sub-Saharan African colonies. A few small territories such as Martinique and Guadeloupe in the Caribbean would remain integral parts, *départements* of France. France would continue to maintain "privileged ties"—termed neocolonialist strategies by some—with some of its former possessions, but, by 1962, the era of empire and unmitigated colonialism was over.

The previous chapter focused on hexagonal or mainland France's liberation from nazi occupation, its return to institutional normalcy and its entry into a period of reconstruction and rapid, sustained economic growth. This chapter retraces the simultaneous shift in status for the vast majority of the French republic's overseas possessions: from territories in a vast colonial empire to independent nations. Although treated in different chapters, the two developments are intimately related. Indeed, even during the war some of the colonies had served as a base for de Gaulle's Free French forces. It was in Algeria, for example, that in November 1943 de Gaulle formed the *Comité Français de Libération Nationale* (French Committee of National Liberation), in fact a provisional government that would come to power once Paris was liberated less than a year later. And it was in the empire that de Gaulle saw the possibility for France of retaining its *grandeur* even as the United States and the Soviet Union emerged as the new superpowers on the world scene. It was also due to the Fourth Republic's inability to deal with Algerian decolonization that de Gaulle would be able to reenter French political life in 1958 as a kind of savior once again, as he had in 1944. Finally, as the empire gave way to the postcolonial world, some of the former colonial subjects of the past became the immigrant workers of the French economic boom (see chapter 8), then its "second-generation immigrants," before becoming a visible part of its "multicultural" population, ironically representing once again, even if years later and in different ways, a challenge to France's ideas about its national identity (see chapters 9 and 10).

★ ★ ★

As parts of mainland France were living through their second harsh winter following the Liberation in 1944, with all of the shortages and deprivations of a country emerging from a devastating war, the rationing of bread, meat, and fuel, among other hardships, the following headline appeared on the front page of a major Parisian newspaper, *Le Parisien libéré* of January 25, 1945:

Loyal and Prosperous
Madagascar Wants to Supply France
One hundred thousand tons of food await cargo ships
[The lead article begins as follows:]
Only those who don't know our overseas populations would think them
capable of ingratitude towards the mother country.

Madagascar holds available the following, but awaits transport:

40,000 tons of coffee

15,000 tons of starches and tapioca

35,000 tons of rice

5,500 tons of frozen meat

4,000 tons of leather and pelts

4 million Malgaches work on their native soil to rescue the French.

Many of the basic ideas that formed the French consensus on empire at the time are present here: the colonies as a vast reserve of supplies (raw material, agricultural goods) and faithful subjects whose attachment to the *metropole* (the "home country") is not to be questioned, for they do not question it themselves, and are ready to give something back to France for what she has given—unstated here but implied and understood: the benefits of civilization. In addition to being populated by faithful subjects now working hard to help the motherland in its time of need, the colonies had also been, earlier, when the war was still raging, a place where France could continue to exist as an independent, democratic republic, away from both Vichy and nazi occupation, while consolidating its forces, the Free French under de Gaulle's leadership. Both during and after the war de Gaulle would repeatedly refer to the empire, as he does in *L'appel* (*The Call*), a war memoir: "In the vast spaces of Africa, France could in fact rebuild its armies and reacquire its sovereignty, while awaiting the alignment of new allies along with the old to change the military balance" (Betts, 50). By considering the empire in this light, de Gaulle was not innovating. Instead, he was connecting with a tradition that harked back to one of the most emblematic moments of France's past in both nation building (turning the peasants of the regions into the Frenchmen of the republic) and empire building (turning the non-European natives into colonial subjects of France): the first decades of the Third Republic. The situation at the time was similar in many ways to the one confronted by France in 1940: defeat in war and loss of territorial integrity (Alsace and Lorraine were annexed in 1870–1871 by the victorious Prussians). At the time, empire appeared as the antidote to the trauma of losing the war and relinquishing a part of France, as well as means of renewal and of resistance to German power. By the late 1930s, as Nazi Germany increasingly became the unavoidable enemy, empire, and the enlargement of France it entailed had become a mainstay of governmental policy: facing the German threat, France, because of its empire, was "transformed from a puny 42 000 000 weakling into an imposing 100 000 000 giant" (Evans, 407). During World War I, the colonies had provided 500,000 soldiers—among them the legendary *tirailleurs sénégalais*, Senegalese infantrymen notorious for their fierceness and bravery; in the same tradition, de Gaulle could count on the empire as a source of fighting men in the war he was waging—300,000 colonial troops from North Africa alone, and 200,000 industrial workers.

As postwar events were to confirm, de Gaulle's vision of the empire thus did not stray from the traditional one of the empire at its height, so that when the leader of the Free French, as early as 1942 declared, "There is an element that, in these terrible trials, has shown the nation that it is essential to her future and necessary for her greatness . . . that element is empire" (Evans, 408), he was perpetuating an imperial tradition that was well entrenched in the national mindset. The enduring combination of elements ranging from economic and strategic imperatives—the latter being the most immediate at the time of de Gaulle's speech—to a more psychological or abstract set of factors ranging from *mission civilisatrice* to exoticism, thus stood in the way of any radical change in the status of empire as World War II entered a decisive phase. At best, imperial policy at the time can be qualified as ambivalent. In some instances, France seemed willing to consider real change. For example, the CNR , which regrouped the different resistance movements, political parties, and trade unions proposed in its *Programme d'action* published in March 1944, "An extension of the political, social and economic rights of the native and colonial populations" (Wieviorka and Prochasson, 400). The limits of this recommendation were already evident in the use of the word "extension" and in the scrupulous absence of any mention of "independence" or even "autonomy." The CNR's "plan of action" was in fact a plan for the liberation and reconstruction of hexagonal France and covered items ranging from the "punishment of [French] traitors" and the reestablishment of trade unions, to industrial and agricultural policies and social security once the war was over. The reference to the colonies occupied two lines in this document and was only considered as merely one item among many, admittedly a crucial one to be taken into account within the framework of *national* postwar policy. This position was confirmed at the Brazzaville Conference held in the capital of French Equatorial Africa, which had rallied to the Free French forces, at the same time as the CNR was drafting its program. The Conference whose goal was to lay out the future evolution of the empire brought together "colonial governors and officials, though significantly not nationalist leaders" (Evans, 408), who nevertheless had already been very active during the war. The conference's closing document contained some declarations that could be interpreted as an acceptance of eventual independence; paragraph 5, for example: "We strongly state our desire to see the different territories evolve, in stages, from administrative decentralization to political personality" (Wieviorka and Prochasson, 392). But, lest any of the declarations in the body of the text should be misconstrued, the participants included a preamble: "The French African Conference of Brazzaville . . . has found it necessary to state the following principle: The objectives of the civilizing efforts accomplished by France in the colonies rule out any idea of autonomy, any possibility of evolution outside the framework of the French Empire; the eventual formation, even in the long term, of *self-governments* [in English in the original] is not to be considered" (Wieviorka and Prochasson, 390). De Gaulle's Commissioner of Colonies, René Pleven, who had organized the Brazzaville conference, was even more lapidary in his own declaration at the end of the conference: "The colonial people do not want any independence other than the independence of France" (Betts, 63). In any case, the territory that would be the scene of the most protracted and murderous scene of French decolonization, Algeria, was not even taken into account in the Conference's deliberations.

When we consider the new national and international contexts in which these declarations were made and documents adopted, French policy at the time can seem shortsighted. France had been vanquished and occupied by Germany and defeated in its Indochinese colony by the Japanese. In both instances the "masters'" weakness had been unequivocally displayed for the "natives." In addition, even when it was an ally who came on the scene, as was the case when the Allied forces landed in North Africa in 1943, or when American troops controlled French colonies, Tahiti, and New Caledonia, during the war, the French seemed decidedly outdone by a superior force and a new ideology. When GIs landed in North Africa they brought with them, translated into Arabic, copies of the Atlantic Charter of 1941 in which the United States and Great Britain, represented by Franklin D. Roosevelt and Winston Churchill, declared that they "respected every people's right to choose its own form of government and wanted sovereign rights and self-government restored to those forcibly deprived of them." More generally, the United States, whose status as world power was confirmed by the same war that marked France's decline, was against the continued existence of the empire. Roosevelt pursued a decidedly anticolonial policy and supported the right to self-determination and independence for territories of the French Empire ranging from Morocco to Vietnam, even if, in the latter case, the United States would support France's policy when the war in Indochina was presented as an anticommunist war rather than an imperial one.

A combination of factors led to increasing demands for autonomy and independence throughout the empire: France's own defeat; the presence during the war of the United States, a powerful country whose policy was anticolonial and whose representatives loudly advocated that policy; the "natives' " own sense that the colonial situation was untenable, accompanied by their perception that there was an opportunity to be seized. In an initial, nonviolent phase, meetings were requested, manifestos were drawn up and presented. In Morocco, where de Gaulle had ignored calls for a meeting, the Manifesto of the Istiqlal, the independence party, was issued in January 1944. It called for the end of the French protectorate, to be followed by independence. The manifesto was accompanied by a letter in which the drafters underlined the link between their sacrifices for France's freedom from fascist occupation and their own freedom: "We think the time has come for France to recognize the blood that Moroccans have shed and will continue to shed if necessary for France's ideals and for its freedom" (quoted in Betts, 63). The universalist claim to liberty, equality, and fraternity for all was being redirected at its source. To use the words of a contemporary collection of essays on postcolonial theory, the empire was writing back.

The same had happened in Algeria where, in the similar context of the Allied landing in 1942, nationalists led by Ferhat Abbas, their requests for a meeting having been ignored, drafted the "Manifesto of the Algerian People." Here, it was not, as was the case in Morocco, a protectorate demanding the end of that status, but a territory that France considered an integral part of the nation demanding for the "condemnation and abolition of colonialism" to be followed by self-government (Betts, 63). De Gaulle's provisional government bypassed the Algerian manifesto, as it had declined a meeting with the Istiqlal in Morocco.

In Indochina, it was the Japanese and not the Germans who had taken over, even if it was the Vichy government that symbolically ruled until 1945. By 1941, the Vietnamese Communists, led by Ho Chi Minh, had declared war against both the Japanese and the pro-Vichy French whom the victorious Japanese had left in charge of the administration. As de Gaulle's provisional government had refused to meet with Abbas in Algeria and with representatives of the Istiqlal in Morocco, it refused to recognize any claim to autonomy and independence from the fighters in Indochina. In December 1943, de Gaulle declared in a speech from Algiers France's plan to regain authority and to rule again over Indochina once the war was over. Here again, the contradiction between universalist claim and historical reality would be used as bitter rhetoric against the colonizer; for example this sentence from a response that appeared in Vietnam, entitled "Franco-Nipponese Fascists": "So the French, themselves struggling against domination, hope to maintain their domination over other peoples!" (Betts, 63).

The new context inaugurated not only by France's defeat and occupation in war but also by the particularly abhorrent nature of the victorious occupier, Hitler and Nazi ideology, made this type of rhetorical analogy particularly effective. Equating fascism and nazism with colonialism laid bare in a particularly glaring manner the contradiction between the proclaimed ideals and the actual practice of the French Republic. This rhetoric was very effective and became a constant in the speeches and writings of anticolonialist writers and militants. Aimé Césaire, like Fanon a Martinican and a Frenchman by virtue of Martinique's being a French *département*, would develop the analogy between fascism and colonialism in his *Discourse on Colonialism* published in 1955 (see dossier 7.1):

> What [the very Christian bourgeois] cannot forgive Hitler for is not his *crime* in itself, the crime against man, it is not the *humiliation of man as such*, it is the crime against the white man, the humiliation of the white man, and the fact that he applied to Europe colonialist procedures which until then had been reserved exclusively for the Arabs of Algeria, the coolies of India, and the blacks of Africa. (Césaire, 14; emphasis in original)

Césaire's *Discourse* was published the same year as the Bandung Conference in Indonesia, which gathered many of the former colonies, now forming what was beginning to be known as the "Third World," and set a framework for the liberation of the remaining colonies.

Dossier 7.1   Aimé Césaire, *Discourse on Colonialism* (1955)

Aimé Césaire was one of the most visible and active members of the *Négritude* movement, formed while he was a student in Paris in the 1930s. His *Cahier d'un retour au pays natal* (*Notebook of a Return to the Native Land*) published in Paris in 1939 reflects the dual influence of surrealism and his (re)claiming of his African roots. As Ronnie Scharfman writes, Césaire's "text was not just a Martinican extension of surrealism. His unconscious use of the surrealist metaphor, which juxtaposes realities that are as distant from each other as possible, is what puts his writing in touch with his black, African, Martinican specificity, what allows the subject to discover those ancestral myths, images, 'my deepest internal vibrations' " (quoted in Hollier, 945).

The *Discourse on Colonialism* retains the acerbic irony of the *Cahier*, but the more personal explorations and stunning images of the latter are displaced in favor of more directly political considerations and of a denouncing of the colonial project. The *Discourse* can be perceived as a dismantling of the idea of colonization as "civilizing mission," and of Marlowe's—Conrad's protagonist in *Heart of Darkness*—view of colonialism as "redeemed" by an "idea at the back of it." It clearly belongs to the general and often violent challenge to colonialism that characterized the postwar.

> *A civilization that proves incapable of solving the problems it creates is a decadent civilization.*
> *A civilization that chooses to close its eyes to its most crucial problems is a stricken civilization.*
> *A civilization that uses its principles for trickery and deceit is a dying civilization.*

The fact is that the so-called European civilization— "Western" civilization—as it has been shaped by two centuries of bourgeois rule, is incapable of solving the two major problems to which its existence has given rise: the problem of the proletariat and the colonial problem; that Europe is unable to justify itself either before the bar of "reason" or before the bar of "conscience"; and that, increasingly, it takes refuge in a hypocrisy which is all the more odious because it is less and less likely to deceive.

Europe is indefensible.

Apparently that is what the American strategists are whispering to each other.

That in itself is not serious. What is serious is that "Europe" is morally, spiritually indefensible.

And today the indictment is brought against it not by the European masses alone, but on a world scale, by tens of millions of men who, from the depths of slavery, set themselves up as judges.

The colonialists may kill in Indochina, torture in Madagascar, imprison in Black Africa, crack down in the West Indies. Henceforth the colonized know they have an advantage over them. They know that their temporary "masters" are lying.

Therefore that their masters are weak.

And since I have been asked to speak about colonization and civilization, let us go straight to the principal lie that is the source of all the others.

Colonization and civilization?

In dealing with this subject, the commonest curse is to be the dupe in good faith of a collective hypocrisy that cleverly misrepresents problems, the better to legitimize the hateful solutions provided for them.

In other words, the essential thing here is to see clearly—that is dangerously—and to answer clearly the innocent first question: what, fundamentally, is colonization? To agree on what it is not: neither evangelization, nor a philanthropic enterprise, nor a desire to push back the frontiers of ignorance, disease, and tyranny, nor a project undertaken for the greater glory of God, nor an attempt to extend the rule of law. To admit once and for all, without flinching at the consequences, that the decisive factors here are the adventurer and the pirate, the wholesale grocer and the ship owner, the gold digger and the merchant, appetite and force, and behind them, the baleful projected shadow of a form of civilization which, at a certain point in its history, finds itself obliged, for internal reasons, to extend to a world scale the competition of its antagonistic economies.

Pursuing my analysis, I find that hypocrisy is of recent date; that neither Cortez discovering Mexico from the top of the great teocalli, nor Pizarro before Cuzco (much less Marco Polo before Cambaluc), claims that he is the harbinger of a superior order; that they kill: that they plunder; that they have helmets, lances, cupidities; that the slavering apologists came later; that the chief culprit in this domain is Christian pedantry, which laid down the dishonest equations Christianity = Civilization, paganism = savagery, from which there could not but ensue abominable colonialist and racist consequences, whose victims were to be the Indians, the yellow peoples, and the Negroes. That being settled, I admit that it is a good thing to place different civilizations in contact with each other; that it is an excellent thing to blend different worlds; that whatever its own particular genius may be, a civilization that withdraws into itself atrophies; that for civilizations, exchange is oxygen; that the great good fortune of Europe is to have been a crossroads, and that because it was the locus of all ideas, the receptacle of all philosophies, the meeting place of all sentiments, it was the best center for the redistribution of energy.

But then I ask the following question: has colonization really placed civilizations in contact? *Or, if you prefer, of all the ways of* establishing contact, *was it the best?*
I answer no.
And I say that between colonization *and* civilization *there is an infinite distance; that out of all the colonial expeditions that have been undertaken, out of all the colonial statutes that have been drawn up, out of all the memoranda that have been dispatched by all the ministries, there could not come a single human value.* (9–12)

By addressing the crucial question of whether there has been a positive aspect to colonialism, Césaire goes to the heart of the notion of "civilizing mission" and answers with a resounding "no." He admits that cross-cultural exchanges are the very basis of dynamic civilizations but unequivocally goes against colonialism as the means of establishing this contact. His Marxist background is also evident in his view of colonialism as an extension of the metropole's markets, and his setting up a parallel between proletariat and colonized populations. Like many French intellectuals, he left the Communist Party in 1956, in the wake of the Soviet repression of the Hungarian uprising; he later founded Martinique's Socialist-leaning Progressive Party. As the mayor of Fort-de-France, the capital of Martinique and as the island's representative to the National Assembly in Paris, Césaire navigated a sometimes ambivalent path between acceptance of the links with France and the possibility of completely independent Martinique. In 1946, he cosponsored the bill that turned Martinique into a *département* of France.

The essayist and novelist Albert Memmi, a Jew born in predominantly Muslim Tunisia, would use a similar analogy in his essays *Portrait du colonisé* (*Portrait of the Colonized*) and *Portrait du colonisateur* (*Portrait of the Colonizer*). The essays were not published in book form until 1966 but sections were published in 1957 in the journals *Les Temps Modernes* and *Esprit* (see chapter 6). These excerpts were especially relevant at a time when the Algerian War had already begun and when many who had served in World War II were fighting in Algeria:

What is fascism if not an oppressive regime for the profit of a few? Yet, the entire administrative and political machine of the colonies has no other objective. There, human relations issue from an exploitation that is as extensive as possible, and are founded on inequality and contempt, made secure by police-state authoritarianism. There is no doubt, for whoever has lived through it, that colonialism is a variant of fascism. One should not admit to one's self that institutions dependant on a liberal central power can be so different from those of the metropole. This totalitarian face that democratic regimes wear in their colonies only seems to be an aberration: represented in the colonies by the colonizer, they can show no other face. (100)

Memmi makes it quite clear in this statement and elsewhere throughout *The Colonized* that although the civilizing mission policy and racism go a long way to explaining the rationale of colonialism, economic imperative rather than any sort of ahistorical fatalism or biological determinism lay at its core: the oppressive regime is "for the profit of a few" in a logic of "extensive exploitation." As Sartre ironically expresses in his introduction to

Fanon's *The Wretched of the Earth*, "Of course there is no question of granting [integration]; the whole system, which depends on overexploitation, as you know, would be ruined" (8). The combination of economic imperative and all of the different rationalizations of colonialism that were subsumed under the heading of "civilizing mission," including the objective of maintaining or recovering "grandeur," thus made it particularly difficult for France to relinquish its colonies.

The paradox of the "republican empire" France continued to be at the end of World War II is vividly illustrated by the events at Sétif, Algeria, that occurred on the very day of German surrender, May 8, 1945. Allied democracy and freedom, including the principles of self-determination that formed the basis of the new world order had prevailed over nazism; as part of France, Algeria was also celebrating. In the small town of Sétif, supporters of Messali Hadj, founder of the nationalist and pro-independence *Parti du Peuple Algérien* (Party of the Algerian People), had also gathered to protest his imprisonment. The police brutally intervened, prompting a Muslim insurrection and a rampage that led to the killing of one hundred Europeans in the area. The French reaction was immediate and overwhelming: thousands of troops were flown in, planes bombed villages. The death toll was estimated at 1,000 by the French authorities, but in fact lies somewhere between 8,000 and 45,000, the latter "a figure that French opponents of the war [that was to begin in 1952] later accepted" (Sowerwine, 286). In 1947, in Madagascar, an armed uprising organized by nationalists was also directed against French military personnel, administration, and civilians. Here again the French reaction was implacable; resistance was brought under control by 1948, and the conflict ended with close to 90,000 dead on the Malgache side. The situation on the island kingdom seemed very far indeed from the one described in the front page of the *Parisien Libéré* in the winter 1945, quoted above, where the Malgaches were touted as "grateful subjects of the mother country."

As France entered the "thirty glorious years" that would see the fastest period of economic growth and modernization in its long history, it was thus also entering a painful and traumatic twenty-year period where its empire appeared in direct contradiction to modernization. Richard Kuissel's comment about the war in Algeria can be extended to France's struggle to hold on to its empire in general:

> In fighting for Algeria, France was still fighting a rearguard action for Empire, for protectionism, for the traditional trappings of great power status. Euratom [the European energy Commision, a joint agency for the development of nuclear energy] and the common market [established by the Treaty of Rome in 1957] by contrast, offered not only innovative ways to remedy the energy problem, to enhance competition and promote trade through economic growth and modernization rather than through war and imperial preference. (233)

It took a while for this redeployment of the French economy to occur, for until 1960 "the empire was France's most important trading partner, reaching a high point in 1952, when the colonies accounted for 42 per cent of French exports" (Alexander, 409).

In the postwar era, in spite of all the signs that the empire could no longer be sustained, France was simply not ready to relinquish part of its history, of its own making as a nation. A nominal change was included in the constitution of 1946, founding the Fourth Republic and gathering all the colonies and mainland France into an all-encompassing *Union française* (French Union). This new configuration consisted of two parts. The first was made up of mainland, metropolitan, hexagonal France, as well as Algeria and other overseas departments like Martinique and Guadeloupe, all considered and administered as an integral part of the French Republic. The second part consisted of the associated territories and states, mainly in North and West Africa, and Indochina. Even if it made concessions to eventual political autonomy *under French guidance*, this left the colonial institution intact, with, at its heart, a hierarchy. The "natives" were citizens but not quite like the French. In any case, it was deemed by the metropole that they were not ready for independence.

At the end of the nineteenth century, France's colonies in Indochina or *Indochine française* comprised the present-day states of Vietnam, Cambodia, and Laos. This territory, Vietnam in particular, had a long history of occupation by the Chinese going back to the third century BC. When Chinese domination receded in the mid-nineteenth century, the result of determined resistance by the Vietnamese and of China's own interior problems, the French filled the gap. Here again the trio of economic interest, exoticism, and the ideology of *mission civilisatrice*—ever more paradoxical in these lands of old civilization and recorded history—proved a powerful mix.

The colonial administration oversaw the building of an infrastructure that was essentially devoted to trading with metropolitan France. A tiny minority of French, between 25,000 and 39,000 in 1940 (Jennings, 137), ruled over the population; peasants' farmlands were confiscated and turned into vast plantations, mostly rubber; former farmers, now without land, worked in mines and marble quarries. Forced labor was a common practice and, often, the situation of the Indochinese population no better than slavery. Facing any form of resistance, common in Vietnam, the French systematically retaliated with "pacification" expeditions. These conditions imposed by the most recent occupier, added to the long tradition of nationalist resistance, and the rise of communist ideology among the urban and Westernized youth of Vietnam led to the formation of a number of nationalist movements in the 1920s. The most important personality to emerge from these movements was, however, the son of a poor country scholar, Nguyen Sinh Cung, better known as Ho Chi Minh, who founded the *Parti Communiste Indochinois* (Indochinese Communist Party) in 1930. The creation of the party coincided with a violent insurrection against the French occupation in Vietnam. The campaign of pacification by the French was brutal. Only in 1936, when the Popular Front came to power in France were local political movements allowed to operate more freely. By 1938, however, the Daladier government that followed the Popular Front reinstated a harsh repression. Between 1939 and 1940, about 7,000 Communists and nationalists were arrested, many of them executed; in 1940, when most of the arrest and executions occurred, "the authorities used wires run through the hands and heels of prisoners when they ran out of handcuffs" (Sowerwine, 256). In this extremely repressive colonial context, the international Socialist and Communist option represented for Vietnamese nationalists a counterdiscourse, even an equally "universal" one, to French universalism and its unevenly and selectively applied precepts.

The year 1940 was also the year France was defeated and occupied by Germany; Ho Chi Minh, planning to use this to his advantage, founded with a few comrades— among them Vo Nguyen Giap, the military strategist who would defeat France in

Indochina and the United states in Vietnam—the *Viet Nam Dop Lac Dong Minh Hoi* (League for the Independence of Vietnam) or Viet Minh. The Viet Minh's message to the population was simple: join us and together we will liberate ourselves from both the Japanese and the French. The movement was active throughout the war, increasingly gathering support and momentum. In 1945, after the Japanese arrested or executed the members of the French colonial administration, and after the Americans dropped atomic bombs on Hiroshima and Nagasaki, the situation changed dramatically for the Viet Minh: the two occupiers had been neutralized or eliminated. Now Ho Chi Minh followed a strategy of cooperation with the American effort against the remaining contingent of Japanese troops in Indochina, contacting and collaborating on missions with the OSS (Office of Strategic Services, precursor of the Central Intelligence Agency). The United States, like communism, represented yet another means of countering French colonialism and universalist doctrine. America represented a new type of internationalism that, at least in 1945, constituted a viable tactical alternative for the Vietnamese independence movement. America was one of the promoters of the Atlantic Charter, which defended all countries' right to self-determination as it "respected every people's right to choose its own form of government and wanted sovereign rights and self-government restored to those forcibly deprived of them." Already, in 1919, at the Versailles Peace Conference Ho Chi Minh had tried to denounce the French selective application of its universalism by addressing an eight-point petition to the international forum, demanding that the French colonial power grant the indigenous population equal rights. Joining forces with the United States against the Japanese thirty years later followed the same logic.

By the time the Japanese surrendered on August 15, the Viet Minh controlled North Vietnam. Its troops entered Hanoi, on September 2, and Ho Chi Minh declared Vietnam independent. Bao Dai, the French puppet emperor abdicated, becoming Ho Chi Minh's "Supreme Counselor." In his speech to the crowd of half a million people gathered in the capital, Ho Chi Minh used words that were reminiscent of the American Declaration of Independence: "All men are born equal: the Creator has given us inviolable rights, life, liberty and happiness."

The Viet Minh seemed to have succeeded in reaching its primary goal: an independent country. But France, now no longer occupied, was intent on reestablishing control over what it still considered its colony. In addition, according to an Allied agreement, Chinese troops were to replace the Japanese troops north of the seventeenth parallel, that is, in North Vietnam; China would surely use this opportunity to reassert control over a territory it had once occupied. In this configuration, Ho Chi Minh's objective was to negotiate with the French in order to be rid of the Chinese whom he considered a far more formidable opponent. As he put it, "The last time the Chinese came, they stayed a thousand years. The French are foreigners. They are weak. Colonialism is dying. The white man is finished in Asia. But if the Chinese stay now, they will never go. As for me I prefer to sniff French shit for five years than eat Chinese shit for the rest of my life" (Sowerwine, 257).

In the negotiations that ensued, the French were able to obtain evacuation of the Chinese troops and Ho Chi Minh signed an agreement in which Vietnam was recognized by France as a "free state with its own government, army, and finances," but was considered part of the "Indochinese Federation" and integrated into the Fourth Republic's "Union française," the French Union, in which France in fact dominated.

The agreement proved to be unsatisfactory to elements on both sides. On the French side, no political party, with the exception of the Communists, was willing to support Vietnamese independence; but, as reconstruction was underway in the metropole in 1946, the French Communist Party's focus was still on participation in and cooperation with the government. In addition, high army and colonial officials, the latter known as the "Saigon clique," lobbied effectively against any concession to the Viet Minh. On the Vietnamese side, Ho Chi Minh had to contend with his own hard-line faction, led by Giap who favored continued guerilla war (rather than the referendum provided for by the agreement) as the only effective means of obtaining Vietnamese unification and independence. The precarious peace was broken in November 1946. The French administration, led by the conservative High Commissioner, Thierry d'Argenlieu, attempted to reestablish its full authority over the entire country. D'Argenlieu ruled out the referendum provided by the agreement of 1945, set up customs agents in Hanoi's port city of Haiphong, and ordered the Viet Minh to evacuate. Facing their refusal, the French navy bombed the city, killing 6,000, mostly civilians. The French then moved quickly and captured Hanoi by 1947, while, once again, the Viet Minh guerilla resistance begun.

The Fourth Republic was facing the first of two colonial wars—the second would begin eight years later in Algeria—that were to test its ability to respond to the challenges to empire that were part and parcel of the new international order emerging from World War II. "Pacification" of Vietnam by the French proved to be illusory. The Viet Minh had very strong support among the population, especially in the north. Ho Chi Minh's organization had acquired enormous popularity during the war through its fight against the Japanese and the application of a number of measures in the territories it had freed and administered: abolition of colonial taxes, establishment of Vietnamese-led local governments, redistribution of land that had belonged to French landlords. In many ways, the Viet Minh were similar to the French Resistance fighters, especially to the French Communist Party, standing as it did for antifascism and social change. Where the popularity of Ho Chi Minh's forces met its limits, the Viet Minh enforced their presence and continued their war effort through reprisals against their local Vietnamese opponents. The French did not hesitate to use all the means at their disposal to wage what was quickly becoming known in the press and among intellectual circles as *la sale guerre*, (the dirty war). Nazi German soldiers who had been smuggled from Europe through a number of "rat lines" were incorporated into the French army; the use of torture by the troops also became a strategic and political issue. Vietnam's distance from France made the war an extremely costly enterprise and a logistical nightmare. To continue to finance the war, France turned to the United States. At first the Americans requested that the French find a nationalist and anticommunist alternative to the Viet Minh. France only came up with Bao Dai whom they set up in Saigon, the southern capital. The former "Supreme Counselor" himself, realizing that army, finances, and foreign affairs would be controlled by the French, went back to his exile in France.

In spite of its reservations regarding this arrangement, the American government began financing a hefty portion of France's Indochina war budget, preferring a continuation of colonialism to the installation of a Communist regime in Vietnam. In the Indochinese peninsula, the old imperial power and the young powerhouse of international capitalism, the rationales of civilizing mission and "containment" of communism could join forces.

It took a major military defeat of the French in 1954 to bring the parties back to the negotiating table. This defeat occurred at the fortress of Dien Bien Phu where 13,000 French troops had retreated after a failed campaign to cut the Viet Minh's supply lines between Vietnam and Laos. Contrary to what the French military command had expected, Giap gathered the bulk of his troops, about 50,000 soldiers, at that location, and, also contrary to expectations, after a siege that lasted several months, the Viet Minh were able to mount a major artillery attack against the surrounded French who surrendered in May 1954 after suffering heavy losses.

The military catastrophe led to the fall of the government in Paris, to the appointment of Pierre Mendès-France as prime minister and to negotiations in Geneva. The new geopolitical context was obvious at Geneva: France, the waning imperial power, depended on American support, while Vietnam relied on the two major Communist states, the Soviet Union and China, to defend its case at the negotiating table. The resulting Geneva Agreement did not produce the united and independent Vietnam the Viet Minh considered the logical outcome of its military victory in the field. Instead, it was forced by its two powerful Allies, who had agendas of their own, to accept a compromise: a temporary line of demarcation would divide the north, where Ho Chi Minh's government would rule, from the south, where Bao Dai would head the government; elections would be held two years later, in 1956, and would determine the government of a united Vietnam. Because the United States would only accept United Nations supervision of these elections, while the Agreement stipulated supervision by an International Control Commission (Canada, India, and Poland), the Americans did not endorse the Agreement. The French and the English, the old imperial powers, opposed UN supervision because it would set an unacceptable precedent in colonial issues: the internationalization of matters they considered to be national and internal. The Americans succeeded in persuading Bao Dai, who remained in France, to appoint Ngo Dien Diem, the kind of anticommunist nationalist they had been intent on finding, as prime minister. The French puppet had been replaced by an American puppet. Buffeted by American support, Diem's government consolidated its position in the south and refused to apply the 1956 elections clause of the Geneva Agreement. By then the first American "advisors" and troops had arrived, replacing the French. The old imperial mission had been replaced by the anticommunist crusade, and Mendès-France had succeeded in extricating his country from a bloody war it had no hope of winning.

Mendès-France continued on his momentum and began negotiations that would lead to independence for France's two North African protectorates, Tunisia and Morocco, in 1956. However, facing the newly formed National Liberation Front's demands for an independent Algeria, he would not negotiate: "One does not compromise when it comes to defending the internal peace of the nation, the unity and integrity of the republic. The Algerian departments are part of the French Republic. They have been French for a long time, and they are irrevocably French . . . Between them and metropolitan France there can be no conceivable secession." As had been the case in Vietnam, the French were thus beginning another drawn out and bloody war that would, like the Indochinese conflict, last eight years. This war would lead to the rapid fall of successive governments of the Fourth Republic, eventually ending in its demise and to the return of Charles de Gaulle to political leadership.

The events at Sétif on May 8, 1945 (see above) were symbolic of the colonial situation in general in the postwar world and of the case of Algeria in particular: as the French were celebrating the victory of democratic and universalist republican values over nazi blood and soil ideology, the French army cracked down on supporters of a pronationalist and pro-independence leader claiming Algeria's right to its own freedom from colonial domination. These events clearly showed that colonial ideology could allow only for a selective application of the principles of liberty, equality, fraternity that lay at the very roots of the French Republic; the result was a paradox: freedom at home and domination abroad. In Albert Memmi's formulation, "This totalitarian face that democratic regimes wear in their colonies only seems to be an aberration: represented in the colonies by the colonizer, they can show no other face." France's incapacity to "show another face" in Algeria was precisely what led to the radicalization of demands. The evolution of someone like Ferhat Abbas, one of the leaders of the Algerian independence movement, is a good example of the results of France's Algerian policy. Abbas began his political activity with the *Jeune Algérien* (Young Algerian) movement during the interwar years and advocated assimilation and coexistence with the French within a context of equal rights for the Algerian population, but ultimately became a fervent partisan of total independence. In an initial phase, Abbas tried to see beyond what Memmi called France's "totalitarian face" by looking beyond the colonialist representatives and seeing the universalist republic.

Until 1936, Abbas and the Jeune Algérien Movement demanded equal rights, but remained within the framework of French sovereignty. As Benjamin Stora summarizes it, this policy was based on a vision of France that was different from, in Memmi's terms, "the face it was showing" in Algeria:

> By not equating the colonial system with France itself, [Abbas] expressed a longing for the true France, which exemplified the principles of 1789. France, the country that had invented democratic culture via the Great Revolution, could impose, on the Europeans of Algeria, respect for the indigenous person deprived of rights. He therefore championed rights equal to enjoyed by what would be later called *pieds noirs* [the close to one million Europeans who lived in Algeria] but remained attached to Algeria's religious personality: for him, a person could be simultaneously and fully French and Muslim. He imputed all the injustices of colonialism to the European colony. For him, there were two Frances and two policies: one a country of colonization and oppression, the other the beacon of civilization and of moral prestige. He hoped that France would choose the right path. (17)

The reasons why France did not or could not choose "the right path" and eventually had to go through a bloody struggle that would shake the foundations of the French Republic itself have to be retraced to the beginning of its involvement in Algeria in 1830. When the French forces conquered Algiers and its surroundings in 1830 after a three-year siege of the city, they were only the latest of a series of occupiers that had begun to arrive in 1100 BC with the Phoenicians, continuing with the Romans and the Byzantines, who were followed by the Arabs who remained there from 755 to 1516, the year when the Turks arrived, remaining until the French arrival displaced them.

The Arab presence had deeply influenced Algeria, turning it into an "Eastern" culture profoundly marked by Islam. The ensuing rule of the Ottoman Empire did not constitute a radical break since the Turks were also Muslims. Thus the French colonial conquest was all the more resented because it was not only occupation but occupation by a Christian European power. In addition, the occupying forces were quickly followed by civilians who rushed to appropriate or buy all manner of property ranging from stores and houses to farms and land. Most of these new arrivals to Algeria in the wake of the French army were from the poor southern regions of France, including Corsica, but also from the southern regions of Italy and Spain, and from Malta. Under pressure from increasingly numerous arrivals hungry for additional land, the army and the colonial administration expanded beyond the territories around Algiers, where the conquest had begun. The objective was simple: to make more land available for colonization. Complex sets of rules that governed traditional land ownership were eliminated; land owned by religious foundations, tribal land or otherwise collectively owned land, was either appropriated or put up for sale. At first, under the *régime du sabre* (rule of the saber), the army controlled and administered the expansion. By 1848, however, the territory was formally integrated into France as three *départements*, as much part of France as Normandy, Burgundy, or Britanny. In 1870, the settlers overthrew the army administration and established a civilian administration. This move was legalized and institutionalized by the metropole, and Algeria sent representatives, deputies, and senators to Paris where they became the kernel of a colonial voting bloc that successive governments would have to contend with. By 1896, what Benjamin Stora calls a "Mediterranean mix," born in Algeria, would outnumber those who arrived through immigration. The needs of this European population, especially those of powerful large business and landowners were scrupulously served by the representatives of the three Algerian *départements* sent to Paris, while the indigenous population was effectively dispossessed, and their inferior status defined and codified in a *Code de l'Indigénat* (Native Code) that made them colonial "subjects" with no formal representation, while those of European descent were full-fledged "citizens," with representatives in Paris.

The massive transfer and appropriation of land led to a gradual dismantling of traditional Algerian society as dispersed farmers and tribal peoples migrated to the cities, forming an urban proletariat, or to the less desirable lands of the high plateaus, where they led a precarious existence. Some even sought exile in France, signaling the beginning of a trend that would accelerate with World War I. The population of European descent was itself far from homogeneous. Some, the "grands colons" (big colonists, owners of large farming estates or businesses) had succeeded in accumulating vast tracts of land or became owners of successful businesses; others, the *petits blancs* (small whites, or poor whites), who owned only small parcels or worked either as farm hands, in factories or as minor civil servant, were often not much better off than the indigenous Algerians. Nevertheless, given the line of demarcation between "citizen" (of the republic) and "subject" (of the empire), between European and indigenous Algerian, the two classes of European origin "were unanimous in defending their privileges which made the most insignificant French government employee superior to any Arab" (Stora, 23). Perceived social superiority, added to the fear of the Muslim Arab majority, led to a virulent racism, all combining to make any change in the colonial structure extremely difficult and, in the eyes of the vast majority of the European population in Algeria, unthinkable.

Both the initial conquest and its extension, followed by the institutionalization of colonial society, met with resistance. At first, from the Ottomans, then from local tribal leaders, most notably Abd al Kadir, who is revered as the first hero of Algerian independence; his green and white standard became the symbol of the Algerian independence movement during the war that would begin in 1954, and later appeared on the national flag of independent Algeria. Gradually, however, tribal leaders were either vanquished by the superior French military strength and technology, or were co-opted. These tribal leaders who often negotiated with the French for personal advantages became derisively known as *Béni oui-ouis*, or "yes men."

Another type of resistance was constituted by the so-called *évolués*, the educated or "enlightened" Algerians, such as Ferhat Abbas, who at first claimed equality but did not question French sovereignty. These *évolués*, often educated in both Arabic and French came from the liberal bourgeoisie that gradually formed under French rule. The first nationalist movement to directly question French sovereignty and actually demand independence was *Etoile Nord- Africaine* (North African Star), founded by Messali Hadj. Unlike Abbas, who was a doctor of pharmacy and belonged to a prominent family, Hadj came from a family of farmers and artisans. He served in the French army during World War I, an event that led to "a 'loss of innocence' among Muslim Algerians, a debunking of the myth of the benefits of Western civilization" (Stora, 12). In addition to the 173,000 indigenous Algerians who served in that war, 119,000 were requisitioned to work in France, replacing French workers who had gone to war. Mesali Hadj, like many of these soldiers and workers would experience in this move from the periphery of empire to its center some of the ideas and trends that would confirm their own desire for a more equitable society in Algeria and, even, independence: the Russian Revolution of 1917, the factory strikes by organized workers in Paris, Lyon, and their working-class suburbs and, more generally, the direct contact with a culture—"Metropolitan" France where the ideals of the republic were clearly more visible—radically different from Algerian colonial society. By 1927, the Star's demands were a combination of independence from France along with demand for a series of immediate reforms: freedom of the press and association, a parliament chosen through universal suffrage, confiscation of large estates, and the establishing of Arabic schools. Mesali Hadj returned to Algeria to organize urban and farm workers around this platform. In addition to Abbas's reformist but integrationist platform and his pro-independence North African Star, there was also a more specifically Islamic movement whose leaders, among them Sheik Abdulhamid Ben Badis, were extremely popular among the Muslim masses. Facing these different strands of Algerian claims ranging from liberal integrationist ideas and recognition of cultural and religious specificity, to total independence, the *colons* remained firmly opposed to any serious reform. In the wake of the Popular Front's victory in 1936, Leon Blum's left-wing coalition attempted, with the Violette Plan, to respond to some of the native Algerian demands by granting political equality to 21,000 people "in a nontransmissible and personal capacity" (Stora, 18). The question of independence was not raised. On the contrary, it became the cause of antagonism with the Popular Front, and ultimately to the dissolution of the North African Star and to the arrest of its leader. Facing vehement opposition from the *colons*, the Violette plan, as timid as it was, was not pursued. The effect of this latest failure in promoting reform was to radicalize more moderate movements and leaders such as Ferhat Abbas who abandoned his policy of assimilation and began to call for the development of a Muslim Algeria in close association with France but retaining "her own physiognomy, her language, her customs, her traditions" (Library of Congress, 19). By the time World War II began in

1939, Algerian nationalism was a reality and the very idea of assimilation seemed to recede in a distant past.

The situation did not improve during the Vichy phase in Algeria, and after the 1942 Allied landing in Algeria, Ferhat Abbas presented the Manifesto of the Algerian People to de Gaulle's representatives. While the Manifesto made a number of demands, including the recognition of Arabic as an official language and legal equality for all Muslims, it stayed short of claiming independence. De Gaulle and his newly appointed governor general recognized the need for change but responded with a set of reforms modeled on the old Violette plan. This return to the past provoked an alliance between Ferhat's assimilationist moderates and Hadj's pro-independence party that agreed on an addendum to the Manifesto, which left no room for doubt that the different movements of Algerian nationalism were now united under the banner of independence: "At the end of hostilities, Algeria will be set up as an Algerian state endowed with its own constitution, which will be elaborated by an Algerian constituent assembly, elected by universal suffrage by all the inhabitants of Algeria" (Stora, 21). When the war was over, the events at Sétif would confirm that the time for cautious reform had indeed passed.

While France dealt with the end of German occupation, political and economic reconstruction, and began a period of unprecedented economic growth, its empire was thus in the process of being challenged from all corners of the globe. The war in Indochina and the evolution of two former protectorates, Morocco and Tunisia, toward independence set a precedent for the Algerian nationalists. The National Liberation Front founded by the "historic nine," including Ben Bella, became the new face of the Algerian struggle for independence, and it is symbolic that the group's first meeting occurred on the day that the fall of Dien Bien Phu was announced. Shortly after, the FLN issued its own manifesto, proclaiming the independence of Algeria and, on the holiday of All Saint's Day, November 1, 1954, began a systematic armed struggle that would end only eight years later. The initial targets were government buildings and police stations. The French response was, as it had been in Indochina, overwhelming: 20,000 troops were sent to crush the rebels. In this initial phase, the French army defeated the FLN, quickly capturing many of its leaders.

At this stage, the FLN opted for the use of terrorism as a political and military tactic in its war against France. These tactics were also used against noncompliant Algerians, those who would not respect the FLN' s ban on prostitution, alcohol, and cigarettes, or join in the struggle, for example, as well as against French civilians, beginning with those who lived in isolated settlements. In August 1955, near the town of Phillippeville, 123 French civilians were massacred by FLN troops. The French retaliation erupted in an orgy of killing by army personnel, the police, and by civilian vigilante groups. The government claimed about 1000 people were killed while the FLN estimated the number of dead at 12,000. Phillippeville constituted a watershed in the escalating conflict. After that, all-out war began in Algeria, with civilian killings and atrocities on both sides. The size of the French Army, made up essentially of draftees, was up to 400,000 troops by 1956.

The fighting, which until then had largely taken place in rural areas, was taken to the cities by the FLN. The objective was to bring their struggle to the attention of the international community as well as to the public opinion of metropolitan France. The

"Battle of Algiers" was the most publicized example of this new tactic; it began in September 1956 when three women members of the FLN placed bombs in the offices of Air France and in two crowded cafés in the capital city. This was followed by an average of 800 shootings and bombings per month. The FLN also called for a general strike to show that it had strong support in the Muslim population. To deal with this new urban guerilla, Paris gave free reign to General Jacques Massu who succeeded in systematically dismantling the FLN organization in Algiers and in breaking the general strike. However, in winning the battle of Algiers he used methods similar to those he was fighting against and against which he had fought in the war against Nazi Germany: intimidation, terror, torture, including the use of electroshock and rape. At first, the French prevailed in Algiers; however, as Tyler Stoval writes, "Politically . . . the Army's repressive tactics merely underlined the bankruptcy of French policy in Algeria. The prospect of a Socialist government permitting a military reign of terror on what was technically French soil showed how little relevance Resistance notions of liberty had in France's colonies" (56). Clearly the selective application of republican principles did not apply in Algeria. Jean-Paul Sartre would point to racism as one of the primary tools used to justify this blatant contradiction: "One of the functions of racism is to compensate the latent universality of bourgeois liberalism: since all human beings have the same rights, the Algerians have to be made subhuman" (*Colonialism and Neocolonialism*, 1964; quoted in Forsdick and Murphy, 72). The French government also claimed that the FLN was a terrorist organization with no real support in the population and that the republic was protecting the majority of the population in Algeria. To this it added that France had the support of the majority of the population of the metropole and, it goes without saying, that of the majority of the *colons* in Algeria who, having everything to lose, wanted even more repressive measures to be adopted. Lastly, the French government pointed to its support in the native Algerian population itself: although French paratroopers acquired particular notoriety, both at the time of the war and, later, in films such as Gillo Pontecorvo's 1964 *Battle of Algiers*, about 170,000 of the regular French army troops in Algeria were Muslim Algerians, the "Harkis," most of whom had volunteered. The situation was indeed complex and in many ways similar to other colonial scenarios, South Africa, for example, where generations of people of European stock had come to think of the land conquered and settled by their forebears as "home." The Algerian settler lobby in all circles of French society ranging from the world of business to the National Assembly played no small part in the determination of policy. In the case of Algeria, there was also the recent loss of Indochina and the military disaster of Dien Bien Phu to contend with. To these considerations at the particular historical juncture of the mid-1950s should be added others who played a role in France's brand of colonialism: its perception of itself as a nation endowed with both a universal culture and with the "civilizing mission" to extend it to the rest of the world, and the perception of the colonies as playing an integral role in France's "grandeur." The character of Colonel Mathieu, the leader of the paratroopers in *The Battle of Algiers*, does not address all of these issues, but his comments do help us understand what was involved in France's decision to wage all-out war rather than negotiate with those the government insisted on calling "rebels." In this excerpt, Mathieu is holding a press conference after one of the recently captured FLN leaders has allegedly made a rope of his bed sheet and hung himself while in custody, even though it had been ordered that his hands and feet be kept tied at all times. The question of the "methods" used by the paratroopers comes up and Mathieu answers:

> OK, fine, let's try to be precise then. The word "torture" doesn't appear in our orders. We have always talked about questioning being the only valid method for a police operation against a clandestine group. The FLN, for its part, asks each of its members to keep silent for twenty-four hours after capture, after which they can speak. The organization therefore has the time necessary to render information useless. And us, what kind of questioning should we adopt? Court procedures that can drag on for months?

> JOURNALIST: Legality isn't always so convenient, Colonel.
> COLONEL MATHIEU: Does someone who drops bombs on public places show respect for legality? Since you asked Mister Ben M'Hidi this question, remember what he said. No, gentlemen, believe me, it's a vicious circle. The problem is that the FLN wants to chase us out of Algeria and we, we want to stay. And even when the rebellion broke out, there weren't any dissensions. All the press, including *L'Humanité* [the Communist Party's official newspaper] asked that it be put down. That's why we were sent here, to do that. We are neither crazy nor sadistic. Those who call us Fascists today tend to forget the role we played in the Resistance. Those who call us Nazis may not know that some of us survived Dachau and Buchenwald. We are soldiers and our duty is to win. Since we are being precise, now it's my turn to ask you all a question: should France remain in Algeria? If you say "yes," then you must accept all the consequences.

Mathieu attempts here to resolve a contradiction. On the one hand, he wants to counter the argument that the army's operation in Algeria is a fascist undertaking. As we have noted, after the war the equation "colonialism = Nazism" was indeed a slogan and a developed argument not only throughout the empire from Saigon to Algiers, but also in France itself in certain circles. Early in 1955, the writer Claude Bourdet published an article entitled "Is there a Gestapo in Algeria?" attacking French brutality there (Stovall, 56). On the other hand, Mathieu must justify torture, the very methods used by the nazis against the Resistance that many soldiers, especially officers, serving in Algeria had belonged to, some having "survived Dachau and Buchenwald." Ultimately he must resort to what can be called the pragmatism of colonialism contained in a single question: are we willing to do what it takes to remain where we are not wanted, and accept the consequences? The consequences, for a time, were indeed accepted even as a growing movement of opposition to the war began to take shape in France, and the Fourth Republic began to fall apart.

The French army won the "battle of Algiers" but France had lost the diplomatic and moral high ground. As rumors of torture spread, they were confirmed by a number of sources ranging from army officers themselves to newspapers and magazines. In March 1957, an army general, Paris de Bollardière, who had been a leading figure of the Resistance published a letter in the weekly news magazine *L'Express* stating that France was "losing sight of moral values . . . under the fallacious pretext of expediency" (quoted in Sowerwine, 293). Torture was also a recurring topic in the Catholic writer François Mauriac's weekly column in the same publication. In Algeria, those who spoke out against the war were targeted for police questioning. Many began to disappear after having been taken in for such "questioning." It gradually became known that far from being an isolated and contained tactic used in the gathering of intelligence, torture had become a widespread practice used not only against members of the FLN but against a much wider public that included suspected sympathizers. In Paris, the publishing houses began to print accounts ranging from Jean-Jacques Servan-Shreiber's *Lieutenant in Algeria*, published by Editions du Seuil in 1957, to Henri Alleg's *La question*, published by Editions de Minuit in 1958 (see dossier 7.2). These works showed the other face of the war, the one the government wanted to keep hidden, wanting at all cost to portray the Algerian uprising as a rebellion by a few violent terrorists rather than an anticolonial war of liberation that had begun to gather support among the French public. Servan-Shreiber was one of the founders of the influential *L'Express* and his book gained widespread attention. One of the issues it addressed was the difficulty of distinguishing the general population from the *fellaghas*, the FLN fighters. This aspect of the war is summarized by the following exchange between two soldiers:

> "I'm suggesting that it's bad business to kill people who may be innocent, and that it's not what we're here for. Once more, all my apologies. I know that since I wasn't in Indochina and I've only been in Algeria for a few days, I ought to just listen." [The reply, is similar to Colonel Mathieu's to the journalists in Pontecorvo's film.]
> ". . . There's only one way [to do your duty honorably]: treat every Arab as a suspect, a possible *fellagha*, a potential terrorist—because that, my dear sir, is the truth. And don't come back at me with words like justice and charity. They have nothing to do with it. I don't say they don't exist: I say that's not in the same boat." (Servan-Schreiber, 33)

Here again, the selective application of the ideals of the French Republic is laid out.

Dossier 7.2   Henri Alleg, *The Question* (1958)

Henri Alleg was the editor of the banned *Alger Républicain*, one of the Algerian capital's main newspapers and the quasi-official publication of the Algerian Communist Party, which had taken a strong pro-independence stand. He was arrested in 1957. His account of his interrogation at the hands of the paratroopers was published in 1958 and revealed the extent to which torture had been organized as a routine operation by the army. The book became a bestseller; 65,000 copies were sold in 5 weeks. It was then banned and seized by the government.

> *In this enormous overcrowded prison, where each cell houses a quantity of human suffering, it is almost indecent to talk about oneself. The "division" for those condemned to death is on the ground floor. There are eight of them, their ankles chained together, waiting for reprieve or death . . . (39)*
> *. . . Torture? The word has been familiar to us all for a long time. Few of those imprisoned here have escaped it. The first question put to new arrivals, when it is possible to speak to them, are these, and in this order: When were you arrested? Have you been tortured? By the "Paras" [paratroopers] or the detectives? My particular case is exceptional in that it has attracted public attention. It is not in any way unique. What I have said in my petition and what I am saying here illustrates by one single example what is common practice in this atrocious and bloody*

war. It is now more than three months since I was arrested. I have survived so much pain and so many humiliations during this time that I would not bring myself to talk again of those days and nights of agony if I did not believe that it would serve a purpose, and that by making the truth known I might do a little towards bringing about a cease-fire and peace. For whole nights during the course of a month I heard the screams of men being tortured, and their cries will resound forever in my memory. I have seen prisoners thrown from one floor to another who, stupefied by torture and beatings, could only manage to utter in Arabic the first words of an ancient prayer. But, since then, I have come to know of other atrocities. I have been told of the "disappearance" of my friend Maurice Audin, arrested twenty-four hours before me, tortured by the same group who afterwards took me in hand. He disappeared like Sheikh Tebessi, President of the Association of Oulamas [religious scholars], Doctor Cherif Zahar, and so many others. At Lodi, I met my friend De Milly, employed previously at the Psychiatric Hospital at Blida, who had also been tortured by the "Paras," by means of a new technique. He was fastened down, naked, on a metal chair through which an electric current was passed; he still has the deep marks of severe burns on both legs. In the corridors of the prison I recognized among the new "entries" Mohamed Sefta, Registrar of the Mahakma [Moslem Court] of Algiers. "Forty-three days with the Paras. Excuse me but I still have trouble in speaking. They burnt my tongue." And he showed me his slashed tongue. I have seen others: a young trader from the Casbah [Moslem quarter of Algiers, as opposed to the European quarter], Boualem Bahmed, showed me, in the prison car in which we were driven to the Military Tribunal, the long scars on the calves of his legs. "The Paras . . . with a knife; I hid a member of the FLN."

On the other side of the wall, in the wing reserved for women, there are young girls, not one of whom has given way: Djamila Bouhired, Elyette Loup, Nassima Hablal, Melika Khene, Lucie Coscas, Colette Grégoire and many others. Undressed, beaten, insulted by sadistic torturers they too have been submitted to the water and the electricity. Each one of us here knows of the martyrdom of Annick Caste, raped by a parachutist and who, believing herself pregnant, dreamed only of death.

On reading this account, one must think of all those who have "disappeared" and those who, sure of their cause, await death without fear; of those who have known torturers and who have not feared them; of those who, faced with hatred and torture, reaffirm their belief in future peace and friendship between the French and the Algerian peoples. This could be the account of any one of them.

The tortures Alleg was subjected to included beatings, electrodes attached to different parts of his body, the nipples and genitals in particular; live electric wires forced down his throat "right to the back of the palate"; his nipples and the soles of his feet burned. The ultimate phase of his torture ended with the use of pentothal, or "truth serum," in a last attempt to have him give the names of his "accomplices."

Feeling that that they were not receiving the necessary support from politicians in Paris, the military increasingly considered the Algerian War to be indeed a "mess." The hard-liners found support among the *colons*, who were afraid that the government in Paris would relinquish Algeria to the rebels. On May 13, 1958, the Army and pro-*Algérie française* (pro-French Algeria) civilians called for a general strike and demonstrations in Algiers. The event turned into a insurrection against the government in Paris, with General Massu named leader of a *Comité de Salut*

Public (Committee of Public Safety). Massu immediately called for the Paris government to name de Gaulle head of a government of national union. Once again, a military crisis had brought de Gaulle, "the savior" of the postwar, to the political arena. He carefully maintained his options open, neither publicly encouraging the revolt nor refusing the possibility of accepting the leadership from the Paris government, declaring: "I hold myself ready to assume the powers of the Republic." By the end of May, the situation had become critical: Massu's paratroopers landed in Corsica, threatening a military coup d'état. To avoid the possibility of a military takeover, the Parliament voted de Gaulle prime minister, with special powers for six months. Many, especially on the left, including Mendès-France and François Mitterand, who saw de Gaulle as endorsing "rebellion and sedition," perceived his return to government as a civilian coup d'état; the Communist Party also firmly opposed him. De Gaulle was nevertheless voted prime minister by the parliament by a comfortable majority. He was also invested with the power to draft a new constitution. The constitution, which provided unprecedented power to the executive, was approved by 85 percent of the electorate. De Gaulle became the first president of this Fifth Republic, leader of a country in full economic expansion, but one for whom he could not begin to realize his dream of *grandeur* before finding a solution to the Algerian problem.

De Gaulle's declaration to the crowd that greeted him when he visited Algeria on June 1958 is a good example of his political savvy: knowing full well that a "French Algeria" had become unworkable, he nevertheless uttered this phrase, with his arms raised to make the victory sign: *Je vous ai compris*, which translates as "I have understood you," but in retrospect could be understood, in fact *should* have been understood to mean, as Sowerwine proposes, "I've got your number" (302). In any case he did not pronounce the words that would have left no doubt in the minds of the cheering crowd: *Algérie française*, French Algeria.

As early as September 1959, de Gaulle made his position publicly clear on radio and television: negotiations and, ultimately, self-determination for Algeria. The fighting nevertheless continued, as did the widespread use of torture. One strategy consisted in "regrouping" villagers in concentration camps as a means of cutting off the FLN from any source of support from the local population. Numerous cases of torture continued to be reported in spite of the government's assurances that this practice had stopped. In June 1960, the country's most respected newspaper *Le Monde*—its editor Hubert Beuve-Méry was a personal friend of de Gaulle, who had supported the paper's founding after World War II—published an article by Simone de Beauvoir containing details of the torture and rape of a young woman member of the FLN, Djamila Boupacha. An account of Boupacha's ordeal was published in *L'Express*. It was written by Françoise Sagan, a young author recently made famous by the publication and huge success of her first novel, *Bonjour Tristesse*, at seventeen. The widely publicized case further brought to light the extent of the resistance to the war in the press, publishing circles, among intellectuals, and in the general public as well. During the same summer, 121 public figures ranging from actors and writers to journalists and doctors signed a manifesto against the war, stating that ". . . it is normal that . . . conscientious objection be resolved concretely through increasingly more numerous acts of insubordination, of desertion, as well as protection of and aid to the Algerian fighters" (see dossier 7.3).

A friend of Jean-Paul Sartre and a leading member of *Les Temps Modernes*, Francis Jeanson, was one of many who actively helped the FLN. The volunteers of the "Jeanson network" who had secretly been collecting funds for the FLN were brought to trial during the same period. In spite of government censorship, which included seizure of an entire print run of *L'Express*, both the trial and the manifesto became widely known, and support became increasingly widespread for the position of manifesto's signatories and for the members of the network.

Dossier 7.3   "Manifesto of the 121" against the Algerian War (September 6, 1960)

A very important movement is developing in France, and it is necessary that French and international opinion be better informed about it, at a time when the new course of the war in Algeria should lead us to see, rather than to forget the depths of the crisis that began there six years ago.

In ever greater numbers, French men and women have been arrested, imprisoned and convicted for having refused to take part in this war or for having come to the aid of the Algerian fighters. Distorted by their adversaries, but also toned down by those very people whose duty should be to defend them, their reasons have generally remained misunderstood. Yet it is not enough to say that this resistance to public authority is honorable. It is the protest of men acting out of a sense of betrayed honor and in defense of their rightful idea of what the truth is, and its significance transcends the circumstances in which it has taken shape, which it is important to understand, no matter how things turn out.

For the Algerians, the struggle, pursued by either military or diplomatic means, is absolutely clear. It is a war of national independence. But, for the French, what is the nature of this war? It is not a foreign war. France's national territory has never been threatened. Furthermore: this war is being waged against men whom the State pretends to consider French but who are themselves fighting precisely in order to stop being French. It would not be enough to say that it is a war of conquest, an imperialist war accompanied, in addition, by racism. There is some of that in all wars, and the ambiguity persists.

In fact, by a decision that constituted a fundamental abuse of power, the government has first of all drafted large numbers of citizens for the sole end of achieving what it itself calls a police action against an oppressed population, a population that has revolted out of a desire for basic dignity, since it demands to be finally recognized as an independent community.

Neither a war of conquest nor a war of "national defense," nor a civil war, the Algerian war has little by little fallen under the control of the army and of a caste that refuses to give way in the face of an uprising whose meaning even civil authorities, becoming aware of the general collapse of colonial empires, seems ready to recognize.

At the present time, it is essentially the will of the army that maintains this criminal and absurd fighting, and this army, through the political role that several members of its high command makes it play, acts sometimes overtly and violently outside the law, betraying the goals conferred upon it by the nation as a whole, compromises and risks corrupting the nation itself by forcing citizens under its command to be the accomplices of a factious and depraved action. Is it necessary to remind our readers that, fifteen years after the destruction of the Hitlerian order, French militarism, responding to the pressures of this war, has succeeded in restoring torture and in once again turn it into something like a European institution?

It is in these conditions that many Frenchmen have come to question the meaning of traditional values and obligations. What is civic responsibility when, under certain circumstances, it becomes a shameful surrender? Aren't there any cases where saying no is a sacred duty, where "betrayal" means the courageous respect of the truth? And when, because those who use it as an instrument of racist or ideological domination have so decreed, the army places itself in a state of open or latent revolt against democratic institutions, doesn't revolt against the army take on a new meaning?

The issue of conscientious objection has been raised since the beginning of the war. Since the war continues, it is normal that this conscientious objection be resolved concretely through increasingly more numerous acts of insubordination, of desertion, as well as protection of and aid to the Algerian fighters. Independent movements have developed outside of all official political parties, without their assistance, and, in the end, in spite of their disapproval. Once again, independently of established frameworks or slogans, a resistance was born through a spontaneous awakening of consciousness, one that searches for and invents new forms of action and means of struggle adequate to a new situation whose meaning and true requirements political groups and journals of opinion have agreed—either as a result of their inertia, ideological timidity, or national or moral prejudices—not to recognize.

The undersigned, considering that each one must pronounce himself on acts that it is now impossible to consider as those of isolated individuals, considering that they themselves, given who they are and according to the means at their disposal, have a duty to intervene, not to give advice to men who have to decide individually in the face of such serious issues, but to ask those who preside at their trials not to allow themselves to be fooled by the ambiguity of words and actions, declare:

—We respect and consider justified the refusal to take up arms against the Algerian people.

—We respect and consider justified the conduct of French people who consider it their duty to bring help and protection to the Algerians oppressed in the name of the French people.

—The cause of the Algerian people, which is making a decisive contribution to the downfall of the colonial system, is the cause of all free men. (Prochasson and Wieviorka, 495–497)

De Gaulle began to speak of an "Algerian republic," a choice of words that reflected his willingness to negotiate with the GPRA (Provisional Government of the Republic of Algeria, Gouvernement Provisoire de la République Algérienne). When de Gaulle had come to power in 1958, a clear majority of the population was against disengagement from Algeria; in a national referendum held in January 1961, 75 percent of the mainland French voted in favor of self-determination. The settlers in Algeria voted against in equal proportion. This turn of the tide in metropolitan public opinion, the prospect of negotiations with the GPRA, and of the eventual withdrawal of the French army led to a radicalization of the French Algeria faction. The most active opponents to negotiation and withdrawal founded the OAS (Secret Army Organization, Organization armée secrète) a paramilitary group whose tactics of bombing, abduction, and execution also included several assassination attempts against de Gaulle himself. The OAS was also behind the military putsch of April 1961 in Algiers, led by "a quartet of retired generals" (de Gaulle's derisive label). De Gaulle addressed the nation and called upon "every Frenchman and above all every soldier, to execute any of the orders" issued by the generals, in open mutiny against his policies. The speech was heard by the troops in Algeria on transistor radios, new arrivals on the market in France. This image of soldiers fighting a colonial war and using one of the new products brought by modernization is symbolic of the dual status of France at the time: a country experiencing an economic boom in a rapid process of modernization, and an empire fighting a backward-looking colonial war. This duality also reflects the contradiction between the universalist values of the republic and the inequities of colonization.

De Gaulle's political savvy, his understanding of the Algerian adversary's determination and the impossibility of a clear and total victory, together led to the collapse of the pro-French Algeria faction. The bulk of the army refused to obey the mutineers and even arrested a number of them.

The violence nevertheless continued, with both the FLN and the OAS pursuing bombings, executions, and campaigns of intimidation not only in Algeria but also in mainland France. In Paris, the police repression of both groups was extreme, especially when it came to the FLN and its partisans. On October 17, 1961, about 30,000 demonstrators, mostly Algerians from the shantytowns in the suburbs of Paris, joined in a march of support for the FLN. The police launched an assault that left over 200 people dead, many beaten or strangled and others tied up and thrown into the Seine. The report commissioned by the prefect of Police, Maurice Papon (see chapter 9), mentions three deaths. As noted by Jim House and Neil MacMaster in an article written in 2002,

> The brutality and killings of 17th October [1961] did not appear out of the blue, but were the culmination of a lengthy period of torture and murder during which police officers had become habituated to both violence and to a feeling of routine impunity. October 1961 represents the moment that levels of systematic violence that were quite widely accepted within the colonial theater erupted into the "civilized" center of empire. (274)

This is exactly the sort of eruption that Fanon had predicted in *Black Skins, White Masks* a decade earlier:

> The violence that has ruled over the ordering of the colonial world, which has ceaselessly drummed the rhythm for the destruction of native social forms and broken up without reserve the systems of reference of the economy, the customs of dress and external life, that same violence will be claimed and taken over by the native at the moment when, deciding to embody history in his own person, he surges into the forbidden quarters. (34)

In the North of Paris, eight people died crushed against the gates of the Charonne metro station after the police charged demonstrators marching against the OAS on February 8, 1962. A few days later, the largest demonstration since the celebrations of the Liberation took place in Paris as half a million people marched in the funeral procession of those who had been killed at Charonne. French public opinion had shifted completely since the first skirmishes that had begun the insurrection, an insurrection that, over the years, had turned into a war for independence. De Gaulle pursued negotiations with the FLN; both parties signed the Evian Agreement on March 18, 1962, followed by a referendum in Algeria in which 99 percent of the population voted for independence, formally recognized by France on July 3, 1962.

Over 300,000 Algerians died in the war, a figure that does not include the estimated 70,000 civilians who were killed by the FLN itself in its campaign to rally the population to its cause. The French military estimated its own losses at 18,000. In the wake of the Evian Agreement, the last *pieds noirs* who were still in Algeria took the ships and planes that would take them to France, a country most had never seen. Some of the *Harkis* were also able to leave with the Europeans, but those who stayed behind became victims of the FLN's campaign of retaliation against those it considered collaborators, traitors to the cause of independence.

Figure 7.1 The "Pieds noirs" Leave Algeria (1962)

May 1962: Arriving in the French port of Marseilles from Mers-El-Kebir in Algeria, the overwhelming majority of the passengers had never been to the *metropole*. (© Hachette Photo Presse)

The decolonization of West Africa occurred in much less violent circumstances. Even before de Gaulle came to power in 1958, the Fourth Republic had already taken some steps toward granting increased autonomy and rights to its colonies in West Africa. The constitution of 1946 established the *Union française*, but, as we have seen, self-rule was out of the question. Ten years later, in 1956, the same year that saw the independence of Morocco and Tunisia in North Africa, the Defferre law, named after the minister for overseas France, created local assemblies and increased the recruitment of civil servants from within the local populations in the sub-Saharan colonies and Madagascar and Mauritius in the Indian Ocean.

Compared to what had been the case in Indochina and North Africa, nationalist movements had been slower to develop in that part of the empire. By the time the Deferre law was adopted, however, a number of parties and movements were already asking for increased autonomy. Léopold Sedar-Senghor and Félix Houphouet-Boigny led these movements in Senegal and the Ivory Coast respectively. When he proposed the new constitution of the Fifth Republic in 1958, De Gaulle continued the trend of gradual relinquishing of colonial power by simultaneously announcing a referendum on the formation of a *Communauté française* (French Community) to replace the *Union française*. The members of this French Community would acquire internal autonomy while France would remain in charge of military and diplomatic issues. Making allowances for the sovereignty of the individual populations, however, the French government would recognize the independence of any colony voting against membership in the Community. Such a vote would also lead to the loss of any aid from the former *métropole*. The population of Guinea, led by Sékou Touré, was the only colony to choose immediate independence while all the others voted by substantial majorities to become members of the Community. The French reaction to the vote in Guinea was not quite as violent as that of the OAS and the departing Europeans when Algeria became independent—blowing up university, school, hospitals, official buildings, and oil refineries, vowing to "leave Algeria as the French had found it in 1830" (Sowerwine, 315)—but economic aid to Guinea immediately stopped. The departing French "[removed] everything in the country that belonged to France, going so far as to unscrew light bulbs and rip telephone wires out of walls" (Stovall, 59). By 1960, all the other remaining colonies opted for full independence, but this time France also opted for a more diplomatic strategy and kept close bilateral relations with the former colonies. Economic aid from France continued to arrive, as well as the *coopérants*, young Frenchmen serving their tour of military duty as technical advisors and teachers. French remained the language of education—which created a different set of issues (see dossier 7.4)—and French companies continued to hold important interests in the former colonies. Immigrants from these newly independent former colonies also represented a substantial proportion of immigrants arriving in France during the years of economic boom. Ultimately, this would also create a new set of issues for France, especially after 1973. By then the years of rapid economic growth would be over, the country would enter a long period of recession, and the foreign workers would no longer be as welcomed as they were earlier. In the early 1960s, the presence of *pieds noirs, Harkis*, and the immigrants from all over the empire reminded one that the stories of modernization and decolonization were not separate.

Dossier 7.4   Kateb Yacine, *The Starred Polygon*, (1966)

In *Portrait of the Artist as a Young man*, Stephen Daedalus, James Joyce's alter ego, reflects on his use of English as opposed to that of the dean of his school, an

Englishman: "That language in which we are speaking is his before it is mine. How different are the words *home, Christ, ale, master,* on his lips and mine! I cannot speak or write these words without unrest of spirit. His language, so familiar and so foreign, will always be for me an acquired speech. I have not made or accepted its words. My soul frets in the shadow oh his language" (189). Here Joyce writes about the colonial relation between his country, Ireland, and England, in particular as it relates to language. Thirty-five years later, Franz Fanon addresses a comparable issue in *Black Skin, White Masks* (1952) as the independence movements throughout the French Empire begin to gain momentum:

> To speak is to exist absolutely for the other . . . To speak . . . means above all to assume a culture, to support the weight of a civilization . . . Every colonized people—in other words, every people in whose soul an inferiority complex has been created by the death and burial of its local cultural originality—finds itself face to face with the language of the civilizing nation; that is, with the culture of the mother country. The colonized is elevated above his jungle status in proportion to his adoption of the mother country's cultural standard. He becomes whiter as he renounces his blackness, his jungle. (17–18)

Fanon's acerbic irony and his lament have the same origin. That French remained the language of education and the language of the educated elite in the former sub-Saharan colonies, as it did in other parts of the former empire, does not eliminate a crucial fact: French had also been the language of the colonizer. It was a language that came from outside and was imposed on the "natives" either as the avowed tool of "modernization," of "access to civilization," or as the unavowed tool of colonial exploitation. The Algerian writer Assia Djebar recently commented in the *New York Times*, by way of an analogy, on this particular type of coexistence of two languages in one person: "Think of the German Jews, writing after the Shoah. German is their language, and yet they suffer in it. Well, little by little I began to question my own relation to French and the memories it carried for me." Other "bilingual writers" already encountered in this study can also serve as a point of comparison. The writers of the *Nouveau Théâtre* (see chapter 6), like Beckett, an Irishman "leaving" English for French, or Ionesco, a Romanian, "reconfiguring" French, had both come to French voluntarily and for reasons of their own. They were writers who came from a European tradition that was more or less that of France, while writers of the first generation to come out of the empire had no choice but to learn the language of a colonizer that belonged to a radically different civilization, the "West." Rather than the voluntary appropriation of a language not originally his own, the encounter of the language of the colonized with the colonizer's language occurs at first on the mode of conflict and shame. Commenting on this conflict "within the colonial individual" Albert Memmi insists on the fact that a hierarchy is created in which the mother tongue invariably appears as inferior: "His [the colonial individual's] mother tongue is that which is crushed. He himself sets out about discarding this infirm language, hiding it from the sight of strangers" (*The Colonizer*, 141). At first, there is a devaluation of the colonized subject's own language vis-à-vis the colonizer's language, especially in the case of French. Indeed French, the language of a culture that perceives itself as universal appears less tolerant of appropriation than, say English. Still, the colonized finds himself in a situation where, having been educated in French, having been introduced to writing culture by way of French, has this language at his disposal only if he wants to partake of writing culture. This is more accurate in the case of France's West African colonies where the language was basically anchored in an oral culture than in the case of Arab-speaking colonies, for example, themselves writing cultures. However, the existence of a previous writing culture does not, as we have seen, prevent the traumatic encounter. It is, precisely, this encounter that, from a writing culture or not, the colonized writers had to negotiate. The writers of the colonial and of the first postcolonial generations in particular, confronted with an entirely new situation, had to find their own way of facing this predicament. The following comments, one by a writer from West Africa and the other from North Africa, indicate the essential characteristic of this strategy, whether the colonized is from an oral or a writing culture. About *Les soleils des indépendances* (*The Suns of Independence*, 1968), his novel set in a fictional territory during the colonial period, Ahmadou Kourouma , the Ivorian author, writes that it was "thought in Malinke and written in French" (Hollier, 1028), while Kateb Yacine, the Algerian, declares in the preface to his novel that "conceived and written in French, *Nedjma* remains a profoundly Arab work" (Hollier, 1021).

The following excerpt is taken from the end of Yacine's *Le polygone étoilé* (*The Starred Polygon*, 1966) that had been conceived as forming one novel with *Nejma*.

But I was still nothing more than a tadpole, happy in his river, content with the nocturnal strains of his batrachian tribe; in short, doubting nothing and no one. I had no love for the Taleb's [Coranic teacher] ferule and goatee, but I was studying at home, and so was not reproached for anything. Yet when I was seven, in another village (my family traveled a great deal because of the frequent transfers of the Muslim justice system), my father suddenly decided, irrevocably, to feed me to the lions, that is, to put me in French school. He did it with a heavy heart:

"Leave Arabic for the time being. I don't want you to be like me, caught between two stools. No, if I have any say in the matter, you will never be a victim of the Medersa [Coranic school]. Under normal circumstances, I could have been your literature teacher and your mother would have done the rest. But where would such an education lead you? The French language is master. You will have to master it, and leave behind everything that we have instilled in you since your innocent childhood days. But once you have become master of the French language, you will be able to return safely with us to your point of departure."

This, in essence, was the paternal speech I got. Did he himself believe what he was saying?

My mother sighed; and when I plunged into my new studies, when I did my homework, alone, I saw her wandering aimlessly, like a hurt soul . . . Farewell to our intimate and childish theater, farewell to the daily plot hatched against my father to reply in verse to his satirical remarks . . . and the tension was building.

After a laborious and hardly brilliant start, I quickly took to the foreign language, and later, deeply in love with a spirited schoolteacher, I went as far as dreaming of solving for her, without her knowledge, all the problems in my arithmetic book!

My mother was too shrewd not to be upset by the unfaithfulness I was showing her in this way. I can still see her, completely wounded, tearing my books from me—"You're going to make yourself sick!"—and then one evening, in a heartfelt voice, not without sadness, saying to me "Since I must no longer distract you from your other world, teach me French . . ." Thus the trap of Modern Times snapped on my fragile roots, and now I am furious when I think of my foolish pride on that day when, a French newspaper in her hand, my mother sat down at my work table, distant as always, pale and silent, as if the small hand of the cruel pupil were making it her duty, since the pupil was her son, to impose on herself the straitjacket of silence, and even to follow him to the ends of his efforts and his solitude—into the lion's jaws.

I never, not even during the time of my success with the schoolteacher, ceased to feel deep within me this second severing of the umbilical tie, this inner exile that brought the schoolboy closer to his mother only to tear them away, each time a little more, from the murmur of the blood, from the reproachful shivers of a language banished, secretly, with a common accord that was broken as soon as it was made . . . Thus I had lost at one and the same time my mother and her language, the only inalienable treasures—and yet they were alienated! (Translated from the French by Alyson Waters)

References

Betts, Raymond F. *France and Decolonization 1900–1960.* New York: Saint Martin's Press, 1991.

Césaire, Aimé. *Discourse on Colonialism.* Translated by Joan Pinkham. New York: Monthly review Press, 1972. Originally published *as Discours sur le colonialisme* (Paris: Présence Africaine, 1955).

Conrad, Joseph. *Heart of Darkness.* New York: Penguin Books, 1973 [1902].

Evans, Martin. "From Colonialism to Post-colonialism. The French Empire since Napoleon." In Martin S. Alexander, ed. *French History since Napoleon.* London: Arnold Publishers, 1995.

Fanon, Frantz. *Black Skin, White Masks.* Translated by Charles Lam Markmann. New York: Grove Press, 1967. Originally published as *Peau noire, masques blancs* (Paris: Seuil, 1952).

———. *The Wretched of the Earth.* Constance Farrington, trans. New York: Grove Press, 1966. Originally published as *Les damnés de la terre* (Paris: Seuil, 1961).

Forsdick, Charles and David Murphy. *Francophone Postcolonial Studies: A Critical Introduction.* London: Arnold, 2003.

House, Jim and Neil Mac Master. "'Une journée portée disparue.' The Paris Massacre of 1961 and Memory." In Martin S. Alexander and Kenneth Mouré, eds., *Crisis and Renewal in Twentieth-Century France.* New York, Oxford: Berghahn Books, 2002, 267–290.

Jennings, Eric T. *Vichy in the Tropics. Pétain's National Revolution in Madagascar, Guadeloupe, and Indochina.* Stanford: Stanford University Press, 2001.

Joyce, James. *A Portrait of the Artist as a Young man.* New York: Viking Press, 1969 [1916].

Kuisel, Richard. *Seducing the French. The Dilemma of Americanization.* Berkeley: University of California Press, 1993.

Lacouture, Jean. *Ho Chi Minh: A Political Biography.* Peter Wiles, trans. New York: Vintage Books, 1968.

Library of Congress, Country Studies. http://reference.allrefer.com/country-guide-study/algeria/algeria11.html, June 16, 2005.

Memmi, Albert. *Portrait du colonisé. Précédé du Portrait du colonisateur.* Paris: Editions Jean-Jacques Pauvert, 1966.

Servan-Schreiber, Jean-Jacques. *Lieutenant in Algeria.* New York: Alfred A. Knopf, 1957.

Sowerwine, Charles. *France since 1870. Culture, Politics and Society.* New York: Houndmills, 2001.

Stora, Benjamin. *Algeria 1830–2000. A Short History.* Jane Marie Todd, trans. Ithaca, London: Cornell University Press, 2001.

Stovall, Tyler E. *France since the Second World War.* Harlow, London: Pearson Education Ltd., 2002.

Wieviorka, Olivier and Christophe Prochasson, eds. *La France du XXe siècle. Documents d'histoire.* Paris: Editions du Seuil, 1994.

Yacine, Kateb. *Le polygone étoilé.* Paris: Editions du Seuil, 1966.

CHAPTER 8

MODERNIZATION, MASS CULTURE, MAY 68, AND LIFE AFTER DE GAULLE (1955–1981)

The public opening of the body's interiority is moreover a general feature of the advertising of toilet products. "Decay is expelled (from the teeth, the skin, the blood, the breath)": France is having a great yen for cleanliness.

—Roland Barthes, *Mythologies* (1957)

There was clothes-washing, clothes-drying, ironing. Gas, electricity, telephone. Children. Clothes and under-clothes. Mustard. Packaged soup powders, canned soup. Hair—how to wash it, how to dye it, how to make it hold a wave, how to make it shine. Students, fingernails, cough syrups, typewriters, fertilizers, tractors, leisure-time activities, gifts, stationery, linen, politics, highways, alcoholic drinks, mineral waters, cheeses and jam, lamps and curtains, insurance, gardening.

Nothing human was alien to them.

—Georges Perec, *Les choses. A Story of the Sixties* (1965)

Yesteryear, to go courting
You spoke of love
To prove your passion
You offered your heart
Today it's not the same
It's changing, it's changing
To seduce the dear angel
You whisper in her ear
Ah Bertha, Come kiss me
And I'll give you A Frigidaire
A pretty scooter
An atomizer
And a Dunlopillo mattress
A stove
With a glass oven
Lots of dishes and cutlery
And cake servers
An eggbeater
To make vinaigrette

A beautiful deodorizer
To lap up smells
Electric sheets
A waffle pistol
An airplane for two
And we'll be happy
            —Boris Vian, *The*
Lament of Progress (1954)

World War II and its aftermath suddenly seemed very far away. The intervening years between a time when "there was nothing," as one commentator summarized the lean years that followed the war, and a time when there seemed to be everything, including a few unheard of objects such as those in Boris Vian's song, had brought massive changes to the French, who were becoming less citizens of the republic and more consumers of these new objects.

The war was the past, especially for the baby boomers who were coming of age, and the "new" was in: new modes of consumption, new music, new criticism, new novel, new cinema. François Truffaut's *The Four Hundred Blows* hit the screens in 1959 signaling, with Jean-Luc Godard's *Breathless* among other films released the same year and in 1960, the beginning of the "New Wave" in French cinema. It is fitting, on the eve of a decade that witnessed the appearance of "youth" as a self-conscious group and the blooming of a "youth culture," that the first scene of Truffaut's groundbreaking film is set in a classroom in Paris where rowdy adolescent boys are being reprimanded by their teacher. Exasperated by their laughter and unruliness he yells out: "What will it be in ten years!" His question turned out to be prophetic: just about ten years later, the very same adolescents of that generation, products of the postwar baby boom, many of them by then university students, would be throwing pavement stones at the charging police in the streets of Paris during the "events of May 68" that shook de Gaulle's Fifth Republic to its foundations. This generation was the first to have grown up exclusively during the *trente glorieuses*, the "thirty glorious" (years), a phrase coined by the sociologist Jean Fourastié to describe the three decade–long period of France's unprecedented economic growth from the postwar to the early 1970s. These rowdy boys in the classroom were the first to already have *argent de poche* (pocket money), a kind of disposable income that reflected the booming economy, new spending patterns, and other repercussions that accompanied that time of plenty. This was the generation that grew up with radio but came of age with television, the generation that "would be immersed in the sound of electric guitars even before being old enough to vote: electrical before being electoral, [the members of that generation] were also consumers before being producers" (Rioux and Sirinelli, 262). This generation was indeed reaping the fruits of France's remarkable economic growth since the end of the war. By the time de Gaulle came to power in 1958, this economic growth had been steady and rapid for over fifteen years and the country was in the process of entering the consumer age in earnest.

The Fourth Republic's poor record in the areas of political stability and decolonization had not prevented it from initiating and developing the major policies—ranging from the economic plan with its reconstruction and consumer phases on the national level, to European economic integration on the international level—that were instrumental in transforming France from a war-devastated country into one of the fastest growing economies in the world. From the moment he came to power, de Gaulle's policies on the economic front were essentially a continuation of the Fourth Republic's even as he proceeded to deal with the Algerian War and with decolonization in general. By 1962, when the Algerian "ball and chain" has been left behind and decolonization achieved with much less violence elsewhere (See chapter 7), France was no longer an imperial power extending from the Caribbean to Asia. Its frontiers took the shape and fit into the much-reduced area of what rapidly became known in everyday language as the "Hexagon." War—the Franco-Prussian War, World War I, World War II, the wars in Indochina and Algeria—and its corollary type of politics had been central to French life since 1870. Beginning in the early 1960s, in this "post-colonial" and consumerist period, the dominant debates in France would be dictated by economics. In the midst of deep changes in French society, including the appearance of mass and youth cultures and the challenges they represented for a country whose identity was singularly predicated on a centralizing, homogenizing impulse and a penchant for hierarchy, grandeur, and high culture, "economics had taken precedence over politics" (Crozier, 100).

Politics reemerged spectacularly in the "events of May 68" as "consumer society" or the "capitalist economy" or "the System" was challenged in its turn, first by students and workers, then by French men and women from all walks of life. May 68 indeed appeared as a counterdiscourse to the republic and the modernization model it had adopted in the aftermath of World War II.

After de Gaulle's definitive departure from politics in 1969, the Fifth Republic endured. De Gaulle was succeeded as its leader by his prime minister, Georges Pompidou, and then by Valéry Giscard d'Estaing, not quite a faithful Gaullist like Pompidou, but still a man of the center-Right. Pompidou and Giscard d'Estaing presided over a "post–de Gaulle" era, 1970–1974 and 1974–1981, respectively, that, at least symbolically, begins with the events of May 68.

The changes in French society either initiated or revealed by May 1968 resulted in attempts by successive governments of the Right to address the transformations that had occurred in France in the quarter century since the end of Word War II. Jacques Chaban-Delmas, Pompidou's prime minister, called his attempt a project for a *nouvelle société* (new society), while Giscard d'Estaing framed his presidency around his program for a *société libérale avancée* (advanced liberal society). Pompidou's presidency ended with the last years of the economic boom as the thirty glorious years came to a sudden halt with the oil crisis of 1973. During Giscard d'Estaing's presidency, the state's attempt to come to terms with the changes brought by modernization, the consumer society, and mass culture occurred, on the international level, against the background of rapidly globalizing economies and, on the national level, in a context of recession and unemployment. During his presidency, structural unemployment remained a visible sign that the modernization model adopted by France was not without its drawbacks or injustices and, after seven years of his presidency, the French would be ready for a change. The change, when it came in 1981, in the form of a Socialist president and a socialist government, was partly the result of economic dissatisfaction at a time when the proverbially politicized French citizen had increasingly become the consumer of a market economy. However, the arrival of the Socialists in 1981 also signaled a major shift in French politics reflected in Giscard d'Estaing's own professed desire for a *décrispation de la politique*, a "de-dramatizing," a "normalization" of politics with alternate governments of the Right and of the Left, on the "Anglo-Saxon model." This normalization of political life, at least in the way it was formulated if not yet practiced during Giscard d'Estaing's presidency, signaled the beginning of the end of a constant in French politics since the postwar years: the Right governing and the Left in the opposition, including a powerful but marginalized Communist party. It was the rigid Left versus Right dichotomy in French politics that made it possible for de Gaulle to defuse the May 68 movement by presenting the situation as one where the only alternative was to choose between his government or what he called "dictatorship" and "totalitarian communism." Once the Left was no longer perceived in those terms, this rhetoric could not be effective. The *décrispation* of French politics, economic dissatisfaction, along with a still vibrant desire for social and political change reminiscent of the May 68 movement, would bring François Mitterand and the Socialists to power in 1981. For the first time since the Popular Front government of 1936, France would be ruled by the Left.

★ ★ ★

As we have seen, in the aftermath of war and foreign occupation the primary objective of the new leadership had been to avoid civil war and to ensure national unity and political stability. Simultaneously, it was also imperative to address the no less urgent task of economic reconstruction. At first the focus was placed on heavy industry and infrastructure at the expense of the consumers waiting on long lines or filling out forms for everything ranging from cars and apartments to butter and heating fuel. The first national economic Plan thus concentrated on areas such as steel, cement, tractors, and the railroad network, among others, rather than on consumer goods. As the war shortages receded into the past, however, France began to enter the consumer age and experience a number of social and cultural repercussions on a scale and at a speed it had never encountered in its long history. As the historian Serge Bernstein summarizes it, "Within a decade the spectacular growth in purchasing power enabled them to buy the goods and services that had been the preserve of the privileged groups in society . . . The consequence was that in the 1960s the principal occupation of the French became their access to all forms of consumption. And one can speak in this respect of a veritable revolution" (146).

This entry into consumer and mass culture took place in the context of a rapidly expanding population. From 40 million in 1946 when de Gaulle left political office and began his long "crossing of the desert," the population increased to 50 million by 1969, the year he left power once again after having served eleven years as the first president of the Fifth Republic he had established in 1958. This increase in population was due not only to the postwar baby boom, but also to immigration and to the decline in mortality rate that accompanies improvements in a population's material well-being. Indeed, one of the Fourth Republic's lasting achievements was "the creation of an extensive social welfare system, including Social Security coverage, subsidized medical care, pensions for the elderly, and a minimum wage" (Stoval, 35).

At first, the influx of foreign workers required by the expanding economy and actively encouraged by the government came essentially from "Mediterranean Europe"—Spain, Italy and Portugal—and then increasingly from North Africa—Morocco, Tunisia, and Algeria, and West Africa, France's former protectorates and colonies. From 1946 to the end of the Algerian War in 1962, which signaled the symbolic and traumatic end of the

French Empire, a total of almost 4 million immigrants, a large portion of whom were born in that empire, including the 1 million *pieds noirs* (French and other Europeans from Algeria) and the *Harkis* of Algeria (Algerians who had sided with the French)—arrived in France and represented about one-third of the postwar population growth. Ironically, as the population of former imperial subjects increased in the Hexagon, France's foreign trade, which had been traditionally dependent on colonial markets—in 1952, the colonies still accounted for 42 percent of French exports—began to be realigned along European and North Atlantic lines. The intersection of these two trends, modernization and decolonization, is very revealing of the intimate relation that exists between France's thirty glorious years of economic expansion and the gradually increasing presence in the Hexagon of immigrant workers from its former empire. As Kristin Ross proposes, the former could not have taken place without the latter: "The immigration that haunts the collective fantasies of the French today [in the mid 1990s when Ross's book came out] is the old accomplice of the accelerated growth of French society in the 1950s and 1960s. Without the labor force of its ex-colonial immigrants, France could not have successfully "Americanized," nor competed in the postwar industrial contest (*Fast Cars, Clean Bodies*, 9)." Ross's comparison between the respective effects of American-style modernization, soon to morph into "globalization," and immigration, specifically from the former colonies, also reflects the dual but unequal challenge both represented for France's discourse of "national identity": "[After the Algerian War] France retreats within the Hexagon, withdraws from Empire, retrenches within its borders at the same time that those boundaries are becoming newly permeable to a whirlwind of economic force— forces far more destructive of some received notion of "national culture" than any immigrant community could muster" (12).

At first, however, as the economy was expanding and the labor shortage remained chronic, it was "Americanization" and its nefarious corollary, "cocacolonization" (see chapter 6), that provoked systematic and generalized debate in the Hexagon rather than the presence of immigrants at first from inside and then from outside Europe. Only after the thirty glorious years had sputtered out would immigration and the question of national identity begin to be paired in national debate, eclipsing, as least for a time, the issue of the "American challenge" to "Frenchness" and to the "French way of life" (see chapter 9).

In the 1950s and 1960s, the decline in the general population of the farmer of rural France certainly represented one aspect of this "French identity" viewed as being under attack by the forces of modernization. Before World War II, 17 percent of the French population worked in farming, which declined to 8.4 percent by 1962 as policy favored larger, more efficient farms, and rural depopulation gathered momentum; today, this population is estimated at below 3 percent of the total. Bernstein's summary of this shift is eloquent:

> The dominant system of social values and mentalities was profoundly impregnated by the idea (which the effects of World War I had reinforced) that France was in essence a rural country composed of small landowners working a land that gave them independence and liberty. The years of growth were to blow this image to smithereens, so that by the end of the 1960s the average Frenchman had become a city dweller who was henceforth divorced from the land and whose social integration required the rejection of the old rural values and the adoption of new norms of profitability and mass production leading to mass consumption. (130)

The same was true of the small shopkeepers who also represented, in their own way, that "certain idea of France" so touted by de Gaulle: they were individualistic citizens of the Republic but nevertheless all partaking of the *grandeur* that is France. Government policy did not parallel this official ideology as it reversed its policy of protecting small shopkeepers against the competition of larger units, and as the first supermarkets began to appear in 1963. The shopkeepers and artisans who perceived themselves as victims of this modernization formed the core of the Poujadist movement, a telling example of the resistance to modernization viewed as a direct attack on "French values." Pierre Poujade, a small book and newspaper wholesaler, founded the movement, which started out as a protest against tax audits. Many of those attracted to the movement came essentially from a section of the lower middle class that perceived the government as well as the economic and intellectual elites as betraying the people. Poujade's movement, named *Union de Défense des Commerçants et des Artisans* (UDCA, Union for the Defense of Shopkeepers and Artisans), gave voice to the anxieties of that segment of the population as it gathered momentum and even obtained 11 percent of the national vote in the parliamentary elections of 1956, winning 53 seats. Around that time Poujade himself became the object of a cult of leadership in the UDCA, making speeches at rallies all over France excoriating the "new men" of postwar France. One of these speeches is quoted in *Mythologies* by Roland Barthes (see dossier 8.2) whose own status as intellectual and academic placed him among those targeted by the Poujadists: "France is stricken with an overproduction of men with diplomas, polytechnicians [the graduates of the Ecole Polytechnique, one of France's prestigious *grandes écoles*, elite institutions of higher education], economists, philosophers, and other dreamers who have lost contact with the real world." The "real world" Poujade refers to here is no doubt the world of small shopkeepers, artisans, and farmers—as opposed to that of the new "American style" managers and technocrats—who, in his view, represent that "real France" threatened by the immense forces of modernization at work in the period. The fact that Poujade is again quoted and is indeed the subject of yet another essay in Barthes's *Mythologies*, one of the most influential books of the period, reflects the scope the movement had for a time. Quoting Poujade, Barthes underscores the ultra nationalist and racist undertones of his discourse: "My forebears, the Celts, the Arvernes, all mixed. I am the fruit of the crossroads of invasion and exodus." For Barthes, Poujade "effortlessly finds the fundamental racist object, Blood (here it is especially Celtic blood, the blood of Le Pen, the *solid Breton*, separated by an abyss from the *Esthetes of the New Left*, or the blood of the Gauls that Mendès [a prominent French Jewish politician of the Left] is lacking") (188). Poujade's rhetoric places him outside the realm of the republic's universalizing and modernizing project. To a state power that oversees modernization in technocratic and republican terms, Poujade opposes a particularist resistance based on race and soil. To the universalism of the republic that would, at least theoretically, extend its principles to include Others, Poujade opposes what Barthes calls an exclusionary "petit-bourgeois universality":

> Monsieur Poujade's language shows, once more, that the whole petit-bourgeois mythology implies the refusal of alterity, the negation of the different, the euphoria of identity and the exaltation of the Same. In general, this equational, reduction of the world prepares an expansionist phase in which the "identity" of human phenomena quickly establishes a "nature" and thereupon a "universality." (52)

It is no accident that Jean-Marie Le Pen, the future founder of the extreme Right political party, the National Front (see chapter 9), was one of the elected deputies and spokesmen of the Poujadist movement. The link embodied by the Poujadist movement between a certain type of racist, anti-Semitic discourse and the refusal of a certain type of modernization perceived as the relinquishing of traditional, "real" France already announces the anti-immigration anti-European Union discourse of the National Front beginning in the 1980s. For its part, the Poujadist movement waned as quickly as it appeared. The group it formed in parliament proved to be without an effective program and its followers themselves, caught up by the consumerism and the new trappings of mass culture grew disenchanted with the movement and joined the general buying spree.

Dossier 8.1   Georges Perec, *Les choses. A Story of the Sixties* (1965)

Jacques Tati's 1958 film *Mon oncle* (*My Uncle*) parodied the managerial class that emerged in France with modernization and American-style consumption. The "uncle" in the film, played by Tati himself, is, with his pipe and perplexity, seemingly stuck in a more lovable and familiar "pre-modernization" France. His sister and her husband, a businessman-manager, inhabit a rectilinear house equipped with the latest gadgets and appliances, a home complete with flowerless garden and antiseptic kitchen. Their young son's sympathy clearly lies with the bumbling uncle, and the film reflects the deep ambivalence with which some French men and women viewed their country's entry into consumer culture. Georges Perec's 1965 novel addresses the same issue, but the protagonists have changed: Sylvie and Jérôme are in their early twenties; they are not managers but aspire to what they see as the managerial class' life of international travel, discerning taste and elegant luxury. They are employed in the newly configured field of market research and are representative of a period in France when the human sciences, sociology in particular, were being tailored to fit economic and business objectives. As the sociologist Edgar Morin notes, "At the same time as sociology was becoming a social myth, the use of the 'expert sociologist' was more and more widely championed in the workings of the Plan, the Administration, the Corporation . . . the opinion survey based on focus group was provoking less and less scornful skepticism, and imposed itself as universal stethoscope" (*L'esprit du temps*, 26).

The first excerpt from *Les choses* focuses on the young couple's job as "psycho-sociologists"; the second on their own pursuit of goods, while the third reflects their perceived affinity with the lifestyle both chronicled and emblematized by *L'Express*, the news weekly founded in 1953 by Françoise Giroud and Jean-Jacques Servan-Schreiber. To the left of center, *L'Express* became an influential publication that took part in the major political and cultural debates of the period and reflected, as did the new lifestyles on which it commented, the influence of the American model: "Frankly copying the format and layout of the American magazine *Time*, it was a form of import-substitution: a conscious attempt to meet the challenge of US cultural dominance by appropriating American methods" (Forbes and Kelly, 147).

Jerome was twenty-four; Sylvie was twenty-two. They were both psycho-sociologists. Their work, which was not exactly a trade, nor yet a profession, consisted of interviewing people, by various techniques, on a number of subjects. (24)

And for four years, perhaps more, they explored, interviewed, analyzed. Why do tank-type vacuum cleaners sell so badly? What opinion do people in modest circumstances have of chicory? Is prepared purée liked, and why? / Because it's light / Because it's rich? Because it's so easy to make—just one thing to do, and there you are? Do baby carriages really seem too expensive? Aren't people always ready to make a sacrifice for the sake of their children's comfort? How will the French woman vote? Do people like cheese in tubes? Are people for or against public transportation? What do people eating yoghurt first notice? The color? The consistency? The taste? The natural flavor? Do you read a great deal, a little, not at all? Do you go to restaurants? Madame, would you like renting a room to a Negro? What's your frank opinion of pensions for old people? What do young people think? What do executives think? What do thirty-year-old women think? What do you think of vacations? Where do you spend your vacations? Do you like frozen foods? How much do you think a lighter like this costs? What qualities do you require your mattress to have? Can you describe to me a man who likes noodles, spaghetti, and macaroni. What do you think of our washing machine? Are you satisfied with it? Doesn't it make too many suds? Does it wash well? Does it tear clothes? Does it dry clothes? Would you prefer a washing machine that would dry your clothes too? Is mine safety adequate, or isn't there enough in your opinion? (Make the subject talk; ask him to recount personal examples, things that he's seen. Has he already been hurt himself? How did it happen? And will his son be a miner like his father? If not, what?)

There was clothes-washing, clothes-drying, ironing. Gas, electricity, telephone. Children. Clothes and underclothes. Mustard. Packaged soup powders, canned soup. Hair—how to wash it, how to dye it, how to make it hold a wave, how to make it shine. Students, fingernails, cough syrups, typewriters, fertilizers, tractors, leisure-time activities, gifts, stationery, linen, politics, highways, alcoholic drinks, mineral waters, cheeses and jam, lamps and curtains, insurance, gardening. Nothing human was alien to them. (28–29)

Then—and it was almost one of the red-letter days in their lives—they discovered the Flea Market. They found marvelous Arrow or Van Heusen shirts with long button-down collars (impossible to come by in Paris at that time, although they were beginning to be popular because of American comedies—at least among that restricted fringe of people who find their happiness in American comedies), piled up there in a big heap, alongside supposedly indestructible trench coats, skirts, blouses, silk dresses, leather jackets, soft leather moccasins. They went there every other week on Saturday mornings for a year or more, to dig around in the boxes, the stalls, the piles, the cartons, the umbrellas turned upside down, amid a crowd of teenagers with spit curls, Algerian watch sellers, American tourists who had emerged from the glass eyes, the top hats, and the wooden horses of the Vernaison market and were wandering about, somewhat terrified, in the Malik market, contemplating, alongside the old nails, mattresses, carcasses of machines, and spare parts, the strange destiny of the tired surpluses of their most prestigious shirt-makers. And they brought back clothes of all sorts, wrapped in newspapers; and knickknacks, umbrellas, leather knapsacks, records. (31)

[On L'Express:] They faced up to it: they were L'Express . . . Where else could they have found a truer reflection of their tastes, their desires? Were they not moderately rich? L'Express offered them all the signs of well-being: thick dressing gowns, brilliant exposés, beaches that were "in," exotic cuisine, useful shortcuts, intelligent analyses, the secret of the gods, little inexpensive holes in the wall, different views, new ideas, little dresses, frozen foods, elegant details, polite scandal, last minute advice.

They dreamed, in a half whisper, of Chesterfield divans, L'Express dreamed with them. (38)

The durable consumer goods people bought in those years were indicative of a privatization of daily life in the sense that couples and families were now more than ever able to retreat into the comfort of the home as cocoon, with the car providing the equally impermeable link between home and the workplace. Television was one of the most symbolic and influential of the new products of those years. Along with the car, that other vector of modernity, TV became an indicator of the profound changes that were affecting French society. In 1958, when de Gaulle came to power, only 9 percent of French homes were equipped with a set. Throughout the 1950s, when the shift from an infrastructure-oriented economy to a consumer-oriented one was underway, radio was still king. By 1965, 42 percent of homes were equipped with a TV set, with 70 percent owning one in the late 1960s and 91 percent by 1984. The evolution of the role played by television in French life is indicative of the shift from " citizen" to "consumer" that paralleled the shift from "Republican culture" to "mass culture" of those years. In its earlier phase, especially until 1963 when there was only one (state-controlled) channel, television was a primary dispenser of "civic pedagogy" as Rioux and Sirinelli formulate it: "In place of the 'Republican catechism' transmitted by the *instituteurs* [teachers] of the Third Republic to schoolchildren, [television] put on a legendary series of programs . . . and amalgamated itself with the school culture common to the greatest number" (268). A number of programs were devoted to the most famous events and people of French history, among them two of the major figures of the French Revolution, Danton and Robespierre. Gradually, however, as television replaced radio as the dominant media, it also reflected the change from a viewing public being "educated" by the media, brought into the folds of republican discourse, to an audience that primarily sought entertainment from the tube. A 1969 survey revealed that more than being educated or informed, 80 percent of the audience wanted *la détente*, to be entertained, to "relax." *Télé 7 jours*, a publication exclusively devoted to television programs was created in 1960; by 1965, it reached sales of 2 million, and was the number one publication in France in the late 1960s. A definitive break with television as "civic cement" occurred when advertising was added to its programs after 1968. The mix of leisure and marketing had found yet another outlet.

Roland Barthes, the literary critic and semiotician, can be considered the primary chronicler and critic of this new age of consumerism and modernization as it began to gather speed. Using as a base the work of Swiss linguist Ferdinand de Saussure whose *Course in General Linguistics* had become an essential reference for a number of intellectuals and scholars of the period, Barthes proceeded to "read" the new mass culture that was taking shape in the France of 1950s. In Saussurian linguistics the spoken or written word is a "signifier" that denotes something—a horse, a house, freedom, love, etc.—that is the "signified"; the two combined form the "sign." One of Saussure's major propositions is that the link between the signified and the signifier is arbitrary, that there is no reason why "cat," rather than any other word, "dog" or "clown," for that matter, should designate the small furry four-legged domestic animal. What matters, according to Saussure, what creates meaning is the convention or the agreed upon system of differences between one word and all the others; "cat" means cat, the small furry four-legged domestic animal, by virtue of not being "bat," "nat," or "dog." Language is structured according to a system of differences rather than having a natural, organic, or even magical origin lost in the sands of time. What Barthes does in his *Mythologies*, a series of short pieces published in the left-of-center journal *Lettres nouvelles* throughout the 1950s and as a book in 1957, is to extend Saussurian linguistics to all aspects of daily life and popular culture, to *read* them as "sign systems." In doing so Barthes wants to display the mechanism by which apparently "objective" meaning is in fact permeated with ideology and "myth." In other words, he wants to show that in addition to the first level of meaning of the linguistic sign, there is an added or overlaid meaning that insinuates itself. While the signifier "bowtie," for example, refers to a signified that is a particular item of men's clothing, it can also denote "sophistication," even an entire "lifestyle." Barthes's bête noire, the running thread of *Mythologies* is indeed a systematic undoing of the myth of "petit-bourgeois universality" he sees taking shape in parallel with the modernization process of the Fifties. In his introduction to a 1970 reedition of *Mythologies*, Barthes writes about the dual objective of his short essays: "On the one hand an ideological critique bearing on the language of so-called mass culture; on the other hand, a preliminary semiological dismantling of that language: I had just read Saussure and I had become convinced that by treating 'collective representations' as so many sign systems, one could hope to go beyond empty denunciation and give a *detailed* account of the mystification that transforms petit bourgeois culture into something natural and universal" (7). And this is precisely what he proceeds to do in *Mythologies*, leveling the "demythification" process at a wide range of cultural trends and objects ranging from cars and music halls to striptease and travel guides.

Dossier 8.2   Roland Barthes, *Mythologies* (1957)

In this essay *"Depth Advertised,"* Barthes focuses on beauty products, more specifically on the advertising of beauty products. After the penury of consumer goods that characterized the postwar years, a time when many women had to resort to drawing a line on the back of their legs in order to simulate the unavailable nylon stockings, looking good and being clean had become a national obsession, and the basis of major industries.

"Depth Advertised"
    Today as I have indicated elsewhere, the advertising of detergents plays essentially on a notion of depth: dirt is no longer stripped from the surface, but expelled from its most secret cells. All advertising of beauty products is similarly based on a kind of epic representation of the intimate. The little scientific prefaces, meant to introduce (and to advertise) the product, ordain that it cleans in depth, relieves in depth, in short, at any price, infiltrates. Paradoxically, it is insofar as the skin is first of all a surface, but a living, hence a mortal surface, likely to dry out and to age, that it readily assumes its role as a tributary of deep roots, of what certain products call the basic layer of renewal. Moreover, medicine makes it possible to give beauty a deep space (dermis and epidermis) and to persuade women that they are the product of a kind of germinative circuit in which the beauty of efflorescences depends on the nutrition of roots.
    Hence the notion of depth is a general one, present in every advertisement. As to the substances which infiltrate and convert within this depth, an utter blank; all we are told is that it is a matter of (vivifying, stimulating, nutritive) principles or (vital, revitalizing, regenerative) essences, a whole Molièresque vocabulary, updated perhaps by a touch of scientism (bactericide agent R-51). Now the real drama of all this little psychoanalysis of puffery is the conflict of two

warring substances which subtly oppose the advance of the "essences" and the "principles" toward the field of depth. These substances are water and grease.

Both are morally ambiguous: water is beneficent, for everyone can see that old skin is dry and that young skins are cool, pure (of a cool moistness, says one product); the firm, the smooth, all the positive values of fleshly substances are spontaneously perceived as made taut by water, swelled like a sheet on the line, established in that ideal state of purity, cleanness, and coolness to which water is the general key. In advertising terms, hydration of the depths is therefore a necessary operation . . .

Greasy substances have the inverse qualities and defects: they do not refresh; their softness is excessive, too durable, artificial; we cannot establish a beauty campaign on the pure idea of creams, whose very density is perceived as an unnatural state. Doubtless, grease (more poetically known as oil, as in the Bible or the Orient) contains a notion of nutrition, but it is safer to exalt it as a vehicular element, a euphoric lubricant, conducting water to the skin's depths. Water is posited as volatile, aerial, fugitive, ephemeral, precious; oil, on the contrary, holds fast, weighs down, slowly forces its way into surfaces, impregnates, slides down along the "pores" (characters essential to beauty advertising). Every advertising campaign of beauty products therefore prepares a miraculous conjunction of these enemy liquids henceforth complementary; diplomatically respecting all the positive values of the mythology of substances, this conjunction manages to impose the happy assurance that grease is conveyed by water, and that there exist certain creams, certain softnesses without luster.

Most of the new creams are therefore nominally liquid, fluid, ultra-penetrating, etc.; the notion of grease, for so long consubstantial with the very idea of a beauty product, is masked or complicated, corrected by liquidity, and sometimes even vanishes, giving way to the fluid lotion, to the spiritual tonic, gloriously astringent if it is to combat the skin's waxiness, modestly special if, on the contrary, it is to nourish these voracious depths whose digestive phenomena are pitilessly exposed. The public opening of the body's interiority is moreover a general feature of the advertising of toilet products. "Decay is expelled (from the teeth, the skin, the blood, the breath)": France is having a great yen for cleanliness. (47–49)

Roland Barthes's *Mythologies* was only one aspect of the influence exerted by Saussurian linguistics in France. More generally Barthes's work can be perceived as part of a wider intellectual trend that was influenced by Saussure and was replacing existentialism as the dominant mode of thought in France at the time: structuralism. Where existentialism had developed in times of war, crisis, and penury, structuralism began to develop as a mode of thought and inquiry in the mid-1950s as France was already experiencing the effects of a decade of economic recovery and growth. Where existentialism, in spite of its dismantling of objectivity and metaphysics, had kept individual human agency as a force to be contended with—man is "condemned to be free" but he can also choose to act or not, to become engaged in history and make a difference—structuralism proposed that human life was ultimately conditioned and determined by "deep structures" independent of man's will. These objective structures are not affected by historical conditions but, instead, function according to their relations with each other, like the signs in Saussurian linguistics. Albert Camus, who had developed the notion of the absurd in his essay *The Myth of Sisyphus* and in his novel *The Stranger*, both published in 1942 (see chapter 6), was not thinking of structuralism when he made the following declaration in an interview in the journal *Demain* in the aftermath of the 1956 Soviet invasion of Hungary. His words, however, certainly reflect the stark opposition between the room for conscious choice in existentialism, and structuralism's application of the basic Saussurian proposition that "the sign is arbitrary": "A newspaper or a book is not true because it is revolutionary. It has a chance of being revolutionary only if it tries to tell the truth. We have the right to think that the truth with a capital letter is relative. But facts are facts. And whoever says that the sky is blue when it is gray is prostituting words and preparing the way for tyranny" (quoted in Stovall, 116).

Camus was leveling his criticism at the Stalinist Left in France, which continued to side with Moscow even after Soviet troops had invaded Hungary. Today, when the notion of "objective facts" unencumbered by either language, ideology, or history has been thoroughly undermined, his comment may appear somewhat naive, but can serve to point out the essentially "unengaged" aspect of structuralism. The purpose of the intellectual or the scholar in the structuralist mode can indeed be perceived as an analysis of "deep structures" and their combinations in order to better understand human behavior and institutions rather than to challenge them or to have a direct, political effect on them.

If Roland Barthes's *Mythologies* can be considered a kind of ethnography of French modernization that applies the structuralist method to petit-bourgeois "myths," Claude Lévi-Strauss' *Structural Anthropology* (1958) is an analysis of myths in general, in particular those of North and South American Indians. Lévi-Strauss' wide-ranging study of these myths led him to the conclusion that "all myths belong to a basic set and each individual articulation of any specific myth [is] a subset or a rearrangement of the elements found in the main set" (quoted in Cook, 24). Like Saussure before him, Lévi-Strauss emphasized that the crucial factor is not the elements themselves but the way in which they are combined.

This emphasis on abstract and supposedly objective structures that seemed beyond the ken of individual human agency led to the perception of structuralism as a deeply antihumanist mode of thought and intellectual inquiry. This was held to be true not only of structural anthropology but of other fields as well, including psychoanalysis, a discipline whose best-known French practitioner, Jacques Lacan, wrote in his *Ecrits* (1966) about "Freud's discovery that the true center of the human being is no longer in the same place assigned to it by a whole humanist tradition" (401). The same relinquishing of the individual subject and the search for new ways of thinking is also evident in the other "intellectual bestseller" of 1966, Michel Foucault's *The Order of Things*. In this work, Foucault writes: "It is no longer possible to think in our day other than in the void left by man's disappearance. For this void does not create a deficiency; it does not constitute a lacuna that must be filled. It is nothing more, and nothing less, than the unfolding of a space in which it is once more possible to think" (342).

"Man," at least as active historical agent, thus seemed to recede and even to disappear in these years where the urgencies of the immediate postwar period had been replaced by the relative opulence of a society more attentive to its material well-being than to specifically political concerns. However, the Marxist heritage of both Foucault and Barthes also displayed an other aspect of modes of thought perhaps too quickly and monolithically subsumed under the label of an abstract and antihumanist structuralism.

Barthes's will to go beyond "empty denunciation" and to actively dismantle the system of petit-bourgeois myths, and Foucault's subsequent involvement in specific political causes such as the *Groupe d'information sur les prisons* (Prison Information Group) in the early 1970s, and his active participation in the homosexual movement in France, which was beginning to gain momentum during the same period, reflect their engagement beyond purely textual practices. In response to the photo exhibit "The Family of Man," for example, in which it is proposed that under the relatively superficial layers of human institutions and the color of their skins, all men are the same, Barthes writes: "Why not ask the parents of Emmet Till, the young negro murdered by whites what *they* think of 'the family of man' " (*Mythologies*, 175).

Others, most prominently Louis Althusser, who taught philosophy at the Ecole normale supérieure, used the tools of structuralism to proceed with a rereading of Marx in order to "distinguish what belongs to ideology on the one hand and to science on the other" (Loyer and Goetschel, 140). This project is contained in essentially two works published in 1965: the collective *Lire le Capital* (*Reading the Capital*, written with a number of philosophers who would later make their personal mark, among them Etienne Balibar and Jacques Rancière) and *Pour Marx* (*For Marx*).

Whether those who were labeled "structuralists" were, by very virtue of their approach and methods of inquiry, less politically engaged than the existentialist generation represented by the still very much active Sartre—who would die in 1981, the year of the Socialist electoral victory—it remains that they came to prominence at a time when the favorable economic situation and the end of war, at least on French soil, "freed" them to a certain extent from the type of direct engagement unavoidable for a member of the Resistance, a soldier on the battlefield, indeed of any civilian in times of war, occupation, or devastation. It must be noted, however, that anticolonialist struggles would provide an arena for engagement that would continue to attract a number of intellectuals.

Politically committed or not structuralism certainly represented the displacement of a system of thought, existentialism, that was increasingly perceived as belonging to another era both in its content and in its form.

The *Nouveau théâtre* had begun earlier to explore new ways of representing the human condition that were startling when compared to the more traditional techniques of existential theater (see chapter 6). The *nouveau roman* or "new novel" of the 1950s and 1960s continued in this direction. The term *nouveau roman*, which appeared in a a magazine article in 1957, came to designate a number of novelists who were being published by Jérôme Lindon's publishing house, Les Editions de Minuit, including Alain Robbe-Grillet, Michel Butor, and Samuel Beckett, who was also associated with the *nouveau théâtre*. Although the the "new novelists" did not constitute a "movement" or a "school," their work reflected a subversion of the conventions of the nineteenth-century realist novel represented by Honoré de Balzac: plot- and psychology-oriented, providing narrative certainty, and organized around a central hero. Robbe-Grillet in particular became the theoretician of the *nouveau roman*. In a series of essays gathered under the title *Pour un nouveau roman* (*For a New Novel*) published in 1963, he was already referring, in different terms, to the "void left by the disappearance of man" announced three years later in Foucault's *The Order of Things*. Here, Robbe-Grillet insists on the fact that the traditional novel has become inadequate in a changed world:

> Our world, today, is less sure of itself, more modest, perhaps, since it has renounced
> the omnipotence of the person, but more ambitious too, since it looks beyond. The
> exclusive cult of the "human" has given way to a larger consciousness, one that is less
> anthropocentric. The novel seems to stagger, having lost its best prop, the hero. If it
> does not manage to right itself, it is because its life was linked to that of a society now
> past. (29)

In the same collection of essays, Robbe-Grillet took existentialism directly to
task and proposed that "'socialist realism' or Sartrean 'engagement' are difficult to
reconcile with the problematic exercise of literature, as with that of any art" (8).
Robbe-Grillet's choice of both existentialism and socialist realism as targets was
revealing: at a time when the cold war was being waged and existentialism had
become the dominant ideology in France, he proposed that, in the realm of literature, both were outdated approaches in a new era. This new era was, precisely, the
era of consumer culture. Like structuralism, the new novel emerged at a time when
improvements in material conditions resulting from rapid economic growth had
become tangible in France. In the absence of war and occupation, writers, intellectuals, and artists could turn their attention in other directions. We can see in the
following declaration the affinities between Robbe-Grillet's apology for a new
novel and the basic tenets of structuralism; structure and form take precedence
over particular situations or individual psychology and agency: "The novel of
characters belongs entirely to the past, it describes a period: that which marked the
apogee of the individual. Perhaps this is not an advance, but it is evident that the
present period is one of administrative numbers. The world's destiny has ceased,
for us, to be identified with the rise and fall of certain men, of certain families"
(11). Rather than a dramatic chronicle of readily identifiable historical and social
contexts, the new novel is presented by Robbe-Grillet as an exploration of form
and structure, of the process of writing itself rather than writing's capacity to realistically reproduce a given reality that would preexist it. In this at least the new
novel was in agreement with existentialism: reality did not preexist man, but took
shape through his perception, subjectively, and in the absence of any overarching
system. As Roland Barthes, one of the early champions of the new novel, wrote in
an essay entitled "Objective Literature: Alain Robbe-Grillet":

> The novel becomes man's direct experience of what surrounds him without his being
> able to shield himself with a psychology, a metaphysic, or a psychoanalytic method in
> his struggle with the objective world he discovers. The novel is no longer a chtho-
> nian revelation, the book of hell, but of the earth—requiring that we no longer look
> at the world with the eyes of a confessor or a doctor, or of God himself (all signifi-
> cant hypostases of the classical novelist), but with the eyes of a man walking in his city
> with no other horizon than the scene before him, no other power than that of his
> own eyes. (11)

The use of the word "objective" in this citation is not to be confused with the existence of an unchanging, removed reality but, on the contrary, with a world in
which there is no such certainty. In the new novel, the narrative breaks—rather

than continuity and classic dramatic structure—the meticulous, even obsessive description of objects—rather than psychological depth or symbolism—are ways for the new novel to depict an uncertain, subjective world. The themes as well as the techniques of the traditional novel are subverted in the process.

Dossier 8.3   Michel Butor, *La modification* (*A Change of Heart*) (1957)

In 1957, Butor's *La modification* won a major literary prize, the Prix Renaudot, reflecting the *nouveau roman*'s success on the literary scene. It is the account of a man's train journey from Paris to Rome, from the city where his wife and family live, to the city where he plans to announce to his mistress that he is leaving them. The substance of the work is not to be found in this rather banal situation but in the way in which it is represented. The narration occurs in the second person plural, the usual polite form of address in French, as if we, in a transposed configuration of the protagonist, rather than any omniscient or God-like narrator-author, were recounting the events. In the late 1950s, as investments in heavy industry and infrastructure were beginning to be complemented by consumer goods, it was fitting that the "you" of the novel is a businessman who works for an international typewriter company. In this "age of administrative numbers" the new novel's depiction of objects is divested of the formerly symbolic quality they had in the realist, psychological novel. The world of *La modification*, as Robbe-Grillet describes the world of the new novel in general, "is neither significant nor absurd. It *is*, quite simply . . . In this future universe of the novel, gestures and objects will be *there* before being something . . . Henceforth, on the contrary, objects will gradually lose their instability and their secrets, will renounce their pseudo-mystery, that suspect interiority which Roland Barthes has called 'the romantic heart of things.' No longer will objects be merely the vague reflection of the hero's vague soul, the image of his torments, the shadow of his desire" (19–21; emphasis in original). Objects that are simply *there*, and a perspective that is limited by the narrator's own subjectivity are at the heart of Butor's novel.

This excerpt is the opening of *La modification*.

Standing with your left foot on the grooved brass sill, you try in vain with your right shoulder to push the sliding door a little wider open.

You edge your way in through the narrow opening, then you lift up your suitcase of bottle-green grained leather, the smallish suitcase of a man used to making long journeys, grasping the sticky handle with fingers that are hot from having carried even so light a weight so far, and you feel the muscles and tendons tense not only in your finger joints, the palm of your hand, your wrist and your arm, but in your shoulder too, all down one side of your back, along your vertebrae from neck to loins.

No, it's not merely the comparative earliness of the hour that makes you feel so unusually feeble, it's age, already trying to convince you of its domination over your body, although you have only just passed your forty-fifth birthday.

Your eyes are half closed and blurred with a faint haze, your eyelids tender and stiff, the skin over your temples drawn and puckered, your hair, which is growing thinner and grayer, imperceptibly to others but not to you, not to Henriette or Cécile or, nowadays, to the children, is somewhat disheveled, and your whole body feels ill at ease, constricted and weighed down by your clothes, and seems, in its half-awakened state, to be steeped in some frothing water full of suspended animalcula.

You have chosen this compartment because the corner seat facing the engine and next to the corridor is vacant, the very seat you would have got Marnal to reserve for you if there had still been time, not the seat you would have asked for yourself since nobody at Scabelli's must know that it's to Rome you are escaping for these few days.

A man on your right, his face level with your elbow, sitting opposite that place where you are going to settle down for this journey, a little younger than you, not over forty, taller than you, pale, with hair grayer than yours, with eyes blinking behind powerful lenses, with long restless hands, nails bitten and tobacco-stained, fingers crossing and uncrossing nervously as he waits impatiently for the train to start, the owner, in all probability, of that black briefcase crammed with files, a few colored corners of which you notice peeping through a burst seam, and of the bound and probably boring books stacked above him like an emblem, like a legend whose explanatory or enigmatic character is not lessened by its being a thing, nor a mere word but a possession, lying on that square-holed metal rack and propped up against that partition next to the corridor.

This man stares at you, irritated at your standing motionless and with your feet in the way of his feet; he would like to ask you to sit down, but his timid lips cannot even frame the words, and he turns toward the window, pushing aside with his forefinger the lowered blue shade with its woven initials SNCF.

On the same seat as this man, next to a place at present vacant but which someone has reserved with that long umbrella in its black silk sheath stretched against the green oilcloth, beneath that green attaché case in its waterproof tartan cover, with its two gleaming locks of thin brass, a fair young man who must just have finished his military service, dressed in light-gray tweed, with a diagonally striped red-and-purple tie, holds in his right hand the left hand of a young woman, darker than himself, and plays with it, passing his thumb to and fro across her palm while she watches him contentedly, raising her eyes for a moment to look at you and dropping them quickly when he sees you watching him, but without stopping his play.

They are not merely lovers but a young married couple, since they are each wearing a new gold ring, on their honeymoon perhaps, and they must have bought for the occasion, or else have been given by a generous uncle, those two big, identical pigskin cases, brand-new, one on top of the other above their heads, with little leather labels fixed to the handles with tiny straps.

They are the only ones to have reserved their seats in this compartment; their brown and yellow tickets, with big black numbers on them, hang motionless from the nickel-plated rail. (1–3)

The will to subvert prior forms and themes and to explore new means of analysis and expression evident in structuralism in the social sciences and the New Novel in literature was at work in the output of the new generation of directors whose films began to appear as the 1950s ended. They became known as the *Nouvelle vague*, the "New Wave," a term coined by Françoise Giroud in an article in *L'Express*. For the new novelists, the nineteenth-century author Balzac became the symbol of everything that was inadequate about classic literature; for the filmmakers of the New Wave, the old forms were subsumed under the label *le cinéma de papa*, "daddy's cinema," or *le cinéma de qualité*, "quality cinema." The derisively and ironically applied labels appeared in an article written by François Truffaut in the newly founded film journal *Cahiers du cinéma (Film Notebooks)* founded by André Bazin and Jacques Doniol-Valcroze in 1951. In this influential article *Une certaine tendance du cinéma français* (A Certain Tendency in French Cinema), which appeared in 1954, Truffaut denounced a type of studio filmmaking that relied heavily on plot and dialogue, often based on classics of French literature such as Claude Autant-Lara's *Devil in the Flesh* (1946), an adaptation of Raymond Radiguet's novel; Jean Delannoy's *La symphonie pastorale* (1946), from a novel by André Gide the grand old man of French literature at the time, or adaptations of popular thrillers such as Henri-Georges Clouzot's *Les Diaboliques* (1955) based on Pierre Boileau and Thomas Narcejac's *Celle qui n'était plus* (1952). "The key figure in this literary/theatrical cinema was the scriptwriter, the director being merely the 'gentleman who added the pictures'" (Cook, 529). By the time Truffaut's influential article appeared, the *Cahiers du cinéma* had become the rallying point for a number of young critics who would later begin to make their own films, among them Jean-Luc Godard, Claude Chabrol, and Truffaut himself.

The generation represented by the "*Cahiers* group" had at least one thing in common with the practitioners of the new novel: they were also critics and theorists of their own medium, which no doubt contributed to the self-reflexive quality of many of their films. Film for the New Wave filmmakers was not only a means of faithful and realistic adaptation of a script but also a way of exploring the medium *as a medium*. Fundamental to the New Wave ethos was the concept of the *caméra-stylo* (the pen—camera) that would enable cinema "to become a means of expression as supple and subtle as that of written language," as Alexandre Astruc wrote in his influential article published in *L'Ecran français* in 1948 (Cook, 528). Indeed it was a medium with which they were thoroughly acquainted, having grown up watching movies in the postwar years, especially at the *Cinémathèque Française* (the French Film Archives) in Paris, an extensive film collection and a public movie house founded by Henri Langlois in 1936, in the days of the Popular Front. The Cinémathèque gave easy access to the future directors of the New Wave to what was essentially the history of world cinema: from early classics by D.W. Griffith and Abel Gance to the American directors of the 1940s whose work had been banned during the German occupation. As they flooded the French market in the postwar period, Hollywood production and especially the American "B" films, mostly Westerns and thrillers, became a major focus of the *Cahier* group's theoretical output. They argued that in spite of the banal and violent subject matter of these films, their directors, who worked in Hollywood's studio system and assembly-line approach to filmmaking, nevertheless managed to leave their imprint or "signature" on their films. This affirmation of personal artistic expression in a body of films is one of the basic tenets of the New Wave and became known as the *politique des auteurs* or "policy of authors," later translated as "auteur theory" by the American film critic Andrew Sarris. This insistence on the director's idiosyncrasies reflects the crucial place of style and form over story in the New Wave approach, an insistence on technique and mood rather than on plot-driven narrative.

Although they were preceded by a number of shorts and by what is generally acknowledged to be the first feature-length films of the New Wave—Agnès Varda's *La Pointe Courte* (*The Short Tip*, 1955) and Claude Chabrol's *Le Beau Serge* (*Handsome Serge*, 1958)—the best known and in many ways the most representative films of the New Wave came out in 1959 and 1960: François Truffaut's *Les Quatre-cents coups* (*The 400 Blows*) and Jean-Luc Godard's *A bout de souffle* (*Breathless*). Truffaut's first feature begins in a classroom where we meet Antoine Doinel, the film's adolescent protagonist, and then follow him around Paris as he copes with school, friends, family, and the difficulties of growing up. The movie sets have disappeared along with the very literary dialogue of the *cinéma de papa*, and Truffaut's camera moves around the streets of Paris, the school, the cramped apartment of Antoine's parents, ends with one of the most celebrated sequences and final shots in film history. Antoine's difficulties with authority and institutions, ranging from family to school and the police, have landed him in reform school. In the film's final minutes we see him, in a long shot, running from the school grounds, and winding up at the sea, which he gazes upon for the first time as the film ends with a freeze frame close-up of his face. *The 400 Blows* won "Best Director" at the Cannes Film Festival that year as well as the New York Critics award for Best Foreign Language Film. The New Wave was definitely on the map.

The success of Godard's *Breathless* would also contribute to the sudden fame of the New Wave. Shot in four weeks for less than 90,000 dollars, it "contained virtually every major technical characteristic of the New Wave film . . . the use of shaky hand-held 35 mm camera shots, location shooting, natural lighting, improvised plot and dialogue, and direct sound recording on location with portable tape machines that were electronically synchronized with the camera" (Cook, 533). All of these characteristics together gave Godard's first feature an immediacy and freshness that it retains to this day. Michel Poicard, the protagonist of *Breathless*, like the *Four Hundred Blows'* Antoine Doinel, does not "fit in" and is always in trouble of some sort. In a scene that features the famed "jump cuts" of the New Wave, Michel shoots a motor-cycle cop who had been pursuing the stolen car he was driving. In jump cuts, the traditional realistic effect is eliminated as a segment of a continuous shot is cut out and the two remaining "ends" are spliced together, creating a "jumping" effect caused by the absence of continuity. In a series of rapid, apparently isolated shots, we see Michel bending to open his car's glove compartment to retrieve a pistol, we hear the off-screen cop's command to stop, we see close-up of the firing gun, the cop falling backward into bushes, Michel running across a field and then arriving in Paris, having hitched a ride. The whole sequence occurs over a few seconds, with the viewers almost completely disoriented, but very much aware that they are watching a film. Godard, the New Wave director, displayed his own, self-reflexive mastery of the medium.

The film's self-reflexive quality is created by elements such as the jump cut, which take the viewers out of the passive comfort of a smoothly told story, or by characters speaking to the audience, looking straight into the camera. This aspect of *Breathless* is also emphasized by an elaborate system of tongue-in-cheek quotations of earlier films and homage to other directors and genres. Even as the credits appear we are informed that *Breathless* is dedicated to Monogram pictures, an American studio that produced many of Hollywood's "B" films; Michel adopts some of the mannerisms of Humprey Bogart, the iconic actor of the American gangster and *noir* films of the 1940s and 1950s; like the director Alfred Hitchcock, one of the New Wave's heroes, Godard makes a very brief cameo appearance and, in true *film noir* form, Michel is ultimately betrayed by the girl he loves, played by American actress Jean Seberg. The American student played by Seberg, the ubiquitous appearance of Bogart, as a model admired and imi-tated by the film's lead character or as the subject of a movie poster, the big American cars and the film's jazz soundtrack all underscore the extent of the presence of things

Figure 8.1   Jean-Luc Godard, *Breathless* (1959)

The actors Jean-Paul Belmondo and Jean Seberg during the filming of *Breathless*; Godard (wearing sunglasses) can be seen in the background following them as they walk up the Champs Elysées. The streets of Paris have replaced the elaborate sets of "daddy's cinema." (© AFP/Getty Images)

American in France in the 1950s. They reflect more generally the simultaneous denunciation and appropriation of American culture in France at a time when modernization and commercial cinema had recently become synonymous with the United States.

In *Contempt* (1963), a film he made four years later, Godard addressed more directly the issue of American cultural influence. Jack Palance, the American actor who had appeared in many gangster films and Westerns plays a brash and cynical Hollywood producer who does not care at all for art films (of the sort being made by the New Wave directors) and has hired a French scriptwriter to commercialize the script of a film to be made from Homer's *Odyssey*. The director is German expatriate to Hollywood Fritz Lang, a director from "old Europe" who had migrated to the United States. On one side, we have the European tradition present in a genealogy that ranges from Homer to the French scriptwriter and the German director; on the other, the materialistic American in his red sports car. The scriptwriter's wife is played by the rising star of the period, Brigitte Bardot. Her contempt for her husband slowly reveals itself, leading to the couple's breakup. The pressure to make money while creating significant works of art is at the core of the film and reflects the more general encounter between France's traditional bourgeois European culture and the mass consumerism being championed and spread by the American presence in postwar Europe. Godard continued to address this issue in increasingly political films in which America is not directly targeted but where the spreading commercialization and commodification of culture and of life in general are denounced. Godard's work displays the paradox of America in France: the source of a vibrant, innovative cinema, and a means of subverting the traditional *cinéma de papa*, but also the emblem of the scorned capitalist modernization model in films such as Godard's *La Chinoise* and *Weekend*, both made in 1967, during the Vietnam war.

Other members of the New Wave like Chabrol and Truffaut took different, more commercial or lyrical paths. Truffaut, for example, continued to chronicle the life of the *Four Hundred Blows'* Antoine Doinel into adulthood. This diverging of paths is what led some critics to situate the "demise of the New Wave as early as 1963," the year of Godard's *Contempt* (Powrie and Reader, 27).

The New Wave, as a cohesive group or not, appeared on the scene as cinema began to be claimed as a form of autonomous culture by the generation that came of age in the 1950s and 1960s. As it was for Sylvie and Jérôme, the protagonists of Perec's *Les choses*, for many of the young people of the time, cinema became their *dada*, their "thing" in opposition to a form of culture that had been derided as "daddy's cinema." As we have seen with the New Wave, American movies could play a crucial role in the subversion of traditional French cinema. Hollywood and youth culture thus appeared as mutually reinforcing discourses that went against the grain of a specifically French cultural production. This can be extended to include other areas such as music where the traditional French *chanson* was being challenged by a new generation of singers with American-sounding names like Johnny Hallyday, Dick Rivers, Lucky Blondo, Sheila, and Eddy Mitchell, among others. The *chanson* or "song," whose best-known practitioners of earlier generations include Maurice Chevalier, Charles Trenet, and Edith Piaf and, later, Yves Montand and Jacques Brel, is a typically French genre. As journalist Marcelle Clement defines it, "The French chanson is a tricky cultural artifact. Its text predominates and its images can arouse intense emotion in both singer and audience. A great chanson evokes a powerful melancholy that can make listeners experience longing and consolation, often simultaneously" (1). Edith Piaf's *Je ne regrette rien* and Jacques Brel's *Ne me quitte pas* (translated by the American poet Rod McKuen as "If You Go Away") are two of the most famous examples of the genre. To a generation of young French people of the late 1950s and early 1960s, the *chansoniers*, or practitioners of the traditional *chanson*, were also becoming representative of tradition, a tradition that these young people were in the process of contesting. The images and sounds coming from the United States represented a new type of music and were claimed or reworked as their own, as signaled by the new American-sounding names of their new "idols."

Dossier 8.4   Figure 8.2 Brigitte Bardot in Roger Vadim's Film *And God Created Woman* (1956) (©Hachette Photo Presse)

Brigitte Bardot, the "sex kitten" of the 1950s and beyond became not only a major film star but also embodied a first wave of sexual liberation that prefigured the

Figure 8.2 Brigitte Bardot in Roger Vadim's Film *And God Created Woman* (1956) (© Hachette Photo Presse)

more subversive and extensive challenge to tradition and authority of the late 1960s. There is no essay in Roland Barthes's *Mythologies* devoted to "BB." However, what Barthes and Simone de Beauvoir write about cars and Bardot respectively is indicative of the way in which the 1950s were indeed an era in which modernization was not only a material improvement in lifestyle, but also a great source of "myths." About the new DS Citroën, Barthes writes: "I believe that the car is today the more or less exact equivalent of the great gothic cathedrals: I mean the large creation of an era, passionately conceived by unknown artists, consumed through its image if not its usage, by a whole people that, through it, appropriates a perfectly magical object. The new Citroën manifestly falls from the sky to the extent that it presents itself first of all as a superlative *object*" (150). In *Brigitte Bardot and the Lolita syndrome* (1959), Simone de Beauvoir ironically underlines the link between the "BB myth" and merchandise. The new symbol of French cinema becomes an export product, like the traditional wines and cheeses, fashion and perfumes—products more congruent with a certain view of France as repository of "good food and high fashion"—and the new cars being sold abroad by France's car industry: "When *And God Created Woman* was shown in first-run houses on the Champs Elysées, the film, which had cost 140 million francs, brought in less than sixty. Receipts in the USA have come to $4,000,000 the equivalent of the sale of 2500 Dauphines [a new model launched by Renault in 1956, the same year *And God Created Woman* came out]. BB now deserves to be considered an export product as important as Renault automobiles (6)". As Rioux and Sirinelli summarize it, *And God Created Woman* "gives birth to the Brigitte Bardot myth" (258).

James Dean, the star of *Rebel without a Cause* (1955) became a figure of reference for the star of the then-shocking *And God Created Women* as well as for some of those new young singers with their American-sounding stage names. As Simone de Beauvoir wrote,

> Brigitte Bardot "professes great admiration for James Dean. We found in her, in a milder form, certain traits that attain, in his case, a tragic intensity—the fever of living [the French title of the film *Rebel without a Cause*], the sense of the imminence of death. She, too, embodies—more modestly than he, but quite clearly—the credo that certain young people of our time are opposing to safe values, vain hopes and irksome constraint. (18)

Johnny Hallyday, *né* Jean-Philippe Smet in Belgium, with his leather jacket, T-shirt, and his flamboyant rejection of what could be called the "daddy's music" of the *chanson* for the simpler, less "written" lyrics and the syncopated beat of Elvis Presley and Chuck Berry, also "professed admiration" for James Dean. "Johnny" was one of the most successful performers of the new music that would become known as *musique yé yé* and that would, for a while at least, and among young people, overshadow an older generation of crooners, such as Charles Aznavour and Gilbert Bécaud or *chansonniers*, such as Léo Ferré and Georges Brassens. The origin of the *yé yé* label varies among cultural historians: a French adaptation of the "yeah, yeah, yeah" from the Beatles' 1963 hit "She Loves You," or a "yeah" derived earlier from the lyrics of late 1950s American blues or rock and roll singers." Mass communication (press, radio, TV cinema)," writes Edgard Morin, "played an important role in the crystallization of this new age group" that was the audience for *musique yé yé*. The *yé yé* singers provided it with myths, heroes, and models to be imitated. At first, it was through the movies that the new heroes of adolescence emerged "around the exemplary image of James Dean," with (American rock music providing the continuation of the trend (Morin, *Le Monde*, 11).

The music was played on the recently marketed transistors and the smaller radio models in young people's bedrooms all over France, rather than on the family radio that had been the centerpiece of home entertainment throughout the postwar into the 1950s. It was also recorded on the new 45 rpm records that had replaced the old 78 format, and it was played endlessly on "pick-ups," the portable record players that had quickly flooded the youth market. The music was played on radio stations that were beyond the control of the French government since their antennas were outside French territory even if the main audience was within French borders: Radio Monte-Carlo, Radio Andorre, Radio Luxembourg, and Europe Numéro 1, whose producer Daniel Filipacchi created the enormously successful program directed at the new youth audience, *Salut les copains* (*Hello Buddies*), in 1959. Radio thus played a crucial role in the spread of this new youth culture symbolized by *yé yé* music, complete with its juvenile market of records, clothes—leather jackets and jeans most prominently—postcard-format photos of the "idols," fan clubs, specialized magazines, and so on.

Figure 8.3   Johnny Hallyday Rehearsing (1962)

The young singer's stage name (his real name was Jean-Philippe Smet), the jeans, the pom-padour hairstyle, and the name of the band, "The Golden Stars," attest to the American influence on the "Johnny phenomenon." (© Hachette Photo Presse)

Television also played a major role; as Susan Weiner writes about Johnny Hallyday,

> His songs written to the tunes of American hits were initially unpopular on the radio, for the Hallyday experience was above all a visual one. When Johnny first appeared on the show "L'Ecole des vedettes" in 1960 at the age of seventeen, clad in tight black leather pants, to sing "T'Aimer Follement," his French version of Elvis Presley's "Makin' Love," he became notorious overnight. Public opinion was divided, and the division ran along the lines of generations. Parents were horrified; teenagers were thrilled. (146)

A new phenomenon, the mass concert–rally, also made its appearance in the early 1960s, most famously the June 1963 concert organized by the teen magazine,

Le Temps des Copains (The Time of Buddies) that gathered 150,000 fans who had come to see their "idols" perform.

As was the case for the New Wave, an American trend had been appropriated and represented in France, creating a counterdiscourse that combined elements from another culture with the newly configured youth culture of the period. However, even if it "horrified" parents, as Weiner writes, *yé yé* culture was far from being socially or politically subversive in any active sense. On the contrary, as Morin suggests, this aspect of youth culture is economically integrated to a "capitalist culture industry that functions according to the laws of the market. It is thus a branch of a system of production and distribution that functions for all of society, carrying in its wake material goods as well as spiritual products, putting forward the values of modernity, happiness, leisure, love, etc" ("Le temps des copains," 11). Yet, in the guise of youth culture it was the very idea of a homogeneous society sharing the same traditional values, the *République des bons élèves* (the republic of good students) (Rioux and Sirinelli, 275), which had prevailed throughout the postwar period and the 1950s, that was being challenged; the challenge was undeniable even if *yé yé* music and the *copains* audience remained essentially part and parcel of the capitalist modernization model. In a study entirely devoted to the "black leather jacket generation," published in 1962, Emile Copfermann comments on the links between youth culture, the entertainment industry, and a type of standardization that in today's terms would be referred to as the globalization of culture:

> The entertainment industry . . . begins by gratifying people's vague aspirations. On the basis of these it provokes artificial needs and then caters for them in abundance, thereby creating its own profits and, at the same time, producing a standardized effect. The youth of towns in Germany, Italy, England and France are all beginning to look the same. From their dress to their drinks—give or take a few details—they represent one anonymous mass! How many Brigitte Bardots and how many "Chaussettes Noires" [The "Chaussettes Noires" or "Black Sox" were an early French rock group whose lead singer was Eddy Mitchel]. (Quoted in Rigby, 166)

The *Salut les copains* concert of 1963 was not the massive strike of May 68 or the Woodstock "love in" of 1969, but the black leather- and jean-clad youth of *le temps des copains* would increasingly turn toward the more subversive garb of the hippie. As the 1960s wore on, youth culture gradually began to be a challenge to capitalist society and to the modernization model that had dominated since the end of World War II. Challenges to authority and to the universal republican discourse of the state concerned a wide spectrum of issues ranging from hairstyles and sexual attitudes to the very core of the modernization model and its very reason for being. In short, youth culture took on a radicalized and politicized edge. If the *yé yé* label originated in the early Beatles, the subsequent phase of youth culture was more in tune with "late Beatles"; the evolution is mapped out in the shift from Sheila's "wholesome hits" (Weiner, 148) such as *Ma première surprise-partie* (My first Party) to Lennon and McCartney's psychedelic "Lucy in the sky with diamonds," the acid rock of Jimmy Hendrix, or Bob Dylan and Joan Baez' s more politically subversive brand of protest songs.

Morin notes that, during that time, the " 'media' remain the same, but 'diverted' [détournés] from their previous function; the objective of the press, cinema, music, radio programs was no longer 'entertainment' [*divertissement*] and no longer partook of the euphoric mythology of pleasure and leisure: from then on, a quasi militant function was bound with this new type of participation" (174). The teenage sentimental crises that provided much of the material for the songs of the *yé yé* period were replaced by other, more political concerns; an ethics of refusal and criticism of the consumerist leisure society emerged.

The evolution from *yé yé* to a more radical phase of youth culture occurred against the background of de Gaulle's presidency and of his policy of grandeur. The aging general and his "certain idea of France," rooted in tradition and "greatness," and the young people who were finding new models and practices in the contemporary and the popular, represented diverging trends in the 1960s. After having extricated France from the Algerian quagmire, de Gaulle's objective was to restore the country's international prestige in a world dominated by the two superpowers, the United States and the Soviet Union. His insistence on developing an independent nuclear capacity—the *force de frappe*—, his 1963 veto of British membership, perceived as an American "Trojan Horse" in the European Economic Community, France's withdrawal from NATO in 1964, his criticism of American involvement in Vietnam, his policy of support for and rapprochement with a nonaligned third world, and his acclamation of the separatists during a state visit in Canada in 1967, with his notorious phrase *Vive le Québec libre!* (Long Live Free Québec!), were all attempts at affirming France's identity and autonomy. They were sometimes merely symbolic initiatives but served an ulterior motive: the creation of a sense of national pride and grandeur around a number of themes and issues. De Gaulle's policy of grandeur was also an attempt to counter some of the effects of the modernization process in which France was engaged: cultural standardization along the model set by the United States, and consumerist attitudes that went against the grain of civic, republican ethos, among other trends. De Gaulle saw French culture itself as a means of maintaining "a certain idea of France" alive in a world where, politically, France was no longer dominant. The founding of a Ministry of Culture, to be headed by his friend, the novelist and critic André Malraux, "sprang from de Gaulle's determination to restore his country's international prestige, and his perception of the role culture could play in achieving this aim. He recognized both that culture was a crucial component of French national identity, and that it was an important asset in establishing France as a country of world rank" (Forbes and Kelly, 151). The very formulation of the new Ministry of Culture's mission statement reflected the grandiose scope of its objectives:

> The objective of the Ministry responsible for Cultural Affairs is to make available the major works of art of humanity, and particularly of France, to the greatest possible number of French people, to ensure the widest possible audience for our cultural heritage, and to promote the creation of works of art and of the mind that can enrich it.

The mission statement was quite clear: the goal was not to redefine the idea of culture itself, but to make "a certain idea" of culture available, the culture constituted by "major works of art" and France's "cultural heritage." In other words, the mission was to extend culture to more people, not to change it. The objective was "to do for culture what Jules Ferry had done for education" (270). Rioux and Sirinelli's comparison with the Third Republic is telling: culture in de Gaulle and Malraux's view would serve as a kind of republican cement by providing a window to the nation's glorious artistic tradition. Just as Jules Ferry's *instituteurs* or teachers were dispatched throughout France to instill the universalist republican ethos and "turn peasants into Frenchmen" (see chapter 2), the new ministry founded *maisons de la culture* (cultural centers) throughout the provinces in order to bring the people into the national fold. Eight *maisons* were established and they were to include theater, cinema, music, painting, sculpture, as well as spaces for lectures and exhibitions. The *maisons* were not as successful as de Gaulle and Malraux had hoped, and the reasons for their relative failure can be traced to a number of factors. On a practical level, the financing of their activities was not adequate to their mission. In addition, this mission, with its focus on high culture, left out popular culture and entertainment at a time when, precisely, they were invading the cultural landscape. Malraux himself "was vehement in his criticism of the mass culture purveyed by cinema and television, since he saw it as appealing only to the basest aspects of humanity" (Rigby, 133). As a result, the audience that constituted the primary target of the democratization of culture à la Jules Ferry was essentially left out of the process. Malraux's declaration, "In ten years, this hideous word 'provincial' will have ceased to exist," also reflects the cultural suppositions behind the Ministry of Culture's "civilizing mission" in the French hinterlands. Paris clearly remained the central purveyor of cultural production, even if cultural decentralization was the official order of the day. On the whole, the attempt to use high culture and the French national heritage in a centralizing and unifying policy ran counter to the cultural trends of the period when "the consumer society had pulled to pieces many of the assumptions behind pop culture . . . [and] television, records, pop radio stations and the other media of the consumerist age all highlighted culture as pluralistic rather than as unitary, popular rather than elitist, and diverse rather than canonical" (Jones, 301–302). As young people were flocking to see their "idols" perform in mass concerts, as the New Wave was dethroning "daddy's cinema," the *maisons de la culture* stood out like "cultural cathedrals," as they were often referred to at the time. It was not so much that these cultural centers failed, but that they were not flexible enough to extend their reach beyond a conception of culture as a monumentalized, even sacred phenomenon. Malraux's own concept of culture was deeply mystical and he perceived it as filling the void left by the decline of religion in modern times. Culture was what people would come to when freed from the vicissitudes of their daily lives.

To the challenges of modernization and the fragmentation and, in their eyes, the debasement of culture, de Gaulle and Malraux offered a redemptive, humanist, and universalist vision. A critical shortcoming of this vision was its neglect of the particularities of popular culture and, more generally, of daily life. These are the aspects of culture, in a wider acceptance of the word, that were being theorized by the French sociologist Henri Lefebvre under the heading of *la vie quotidienne* (everyday life). As early as the 1940s, Lefebvre began to delineate the tensions that would lead to the explosion of May 68. In his masterwork *The Critique of Everyday Life*—three volumes published in 1947, 1961, and 1981—Lefebvre extends Marx's concept of the alienation of labor to encompass all aspects of daily life; he argues that it is not only the worker who is alienated from his work because of the exploitative organization of labor, but also human beings in general whose lives are emptied of meaning or relevance, which are then spuriously replaced by "spectacular commodities."

Lefebvre had an enormous influence on a group of thinkers and artists organized into the avant-gardist movement known as the "Situationist International" in 1957.

Lefebvre's notion of a daily life that was emptied of meaning in the midst of plenty resonated with this younger generation of intellectuals who had grown up during the thirty glorious years. The opening paragraph of Situationist Guy Debord's *La société du spectacle* (*The Society of the Spectacle*), published in 1967, is representative of the general critique of consumerism, and of the exploitation, alienation, and boredom with which it was associated by the Situationists:

> The whole life of those societies in which modern conditions of production prevail presents itself as an immense accumulation of *spectacles*. All that was once directly lived has become mere representation . . . The spectacle is not a collection of images; rather it is a social relationship between people that is mediated by images . . . Understood in its totality, the spectacle is both the result and the goal of the dominant mode of production. It is not something *added* to the real world—not a decorative element, so to speak. On the contrary, it is the very heart of society's real unreality. (12–13)

When *The Society of the Spectacle* came out in 1967, its relevance in the context of French modernization was clear. Decades later, a film like Andy and Larry Wachowsky's *The Matrix* (1999), with its depiction of a society totally controlled by computerized images, attests to the prophetic quality of Debord's book.

The Situationists drew from previous avant-gardes such as Dada and surrealism (see chapter 5) and proposed to do away with conventional forms of art and, further, to reintroduce in daily life itself the elements of spontaneity, imagination, and creativity, of a truly lived experience, to reintroduce a kind of energy and authenticity that had been drained from it by the new consumerist modes of behavior. This challenge to "the System," or to the "Matrix," was not limited to France and had already gathered momentum in other countries such as Japan and the United States. In his aptly titled *Traité du savoir-vivre à l'usage des jeunes generations* (*Treatise on Living for the Young Generation*), also published in 1967, another Situationist, Raoul Vaneigem, predicted that the revolution that had to result from this world situation was not far away (see dossier 8.5)

Dossier 8.5   Raoul Vaneigem, *Treatise on Living for the Use of the Young Generation* (1967) Excerpt from Chapter 25: "You're Fucking around With Us?—Not For Long!"

The subtitle of this section is "The Sans-Culottes' Address to the Convention, December 9, 1792," establishing a link between Vaneigem's propositions for the late 1960s and the Sans-Culottes' call for a radicalization of the French Revolution of 1789.

In Watts, Prague, Stockholm, Stanleyville, Gdansk, Turin, Port Talbot, Cleveland, Cordoba, Amsterdam, wherever the act and awareness of refusal generates passionate break-outs from the factories of collective illusion, the revolution of everyday life is under way. The struggle intensifies as misery becomes universal. What for years were reasons for fighting specific issues—hunger, restrictions, boredom, illness, anxiety, isolation, deceit—now reveal misery's fundamental rationality, its omnipresent emptiness, its appalling oppressive abstraction. For this misery, the world of hierarchical power, the world of the State, of sacrifice, exchange and the quantitative—the commodity as will and representation of the world—is held responsible by those moving towards an entirely new society that is still to be invented and yet is already among us. All over the globe, revolutionary praxis, like a photographic developer, is transforming negative into positive, lighting up the hidden face of the earth with the fires of rebellion to ink in the map of its triumph.

Existential conflicts are not qualitatively different from those inherent in the whole of mankind. That's why men can't hope to control the laws governing their general history if they can't simultaneously control their own individual histories. If you go for revolution and neglect your own self, then you're going about it backwards, like all the militants. Against voluntarism and the mystique of the historically inevitable revolution, we must spread the idea of a plan of attack, and a means, both rational and passionate, in which immediate subjective needs and objective contemporary conditions are dialectically united. In the dialectic of part and totality, the curved slope of revolution is the project to construct daily life in and through the struggle against the commodity form, so that each phase of the revolution is carried in the style of its final outcome. No maximum program, no minimum program, and no transitional program—instead a complete strategy based on the essential characteristics of the system we want destroyed. (Translated by John Fullerton and Paul Sieveking http://library.nothingness.org/articles/SI/en/display/216)

May 68 in France was thus not an isolated phenomenon. It took place in an international context of challenge to the international economic system that had emerged from World War II and to the types of societies this economic system had fashioned. The trappings of the consumer "society of the spectacle" were denounced for their alienating effects on the population of advanced industrialized societies. The international capitalist system itself that produced these societies was also denounced for its imperialist policies in the Third World. In the late 1960s much of this critique was directed at the American presence in Vietnam. The Soviet Union, too, was denounced for its repressive Stalinist policies, especially after the repression of the Hungarian uprising of 1956. Both countries increasingly came to be perceived as representing an outdated cold war bipolar system, and the French New Left looked for models of revolution elsewhere. These were found in personalities as varied as Che Guevara in Cuba, Ho Chi Minh in Vietnam, and Mao Zedong in China. Like Debord's and Vaneigem's anticapitalist treatises, Mao's *Little Red Book* was published in French in 1967; it was one of the founding texts of an emerging "Third Worldism" in French radical politics.

The state of the university system in France made it particularly receptive to the widespread challenge to the "Establishment" that was the order of the day in the late 1960s. The baby boomers had reached college age by the middle of the decade; between 1960 and 1968, the university population increased from 200,000 to over 500,000. On the eve of the student revolt the number of people attending college was about ten times what it had been twenty years earlier. To say that the classrooms and lecture halls were overcrowded is an understatement: many students routinely sat on the floor in hallways and could not even see the professor on his podium dispensing a lecture in the traditional *cours magistral* mode—nonstop lecture from a podium without any interaction between the professors and students. In addition, the education most of these students received, in the "classical, rationalist, and humanist cultural tradition" was "despite its continuing prestige, wholly inadequate to the contemporary world." The inadequacy of this education dispensed in the context of the university's "suffocating Napoleonic centralization" (Crozier, 114) and of diminishing prospects on the job market made the French university system fertile ground for throwing into question society as a whole. There was no autonomy because all universities reported directly to the Ministry of Education in Paris; yet, in spite of this centralization, the inequality of a system reputed to be based on democratic republican principles also added to the university population's anxiety and frustration. The university came only a distant second to the *grandes écoles* system that had been instituted by the French Revolution and consolidated under Napoleon. This system, access to which was sanctioned by entrance examinations, formed the elites of France, and its top graduates received the most prestigious positions in both the public and private sectors. What existed—and to a great extent continues to exist in France—was a de facto two-tier system that perpetuated inequalities. As Michel Crozier writes in his influential *La société bloquée* (*The Stalled Society*) published in 1970,

> These problems were common to all Western countries but no other country has organized social selection through the educational process so severely and so humiliatingly as France. No other society has squandered so much human potential so indifferently, nor sought to hide its conservatism behind such demagogic egalitarianism. This situation is what gave the student revolt its large social dimension and led to its making such a striking impact upon the conscience of France. (117)

In response to the massive increase in the student population, the government hastily built branches of the university system outside the big cities. The Nanterre campus, in the suburbs of Paris, built on an abandoned lot next to a slum where immigrants lived in terrible conditions, was where the events of May 68 would begin.

The international background to events that were seemingly confined to a suburban branch of the University of Paris was evident in the bombs that exploded on March 18 at the offices of the Bank of America and of TWA, two American companies in the French capital. These companies were considered to be outposts of the United States as both a bastion of capitalism and an imperialist power waging war against Vietnam. Two days later, student demonstrators, many from the Nanterre campus, shattered the windows of the American Express office in Paris. On March 22, a group of Nanterre students occupied the university's administration building. Led by a sociology student, Daniel Cohn-Bendit, they came to be known as the "Movement of March 22" and also as the *enragés*, a term originally applied to the Sans-Culottes of the French revolution in its 1793–1794 phase (a clear link between Vaneigem's *Traité* and the May 68 movement). They denounced the university as capitalism's tool to propagate its ideology by creating servants and watchdogs of the system. Very quickly the *enragés* of the March 22 movement were joined by a number of other groups, among them the Trotskyist *Jeunesse Communiste Révolutionaire* (Revolutionary Communist Youth), the Maoist *Union des Jeunesses Communistes* (Union of Communist Youth) and the *Comité Vietnam National*, the main antiwar student organization (Sowerwine, 347). All came together in a series of discussion groups. The *enragés* had created an atmosphere that would permeate May 68, one in which hierarchy and recognition of specialized places were, to a great extent, abolished: "The *enragés* of the Nanterre campus of the university of Paris who suddenly emerged around the figure of Daniel Cohn-Bendit effectively managed for at least a moment in the paroxysm of their revolt, to square the circle of direct democracy: they created a crowd in which individuals could express themselves, an action without organization, permanent spontaneity" (Crozier, 117). This was the kind of spontaneity and openness the Situationists had advocated in their work.

The student actions reflected widespread discontent with the rigid, stratified system that existed in the university. Beyond the confines of the educational system, these actions demonstrated that traditional, nineteenth-century modes of behavior had been made obsolete by the capitalist modernization model on which France had embarked. The objective of the *enragés*, and here we can see the influence not only of the Situationists but also of Mao and Trotsky, was not only university reform but the dismantling of capitalist society itself.

Facing the impossibility of continuing to operate the university without at least discussion and negotiation with the student groups, the administration chose to close its doors. In shutting down the Nanterre campus, the rector had hoped to defuse what he saw as localized student agitation. The decision had the opposite effect: rather than losing momentum, the movement was extended to Paris. On May 3, student militants occupied the courtyard of the Sorbonne, France's oldest and most prestigious university, in the heart of the Latin Quarter. There, the administrators immediately called in the police to remove the students. For many observers, this event signaled a major shift in the balance of power, the day when "everything fell apart as the Nanterre microcosm exploded into the crisis of May 68" (Bernstein, 215). Even at that point the government still thought it was dealing with "a few trouble makers" rather than with a generalized upheaval: the day before, de Gaulle's prime minister, Georges Pompidou had left with the minister of foreign affairs for a state visit to Iran.

The removal operation was performed with a certain amount of brutality. The police, especially the CRS, many of whom had been trained during the repressions of Algerian demonstrations, used teargas and bludgeoned the protesting students; they also extended their activity to the area around the Sorbonne in pursuit of retreating students. The students dislodged and heaved pavement stones; they erected barricades. Passersby, commuters coming out of the metro, and others sitting at cafés near the Sorbonne became the targets of the police and were even taken away in police wagons along with the students. One clear result of the Sorbonne operation was public sympathy for the student movement. After May 3 the movement continued to spread, becoming increasingly violent, up to the "night of the barricades," May 10–11, when cars were burned, storefronts were smashed, and hundreds of police and students were injured. Police brutality became a central issue as the students continued to gain support from the general public as well as the opposition parties. When Pompidou returned from Iran, the government responded to the mounting crisis by allowing the reopening of the Sorbonne. It was, however, too little and too late. The gesture appeared as a sign of weakness, giving additional impetus to the movement. May 13 proved to be a major turning point as the trade unions joined the fray by declaring a one-day strike in support of the students. In Paris, 800,000 people, including workers, students, and the public marched to the shouts of "Ten years of de Gaulle, that's enough!" The demonstration was accompanied by others throughout the country. The student movement had become a national crisis.

Figure 8.4   Paris, May 68

Protesting students and the *Compagnies républicaines de sécurités* (CRS) the riot control police, face off in the Latin Quarter. The police used tear gas and bludgeons while the students' weapon of choice were the *pavés*, or pavement stones they dislodged from the streets. (© Hachette Photo Presse)

The student discussion groups became veritable mass meetings where the *prise de parole* (taking the floor, speaking out) that, in academia, had been the privilege of the professor delivering his lecture, became possible for all in a generalized disruption of roles and a subversion of hierarchy at all levels. Beyond their dissatisfaction with their share of the benefits of the thirty glorious years, the workers demanded more active participation in the decisions affecting their labor. Sometimes going against the trade union leadership, especially the Communist-oriented CGT whose demands were restricted to classic "wage and benefits" packages, the rank and file went on strike throughout France. As Kristin Ross describes,

> New political practices were being invented . . . Thus came the return throughout the culture of May to what we could call a thematics of equality: overcoming the separation between manual and intellectual work, refusing professional or cultural qualification as a justification for social hierarchies and systems of political representation refusing all delegation, undermining specialization—in short, the violent disruption of assigned roles, places, or functions. By starting with a refusal of the roles or places predetermined by the social system, the May movement veered throughout its existence toward a critique of the social division of labor. (*May 68*, 78–79)

The movement came to include not only blue-collar workers and students but also a veritable cross-section of French society, ranging from employees at the

ORTF (National Radio and Television Office) protesting government control and censorship, to public servants and managers. The Cannes film festival closed down, bus and metro workers went on strike, high school students went on strike and even the soccer players occupying the offices of the national federation chanted "Soccer to the soccer players!" Other slogans of May 68, some shouted during demonstrations, some spread across posters being printed out most famously by the students of the Ecole des Beaux Arts in Paris, some in the shape of graffiti in the streets, reflected the simultaneously humorous, political and utopian quality of May 68:

> Boredom is counter-revolutionary!
> Barricades close the streets but open up the Way!
> They're buying your freedom. Steal it!
> It is forbidden to forbid!
> Take your desires for realities!
> Don't negotiate with the bosses. Get rid of them!
> Under the paving stones, the beach!

The very basis of bourgeois capitalist French society was being subverted, and what had originated as a localized student protest had ballooned into the largest strike in French history: 10 million people from all walks of life had joined and stopped work; by the third week of May France had come to a standstill.

Dossier 8.6   Louis Malle, *Milou en mai* (*May Fools*) (1990)

Thirty years later, the film director Louis Malle recounted the events of May 68 from the vantage point of an upper middle class family and assorted acquaintances and servants gathered for the funeral of the matriarch in the family home in southwestern France, far from the riots and the violence in Paris. One of the family members, Alain, is a student in Paris and has managed to join them by hitching a ride with a trucker. That evening, they sit down to dinner and Alain attempts to convey to them what is happening in the capital.

ALAIN: I'm talking about the students; they started it. It's really simple you know, they say they are sick of the wealthy, rich powerful nations, consumerists, the depletion of the earth. And they say, let's stop! It's so pointless! It's absurd! We're like rats, led to our deaths by the pied piper; we're just going to drown for sure. Let's just stop!
HIS FATHER: Stop? And then do what?
ALAIN: To talk things over, to try to imagine other things . . . You're far from Paris . . . everything is probably exaggerated for you. There's no way you'd know what's going on . . . Simply because it doesn't seem like anything that's ever happened before. This is completely new! People are just talking, freely, spontaneously!
FATHER: Spontaneous . . . yeah sure, with lots of committees, Marxists, Maoists, Situationists . . .

De Gaulle had left Paris for an official visit to Romania on May 14, the day after the mass student-worker demonstration in Paris. The president of the republic was thus showing his disdain or, differently interpreted, his inability or even refusal to understand the gravity of the situation. As Crozier puts it, "De Gaulle insisted on playing Richelieu and Louis XIV. The *enragés* of May 68 responded by acting out the great scenes of 1793 and 1848" (135). To those dates should be added 1871 and the Commune (see chapter 2), and 1936 and the Popular Front (see chapter 5). These dates and events of French history have in common with May 68 that they represent mass challenges to the universalist republican model; they point out its shortcomings and even injustices, and constitute its ruptures and exceptions.

Facing the deterioration of the situation de Gaulle wound up cutting short his visit and returned to France on May 18. His own lapidary pronouncement seemed a counter slogan: *La réforme oui, la chienlit non* (Reforms, yes, havoc no). He announced reforms in higher education and had his prime minister negotiate with the workers. More particularly, Pompidou negotiated with the CGT in an effort to limit the talks to classic worker demands, wages, and benefits, while bypassing the "qualitative" demands of the more progressive CFDT that involved issues concerning worker participation, comanagement, and internal transformations of labor relations in general. The negotiations between the government and the CGT resulted in the Grenelle Accords that proposed a "35 percent increase in the minimum wage, a two-stage wage increase of 10 percent, a reduction in social security payments by workers, a reduction of one-hour in the work week . . . , the recognition of trade union workplace branches and half pay during strikes" (Bernstein, 219). The proposal was rejected by the rank and file. The attempt to deal with classic demands while bypassing the qualitative ones that had become an integral part of the movement had failed. The government and the CGT seemed to have offered all they could on a traditional front and yet the movement continued. It seemed as though a power vacuum had been created. The opposition political parties began to ready themselves for the succession and called for new elections. This was the moment de Gaulle chose to "disappear." The interpretations of this "disappearance" vary between a crisis of confidence on de Gaulle's part, to a tactical move. Since de Gaulle had in fact gone to visit General Massu, the commander of French forces in West Germany and his old comrade from the days of the Algerian crisis that had brought him to power, it can be assumed that he had gone there to assure himself of the army's support. When he returned from Germany, de Gaulle made a forceful speech in which he affirmed his resolution to remain in power and warned against the danger of a Communist takeover; he dissolved the National Assembly and called for new elections in June: "France is indeed threatened with a dictatorship. They want to force her to accept a power that will impose itself against the backdrop of national despair, and the power will obviously be that of the winner, that is the power of totalitarian communism" (Wieviorka, 536). In his speech, de Gaulle had found the perfect strategy: two decades before the fall of the Berlin Wall, at a time when the Left still appeared to be exclusively a radical or revolutionary alternative to the center-Right government, at a time when the possibility of Soviet tanks rolling down the Champs Elysées was not out of the question for a sizable section of the French population, he raised the specter of Communist seizure of power in the classic Marxist mode of a proletarian revolution. In addition, after weeks of protests and strikes and the disruptions in the daily life of the general population (the absence of public transportation, the long gas lines, the difficulty of obtaining basic necessities, etc.), de Gaulle's speech offered the possibility of a return to normalcy through a reaffirmation of state power. On the evening of May 30, some 300,000–400,000 supporters of de Gaulle marched in the streets in a show of solidarity with the proposals made in the speech in particular and with the Gaullist program in general. By calling for elections, de Gaulle had in fact neutralized all discourses and positions that were beyond the traditional patterns and placed them squarely in the political arena. The massive challenge to bourgeois capitalist society and to the centralized French republican model represented by the May movement implied a questioning and even elimination of the very terms of social and political debate, while de Gaulle's proposal of a return to "normalcy" offered the possibility of continuing on familiar ground. The government, of course, the political parties, the trade unions were all in support of the elections that provided them with familiar terms and objectives. There remained an important segment of the trade unions, the students and the leftist groups (*groupuscules*), who were opposed to the elections and perceived and denounced them as a betrayal of the movement. In the aftermath of the march in support of de Gaulle and in the expectation of elections in June, for which the parties were all actively preparing, they became increasingly isolated.

Whether "massive carnival," "counter-cultural revolt," as some saw it, "failed revolution" or the "largest strike in the history of France," as others have perceived it, May 68 certainly constitutes a watershed in French life. The Gaullists won the June elections by a landslide, obtaining an unprecedented majority that seemed to leave them in complete control. The workers went back to the factories, and the students back to school after the turbulent spring of 1968, but something had irrevocably changed. On the institutional, political level France seemed to be back to the status quo but, in the years that followed, the imprint of May 68 remained clearly visible: "During the 1970s conservatives dominated politics, but they could not stop change" (Sowerwine, 361).

De Gaulle had returned the debate to the political arena in order to defuse the crisis and, in the short run, he seemed to have succeeded. Yet, "beyond May 68 it is the very idea of the Republican model that [was] once again thrown into question" (Rioux and Sirinelli, 286). In spite of the Right's electoral victory, and as the events of May 68 had shown, the government, and, beyond it, an entire system of authority and hierarchy was now out of tune with a society that, after a quarter century of economic growth and modernization had itself changed radically. As a result, even if the May movement had been short circuited in the political arena, its themes and issues reemerged in a multiplicity of places and organizations ranging from factory floor and theater stage to the media and academia.

The fact that, less than a year after the elections, de Gaulle resigned after failing to obtain a majority of votes in his proposed referendum on regional reform and a restructuring of the Senate in April 1969 indicates that May 68 was having a lasting effect. Beyond the measures proposed by the referendum, de Gaulle was attempting to reaffirm his personal authority, but the vote, 47 percent "yes" against 53 percent "no," was a clear disavowal of his presidency. On April 28, he announced his resignation in a laconic communiqué: "I cease to exercise the functions of President of the Republic." He retired to his village of Colombey and, this time, there would be no triumphal return to politics after a "crossing of the desert." De Gaulle died a year later, shortly before his eightieth birthday. On this occasion, the provocative headline of a satirical weekly that had been created in 1969, *Hara-Kiri Hebdo*, was symbolic of the challenge to authority that would be commonplace in France throughout the 1970s: "Tragic ball at Colombey: 1 dead."

The weekly was parodying the headlines and editorials that had appeared throughout the press following a fire in a dance club where 146 people had died. The phrase "tragic ball" had been used relentlessly by the media. The death of the leader of the Resistance and the first president of the Fifth Republic was being reduced to the level of a human interest story. The minister of the interior shut down the paper, citing as his reason cartoons depicting naked men that had previously appeared in *Hara Kiri Hebdo*. It reappeared, however, the following week with the same editorial staff but under a different title, *Charlie Hebdo*. The staff included the guilty cartoonists, Wilem and Cabu, as well as a number of other cartoonists, among them Georges Wolinski whose two nameless figures, a loud, tubby one and a thin, shy one were among the most popular to appear in *Charlie Hebdo*. Wolinski's figures represented the conservative and nationalistic "regular guy." They appeared in a weekly *bande dessinée* (comic strip), *L'évolution de la situation* whose sardonic tone was representative of the *Charlie Hebdo* style: "Monsieur, I'm for freedom of the press, as long as the press does not take advantage of this to say anything it wants" or "Monsieur, there are times when I wonder if it was worth it to win the war against a man who could have rid us of communism," and "Socialism is like marijuana: it may be harmless but it leads to harder drugs like communism."

Other contributors to the paper included Jean-Patrick Manchette, who wrote a film column for *Charlie Hebdo* and would become known as the "father of the *néo-polar*" or the "neo-detective novel," which became an important popular channel of social and political criticism in the 1970s (see dossier 8.7).

Dossier 8.7   Jean-Patrick Manchette, *Le petit bleu de la côte ouest (Three to Kill)*, (1976)

Jean-Patrick Manchette's *néo-polars* or neo-detective novels began to appear in the early 1970s. For Manchette, the popular genre was a tool of social and political criticism. In his gallery of characters, the ex-leftist who has "sold out" and the leftist who has gone underground and into armed struggle are common. Georges Gerfault, the main character of *Three to Kill*, with his "clutch of left-wing ideas" that "may just be discerned" is clearly a representative of the former. Georges, like the characters of Claire Bretécher's comic strip *Les Frustrés*, which began to appear at the same time, belongs to that peculiarly 1970s category, *la gauche caviar*, the "caviar left" or "radical chic" who, as another expression of the period had it, "carried its heart on the left and its wallet on the right." In *Nada* another *néo-polar* he published in 1972, Manchette focuses on those who, like the Baader-Meinhoff group in Germany, the Red Brigades in Italy, or the Weathermen in the United States had, instead, gone into urban armed guerilla combat. In *Nada*, the plot revolves around the kidnapping of the American ambassador to France and ends in a bloodbath as the system wins out against a motley band of anarchists, ex-members of *groupuscules* (small revolutionary groups that had been active in the May 68 movement) and even an ex-member of the "Jeanson network," a group of FLN sympathizers from the time of the Algerian War.

In this excerpt from *Three to Kill*, the "System"'s victory is less dramatically depicted. American bourbon and jazz and the German Mercedes that Georges is driving—a product of the "German economic miracle" of the post war period— belong to that series of "objects" that appeared in Boris Vian's "Lament of Progress" and in Georges Perec's *Les choses*. A decade after Vian's song and Perec's novel, they represent more than ever the changes in consumer patterns brought by modernization and "Americanization." The Paris *périphérique* or ring road on which George is speeding is itself a sign that the *civilization de la voiture* (the car civilization) has definitely arrived. The road was completed in 1973.

And sometimes what used to happen was what is happening now. Georges Gerfaut is driving on Paris's outer ring road. He has entered at the Porte d'Ivry. It is two-thirty maybe three-fifteen in the morning. A section of the inner ring road is closed for traffic, and on the rest of the inner ring road traffic is almost nonexistent. On the outer ring road there are perhaps two or three or at the most four vehicles per kilometer. Some are trucks, many of them very slow moving. The other vehicles are private cars, all traveling at high speed, well above the legal limit. This is also true of Georges Gerfaut. He has had five glasses of Four Roses bourbon. And about three hours ago he took two powerful capsules of a powerful barbiturate. The combined effect on him has not been drowsiness but a tense euphoria that threatens at any moment to change into anger or else into a kind of vaguely Chekovian and essentially bitter melancholy, not a very valiant or interesting feeling. Georges Gerfaut is doing 145 kilometers per hour.

Georges Gerfaut is a man under forty. His car is a steel-gray Mercedes. The leather upholstery is mahogany brown, matching all the fittings of the vehicle's interior. As for Georges Gerfaut's interior, it is somber and confused; a clutch of left wing ideas may just be discerned. On the car's dashboard, below the instrument panel, is a mat metal plate with Georges's name, address, and blood type engraved upon it, along with a piss-poor depiction of Saint Christopher. Via two speakers, one beneath the dashboard, the other on the back-window deck, a tape player is quietly diffusing West Coast—style jazz: Gerry Mulligan, Jimmy Giuffre, Bud Shank, Chico Hamilton. I know, for instance , that at one point it is Rube Bloom and Ted Koehler's "Truckin" that is playing, as recorded by the Bob Brookmeyer Quintet.

The reason why Georges Gerfaut is barreling along the outer ring road, with diminished reflexes, listening to this particular music, must be sought first and foremost in the social relations of production. The fact that Georges has killed at least two men in the course of the last year is not germane. What is happening now used to happen from time to time in the past. (3–4)

The type of tactic—challenge and skirmish, with withdrawal and regrouping of forces—used by *Hara Kiri Hebdo*, resuscitated as *Charlie Hebdo*, was also used against the government by a number of groups that were appearing in the wake of May 68. The resistance to the government's decision to extend a military base in the Larzac region in south-central France followed a similar pattern. This movement became symbolic of the ecological movements that were developing in the early 1970s. The group *Survivre* (Survive) was created in Alsace where the first ecological candidate ran for local elections in 1971 while, in 1974, René Dumont, a well-known agronomist and champion of the Third World became a presidential candidate. The Larzac movement reflected May 68 not only in its challenge to the central government but also in the eclectic character of the participants: small farmers, large landowners, *établis* (see dossier 8.8), *paysans installés*, people who had left other occupations for the farming life in the Larzac—José Bové, future leader of the *alter-mondialiste* (antiglobalization) movement, Confédération paysanne (see chapter 10) was such *a paysan installé*—, Parisian activists and intellectuals. There was even the establishment of a Larzac-Université—a "site where locals, militants, farmers and Parisians and other outsiders could come together and organize sessions and other cultural and educational projects" (Ross, *May 68*, 122). As had happened during the events of May 68, the hierarchy of recognized places and functions was disrupted as farmers protested on their tractors and even left their land to *monter sur Paris* (take the struggle to Paris). In October 1970, they walked sixty sheep all the way to the manicured lawns of the Champ de Mars, near the entrance to Napoleon's tomb at the Invalides. Methods that became common in the 1970s were used by the Larzac activists: hunger strikes, the squatting of the lands targeted for the extension of the military base, rallies, and marches. The struggle would last until 1981 when the new Socialist president cancelled the extension of the military camp, as promised during his presidential campaign.

Dossier 8.8   Jean-Pierre Thorn, *Témoignage* (Bearing Witness) (1970)

As early as 1967, a number of young militants, often members of Maoist and Troskyist *groupuscules* decided to "establish" themselves in factories. Often, their objective was to "raise worker consciousness," to mobilize the proletariat by freeing it from the control of communist organizations, viewed as reactionary or not militant enough. In the wake of May 68, the number of *établis* increased as the revolution many of these Maoist and Troskyist militants had hoped for did not materialize. In this excerpt, Jean-Pierre Thorn gives an account of his experience as an *établi* to Valérie, the daughter of Robert Linhart, a militant made famous by his account of his experience at the Citroën car factory, *L'établi*, published in 1978.

> Until 1968 I wasn't acquainted with either the working class or the factory. At that point, I discovered that an impressive world existed around us, with the power to bring the country to a standstill by stopping work. Red flags were floating at factory doors. I was twenty, I was astonished.
>
> I'd been wary of the student movement and had not gone along with it, being certain, without saying so to myself, that real life could not be in the Latin Quarter. The movie people had gone on strike and I had gone to the CGT to offer my services to film the factories. Negative. One day, friends from Ulm [The Ecole normale supérieure, called by the name of the street in Paris where it is located] took me to Flins [where workers from the Renault plant had gone on strike]. I discovered the intelligence, the warmth of militant workers, the risks they were taking. My desire to establish myself is directly linked to the film Oser lutter, oser vaincre [Dare to Fight, Dare to Win] that I made at the time. Sometimes, I would stop shooting because what was happening around me seemed so much to be real life. Between two takes, I read Mao's Little Red Book, Of Practice: "If one wants to know what a pear tastes like, one must transform it, by taking a bite . . . If one wants to know theory and revolution, one must take part in the revolution."
>
> I left to establish myself without any organization behind me. I lived those first years in the factory in great bliss. The discovery of another cultural universe, the questioning of all my modes of behavior, even the most intimate, jostled me about, like in a western. . . .
>
> At the factory, I did a very boring job. I had to cut copper bars into different round pieces and spray the machine's teeth with a milky liquid to cool them down. The only advantage that I had was to take these pieces afterwards wherever they were needed throughout the factory. I crossed through the shops fascinated; it was like being at the movies . . .

I had decided with two friends, one Maghrebi, the other Italian, to organize the immigrant workers in order to improve their work conditions. The CGT was not interested then in OS [assembly line workers] . . . So we organized a CFDT section, a practical way to discuss things with others during work time . . .

I spent seven years in that factory; I stayed there from 1971 to 1978. Gradually, I became more self-assured. I loved to speak out, to convince the workers to go on strike using straight forward slogans, to arrive in the director's office and say: "Enough of your bullshit . . ." To avoid the firing of those who headed the marches, I suggested wearing masks during demonstrations. A buddy took it a step further and arrived at a march disguised as a monkey. There are extraordinary pictures from that time . . . It was exhilarating; I was living an adolescent dream . . . I was living for the factory. My only problem was the terrible, crushing fatigue, especially after political meetings in the evenings.

I started cracking up after the big strikes of 1977. I could no longer understand the objective of my action . . . In 1978, I relinquished my union mandate. Once again a simple rank and file worker, I wondered: what am I doing here? I could no longer bear the types of relations I had with the workers, relations of power and dependence that I myself had established and that had so exhilarated me. As soon as something was going on, they would say to me: "Jean-Pierre, speak out, you speak better than we do!" I had become the "savior," which allowed them not to take charge themselves . . . Throughout all these years, I suffered from concealing things . . . I hid that I was an intellectual without fooling anyone . . .

My regret with regard to établissement is to have experienced it through this dimension of renunciation, of mortification. I came from a petty-bourgeois background, I knew nothing about manual labor, it did me a lot of good to be confronted with reality, to meet guys who were not always altar boys. Why did I have to live through this experience in this fashion? That's the big question.

Six months after I left, my buddies occupied the factory. They came to get me so that I could film. I made Le dos au mur *(Back against the Wall) in complete happiness. Finally I accepted my role as a filmmaker, among my worker comrades and in the factory! Since then, I dream about filming the shops, all the little stories that take place there, the conflicts from a daily vantage point . . .*

I still ask myself why I left the factory. In the evenings, with the exception of a film I make every five years I have nothing to say about my long empty days. At the end of my days on the assembly line, everyday, I had fantastic films to talk about. Today, it's more difficult for me to find meaning in my life. (190–195). (From *Volontaires pour l'usine [Volunteers for the Factory]* by Virginie Linhart [Paris: Editions du Seuil, 1994]. In Wierviorka and Prochasson, 565–569)

The tensions between the Giscard d'Estaing presidency and the Larzac activists were indicative of the contentious relations between the central republican power and the regions in general. As far back as the prerevolutionary period, some of the territories and provinces of what was to become the Hexagon had resisted their incorporation into a single entity under the king. The language issue is a convenient means of delineating this centuries-old opposition between a centralizing power and the particularities embodied by the various regions. As Alec Hargreaves proposes, "What was to become modern French gained its ascendancy because of the privileged status accorded to it by the unifying power of the state, rather than by simple weight of numbers" ("Challenges," in Kidd and Reynolds, 97). Before 1789, it was the monarchy that imposed a standardized form of French as the official administrative language, while other languages were relegated to the status of dialects or "patois." The no less centralizing Jacobins of the Revolution who "regarded regional languages and dialects as reactionary" (Hargreaves, 97) perpetuated and reinforced this policy. The Third Republic's own version of this centralizing and homogenizing practice was embodied most famously by the *instituteurs* it sent throughout the regions to spread the republican gospel of modernization and allegiance to the state represented by the Paris-based government. This centripetal feature of nation building was not unique to France, as we can see in the examples of German and Italian unification of the nineteenth century, but the universalist component of the French model made it even more difficult than it was elsewhere to sustain any type of regional identity. The ruling and systematically enforced credo was that people were French citizens above and beyond being Breton, Corsican, or Basque.

The general upheaval of May 68, with its decentralizing ethos and its shake-up of hierarchies gave renewed impetus to regionalist claims. These claims manifested themselves partly in demands for increased state support for the teaching of regional languages in the republic's schools. Some languages—Breton, Basque, Catalan, and Occitan—had already been granted a reduced form of state subsidy by the 1951 Deixonne Law, but now the demands were for an extension of these measures and of the list of recognized languages. The impact of May 68 on regional identity also manifested itself in a flurry of cultural activities and political positions. The success of Breton musician/singer-songwriter Alain Stivel and Corsican demands for increased autonomy were two poles of a general affirmation of regional identity in the 1970s. The teaching of the Corsican language, or dialect, depending on the perception, gained the approval of the Giscard d'Estaing administration in 1974, but the demands of the newly formed the *Action Régionaliste Corse* (ARC, Corsican Regional Action) went well beyond the language issue. On the whole, the ARC viewed the relation between the mainland and the island as "colonial." Ironically, the incident that would trigger the radicalization of the autonomy movement in Corsica took place on the farm of repatriated *pied noir*, one of the hundreds of thousands who had had to leave in the wake of the Algerian War of independence. The *pieds noirs* had settled en masse in Corsica and were viewed as outsiders whose know-how as farmers and wine growers had enabled them to gain a stronghold on the island. Two policemen died in the shootout that took place between the police and the militants of the ARC who had positioned themselves in the *pied noir* winegrower's cellar near the Corsican city of Aleria in the summer of 1975. If the French government was willing to negotiate on the language issue, it was much less reluctant to approve any real autonomy for the island. The creation of the *Front de Libération National Corse* (FLNC, National Liberation Front of Corsica) represented a radicalization on the Corsican side since now, beyond autonomy, the objective was independence. The *cas corse* (Corsican case) has continued to test the capacity of successive governments of both the Left and the Right to find a solution to this regionalist challenge to central republican authority. The killing of Claude Erignac, the republic's prefect in Corsica, in 1998 is only one of several spectacular and violent signs that the centralizing and homogenizing policy that has been applied by kings, Jacobins, and republican nationalists, of the Left or the Right, is still contested by some. The *cas corse* remains very much part of the national debate on French identity, republicanism, and universalism, with some politicians and opinion-makers advocating force to make Corsica fully and unquestionably integrate the republic and respect its laws, while others see in an extension of regional rights a way out of the confrontation. In 1994, a proposal to grant the Corsican assemblies the right to amend certain national laws led to the resignation of the minister of the interior, Jean-Pierre Chevènement, who "denounced a special status for Corsica as fundamentally un-republican—a challenge to the Jacobin tradition and the indivisibility of the Republic" (Howarth and Varouxakis, 66).

If the Larzac came to symbolize the ecological trend of "post-68," the worker takeover of the Lip watch factory in Besançon, a town in eastern France, came to symbolize the importance *autogestion* (the principle of worker-run companies) had taken in the period. Oddly enough, Napoleon provides a link between the Larzac protesters and the workers of the Lip watch factory: when the farmers of the Larzac plateau walked their sheep to Paris and arrived at the Invalides esplanade, they had reached the resting place of the emperor to whom Emmanuel Lippman, the founder of Lip, had made a gift of the first watch chronometer, which his company had built. Lippman's company thrived in the century and a half that followed and began to market an electric watch in 1971 and the first French quartz watch in 1973. In these first few years of the 1970s, before "globalization" and "outsourcing" became everyday words, competition from Asia was already leading to massive layoffs in entire sectors of the European economies. The Lip company management, facing the flooding of the French market by much cheaper quartz watches from Asia, filed for bankruptcy. The workers seized the stock as "war treasury" and continued to operate the factory and to manage the company. This was *autogestion* in practice, and it gained the support of much of the population; people from all over France showed their solidarity with *les Lip* (the workers from Lip) by buying the watches that were still being manufactured and sold by the workers. The Lip factory became a cause célèbre, due to a great extent to the CFDT representative, the very articulate Charles Piaget who effectively used the media to make the case for continued occupation and operation of the factory. The struggle of *les Lip* would last nine months, at the end of which they would be removed from the factory by the police in August 1973.

The events at Lip were closely covered by a recently created newspaper called *Libération*. Its journalists were warmly welcomed by the striking Lip workers: "A page of the newspaper was offered daily to the striking workers, who used it with a devastating sense of humor" (Bois, "French Lib," in Hollier, 1042). It made sense that the journalists from *Libération* were more welcomed by the Lip workers than other journalists: they too represented an effective example of *autogestion*, and they provided the striking workers with a forum in the paper. *Libération* started as a news agency, the *Agence de Presse Libération* (APL) by a group of Maoist militants. It became a respected source of information after it "scooped" an event that some consider one of the major turning points of the workers' movement in France: the killing of a worker, Pierre Overney, by the private security guard of the government-owned Renault factory at Billancourt, in the suburbs of Paris. The killing did not provoke mass protests on the part of workers, but APL released a series of photographs "displaying the cold-blooded assassination step by step . . . and overnight [it] became a respected source of information concerning all censored issues" (Bois, "French Lib," in Hollier, 1042).

Government censorship was indeed widespread in the early 1970s, from the censoring of dozens of Maoist and *gauchiste* newspapers to the ludicrous ban on singer-songwriter Serge Gainsbourg's *Je t'aime, moi non plus* (I Love You, Me Neither), with its breathy sounds of love-making against the background of slow organ riffs. The events of May 68 remained tangible in the ubiquitous police presence in the capital, with its wagons of CRS in central neighborhoods in Paris and in other cities throughout France. It was a time when, in order to circumvent censorship, Jean-Paul Sartre and Simone de Beauvoir, now veritable institutions, became the official directors of many of the *gauchiste* papers that sprouted in the "post-May" years. When APL became *Libération* in 1973, Sartre was its official director. The "existentialist activist" and ex-"fellow traveler" of the Communist Party did not share all the ideas or vocabulary of these groups of Maoists but he was attracted by their blurring and even dismantling of the division between manual and intellectual labor. Indeed *Libération* was not organized along the lines of the institutionalized press: no specialized journalists, no attribution of specific tasks, no advertising, no outside capital. This is why when the journalists of *Libération* showed up at the Lip factory, they were on both familiar and friendly ground.

Libération mixed irreverence with solid reporting. In 1974, when Raymond Queneau, the famous French writer and poet, died, *Libération*'s headline paid homage to him but included an exuberant reference to one of his fictional heroines, the young Zazie of *Zazie dans le métro*, Queneau's best-known novel: *Le grand pataphysicien Raymond Queneau est décédé . . . Mon cul! Vive Zazie!* (The Great Pataphysician Raymond Queneau Is Dead . . . My Ass!!! Long Live Zazie!!!). When Mao Ze Dong died, along with detailed reporting on the life and times of the Chinese revolutionary leader, the paper carried a front page cartoon of a Belgian—the butt of jokes in France—eating fries and stolidly asking: "Mao died, did you know?" The headline was accompanied by an editorial commenting on the aged Mao's inability at the end of his life to "fart and to screw." *Libération* remained an *autogestioné* newspaper throughout the 1970s but in 1982 it adopted the practices of the institutionalized press: specialized tasks, a salary scale, the introduction of exterior capital. It did not lose, however, its mordant irony and investigative spirit. The institutionalization of a paper that had been founded on Maoist and *autogestionaire* principles was also indicative of an overall shift in French society: the depolarization or, in Giscard d'Estaing's formulation, the *décrispation* of politics that was developing in France in the late 1970s. Behind this evolution lay the integration of France in the North Atlantic economic sphere and the resulting liberalization of its national economy. The example of *Libération* in its two phases reflects both the general challenge to authority and hierarchy that was at the heart of the May movement, and the modernization of the French economy along the lines of a neo–liberal capitalist model.

In fact, both the ideology, or ideologies, of the May movement and the "Americanization" of France, either in cultural or economic terms, represented challenges to "a certain idea of France" and to the universalism that lay at its core.

This questioning of universalism was very much the order of the day in academia where the May movement had begun. As Denis Hollier proposes, the intervention of the police within the confines of the university symbolized the end of knowledge conceived in terms of a universalism-based model. As had been the case for a wide range of activities from factories to football, the subjective, historical aspect of the university and of the knowledge it dispensed were laid bare by the police action at the Sorbonne:

> Traditionally, the impartiality of the scholar, theorist, or writer had endowed him or her with moral prestige. The specialist in universal truths was held to be above partisan interests; and this detachment from the practical world was precisely the source of theory's authority in non-theoretical matters. But once the police intervened to maintain order on the campuses, this became an untenable illusion. The production of knowledge now itself appeared to be an arena of activity in which multiple strategies were played out, submitted to competition between diverse interests. There is a politics of science, of truth. Knowledge was fractured into local knowledge. (Hollier, 1036)

This fragmentation of knowledge was apparent in the theory and philosophy of the post-68 era. In its Saussurian linguistics-based exploration of "deep structures" and the laws that govern the sign systems that organized life, the reigning intellectual approach of the preceding decade, structuralism, at least in its "hardest forms" (Eagleton, 108) had left universalism relatively intact. The sign systems it surveyed could vary from one culture to another, opening a door to the dismantling of universalism, but the deep structures that ultimately governed these systems were invariable, and thus . . . universal, closing the door.

The philosopher Jacques Derrida had begun the work of dismantling this paradigm even before the labels "poststructuralist" or *la pensée 68* (the philosophy of May 68, or the thought of May 68), as the philosopher and future minister of education Luc Ferry called it, had gained currency (see below). Derrida laid the groundwork for "deconstruction," the operation by which the dismantling he practiced was called, in two books, *De la Grammatologie* (*Of Grammatology*) and *L'écriture et la différence* (*Writing and Difference*) both published in 1967. In these two works, Derrida "deconstructs" the binary systems upon which structuralism relied to map out myths and sign systems: rather than the classic structuralist opposition of elements such as self and nonself, sense and nonsense, center and margin, Derrida suggests that these oppositions are not as clearly contained as they seem and mask inconsistencies, ruptures, and discontinuities. In other words, the rigid line separating one term of the binary structure from the other in structuralism is invalid because it hides the necessary *contamination* that occurs from one to the other, since one pole is always part of the other and needs that other for its own definition. The task of deconstruction is to tease out the inconsistencies, the discontinuities in the apparently ordered opposition. In Derrida's scheme, meaning, like the line that would separate binary structures, is not stable or rigid; instead, there is "a continual flickering, and defusing of meaning—labeled *dissemination* by Derrida—which cannot be easily contained within the categories of the text's structure, or within the categories of conventional critical approaches to it." Ultimately, deconstruction challenges the very basis of a structure because a structure is a concept that "presumes a center, a fixed principle, a hierarchy of meaning and a solid foundation" (Eagleton, 134). Deconstruction disrupts the very basis of an objective, metaphysical realm that would define things once and for all; in doing so it also throws into question the possibility of universalism. We can see that this theoretical and philosophical challenge to universalism is reflected not only in the general challenge to the authority of the republican government in May 68 but also in the post-68 examples of the Larzac farmers, the Corsican autonomists, the Lip watchmakers, and the journalists of *Libération*. Deconstruction would have a more directly traceable impact on the women's movement and its challenge to male authority and power posited as the top of a hierarchy (see below).

Roland Barthes, whose *Mythologies* certainly relied on a structural approach to mass culture and modernization, also evolved in the direction of "poststructuralism." In a famous essay published in 1968, "The Death of the Author," Barthes proceeds to replace the very idea of literature conceived as a collection of original texts produced by original, individual authors, with the concept of *writing*: "Literature (it would be better from now on to say *writing*), by refusing to assign a 'secret,' an ultimate meaning, to the text (and to the world as text) liberates what may be called an antitheological activity, an activity that is truly revolutionary since to refuse to fix meaning is, in the end, to refuse God and his hypostases—reason, science, law." As in Derrida's deconstruction, at work again here is a will to undo the very notion of an ultimate meaning based on the positing of a stable point of reference, in this case the author's intended and restricted meaning. Rather than stable meaning originating in a single author there is an "intertextuality"—a concept associated with the work of the literary critic and psychoanalyst Julia Kristeva—a network of texts where words are recycled with no possibility of ultimately ascribing originality to any particular author. Here again, we encounter the refusal of an underlying and ultimate point of reference that could serve as the basis of a stable hierarchy.

Like Barthes, the historian and philosopher Michel Foucault taught at the prestigious Collège de France where he was professor of the history of systems of thought and, like Barthes, he was at first associated with structuralism, a label he did not refuse initially. However, his work contains a historical dimension that goes against the grain of the structuralist method. What he does have in common with the "later Barthes," the poststructuralist Barthes, is a questioning of the very conditions of discourse that give rise to concepts and institutions. In *Madness and Civilization* (1961), he delineates the ways in which civilization constructs the notion of the "mad" and, more generally, construct its "others." Foucault's concrete interest in these "others" would later lead him to participate in the foundation of the Prison Information Group that would give prisoners a voice. This reflected a marked politicization of his work, as made obvious in his 1975 book *Discipline and Punish: The Birth of the Prison*. Politics, or rather, power and mechanisms of control and the means by which they take shape and evolve were also central to his *History of Sexuality* (the first volume was published in 1976). In this history, Foucault argued against the generally accepted notion that Western societies repressed sexuality. Instead, he proposes that there was a fixation with sexuality reflected in the multiplicity of discourses about it. The discourses themselves gave shape to sexual identities. There would not have been "sexual minorities" without the discourses that gave rise to them. Indeed the concept of "sexuality" would not have existed without the discourse that created it. Foucault's work is not a "deconstruction" in a textual Derridean mode. Rather, by showing how mechanisms of power are constructed historically, through discourse, he empowers those who would challenge the institutions that are based on these constructions. In this, he is squarely in the subversive lineage of what came to be called *la pensée 68*.

Before going to the Collège de France, Foucault taught for a short period at the University of Vincennes, which opened its doors in January 1969. Vincennes was a direct result of an attempt to liberalize higher education in the wake of the May 68 movement. Its open-admissions policy and its genuine will to democratize and inno-vate attracted a number of libertarian and left-wing academics. It was at Vincennes that Foucault taught for a while with someone he considered to be the most impor-tant philosopher of his times, Gilles Deleuze, proposing that "Maybe someday this century will be Deleuzian" ("Theatrum philosophicum," 885). Arguably the most influential work of the post-68 period is Gilles Deleuze and Félix Guattari's *Anti-Oedipus: Capitalism and Schizophrenia*, published in 1972. The May movement had not ultimately led to revolution; the people had gone into the streets, authority had been questioned, challenged, but the traditional capitalist hierarchy and state power had reaffirmed themselves. One of Deleuze and Guattari's objectives in *Anti-Oedipus* is to go beyond both Marx and Freud in order to arrive at an understanding of and a response to this dual process of subversion and control. Two of the crucial concepts developed in this complex book are those of *deterritorialization* and *reterritorialization*, which the authors see as the two movements, in tandem, of capitalism. On the one hand, capitalism steamrolls tradition in all its manifestations, including the sacred, the state, the family. This dismantling of institutions of control results in the appearance of the private individual, owner of his labor and of his body. In this sense, capitalism acts as a liberator of individual energy because it goes against any form of ritualized, familial, or state control. To paraphrase an author and a philosophy from a earlier generation, Sartre and existentialism, in this first movement "Man is free(d)." But since capitalism needs the very structures, the territorial groupings it had swept away, in order to function and thrive, these reappear, albeit in modified form and continue to oppress and control the individual. *Deterritorialization* is followed by *reterritorialization*, the reappearance of codes that control and dominate. This double movement is what Deleuze and Guattari see as the "schizophrenic" nature of capi-talism. In this situation the subject is always between two poles of repression and desire and can only move beyond this neurotic state, which is the state of any "nor-mal individual," through what Deleuze calls "nomadization." In the Deleuzian understanding of the word, it is not a question of leaving, never to come back, which would be a relinquishing but, instead, of constantly negotiating some space between the two movements of *deterritorialization* and *reterritorialization* for, as Deleuze points, "There are stationary voyages, voyages in intensity and, even his-torically, nomads are not those who move as migrants do; on the contrary, they are those who do not move and begin to nomadize in order to remain in the same place while escaping the codes" (*Nietzshe aujourd'hui*, 174).

Many of the movements and trends that followed May 68 can be perceived in those terms: since the revolution has not taken place, new strategies have to be devised that would allow a continuation of the challenge to authority while remain-ing within its purview. Rather than the frontal, unified assault of revolution by "the people" in its classic, Marxist mode, *Anti-Oedipus* proposed a strategy of continuous and atomized challenge to power that took into account that power's own con-stantly evolving and fragmented form. Beyond the prison, the courtroom, the police, and other traditional instances of state power emerge the figures of the multinational corporations, the entertainment industry, the media, and an entire array of postnational and postindustrial institutions. This new configuration of power as a force distributed in a multiplicity of locations, rather than contained essentially in the universal republican state apparatus, corresponded to a paradigm that Jean-François Lyotard, a colleague of Deleuze's in Vincennes's philosophy department, would call the "postmodern condition," the title of a book he published in 1979. In his preface to Lyotard's *The Postmodern Condition*, the American philosopher Fredric Jameson points out a basic similarity between that work and *Anti-Oedipus*:

> Lyotard's affiliation would seem to be with the *Anti-Oedipus* of Gilles Deleuze and Félix Guattari who also warned us, at the end of that work, that the schizophrenic ethic they proposed was not at all a revolutionary one, but a way of surviving under capitalism, producing fresh desires within the structural limits of the capitalist mode of production as such. (xviii)

Jameson argues that the thrust of Lyotard's argument in *The Postmodern Condition* is not "revolutionary" because, like Deleuze and Guattari's "schizophrenic ethic," it does not entail a revolution in the Marxist sense of a takeover by the proletariat resulting from class struggle. However, Lyotard's analysis does provide alternatives and modes of resistance to the state by analyzing, questioning, and ultimately refuting, as did Foucault, Barthes, and Deleuze, the very basis of its power in a claim to universalism.

Lyotard describes the postmodern as "the crisis of narratives." In other words, how do we know that a narrative is true, how does it legitimate itself? In an era where the police has already broken down the doors of the university, taken off the veil of universality from a certain type of academic discourse—among other discourses, whether scientific or in the humanities—how do discourses then legitimate themselves? Lyotard proceeds with a questioning of the power that guarantees the validity of a narrative. "By the yardstick of science," Lyotard writes in the introduction, "the majority of [narratives] prove to be fables." This is why science "then produces a discourse of legitimization with respect to its own status" (xxiii). Lyotard designates this operation as "modern": "I will use the term *modern* to designate any science that legitimates itself with reference to a metadiscourse of this kind making an explicit appeal to some grand narrative" (xxiii; emphasis in original). This grand narrative relies on a consensus between sender and receptor of a statement, a statement whose "truth value is deemed acceptable if it is cast in terms of a possible unanimity between rational minds . . . This is the Enlightenment narrative" (xxiii). And it is precisely this type of consensus that is at the core of Lyotard's definition of the postmodern: "incredulity towards metanarratives." These "metanarratives" entail a "consensus that does violence to the heterogeneity of language games." Lyotard is opposed to the (unfounded) universal quality of this consensus, and proposes a type of postmodern knowledge, one that is "not simply a tool of the authorities; [that] reinforces our sensitivity to differences and reinforces our ability to tolerate the incommensurable" (xxv). In a concrete sociopolitical context, this "incommensurable" could be located in the multiplicity of discourses that continuously overspill the limits and rules of universalizing grand narratives—the discourses of students, the mad, homosexuals, foreigners, prisoners, the young, and, in this necessarily incomplete list, one of the most important "differences" to emerge from May 68: the women's movement.

In the aftermath of the barricades where women had challenged the bourgeois capitalist order alongside their male counterparts, *phallo*, short for *phallocrat*, was a commonly heard barb in France. It was directed at men by women who, having taken part in the May 68 movement, had come to the conclusion that while the entire social and political order was being challenged one essential aspect of it had remained intact: it remained male-dominated. In the psychoanalytically inflected vocabulary of the 1970s this was referred to as the "phallic order." In other words, this was an order where men constituted the central or highest point of reference in a hierarchy. This hierarchy was similar in its structure to what Derrida had called the "transcendental signifier," a point beyond the reach of questioning or challenge, beyond the reach of "play," in the sense of room for maneuvering or negotiation. In Lyotard's terms, this system would rest squarely on a bogus legitimization system that "does violence to the heterogeneity of language games." The burgeoning women's movement represented the possibility of a discourse that would *not* have as point of departure or reference the phallus as transcendental signifier.

Some of the theoreticians of the movement found in Derrida's work a useful point of departure. Hélène Cixous, who had joined the faculty at Vincennes in the aftermath of May 68 and today directs one of the very few women's studies departments in the French university system, used Derrida's coinage, "logocentrism," to arrive at her own term, "phallogocentrism." Derrida had coined his term to designate the hierarchy in which the spoken word was perceived as a more direct, unmediated link to "truth" than writing. In a move reminiscent of Simone de Beauvoir's use of Sartrean existentialism for a woman-specific critique, Cixous used Derridean deconstruction to subvert the male-dominated system of her time. She used the term "phallogocentrism" to refer to "these forms of thought which posited the male principle, symbolized by the phallus, as the positive term in a series of binary oppositions between male and female, activity and passivity, and so on" (Lane, 296). Cixous' attack on the "phallic order" is an attack on yet another system based on a historical contingency raised to the status of a universal truth. To monolithic phallic discourse, she opposes one based on heterogeneity and differences originating in a feminine realm. Cixous' contemporary, the psychoanalyst and philosopher Luce Irigaray (see dossier 8.9), was also perceived "as typifying French feminism's focus on sexual difference as a force which disrupts a symbolic and social order organized around the power of the phallus" (Lane, 296).

Dossier 8.9   Luce Irigaray, *This Sex Which Is Not One* (1977)

Luce Irigaray belongs to the generation of feminists that emerged from the May 68 movement. Although centered on the specific figure of woman, her work shares with that of other intellectuals of the period a will to dismantle the very basis of dominant discourses by delineating the mechanisms of their construction, the better to reveal their relative status. Irigaray's work is in a tradition that includes Roland Barthes's earlier analysis of "myths," Michel Foucault's "archeology" of power, Jacques Derrida's "deconstruction" of Western metaphysics, Deleuze and Guattari's "nomadic thought" and Jean-François Lyotard's critique of "grand narratives." Where Barthes, for example, denounces "petit-bourgeois universalism," which relegates difference to the status of aberrations, Irigaray denounces the tradition of Western discourse that posits the male as the "origin," dictating the terms of woman's definition in a "phallic order." In this excerpt she focuses on woman's sexuality as a primary means to challenge this hierarchy.

Female sexuality has always been theorized within masculine parameters. Thus, the opposition "virile" clitoral activity/"feminine" vaginal passivity which Freud—and many others—claims are alternative behaviors or steps in the process of becoming a sexually normal woman, seems prescribed more by the practice of masculine sexuality than by anything else. For the clitoris is thought of as a little penis which is pleasurable to masturbate, as long as the anxiety of castration does not exist (for the little boy), while the vagina derives its value from the "home" it offers the male penis when the now forbidden hand must find a substitute to take its place in giving pleasure.

According to these theorists, woman's erogenous zones are no more than a clitoris-sex, which cannot stand up in comparison with the valued phallic organ; or a hole-envelope, a sheath which surrounds and rubs the penis during coition; a nonsex organ or a masculine sex organ turned inside out in order to caress itself.

Woman and her pleasure are not mentioned in this conception of the sexual relationship. Her fate is one of "lack," "atrophy" (of her genitals), and "penis envy," since the penis is the only recognized sex organ of any worth. Therefore she tries to appropriate it for herself, by all the means at her disposal: by her somewhat servile love of the father-husband capable of giving it to her; by her desire of a penis-child, preferably male; by gaining access to those cultural values which are still "by right" reserved for males alone and are therefore always masculine, etc. Woman lives her desire only as an attempt to possess at long last the equivalent of the male sex organ.

All of that seems rather foreign to her pleasure however, unless she remains within the dominant phallic economy. Thus, for example, woman's autoeroticism is very different from man's—he needs an instrument in order to touch himself: his hand, woman's genitals, language—and this self-stimulation requires a minimum of activity. But a woman touches herself by and within herself directly, without mediation, and before any distinction between activity and passivity is possible. A woman "touches herself" constantly without anyone being able to forbid her to do so, for her sex is composed of two lips that embrace continually. Thus, within herself she is already two—but not divisible into ones—who stimulate each other. (99)

. . . Whence the mystery that she represents in a culture that claims to enumerate everything by units, inventory everything by individualities. She is neither one nor two. She cannot, strictly speaking, be determined either as one person or as two. She renders any definition inadequate. Moreover she has no "proper" name. And her sex organ, which is not a [or: one] sex organ, is counted as no sex organ. It is the negative, the opposite, the reverse, the counterpart, of the only visible and morphologically designatable sex organ (even if it does pose a few problems in its passage from erection to detumescence): the penis. (101)

. . . In order for a woman to arrive at a point where she can enjoy her pleasure as a woman, a long detour by the analysis of the various systems of oppression which affect her is certainly necessary. By claiming to resort to pleasure alone as the solution to her problem, she runs the risk of missing the reconsideration of a social practice upon which her pleasure depends. (105)

Let women tacitly go on strike, avoid men long enough to learn to defend their desire notably by their speech, let them discover the love of other women protected from that imperious choice of men which puts them in a position of rival goods, let them forge a social status which demands recognition, let them earn their living in order to leave behind their condition of prostitute—These are certainly indispensable steps in their effort to escape their proletarization on the trade market. (106)

There was no unified, national Women's Liberation Movement in France in the late 1960s, but a number of small organizations and groupings that had been formed in the aftermath of the May movement. The term MLF was coined by the French press as these disparate groups began to be noticed. One of the events that brought the women's movement to prominence took place when a group of women attempted to place a wreath on the tomb of the "unknown soldier's wife" at the Arc of Triumph in Paris in August 1970. This event, with its setting in one of the most emblematic historical landmarks of the French capital, is a revealing example of the way in which the women's movement constituted a refusal to accept the subservient position of women in society as well as a challenge to very idea of the universal republic under which all identities are equally subsumed: "The Arc de Triomphe is one of the most explicit signs of a French, and by extension, of a victorious, universal, male order . . . the wreath not only challenged these value . . . [it] raised the possibility of another series of values, those, unknown, that might have come, that might now come into being through the absent women" (de Courtivron and Marks, 31).

Throughout the 1970s, much of the feminist discourse was highly theoretical, but reproductive rights provided the Women's Movement with a concrete rallying cause in the sociopolitical arena. The execution of Marie Latour in July 1943 by the Vichy regime for performing abortions—she became the subject of Claude Chabrol's 1988 film *Une Affaire de femme* (*Story of Women*)—provides a background to the general state of reproductive rights at the time. The law in effect at the time of the execution, and still in effect fifty years later, had been adopted in 1920. The execution of Marie Latour took place at a time when the image of woman was essentially that of the wife and mother. During the Occupation, however, this image was counterbalanced by the millions of women who had gone beyond the limits of the home and become visible in the workplace, replacing the men who had gone to war. Many women also actively participated in the Resistance, which led, in part, to women being granted the right to vote by the de Gaulle-led provisional government in 1944. Two years later, the constitution of the Fourth Republic recognized the equality of women in most areas. "This was followed in the early 1960s by a series of laws undoing the gynophobic strictures of the Napoleonic code. Women were no longer officially subordinate to men in marriage, in financial arrangements women needed their husband's permission to open a bank account [a situation that obtained until 1965] or as parents" (de Courtivron, 28). The years of modernization, the massive irruption of women as economic decision makers in the purchase of consumer goods, and the more permissive mood of the late 1960s contributed to the legalization of contraception by the Neuwirth law voted in 1967. Even after it was adopted, however, there was widespread resistance to its actual application. The Neuwirth law went into effect only gradually from 1969 to 1972, while abortions remained illegal.

"The Manifesto of 343," which appeared in the major news weekly *Le Nouvel Observateur* in 1971, was instrumental in challenging this illegality and placing the issue of abortion on the national agenda. Its text was simple and to the point:

> A million women have an abortion every year in France. They do so in dangerous conditions as a result of the clandestinity to which they are condemned, even though, under medical supervision, this is a very simple procedure. There is total silence regarding these

millions of women. I declare that I am one of them. I declare having had an abortion. And, as we demand free access to contraception, we also demand free access to abortions.

The manifesto was signed by a number of high-profile women including writers, actresses, lawyers, journalists, and intellectuals. Some of the names were among the best-known in France: Simone de Beauvoir; the actresses Stéphane Audran, Catherine Deneuve, and Delphine Seyrig, the writers Marguerite Duras, Christiane Rochefort, and Françoise Sagan, and theater director Ariane Mnouchkine. Those who signed the manifesto were publicly admitting to having broken the law. In order to protect and defend them in the event of prosecution—which of course the signatories were hoping for in order to bring the issue to further public attention—Gisèle Halimi, who had defended Djamila Boupacha, the young Algerian FLN member who had been tortured and raped by paratroopers during the Algerian War (see chapter 7) and de Beauvoir founded the group *Choisir* (*To Choose*). None of the signatories was prosecuted and *Choisir* did not have to intervene, but the proabortion movement found its test case when the mother of a seventeen-year-old girl from the working-class suburb of Bobigny helped her daughter arrange for an abortion. The two women and the doctor who had performed the abortion were brought to trial. The case became a cause célèbre. Halimi was the defense lawyer and her argument went well beyond the particular case to become an indictment of the law itself. Signatories of what came to be known as the *Manifesto of the 343* came to testify, as did prominent gynecologists. The court's ruling resulted in suspended sentences for the girl and her mother and in a nominal fine for the abortionist, whose conviction was later overturned.

It became obvious that the outdated law could not be enforced and the case constituted a milestone toward the legalization of abortion. It would take another four years before a law was adopted by the government, and not until 1982, under the socialist government, would the cost of abortions be reimbursed by the national health care system. The Veil Law of 1975, named after Simone Veil, Giscard d'Estaing's minister of health, and the first woman to hold a senior ministry in France, was adopted in 1975. Veil was one of the six women ministers in Giscard d'Estaing's government, including Françoise Giroud's post as secretary of state for the condition of women. These official appointments certainly contributed to further empowerment of women in French life, although many inequities continued, whether in the workplace or in general attitudes. Even at the end of the "socialist years," in 1995, only 5 percent of those who held public office in France were women (Celestin, DalMolin, and de Courtivron, 3). This figure is only one of the indications that a new wave of activism would be necessary in order for the condition of women in both the private and public spheres to improve. As reproductive rights had been in the 1970s, the *parité* (parity) debates—around the issue of the proportion of women among elected officials—would be a rallying point for women's rights in the late 1990s (see chapter 10).

As we can see in the excerpt from Luce Irigaray's "This Sex Which Is Not One" (dossier 8.9), some of the feminist theorists and activists saw in homosexuality a means out of countering male dominance and of escaping its codes. While this type of "secession" was very much part of the post-May period, it represented a marked difference from the objectives of earlier homosexual groups. *Arcadie* (Arcadia) for example, the first organized homosexual organization in France, founded in 1955, advocated assimilation into the mainstream. The name alone of the *Front Homosexuel d'action révolutionaire* (FHAR, Homosexual Front for Revolutionary Action) founded in 1971, reflects the radicalization of the movement: from assimilation to challenge of the system as a whole. With his first book, *Le désir homosexuel* (*Homosexual Desire*), published in 1972, the philosopher Guy Hocquengem, one of the founders of the FHAR, became one of the first intellectuals to produce a sustained critique of institutionalized homophobia. The influence of both Foucault and Lacan is obvious in his dismantling of a hierarchy in which some types of desire would be more or "justified" than others. In Hocquengem's view there is no universal definition of normality, only different manifestations of a diffuse, generic *desire*.

Max Ophul's documentary on the Holocaust, *The Sorrow and the Pity*, made for television in 1968, was released in 1971, the same year Hocquengem's groundbreaking work was published. This is not simply a chronological coincidence, for both partake of the general questioning of official, established narratives that characterized the early 1970s. In the case of *The Sorrow and the Pity* and *Le désir homosexuel*, a more specific link can also be found in the fact that "Vichy France implemented what has been described as a 'gay Holocaust' during World War II, deporting homosexual men as well as Jews, gypsies, communists and other 'undesirables.'" (Cairns, in Kidd and Reynolds, 87). Ophul's film challenged the myth of a unified Resistance and of a French population that had played no part in the Holocaust. The four-hour long documentary is set in the town of Clermont-Ferrand and mixes newsreel footage from the years of the Occupation with contemporary interviews. *The Sorrow and the Pity* contradicted the then-dominant narrative of a valiant and resisting French population, with a few traitors and collaborators as the exception that confirmed the rule. Instead, the documentary made it obvious that many French people approved the German occupation and that anti-Semitism was not only a wartime phenomenon but "deeply ingrained" in the population (Stoval). "The overall impression given by the film was that all the elites had collaborated and that only some workers and peasants had resisted. The Gaullist contribution was totally neglected" (Sowerwine, 362). There is no unifying voice-over in the documentary, what Lyotard would call a grand narrative providing legitimization, only the opposition of past images with contemporary interviews. The film is not presented as "the Truth" or "the Only version," but, instead, leaves blanks, a space for the viewer to form an opinion. Thus, *The Sorrow and the Pity* "stands as a work of revolutionary impact because it offered aesthetic as well as a political fissure in the narrative of contemporary French history that had been imposed by the Gaullist-controlled media and demonstrated that there was more than one way of telling a story, that the 'truth' had multiple facets" (Forbes and Kelly, 240).

American academic Robert Paxton's book, *Vichy France: Old Guard, New Order* was published a year later and also contributed to disrupt official discourse on the period of the Occupation. Its sober and meticulously researched account of the French participation in decision making during those years contradicted the hitherto sanctioned version of an administration and a population forced to comply with the enemy and never taking initiatives. Highly publicized trials in the 1980s and 1990s, first of the "Butcher of Lyon," the Nazi officer Klaus Barbie, and then of high-profile French collaborators, would continue the process of coming to terms with the "dark years" (see chapters 9 and 10).

The spirit of challenge to official institutions and traditional modes of representation were also present in the theater of the post-May period. The combination of derision and social and ideological criticism that had been at the heart of the May movement found its way on the stages of the numerous *café-théâtres* that appeared in the early 1970s. The *cafés-théâtres* were small venues and reminiscent of the cabarets that had flourished in the Montmartre neighborhood of Paris at the turn of the century. As had been the case then, the order of the day in the *cafés-théâtres* of the 1970s was often political and social satire. In a France coming to the end of the economic boom of the *trente glorieuses*, the new modes of consumption and the "new middle class" of white collar workers and their families that had resulted from that boom were prized targets. One of the most celebrated sketches of the period, *Amours, coquillages et crustacées* (*Love, Shells and Shellfish*), was performed by the Splendide group. It was a satire of the "Club Med" vacation, which had become a very successful enterprise in the 1960s.

The "anti–Club Med" trend of those years also took the shape of the travel agency *Nouvelles frontières* (New Frontiers), founded in 1967, whose motto *On ne veut pas bronzer idiot* (We don't want to just stupidly get a sun tan) reflected its antiestablishment, antibourgeois take on travel to other countries. Where Club Med prided itself on the contained and protected quality of its "villages" that were completely cordoned off from the local populations, the *Nouvelles frontières* ethos was one of a discovery of and exchange with the people whose countries the traveler was visiting. Interaction rather than consumption was the driving force.

Ariane Mnouchkine's *Théâtre du Soleil* took this interactive or participatory principle to the stage, or, rather to the elimination of the stage as traditionally conceived. The *Théâtre du Soleil* was founded in 1964 on what could be called the *autogestion* principles that would be manifest years later in other instances such as the newspaper *Libération* in its "1970s phase" and in the Lip watch company takeover by the workers in the spring of 1974: equal salaries and shared profits for the members of the company; everyone to have a vote in decision making; absence of a specialized hierarchy, since "actors were to be technicians and vice versa, as well as cleaners, sweepers, ushers and bar staff, box office attendants, telephone receptionists, etc. And everybody was to take part in the process of creating a production—not writing it" (Cook, 69).

The *Théâtre du Soleil* came to prominence in 1971 with a production entitled *1789*. What the play, about the first year of the French Revolution, had in common with Ophul's *The Sorrow and the Pity* was that it offered no thesis, and passed no judgment. Instead, the physical set-up and the narrative structure of the production encouraged the spectators to come out of a passive consumption and to think for themselves about historical events and their presentation. The company performed at the Cartoucherie de Vincennes, a reconverted ammunition storage warehouse in the Bois de Vincennes on the outskirts of Paris. For *1789*, there was no main stage to speak of; instead the different scenes were presented on five different wooden stages that were linked to each other by walkways. Rather than sitting down, the audience had to move around the large space of the Cartoucherie in order to proceed from one scene to the other, using the walkways. Having been taken out of the usual position of static observer, the spectators were also offered a shifting view of the events of 1789:

> The way in which the episodes were introduced and commented revealed the company's intention to create a distancing effect that would encourage the audience to think critically about the historical events being represented. Occasionally different readings of events were offered, as at the very beginning, when the play seemed to be launching

itself with a predictable account of the flight to Varenne of the King and Queen, only to stop, pass comment and start again on a different track. (Cook, 71)

Accompanying this invitation to interpret and think rather than simply absorb, were reminders that this was a theater, a performance: some of people who were ushering in the audience or serving them food and drinks would reappear as actors in the performance; the actors also put on and removed their makeup in full view of the arriving or departing audience. During the performance, the actors sometimes went into the audience, turning them into participants, at one point having them take part in the storming of the Bastille. The *Théâtre du Soleil's* production of *1789* launched the company's national and international success. It continued its innovative approach in a number of major productions that ranged from *L'Age d'or* (*The Golden Age*) of 1975—already addressing the issue of immigration that was quickly coming to the fore with the end of France's economic boom—to *Le dernier cavaranserail* (*The Last Caravanserai*) produced in 2003 and also centered around the mass migratory movements from non-industrialized to industrialized world.

The *Théâtre du Soleil*, like many of the initiatives of the 1970s on the cultural and social fronts, reflected a desire for *une vie et une culture autre* (another kind of life and another kind of culture) that had been at the core of the May movement. As we have seen, these initiatives came from a variety of fields ranging from the new type of newspaper represented by *Libération*, the Larzac movement, the attempt to enact *autogestion* at Lip, to the women's movement, and the challenge to the official narrative of the Occupation. These disparate trends, organizations, and movements had at least one thing in common: they originated in a rebellious desire to question and to change that identified with the Left. The same was true of the philosophy and literary theory of the period in which Barthes, Foucault, Deleuze, Lyotard, Derrida, and Cixous, among others, were celebrities. Much of this thinking was directed at throwing into question or, as Derrida called it, a "deconstruction" of the Western philosophical tradition associated with Enlightenment and universalism.

The critique of the capitalist modernization model that was inherent in the writings of these philosophers and literary theorists was in tune with the May movement and, in many ways, was associated with it. The May movement did not bring about a revolution in France in the classic, Marxist sense, but it nevertheless created an unprecedented and massive challenge to the established order. The political Right's response to this challenge and its aftermath was reflected by a swing from the Left to the Right in French intellectual life. The shift came most spectacularly in 1974 in the shape of the self-proclaimed *nouveaux philosophes* (new philosophers). These *nouveaux philosophes*, most notably Bernard Henri-Lévy and André Gluscksmann, ex-Maoists, and, ironically, ex-students of Foucault and Derrida, respectively, gathered around the arrival in France of the famous Soviet dissident Alexander Solzhenitsyn, and the publication in French of his *Gulag Archipelago*, "an essay of literary investigation" of the Soviet prison system. The book became a bestseller, something close to a remarkable event in France. Although the existence of the "Gulag" had already been revealed in the past, this time around the revelation served not only as a means of discrediting the Soviet Union as a viable social model, something that had also been done before, but to denounce the Communist Left in France and, beyond it, the very idea of revolutionary politics. The *nouveaux philosophes* were at the forefront of this development, which was also a claim for a return to liberal Enlightenment values and, behind them, the French liberal tradition. The "totalitarian state" represented by the Soviet Union and, with it, what was going to be named "the thought of May 68" became the target. The Enlightenment-based universalism that had been itself under attack or "under deconstruction," came back in the vocabulary of the *nouveaux philosophes*. In Bernard Henri-Lévy's *Barbarism with a Human Face* (1977), we read:

> Everyone knows for example that the classless society is in a certain sense the practical embodiment of the totalitarian dream of the advent of the universal . . . that Marxist theory itself, because it sanctifies the Hegelian dream of the truth becoming the world and the world becoming the truth, ends up with an ideal which is, as we shall see, one of the definitions of modern tyranny . . . What is the Gulag? The Enlightenment minus tolerance. (121)

The Gulag and "anti-Enlightenment" thought were conflated. The term *pensée 68*, which would also become known as "French theory" on American campuses, had not yet been coined, but in the critique of the Gulag lay a critique of the "antifoundationalist," and thus "anti-Enlightenment" philosophy of thinkers such as Foucault, Derrida, and Deleuze. A full decade after the publication of *The Gulag Archipelago*, the term *pensée 68* was consecrated in a book published by the philosophers Luc Ferry and Alain Renaut, entitled *La pensée 68. Essai sur l'anti-humanisme contemporain (French Philosophy of the Sixties, An Essay on Anti-humanism)*. As the title indicates, the philosophy of the *maîtres à penser* (mentors) of the 68 generation is viewed, as existentialism had been in the postwar period, as an antihumanist, even nihilist philosophy and is unfavorably compared by Ferry and Renaut to the thought of the Enlightenment. In a new introduction to the book, this comparison is somewhat tempered by the intervening years but the opposition Enlightenment versus *pensée 68* remains intact:

> If we cannot today (this is obvious but also has to be emphasized in view of the predictable criticism) simply return to the values of the philosophy of the Enlightenment, it is equally impossible not to refer to them, as 68 philosophy tried to do, and to effect a *tabula rasa* of the tradition. (Ferry, xxvii)

According to Ferry and Renaut, the view of modernity as a simultaneously repressive and ordering movement is flawed, because it does not take into account the positive aspects of the Enlightenment in which modernity originates. According to them, there is a refusal in *la pensée 68* to acknowledge the Enlightenment's progressive quality, and, according to them, this refusal is evident in

> . . . Foucault's *Madness and Civilization*, with his interpretation of the birth of modern reason as imposing the negation/expulsion/reduction of everything viewed as external in terms of a *universal* norm, in spite of the apparent emancipating intention of the Enlightenment; in Derrida, with his designation of the "violence" necessarily hidden within the modern emergence of reason based on identity, constrained to reject anything that threatens it from within, whether it is ontological or sexual *difference* (logocentrism as well as phallocentrism). (xxvi; italics added)

The critique of universalism that had been at the core of Foucault and Derrida's philosophy was precisely what Ferry and Renaut were criticizing, and behind this criticism lay a defense of the universalist French Republic itself. In the mid-1970s, at the height of the *nouveaux philosophes'* fame, there was a call to replace revolutionary thought with a more pragmatic concern for human rights, whether protesting against Soviet repression or organizing rescue operations for the boat people fleeing South Vietnam in the wake of the communist victory and the American evacuation. Those who were perceived as remaining faithful to the ideals of revolutionary or utopian thought were then relegated to the status of supporters of totalitarianism. There reigned then, as François Cusset proposes in a recent work entitled *French Theory* (2003), a "new moral blackmail imposed on intellectuals—to convert immediately or soon suffer general opprobrium" (324). Cusset goes on to give two examples of the link between the attack on *la pensée 68* and the defense of the universalist republic. First, "It is necessary [according to the *nouveaux philosophes* and their followers] to put an end to the great masters and to ukases in the intellectual sphere, as called for by Pierre Nora who created [the journal] *Le débat* in order to make what he calls 'the Republic *in* literature and philosophy [*les lettres*].'" Explicit in this phrase is the proposition that the "pensée 68" was *outside* of or could not be reconciled with the idea of the universalist republic. Cusset also refers to André Glucksmann's phrase, quoting Hegel, "to think is to dominate," and comments wryly that "Thinking [became] the last idol to be slain by the secular Republic" (325). The secular republic and the defense of human rights were proposed as the alternatives to the discredited revolutionary and utopian *pensée 68*.

It is no accident that the beginning of this shift in French intellectual life, from the utopian and revolutionary Left to a philosophy that accommodated rather than challenged republican universalism, occurred during the years of Valéry Giscard d'Estaing's presidency and of his program for "advanced liberal society." This presidency began as the thirty years of economic boom and modernization were ending and *la crise* (the economic crisis and period of recession inaugurated by the oil embargo of 1973) was about to become a ubiquitous term. However, even as the recession started, the rapid spread of electronic technology and communication had already become part of daily life, and intellectual life was no exception. The media, especially television, and journalism were in the process of replacing the university and the publishing houses at the symbolic epicenter of intellectual life in France. It is thus also no accident that the *nouveaux philosophes'* first public appearance under that label took place on television in the newly created literary program, *Apostrophes*, one of the most popular programs on French television from the first year of its appearance in 1975. *Apostrophes* was exclusively dedicated to books—its host Bernard Pivot invited authors to discuss their newly published works—and an appearance on the program could result in massive sales for the most specialized books; however, for a large segment of the audience, watching the program came to replace the actual reading of the books being discussed. Gilles Deleuze, whose *Anti-Oedipus* was one of the principal targets of the *nouveaux philosophes*, did not immediately comment on their sudden fame and on their work, but in 1977, he published a short text in which he took to task the *nouveaux philosophes* for what he saw has their shallow philosophy and media opportunism (see dossier 8.10). At least one British cultural historian would later refer to the *nouveaux philosophes'* "media gold-digging" (Forbes and Kelly, 216) while in his *Le pouvoir intellectuel en France* (*Intellectual Power in France*), published in 1979, Régis Debray, the French philosopher who had fought alongside Che Guevara in Bolivia, proceeded with an extensive critique of the "mediatization" of intellectuals in France. In this critique, we can also observe a stand against what was called "cocacolonization" in the 1950s, as Debray equates "mediatization" with "Americanization"; in addition, as a *républicain de gauche*, a Left-wing supporter of the republic and of its values, Debray also includes Europe as a threat to the independence and national integrity of France. "An Americanized intelligentsia in a Europeanized France puts the emphasis on smiles, good teeth, nice hair and the adolescent stupidity known as petulance" (quoted in Howarth and Varouxakis, 137). Others saw in the *nouveaux philosophes'* appropriation of the media a means of reclaiming the type of authority and status that had been thrown into question by the May movement and its aftermath. In Kristin Ross's acerbic evaluation, the "New Philosophers represented intellectuals who in the old Maoist phrase, had once gotten off their horses in May [68] to gather the flowers, but who were once more firmly back in the saddle, reclaiming the specificity and prestige of a social category that May had disrupted and put into question" (*May*, 174).

Dossier 8.10   Gilles Deleuze, Regarding the nouveaux philosophes (Plus a More General Problem) (1977)

An addition to *Minuit*, no. 24, May 1977. The full text, dated June 5, 1977, was offered free of charge in bookstores where numerous polemical works, billed as "the new philosophy," were being distributed and sold. The following is an excerpt.

　—What do you think about "the new philosophers"?

　—Not much. I can think of two reasons why their thought is empty. First, they work with big concepts, all puffed up like an abscess: THE law, Power, Master, THE world, THE revolution, Faith, etc. Then they create these monstrous packages, gross dualisms: THE law and THE rebel, Power and Angels. Second, the weaker the thought, the more important the thinker. The expressing subject takes itself all the more seriously in relation to empty propositions ("It is I who speak, and I am courageous and lucid . . . , I am a soldier of Christ . . . , I belong to the lost generation . . . , We were there in May 68 . . . , We won't get fooled again . . ."). These two rhetorical procedures spoil the work. For a long time now, people in every discipline have been working to avoid these very pitfalls. We've been trying to create concepts with fine articulations, extremely differentiated concepts, to escape gross dualisms. And we've been trying to uncover creative functions that would no longer require an author-function for them to be active (in music, painting, audio-visual arts, film, and even philosophy). This wholesale return to the author, to an empty and vain subject, as well as to gross conceptual stereotypes, represents a troubling reactionary development . . .

　In any event, however bad a school may be, we cannot say that these new philosophers are a school. They do have a certain newness about them: rather than form a school, they have introduced France to literary or philosophical marketing. Marketing has its own particular logic: 1) You have to talk about the book, or get the book talked about, rather than let the book do the talking. Theoretically, you could have all the newspaper articles, interviews, conferences, and radio shows replace the book altogether, it needn't exist at all. The work that the new philosophers do has less to do with their books than with the articles they can obtain, the newspapers and TV shows they can monopolize, an interview they can give, a book review they can do, or an appearance in Playboy. The effort they put into it, at this level anyway, and with this degree of organization, implies an activity exclusive of philosophy, or at least excluded from it. And

2) from a marketing perspective, the same book or product should have several versions, so as to appeal to everyone: a pious version, an atheist version, a Heideggerian version, a leftist, a centrist and a neo-fascist version, a Jacques Chirac version, a nuanced "unity of the Left" version, etc.

—If it really is a question of marketing, why did we have to wait for the new philosophers, why is it only now that their thought has arrived?

—For several reasons which are beyond the control of any one person. Andre Scala recently analyzed the reversal of the relationship between journalists and writers, between the press and books. Journalism, through radio and television, has increasingly realized its potential to create events (controlled leaks, Watergate, polls, etc.). And just as journalism needs to refer to external events less and less, since it already creates many of them, it also needs less and less to refer to external analysis, including polls of "intellectuals" or "writers." Journalism has discovered an autonomous and sufficient thought within itself. *This is why, if we pursue this line of argument to its limit, a book is worth less than the newspaper article written about it or the interview which comes after it. Intellectuals and writers, even artists, are thus forced to become journalists if they want to conform to the norm. This is a new type of thought, the interview-thought, the conversation-thought, the sound bite-thought. We can imagine a book that would be about a newspaper article, and not the reverse. The power relations between journalists and intellectuals have totally changed. It all began with television, and the special editions that sought to tame willing intellectuals. The media no longer needs intellectuals. I'm not saying that this reversal, this domestication of the intellectual, is a disaster. That's how things go: precisely when writing and thought were beginning to abandon the author-function, when creations no longer required an author-function for them to be active, the author-function was co-opted by radio and television, and by journalism. Journalists have become the new authors, and those writers who wanted to become authors had to go through journalists, or become journalists themselves. A function that had been somewhat discredited has managed to recapture some modernity and find a new conformity by changing its place and its object. This is what made the enterprise of intellectual marketing possible.*

To sum up, my problem with the new philosophers is that the work they do is manure, and this work partakes of a new relationship between book and press that is fundamentally reactionary. They are new, yes, but conformist in the highest degree. But the new philosophers themselves are not important. Even if they disappear tomorrow, their marketing enterprise will be repeated again and again. This marketing enterprise represents the submission of thought to the media. By the same token, thought offers the media a minimum intellectual guarantee and peace of mind to stifle any attempts at creation that would make the media themselves evolve. The lame debates we see on TV, and the stupid narcissistic director's films, lessen the chances of any real creation on television and elsewhere.

The *nouveaux philosophes* were just one manifestation, albeit a very visible one, of a trend that would become increasingly more widespread in France as the 1970s wore on: massive and rapid modernization had been accompanied by the "mediatization" of life that had already been referred to in works such as Guy Debord's *Société du Spectacle* a decade earlier, as well as in the work of the Canadian sociologist and media historian, Marshall McLuhan, on the media during the same period. What McLuhan called the "Gutenberg galaxy," also referred to as "print culture," was being superseded by visual media. This was of course also occurring in other advanced industrial societies, but in France, with its long, prestigious, and centralizing cultural and linguistic tradition, the effects of this shift were perceived and experienced as a *more* threatening and destabilizing development. This perception can be traced in part to the fact that France had been instrumental in the creation of the modern paradigm that was in the process of being bypassed and that the end of its own dominance as a nation on the world scene was relatively recent. Because of this chronological proximity, some of the particular characteristics of French modernity remained very much part of the country that had emerged from thirty years of rapid modernization and all of the disruptions this entailed. The very strength of the centralized, universalist, and republican model of modernity embodied by France remained manifest in the midst of, indeed in spite of post-1945 modernization, Americanization, and mediatization: *Apostrophes*, for example, was a popular television program, but it was also a program devoted to the celebration of writing culture; its host, Bernard Pivot, also presided over the annual and televised *dictée* (dictation), an exercise in which millions of French-speaking people throughout the world participate every year. To see all of these people of all ages quietly taking a dictation is to witness the continued relevance of a ritual that harks back to the monarchy's standardization of French and to the Third Republic's *instituteurs*. The *dictée de Bernard Pivot* (Bernard Pivot's dictation) is a peculiarly French exercise in the midst of the media age; it is the audiovisual with a republican educational edge. The *nouveaux philosophes* may well have been (and continue to be) media personalities, but they were also perpetuating a trend of public intellectual debate that was very much part of a well-entrenched French tradition, even if it was taking place in a medium and at a level which some, Gilles Deleuze most prominently, found lacking in rigor.

The "Pompidou Center," the museum of modern art and multipurpose exhibition space—it included a library and a cinema—that opened in 1977 and was named after President Georges Pompidou was also *spectacularly* representative of France's particular response to the age of mediatization and mass culture that had come to the fore. On the one hand, the "Pompidou Center," popularly known as "Beaubourg," after the neighborhood in which it is located, was a project initiated and supported by the president of the republic himself. This type of active and personal involvement of a premier in cultural matters was a reflection of the mix of republican practice and acknowledgment of the forces of mass culture that characterized the 1970s. One historian who called the actual structure "modernism turned inside out" (Jones, 301) was also inadvertently referring to a state-supervised extension of the audience for culture represented by the project: modernism, essentially a paradigm of the few, was given an architectural structure opened to the masses. As had been the case for André Malraux's *maisons de la culture*, the objective was not to modify or extend the concept of culture, but to bring the people to high culture, in this instance modern art. At a time when mass culture was becoming dominant, the French state built a public building that was designed to attract the masses, but to a concept of culture that, itself, had not changed. The philosopher Jean Baudrillard, one of the best-known French theoreticians of the postmodern declared in an interview that the Pompidou center was a sign of the encounter between a mass audience and elitist culture "parachuted from the top"; according to Baudrillard, the crowds came but did not understand what was being offered to them (Celestin, "From Popular Culture to Mass Culture," 13). The Pompidou Center, whose construction entailed the destruction and ensuing "gentrification" of one of Paris' oldest neighborhoods can also be perceived in the tradition of the nineteenth-century "Haussmannization" of Paris when old, working-class neighborhoods were razed to make room for the wide avenues and public buildings that reflected the imperial capital's and, later, the republic's grandeur.

Figure 8.5   The Pompidou Center (1977)

The Pompidou Center, named after the French president who initiated the project, was opened in 1977. It quickly became the most popular museum and public building in Paris. The unexpected turnout of visitors placed enormous strain on the building, which had to be closed for repairs in 1994. In 2001, 150,000 artificial poppies were "handplanted" on its esplanade as a symbol of designer Kenzo's latest perfume. Today, the giant perfume bottle still stands on the esplanade, a reminder of the conflation of culture and commerce that characterized the "postmodern." (© Manoocher Deghati/AFP/Getty Images)

By the time the Pompidou Center opened its doors in 1977, Valéry Giscard d'Estaing had been president for three years and France was experiencing the recession that had begun with the OPEC oil embargo of 1973. Other factors, such as the economic downturn in the United States, traditionally a motor of world economy, contributed to the continuation of the recession. By 1975, the symbolic number of one million unemployed had been reached in France. In 1977, Giscard d'Estaing appointed the economist Raymond Barre as prime minister to replace Jacques Chirac, officially a Gaullist, but in fact a member of the generation that came after de Gaulle and never knew him or served during his presidency. Barre's austerity program—wage and price freezes and cuts in government spending and in business taxes with a view to boost the economy—had some temporary success that showed in the slightly higher growth rates, but inflation and unemployment remained high.

During these economic hard times, the Left was in the process of reorganizing and regrouping. François Mitterrand became First Secretary general of the newly founded

Socialist Party in 1971 and signed the *Programme commun de la Gauche* (a joint program for government by the Left) with the Communist Party one year later. Realizing that his political future lay with the Left rather than with the center, Mitterand committed the Socialist Party to a "radical break with capitalism." As the candidate of the united Left in the presidential elections of 1974, Mitterand lost to Giscard d'Estaing by a very thin margin. This loss is explained by several factors: the fear of a "dictatorship of the proletariat," of "commissars at the helm," used so effectively by de Gaulle to regain control of the political situation in 1968, was still very much a factor: "Fear of a Mitterand victory produced the highest voter turnout in French history—87.33 percent" (Sowerwine 375); Giscard won with 50.8 percent of the vote to Mitterand's 49.2 percent. In addition, when the elections took place the *crise* was not yet in full swing as wages were still rising and unemployment had not yet become a factor. By 1981, the year of new presidential elections, however, the situation had changed dramatically on both the economic and political fronts. Unemployment, which had reached over one and a half million by 1981, showed no sign of slowing down. The tools of the market economy were proving to be ineffective. On the political front, the Right was fragmented. Jacques Chirac, who had founded his own party, the *Rassemblement pour la République* (RPR, Rally for the Republic), after having been Giscard d'Estaing's prime minister, went on to become mayor of Paris. A new law had reinstated the position, which had been abolished since 1800. Chirac won the high-profile position by running against a Giscard d'Estaing protégé and would continue to occupy it until he was elected president in 1995.

On the Left, François Mitterand's Socialists came to dominate the coalition with the Communists who proved to be unable or unwilling to follow a strategy of courting voters of the center. The Union of the Left broke down in 1977, but Mitterand had shown both his commitment to make major reforms and his ability to resist "unreasonable" demands from the Communist Party. When the presidential elections came up in 1981, Chirac's tepid support of Giscard d'Estaing's candidacy, the continued economic woes of Giscard's center-Right government, the Socialists' aura as reformist party, a party whose candidate the Communists had no choice but to support in the second round of the elections, all combined to give François Mitterand the victory with 51.75 per cent of the vote. The Socialist president had been elected on a platform of "110 propositions" that promised a "radical break with capitalism." It remained to be seen whether he would be able to enact this program in the France of the 1980s.

References

Barthes, Roland. *Mythologies*. Paris: Editions du Seuil, 1957.

———. "Objective Literature: Alain Robbe-Grillet." Richard Howard, trans. In *Two Novels by Robbe-Grillet. Jealousy & In the Labyrinth*. New York: Grove Press, 1965.

———. *The Eiffel Tower and Other Mythologies*. Richard Howard, trans. New York: Hill and Wang, 1979.

———. "The Death of the Author." In *Image, Music, Text: Essays Selected and Translated by Stephen Heath*. New York: Noonday Press, 1988.

Bersntein, Serge and Jean-Pierre Rioux. *The Pompidou Years. 1969–1974*. Paris, Cambridge: Editions de la Maison des Sciences de l'Homme and Cambridge University Press, 2000.

Bois, Yves-Alain. "French Lib." In Hollier Denis, ed., *A New History of French Literature*. Cambridge, MA and London: Harvard University Press, 1989, 1040–1045.

Butor, Michel. *A Change of Heart*. Jean Stewart, trans. New York: Simon and Schuster, 1959. Originally published as *La modification* (Paris: Gallimard, 1957).

Célestin, Roger. "From Popular Culture to Mass Culture: An Interview with Jean Baudrillard." *SITES: The Journal of Contemporary French Studies*, 1, 1 (Spring 1997): 5–15.

Célestin, Roger, Eliane DalMolin, and Isabelle de Courtivron. *Beyond French Feminisms. Debates on Women, Politics and Culture in France. 1981–2001*. New York: Palgrave-McMillan, 2003.

Cerny, Philip G. *Une politique de grandeur: Aspects idéologiques de la politique extérieure de de Gaulle*. Anne Krief, trans. Paris: Flammarion, 1986.

Clément, Marcelle. "Sighing, a French Sound Endures." *New York Times*, October 18, 1998, Section 2.

Cook, David A. *A History of Narrative Film*. London and New York: W.W. Norton & Co., 1981.

Cook, Martin, ed. *French Culture since 1945*. London, New York: 1993.

Copfermann, Emile. *La génération des blousons noirs: Problèmes de la jeunesse française*. Paris: Maspero, 1962.

Courtivron, Isabelle de, and Elaine Marks. *New French Feminisms. An Anthology*. New York: Schocken Books, 1981.

Crozier, Michel. *The Stalled Society*. Rupert Swyer, trans. New York: Viking Press, 1973. Originally published as *La société bloquée* (Paris: Editions du Seuil, 1970).

de Beauvoir, Simone. *Brigitte Bardot and the Lolita Syndrome*. Bernard Fretchman, trans. New York: André Deutsch, Weidenfeld, and Nicolson, 1960.

Debord, Guy. *The Society of the Spectacle*. Donald Nicholson-Smith, trans. New York: Zone Books, 1995. Originally published as *La société du spectacle* (Paris: Buchet Castel, 1967).

Deleuze, Gilles. *Nietzsche et la philosophie*. Paris: Editions de Minuit, 1962.

Guattari, Felix. *Anti-Oedipus. Anti-Oedipus: Capitalism and Schizophrenia*. Robert Hurley, Mark Seem, Helen R. Lane, trans. Minneapolis: University of Minnesota Press, 1983. Reprint. Originally published by New York: Viking Press, 1977.

———. *Regarding the* nouveaux philosophes *(Plus a More General Problem)*. In David Lapoujade, ed., Ames Hodges and Mike Taormina, trans. *Two Regimes of Madness: Texts and Interviews 1975–1995*. Los Angeles, CA : Semiotext(e); Cambridge, MA: Distributed by MIT Press, 2006.

Deleuze, Gilles and Félix Guattari. *Anti-Oedipus: Capitalism and Schizophrenia*. Robert Hurley, Mark Seem, and Helen R. Lane, trans. New York: Viking Press, 1977.

Ferry, Luc and Alain Renaut. *French Philosophy of the Sixties. An Essay on Antihumanism*. Mary H.S. Cattani, trans. Amherst: University of Massachusetts Press, 1990. Originally published as *La pensée 68. Essai sur l'anti-humanisme contemporain* (Paris: Gallimard, 1985).

Forbes, Jill and Michael Kelly, eds. *French Cultural Studies. An Introduction*. Oxford, New York: Oxford University Press, 1995.

Foucault, Michel. *The Order of Things. An Archeology of the Human Sciences*. New York: Pantheon Books, 1970. Originally published as *Les mots et les choses* (Paris: Gallimard, 1966).

———. 1970. "Theatrum philosophicum." *Critique* 282: 885–908.

Hargreaves, Alec G. "The Challenges of Multiculturalism: Regional and Religious Differences in France Today." In Kidd and Reynolds, 95–110.

Hollier, Denis, ed. "Actions No! Words, Yes!" In Denis Hollier, ed. *A New History of French Literature*. Cambridge, MA and London, UK: Harvard University Press, 1989.

———. *A New History of French Literature*. Cambridge, MA and London: Harvard University Press, 1989.

Irigaray, Luce. "This Sex Which Is Not One." Claudia Reeder, trans. In Isabelle de Courtivron and Elaine Marks, 99–110.

Jones, Colin. *The Cambridge Illustrated History of France*. Cambridge: Cambridge University Press, 1994.

Kidd, William and Sîan Reynolds. *Contemporary French Cultural Studies*. London: Arnold, 2000.

Kuisel, Richard. "The French Search for Modernity." In William Cohen, ed. *The Transformation of Modern France*. Boston, NY: Houghton Mifflin, 1997, 28–46.

Labro, Michel. "Comment on en est arriveé là." *L'Express*, December 2, 1998.

Lacan, Jacques. *Ecrits*. Paris: Editions du Seuil, 1966.

Lane, Jeremy F. "The French Contribution to Contemporary Cultural Analysis." In Kidd and Reynolds, 287–299.

Lefebvre, Henri. *Critique of Everyday Life*. John Moore, trans. London: New York: Verso, 1991.

Lévy, Bernard Henri. *Barbarism with a Human Face*. New York: Harper and Row, 1979. Originally published as *La barbarie a visage humain* (Paris: Grasset et Fasquelle, 1977).

Loyer, Emmanuelle and Pascale Goetschel. *Histoire culturelle et intellectuelle de la France au XXe siècle*. Paris: Armand Colin, 1995.

Lyotard, Jean-François. *The Postmodern Condition: A Report on Knowledge*. Geoff Bennington and Brian Massumi, trans. Minneapolis: University of Minnesota Press, 1979. Originally published as *La condition postmoderne: Rapport sur le savoir* (Parris: Editions de Minuit, 1979).

Manchette, Jean-Patrick. *Three to Kill*. Donald Nicholson-Smith, trans. San Francisco: City Lights Books, 2002. Originally published as *Le petit bleu de la côte ouest* (Paris: Gallimard, 1976).

Morin, Edgar. "Le temps des copains." *Le Monde*, July 6, 1963.

———. *L'esprit du temps*. Vol. 1: *Nécrose*. Paris: Bernard Grasset, 1975.

Perec, George. *Les choses. A Story of the Sixties*. Helen R. Lane, trans. New York: Grove Press, 1967. Originally published as *Les choses. Une histoire des années soixante* (Paris: Juillard, 1965).

Rigby, Bryan. *Popular Culture in Modern France. A Study of Cultural Discourse*. London, New York: Routledge, 1991.

Rioux, Jean-Pierre and Jean-François Sirinelli. *Histoire culturellle de la France. Vol. 4. Le temps des masses. Le vingtième siècle*. Paris: Editions du Seuil, 1997.

Robbe-Grillet, Alain. *For a New Novel. Essays on Fiction*. Richard Howard, trans. New York: Grove Press, 1965. Originally published as *Pour un nouveau roman* (Paris: Editions de Minuit, 1963).

Ross, Kristin. *Fast Cars, Clean Bodies: Decolonization and the Reordering of French Culture*. Cambridge, MA; London, UK: MIT Press, 1995.

———. *May '68 and Its Afterlives*. Chicago, London: University of Chicago Press, 2002.

Stovall, Tyler E. *France since the Second World War*. Harlow, London: Pearson Education Limited, 2002.

Thorn, Jean-Pierre. "Témoignage." In Virginie Linhart, ed. *Volontaires pour l'usine*. Paris: Editions du Seuil, 1994, 190–195. In Wieworka, 565–569.

Vaneigem, Raoul. *Traité de savoir-vivre à l'usage des jeunes générations*. Paris: Gallimard, 1967.

Weiner, Susan. *Enfants Terribles. Youth and Femininity in the Mass Media in France, 1945–1968*. Baltimore and London: Johns Hopkins University Press, 2001.

Wieviorka, Olivier and Christophe Prochasson, eds. *La France du XXème siècle. Documents d'histoire*. Paris: Editions du Seuil, 1994.

CHAPTER 9

THE SOCIALIST REPUBLIC (1981–1995)

This victory belongs to the forces of youth, of labor, of creativity, of renewal who have come together in a great national movement for jobs, peace, freedom, themes that were those of my presidential campaign and will remain those of my administration.

—François Mitterand, from a speech made on the night of his election as president of the republic on May 10, 1981

Immigrants from across the Mediterranean, back to your shacks!

—Jean-Pierre Stirbois, high official of the National Front, from a speech made at the National Front's convention on October 20, 1982

François Mitterand, former first secretary of the French Socialist Party, became president of the republic the same year the American series *Dallas* began broadcasting on French television. Although unrelated, the simultaneous occurrence of the two events reflects the fact that the first government of the Left in France since the Popular Front of 1936 was coming to power in a world where market forces and the media symbolized by the American series had become ubiquitous. Whether a "Socialist island" could exist in such an international context would become an issue the new government would rapidly have to confront. Inside French frontiers, frontiers made increasingly porous by this internationalization (soon to be the "globalization") of national economies, Mitterand and the socialist government would also have to contend not only with opposition from the traditional Right, but also with the rise of an extreme right-wing party, the National Front, whose growing success was posited on a challenge to the very principles that had brought the Left to power. Overall, the years of Mitterand's presidency would coincide with a national debate on some of the most basic notions constitutive of the "French Republic" and "French identity." The principles of universalism and secularism (*laïcité*) that had been at the core of the national narrative would be part of this debate. The French Revolution itself, the founding event of modern France, with its roots in the Enlightenment, would be variously and fractiously reinterpreted. In an era where second-generation immigrants had made France a more "multicultural" society *à l'américaine*, and Socialists applied neoliberal economic policies, the question of the end of "French exceptionalism" would also arise.

★   ★   ★

On the night of May 10, 1981, however, the mood was that of celebration as huge crowds of supporters joyously took to the streets of Paris and other cities in France to celebrate Mitterand's victory. The new president dissolved the National Assembly and called for new elections, which would give his party an absolute majority. The Socialists would not need a coalition in order to apply their program. Nevertheless, the new government included four communist ministers, the first Communist cabinet members since 1947, when the cold war was beginning. Six women were also appointed, including a minister of women's rights; the death penalty was abolished; one hundred and thirty thousand illegal immigrants were amnestied and family reunifications were made easier; the Auroux laws, named after Mitterand's Minister of Labor Jean Auroux, resulted in a higher minimum wage, more paid vacation (from four to five weeks), and a shorter work week (from forty to thirty-nine hours) with no loss in salary. The retirement age was lowered to sixty, family allowances and pensions were increased, and a tax on the wealthiest was adopted. On the economic front the government proceeded with the nationalizations that had been announced during the presidential campaign. The state became the major shareholder in a number of important sectors ranging from banks and insurance companies to the steel industry as well as air and space, arms, chemistry, and electronics. This was a wave of nationalizations unseen since the immediate postwar years. Decentralization was also on the agenda as the regions, departments, and communes were given increased power and responsibilities. The adopted measures on the economic, social, and political fronts signaled that Mitterand was indeed keeping his campaign promises.

For about a year after Mitterand's election, his government and his presidency were in a "state of grace" and the "110 propositions" that had been the core of his election campaign were being applied. But this would change quickly and drastically. The socialist economic program was based on a Keynesian policy where, in principle, the increase in government spending and wages would lead to increased consumption that would jumpstart the economy, and, in turn, lead to increased employment and investment. However, the socialist government had counted on an international economic context, with an American recovery that would stimulate the European economy; this recovery did not materialize. In addition, the French increased purchasing power resulting from the wage hikes, went to purchase foreign goods rather than French ones, which had become less affordable due to high inflation; France's balance of payment deficit had increased; the massive funds needed to pay for the nationalizations could have come from investments, but fear of socialist policies led to a crisis in investor confidence and capital flight. Unemployment continued to rise.

By November 1981, not quite six months after Mitterand's election, his minister of the economy and finance declared: "It will be necessary to pause before announcing further reforms" (Sowerwine, 388). The state of grace was over and the socialist government began to apply an austerity program that included cuts in public spending, a tax increase, a wage and price freeze, and tax cuts for businesses. Profits were encouraged at the expense of wages in order to stimulate investments, a policy very similar to the Reagan administration's "trickle down economics" in the United States. In general, the focus shifted from leftist reforms to a new crusade for economic "modernization," the term used by Mitterand when in November (1983) he presented his first elaborate picture of the new strategy. On the occasion, *Libération*, a newspaper that had come out of the May 68 movement and whose leftist sympathies were no secret (see chapter 8), used the following headline, a timely reference to the season when the new Beaujolais wine arrived on the market: *Le Mitterand Nouveau est arrivé* (the New Mitterand vintage has arrived) (Daley, 36).

De Gaulle had gone against the grain of the vision of France he publicly symbolized, the France of tradition, high culture, empire and *grandeur*, and had overseen the country's economic modernization and its entry into consumer culture; Mitterand was in the process of going against the grain of traditional Left politics and ideology and overseeing France's continued modernization through its alignment on globalization and neoliberal economics. What his predecessor, Valéry Giscard d'Estaing, had referred to as *décrispation*, or the normalization of French politics on a model on nontraumatic transfers of power from the Left to the Right and vice versa, seemed to be playing itself out in the socialist republic.

The nationalizations themselves belonged to the long tradition of an interventionist and centralized state that was, in France, a feature of governments of both the Left and the Right. In the socialist mold, however, there was a claim to use this power of the state for a more active policy of democratization, a more concerted effort to get beyond what sociologist Michel Crozier had called the "stalled society." The Savary Law, for example, named after Mitterand's minister of education, proposed the creation of a unified and secular school system that would put the private schools (essentially Catholic schools) of France under the jurisdiction of the Ministry of National Education. The proposal was presented as a means of leveling the playing field for all students, and quickly became a lightning rod for the Right's protest against the socialist government. When over a million people marched in the streets of Paris—among them the representatives of the two parties of the traditional Right, the UDF (*Union pour la Démocracie Française*) and of the RPR (*Rassemblement pour la République*), led by its founder, Jacques Chirac, the mayor of Paris, as well as representatives from the National Front. The Savary law was withdrawn. Thus disavowed, the prime minister resigned and was replaced not by a traditional Socialist like himself but by an ENA (*Ecole Nationale d'Administration*, the institution that traditionally produces France's political and business elites) graduate from a wealthy background, more of a "bourgeois technocrat . . . who resembled Valéry Giscard d'Estaing physically as well as politically" (Stovall, 89).

The new prime minister, Laurent Fabius, oversaw an extension of the austerity plan and a policy of providing government support for sectors and companies deemed competitive while withdrawing that support from others such as steel, shipyards, and coal mining. During his presidential campaign in 1995, Jacques Chirac would famously label *la fracture sociale* (the social schism), the growing gap between those who had successfully integrated modernized France and those who had not. This gap had widened radically beginning in the mid-1970s. Unemployment was on the rise and the *sans abris* (homeless) began to be a common sight in French cities. "Want and need in an increasingly materialistic consumer society produced a backlash of delinquency—the crime rate increased by 250 percent between the mid-1970s and the mid-1980s"

(Jones, 324). In this climate of rising unemployment and *insécurité*, the National Front, led by Jean-Marie Le Pen, began to score its first electoral victories.

Figure 9.1   The Leadership of the National Front Marching in Paris (1984)

The National Front. Jean-Marie Le Pen, flanked by his wife and daughter, leads a march against *l'insécurité* in Paris' eighteenth arrondissement in December 1984. The Front blamed rising unemployment and the increased crime rate on immigrants, especially those from North Africa. (© Hachette Photo Presse)

The party was founded in 1972 when several far right-wing organizations joined forces in a "united nationalist federation" under the leadership of a "quartet of revengeful elements still yearning for a colonized Algeria and nostalgic for the shriveled France of Vichy" (Plenel and Rollat, 7). The National Front belongs to the tradition of extreme right-wing and populist movements in France that include Boulangisme (see chapter 3), the Action Française, the Leagues of 1936, Vichy (see chapter 5), and the Poujadist movement (see chapter 8). However, Jean-Marie Le Pen "succeeded where none of his predecessors had managed: the union of all protesters, traditionalist and conservative Catholics, those nostalgic for the Action française, neo-nazis, neo-Poujadists, anti-Semites, nationalists, people of modest means frightened by socioeconomic upheavals, by the rise of delinquency and by the violence of urban civilization" (M. Winock, quoted in Plenel and Rollat, 9). Central to the National Front's strategy was the focus on immigrants, particularly on those from North Africa, as the major source of the problems facing the nation. This strategy found a responsive public in France for several reasons: it connected with fears and anxieties regarding Islam that go as far back as the medieval literary text, the *Chanson de Roland*, and the Crusades. Among North Africans, Algerians in particular symbolized one of the most traumatic moments of French history: the Algerian War. In the 1970s, two events contributed to reinforce the image of "the Arabs" as a threat to the West in general and, for the Front's use, to France in particular: the oil crisis of 1973 and the rise of Islamic fundamentalism after the Iranian Revolution of 1979.

Dossier 9.1   Jean–Marie Le Pen and the National Front 1984 (Jean–Marie LePen's Speech of May 13, 1984)

Joan of Arc Day has become the National Front's traditional day of celebration. By laying claim to the figure of the young peasant girl who had led King Charles VII's forces and defeated the British during the Hundred Years War, and was later canonized by the Catholic Church, the Front was displaying its own connection to tradition, a strategy that has well served parties from the entire spectrum of French politics. On the day of his investiture, Mitterand had placed a red rose (the Socialist Party's symbol) on the tombs of three men at the Panthéon, the façade of which is emblazoned with the following inscription: *Aux grands hommes, la patrie reconnaissante* (To great men, the grateful fatherland). Mitterand entered the Panthéon alone and placed his offering on the tombs of Victor Schoelcher, who had authored the decree liberating the slaves in 1848, Jean Moulin, the leader of the inside Resistance, de Gaulle's representative during the Occupation, and Jean Jaurès, the Socialist leader assassinated on the eve of World War I. While Mitterand's symbolic choices at the Panthéon connect his party to a progressive republican past, the National Front's claim of Joan of Arc reflects its attachment to a tradition that is older and more bound to "the soil" through Joan of Arc's peasant roots. On this particular commemoration, the leader of the National Front has chosen to dedicate his speech to the "youth of France."

Ladies and Gentlemen,
    [. . .]
    Beautiful minds and beautiful souls in Paris and elsewhere claim that the policy we follow is a selfish, xenophobic, and racist policy. This is not the case at all, for in fact we only follow in politics what is the most elementary rule of common sense, one whose first duty is to one's self and to those close to one. I have said this several times, I prefer my daughters to my nieces, my nieces to my cousins, and my cousins to my neighbors. The same is true in politics, I prefer the French.
    Let me take one example, one that I refer to often. In the Maghreb, Algeria-Tunisia-Morocco, there were 20 millions inhabitants 20 years ago; today there are more than 50 and they will be more than 100 million 16 years from now, that is in the year 2000, 60 percent of whom will be under 18 years of age, and I ask you to think about this warning that, like Hitler who spoke of his vital space, Houari Boumedienne [President of Algeria from 1965 to 1978] sent us before leaving for Allah's paradise: "The people of the South will go on the assault against those of the North to conquer their livelihood there, and this immigration will be neither brotherly nor peaceful." Who dares say or write that this legitimate self-defense of our people, of our country, and of Europe is racism? It is only the application of a right we all have to be at home in France, and our duty to protect our people first of all. For, and I say this to the intellectuals suffering from a need to embrace the world and from irresponsible generosity, "when Syracuse is taken, Archimedes throat is slit and too bad for the theorem"; if tomorrow the Third World on the on the assault against France and Europe swept them away under one of those

waves of invaders that our continent has known throughout the centuries, and that it stopped at Marathon, at Salamis, at Lepanto, at Poitiers, this submersion would be to no one's advantage. Even if it sacrificed our civilization, for the rest of the world our sacrifice would be that of the hen with the golden eggs, once killed, she would no longer lay them. And our comments include generosity, France's and Europe's responsibility towards the world. The world needs us, the Third World needs us in order to survive and if a solution to these problems is found, once again it will come from the tutelary spirit of our humanist civilization.

Throughout the National Front's campaign for the municipal elections of 1983, "immigrants," a word that essentially referred to the North African population, were systematically targeted as the source of both crime and unemployment in France, and as a major drain on the system of social benefits. The strategy of blaming "the foreigners" led to the first major electoral success of the National Front in elections: the party garnered 10 percent of the vote overall and one of its candidates won the deputy-mayor post in Dreux, a small city about forty miles from Paris. The following year, the National Front would achieve a similar score during the European parliamentary elections. Throughout, the party platform remained unchanged: anti-immigration as a means of advocating its "national populism" (Taguieff, 12).

Several factors explain the National Front's emergence in the early 1980s. As we have seen, during the first two decades or so of economic boom, the immigrants came mainly from Southern Europe, Portugal, Spain, Italy; and then increasingly from the former colonies and protectorates of France, especially North Africa. During the economic boom years, they were ignored if not given a warm welcome, and did not constitute a visible community. By 1974, France had entered a long period of recession accompanied by unemployment rates hovering around 10 percent. Legal immigration was suspended during the Giscard d'Estaing administration. However, illegal immigration continued. In addition, many of the single men who had formed the first waves of immigrant labor had been joined by their families. Some of their children were born in France and were French citizens. There was a shift from a temporary immigration of single men to permanent communities living in France. Usually these communities lived, and continue to live, in the housing projects on the outskirts of large cities; some of these projects had been built during the boom years (Sarcelles in the Paris region, Vaulx-en-Velin in the Marseille region) and some had been areas where earlier generations of European working-class immigrants had lived (Saint-Denis, Gennevilliers in the Paris region). As this earlier wave shows, immigration was not a new phenomenon in France. "It was as French as croissants . . . it has been estimated that in the 1990s, one third of the French population is a first- second- or third-generation immigrant" (Jones, 325). One major difference between the immigration of the boom years and the recent waves of immigrants is that, in those years of economic plenty and rapid modernization, there were jobs in mining, agriculture, and assembly plants in activities ranging from textiles to cars that provided immigrants with stable income and a means of integrating into French society. Mass unemployment and "deindustrialization" beginning in the 1970s made this integration through work increasingly difficult.

The new immigrants were becoming "visible" at a time when the old "smokestack industries" and assembly plants were being *délocalisé* (outsourced—a word not yet in vogue in the 1970s and early 1980s) and advanced industrial countries like France were becoming service and information-based "post-industrial" economies. Whereas industry accounted for 39 percent of the working population in 1975, it had diminished to 29 percent by 1992. In terms of the working population this shift resulted in a decrease in employment figures: notwithstanding what politicians throughout the political spectrum were advocating in political campaigns, the "postindustrial" economies required less labor than the old industrial ones. As a result the *Français de souche* or "native French"—admittedly a problematic term, given the statistics—perceived themselves as competing for jobs with others they considered "undesirable foreigners." Independently of issues of racism and xenophobia, these "native French" were reacting to new economic forces that were leaving them behind. They felt that the traditional structures were no longer adequate in representing them. The proportion of the labor force that made up trade unions in the 1970s fell from 20 to 15 percent by the late 1980s, and the Communist Party, traditionally a major organizing structure for industrial workers went from obtaining a quarter of the national vote in the postwar to just about 5 percent by the presidential elections of 1988. The connection between deindustrialization, structural unemployment, and the defection from the Communist Party and the trade unions in favor of the extreme Right, have led some to consider the National Front itself as a "postindustrial party":

> What is specific to postindustrial capitalism is not so much that it generates material poverty for a substantial segment of the population: blue-collar workers, the unemployed, small traders or farmers whose economic position has been eroded by global competition and unskilled young people without a stable professional future are the expected victims of any capitalist regime. More importantly, these "modernization losers" feel "alone," "alienated," and "powerless," and these feelings are also shared by those whose material conditions are comfortable, but who nonetheless feel insecure, uprooted or unable to climb any further up the social ladder. (Godin, 65–66)

As a result, the National Front was able to recruit its voters not only among the unemployed, but among people who were relatively well to do yet were anxious about their prospects. Economic uncertainty provoked a reaffirmation of identity in the national context through the designation and exclusion of others. As the sociologist Pierre-André Taguieff notes, "Far from provoking the fading away of national/nationalist passions, economic globalization gives rise to national reactions, ethnic resistance, localized or individual, identity-based [*particulariste*] counter-movements" (60).

The National Front's emergence is thus indicative of a more fragmented political culture in general. At a time of considerable economic and social transformations and mass consumption, at a time when private concerns rather than allegiance to party or trade union or even "the nation" became more constitutive of one's identity, the traditional political parties seemed out of touch; "Green" or "homosexual" or "woman" or "Beur," the name the second-generation immigrants of Arab origin called themselves (see below), began to mean more than "Left" or "Right." The Socialists came to power at a time when this rallying around new concerns and new themes had become generalized.

The Green Party, for example, emerged from the ecological movement of the 1960s. The *Parti des Verts* was born in 1984 when the *Partie Ecologiste* merged with the *Confédération Ecologiste*: grassroots movements were becoming a political party to take concerns that had not been traditionally part of the political arena into the national narrative, and sometimes they clashed with this narrative. During Mitterand's presidency, the *"Rainbow Warrior* Affair" illustrates this divergence between the interests and objectives of the republican state and those of groups and organizations such as the ecology movement. In July 1985, the ship *Rainbow Warrior,* which was manned by members of the international ecology movement Greenpeace and had been engaged in a protest against French nuclear tests in Polynesia, was sunk by explosives in New Zealand; a Greenpeace photographer was killed in the explosion. It was later revealed that a team of agents of the DGSE (*Direction générale de la sécurité extérieure,* Office for Exterior Security), the French equivalent of the CIA, were responsible and had been arrested and arraigned by the New Zealand authorities. The ensuing scandal led to the resignation of the director of the DGSE, Admiral Pierre Lacoste, and then of the minister of defense, Charles Hernu. Mitterand emerged unscathed from the affair. The president of the republic had been able to remain "above politics" by playing on the patriotism of the French people. He bemoaned the death of the journalist, but put forward the importance of the French nuclear program and qualified Greenpeace's "interference" as illegal. Twenty years later, *Le Monde* published the "secret report" of Admiral Lacoste in which the former director of the DGSE revealed that he had obtained the "personal authorization" of the president before proceeding with the operation. A cartoon on *Le Monde's* front page shows Mitterand wearing a diver's suit (the explosives that had sunk the *Rainbow Warrior* had been placed by divers), with a small French flag floating from his snorkel, and carrying a bomb; he faces a classroom where French children are holding a book entitled *History of France 1985.* He says "In those days, only presidents had the right to engage in acts of terrorism" (*Le Monde,* July 10–11, 2005). The message of the cartoon was particularly scathing with its allusion to the terrorist bombs that had exploded in London the same week of July 2005, causing dozens of deaths. Lacoste's "secret report" had in fact been circulating as early as 1986, but the political opposition decided not to make use of it against Mitterand. The Right had just won a majority in parliament and, for the first time in the history of the Fifth Republic, a prime minister who was of a different party from the president's would head the government, thus beginning a delicate period of "cohabitation." The *Rainbow Warrior* Affair reflects the particular strength of the *raison d'etat* in the French republican tradition, as well as the growing fragmentation of traditional Right/Left politics. The Green candidates received 3.8 percent of the vote in the legislative elections of 1988 and 5.25 percent in the 2002 presidential elections.

The "scandal of AIDS-infected blood transfusions" represents another instance of the diverging interests of particular groups and state policy. In 1985, stories were released in the press revealing that hundreds of hemophiliacs had been infected with HIV by blood transfusion stocks, some of which had been acquired from "high risk donors" and had not been screened for the virus. National and financial considerations were behind the decision: "Ministry of Health officials had decided to delay the launch of American testing kits in order to allow the commercialization of French ones" (Howarth and Varouxakis, 33). The trials took two decades and while the health minister was found to be partly responsible, he received no penalty with his sentence.

ACT UP-Paris or the Aids Coalition to Unleash Power was another instance of groups gathering around issues beyond the Right/Left political arena in the 1980s. ACT UP was originally founded in New York City in 1987 by the gay community to "defend all populations affected by AIDS" (http://www.actupparis.org/). ACT UP-Paris was thus founded on an American "grass roots model" and so removed twice from traditional national political structures. In the French context, the word that came to qualify such groups ranging from immigrant organizations to ACT UP was "communatarian," reflecting the idea of a "community" advocating a nonnational, *particularist* (identity-based) agenda. In the case of ACT UP-Paris, the agenda may not be linked to the concept of "losers of modernization"; however, what the group had in common with the unemployed, for example, was the perceived inability of the state or other existing structures, such as the traditional political parties of the Left or the Right, or the trade unions, among others to respond to their needs and concerns. As the group's Webpage states, "ACT UP-Paris brings to the public forum a discourse, as well as the demands of people affected by AIDS. This discourse is complementary and sometimes contrary to those of doctors, public services, and pharmaceutical companies. Information is power." The objective was to increase the flow of information or even to force a new conceptualization of issues in the national mindset. In the face of reactions such as Le Pen's 1987 public proposal to isolate those infected with the AIDS virus ("SIDA" in French) in a national *sidatorium*, a coinage that echoes "crematorium" (the gas ovens used in the Nazi concentration camps), the necessity and even urgency of creating such groups was self-evident to many people.

Beyond issues of financial or political liability, the opposition between Act-Up-Paris and some government policies called into question the foundations of French national discourse. David Caron, the author of *AIDS in French Culture*, frames the issue as follows:

> When Mathieu Duplay [a former spokes spokesperson of Act Up-Paris Paris] states that "Act UP provides a structure to rethink a citizen's global position from his/her HIV-positivity . . ." doesn't that automatically entail a rethinking of how citizenship is defined for all? And doesn't that, therefore, imply a rethinking of what defines the nation as a whole? In fact, by bringing the question of communities to the forefront of the current debates of French identity, the AIDS crisis and its responses may already have contributed to triggering a political change in France's definitions of citizenship and manhood. (150)

What became known as the *affaire des drapeaux* (the affair of the flags) also serves to underline the problematic position occupied by "particularist" discourse in the definition of "French identity." In 1996, a neighborhood association in the Marais section of Paris—the city's oldest neighborhood and one where a high concentration of gay men live—circulated a petition opposing the mass display of the rainbow flag, the international gay emblem, by businesses. Eventually, a compromise was reached between the city of Paris and gay business owners: rainbow flags were allowed to hang only during gay pride celebrations. Caron's comments on this controversy place the international gay emblems in the logic of what have been called the "culture wars" between France and the United States: "Not unlike fast food franchises and imported English words, the rainbow flags are criticized as signs of Americanization threatening to turn the oldest Parisian neighborhood into the Castro [San Francisco's gay neighborhood]. The flag controversy, then, may be a recent chapter in what many in France see as a cultural showdown against the United States" (155).

Figure 9.2 Giant Pink Condom over the Obelisk at Place de la Concorde in Paris (December 1993)

ACT UP, the anti-AIDS organization and Benetton, the Italian clothing company sponsored the operation. The use of the obelisk at Place de la Concorde is reminiscent of the use of the Arc of Triumph by feminist activists who wanted to place a wreath on the tomb of the "Unknown Soldier's Wife" in August 1970. The dual sponsoring by an activist group and a business concern is also indicative of the blurring of the private, the corporate, and the political in the postmodern age. The Kenzo perfume advertisement in the shape of 150,000 artificial poppies and a giant bottle of perfume on the esplanade of the Pompidou Center in 2001 also reflected the mix of state-sponsored cultural activity and commercial ventures. (© Gérard Julien/AFP/Getty Images)

The "headscarf affair" of 1987 and the "flag affair" of 1996 share the fact that they both went against the grain of a basic tenet of republican universalist discourse: the French are, above all, citizens of the republic, before being women, Breton or Corsican, gay, or private individuals with particular agendas; before being any of these particular identities, they all partake of the universal and intangible identity of the French citizen. The headscarf affair was particularly symbolic and sensitive because it involved that privileged site of nation building: *l'école laïque et républicaine*, the secular public school of the republic that had proved to be such a powerful tool of the Third Republic in its mission to "turn peasants into Frenchmen." Another aspect of the centralizing and modernizing mission of the Third Republic had also been the "civilizing mission" of France in its colonies (see chapter 7). Now, however, the children of these former colonial subjects, born in France and French citizens themselves, were claiming some aspects of their parents' original culture in the very midst of that Republican institution. In 1987, in the town of Creil, three girls were suspended by the principal for insisting on wearing the traditional Muslim headscarf to school. The principal was in a sense applying the rules of France's secularist tradition in which the school is considered a neutral Republican space where religion and religious affiliation are not to play a role. The case was brought before the *Conseil d'Etat*, the judicial institution responsible for judging cases where the state is involved. In November 1989, the *Conseil* ruled that wearing the Islamic scarf was compatible with the principle of *laïcité* as long as students did not claim religious exception in order to avoid fulfilling their educational obligations. This rather vague ruling ultimately left it to individual school principals to decide on the issue, and it would continue to surface in schools throughout France. Not until 2004 would an actual law addressing the issue be adopted by the government (see chapter 10).

Beyond the educational realm, the headscarf affair ignited a debate on the idea of the republic itself and of its core principles of universalism and secularism. For some observers it was only one example of the more general threat to the republic represented by any claim to a particular identity. The *parité* (parity) debates on the proportion of women among elected officials, for example, would raise similar passions in the late 1990s (see chapter 10). Philosopher Alain Finkielkraut does not specifically address the headscarf affair in his 1987 *The Defeat of the Mind*, but the book constitutes a general critique of what he sees as the abandonment of "Enlightenment values," values that are traditionally disseminated by the republic's schools (see dossier 2).

Dossier 9.2   Alain Finkielkraut, *The Defeat of the Mind* (1987)

Philosopher Alain Finkielkraut's essay can be perceived as an apology for an Enlightenment-based paradigm versus a postmodern paradigm. The former upholds an ethics of responsibility or "enlightened self-interest," while the latter, as he writes, "the pleasure principle—self-interest in its postmodern form." Finkielkraut bemoans the general blurring of the boundaries between high and low culture, the appearance of an eclectic, "self-service" "anything goes" attitude that undermines republican values. In his view, the postmodern era is dominated by consumerism, which gives rise to the "idolatry of juvenile values." This view can be usefully opposed to another work of the 1980s, Gilles Lipovetsky's 1983 *L' Ère du vide* (*The Era of Emptiness*). Lipovetsky argues that "post-modernism is essentially a liberating democratization of the exploration of individual freedom and self-expression associated with modernism, an indicator of an increasingly open and democratic society" (quoted in Kelly, 208).

"A Pair of Boots Is Worth a Play by Shakespeare"

By saying: "we must do for culture what Jules Ferry did for public education," André Malraux placed himself explicitly in the Enlightenment tradition that tried to generalize the knowledge of the great works of mankind; today the great works of Flaubert find themselves relegated to the peaceful world of leisure, together with pulp novels, TV shows, and schmaltzy films intoxicated with contemporary incarnations of Emma Bovary. (116)

But the fact that an individual has broken ties that used to attach him to old communatarian structures (corporations, churches, castes, or hierarchical rankings) and has managed his affairs with no restrictions, does not ipso facto give him new direction in the world. He can cut himself off from society without being free of its prejudices. Limiting authority does not guarantee independence of judgment or will. When inherited social constraints disappear, there is no assurance that freedom of the spirit will follow. It is still necessary to have what people called enlightenment in the eighteenth century: "As long as there are people who do not think for themselves, who let others make up their minds for them, breaking the chains is all in vain."[1. Condorcet, Rapport et projet pour l'organisation générale de l'Instruction publique, avril 1792, quoted in Bronislaw Bracko Une éducation pour la démocratie (Textes de l'époque révolutionnaire). (Paris: Garnier, 1982)]

In a single breath, the Enlightenment philosophers fought to give everyone access to culture while releasing the individual from the power of the state and the control of tradition. They wanted men to be free to do what was good for themselves but also to think about matters beyond the limits of their own self-interest.

We see today that the philosophers won only half the battle. Despotism has been vanquished, but not obscurantism. While traditions have lost their power, so has culture. People, it is true, are not deprived of knowledge. Quite the reverse. In fact we might say that in the West and for the first time in history, the spiritual and intellectual heritage of mankind is available immediately and in its entirety. Now that paperbacks, videocassettes, and data banks have taken over the cottage industry created by the Encyclopédistes, there are no longer any material obstacles standing in the way of spreading the Enlightenment. However, just as technology—television and computers—is able to introduce all forms of knowledge into every home, the logic of consumption destroys culture. The world lives on but emptied of any idea of education, of the possibility of opening up to the world and caring for the soul. From now on in, the pleasure principle—self-interest in its postmodern form—dominates the individual's spiritual life. It is no longer a question of representing men as autonomous subjects, but of gratifying their immediate desires and providing them with entertainment for very little cost . . .

. . . School in the modern sense of the term, was born in the Age of Enlightenment. Today it is dying, as people question the values of that period. There now exists a huge gap between a common code of ethics and that place governed by the strange idea that there is no autonomy without thinking and no thinking without self-discipline. "The mental life of society develops in a middle zone of personal eclecticism," [2. Georges Steiner. In Bluebeard's Castle (London: Faber and Faber, 1971)] everywhere, that is, except between the four walls of educational institutions. School is the ultimate exception to the generalized rule of self-service. Thus the misunderstanding is growing separating the institution from those who use it: the school system is modern, the students postmodern. The school wants to educate minds, but the students bring to it the attention span of young people raised on television.

The headscarf affair was also linked to immigration since the girls were second-generation immigrants who were calling themselves the *Beurs* (according to this denomination, girls are *Beurettes*), a generation that had become visible after the wave of attacks by the extreme right in the early 1980s. The origin of the name was in *verlan*, a slang of the *banlieues*—a word that simply meant "suburbs" but now implies working-class suburbs where a high concentration of ethnic minorities live—in which words are spelled backward with some elisions to make them easier to pronounce: "Arab" pronounced backward, with slight modification of syllables became *Beur*. The word entered the public sphere when *Radio Beur* became one of the first local radio stations to be licensed in Paris (Hargreaves, 105). "Beur" was a name that valorized these young people, unlike the word "Arab" with its colonial and racist overtones, in the mouth of the ex-colonizer. The denomination was a way to signify their difference from their parents while at the same time affirming an identity that can be variously interpreted as *neither* French *nor* Arab, or as a *particular* kind of French citizen. In any case, the name represented a destabilization or fragmentation of the homogeneous and virtual universal space that the republican discourse aims to create. As Alec Hargreaves proposes, "the term served its purpose and the *génération beure* gained valuable public visibility and a political platform" (20).

The *Marche pour l'égalité et contre le racisme* (march for equality and against racism) a march from Marseilles to the center of Paris in 1983 was a founding moment in the constitution of a Beur identity. The march was prompted by a wave of racist violence in the preceding year. The founding of *SOS Racisme* by Harlem Désir, the son of Alsatian and Caribbean parents, was also a response to the racist climate of the early 1980s, most prominently reflected in the rise of the National Front on the political scene. *SOS Racisme*'s slogan *Touche pas à mon pote* (Hands off my buddy), written on a raised defensive/protective bright yellow hand, became well known after *SOS Racisme* organized a concert attended by 300,000 people at Place de la Concorde in 1985. The yellow hand, symbol of SOS's antiracist campaign and the ACT UP-Paris' giant pink condom that would cover the obelisk at the same square a decade later were both symbols of minority groups' ability to use public space and monuments to put their agenda on the national map.

The visibility of the "Beur generation" in France was not confined to its reaction to racism. In the 1980s, that generation came of age as a group that would produce a vibrant culture recognizably its own. Often the terms "Beur culture" and "*banlieue* culture" were used interchangeably, indicating the conflation between the place where most of these young people lived and the identity they were claiming for themselves. One of the best examples of this "crossover" culture is the success of *raï* music, a blend of Arab and Western forms that originated in the Maghreb. The mix of traditional Arab melodies with a background of syncopated rock made a splash among the Beurs with stars like Chek Khaled and Cheb Memmi, at first on imported records and cassettes, especially from Algeria, and then at a number of festivals in France, most notably the 1986 festival at Bobigny, in the north of Paris. Very quickly *raï* performers born in France began to make their mark both in and outside of the *banlieues*. The increasing popularity of *raï* in the 1980s can be traced from French-born Karim Kacel's 1983 hit, *Banlieue*, to Algerian-born Faudel, the "little prince of *raï*" winning the "Revelation of the Year" prize at the fourteenth annual *Victoires de la Musique* (equivalent of the American "Grammies") ceremony in 1988.

The Beurs also began to make their mark in literature in the 1980s with dozens of novels published in the decade. The setting was usually the *banlieue* while the main characters often confronted the difficulties of their dual heritage: North African parents from a traditional village culture, and the French Republic in which they were born. One of the earliest and best-known novels of the Beur generation was in fact written by a young man who was born in Algeria but came to France at eleven with his family to join his father who had been working there for years. In his 1983 novel *Le thé au harem d'Archi Ahmed* (a word play that transforms "Archimedes' theorem" into "Tea in Archi Ahmed's harem"), Mehdi Charef describes the life of a group of boys in the *banlieue* and in particular the relationship between a *Français de souche* (native French) and his Algerian-born friend, modeled after Charef himself. The novel was among the first to depict the lives of a segment of the French population that had remained relatively absent from literary representation. Charef's appearance on Bernard Pivot's popular literary television show, *Apostrophes*, made him "the first Beur artist to reach a genuinely national audience" (Forbes and Kelly, 272). The novel's success would lead to the production of a film for which Charef wrote the scenario.

Dossier 9.3   Azouz Begag, *Le gone du Chaâba* (*The Kid from Chaâba*) (1986)

Azouz Begag's *Le gone du Chaâba* belongs to the first wave of Beur literature that began in the 1980s. Born in France of Algerian immigrants, Begag grew up in the shantytown described in the novel, and is today a recognized author and filmmaker. He was appointed minister for equal opportunities in the de Villepin government in June 2005. In the novel, he describes the turmoil of a character caught between the world of his Algerian family and friends, and his own desire to become successful in the country in which he was born. While some of his classmates from the Chaâba neighborhood accuse him of "selling out" when he performs well in school, he is compelled to show that he is "capable of being like them [the French students]. Better than them even." As Alec Hargreaves suggests, even the novel's title reflects Begag's ability to successfully claim both identities: "The emphasis on local roots is exemplified in the title: while the author's Arab ancestry is signaled in *Chaâba*, the Arabic name of the shanty town where Begag was brought up in the city of Lyon, *gone* (kid) is part of the local slang indigenous to the town. Only those who really belong to a locality can fully master its slang. Begag was born in Lyon, and by calling himself a *gone*, he signals the depths of his roots in France's second city" (Hargreaves, 106).

The school janitor opened the heavy iron gates and moved aside to let in all the multicolored pinafores. It was like a dam giving way. The tide swept into the different playgrounds, carrying the boys into one and the girls in little ones into the other.

Between eight in the morning and eleven thirty total silence reigned: knowledge was being imbibed.

We entered the classroom in rows, two by two. The schoolmaster sat at his desk.

"This morning we will have a lesson in correct behavior," he said, after calling the register and stumbling over all the Arab names.

He started talking about correct behavior, as was his habit every morning since I had moved up to his school. And, as every morning, I blushed as I listened to his words. There was a veritable oued *[river] separating what he said from what I was used to doing in the street.*

I was simply a disgrace where correct behavior was concerned.

A discussion started between the French pupils and the teacher. They all put their hands up to say something, to talk about their experience, to show their moral compliance with today's lesson.

We Arab kids had nothing to say.

With my eyes and ears wide open, I listened to the debate.

I knew that I lived in a shantytown of shacks made of planks of wood and corrugated iron roofs and that it was the poor who lived that way. I had gone several times to Alain's home in the middle of the Avenue Monin, where his family lived in a real house. I could see that it was much nicer than our shacks. And there was so much space. His house alone was as big as the whole of Le Chaâba put together. He had his own room, with a desk and books and a wardrobe for his clothes. At each visit my eyes nearly came out of their sockets with astonishment. I was too ashamed to tell him where I lived. That is why Alain had never been to Le Chaâba. He was not the sort who would enjoy rummaging in the garbage dumped on the embankment, or hanging on to the sides of the garbage truck, or getting involved in extorting money from hookers and the homos. Besides, did he even know what homo meant?

In class the discussion was getting livelier. Pupils were saying words I had never heard before. I felt ashamed. I often used to come out with words straight out of our Chaâba vocabulary when I spoke to the teacher. One day I had even said to him:

"Sir, I swear to you on my mother's life that it's not true."

Everybody around me burst out laughing.

I had also realized that there was some words that I knew only in Arabic, such as kassa *[facecloth].*

I was ashamed of my ignorance. For a few months now I had been resolved on changing sides. I did not like being with the poor and the weak pupils in class. I wanted to be among the top of the class alongside the French children.

The teacher was pleased with the debate on cleanliness that he had started that morning. He encouraged the pupils by giving pictures and merits to those who had participated actively in it.

At the end of the morning the bell rang. Half stunned by the noise, I left the classroom in a thoughtful mood. I wanted to prove that I was capable of being like them, indeed, better than them. Even though I lived in Le Chaâba. (—Translated by Alec Hargreaves)

Mehdi Charef's 1985 film *Le thé au harem d'Archimède* and Mathieu Kassovitz' *La Haine (Hate)* made a decade later, were both set in the *banlieues* and depicted the lives of these second-generation immigrants caught between the hopelessness of the housing projects and their desire to live lives like other, "normal" young people. Both films portray an ethnic mix of young people, *black- blanc-Beur* (black, white, and Beur) to use an expression that would become common in the early 1990s. Charef's film refers to the New Wave, François Truffaut's *The Four Hundred Blows* in particular, reflecting his immersion in a French cinematic tradition (S. Lee, in Celestin, DalMolin, Hargreaves, 185–191). At the end of the film, the boys arrive at the seashore and confront the limits of their ability to escape the *banlieue*, much like Truffaut's Antoine Doinel, thirty year earlier, was forever caught in that final freeze frame in front of the ocean in *The Four Hundred Blows*.

Kassovitz's *Hate* gives wide coverage to the hip-hop culture of the *cité* (the projects) reflecting the appropriation of American "inner-city culture" by French "*banlieue* culture" in the decade that had passed since Charef's film. Kassovitz, who is not a Beur, but a descendant of Eastern European Jewish immigrants, has been criticized for using a highly stylized approach and for depicting an unrealistic setting in which the "black-blanc-Beur" trio of young men does not accurately reflect the actual ethnic composition of the *cité*. He has also been praised for directing a film that accurately depicts the tense and often violent relations between the population of the *cités*, especially its young people, and the rest of the population, especially the police. Images reminiscent of those of *Hate* were to be broadcast on television screens throughout the world when an incident involving young men very much like the trio in the film ignited violence throughout France in the fall of 2005 (see chapter 10).

The pervasiveness of American hip-hop culture in the film signals the continuation of a trend whose beginnings coincide with the socialist liberalization of the legislation overseeing the media in the early 1980s. Until 1981, the French state was the only entity with legal authority to broadcast inside French borders. *Radios libres* or "free radios" had been broadcasting in France since the late 1970s but they were not legal and had no government support. By the time of Mitterand's victory, however, it had become clear that these stations would have to be legalized if the state were to keep any sort of influence over broadcasting. In 1982, a new law legalized scores of "pirate stations" that had appeared on the FM band. Dozens of others appeared. One of the first to begin operating was *Carbone 14* in the 14th arrondissement of Paris, and its music, broadcast twenty-four hours a day, was primarily American hip-hop. "Two of its most popular disc jockeys were Phil Barney and Dee Nasty—the latter was familiar with African American hip-hop because he had contacts in the United States who told him how to develop his 'spinning' style'" (Durand, 2). Yet another American-influenced "youth culture" was making its appearance in the hexagon. In the early 1960s, the models of the *yé yé* generation were Elvis Presley and Chuck Berry, while for the generation of the 1960s and 1970s, they were replaced by the protest folk music of Bob Dylan and Joan Baez, and then the acid rock of Jimmy Hendrix and Janis Joplin; for the Beurs and other ethnic minorities of the *banlieues* of the 1980s, and soon for a much wider segment of the French population, the models were to be found in the rap rhythms of Run DMC and Grandmaster Flash. In one of *Hate*'s most memorable scenes, a "spinner" "remixes" Edith Piaf's classic *Je ne regrette rien* on two turntables in a room overlooking the courtyard of a housing project that could be on the outskirts of any of France's major cities. Hip-hop and rap had become dominant musical forms on the French popular music scene.

This development—the crossover of a cultural production that begins in a localized, "ethnic" segment of the population to reach a national public audience—is symbolic of the inevitable negotiations that the French Republican model has had to undertake in an increasingly "multicultural" and market-driven population. On the one hand, the socialist government, like other governments of the Fifth Republic that preceded it, was the government of a nation built on universalist and centralizing principles; yet it had to contend with the challenge to that model represented by a variety of trends that had already begun to accelerate in the early 1960s. The response to this challenge was evident in the Mitterand administration's attempt to both legalize the multiplication of radio stations *and* to keep some form of state intervention and control. According to the law of 1982, commercial advertising was not allowed and the newly legalized stations had to be run by community groups: both were indicative of an attempt to give some form of republican structure to the newly liberalized media. The absence of advertising was the government's attempt to keep the new radio stations free of market pressures, but even the condition of community group ownership and operation was already an acknowledgment that the state could not speak for the multiplicity of groups that composed contemporary France, as "community groups, from Moslems to homosexuals began to operate radio stations" (Wachtel, 65). In the end, a combination of market forces and personal tastes that were beyond the ken of "citizenship" displayed the difficulty of maintaining the kind of control and civic imperatives that had characterized the "French exception." The example of one private radio station illustrates this point: "Although the law was intended to impede the creation of powerful FM networks, the Paris rock station NRJ built up a series of affiliates throughout France. When the government tried to challenge the NRJ network, protest marches by young people forced it to back down" (Wachtel, 65). This example is also symbolic of the shift in the general attitudes of young people who, thirty years earlier, had been at the forefront of a general rejection of the "consumer society" and "the society of the spectacle," but were now marching to claim their rights as consumers.

Still, the attempt to retain aspects of an "exception" in the face of the "Americanization," "globalization," or "popularization" of culture—three words that are often considered interchangeable—was evident in the governments' continued action in favor of cultural production *in French*. The 1994 Toubon Law, for example, contains specific provisions regarding the use of the French language in the media: since 1996, "a minimum of 40 percent of songs broadcast must be in French" (Kidd and Reynolds, 134). However, the law excluded "'communitarian' radio stations, like Beur-FM and Radio Latina, which represent particular immigrant communities" (Durand 53). Ironically, a law of the republic adopted in order to protect the French language gave a boost to a particular type of music that, given the American and *banlieue* inflections of its lyrics, was far from what politicians, especially conservative politicians, have in mind when they think of *la langue de Molière*, the language of Molière.

"The language of Molière," the great seventeenth-century playwright, is indeed an old coinage used by the French to refer to what they consider the greatness, clarity, and universal quality of their language. Even before Molière's lifetime, however, treatises, manifestoes, prefaces, and other types of texts such as Joachim du Bellays' *Défense et illustration de la langue française* published in 1549, attest to the particular role played by the French language in the construction of the French nation and of French identity. The Toubon law itself should be perceived in a long tradition of royal and then republican intervention in the codification and protection of French. This is a policy that harks back at least to the *Académie française* founded by Cardinal Richelieu in 1635 to codify and regulate the language through established rules of grammar and spelling. The mission of the academy was "to make the French language not only elegant but capable of addressing all the arts and all the sciences." The centralizing and homogenizing policy concerning the French language and the provinces was initiated by the monarchy and has been pursued essentially without interruption to this day, whether by the Jacobins of the French Revolution in the eighteenth century or, more famously, by the Third Republic in the nineteenth century (see chapter 3). Today the

"Forty Immortals" of the French Academy are working on the ninth edition of the *grand dictionnaire*, and the hope is that their work will be completed before 2010.

Where regional languages and the "backward provinces" within France were the primary targets of earlier codifying and centralizing linguistic policies, now English, especially its American variant, became the bête noire of policy makers beginning with France's rapid entry into consumer culture in the early 1960s. When, in 1964, René Etiemble published *Parlez-vous franglais?* his essay against what he perceived as the invasion of the French language by English—the appearance of words mixing French and English (*français* + *anglais* = *franglais*) or of English words simply given a French pronunciation, such as "le living room"—France was in the throes of modernization *à l'américaine*. With the Hollywood films and the new modes of consumption came a language that proved as invasive as the new products. In the following decades, as French industrial consumer society became French postindustrial society in a globalized economy, media, advertising, marketing, science and technology— precisely those sectors that were "English intensive"—occupied an increasingly larger part of daily life. It is not a coincidence that the end of the "thirty glorious years" in the mid-1970s was also a time when the authorities were taking stock of the advances made by English during those three decades. The *Loi Bas Auriol* (Bas Auriol Law) was adopted in 1974; it regulated the use of foreign languages and enforced the use of French in business, the media, and the workplace in general. The previously mentioned Toubon Law of 1994 provided an extension of these provisions and focused on unnecessary or excessive use of foreign words, essentially English. It included provisions for foreign companies operating in France. The very detailed quality of the law's provisions reflected the importance of the issue. The following documents had to be written in French: individual work contracts; bylaws and handbooks; collective labor contracts signed with trade unions; any corporate procedure that includes a compulsory provision for the employee such as accounting procedures and maintenance manuals. In addition to laws, a number of committees, *commissions de terminologie*, were set up in the 1970s and 1980s specifically to provide equivalents and alternatives to foreign, especially English, words and expressions in French (Kidd and Reynolds, 134). On the whole the "defense and illustration" of the French language became a more pressing and official issue as France became increasingly "modernized" and "globalized" after World War II. At first, official policy focused on French in and for itself, but gradually, the defense of the French language and of French exceptionalism was conducted under the banner of the defense of diversity *tout court*.

This shift from France and its language forming a universal—and imperial—whole to be extended throughout the world, to France and the French language as a bulwark against the domination of (American) globalization and English became obvious in the international trade negotiations in the context of the GATT (General Agreement on Tariffs and Trade founded in the aftermath of World war II to promote free trade) in the 1990s. During the "Uruguay round" in 1993, France led the movement to make cinema and other national audiovisual products a "cultural exception" to free trade. France successfully argued the point that the types of support accorded to these industries, ranging from subsidies to imposed quotas on the showing of foreign films on national television, were necessary in order to maintain their existence in the face of global competition, especially the numerous films coming from Hollywood. "Cultural exception" became an accepted rule of the GATT that year, and, shortly after, the term was replaced by "cultural diversity." It remains to be seen whether this type of state intervention can withstand the pressures of the global market. In the case of France in particular it has helped the film industry to remain vibrant, and to hold its own in the national market (35 percent of ticket sales). On the international front, France ranks third, after India and the United States in the number of films made annually (Kidd and Reynolds, 48).

In arguing for "cultural exception" at the GATT, France had relied not only on the support of the European Union, but also on that of a number of non-European countries, many of them former French colonies. In 1993, the call for "cultural exception" was made by Mitterand at the Fifth *Francophonie* Summit held in Mauritius, a former French possession in the Indian Ocean.

By the time of Mitterand's appeal, *Francophonie* had already become an organization, but it had begun as a movement in the aftermath of French decolonization. Its founding text is traditionally considered to be an article published in the journal *Esprit* in 1962, the year of Algerian independence, by the Senegalese poet, president, and grammarian Leopold Sedhar Senghor, who was also the first black member of the French Academy. Senghor's words reflected the perception of French as a universal language that could continue to serve as a link between former colonizer and former colonized:

> At a time when the Civilization of the Universal is coming into being it is, in short, a matter of using this marvelous tool, found in the ruins of the colonial Regime. It is a matter of using this tool that is the French language. *Francophonie*, this integral human-ism which is weaving its threads around the globe, this symbiosis of dormant sources of energy arising from all the continents, all the races that are awakening to their shared warmth. (844)

"Universal" is indeed the key word here: Francophonie was, at first, a disembodied forum, or as Margaret Majumdar writes, "a virtual space, not linked to any particular territory" (22). If, within the republic, one is a French citizen who partakes of the universal attributes of the French Republic *prior to* being a woman, a homosexual, an Arab, or a Jew, in *Francophonie* in its first phase, noncitizens from former colonies as well as from other countries where French is spoken partake of the disembodied universal incarnated by France and its culture through the French language as a medium of communication. This is what Majumdar calls "an idealistic vision of a community sharing the French language and culture, based on the core universalist values of Enlightenment and republican philosophy" (22). Only gradually did this "virtual" entity become an organization complete with objectives, bylaws, and, even, a cultural, political, and economic agenda, as became evident in 1993 when Mitterand made his appeal for cultural exception at the Mauritius summit. The Socialist president had also hosted the first summit of Francophonie at Versailles in 1986, signaling the increased and active involvement of France in the organization. The trend to turn *Francophonie* from a "virtual" entity into an active forum for inter-national change dates from that summit and culminates in 1993, the year when "cul-tural exception" became an issue at the GATT and also the year of the Mauritius summit of Francophonie when Mitterand made his appeal to the members of the organization to support France's bid for that "exception." Beginning that year the focus on French as "universal" language linking a number of member states in a common humanist endeavor shifted to *Francophonie* as a bulwark against "Anglo-Saxon" hegemony and a means of defending and nurturing cultural diversity ". . . in the face of the homogenizing, steam-rolling tendencies of globalized U.S. mass culture, which was imposing Disney, McDonalds, Coca-Cola and other products and cultural phenomena on the entire planet" (Majumdar, 25). Mitterand's policy of cultural exception and the perception of Francophonie as a force countering "globalized U.S. mass culture" would remain constants of French policy even as a president of the Right, Jacques Chirac, succeeded Mitterand the Socialist in 1995. This continuity is reflected, among many other instances, in the following excerpt from a speech made by Chirac in Hungary in 1997:

> The calling of *Francophonie* is to bring together all the other languages of the world in order to ensure the survival of cultural diversity, which springs from linguistic diversity . . . It is our duty to be militants for multiculturalism in the world in order to prevent one single language from stifling the various cultures which constitute the wealth and dignity of humanity. (Quoted in Kidd and Reynolds, 136)

In a world where the French Republic was no longer a dominant power, *Francophonie* was reconfigured as a means of countering globalization and of championing diversity. This evolution reflects what can be called a pragmatism of French exceptionalism and universalism: the concrete manifestations of the universalist republic had been increasingly difficult to maintain in an era when humanist, Enlightenment values were clearly being superseded by market forces, where the consumer had to a great extent replaced the citizen, where the former colonial subject had been replaced by independent people and by "second-generation" immigrants who were also French citizens, where groups ranging from these "second-generation immigrants" and ecologists to homosexuals and feminists were challenging the supposedly neutral basis of the republic's "universalism." In this world, which begins to take shape at first with the modernization of France and its entry into consumer society and continued to evolve into the postmodern, postindustrial planet, successive French governments found different strategies to both maintain a certain vision of France that would, as much as possible, remain in harmony with the republican and universalist principles. Simultaneously, these successive governments also had to find other strategies to deal with change, whether this change was the transformation of colonies into independent countries, economic globalization, or the increased visibility and activism of "particularist" or "communitarian" groups in French society. *Francophonie* itself has been perceived as just such a strategy. Here the logic, at least from France's vantage point, would be as follows: since France can no longer ensure the continued existence of a colonial empire, it can nevertheless continue to maintain privileged relations with former colonies on the basis of a shared language and culture. This is one way of retaining a universalist paradigm in a world where it is systematically challenged and often belied by the concrete facts. A good example of this is a statement made by Tahar Ben Jelloun, a Moroccan writer living in France and the winner of the Goncourt, in 1987 for his novel *The Sacred Night*: "We know that *Francophonie*—this political project based on a language—is supported and represented by writers throughout the world. We also know that these militants of *Francophonie* experience major difficulties in obtaining a visa to enter France" (29).

The challenge to the French idea of universalism and to the French language by a diverse, fragmented conception of the world, culture, and language is reflected in the emergence of the *Créolité* movement in Martinique. Creole languages are spoken throughout the ex-colonies of France from the Caribbean to the Indian Ocean. They evolved from the mix of French and different African dialects spoken in the colonies. At first a simplified means of oral communication between groups who did not know each other's language and between masters and slaves or indentured workers, Creoles became codified, written languages with a grammar in the 1960s and 1970s. The Créolité movement originated in the Caribbean, with a founding text, *Eloge de la Créolité*, written in 1989 by three Martinicans, the linguist Jean Bernabé, and the novelists Raphaël Confiant and Patrick Chamoiseau. In this work, *Créolité* is defined an "an open sensibility," an "annihilation of false universality, of monolinguism, of purity" (McCusker,113).

In an earlier response to the "false universality" of imperial France, the Negritude movement of the 1930s—in which fellow Martinican Aimé Césaire had been a leading figure (see chapter 4)—proffered the figure of a monolithic Africa. Central to Negritude was an identity that would reclaim its authenticity by (re)claiming its African roots. In this instance, the idea of an "authentic" and "pure" origin was opposed to the colonizing power: Africa, instead of or against France/Europe. As revolutionary and subversive as Negritude was in its time, it nevertheless left intact the very idea of "uncontaminated" and "authentic" cultures; another "origin" was opposed to the colonizing power. *Créolité* undoes this binary opposition, which can also be seen as the opposition of one type of universalism to another. Instead, *Créolité* proposes a multiplicity of identities mutually reinforcing, affecting, and feeding one another. This idea is taken up again by Chamoiseau in *Ecrire en pays dominé* (*Writing in a Dominated Country*) published in 1992:

> Amerindians, békés [white settlers in Martinique and Guadeloupe], Indians, Negroes, Chinese, Maderians, SyroLebasese . . . all wanted to preserve original purities, but we saw ourselves crisscrossed by each other. The Other changes me and I change it. Its contact animates me and I animate it . . . Every Other becomes a component of me while remaining distinct. I become what I am in my open support for the Other. (Quoted in McCusker, 116)

The reference is no longer Africa but the varied, hybrid population of the Caribbean; the "origin," if it can still be called that is not the African village or the great civilizations of Africa, but the Caribbean plantation. Derek Walcott, the Saint Lucian poet, winner of the Nobel Prize for literature, refers to the "deep amnesiac blow" the African slaves suffered during the Middle Passage and the ensuing impossibility of a "return" ("Laventille," in *Collected poems*, 1986). The Créolité movement extends this concept to all the people of the Caribbean, proposing that their identity is to be located in a "Creoleness" that knows no origin or purity, no absolutely retraceable roots. Promoting this ethics of diversity, Martinican poet and novelist Edouard Glissant (see dossier 9.4) asserts that ". . . it is a sickness to believe that there are universal languages . . . at a time when . . . we are done with five year plans . . . [when] the world is becoming creolized" (Stovall and van den Abbeele, 108).

Dossier 9.4 Edouard Glissant, "The French Language in the Face of Creolization" (2005)

Edouard Glissant belongs to the generation of Martinican writers that precedes the "generation of *Créolité*," Jean Bernabé, Patrick Chamoiseau, and Raphaël Confiant. He shares with them, however, an ethics of diversity to be posited against any claim to universality. All of Glissant's work, whether the theoretical essays, novels, plays, or poems, reflects a will to affirm the fragmentation of languages and cultures against any claim to a unified or dominant worldview. The following excerpt is from a 2005 essay entitled "The French Language in the Face of Creolization" published in *French Civilization and Its Discontents. Nationalism, Colonialism, Race*, edited by Tyler Stovall and Georges van den Abbeele.

There is one condition, one characteristic that is striking when we examine France's part in the colonization of what was called the New World, that is, the Americas. There is something striking about the fact that wherever the French intervened in an American land, a Creole came into being. Francophone Creole languages emerged under the condition I shall describe, in Haiti, in the lesser Antilles, in Louisiana and in French Guyana, not to mention the islands of the Indian Ocean. But the other condition for there to be a Creole is that there be a peoplement by Africans. For example, in Quebec, there is no Creole. So the presence of an African population is a requirement.

And why should the French language have so often authorized the appearance of Francophone Creoles? I think there are two reasons. The first is that at the time of colonization, when it was not yet the universal language it subsequently claimed to be, the French language, in the Antilles for instance, and throughout the Caribbean, was primarily represented by the ways of speaking of French sailors from Norman and Breton ports. It seems to me that at the time the West Indies were colonized the French language had not yet confectioned its organic unity. In other words, at the time Montaigne was writing the famous chapter of his Essays, "On Cannibals," Cervantes had already written Don Quixote and Shakespeare was in the process of producing his opus. But Montaigne's language—I'm going to shock you— and Rabelais' language are also Creole languages. They are not the language of Malherbe, and even less the language of Racine. They are languages that are still grappling with the world, that are not yet locked into their own purity and organicness. Rabelais and Montaigne, I maintain, are Creole authors. Things happen there: they borrow from all over the place, they pile things up and then mix them together, and then we see something taking place, and it all comes out a certain way, leaving folks astonished—"but what does this word mean there?" and so forth. They are also Creole authors because Montaigne has at least ten ways of writing, for instance, the word "donc" [thus]: donc, adonc, donque, doncque, etc. It is magnificent, and it is beautiful because it has not yet been purified. It has not yet been sifted through Malherbe's grim sieve. And let's suppose this language was available, that the Breton and Norman sailors who trafficked in the Caribbean and the Indian Ocean were speaking a kind of jargon or awful gibberish, which was awful but open, and which allowed, in my opinion, for this kind of osmosis with what people of African descent in those lands brought to bear in the way of lexical and syntactical elements. (108—Translated by Georges van den Abbeele)

Paradoxically, such a concept, subversive as it is of the entire tradition of codification and protection of the French language comes from Martinican writers and intellectuals who hail from what is a *département* of France, an integral part of the republic, like the Vaucluse or the Vendée. Further, far from being perceived as a threat to this French tradition, these writers of *Créolité* are celebrated in the media and garner some of France's most prestigious literary prizes. Chamoiseau, for example, received the Goncourt for his novel *Texaco* in 1992. On the other hand, official literary recognition of a novel, after all written in French, in spite of its Creole inflections and use of Creole words, can be seen as a way of reinscribing and metabolizing any subversive or dissonant voice in the French literary tradition. Awarding the Goncourt to Chamoiseau becomes a means of incorporating the Martinican author and *Créolité* into the *French* literary tradition, a means of claiming him by *extending* the limits of what constitutes that tradition.

The same ability to *extend* traditional parameters in order to cope with change and the appearance of new cultural production was evidenced by the socialist government's policy under Mitterand's appointed minister of culture, Jack Lang. When the Socialists came to power they nearly tripled the cultural budget, and a major shift in cultural policy took place. For the first time since 1958, when the Ministry of Culture was created by de Gaulle, and André Malraux was appointed as its first head, the founding decree was reworded. The new decree of May 10, 1982 read:

> The Ministry's mission is to enable all French people to cultivate their capacity to invent and to create, to freely explore their talents, and to receive the artistic training of their choice; to preserve the cultural heritage of the nation, the regions and different social groups for the common good; to facilitate the creation of works of art and of the mind, and to provide them with the widest possible audience; to contribute to the free dialogue of the word's cultures.

Socialist cultural policy had something in common with both the Popular Front's and Malraux's objectives: a democratization of culture. Something crucial had changed, however: the objective was no longer exclusively to make high culture available to an increased number of citizens, but, also, to extend the definition of "culture" itself. As one commentator formulated it,

> The transition from elitist to popular culture was probably the brightest spot of the cultural projects . . . rather than concentrate on removing the barriers that separate the vast majority of the public from understanding and enjoying traditional culture, the Lang ministry concentrated on legitimizing popular practices, thus reducing the distinction previously drawn between them. (Wachtel, 94–95)

In this sense, the state, although more "interventionist" than ever, stopped being a conveyor of high culture and became active in modes of culture that had been hitherto neglected or simply not included in the traditional definition—and public financing—of culture. During the Lang years, these new modes of cultural production ranged from rock and roll and graffiti (*le tagging*) to rap and comic strips. The *Fête de la musique* inaugurated in 1982 was exemplary of this new trend: a government-sponsored national event where on the evening of the summer solstice, June 21, "anyone who knows how to play an instrument is encouraged to come out into the streets and make music" (Wachtel, 45), from Mozart and Monteverdi to rap and rock. An event like the Techno parade, Paris' answer to the carnival parade in Rio, and yet another government-sponsored initiative, has also become extremely popular. During the "Lang years" the state thus embarked on a redefinition of cultural policy that seemed paradoxical when viewed through the prism of traditional republican and universalist practice. Nonetheless, this new policy also represented a way for the interventionist state to remain actively involved in the lives of its citizens. On the one hand, the idea of a French exception where *grandeur* and high culture dominate seems to be jettisoned, but on the other, the continued presence of the interventionist state in the midst of the popularization and fragmentation of culture perpetuates that exceptionalism. In fact, the continued and active involvement of the government in either paradigm— bringing the people to high culture, as in the Malraux ministry, or extending the definition of culture itself, as in the Lang ministry—partakes of the "the French exception." The intense participation of the state in the definition and financing of culture during the socialist years thus clearly belongs to a long tradition that can be traced as far back as to court poets and playwrights under the Old Régime. Lang diverted from this tradition, however, by increasingly blurring the lines between culture and commerce. As he famously declared in the early 1980s, *Économie et culture, même combat* (Economy and culture: one struggle). As the state of the economy worsened, Lang was indeed under pressure to make culture economically viable: "These two domains had traditionally been considered as belonging to quite separate logics. Now cultural activity was seen as an important factor encouraging economic development: cultural industries (such as the cinema, book publishing, video, multimedia, etc.) received a whole range of supportive state measures, but private business sponsorship was also encouraged (Kidd and Reynolds, 44). The trend can also be seen as part and parcel of the more generalized expansion of the market economy in French daily life. Culture, whether in its "grandeur" or its more "popular" guise, was no exception.

If official state financing of more popular practices such as rap or rock, and the more pervasive role played by corporate financing represented an innovation in French cultural life, at the other end of the spectrum the grands *projets*, major architectural projects located in Paris, belong to an old tradition of France's leaders leaving their tangible mark on the capital and on the nation in general. This tradition goes back most famously to Louis XIV, the Sun King, and to Versailles as well as to the creation of royal academies of music, and painting, or royal manufacturing establishments such as the Gobelins carpet and Sèvres porcelain manufacturing plants.

The Louvre Pyramid was one of the president's *grand projets*, which were all architectural projects located in the capital. The projects sometimes led to heated national debate. Those in favor considered them to be important contributions to Paris' standing as international cultural capital. Others did not hesitate to criticize them as projections of presidential megalomania. The news magazine *L'évènement du Jeudi* of June 26, 1986, for example, contained the following headline: "Does the President think he is Ramses II?" Others opted for a more balanced view and perceived the projects as both emblems of nostalgia for former glory and as possible signs of cultural rebirth. In a special issue of the academic journal *SubStance* devoted to the theme "France's Identity Crisis," sociologist Philippe Genestier's comments reflect both interpretations:

[France] is filled with nostalgia for the period when the enlightened European despots unanimously followed the caprices of the Prince of Versailles in defining the

Figure 9.3 François Mitterand, in Front of the Louvre Pyramid, on the Day of Its Inauguration (March 29, 1989)

To the right, his minister of culture, Jack Lang. (© AFP/Getty Images)

"grand style . . . The seventeenth and eighteenth centuries were the blessed era in which the French state dictated the international norm; since the end of the First Empire [1815] it has no longer had the clout to do so. So, periodically, it aspires to exorcise this decline. Will *les grands projets du président* represent the last avatar of these attempts to prolong the

French monarchic tradition? Perhaps, for these projects, by their monumental ambition, by their determination, present themselves as the manifestoes of a new architecture, and seek to serve as a beacon in contemporary creativity. (In Kritzman, 63)

As had the Sun King, Mitterand took an active part in the realization of these projects: the Bastille Opera, the Louvre Pyramid—part of the "Grand Louvre" project—the Cité de la Musique at la Vilette, the Arche de la Défense, the Institut du Monde Arabe, the Ministry of Finance, and the Bibliothèque de France on the quays of the Seine. While judged "pharaonic" or "prestige operations" by some of their critics, the projects were defended by the administration as a means not only of reaffirming France's cultural greatness and creativity but also of enacting an architectural policy that would reflect the world's and the country's diversity. The apologists of the projects pointed to the different nationalities of the architects chosen, from Chinese-American I.M. Pei's pyramid for the Louvre to Canadian Carl Ott's Opéra Bastille and Frenchman Dominique Perrault's Bibliothèque de France. In an interview published in the magazine *L'Architecture Aujourd'hui* (*Architecture Today*), Lang focused on the wide appeal of these projects for a changed French society: "French society is pluralist today; sensibilities, aspirations, tastes are different, often contradictory" (quoted in Wachtel, 72).

Some of the *grands projets* were also defended as a continuation of the socialist administration's general policy of inclusion, of making culture more accessible to those who had been previously denied access, of creating a new "national culture." The Cité de la Musique at la Vilette is a case in point. The complex includes a "dance and music conservatory, concert halls, a music museum, a student residence and office space as well as a computerized information center where visitors can access music from around the world" (Norindr, 95). When it opened in 1995, the Cité's director proudly declared to an American journalist that "The Cité's target audience is the low-income multicultural population that lives nearby . . . We want to be very democratic . . . we want top draw people who have never been to a concert" (quoted in Norindr, 95). The Cité's appeal is indeed reflected in its power to attract a new public by providing easy access to a wide range of musical offerings; in this respect it is a vector for disseminating cultural difference. However, in the very process of extending the definition and the reach of culture, the republican state was also remaining within a universalist tradition that incorporated any difference it encountered. As Panivong Norindr formulates it,

> While the Cité de la Musique puts an official stamp on these various "performances," sanctioning the legitimacy of these "other" types of music (all too often merely subsuming them under the category of "world music"), it also has the paradoxical effect of recuperating these "local," "minor" musical genres into and for the dominant French culture, assimilating their differences and neutralizing their potentially contestatory force. (96)

The *grands projets* and socialist cultural policy in general were also criticized from another vantage point by a number of commentators who saw in what was presented by the Socialists as the democratization of culture only its commercialization. Among the many books and articles on the topic published at the time, Marc Fumaroli's *L'etat culturel, essai sur une religion moderne* (*The Cultural State: Essay on a Modern religion*), which came out in 1992, had a particularly wide circulation. In this long essay, Fumaroli, a university professor and Renaissance specialist, took the socialist administration to task for what he considered a degradation of culture:

> Ultimately the cultural state should recognize its own obsolescence in the innumerable advertising "spots" that link Verdi and scouring powder, Victor Hugo and washing machines, and that put the "masterpieces of humanity" at everyone's disposal. Culture seems to be nothing more than the official emblem of tourism, leisure, and shopping . . . part of the Ministry of Culture's activities belongs to the Ministry of Tourism and Recreation. (338–339)

Elsewhere in his essay, Fumaroli proposes that the most perfected example of such a conception of culture is symbolized by the United States and, in particular, by Las Vegas. In that "city in the desert," with its replica of monuments ranging from the Eiffel Tower to the Taj Mahal, he sees the "inversion of work and leisure that characterize commercial democracies and having reached its ultimate excess . . . [a site] where, of the entire history of humanity, there only remains a city of standardized and fully commercialized memories and illusions."

Fumaroli's references to the United States in his essay reflect a tradition of intellectuals of both the Right and the Left in France to use American culture as a "countermodel." In the age of globalization—conflated with "Americanization"—in which the essay is written, American culture embodies the most direct threat to a certain conception of culture as high culture or humanist culture. Fumaroli may not be quite as acerbic, but his references to the United States echo the words of Aragon, the surrealist poet and high-profile "cultural czar" of the Communist Party during the cold war when a statue of Victor Hugo was temporarily removed from a public square in Paris to make room for the display of a new Ford model:

> A Ford automobile, the civilization of Detroit, the assembly line, the atomic danger, encircled by napalm . . . here is the symbol of this subjugation to the dollar applauded in the land of Molière; here is the white-lacquered god of foreign industry, the Atlantic totem that chases away French glories with Marshall plan stocks . . . The Yankee, more arrogant than the Nazi iconoclast, substitutes the machine for the poet, Coca-Cola for poetry, American advertisement for la *Légende des siècles*, the mass manufactured for the genius, the Ford for Victor Hugo . . . a civilization of bathtubs and Frigidairs. (Quoted in Kuisel, 41)

In the half-century that separates this statement and Fumaroli's essay, the mass culture and popular culture emblematized by the United States have spread exponentially, to the extent that in some criticisms of the *grands projets* the United States is no longer the central point of comparison, and has been replaced by a more diffuse target that could be called "international" or "global" culture. In an article entitled "Great projects or mediocre designs," sociologist Philippe Genestier writes that these projects "contribute to propelling into charter flights larger and larger numbers of lazy conformists who aspire to nothing more than responding to the pressing call of the consumption of signs . . . Thus history is brought back to an ensemble of patrimonial values, and space is considered as an open expanse whose only beacons are the curiosities duly reported in guidebooks" (70). Aragon's "civilization of Detroit" has been replaced by what Fumaroli calls the civilization of "the traveler with his Kodak and Walkman." For other French thinkers this civilization has also provoked a "first" in European history, as the philosopher Alain Finkielkraut argues, "The absence of thought [*la non-pensée*] has of course always coexisted with the life of the mind, but this is the first time in European history that the two share the same name (culture) and enjoy the same status. Those who believe in "high culture" and dare make the distinction are called racists or reactionaries (117).

Behind these different criticisms of socialist cultural policy in particular, and of the general state of culture in the 1980s and 1990s in general, lies regret for what is perceived as a better, "higher" form of culture, and for an era in which France was the most powerful vector of that culture. The idea of "great culture" that, in the period covered in this book, takes root in the Second Empire is, for conservative thinkers like Fumaroli and Finkielkraut, besieged by what has been variously called "post-modernity," "globalization," and "Americanization." This last label, as we have noted, masks the fact that the United States is no longer the exclusive and all-powerful origin of this development, but only, as Jean Baudrillard has noted, only one of its "strongest poles" ("Interview," in Célestin, 6). Indeed the thesis developed by Fumaroli and Finkielkraut also had its advocates in the United States, as noted by Jean-François Fourny: "In many respects Fumaroli's indictment follows the tradition of Adorno and Horkheimer, who were appalled by the development of 'mass culture.' It thus echoes the neo-Spenglerism made fashionable in the 1980s by Allan Bloom in the United States (*The Closing of the American Mind* and *Cultural Literacy*) and by Alain Finkielkraut in France (*The Defeat of the Mind*, 1987)."

It may seem strange that there should have been a conflation of socialist cultural policy with this "Americanization" of culture for, in a well-publicized speech delivered in Mexico City in 1982, Mitterand declared that "mass culture," by which he implied American culture, constituted interference in the internal affairs of states; in this speech Mitterand also claimed the right to "cultural self-determination," positioning France as the world leader of "culturally non-aligned countries" (Forbes and Kelly, 189).

This speech precedes the socialist government's economic turn about. Mitterand had "normalized" French politics by overseeing the application of neoliberal economic policies by a government of the Left. However, even this change of direction did not manage to produce a drop in unemployment or a more vibrant economy. In the traditional political arena, the socialist government had to contend with the two major center-Right parties, of which the most visible leader was the RPR's Jacques Chirac, also the mayor of Paris. A coalition of these parties won the legislative elections of 1986, which led to an unprecedented event in the history of the Fifth Republic: for the first time, the majority in parliament was in the opposition and the president of the republic would have to choose his prime minister from that majority. Mitterand appointed Jacques Chirac and a period of "cohabitation" began.

During the two years between his appointment as prime minister and the presidential election of 1988, Chirac oversaw a program to undo the socialist nationalizations by privatizing a number of state enterprises (in fact, of the dozen companies involved, only one that had been nationalized by the Socialists was "re-privatized"), and the tax on the wealthiest was abandoned. Chirac also took a harder stance against issues of immigration and naturalization, hoping to gain the vote of some of the far Right electorate. The "Pasqua Laws," named after the center-Right government's minister of the interior, made the acquisition of French citizenship more difficult for the children of noncitizens living in France; where they had automatically become citizens at eighteen, this was no longer the case. This change from a law based on *droit du sol* (those born on French soil have the automatic right to French citizenship) to a law based on *droit du sang* (on blood or ethnicity) was widely perceived as a break with France's tradition of hospitality and also a return to Vichy-era practices. It led to heated national debates, and was ultimately abandoned, while Mitterand, keeping to foreign policy and defense, the "reserved domain" of the president, seemed a nonpartisan observer. His approval ratings, which had plummeted in the two years leading to the 1988 elections, begin to rise again, while Chirac became increasingly perceived as a divisive law and order type whose economic policies were not even successful. In spite of his government's neoliberal economic policies, unemployment continued to rise. Beginning in December 1986 Chirac had to face the longest strike since 1968. Involving transportation and national utility companies, and causing massive disruptions, the strike was a clear disavowal of the Right's economic policies. In addition, pragmatic use of the established Fifth Republic institutions that made of the president a removed figure ruling above political parties enabled Mitterand to remain above the fray; indeed, his election campaign was focused on the image of a wise leader who would preside over *une France unie*, a united France.

In the first round of the 1988 presidential elections, Mitterand won 27.2 percent of the vote against Chirac's 15.9 percent. Le Pen, however, scored 11.5 percent and the communist candidate only 5.4 percent. In the second round, Chirac's strategy of gleaning votes from the extreme right did not prove successful since Mitterand was reelected with 54 percent of the vote against Chirac's 46 percent in the second round.

Mitterand's reelection for a second seven-year term confirmed that a "normalization" of French politics had taken place. The institutions of the Fifth Republic could not only withstand alternate governance from the Left and the Right but also "cohabitation," the coexistence of a president of the Left and a prime minister and an Assembly of the Right. Economics, rather than ideology, seemed to dominate the political scene as, in this respect at least, the policies of governments of the Socialists and the Center became increasingly similar. On the whole, however, socialist policies remained more faithful to an interventionist state and *l'état providence* (the welfare state) while the Right leaned more toward a pure neoliberal economy that was variously denounced as *mondialization à outrance* (excessive globalization) and *capitalisme sauvage* (out of control or savage capitalism). In the wake of modernization *à l'américaine*, and then of deindustrialization, the traditional division of classes along lines separating *le peuple* (the people, the working class) from the "bourgeoisie" had become blurred. Nevertheless, the presence of the millions of unemployed and of a class of people living in quasi-structural *précarité* (precarious conditions) and *exclusion*, a segment of the population dependant on the state's social policies to survive, were ostensible signs that traditional class divisions were far from an anachronism.

After the thirty glorious years, the degree of success of the Left was no longer measured by its willingness to advance the proletariat toward revolution but by its ability to make use of the interventionist state to redistribute wealth more equitably while keeping the country as a whole economically viable in an increasingly globalized world. Mitterand faced the difficulties of achieving both goals simultaneously very early in his first term in office. Once neoliberal economic policies, even when applied by a government of the Left had failed, and once *cohabitation* had taken place and the Right had applied similar policies with more or less the same results, the political scene thus became "normalized." The Right and the Left faced-off in increasingly more symbolic and "mediatized" arenas. Claims to embody the republic, whether in its Gaullist tradition as was the case for Chirac, or in its socialist tradition, as was the case for Mitterand, became more crucial than ever, especially with the National Front still a key player on the political scene. After the elections of 1988, one of the crucial objectives of the Mitterand administration was to present itself as inheritor and perpetuator of republican universalism in its specifically socialist tradition just as it was being challenged by globalization and the "society of the spectacle." Soon after these elections, the celebration of the Bicentennial of the French Revolution reflected the extent to which Mitterand was able to advance this claim while presiding over the advent of what some observers called the "Republic of the Center." The latest electronic technology, complete with giant screens and lasers, mixed with more traditional celebration of the republic and of socialism. The event "had as its centerpiece an extravaganza designed by art illustrator Jean-Paul Goude called *La Marseillaise*, which commemorated the moment under the Third Republic when the anthem came to signify the republican unity of the nation and thus the continuity of the republican and socialist heritage from 1789 to 1870 to the Popular Front of 1936 and so on to 1981" (Forbes and Kelly, 189). The Mitterand administration's socialist credentials were thus being reaffirmed in a celebration of the founding event of the republic. For others, however, the Bicentennial commemoration was pure spectacle rather than a reaffirmation of the progressive or radical tradition of French socialism. "Depoliticized and cleansed of all references to the historical Revolution, the parade up the Champs Elysées was an American-style event in which the very American Jessye Norman sang the Marseillaise draped in the tricolor" (Sowerwine, 406). Others went further and saw in the "extravaganza" a sign of the end of the republican tradition inaugurated by the Revolution of 1789, and even the end of the "French exception" and of the universalist republic rooted in the principles of 1789. Journalist Serge Halimi refers to the opinion of some historians, among them Francois Furet, revisionist historian of the Revolution, and concludes that the Revolution has disappeared under the weight of concessions to capitalism and spectacle, confirming the appearance of a "market economy Socialism":

> In 1988, a few weeks after the reelection of President François Mitterand, three prominent French authors heralded the "Republic of the Center" and announced "The end of the French Exception." A year later, Paris celebrated the bicentennial of the fall of the Bastille amid a gathering of world aristocrats—the heads of delegations of the Group of Seven Industrial Nations (G-7). Mitterand, the triumphant leader of the French Left, a movement whose symbolic birth coincided with the victory of the sans culottes, had invited Georges Bush, Helmut Kohl and Margaret Thatcher to join him in burying the 200-year old corpse called the Revolution. (Halimi, 83)

The Bicentennial celebration could thus be interpreted as the exact opposite of what it purported to be: not the reaffirmation of progressive socialist principles rooted in the Revolution but, rather, the endorsement of mediatized politics and of a market economy symbolized by the presence of the Bush-Kohl-Thatcher trio; rather than the principles of a socialist republic, the alignment of the national economy with the globalization of the world economy.

Mitterand's European policy seemed to confirm this view. There was no apparent difference between the policy he conducted in this area and the one followed by his predecessors on the Right. In fact, like de Gaulle, Mitterand made wide use of the "reserved domain" of defense and foreign policy attributed to the president by the constitution of the Fifth Republic to offset difficulties he and his party were experiencing on the domestic front, especially after the ideological turnaround represented by his economic policies in the early 1980s. Mitterand had always been a Europeanist, but after the fall of the Berlin Wall in 1989 and the prospect of a powerful reunified Germany, advancing European integration became an even more important and urgent objective for him. France played an active part in establishing the Schengen convention of 1991 that established the free circulation of people within the European Economic Community. The following year, the twelve members of the EEC met at Maastricht and approved a treaty on economic, political, and monetary union. True to his tactic of using foreign policy as a tool of domestic politics, Mitterand insisted on submitting the Maastricht treaty to approval by referendum even though he was not required to do so by law. The substantial margin the president had counted on did not materialize; many French people perceived the consolidation of the EEC as a relinquishing of the republic's sovereignty, a loss of French identity in a European sea, and a further step toward the globalization of the economy and increased unemployment. The treaty was barely approved by a majority of less than 51 percent. European construction and extension would continue to be a major issue in the following years and some of the same problems faced by Mitterand in this area would plague his successor, Jacques Chirac. Jean-Marie Le Pen and the National Front would not be alone in opposing further European integration during Chirac's presidency, but the far Right party would be particularly effective in capitalizing on the population's fear of a loss of the republic's sovereignty, of the French people's "loss of identity," and of increased economic woes in a more federalized Europe, as did Le Pen in this speech in May 1998: "In exchange for the false promises of the euro [the common European currency created in 1997 and put in circulation in 2001], they are deprived of their fatherland, of their territory, of their identity, of their patrimony, and when they suspect they've been had, the thieves, the traitors tell them: 'It's too late. You've signed a pact: the Maastricht pact'" (Le Pen speech, May 1998).

Mitterand also supported the American-led war against Iraq in 1991. France committed 10,000 troops as well as airplanes and aircraft carriers to "Operation Desert Storm." There was sizeable opposition in France to the war and to the country's participation in it. However, the rapidity of "Operation Desert Storm," which barely lasted five weeks and the fact that it was not followed by an actual occupation of Iraq, did not provide enough time for a concerted and massive opposition to take shape. The situation would change drastically on the occasion of the second Iraq war in 2002 (see chapter 10).

On the domestic front, the socialist government continued in its attempt to find an effective mix of social and economic policies. The *Revenu minimum d'insertion* or RMI— an allocation of 2000 francs per month to those "between two jobs" as well as to those who were unemployed longer than the usual six months covered by unemployment allocations, and to those or had never held a job—was adopted in 1988. The RMI was financed by the reinstated tax on the wealthiest that Chirac had abrogated when he served as Mitterand's prime minister during the period of *cohabitation*. The RMI was yet one more attempt by the socialists to use the interventionist state's power to palliate the effects of the neoliberal economic policies it had also been adopting since the early years of the Mitterand presidency. The success of this policy was limited, as unemployment reached 3 million by 1993, on the eve of new legislative elections. The globalization of the word economy had begun to gather speed in the early 1970s just as France was ending its long period of economic growth and structural unemployment made its appearance. The issues that had plagued the Right when it was in power throughout the 1970s were continuing to plague the socialists in the 1980s and 1990s.

The same was true of the issue of collaboration and of France's role in the Holocaust, which had surfaced during the Pompidou administration, most notably in Max Ophul's documentary *The Sorrow and the Pity* and Robert Paxton's book *Vichy France: Old Guard, New Order* (see chapter 8). This time, the issue resurfaced not only in books or on film, but also in the form of high-profile trials for "crimes against humanity." The extent to which the republic could be kept separate from the happenings under the Vichy regime was an issue that reappeared with new force as it was not only a German Nazi officer, Klaus Barbie, who was put on trial but also three Frenchmen, René Bousquet, Paul Touvier, and Maurice Papon, two of whom had successful business and political careers after the war.

Barbie's trial took place in 1987. As head of the Gestapo in Lyon, he had personally tortured and killed de Gaulle's representative to the Resistance, Jean Moulin, and was directly responsible for numerous torture sessions and executions of resistance fighters during the Occupation, but he could only stand trial for "crimes against humanity," for which there was no statute of limitations. He was charged with the roundup and deportation of Jews to Auschwitz. Barbie's defense lawyer, Jacques Vergès, "the son of a Vietnamese woman and husband to an Algerian freedom fighter" (Sowerwine, 407) based his defense on an offensive against France's own role in the colonial war in Algeria where French soldiers had engaged in repression, torture, and assassination in the name of the republic. Vergès proposed that logic and justice required that they too be put on trial. Although Vergès' defense strategy did raise the question of the republic's responsibility, he was not successful in obtaining his client's acquittal. Barbie was condemned to life imprisonment, and died of leukemia in prison in 1991.

The case of the three Frenchmen would bring the issue of the republic's responsibility closer to home. The case of Paul Touvier was arguably the least problematic of the three since the former member of the *Milice* (Militia), the paramilitary organization that collaborated with the Germans, had already been sentenced to death in absentia at the Liberation for the execution of seven Jewish hostages. However, with the help of the high clergy of the Catholic Church at Lyon he had obtained a pardon from President Georges Pompidou in 1971. Since Pompidou was no longer alive to be questioned on this decision and since Touvier had been charged with acting on the orders of the Gestapo rather than on those of the Vichy government and had been in relative hiding since the war, the issue of the republic's responsibility was not raised as acutely as it would be in the cases of Bousquet and Papon. Bousquet had retired comfortably after a career in banking; Papon had held high public office, first as de Gaulle's police chief until 1968 and then as budget minister during the Giscard d'Estaing presidency.

Touvier was arrested in 1991 and brought to trial in 1994 on the charge of crimes against humanity. He was sentenced to life imprisonment and died in a prison hospital in 1996. Bousquet had been Vichy's Police chief and it was under his authority that French police officers rounded up 13,000 Jews at the Vélodrome d'Hiver, an indoor bicycle track in Paris, before being transferred to Drancy, a camp outside the capital, and from there to Auschwitz, where most of them died. Bousquet was assassinated by a deranged man in 1993 before he could come to trial. The procedural delay in his coming to trial (he was arrested in 1991) was widely thought to be a governmental tactic to avoid facing up to France's own responsibility in the Holocaust. In addition, this type of trial would have further discredited the myth of "resistancialism" that had, to a large extent, dominated the official narrative of the Occupation: only a "few traitors" (de Gaulle's phrase) had collaborated while the immense majority had resisted. At the Liberation, de Gaulle had also dealt with the issue of France's role during the Occupation by declaring that Vichy had been "null and void," an illegal interlude in the normal functioning of the republic. Mitterand would continue this tradition by refusing to acknowledge that the republic had played any part in the Holocaust. In 1992, the National Assembly designated July 16 as the official day of commemoration for the Vélodrome d'hiver roundup. In the traditional presidential press conference that takes place on July 14, Bastille Day, Mitterand declared that the republic "had nothing to do with the crimes of Vichy" but promised that a monument would be built to commemorate the event. At the ceremony, the prime minister, not the president, made a short solemn speech in which he declared that France "was in mourning" and repeated Mitterand's promise that a monument would be erected "to perpetuate the memory of what took place here." Mitterand himself made no declaration at the ceremony (*Financial Times*, July 25, 1993).

Mitterand's own past record was brought to public attention by a book published in 1993. It was already known that the president had served in the Vichy administration as head of the Prisoner Reclassification Section, a position he kept until 1943 (see chapter 6), but he had emerged from the war with impeccable Resistance credentials, having left his post to join de Gaulle in Algiers. The book did not go into the subtleties of wartime allegiances and many were in fact shocked to learn of Mitterand's Vichy past. The *Canard enchaîné*, the satirical political weekly, had also revealed that every year on November 11, Armistice day—the day commemorating the end of World War I—Mitterand had been sending a wreath to the tomb of Marshall Pétain. In this instance also Mitterand maintained a clear division between paying homage to a hero of the republic, and to a figure discredited by collaboration with Nazi Germany: he was, he declared, honoring the hero of Verdun, not the Vichy leader.

Maurice Papon, the third Frenchman to be put on trial, was the most problematic figure. On the one hand, he had been active in the collaborationist Vichy regime; as head of the Gironde region in southwestern France, he was in constant contact with the nazi command, in particular with the SS corps, which was responsible for the deportation of Jews; he himself was directly responsible for the deportation of 1560 Jewish men, women, and children to concentration camps where most of them died; on the other hand, by switching sides at the last minute he was able not only to evade accusation and prosecution, but also managed to appear as a wartime resister at the Liberation. In the following years Papon became an active and well-known politician, first as a deputy in 1968 and subsequently as Charles de Gaulle's police prefect for ten years, from 1958 to 1968, and finally as Valéry Giscard d'Estaing's budget minister from 1978 to 1981, the year of the socialist victory and the start of Mitterand's presidency. Beginning that year, a number of incriminating documents were leaked to the press and published in *Le canard enchaîné*. Papon was accused of crimes against humanity; although he managed to avoid going to trial for years, he had to leave public life. Not until 1995 would he have to face charges of "complicity in crimes against humanity." By the time he was brought to trial two years later and found guilty, Mitterand was no longer in power.

Rather than any association French voters made between Mitterand and Vichy, collaboration, or the Holocaust, the state of the economy and the continued rise of unemployment were at the core of the socialist rout in the legislative elections of 1993. However, the well-publicized trials did contribute to discrediting the political class as a whole. A series of corruption scandals centered on campaign financing reached the highest echelons of the Socialist party, including Mitterand and his prime minister, Pierre Bérégovoy. This was the most important wave of corruption since the Panama scandal (1889–1893), during the Third Republic (see chapter 3). The political class attempted to whitewash its involvement by voting a law in 1990 that stipulated that "all infractions committed before June 15, 1989 in relation with the direct or in direct campaign financing or of political parties are amnestied." The political establishment as a whole was discredited by the scandals and the supposed "servants of the republic" appeared more as self-serving promoters of their own, private agendas. The scandals reflected the increasingly less "republican" and more market- and media-driven quality of French politics in the 1980s and 1990s. The citizens themselves were part of this general trend as they tended to vote more and more along economic rather than ideological lines. The results of the legislative elections of 1993 were, once again, a warning to the ruling party that its economic policies were found to be wanting.

The Socialists obtained 67 seats, the Communists 24 seats, while the Right coalition of the RPR and UDF obtained a combined 449 seats. This election was reminiscent of the Right's crushing victory in the aftermath of May 68; but a significant change had occurred in the quarter century that had passed. The majority that voted for the Right in 1968 had voted to a great extent in response to de Gaulle's positioning the Right as a rampart against "dictatorship" and "totalitarian communism" (see chapter 8). However, between de Gaulle's rousing speech in the summer of 1968 and the elections of 1993, the Socialists had come to power and proved to be as adept, or inefficient, at conducting economic and social policy as the Right, Communist ministers had occupied cabinet positions for the first time since 1947, and the "dictatorship" did not materialize. In short, the *décrispation* of politics touted by Valéry Giscard d'Estaing in the 1970s had taken place with a vengeance in the 1980s and 1990s: Mitterand and the Socialists had "made France normal" (Collard, 33). When Mitterand died in 1996, a few months after the presidential election that put a politician of the Right, Jacques Chirac, in power, opinion polls showed that Mitterand was the most respected president in France since Charles de Gaulle, the resistance leader and first president of the Fifth Republic. Chirac, the first president since the end of the war "without resistance credentials" (Stoval) would take a much changed France into the third millennium.

References

Ben Jelloun, Tahar. *Hospitalité française*. Paris: Editions du Seuil, 1974.

Bernabé, Jean, Patrick Chamoiseau, and Raphaël Confiant. *Eloge de la créolité*. Paris: Gallimard (Presses universitaires créoles), 1989.

Caron, David. *AIDS in French Culture. Social Ills, Literary Cures*. Madison: The University of Wisconsin Press, 2001.

Célestin, Roger. "From Popular Culture to Mass Culture: An Interview with Jean Baudrillard." In Roger Célestin and Eliane DalMolin, eds. *SITES: The Journal of Contemporary French Studies, 1*, 1 (Spring 1997): 5–15.

Colard, Sue. "The Elusive French Exception." In Chafer and Godin, 30–43.

Chafer, Tony and Emmanuel Godin, eds. *The French Exception*. New York and London: Berghahn Books, 2005.

Daley, Anthony, ed. *The Mitterand Era. Policy Alternatives and Political Mobilization in France*. New York: New York University Press, 1996.

Debord, Guy. *The Society of the Spectacle*. Detroit: Black & Red, 1977. Originally published as *La société du spectacle*, Buchet-Chastel (Paris, 1967).

Durand, Alain-Philippe. *Black, Blanc, Beur. Rap Music and Hip-Hop Culture in the Francophone World*. Lanham, MD and Oxford: Scarecrow Press: 2002.

Finkielkraut, Alain. *The Defeat of the Mind*. Judith Friedlander, trans. New York: Columbia University Press, 1995. Originally published as *La défaite de la pensée* (Paris: Gallimard, 1987).

Forbes, Jill and Michael Kelly, eds. *French Cultural Studies. An Introduction*. Oxford, New York: Oxford University Press, 1995.

Forsdick, Charles and David Murphy. *Francophone Postcolonial Studies. A Critical Introduction*. London: Arnold, 2003.

Fourny Jean-François. *France's Identity Crisis. Special Issue of SubsStance*, In Kritzman, 24, 1 and 2 (1995): 62–72.

Fumaroli, Marc. *L'etat culturel. Essai sur une religion moderne*. Paris: Editions de Fallois, 1992.

Genestier, Philippe "Great Projects or Mediocre Designs?" In Kritzman, 24, 1 and 2 (1995): 62–72.

Glissant, Edouard. "The French Language in the Face of Creolization." In Tyler Stovall and Georges van den Abbeele, 105–114.

Hargreaves, Alec. *Immigration, "Race" and Ethnicity in Contemporary France*. London: Routledge, 1995.

Halimi, Serge. "Less Exceptionalism than Meets the Eye." In Daley, 83–96.

Howarth, David, and Georgios Varouxakis. *Contemporary France. An Introduction to French Politics and Society*. London: Arnold, 2003.

Jones, Colin. *The Cambridge Illustrated History of France*. Cambridge: Cambridge University Press, 1994.

Kidd, William and Siân Reynolds. *Contemporary French Cultural Studies*. London: Arnold, 2000.

Kritzman, Lawrence D., ed. *France's Identity Crisis. Special issue of SubsStance*, 24, 1 and 2 (1995).

Kuisel, Richard. *Seducing the French. The Dilemma of Americanization*. Berkeley: University of California Press, 1993.

Lee, Sonia. "Medhi Charef et le cinéma de l'intégration." *Contemporary French & Francophone Studies: SITES*, 8, 2 (Spring 2004): 185–191.

Lipovetsky, Gilles. *L'ére du vide.Essais sur l'individualisme contemporain*. Paris: Gallimard, 1983.

Majumdar, Margaret A. "Exceptionalism and Universalism: The Uneasy Alliance in the French-Speaking World" In Tony Chafer, and Emmanuel Godin, 16–29.

McCusker, Maeve. "This Creole Culture, Miraculously Forged: The Contradictions of 'Créolité.'" In Charles Forsdick and David Murphy, 112–121.

Norindr, Panivong. "'Popularizing' French Culture: The Bibliothèque de France." *SITES: The Journal of 20-th Century/Contemporary French Studies*, 1, 1 (1997), 93–108.

Plenel, Edwy and Alain Rolat. *La République menacée. Dix ans d'effet Le Pen*. Paris: Editions *Le Monde*, 1992.

Senghor, Léopold Sédar. "Le français, langue de culture." *Esprit*, 311 (November 1962): 837–845.

Silverman, Maxim. *Deconstructing the Nation. Immigration, Racism and Citizenship in Modern France*. London, New York: Routledge, 1992.

Stovall, Tyler E. *France since the Second World War*. Harlow, London: Pearson Education Limited: 2002.

Stovall, Tyler E. and Georges van den Abbeele. *French Civilization and Its Discontents. Nationalism, Colonialism, Race*. Lanham: Lexington Books, 2005.

Taguieff, Pierre-André. *La République menacée. Entretien avec Philippe Petit*. Paris: Les éditions Textuel, 1996.

Wachtel, David. *Cultural Policy and Socialist France*. New York, WT: Greenwood Press, 1987.

Walcott, Derek. *Collected Poems 1948–1984*. New York: Farrar Straus Giroux, 1988.

CHAPTER 10

THE REPUBLIC IN THE THIRD MILLENNIUM (1995 TO THE PRESENT)

Sovereignty, like the Republic, is one and indivisible, and so . . . when I hear . . . that this sovereignty shall be embodied by the two halves of humanity, by women and by men, I admit that I cannot follow this argument. I cannot conceive what a sovereignty embodied in two parts would be . . . universalism is universalism, period.

—Robert Badinter, French Senator intervening
at a Senate session on January 26, 1999

One does not have to be a radical feminist to point out the mystification that can accompany the "universal."

—Michelle Perrot, historian, *Women: A French Singularity?* (1995)

France's universalist vocation seems to have dissolved in the restless search for "proximity." France cultivates a hexagonal vision of the world. It no longer looks to conquer, but to preserve.

—Gérard Mermet, sociologist,
Francoscopie 2005

In the spring of 2005, with two years still remaining in his second term, President Jacques Chirac heard the same slogan that one of his predecessors, Charles de Gaulle, had heard chanted in the streets of Paris during the events of May 68: "Ten years, that's enough!" In May 2005, the French had just voted a clear "non" (54.87 percent) in the referendum on the European Constitution, Chirac's approval ratings had fallen to an abysmal 26 percent, and journalists from right-leaning as well as left-leaning publications were already writing assessments of his presidency that sounded like obituaries. The Right of center *Le Figaro* published a poll in which only 18 percent of those questioned approved of the government's policies. To the Left of the political spectrum, an editorialist of the pro-Socialist weekly *Le Nouvel Observateur* unfavorably compared Chirac to *all* of his predecessors who had been presidents of the Fifth Republic. Referring to the fact that the slogan that had been used against de Gaulle was being used once again against Chirac, Robert Schneider wrote:

Granted, [Chirac] is not the first one. The Left used it in 1968 against de Gaulle, who did not recover from it. The Right attempted to use it against Mitterand whose end-of-reign was difficult. But both, during their tenure at the Elysée, left their mark on History. De Gaulle founded the Fifth Republic and put France back on its feet again. Mitterand made it possible for the Left to come to power, abolished the death penalty, gave the media back their freedom, advanced the construction of Europe, most notably by having the people adopt the euro. The other predecessors of Chirac have also left their mark. Pompidou modernized the economy, Giscard [d'Estaing] unlocked society with the adult age at 18 and the law on abortion. They too advanced the cause of Europe.

What will remain of the Chirac years? Nothing or almost nothing! Neither grand design as with de Gaulle, nor grand projects as with Mitterand. We will only take note of his resistance to Bush during the Iraq war and the controversial recognition—neither de Gaulle nor Mitterand had thought it opportune—of the French State's responsibility during the Occupation. It doesn't amount to much. (46)

This particularly severe summing up of "the Chirac years" was no doubt influenced by the journalist's own political convictions and by the gloomy mood that reigned in France in June 2005 when the editorial was written. However, Schneider's harsh evaluation reflects a more generalized moroseness that seemed to characterize France and the French in these first few years of the millennium. When asked in a 2004 survey to choose the word that best exemplified for them the present state of their society, 40 percent chose "decline," 28 percent chose *immobilisme* (stagnation), and only 32 percent voted for "progress" (Mermet, 9). If in 1968, prior to the events, of May, with the economy booming and de Gaulle in power, *Le Monde* had as a front-page headline "France is bored," in May 2005, with unemployment at about 13 percent and Chirac in power, a possible key phrase describing the mood in France could indeed be *le déclin français* (French decline). The phrase had become ubiquitous after the publication in 2003 of French historian and economist Nicolas Baverez's *La France qui tombe (Falling France)*, in which the author describes France as a country "facing a social and economic crisis with growth nearing a stand-still, a high level of unemployment, the heaviest social charges and the greatest number of strikes in Europe." The general sense of malaise and dissatisfaction evident in Schneider's editorial was perhaps best symbolized and perpetuated when, a mere two weeks after the French *non* to the new European constitution, London was chosen over Paris to host the 2012 Summer Olympics. The disappointment throughout France was palpable and, to outsiders at least, seemed disproportionate. The reaction, however, was indicative of a kind of national desperation and a need for an event, a project that would reassure the French about their own future and their president's ability to conduct a successful policy on both the domestic and international fronts. Chirac had staked his own political reputation on the French vote on the European constitution as well as the International Olympic Committee's vote for Paris as host city. He was disavowed on both counts and, in the spring and summer of 2005, his succession and the presidential elections of 2007, whichever came first, were already being hotly debated. Whether the *Nouvel Observateur's* editorialist was too severe or, on the contrary, prescient, in proposing that "nothing or almost nothing" would remain of the Chirac years remains to be seen, for the period is still too close to us to allow for this type of evaluation. What we propose, instead, is a recapitulation of the past ten years in France through some of the salient events and trends of the decade. In the process it will become evident that the major issues that had taken shape during the Mitterand era remained during Chirac's presidency: the question of "French identity" and its links to immigration and to the idea of a more "federalist" Europe; the role of the interventionist welfare state in the age of globalization; the continued crystallization of "particularist" groups and of a more ethnically diverse population, and the republic's ability—or not—to be inclusive in the process of adapting to the world of the third millennium. In short, as we have encountered throughout the second part of this study, the question of France's ability to maintain the values of the universalist republic in a world where they are no longer dominant.

★ ★ ★

When Chirac was elected to the presidency in 1995, the "normalization" of French politics, which some equated with "the end of the French exception," had taken place with a vengeance: after a quarter century of presidents of the Right since the beginning of the Fifth Republic, France had had a Socialist president for fourteen years, the longest period in office served by a French leader since Napoleon; there had been several periods of *cohabitation* between a president of the Left and a prime minister and parliamentary majority of the Right; Socialist prime ministers had applied neoliberal economic policies, and Mitterand, a Socialist president, had supported the U.S.-led war with Iraq in 1991 with French troops and planes. Chirac's own campaign for the presidency seemed to be that of a candidate of the Left. Indeed, it was focused on putting an end to what he famously called *la fracture sociale*, the riff between haves and have-nots that had been widening since the end of the economic boom in the mid-1970s and had produced structural unemployment and precarious economic conditions for a substantial portion of the population. Those who traditionally voted for the Right were perplexed by the candidate's vocabulary and his denunciation of "the technostructure" and of "the privileged class." Nevertheless Chirac's strategy of attracting voters from the center and the Left succeeded, and he was elected with 52.63 percent of the vote against the Socialist candidate Lionel Jospin, while the National Front's score of 15 percent in the first round for its candidate Jean-Marie Le Pen, and the 20 percent abstention rate of the second round were signs that the traditional parties and politics were losing ground.

Shortly after his election in 1995, Chirac's "social" campaign platform was replaced by a plan that seemed its exact opposite: the objective of reducing the *fracture sociale* was replaced by that of reducing budgetary deficits. Chirac's prime minister, Alain Juppé, announced a plan to finance the social security deficit through an additional income tax. The "Juppé plan" also involved cutting health benefits and raising the retirement age for state workers, effectively delaying access to their pensions. On the whole, the plan was an attempt to dismantle a number of *acquis sociaux*, social benefits and state-controlled programs, in order to "streamline" the French economy according to more "competitive," that is, neoliberal, economic criteria. The reaction was immediate: at first workers from the public sector, led by the national railway and public transportation sectors, went on strike. This initial wave of strikes spread rapidly as workers from the private sector as well as teachers and university faculty joined in. Barely a few months into his presidency Chirac was facing the largest strike in France since 1968. As American historian Georges Ross writing in *Le Monde Diplomatique* in January 1996 noted, "The formidable spectacle of wage earners in the private sector supporting their colleagues in the public sector, refusing to lend themselves to the government's efforts to isolate the strikers, demonstrated fully the extent of popular discontent" (quoted in Sowerwine, 419). The massive movement was also considered by many as a refusal to accept the dismantling of the republic's traditional interventionist role, both as economic and as social agent; in other words, a refusal to accept the alignment of national economic and social policy along the demands of the globalized economy: "For the first time in a rich country, we are witnessing today a strike against globalization, a massive collective reaction against economic globalization and its consequences" (Izraelewicz, 1).

In France in particular, the label "strike against globalization" meant that the strikers of 1995 and their supporters had acted against measures that would reduce the role of the state in overseeing and legislating in the economic sphere. They had been against the privatization of the various areas subsumed under the phrase *acquis sociaux*. The Juppé plan had revealed the extent to which the Chirac-Juppé government was willing to revise a constitutive notion of the French exception, the interventionist welfare state, and to comply with a constitutive notion of globalization, the free play of market forces. The strikers of 1995 had not only been protesting a particular government "package" or "plan" but against a wider trend to align national policy—decried for this purpose as "artificial" and "backward"—with the international parameters of globalization—touted by its proponents as "natural" or "forward looking."

From this vantage point, globalization can be perceived as a kind of "postmodern universalism" in direct opposition to some of the basic principles of French "modern universalism." In the French model, the strong centralizing republican state acts to bring the citizens within the folds of policies designed within the scope of the nation-state. When this policy does extend beyond the borders of the nation, it is only to extend the national ethos perceived as universal. This aspect of France's universalism was at the core of its colonial project (see chapter 7). In the type of postmodern universalism represented by globalization, which is also posited as a planetary model, the nation-state gives way to a diffuse and international series of forces. By definition, this new universalism, like French universalism in its ascending phase, extends itself beyond national borders. However, unlike French universalism, which, at one point, no longer had the material means to continue this extension, globalization, the "new universalism," does not seem to have yet met its limits. The striking workers of 1995 may not have formulated it quite this way, but it was precisely against the extension of another, necessarily conflicting, universalism within France that they were protesting. It is both ironic and fitting that, in the 1950s, when France was in the process of opting for American-style modernization, one aspect of this extension—not yet labeled globalization—was referred to as "cocacolonization," or that the introduction of Halloween, an American custom, in France in 1998, could be denounced by the president of a major political party as "neo-colonialism" (Sowerwine, 434). The expression "cocacolonization" was coined in the 1950s, but was still very much present in the national memory in 1998. In both instances, American-style modernization was forcing onto the French themselves an experience of national disruption that the French *mission civilisatrice* had taken to the far reaches of the globe when France was itself a dominant world power. The strikes of 1995 were thus not only the protest of a population that felt threatened by a particular governmental plan; these strikes were also emblematic of the encounter between two models, two universalisms, one having ostensibly reached its limits, the other in an ascending phase. The strikers were acting against a government policy, but they were in favor of continued state intervention as a means of countering the supposedly irrepressible forces of globalization. The strikers ultimately "won'" as the "Juppé Plan" was withdrawn a few months after it was introduced, but the relations between a French population accustomed to a socially and economically interventionist republic and the demands of globalization remained contentious. The strikes and student protests of winter and spring 2006 against a government proposal to make it easier to fire first-time employees would be a continuation of this antagonism.

Among the many organizations against globalization in France, farmer and activist José Bové's *Confédération paysanne* (Farmers' Confederation) has become one of the most visible. While in the postwar and in the 1950s, France's adoption of the American modernization model was denounced as "cocacolonization," for Bové and his organization, the prime emblem of globalization was McDonalds and *la malbouffe*. There is no one word in English that fully renders the meaning of the French *malbouffe*. "Junk food" has been used as an English equivalent, but in France, *malbouffe* has overtones of unhealthy, processed, and contaminated food. Bové, who coined the word, gives a definition:

> The first time I used the word was on August 12, 1999, in front of the McDonald's in Millau [in the Midi-Pyrenees region]. While I was discussing my speech with friends, I initially used the word "shit-food," but quickly changed it to *malbouffe* to avoid giving offence. The word just clicked—perhaps because when you're dealing with food, quite apart from any health concerns, you're also dealing with taste and what we feed ourselves with. *Malbouffe* implies eating any old thing. (53)

The Confédération's "attack" on a McDonald's franchise in Millau became one of the most celebrated symbols of a grassroots "French resistance" (Mathy) to globalization (see dossier 10.1).

Dossier 10.1   José Bové, *This World Is Not For Sale. Farmers against Junk food* (2001)

In late June 1993, French military police forced their way into the home of José Bové in the Larzac region in order to arrest him and have him begin his prison term for destroying a field of genetically modified rice. The destruction of the field was one of the first actions against the globalization of food production and protest against what would become known as *malbouffe*. The dismantling of a McDonalds franchise in Millau in 1999 as well as the *Confédération*'s presence at the World Trade Organization meeting held in Seattle the same year, represent continuations of a strategy of spectacular protests against globalization. In 2001, Bové described some of these actions in the form of a long interview in *This World Is Not For Sale*. The following excerpt focuses on the "McDonald's episode" of 1999.

Agence France Presse. August 12, 1999, 11:41 GMT
McDonald's construction site ransacked by farmers.
Millau- August 12. A group of farmers ransacked a McDonald's under construction in Millau (Aveyron) during a demonstration on Thursday against the American-imposed sanctions against the ban against the import of hormone-treated beef, according to police sources.

At 11 a.m. on Thursday, August 12, 1999, the Union of Ewe's Milk Producers (SPLB) and the Farmer's Confederation called a rally in front of a McDonald's which was being built on the site of a former gas station, on the road south out of Millau. Three hundred people turned up— half from the countryside, half from the town.

How long had you been thinking of taking on McDonald's?

José Bové: You've got to link McDonald's to the issue of hormone-treated meat. At our Congress in Vesoul, in April 1999, we'd already raised the question of preparing ourselves for the American retaliation against Europe's ban on the import of hormone-treated beef. In February 1998, the World Trade Organization had condemned the European Union's ban, and given it fifteen months to get its house back in order—that is to reopen its frontiers. This deadline had expired on May 13, 1999, so the American move came as no surprise. We had already envisaged linking the issue of hormones and McDonald's. What we had not foreseen, however, was that Roquefort, the main produce of the farmers in my area, would be included in the hundred or so products affected by a 100 per cent customs surcharge on entering the states.

In Washington, the price of Roquefort shot up from $30 a kilo to $60, effectively prohibiting its sale. Around the same time, we found out that a McDonald's was being constructed in Millau. The professional association of Roquefort producers decided to lobby the Minister of Agriculture on August 5th. The Minister, Jean Glavany, informed us that there was nothing he could do, that he was unable to obtain direct financial compensation, that Europe was powerless and there was no other way out. He could promise only to finance publicity for the campaign on the produce affected by the surcharge.

How did you prepare for this action, and how did events unfold?

JB: The objective was to have a non-violent but symbolically forceful action, in broad daylight and with the largest possible participation. We wanted the authorities to be fully aware of what was going on to happen, so we explained to the police in advance that the purpose of the rally was to dismantle the McDonald's. The police notified the regional government, and they called back to say that they would ask the McDonald's manager to provide a billboard or something similar for us to demolish. This, he said, would allow for a symbolic protest. We replied that this idea was ludicrous, and that it remained our intention to dismantle the doors and windows of the building. The police deemed it unnecessary to mount a large presence. We asked them to make sure that the site would be clear of workers, and that no tools were left lying around.

It all happened as we'd envisaged. The only odd thing was the presence of some ten plainclothes police officers armed with cameras. The demo took place and people, including kids, began to dismantle the inside of the building, taking down partitions, some doors, fuse boxes, and some tiles from the roof—they were just nailed down and came off very easily; in fact the whole building appeared to have been assembled from a kit. The structure was very flimsy. While some people started to repaint the roof of the restaurant, others began loading bits of the structure on to a tractor-trailer. One of the trailers was a grain carrier. As soon as the trailers were loaded, everyone left the site. Children clambered on the grain wagon and used wooden sticks to bang on the sides, and the whole lot proceeded in the direction of the prefecture, seat of the regional government. As the procession wound its way through the town, the festive atmosphere was further heightened by the cheering of local people who had gathered to watch us go by. We unloaded everything in front of the prefecture. It was a beautiful day, everyone was having a good time, and many people ended up on the terraces of Millau's restaurants. (3–7)

La demande sociale, the social unrest, that had erupted in 1995 continued the following year and, in 1997, led to Chirac's dissolution of the National Assembly in an attempt to find new legitimacy. The electoral campaign was conducted on issues—European construction and the modernization of the economy—that seemed abstract to voters who were much more concerned, as the strikes had shown, with jobs, social inequalities, and health and retirement plans. The ill-conceived dissolution and the resulting vote ended in a defeat of the Right majority and a victory for a "pluralist Left" ranging from the Greens to the Communists gathered around a reinvigorated Socialist Party led by Lionel Jospin. Once again a period of "cohabitation" began as Chirac had to name Jospin as prime minister. "Cohabitation" was not new since it had occurred three times during the Mitterand presidency, but for the first time, a president of the Right would have to cohabit with a prime minister and a parliamentary majority of the Left. This period of cohabitation would last until the presidential elections of 2002, which would send a shockwave through France, resulting as they did in a runoff between Jacques Chrirac and Jean-Marie Le Pen the candidate of the extreme Right National Front, who gathered more votes in the first round than the Socialist Party's candidate, Lionel Jospin.

In the five intervening years of "cohabitation," some of the issues that had come to the fore in the 1970s and 1980s resurfaced. The role of women in French society had already been at the core of post-68 debates, mainly in the context of the "first wave" of French feminism, but at that time the concerns had remained largely theoretical and literary (see chapter 8). In the 1990s, a more pragmatic and sociopolitically oriented movement emerged, especially around the issue of *parité* or the equal representation of men and women holding political office. The proposal was that political parties present an equal number of men and women on their electoral lists in national elections.

The question of *parité* provoked acrimonious debate because it subverted basic notions constitutive of French republican universalism. For the "universalists," there are no particular identities, only citizens, and any attempt to claim attributes of a specific identity in the public sphere constituted an attack on this tradition of abstract universalism rooted in the revolutionary notion of *liberté, égalité, fraternité* for *all* citizens. In addition, the United States, the nation most emblematic of globalization, also represented a countermodel to be avoided. The universalist side of the debate is succinctly summarized in the following declaration by the philosopher and historian Elisabeth Badinter in an article published in *Le Monde* in June 1996, entitled "No to Quotas for Women": "The ideology of quotas creates sordid and humiliating calculations. For example, there would not be enough Muslim representatives and senators compared to the number of Jews in the Assemblies. And what about gays, 20–30 year olds, or handicapped people, and so on? In the United States, this kind of war has already begun in all spheres of society. Quotas are politically correct" (1). The reference to "political correctness" pointedly establishes the link between *parité* and what are perceived as peculiarly American practices. On the opposing side, the supporters of *parité*, also referred to as *differentialists*, argued that universalism was in fact a veil hiding the de facto inequalities in French society, ranging from the blatant exclusion of ethnic minorities from political life to the equally blatant underrepresentation of women in parliament. The supporters of *parité* demanded the passing of a law that would remedy these inequalities.

Philosopher and historian Sylviane Agacinski, an advocate of *parité*, proposed that it did not go counter to universalism, but only redefined it. Combining "universalism" and "differentialism," she proposed the concept of a "universal difference": "Parity replaces republican universalism with a double universalism, which is neither man or woman, but man and woman at the same time" (18). The opposing camps' arguments were thus laid out.

The parliamentary debate on *parité* was long and drawn out. On June 28, 1999, the members of France's lower and upper chamber, meeting in congress at Versailles, endorsed by a very substantial majority—745 in favor and only 43 against—a double amendment to the constitution's preamble introducing the principle. The irony was flagrant; a country that had long scorned "positive discrimination" (the French term for "affirmative action") as fundamentally contrary to the equal treatment of citizens had become the first in Western Europe to embrace a limited form of such discrimination in its constitution. Legislation instituting *parité* was adopted less than a year later (Howarth and Varouxakis, 97).

In the aftermath of the *parité* debates a new generation of activist young women set up a number of organizations, such as the *Chiennes de Garde*, or Watch Dogs (but the dogs were female, or "Watch Bitches"—see dossier 10.2) and *Mix-Cité*, an organization made up of men and women, and became active in the struggle against sexist advertisement, the harassment of women politicians, and economic and legal discrimination and violence against women.

Dossier 10.2   *The Bitch Manifesto* (March 8, 1999)

The *Chiennes de Garde* (literally "Watch Bitches") group was originally created in 1999 in response to sexist insults aimed at women in public office. Its "Manifesto" was signed by many prominent French men and women who thus displayed their support for an organization fighting against verbal violence against women in general. Beginning in 1999, groups of women wearing dog-masks and protesting issues ranging from sexist declarations made in political institutions such as the Senate and the National Assembly, to certain types of advertising campaigns, became very visible in the media and on the streets of French cities.

We live in a democracy. There is freedom of speech, but not all debates are equal.

Any woman who asserts herself or puts herself forward, runs the risk of being called a "whore." If she is successful, she is suspected of having played couch politics. Every woman in the public eye is judged on her appearance and labeled "motherly," "the maid," a "dyke," a "bimbo" etc.
ENOUGH IS ENOUGH!!

We, members of bitches, have decided to bare our teeth.

Sexist remarks about a woman in the public eye insult all women. We undertake to show our support to women in public life who are insulted as women. We contend that all women must be free in both action and choice. Bitches defends something of great value: the dignity of women.

WARNING

We intend to place the debate on a higher level!

Together! For there is strength in unity. March 8th 1999

No More Sexist Violence!

*Every woman in French politics today has received **sexist** insults, such as "stupid cow," "slag," "bitch" etc., scrawled on their campaign posters, shouted in public or over the telephone: insults in a country which is proud of its tradition of gallantry (which could be viewed as the polite face of sexism); any woman taking an initiative is likely to be treated in this way (the word prostitute originally meant "exposed").*

When Simone Veil defended a French law on abortion, the key to women's freedom, in 1974, she was insulted; then other women in the public eye, such as Yvette Roudy in 1983, when she wanted to pass an anti-sexist law; Edith Cresson, who was Prime Minister in 1991 and, more recently, Nicole Notat, the general secretary of one of France's largest trade unions, were all subjected to sexist attacks whose violence was directed at their womanhood.

Recently, machos made sneering remarks such as "vaginal verbosity" when Roselyne Bachelot, a member of Parliament, stood up to make a speech, and others told the "Green" minister Dominique Voynet to "take her panties off."

Women politicians—and indeed most other women—are not judged on their capabilities, but too often on their physical appearance alone (adjectives such as "sultry," "charming," "portly," "sensible," etc. are bandied about) and assimilated with a sexual function: "motherly," "big sister," "dyke," "slag," etc.

*The very rare women in politics before 1974 were not treated with such violence. Most of those in politics shortly after the War had been active in the Resistance, which probably contributed to the respect they received. The feminism of the seventies, with slogans such as "our bodies ourselves" and "the personal is political" caused a backlash in the anti-feminist current, which has always been virulent in France. Now, as in the past, and in France, as elsewhere, those who cannot accept the legitimacy of **female** participation **in** decisions **on** a **par** with **men** use violence as a method of reducing all women to invisibility and silence.*

*In other developed countries, women politicians are not attacked with such machismo. **Why** is **France** an **exception?** Is it because women were originally excluded from the French Republic? It was only on April 21st 1944 that French women obtained the vote, 96 years after the French Republic declared so-called "universal suffrage." Unlike in neighboring countries, the number of women elected to parliament is still ridiculously small.*

The Caillaux case in 1914 and the suicide of Roger Salengro in 1936 are two examples of how violent insults and public mud-slinging between male politicians could, in the past, be used to gun down enemies. Evolving attitudes and a growing trend towards lawsuits encouraged a measure of self control in democratic debate amongst men in politics. But what about women? Well, from 1981 to 1986, the then Minister of Women's Rights, Yvette Roudy, accomplished great work, but failed to obtain an anti-sexist law along the lines of the anti-racist law of 1972.

*Today, it is up to us, **women** and **men**, to make our voices heard in the name of liberté, égalité, fraternité and tolerance. We demand a law against sexism. We demand an in-depth analysis, educational resources and preventive measures. We want to live in a society in which we can act freely, respecting others and being respected by them.*

It would probably be wiser to être économe de son mépris, en raison du si grand nombre de nécessiteux ("be thrifty with contempt, for there are so many in need of it"), but is it reasonable to hope that mentalities will change uniquely of their own accord, under the beneficial influence of civilization? What if we gave civilization a helping hand?

A sexist insult to a woman in public office insults all women.
It is time we said no and bared our teeth.
Contact us at: *bureau@chiennesdegarde.org*
Sign the Manifesto! Join our organization! Men welcome.
Chiennes de Garde
The Bitch Manifesto

The increased visibility of women on the French scene was not restricted to the sociopolitical arena in which they made claims under the banner of feminism. In the past twenty years or so a new generation of women has also acquired unprecedented visibility in literature and film. In literature, the works of women who distinguished themselves in the twentieth century—Simone de Beauvoir, Marguerite Duras, and Hélène Cixous, among others—were unavoidably concerned with the feminine and, more specifically, with their own status *as women* or *as* women writers and intellectuals. De Beauvoir's monumental *The Second Sex* (see chapter 6) published in the postwar period and the work of women intellectuals and writers of the post-68 generation (see chapter 8), for example, could not but explicitly address issues centered on the place of women in male-dominated history and society. In contrast, a new generation of women writers is far less concerned with feminism—radical or not—than with a shared sense of renewed literary style and subject. In the 1990s and in the first few years of the millennium, a number of women writers, like the male writers before them, from the Marquis de Sade to Georges Bataille, have focused on the sexual as a means of pushing the limits of fiction. Sometimes sex appears in the forefront of these women's writing, sometimes it remains peripheral, as a form of social violence sublimated in the writing itself. In some instances, although these writer's books are published as "novels," that is as fiction, the protagonist is clearly recognizable as the author herself. This is the case in Annie Ernaux's *A Simple Passion* (1991), in which she describes her affair with an Eastern European diplomat posted in Paris; Catherine Millet's *The Sex Life of Catherine M* (2001), in which the well-known art historian recounts explicitly her numerous sexual encounters; or Marie Nimier's *La nouvelle pornographie* (*The New Pornography*, 2002), where the author proposes a "new pornography" that would replace the old one much in the way "nouvelle cuisine" replaced traditional cuisine. While the notorious opening page of *A Simple Passion*, with its description of a scene from a pornographic film, is the only sexually explicit moment in Ernaux's novel, which focuses instead on the recounting of obsessive desire and its relation to writing, Millet's book is a succession of graphic scenes in which no detail is spared, including her own fondness for pornographic films and the uses made of them in her own sexual explorations. Nimier's *La nouvelle pornographie* adopts a more playful tone as the author-heroine has undertaken to write pornographic short stories in order to earn extra income. Inspired by an ad for an ironing table, she decides to invite to her apartment the manager of the company that manufactures these tables. There, with her uninhibited roommate, Aline (named after one of Sade's heroines), and with an ironing table as prop, the three proceed to illustrate that "new pornography," rendered in a vigorous prose that combines reality and imagination. The three novels were among the best sellers of the decade. As Catherine Cusset, another of the successful women novelists of the past two decades sardonically writes, "Women, it would appear, have appropriated for themselves the erotic bastion in order to more easily assassinate the dying novel—and, in passing, to swell the pockets of their publishers, thanks to the commercial viability of their literary prostitution" (161). However, what many of these writers claim, like the men who ventured into sexual territory before them, is the freedom and the license to explore not only the limits of sexuality itself, but also the language of that exploration. As novelist and filmmaker Catherine Breillat formulates it, "We are led to believe that talking about sex and sexuality is a sign of lust. By no means. Sex is the territory of an identity" (quoted in Gillain, 205).

Breillat also belongs to this new generation of women filmmakers and writers who have made a name for themselves in the past two decades. Her statement on sex as the "territory of an identity" is a reminder that in the process of extending the limits of representation in fiction and film, these women are also grappling with the issue of gender, even if no longer in quite the same way as their predecessors in the postwar period and in the 1970s. What they do have in common with theses previous generations of women is that their subversion of a supposed universalist artistic vision is enacted from a particular point of view that is, unavoidably, a woman's. Their objective, though, is no longer the "liberation" of women or a claim to "equality," but the concrete dismantling—through books and films, and with sexuality as a crucial tool—of some of the most fundamental aesthetic and moral categories that have been accepted as "given" or "universal." In her film *Romance* (2000), Breillat depicts a young woman whose husband refuses to have sex with her. She embarks on a series of sexual escapades ranging from encounters with a stranger met in a café, to bondage sessions with the principal of the school where she teaches. The film ends with the heroine giving birth—a scene depicted in close up—to a son named after his father, her husband, who dies in their apartment where she had left the gas on while he slept. In an interview after *Romance* was released, Breillat gave the following answer to a journalist who wanted to know "where she stood": "Basically, normal film focuses on the soul and pornography on the body. My goal is to go beyond this dichotomy" (quoted in Gillain, 204). Breillat does not specifically mention here that the attempt to go beyond the traditional dichotomy is effected from the standpoint of a woman, but the fact that female sexuality is at the center of the attempt reflects its gender-specific attribute. In their work as filmmakers, the women of this new generation may not be operating under the banner of "feminism," but neither are they relinquishing their identity as women.

We can see Breillat's point about subverting traditional categories reiterated in what is perhaps the most notorious French film in recent memory, Virginie Despentes' and Coralie Trin-Thi's 2000 feature *Baise-moi* (*Fuck Me*), based on Despentes' novel. Trin-Thi's answer to a journalist questioning her about how she would categorize the film clearly echoes Breillat's own declaration to the press about *Romance*: "In my view, an art film is one of those pain-in-the-ass French films where nothing happens, and porno is like masturbation. Our film is neither one nor the other" (quoted in Gillain, 203). One of the objectives, then, is to dismantle given traditional categories in which the "pornographic" and the "artistic" are clearly separated, and, in this respect at least, Despentes and Trin-Thi's film is similar to comparable works produced by men in the past, in the "Sade to Bataille" tradition. However, in addition to disrupting aesthetic or formal categories, *Baise-moi*, like Breillat's *Romance*, also disrupts traditional gender roles. Not only sexuality, but sexuality *and* gender are the operative categories here. The premise of Breillat's film is telling in this respect: after a brutal rape at the beginning, the victim and a female companion go on a sex and killing spree. Referring to film theorist Noël Burch's synopsis, "[*Baise-moi*] is about two very ordinary women using men like disposable dildos, buggering them with magnum bullets after they're done," Anne Gillain writes: "We have it figured out: *Baise-moi* is the hardcore *Thelma and Louise*" (202). However, as opposed to Ridley Scott's R-rated *Thelma and Louise* in which two women characters are literally driven over the edge by their pursuers, *Baise-moi* was directed by two women, and its graphic, hardcore quality made it a cause célèbre. This hardcore aspect went hand in hand with the film's disruption of traditional gender, aesthetic, and moral categories. As Catherine Cusset wrote, "What the two heroines of *Baise-moi* put to death is not only men, assholes, bastards, cops, the bourgeois, but also humanism itself" (166). First released as a film *interdit aux moins de seize ans* (no one under sixteen admitted) it subsequently received an "X" rating from the rating commission under pressure from conservative groups. This decision was rejected by a group of leading artists who gathered support in the name of civil liberties. The solution ultimately adopted was to bring back the *interdit aux moins de dix-huit ans* rating (no one under eighteen admitted), one that had disappeared from the French rating system and required an amendment to the existing law. The *Baise-moi* case can thus be perceived as an instance of "exceptionalism making exceptions" in order to continue to exist. In allowing the film to continue to be shown without an "X" label that would effectively remove it from the normal distribution circuit, the universalist republic was accepting a de facto extension of what constituted the "acceptable." If we consider the period ranging from the postwar, beginning with women's right to vote granted by de Gaulle's *Comité français de libération nationale* in 1944, followed by de Beauvoir's *The Second Sex*, the feminist generation of post-68, and then the "second-wave" of feminism, and finally these new women authors and filmmakers, a shift has clearly occurred in the perception and representation of women. As Anne Gillain writes,

> In this respect, *Baise-moi* is as symbolic a film as *Et Dieu créa la femme* [*And God Created Woman*] was at the dawn of New Wave cinema [see chapter 8]. An aesthetically mediocre film, *Et Dieu créa la femme* is an important turning point in the perception of the feminine and of sexuality. Bardot, with her hair cascading down and dancing a wild mambo in bare feet, replaced the "dolls" in minks, high heels, and permanents of the 1950s. Just like *Et Dieu créa la femme*, in its day and time, *Baise-moi* violates a taboo in the perception of the feminine. (203)

The taboo, however, is in the process of entering the public sphere, just as Brigitte Bardot had suddenly replaced the "dolls" of the 1950s when she appeared in Roger Vadim's 1956 film.

In their, often graphic, reappropriation of sexuality in artistic discourse, these women authors and filmmakers go against the grain of a supposedly universalist male tradition, thereby forcing a rethinking of established sexual and gender categories. The debates and criticism surrounding these films and novels were not explicitly framed in universalist terms, as had been the case for the the *parité* issue; however, the question of women's political presence in the public sphere as elected officials and the representation of women in artistic production have in common a challenge to the established order through sexuality and gender.

The challenge to universalism embodied by *parité* was also present in the *"PaCS"* issue. Although not strictly a "gay issue," the PaCS (*Pacte civil de solidarité, Pact of Civil Solidarity*), was perceived by gay and lesbian couples as the only way for them to receive a number of benefits associated with heterosexual marriage. For nonmarried heterosexual couples, it also represented the possibility of benefiting from existing marriage laws without going through an actual marriage, whether religious or civil. The idea of the *PaCS* was raised in 1991 as a result of a news item about a young man whose male partner had died of AIDS and who was evicted from the apartment he had shared with his partner by the latter's parents. This event signaled the beginning of a campaign that attracted support from an increasing number of Communists and Socialists and provoked the ire of the Right and of the Roman Catholic Church. As the prominent sociologist Pierre Bourdieu noted,

> Indeed, paradoxically, just as they are mobilizing to demand universal rights, which they are in effect denied, symbolic minorities are called back to the order of the universal; thus the particularism and *communautarisme* of the gay and lesbian movement is condemned, precisely when that movement is asking for the common law to be applied to gays and lesbians. Notably with the *contrat d'union sociale*. (Quoted in Cairns, 92)

The *contrat d'union sociale* mentioned by Bourdieu was to become the *PaCS*, a bill proposed by the government in 1998. Once voted into law, it would enable two people, whether homosexual or not, to be legally linked and to enjoy many of the benefits associated with traditional marriage in areas ranging from taxation rates to health and welfare benefits, and rental agreements. The bill, whose provisions were somewhat reduced in order to reach a consensus, was voted into law by parliament in July 1999.

The *PaCS* is not a "marriage" but it enables the secular and universalist republic to recognize the validity of the demands of a "particularist" group, same-sex couples in this case, while maintaining the idea of universalism by extending its purview. On the one hand, the *PaCS*, touted by some as a "gay marriage," is in fact a "secular union," that consolidates the republican notion of the separation of church and state that is at the root of the modern French state. On the other, the *PaCS* also signaled a recognition by the republic that universalism, an abstract notion, could not concretely accommodate the particular case represented by its homosexual population unless this was done explicitly through the enactment of a law. As we proposed in the introduction to this book, in the case of *parité* and *PaCS*, French exceptionalism had to make exceptions.

The *PaCS* and *Parité* issues can be considered crucial "test cases" for France as the country was about to enter the third millennium. Both debates were framed in universalist terms and both involved the republic's ability to reconcile so-called *particulariste* and *communautariste* agendas and its own claims to universalism. In this instance, gender and sexual preference were at the center of the debate. Often, opponents to the adoption of the *PaCs* and *parité* laws also pointed to their resemblance to practices in the United States. The objective was to show that "quota systems," for example, as one opponent to *parité* called it, went against the grain of the republic's practices and represented a threat to its tradition. Viewed in this manner, the politics of gender and of sexual preference joined a larger category of threats to the republic or to "French identity" that also included "savage capitalism" and "globalization out of control," both emblematized by the United States. In this perception, the contemporary world becomes one where even sexual and gender politics and debates are being commodified, and this represents a new set of challenges to the republican universal ethos. Paraphrasing Catherine Cusset's comment above, beyond their artistic and subversive quality, the bestselling novels by women authors, with their often graphic representation of sexuality, were also filling the coffers of their publishers. The values of the republic where one was a citizen before any other *particulariste* identity—"woman," "gay," "lesbian," "black" "Jewish," "Arab," and so on—had already been eroded during France's rapid modernization *à l'américaine* throughout the thirty glorious years as its population entered consumer society. Now these values were being further eroded by the continuation of the same process in the world of postcapitalist globalization. The claims or mottos "I am a woman and a citizen" or "I am a homosexual citizen," for example, which already present a challenge to the "citizen of the republic" identity, are themselves superseded by a motto that could be "I shop, therefore I am." The challenges to civic identity within the universalist republic are themselves becoming even more subversive and threatening by their transformation into a generic, amorphous marketability. New categories are replacing the old ones, or, as Michel Houellebecq, one of the most controversial and successful French writers at work today put it in his latest novel, *The Possibility of an Island* (2005), "In the modern world you could be a swinger, bi, trans, zoo, into S&M, but it was forbidden to be old" (quoted in Smallwood, 50). In his first novel, *Extension du domaine de la lutte* (see dossier 10.3), translated into English as *Whatever*, Houellebecq has one of the sexually unsuccessful characters declare: "I feel like a shrink-wrapped chicken leg on a supermarket shelf" (98): here, failure to succeed sexually is represented as merchandise, and sexuality and sexual preference in general are represented in postcapitalist economic terms. Even before the adoption of the PaCS, the developing "homosexual market," for example, was already being commented on as gays and lesbians became targets of a wide array of commercial ventures from car and telephone companies to hotel chains and tour operators. Dennis Altman, a professor of politics and the author of *Global Sex*, commenting on a 1996 cover story from *The Economist* entitled "Let Them Wed," writes about a "global shift in attitudes towards homosexuality and the rapid spread of new concepts of homosexual identity and acceptance" (1). Altman quotes *The Economist's* three-page article in which the journalist concludes, "In effect, what McDonald's has done for food and Disney has done for entertainment, the global emergence of ordinary gayness is doing for sexual cultures." It is no accident that the two companies, Disney and McDonalds, are themselves often considered to be primary emblems of globalization *à l'américaine*. The so-called *particulariste* agendas of PaCS and *parité*, for example, are being bypassed by the continued spread of globalization and its de facto transformation of identities subsumed by the label "lesbians" and "gays" into "consumers" or "identifiable marketing targets."

Dossier 10.3   Michel Houellebecq, *Extension du domaine de la lutte* (*Whatever*) (1994)

When Houellebecq's *Extension du domaine de la lutte* came out, it rapidly became a cult novel for a generation whose parents had come of age as France was entering consumer culture and experienced "the 60s," with its war protests, sexual liberation, and the "counter culture." In this, his first novel, Houellebecq portrays a generation, his own, the "80s generation," or the "me generation," whose outlook is characterized by disillusionment rather than subversion, cynicism, and materialism rather than any sort of revolutionary agenda. Houellebecq himself has been alternately praised as one of the most gifted writers of his generation and decried as a racist and a misogynist with a mediocre writing style. On the cover of the English translation of *Extension*, the novel is hailed as "*L'étranger* for the info generation." The phrase takes notice of the existential quality of *Extension* with its numerous references to Albert Camus's classic 1942 novel. Here, however, the sea and heat of *L'étranger*, and Meursault's sensuous relation to the world, in spite of his refusal to comply with social strictures, have been replaced, fifty years later, by a world in which technology and the market economy have invaded the most private spaces. In *Whatever*, as the translated title suggests, there is no longer any question of a lyrical "happy death" for Houellebecq's central character, only simultaneously lucid and sarcastic musings on a society ruled by "bands" of consumers and crooked politicians. The "domain of the struggle" of the original title is the territory in which vestiges of lucidity are confronted with generalized commodification. In the first passage, sexuality—Houellebecq's topic of predilection—and its place in the neoliberal market economy occupy center stage. The second passage, in which the main character walks through a provincial town on a Sunday afternoon, recalls Meursault's Sunday in Algiers as he watches the world go by from his balcony.

It's a fact, I muse to myself, that in societies like ours sex truly represents a second system of differentiation, completely independent of money; and as a system of differentiation it functions just as mercilessly. The effects of these two systems are, furthermore, strictly equivalent. Just like unrestrained economic liberalism, and for similar reasons sexual liberalism produces phenomena of absolute pauperization. In a sexual system where adultery is prohibited, every person more or less manages to find their bed mate. In a totally liberal sexual system certain people have a varied and exciting erotic life; others are reduced to masturbation and solicitude. Economic liberalism is an extension of the domain of the struggle, its extension to all ages and all classes of society. Sexual liberalism is likewise an extension of the domain of the struggle, its extension to all ages and all classes of society. (99)

I don't really want to see the town.

And yet here are very fine medieval remains, some ancient houses of great charm. Five or six centuries ago Rouen must have been one of the most beautiful towns in France; but now it's ruined. Everything is dirty, grimy, run down, spoiled by the abiding presence of cars, noise, pollution. I don't know who the mayor of this town is, but it takes only ten minutes of walking the streets to realize that he is totally incompetent, or corrupt. To make matters worse there are dozens of yobs who tear down the streets on their motorbikes. They come in from the Rouen suburbs, which are nearing total industrial collapse. Their objective is to make a deafening racket, as disagreeable as possible, a racket that should be unbearable for the local residents. They are completely successful.

I leave my hotel around two. Without thinking, I go in the direction of the Place du Vieux Marché. It is a truly vast square, bordered entirely by cafés, restaurants and luxury shops. It's here that Joan of Arc was burnt more than five hundred years ago. To commemorate the event they've piled up a load of weirdly curved concrete slabs, half stuck in the ground, which turn out on closer inspection to be a church. There are also embryonic lawns, flowerbeds, and some ramps which seem destined for lovers of skateboarding—unless it be for the cars of the disabled, it's hard to tell. But the complexity of the place doesn't end here . . .

I settle on one of the concrete slabs, determined to get to the bottom of things. It seems highly likely that this square is the heart, the central nucleus of the town. Just what game is being played here exactly?

I observe right away that people generally go around in bands, or in little groups of between two and six individuals. No one group is exactly the same as another, it appears to me. Obviously they resemble each other enormously, but this resemblance could not be called being the same. It's as if they'd elected to embody the antagonism which necessarily goes with any kind of individuation by adopting slightly different behavior patterns, ways of moving around, formulas, for regrouping.

Next I notice that these people seem satisfied with themselves and the world; it's astonishing, even a little frightening. They quietly saunter around, this one displaying a quizzical smile, that one a moronic look. Some of the youngsters are dressed in leather jackets with slogans borrowed from the more primitive kind of hard rock; you can read phrases on their backs like Kill them all! Or Fuck and destroy!; but all commune in the certainty of passing an agreeable afternoon devoted primarily to the consolidation of their being.

I observe, lastly, that I feel different from them, without, however, being able to define the nature of this difference. (67–69)

In the 1990s, as *parité* and *PaCS* were about to become national issues, France's non-European ethnic minorities, essentially from its former colonies, also constituted a visible exception to the universalist ethos. Indeed, a number of historians and cultural critics have noted that the debates around the representation of women in public office, and "gay marriage," had repercussions beyond the concerned groups and directly perceivable issues. Eric Fassin, a sociologist who teaches at the prestigious Ecole Normale Supérieure in Paris, was among those who commented at length on this "ripple effect":

> In theory, *parité* is only about political representation. But the absence of women on the boards of major companies became visible, as well as the lower pay of women at all levels: economic participation became an issue: *parité* goes beyond *parité*. In theory *PaCS* has to do mostly with the discrimination endured by gay and lesbian couples. But racial or ethnic discrimination immediately became more visible, both in the *PaCS* (in the case of immigrants) and outside the *PaCS* (for example, the absence of "visible minorities" on French television, their exclusion in housing and employment, and so on, became issues). *PaCS* goes beyond the *PaCS*. (35)

We noted in an earlier chapter that France experienced a fragmentation of identity as it approached the late 1960s and the end of its postwar economic boom. The disappearance of the traditional peasantry and of a class structure inherited from the nineteenth century; the appearance of "youth" as a self-conscious and identifiable class of citizens, or consumers; new modes of consumption; more individualist notions of identity and of political participation, ranging from the women's movement to the ecology movement; the internationalization of the economy: all these factors contributed to the erosion of the conventional or republican definition of "being French." The "peasants had been turned into Frenchmen," but the Frenchmen—and French women—had, in turn, morphed into something else. These new identities gradually took shape during the years of economic plenty, and became increasingly more active and visible in the aftermath of May 68. Ethnic minorities, on the other hand, remained essentially invisible, as long as the economic boom lasted, that is, into the mid-1970s. It is only with the end of the "thirty glorious years" that the presence of a sizable population of first- and second-generation people of non-European origin became part of the national debate. From the rise—and electoral success—of the National Front on a racist and anti-immigrant platform, to the appearance of the "Beur generation" (see chapter 8), the visibility of this group increasingly challenged established notions of French identity. In the time of empire, the non-European "natives" were colonial "subjects," but now their children, born in France and French citizens themselves, were demanding to be considered in the universalist republic. As we saw in the case of the headscarf affair involving three Muslim students in a French high school, the founding of *SOS-Racisme* and the national marches of the 1980s (see chapter 8), the secular republic had to confront a new set of challenges to its self-definition.

France's victory in the soccer World Cup of 1998 spectacularly pointed to the possibility of a French identity that would no longer be conceived of in terms of ethnic homogeneity. "Black-blanc-Beur," a phrase that had been coined in the early 1980s, made a comeback on the national scene as it was used to describe the composition of France's victorious multiethnic national team. In addition, the hero of the World Cup was Zinedine Zidane, the son of Algerian immigrants (Howarth and Varouxakis, 33).

The World Cup victory belonged to the category of moments de Gaulle had famously characterized as moments of grandeur that provide a "national cement" against the "seeds of dissent" that continually affect the notoriously fractious French population. For a while it seemed that France would be able to partake of a post-modern notion of identity in which ethnic particularity would be recognized, even if this went against the grain of long-held principles of a nation of citizens of the republic before and above all.

The presidential elections of 2002 showed that this particular entry into postmodernity was far from assured. What *had* been taken for granted in those elections, mainly that the two candidates in the second round of elections would be Jacques Chirac, the candidate of the Right, and Lionel Jospin, the Socialist candidate, instead turned into what *The Economist* titled "France's Shame": the second-place finish of Jean-Marie Le Pen, the leader of the extreme Right National Front in the first round. Prior to the first round and facing the Socialist Jospin, the candidate he perceived as his most dangerous opponent, Chirac focused his campaign on *l'insécurité*, a term synonymous with urban tension and, more specifically, with the officially unacknowledged perception of ethnic minorities as the principal cause of dangerous urban conditions and social unrest. Chirac presented himself as the "law and order" candidate, a theme the Left had abandoned. The implications went well beyond the issue of safety: in addition to being associated with *l'insécurité*, the ethnic minorities, those of Arab descent in particular, continued to be perceived by some as a major cause of France's economic woes. For a substantial portion of the population, immigration continued to be associated with unemployment, as it had been beginning in the mid-1970s. In addition, the continued expansion and federalization of the European union was perceived as a supranational project in which "French values" and "French identity" would be lost. Finally, globalization and its links to unemployment and erosion of national identity contributed to

Figure 10.1　France Wins the Soccer World Cup (1998)

Players of the victorious French national soccer team wave from an open-topped bus to supporters during a parade on the Champs Elysées where hundreds of thousands of wildly happy
people greeted them on July 13, 1998. The event was variously perceived as the country's celebration of an all too rare opportunity to shine on the international stage, the joyous display of
France's multiethnic population, as well as a reminder of de Gaulle's victory march at the
Liberation, which had also taken place on the Champs Elysées. (© Jack Guez/Getty Images)

widespread disappointment with the policies of the traditional Left and Right parties. The Gaullist or neo-Gaullist parties, the Communist Party, and the Socialist Party all seemed unable to cope with the transformations undergone by French society in the previous two decades; they also seemed unable to allay the fears of a segment of the population that perceived itself as under attack by an array of forces ranging from *multiculturalisme à l'américaine* to structural unemployment. The electoral middle ground thus seemed to be abandoned by the traditional political parties on both the Left and the Right. This, added to the decline of trade unions as channels of negotiations for industrial workers, enabled the Front National to exploit the new political configuration in the presidential elections of 2002. Its candidate obtained a greater share of the vote in the first ballot (almost 17 percent) than the Socialist candidate (16.2 percent) and second to Chirac's 18.9 percent. It was at this point, between the two rounds of voting, that the call to rally around the values of the universalist republic were heard from the traditional Left and Right in order to galvanize voters against Le Pen's racist and xenophobic platform. Chirac was reelected with an unprecedented 82.21 percent of the vote in the second round.

The difficulties and traditional divisions nevertheless remained. Perhaps the only "moment of grandeur" experienced by the Chirac administration up to this point was on the international scene as France became a leader in the refusal to endorse the invasion of Iraq in 2003. For a while at least France became a manifest presence on the diplomatic scene and it seemed as if the Gaullist dream of grandeur had materialized in the fiery speeches of the French envoy to the United Nations Security Council in which the United States was castigated for going against the principles of international law. In the past twenty years, France had already presented itself as the champion of resistance to American cultural hegemony; the members of the Organization Internationale de la Francophonie (see chapter 9), as well as the European Union, had been enlisted by France as allies in the fight for "cultural exception" at the GATT by Mitterand in 1993. The policy of presenting France and the French language in particular as bulwarks of multiculturalism and diversity against "Anglo-Saxon" linguistic and cultural hegemony was pursued by Chirac who now took "French resistance" from the cultural and economic fronts to the diplomatic front as the second war in Iraq was beginning. In the immediate aftermath of 9/11 *Le Monde*'s front-page headline "We Are All Americans" reflected France's condemnation of the attack on the Twin Towers, but as the United States moved from war in Afghanistan—for which France provided support—to the invasion of Iraq, the French government distanced itself and clearly stated its disapproval. That "French fries" would be renamed "freedom fries" in the U.S. Senate cafeteria in the process was symbolic of the generalized "French bashing" that occurred in the United States on all levels ranging from media and political circles to American restaurants where French wines were often boycotted. The fact remained that France's opposition to the invasion and its alignment with the United Nations position that further negotiations were necessary before any armed intervention could occur, gained enormous political prestige for France abroad.

The government's position gained wide support among the French population as well. This did not prevent the attacks of September 11 and the ensuing war from creating an opportunity for many in France of Arab descent to proclaim their support for Al Qaeda. This support was also the sign of a deeper national problem: by

Figure 10.2   Housing Project Outside of Lyon (2001)

In the aftermath of the September 11 attacks, graffiti in support of Osama Bin Laden in a housing project on the outskirts of Lyon, France's second-largest city. The French phrase: "Long Live Osama Ben Laden." The caption, in Arabic: "There is only one God [Allah] but God, and Mohammed is his prophet." The French government has had increasing difficulty in bringing into the republican universalist project a segment of the population that perceives itself as discriminated against, a claim borne out by extremely high unemployment figures and constant police identity checks, among other factors. The September 11 attack became a rallying theme for a number of disaffected French youth of Arab descent, a means of affirming a scorned identity. (© Jean-Philippe Ksiazek/AFP/Getty Images)

claiming an affiliation above and beyond French citizenship, they challenged the abstract homogeneity that is the basis of French republican universalism. In the graffiti that covered the walls of housing projects throughout the suburbs of French cities could be discerned the elements of an issue that this book has traced over a period of 150 years: with the intensification of *particularist* identities—whether ethnic, religious, class-based, or gendered—and the gradual replacement of the "citizen of the nation state" by the "global consumer," how can the republic continue to exist without discarding its constitutive notions? Short of a confrontation based on an absolute refusal to accommodate *any exceptions to exceptionalism*, or a complete relinquishing of basic principles, the only option may well be to compromise. The proposition that France must adapt while preserving the constitutive notions that differentiate it from other nations has made its way in both the political and intellectual spheres in the past decade. Prominent among intellectuals of his generation, the sociologist Pierre-André Taguieff (see dossier 10.4), for example, has supported the idea of a "redeployment" of the "universalist and republican idea."

Dossier 10.4 Pierre-André Taguieff. *La République menacée (The Threatened Republic*, 1966)

Taguieff, who has written extensively on contemporary issues, considers the challenge to universalism represented by trends in the past ten years, ranging from the crisis of education to the rise of the National Front. This particular work is presented in the form of a book-length interview.

How can the Republic hold on to its integrationist universalist project and, at the same time, guarantee the diversity dear to you?

That's the whole question right there. It's the crucial question. The French version of the Republic and the Jacobin model (which is one of its harder aspects) are not simply—"simplistically"— universalist. We must approach them as the historical illustration of a will to synthesize, to compromise between the necessity for universalism and the respect of cultural identities or specificities, inasmuch as they remain within the private sphere. We must thus posit a distinction between private and public space, a distinction that the Republic in its French variant has taken up. What complicates matters or creates an issue is that if the cultural identity of Franc—if this identity exists—is a political identity, then it exists within republicanism. French identity is the republican idea. But such a proposition is not acceptable for a historian. I do not summarily oppose French universalism to multiculturalism. When I speak of cultural diversity, I suppose, on the contrary that, in recent modernity—especially in the industrialized world—this diversity is to a great extent guaranteed by the model of the Nation State. This may appear paradoxical. But let us take the example of French cultural identity. It was to a great extent dictated from above at the expense of local cultures. Which does not prevent it from existing. That it has been built historically is one thing, that it now functions is another. Yet it is no longer exclusive of a certain cultural or ethnic diversity. A constituted national identity can afford the luxury of tolerating the existence of forces that threaten the cultural homogeneity it entails. It is this politico-cultural specificity of France that I think is worthy of being defended. (77–78)

The continuation of what Taguieff calls the "politico-cultural specificity" of France, and which we have called French exceptionalism in this study, has relied indeed on the republic's ability to navigate between strict enforcement of a perceived sine qua non—the core principles of the secular and universalist republic—and the recognition that the very notion of universalism must be reconsidered and extended if the French nation is to endure.

Several recent events illustrate the complexities and pitfalls of this dual policy. In one way or another they all involve France's non-European ethnic minorities. "Americanization" in all the variants and labels we have encountered in this study, "cocacolonization," "Dysneyfication," and "globalization," among others, can be seen as challenges to "a certain idea of France" from without, while the population of France with ancestry in its former colonies represents a challenge from within. At present, the different ways in which issues involving France's ethnic minorities are addressed are perhaps the most revealing of the republic's capacity to adjust and adapt.

First, there was the adoption of the "Stasi law" in March 2004, effectively proscribing the "wearing of any object or item of clothing displaying religious affiliation in public elementary, junior and high schools"(*Journal Officiel*, 5190). The stated objective of the Stasi law is to preserve the public and secular space of the French schools by prohibiting the "ostentatious display" of *any* religion. However, the law has also been perceived as singling out Muslim students. The presence of religion in the public schools had in fact become a national issue beginning with the "affair of the veil" in 1989 when three students were refused entry to their schools for wearing the *foulard islamique* (see chapter 8). In the case of the "Stasi law," the republic can be perceived as having opted for a "reductive" version of universalism, one that holds on to an abstract homogeneity at its core when considering the adoption of concrete measures. For some observers, the refusal to acknowledge any kind of ethnic or religious particularity in the midst of the secular republic is equivalent to choosing abstraction over historical reality, resulting in a kind of blindness. In a collection of essays on postcolonial France, aptly entitled, *French Civilization and Its Discontents*, Hafid Gafaiti, a professor of French and postcolonial studies, writes about a veritable "historical amnesia" in France when it comes to immigration:

> As in all countries, immigration is at the heart of the constitution of France as a nation. In this sense, the history of France is the history of the denial of fundamental elements of its own identity. It is precisely the model of the nation upon which republican France is founded that has led to the historical amnesia concerning the role of immigration in the formation of French society. (190)

The historical amnesia, or denial, to which Gafaiti refers could also be said to have played a role in the French Parliament's passage of a bill in 2005 mandating that the historical curriculum in French schools place more emphasis on the "positive aspects of French colonization." The bill calls for French school curricula to "recognize in particular the positive role of France's presence overseas, notably in North Africa, and give due prominence to the history and sacrifices of French army fighters from these territories" (quoted in Anderson, 14). The bill, adopted by the ruling center-Right majority, was roundly denounced by civil rights groups and by politicians from the Left who viewed it as an attempt to whitewash France's colonial past. Victorin Lurel, a Socialist deputy from Guadeloupe, one of France's *département d'Outre-mer*, spoke of a clear a link between the present treatment of the France's ethnic black and Arab population and the country's colonial past. The link between the eras "is very, very great discrimination . . . The youngsters in the suburbs are sons of immigrants—they are colored and blacks and Algerian, and their parents were discriminated against in French society, and that is one motivation that was at the foundation of the violence and riots in the suburbs" (quoted in Anderson, 14).

Lurel was referring in particular to the riots that shook France in fall 2005. The riots in the suburbs in October and November 2005 began when three teenagers, two of Arab and one of West African descent, attempted to escape police pursuit by climbing a fence into an electrical substation where two of them were electrocuted. A security guard from a nearby construction site had called the police because he believed the teens were trespassing. Protest took the form of peaceful marches as well as car burnings and the smashing of store windows. The riots resulted in 8,400 scorched vehicles and over 2,600 arrests in nearly 100 towns across France, as well as one death. Early on in the violence, Interior Minister Nicolas Sarkozy went on national television to promise "zero tolerance" for the *racaille*—usually translated by "scum" in the English-language press, but more accurately rendered as "riffraff." After nearly two weeks of confrontations in housing projects and *banlieues* throughout France, the prime minister, Dominique de Villepin, announced a state of emergency that temporarily gave extended powers to regional prefects, including the power to close public spaces and order search-and-seizures, house arrests, and press censorship. Ironically, this measure was based on a law adopted in 1955, at a time when the French government was attempting to eradicate the burgeoning Algerian War of independence. Before being invoked by de Villepin in November 2005, the law had only been applied once in Algeria proper, twice in the Hexagon—but during the Algerian War—and once in 1984–1985 when an indigenous movement for independence led to an uprising in the French colony of New Caledonia, in the South Pacific. The claim made by the Socialist deputy from Guadeloupe of a link between colonialism and the violence that took place in France in fall 2005 seems substantiated by this "return of the repressed" in the guise of a law from the colonial past. Some observers have even gone as far as to claim that there is a veritable "colonial logic" at the heart of the French state's treatment of its ethnic non-European population:

> The colonial law's deployment in response to the present crisis points to an enduring logic of colonial rule within post-colonial metropolitan France. Like settler cities of the colonial period, contemporary French urban centers function in opposition to their impoverished peripheries, the latter being consistently presented in the media, state policy and popular speech as culturally, if not racially, different from mainstream France. (Silverstein and Tetreault, 2)

The president's attempt to remain above the fray during both the riots in the fall and the stormy debates around the "law on the positive effects of colonialism" reflects a constant in the country's postwar history: the appeal to an abstract republican, secular, and universalist entity above politics and "aberrations." The period of the Occupation, the "dark years," is particularly illustrative of this practice. De Gaulle had declared the Vichy government "null and void" and refused to recognize any responsibility of the republic in collaboration with the Nazis and in the Holocaust. In a television interview in 1994, the Socialist president, François Mitterand, pursued this policy, clearly distinguishing the republic from an "active minority": "The Republic had nothing to do with all that. I do think that France is not responsible. Those who are accountable for those crimes belong to an active minority who exploited the [French] defeat. Not the republic and not France. I'll never ask for forgiveness in the name of France" (Di Paz, 1). Chirac spectacularly deviated from this policy when, two months after his election in 1995 he attended a ceremony commemorating the round up and deportation of 13,000 Jews from France to the death camp at Auschwitz. At a monument located near the Vélodrome d'Hiver, a now demolished cycling stadium, where the 13,000 had been held by French police, the president of the republic declared:

> It is difficult to evoke them, because those dark hours tarnish forever our history, and are an insult to our past and our traditions. Yes, the criminal folly of the occupier was assisted by French people, by the French state. France, homeland of the Enlightenment and of human rights, land of welcome and asylum, France, on that very day, accomplished the irreparable. Failing her promise, she delivered those she was to protect to their murderers." (Di Paz, 1)

By clearly recognizing the French state's responsibility in the Holocaust, Chirac was thus breaking with a tradition of keeping the republic above the fray and of relegating certain traumatic events to the status of "aberrations" in which the republic played no part. In a nationally radio-televised speech during the debates around "the law on the positive effects of colonialism," the president returned to a more traditional mode in which abstract pronouncements about "history" replaced concrete recognition of any wrongdoing on the part of the republic: "History is the key to a nation's cohesion, but it only takes a little for history to become an agent of division, for passions to inflame and the wounds of the past to re-open . . . The law's job is not to write history. The writing of history is the task of historians." The speech reflected a return to the "dual track" policy of admitting the occurrence of negative events but stopping short of ascribing specific blame to the republic. The idea of "France's *mission civilisatrice*" in Asia and Africa, especially as defined during the height of the Third republic's imperial project (see chapters 3 and 7) is claimed once again by the law, while the negative aspects of the colonial period are occulted. Nevertheless, another part of Chirac's speech on this occasion points to an evolution in the government's willingness to acknowledge the "dark" aspects of the republic's history and to assume responsibility, this time in the case of colonialism, as Chirac had, in the name of France, in the case of the Holocaust: "Like all nations France has known greatness but also difficult times. There have been moments of light but also moments of darkness. It is a legacy which we must assume in its entirety." More specifically, Chirac appointed a committee to reexamine the law, which was repealed a few months later. This outcome may have been provoked by political expediency and pragmatism in the face of heated debate and protest, but it nevertheless signaled once again an admission that the Republic could not remain an abstract notion devoid of any concrete historical responsibility if it is to endure.

Chirac's decision to appoint a Slavery Remembrance Committee on the occasion of the centennial of the abolition of slavery in France (May 10, 2006) can be inscribed in the same tradition of recognizing responsibility while keeping intact de Gaulle's "certain idea of France." In a speech made in honor of the committee in January 2006, Chirac, the neo-Gaullist, emphasized the republic's position against slavery and even referred to a "republican spirit" *avant la lettre*:

> In France, those who, even before the Republic, had the Republican spirit, took up the battle for emancipation. It is to the honor of the First Republic that in 1794 it abolished slavery in the French colonies. Restored by the Consulate in 1802, it was, on Victor Schœlcher's initiative, definitively abolished by the Second Republic on 27 April 1848. We have to say, with pride: from the outset, the Republic has been incompatible with slavery.

In Chirac's declarations, in which the republic is portrayed in all its universalist glory and as a champion of human rights, there is a tendency to refer to tradition, with a hint of pomp and circumstance. This tendency is not exclusively French, but it reflects a peculiarly French tradition of what the philosopher Jean Baudrillard refers to as policy and culture "parachuted from the top," a channeling of decisive moments and shifts in policy through old and venerated institutions. The Panthéon and the French Academy, both located in Paris, are foremost among these institutions emblematic of "a certain idea of France" and they both recently played a role in what can be seen as two official displays of the republic's universalism. The Panthéon is where France, that most literary of countries, lays to rest its great men (and, sometimes, women). Built as a church by Louis XV, it was turned into a public building by the revolutionaries of 1789 even before it was completed and became the resting site where the new republic, the "grateful fatherland," honored its illustrious dead. Voltaire and Rousseau are buried there, as are Victor Hugo and Marie Curie. In 2002, exactly two centuries after the year of his birth the remains of Alexandre Dumas, the author of *The Three Musketeers* and *The Count of Monte Cristo*, were taken to the Panthéon to be put to rest. On this occasion, Chirac declared in a speech made on the Panthéon's esplanade that, in bringing Dumas's remains to this final resting place, "the Republic is not only honoring Dumas's genius . . . it is righting a wrong. A wrong that has branded him since his childhood, as it had already branded his slave ancestors with an iron." The reference to Dumas's slave ancestors harks back to his grandmother, a black *affranchie*, or freed slave, from Haiti, a French colony until 1804. The president was engaged in a process of reconciling the republic's abstract universalism with its concrete history. The difference symbolized by Dumas—not Dumas the celebrated author, but Dumas the descendant of slaves—was assimilated into official discourse and practice. *Le Monde's* front-page headline laid out on four columns the next day is indicative of this process of republican and universalist acknowledging and metabolizing of difference: *Avec Alexandre Dumas, le métissage entre au Panthéon*" (With Alexandre Dumas, *métissage* enters the Panthéon). *Métissage* or ethnic blending belongs to a discourse that goes against abstract homogeneity and uniformity; the word had gained currency in the context of the Créolité movement spearheaded by writers from Martinique. *Métissage* and *créolité* belong to the category of *differentialism*, as do the supporters of *parité* and *PaCS* but, by being thus *Pantheonized*, by way of Dumas, the concept and the movement were incorporated into the republic's discourse of universalism.

The election of the Algerian-born author Assia Djebar to the august *Académie française*, on June 16, 2005, represents another facet of the universalist ethos as it manifests itself institutionally. The presence of Djebar, a woman, an Arab, and a worldrenowned author and contender for the Nobel Prize in Literature, among the "Forty Immortals" (the members of the Academy, elected for life) emblematizes both a recognition of a particular identity, of a particular talent, and the application of universalist principles by the republic. The Algerian War was unquestionably one of the most traumatic episodes in twentieth-century French history, and Djebar, while writing in French and having received a French education, remains an Algerian who has written about Algeria, including the colonial period that ended in a brutal war, with atrocities committed by both sides (see chapter 7). A graduate of the prestigious Ecole normale, Djebar also supported Algerian independence, and denounced the practice of torture by French paratroopers. Four decades after the end of the war, the French minister of culture's declaration on the occasion of her election to the academy, accurately reflects the dual nature of French universalism in these first years of the third millennium: "June 16 will remain a memorable date for the French Academy, for French culture and for the French language . . . Throughout her itinerary, and through her destiny and her tireless struggle for justice and righteousness, [she] has been the precious ally of freedom in its most human acceptation, that is, its *universal* acceptation . . . At the crossroads of her identities, the oeuvre and the person of Assia Djebar are the marvelous reflection of our own *multiplicity* (*Déclarations Officielles*, 2; italics added). Assia Djebar's official reception under the grand cupola of the French Academy took place with pomp and circumstance on June 22, 2006.

We have added these italics at the very end of this study as a means of simultaneously opposing and emphasizing the two notions that, throughout, have been central to our exploration of France's evolution from a period of dominant universalism that begins in the mid-nineteenth century. The presence of both terms, *universal* and *multiplicity*, in a single official speech well encapsulates the issues faced by a nation that was instrumental in the creation of modernity but has had to reassess its most basic attributes as a nation in order to enter postmodernity.

References

Agacinski, Sylviane. "The Turning Point of Feminism: Against the Effacement of Women." In Celestin, DalMolin, and De Courtivron, 17–22.

Altman, Dennis. "On Global Queering." *Australian Humanities Review*. http://www.lib.latrobe.edu.au/AHR/archive/Issue-July-1996/altman.html, May 5, 2005.

Anderson, John Ward. "Law on Teaching Rosy View of Past Is Dividing France." *Washington Post*, December 17, 2005.

Badinter, Elisabeth. "Non aux quotas pour les femmes." *Le Monde*, June 12, 1996.

Baverez, Nicolas. *La France qui tombe*. Paris: Perrin, 2003.

Bové, José and François Dufour. *The World Is Not for Sale. Farmers against Junkfood*. Interviewed by Gilles Luneau. Anna de Casparis, trans. London, New York: Verso Books, 2001.

Cairns, Lucille. "Sexual Fault Lines: Sex and Gender in the Cultural Context." In Kidd and Reynolds, 81–94.

Celestin, Roger, Eliane DalMolin, and Isabelle de Courtivron. *Beyond French Feminisms. Debates on Women, Politics, and Culture in France. 1981–2001*. New York: Palgrave, 2003.

Cusset, Catherine. "The Nieces of Marguerite: Novels by Women at the Turn of the Twenty-First Century." In Célestin, DalMolin, and de Courtivron, 161–175.

Déclarations Officielles. Ministère des Affaires Etrangères. http://www.diplomatie.gouv.fr/actu/bulletin.asp?liste=20050617.html, May 2, 2006.

Di Paz, Michel. "Chirac Hailed for Citing Fance's Role in Holocaust." *The Jewish News Weekly of Northern California*, July 21, 1995.

Fassin, Eric. "The Politics of PaCS in the Transatlantic Mirror. Same-Sex Unions and Sexual Difference in France Today." In Célestin, DalMolin, and de Courtivron, 27–38.

Finkielkraut, Alain. *Au nom de l'autre. Réflexions sur l'antisémitisme qui vient*. Paris: Gallimard, 2003.

Gafaiti, Hafid. "Nationalism, Colonialism, and Ethnic Discourse in the Construction of French Identity." In Tyler Stovall and Georges van den Abbeele, 190–212.

Gillain, Anne. "Profile of a Filmmaker: Catherine Breillat." In Celestin, DalMolin, and de Courtivron, 201–212.

Houellebecq, Michel. *Whatever*. Paul Hammond, trans. London: Serpents' Tail, 1998.

———. *The Possibility of an Island*. New York City: Knopf, 2006.

Howarth, David and Georgios Varouxakis. *Contemporary France. An Introduction to French Politics and Society*. London: Arnold, 2003.

Izraelewicz, Erik. "La première révolte contre la mondialisation." In *Le Monde* December 9, 1995 Quoted in Kristin Ross, "The French Declaration of Independence." *Contemporary French and Francophone Studies/SITES: "France-USA,"* 8, 3 (Summer 2004): 273–284.

Kidd, William and Siân Reynolds. *Contemporary French Cultural Studies*. London: Arnold, 2000.

Mermet, Gérard. *Francoscopie 2005. Pour comprendre les Français*. Paris: Larousse, 2004.

Ross, Kristin "The French Declaration of Independence." In *Contemporary French and Francophone Studiers/SITES: "France-USA,"* 8, 3 (Summer 2004): 273–284.

Schneider, Robert. "La dernière arnaque." *Le Nouvel Observateur*. No. 2118, June 9–15, 2005, 44–48.

Silverstein, Paul and Chantal Tetreault. "Urban Violence in France." *Middle East Report*. November 2005. http://www.merip.org/mero/interventions/silverstein_tetreault_interv.htm, June 2, 2006.

Smallwood, Christine. "The Book of Daniels: Michel Houellebecq's *The Possibility of an Island*." *The Nation*, May 29, 2006.

Sowerwine, Charles. *France since 1870. Culture, Politics and Society*. Houndmills, NY: 2001.

Stovall, Tyler, Georges van den Abbeele, eds. *French Civilization and Its Discontents. Nationalism, Colonialism, Race*. Lanham: Lexington Books, 2003.

Taguieff, Pierre-André. *La République menacée*. Paris: Les Editions Textuel, 1996.

INDEX